Time Out

Las Vegas

timeout.com/las vegas

D1473145

Published by Time Out Guides Ltd, a wholly owned subsidiary of Time Out Group Ltd.
Time Out and the Time Out logo are trademarks of Time Out Group Ltd.

© Time Out Group Ltd 2005
Previous editions 1998, 2000, 2001, 2003.

10 9 8 7 6 5 4 3 2 1

This edition first published in Great Britain in 2005 by Ebury Publishing
Ebury Publishing is a division of The Random House Group Ltd,
20 Vauxhall Bridge Road, London SW1V 2SA

Random House Australia Pty Limited, 20 Alfred Street, Milsons Point, Sydney, New South Wales 2061, Australia
Random House New Zealand Limited, 18 Poland Road, Glenfield, Auckland 10, New Zealand
Random House South Africa (Pty) Limited, Endulini, 5A Jubilee Road, Parktown 2193, South Africa

Random House UK Limited Reg. No. 954009

Distributed in USA by Publishers Group West
1700 Fourth Street, Berkeley, California 94710

Distributed in Canada by Penguin Canada Ltd
10 Alcorn Avenue, Toronto, Ontario, Canada M4V 3B2

For further distribution details, see www.timeout.com

ISBN 1-904978-41-X

A CIP catalogue record for this book is available from the British Library

Colour reprographics by Icon, Crowne House, 56-58 Southwark Street, London SE1 1UN

Printed and bound in Germany by Appl

Papers used by Ebury Publishing are natural, recyclable products made from wood grown in sustainable forests

Time Out Guides Limited
Universal House
251 Tottenham Court Road
London W1T 7AB
Tel + 44 (0)20 7813 3000
Fax + 44 (0)20 7813 6001
Email guides@timeout.com
www.timeout.com

Editorial
Editor Will Fulford-Jones
Deputy Editor Janice Fuscoe
Consultant Editor James P Reza
Sub Editors Edoardo Albert, Lily Dunn
Researchers Maria Phelan, Michael T Toole
Proofreader Simon Coppock
Indexer Jonathan Cox

Editorial/Managing Director Peter Fiennes
Series Editor Ruth Jarvis
Deputy Series Editor Lesley McCave
Business Manager Gareth Garner
Guides Co-ordinator Holly Pick
Accountant Kemi Olufuwa

Design
Art Director Scott Moore
Art Editor Tracey Ridgewell
Senior Designer Oliver Knight
Designer Chrissy Mouncey
Digital Imaging Dan Conway
Ad Make-up Charlotte Blythe

Picture Desk
Picture Editor Jael Marschner
Deputy Picture Editors Tracey Kerrigan, Monica Roche
Picture Researcher Helen McFarland

Advertising
Sales Director Mark Phillips
International Sales Manager Ross Canadé
International Sales Executive Simon Davies
Advertising Assistant Lucy Butler

Marketing
Marketing Director Mandy Martinez
Marketing & Publicity Manager, US Rosella Albanese

Production
Production Director Mark Lamond
Production Controller Samantha Furniss

Time Out Group
Chairman Tony Elliott
Managing Director Mike Hardwick
Group Financial Director Richard Waterlow
Group Commercial Director Lesley Gill
Group General Manager Nichola Coulthard
Group Circulation Director Jim Heinemann
Group Art Director John Oakey
Online Managing Director David Pepper
Group Production Director Steve Proctor
Group IT Director Simon Chappell

Contributors
Introduction Will Fulford-Jones. **History** Will Fulford-Jones (*Viva Vegas Vic* Gregory Crosby). **Las Vegas Today** Kate Silver.
Architecture Phil Hagen (*Looking up* James P Reza). **Celluloid Vegas** Geoff Carter. **Sex & the City** James P Reza (*Rooms for manoeuvres* Dayvid Figler). **Gambling** Deke Castleman (*Sucker bets* Matt Weatherford). **Casinos & Hotels** Norine Dworkin-McDaniel, Will Fulford-Jones, Phil Hagen, Amy Schmidt; *gambling content* Deke Castleman (*The biggest and the best?, All through the night, Fame makes a man take things over* Phil Hagen; *Games without frontiers* Mark Sinclair).
Sightseeing: Introduction Will Fulford-Jones. **The Strip** Amy Schmidt (*Walk this way* Mark Sinclair; *Harry, can you hear us?* Kate Silver). **Off-Strip** Amy Schmidt (*Only in Vegas?* Kate Silver). **Downtown** Dayvid Figler (*Viva Oscar Goodman* Mark Sinclair).
The Rest of the City Jennifer Prosser. **Restaurants & Buffets** Will Fulford-Jones, Phil Hagen, James P Reza, Amy Schmidt; *additional reviews* Kate Silver (*Viva Elizabeth Blau* James P Reza; *Hold the pickle!* Matt Weatherford). **Bars & Lounges** Kate Silver; *Lounges* Norine Dworkin-McDaniel (*Casino malls at a glance, Brits abroad* Will Fulford-Jones; *Come the revolution* Amy Schmidt; *Star spas* Norine Dworkin-McDaniel). **Festivals & Events** Jennifer Prosser (*Viva Cindy Funkhouser* Kate Silver). **Adult Entertainment** James P Reza (*Dirty secrets* Dayvid Figler).
Casino Entertainment Norine Dworkin-McDaniel, Will Fulford-Jones; *additional reviews* Jaq Greenspon (*Viva Sandy Hackett* Norine Dworkin-McDaniel). **Children** Michael T Toole. **Film** Michael T Toole. **Galleries** Erika Yowell. **Gay & Lesbian** Stacy Willis. **Music** Robert Kimberly (*Viva Rob Ruckus* Dayvid Figler). **Nightclubs** James P Reza. **Sports & Fitness** Jaq Greenspon (*Making the bigs* Matt Weatherford). **Theatre & Dance** Jaq Greenspon. **Weddings** Cheri Watkins (*Car trouble* Renée Battle).
Trips Out of Town: Getting Started Will Fulford-Jones. **Arizona** Ruth Jarvis. **California** Will Fulford-Jones. **Nevada** Will Fulford-Jones. **Utah** Will Fulford-Jones. **Directory** Will Fulford-Jones.

Maps JS Graphics (john@jsgraphics.co.uk), except: page 315, used by kind permission of the Regional Transportation Commission of Southern Nevada.

Photography Heloise Bergman, except: pages 10, 13, 128 Corbis; page 15 Bettmann/Corbis; page 16 Hulton Archive/Getty Images; page 17 Popperfoto/Alamy; page 18 Reuters/Corbis; pages 23, 29 Elan Fleisher; page 30 Kobal; page 33 Channel 5; page 84 PA Photos/ABACA; pages 172, 238 Geoff Carter; page 203 Getty Images; pages 208, 222-223 MGM Grand; page 213 Bryan Haraway; page 219 Tropicana Resort & Casino; page 245 Topfoto; page 274 Amanda C Edwards. The following photographs were supplied by the featured establishments/artists: pages 55, 95, 102, 108, 140, 145, 153, 252.

The Editor would like to thank Nyx Bradley, Simon Cropper, Ingrid Reisman at the Regional Transportation Commission of Southern Nevada, John Watson, Erika Yowell at the Las Vegas Convention & Visitors Authority, and all contributors to previous editions of *Time Out Las Vegas*, whose work forms the basis for parts of this book.

Contents

Introduction

Given that the most compelling images of it all date back 40 years, Las Vegas sure knows how to look to the future. The old Vegas icons that everybody knows and most bodies love – as seen in *Viva Las Vegas* and Sinatra's *Ocean's 11*, as mythologised by *Honeymoon in Vegas* and Clooney's *Ocean's Eleven* – may have drifted out of focus during the 1990s, but they've all but vanished in the last half-decade. The Desert Inn, home for three years to Howard Hughes, has followed the Dunes, the Sands and the Hacienda into obliteration, much like the Glass Pool and Algiers motels. Binion's Horseshoe, for years the most characterful casino not just in Downtown Las Vegas but in the entire city, has been sold by the Binion family to Harrah's, who've dropped the 'Horseshoe' and diluted the atmosphere. And over at the Hilton, the showroom owned by Elvis Presley for his record-breaking run of 837 sell-out shows, has recently been given over to... Barry Manilow?

Old-schoolers may not be too happy about the winds of change gusting through this desert town, but they shouldn't be surprised. There's never been much 'yesterday' in Las Vegas, a city that lives on the cusp of tomorrow. Save for a brief and ugly spell in the late 1970s and 1980s, the city has long operated on the 'adapt or die' principle of capitalism. From the late 1960s to the end of the '70s, this entailed a gradual dissolution of the much-pilloried Mob involvement in the casino industry. The early 1990s saw a rush to open family-friendly resorts; the mid '90s saw this façade gradually dissolve amid the construction of a slew of heavily themed, parent-slanted casinos. And in the last seven or eight years, the town has returned to its adult-oriented roots with the likes of the Bellagio and the Venetian, operations aimed at those who, like the Rat Packers of the early '60s, want sophistication, or at least the illusion of it. All this image shifting has seen casualties galore, but so brightly does the new Vegas dazzle the visitor that only pop-culture historians seem to notice the losses.

The change that swept through the city in the '90s was so dramatic – in the 11 years that followed the opening of the Mirage in November 1989, more than a dozen new resorts and well over 40,000 guestrooms were built on the Strip alone – that the first few years of the 21st century saw stasis. The major resorts looked to consolidate, and sat back as visitor numbers soared to unprecedented levels: 37 million came here in 2004. But in 2005 and 2006, the town seems to be on the verge of a new era. Where once squatted the Desert Inn now stands the glossy form of Wynn Las Vegas. Huge and hugely expensive condo towers are planned for the sites of the old '50s motels. The Downtown casinos, among them Binion's, are in a constant state of flux, with ownership changing almost by the month. And a glamorous new production show opens seemingly every week, taking the town further from its lounge-act roots. We'd suggest that there's never been a more exciting time to visit this most ridiculous, unmanageable and wonderful of cities, were it not for the fact that we've said the same thing in the last four editions of *Time Out Las Vegas* and will doubtless say it in the four that follow this one. Have a ball, why dontcha?

ABOUT THE TIME OUT CITY GUIDES

This is the fifth edition of *Time Out Las Vegas*, one of an expanding series of *Time Out* guides produced by the people behind the successful listings magazines in London, New York and Chicago. Our guides are all written by resident experts who have striven to provide you with all the most up-to-date information you'll need to explore the city or read up on its background, whether you're a local or a first-time visitor.

THE LIE OF THE LAND

For many visitors, Las Vegas is an easy city to negotiate, if only because they rarely leave Las Vegas Boulevard. However, there is a city beyond the Strip, and to make both book and city easier to navigate, we've divided Las Vegas into areas and assigned each one its own chapter in our Sightseeing section. While these area designations are a simplification of Las Vegas's sprawling geography and most are not official names you'll see on signposts, we hope they'll help you to understand the city's layout and to find its most interesting sights. For consistency, the same areas are used in addresses throughout the guide; we have not included an area name in the addresses of businesses located on the Strip. We've also included cross-streets, phone numbers, website

addresses, zip codes for those venues to which you might want to write, map references that point to our street maps at the back of the guide and, in the case of any business or show housed within one of the major hotel-casino resorts, a cross-reference back to the hotel's main review. For further orientation information, *see p110*.

ESSENTIAL INFORMATION

For all the practical information you might need for visiting the area – including visa and customs information, details of local transport, a listing of emergency numbers, information on local weather and a selection of useful websites – turn to the Directory at the back of this guide. It begins on page 290.

THE LOWDOWN ON THE LISTINGS

We have tried to make this book as easy to use as possible. Addresses, phone numbers, bus information, opening times and admission prices are all included in the listings. However, businesses can change their arrangements at any time. Before you go out of your way, we'd strongly advise you to phone ahead to check opening times and other particulars. While every effort and care has been made to ensure the accuracy of the information contained in this guide, the publishers cannot accept responsibility for any errors it may contain.

Advertisers

We would like to stress that no establishment has been included in this guide because it has advertised in any of our publications and no payment of any kind has influenced any review. The opinions given in this book are those of Time Out writers and entirely independent.

PRICES AND PAYMENT

We have noted where venues such as shops, hotels, restaurants, bars, museums and theatres accept the following credit cards: American Express (AmEx), Diners Club (DC), Discover (Disc), MasterCard (MC) and Visa (V). Many of these establishments will also accept travellers' cheques, as well as other cards such as Carte Blanche.

The prices we've listed in this guide should be treated as guidelines, not gospel. If prices vary wildly from those we've quoted, ask whether there's a good reason. If not, go elsewhere. Then please let us know. We aim to give the best and most up-to-date advice, so we want to know if you've been badly treated or overcharged.

TELEPHONE NUMBERS

The area code for Las Vegas is 702. All telephone numbers listed in this guide take this code unless otherwise stated. For more on telephones and codes, *see p300*.

MAPS

The map section at the back of this book includes street maps of the Strip and Downtown areas, a guide to bus routes around Las Vegas, and maps relating to the Trips Out of Town section. The maps start on page 311.

LET US KNOW WHAT YOU THINK

We hope you enjoy the *Time Out Las Vegas Guide*, and we'd like to know what you think of it. We welcome tips for places that you consider we should include in future editions and take note of your criticism of our choices. You can email us at guides@timeout.com.

There is an online version of this book, along with guides to over 45 other international cities, at **www.timeout.com**.

In Context

Features

History

From oasis to supertramp to chic.

Around 25,000 years ago, at the tail-end of the last ice age, the large valley in which Las Vegas now sits was partially underwater. Glaciers were retreating from the mountains that surround the Las Vegas Valley, and the glacial run-off fed a vast lake, 20 miles wide and thousands of feet deep. The lake's outlet was a river known now as the Las Vegas Wash, today a wetlands park; it flowed for only 40 miles, but was larger than anything that remains in the western United States. At its mouth, the Wash was swallowed by the same monster waterway that had been carving the Grand Canyon for a couple of hundred million years (it was later named the Colorado River). The Strip was built at what was once the deepest part of the lake.

Palaeo-Indians lived in caves near the lake's shoreline, which shrank as the climate changed gradually from cold and wet to warm and dry. The first Las Vegans shared the tule marsh at the edge of the lake with prehistoric horses, giant ground sloths, American camels and massive condors, and hunted big Pleistocene mammals such as woolly mammoth, bison, mastodon and caribou as early as 13,000 BC.

Little is known about these early inhabitants, but from 5,000 years ago, a clearer picture of the local prehistoric people begins to emerge.

Hunter-gatherers known as Archaic Indians introduced an Indian culture that evolved over four millennia. The area they occupied was by then desert, though plentiful spring water bubbled to the surface and flowed down the Las Vegas Wash (now a creek) to the canyon-carving Colorado River. However, it wasn't until the first centuries AD that there were signs of civilisation in and around Nevada's southern desert. The native Anasazi resided in pit houses (holes in the ground, topped with brush roofs) and lived basically. By around AD 500, they had evolved into an organised people who hunted with bows and arrows, made pottery, mined salt and traded with their neighbours. They had also refined their building techniques: their dwellings now had adobe walls.

Three centuries later, the tribe was cultivating beans and corn in irrigated fields, living in 100-room pueblos, fashioning artistic pots and mining turquoise. Mysteriously, though, the Anasazi disappeared from the area around 1150: perhaps due to disease, drought, overpopulation or war, though no one really knows for sure. A large Anasazi village was discovered in 1924, parts of which are now commemorated at the Lost City Museum in Overton, 45 miles north-east of Las Vegas.

Southern Paiutes, hunter-gatherers more like Archaic Indians than the Anasazi, claimed the abandoned territory, but they never regained the advanced elements of their predecessors' society. For the next 700 years, the Paiute remained semi-nomadic, establishing base camps of movable 'wickiups' (similar to teepees), cultivated squash and corn at the springs and creeks, and travelled seasonally to hunt and harvest wild foods. A frequent stopover on their travels was the Big Spring, the centre of a lush riparian habitat and, now known as the Las Vegas Springs Preserve, still the largest area of undeveloped land in the city.

MEXICANS AND MORMONS

The Paiutes greeted the earliest European explorers and settlers in the mid 19th century. The first white men to enter the region were Mexican traders, travelling along the Old Spanish Trail blazed by Franciscan friars to connect Spanish-Catholic missions scattered between New Mexico and the California coast. Then in 1830, three decades before the Civil War, Antonio Armijo set out from Santa Fe to trade goods along the trail. An experienced scout in his party, Rafael Rivera, found a short cut, by way of the Big Spring, and became the first non-native to set foot on the land. He named the area Las Vegas, or 'the Meadows'.

By the time John C Fremont, a legendary surveyor and cartographer for the Army Topographical Corps (his name lives on as the main street in Downtown), passed through Las Vegas Valley in 1845, the Old Spanish Trail had become the most travelled route through the Southwest. The area was by then a popular camping spot, thanks to Big Spring offering the only fresh water within a day's march. Latter-Day Saints, who had settled at the shore of the Great Salt Lake a few hundred miles further north-east, passed through Las Vegas regularly on their way to Los Angeles. Indeed, by the early 1850s, Mormon pioneer parties, wagon trains and mail carriers travelling between central Utah and southern California stopped at Big Spring with such frequency that Church elders decided to colonise the area.

In 1855, a party of Mormon missionaries was dispatched from Salt Lake City to establish a community at Las Vegas that would serve the travellers on the trail and convert the Paiute people. The missionaries erected a fort, dug irrigation ditches, cultivated crops and even

managed to befriend some Indians. But the rigours of domesticating a vast desert proved beyond them. Crops failed and rations were meagre. Timber had to be hauled from the nearest mountainsides, 20 miles away. The isolation further sapped morale.

Still, the mission might have succeeded had the colonists not located deposits of lead nearby. The discovery attracted miners from Salt Lake City, whose need for food, lumber and shelter taxed the colonists' already inadequate supplies to breaking point. Despite the miners' vociferous objections, the colonists petitioned Salt Lake City to be recalled, and the mission was abandoned in 1858. A small remnant of the Mormon fort survives as the oldest standing structure in Las Vegas.

OD GASS AND HELEN STEWART

Soon after the Mormons abandoned Las Vegas, prospectors picked up where the lead miners left off and discovered that the ore averaged a rich $650 per ton in silver. A small mining boomtown mushroomed in the desert around Big Spring. Miners who arrived too late to get in on the action fanned out from the settlement and found gold along the Colorado River, about 50 miles south-east of Las Vegas.

One of the gold seekers, Octavius Decatur Gass, saw a better opportunity in homesteading the well-watered valley. Gass appropriated the Mormon fort in 1865, using the lumber to build a ranch house and utility shop. He dug irrigation canals, planted grain, vegetables and fruit trees, and ran cattle on a chunk of land known as Las Vegas Ranch. Over the next ten years, Gass expanded his land and water holdings, assumed civil duties such as justice of the peace, and helped other homesteaders get established.

However, Gass was in financial trouble by the mid 1870s and took a loan from Archibald Stewart, a wealthy Scottish rancher from Pioche, another mining boomtown to the north. When Gass couldn't repay the loan, Stewart foreclosed and took Las Vegas Ranch, expanding the property until he was shot dead in 1884 after an argument with a ranch hand from a neighbouring spread. Stewart's wife, Helen, ran the ranch for the next 20 years, buying up more acreage, making a living in the livestock business, and running a resort for nearby ranchers and a campground for travellers on the Mormon Trail.

LONG TRAIN COMING

The San Pedro, Los Angeles and Salt Lake Railroad arrived in 1903, its planned route running through the heart of the ranch. Thanks to its strategic location and plentiful water, Las Vegas had been designated a division point for crew changes, a service stop for through trains and an eventual site for maintenance shops. Ready to retire, Mrs Stewart sold most of her 2,000-acre shootin' match for $55,000, but deeded ten acres to the Paiutes, who'd been reduced to living on the edge of town, dependent on government largesse. For this and other civic-minded deeds, Stewart is considered the First Lady of Las Vegas.

In preparation for the land sale, Stewart hired JT McWilliams to survey her property. The canny McWilliams discovered and immediately claimed 80 untitled acres just west of the big ranch, planned a town site and began selling lots to a steadfast group of Las Vegas 'sooners' (the earliest speculators on the scene). In late 1904, two railroad construction crews, one from the north-east and one from the south-west, converged on Las Vegas Valley; in January 1905, the golden spike was driven into a tie near Jean, Nevada, 23 miles south of Las Vegas.

McWilliams's settlement, known as Ragtown, was one of a long line of boomtowns that had been erupting from the desert floor across the state of Nevada for the preceding 50 years. On the day the first train travelled through Big Spring on its route between Salt Lake City and Los Angeles, Ragtown's saloons, banks and tent hotels teemed with settlers, speculators, merchants, tradesmen and itinerants. But the San Pedro, Los Angeles and Salt Lake Railroad had other plans for the fledgling settlement. It organised a subsidiary, Las Vegas Land and Water, to build its own town of Las Vegas. Officials laid out the town site, scraped the scrub from 40 square blocks, and staked 1,200 lots. The new town received enough national publicity to create demand for the land, with prospective buyers coming by train from Los Angeles ($16 return) and Salt Lake City ($20).

GAMBLING ON PROSPERITY

Competition for the prime locations proved so overwhelming that, in order to handle the hordes of hopefuls, the railroad scheduled an auction to sell the remaining lots. The auction pitted eager settlers, hoping for jobs with the railroad, against Los Angeles real estate speculators and East Coast investors. All were gambling on the initial prosperity of yet another Western railroad boomtown.

The auction was held on 15 May 1905 at the intersection of Main and Fremont Streets, on the site of today's Plaza Hotel in Downtown. The bidding quickly inflated the price of choice lots to more than double their listed values. The locals, who lived across the tracks in JT McWilliams's Ragtown, grumbled about the railroad tactic of encouraging out-of-town investors to heat up the prices; as one

participant observed, 'the auction was a nice clever scheme – the simplest way of giving everyone a fair shake (down)'. When it was over, nearly 1,000 lots had been sold for the grand total of $265,000, which was $195,000 more than the railroad had paid for the entire Las Vegas Ranch only three years earlier.

Immediately, the proud new property owners searched out the stakes sticking out from the desert sand that marked lot boundaries and erected makeshift shelters. Ragtown residents rolled their possessions over to the new Las Vegas on horse- and ox-drawn wagons; what remained of the first town site burned to the ground four months later, and the first Las Vegas building boom followed.

SETTLING IN

Saloons, honky-tonks and cribs were the first to go up, in the designated nightlife and red light district on Block 16 between Ogden and Stewart and 1st and 2nd Streets (now the parking lot at Binion's). Hotels, restaurants, banks and shops were erected along Fremont Street; railroad and town administrative offices, a school, a post office and two churches surrounded the core. The railroad company built the infrastructure: gravel streets and plank sidewalks, water service and sporadic electricity. Houses went up on the residential streets of the eight-block-long and five-block-wide town; supplies arrived daily by train. By New Year's Day 1906, 1,500 pioneers were calling Las Vegas home.

> ## 'The town was a slice of the Wild West, with legal casinos, legal prostitution and legal everything else.'

But the initial boom was short-lived. Barely a year passed before the railroad town managers showed their true colours, concerned first with operating the main line and last with servicing the town. Their refusal to extend water pipes beyond the town site stunted growth and forced the rural dwellers to dig wells and tap into the aquifer. Fires, conflicts and the usual growing pains of a young settlement slowed the influx of new residents, reducing both property values and optimism; the heat, dust and isolation contributed to the consensus of discomfort.

A rare bit of good news arrived in 1909, when the Nevada Legislature created Clark, a new county in the south of the state named after William Clark, the chairman of the San Pedro, Los Angeles and Salt Lake Railroad; Las Vegas was installed as its seat of government. Soon after, the railroad gave the new town a boost by building a shop for maintaining the steam locomotives, passenger coaches and freight cars along the line. When the facility opened in 1911, it created hundreds of jobs; by the time the shop was fully staffed, the population of Las Vegas had doubled to 3,000. Telephone service arrived when the first phone – boasting, of course, the number '1' – was installed at the cigar counter in the lobby of the Hotel Nevada (now the Golden Gate, the oldest hotel in Las Vegas) at the corner of Main and Fremont Streets. In 1915, the big town generators began supplying electricity to residents 24 hours a day.

But it was all downhill for the next 15 years. The railroad found itself losing business to car and truck traffic, and workers were laid off. A nationwide railroad, Union Pacific, bought up the San Pedro, Los Angeles and Salt Lake, relegating it to the status of a small siding on its vast network, shutting down maintenance shops, eliminating jobs and driving out locals. It also implemented policies, in particular concerning water delivery, that severely inhibited the town's growth. Las Vegas would have dried up and blown away by the late 1920s if it hadn't been for a monumental federal dam-building project gearing up nearby.

THE HOOVER DAM

The 1,450-mile Colorado River, the main waterway of the arid Southwest, had been gouging great canyons and watering lush valleys for aeons, when the US government became determined to harness its flow in the service of irrigation, electricity, flood control and recreation. The Bureau of Reclamation began to consider damming the Colorado in 1907; 17 years later, it had narrowed the location for the dam to two canyons east of Las Vegas. In 1930, Congress appropriated the $165 million necessary to build it.

Anticipation of the dam project began to fuel noticeable growth in the railroad town. By the time construction began in 1931 (the name change, from the Boulder Dam to the Hoover Dam, was announced at the spike-driving ceremony), a long-distance phone service, a federal highway linking Salt Lake City to Los Angeles and regular air-passenger services had arrived. The population soared to 5,000, with thousands more passing through Las Vegas en route to the soon-to-be-tamed river.

Even today, the building of Hoover Dam is mind-boggling in its immensity. The nearest power plant was 200 miles away in southern California, from which wires had to be strung to supply the necessary electricity. Some 5,000 workers had to be hired and an entire town (Boulder City) built to house them and their families. Most daunting of all, the mighty Colorado River had to be diverted. It took 16

Round-the-clock work on the **Hoover Dam**.

months to hack four diversion tunnels through the canyon walls before the river could be routed around the construction site. Finally, the great dam itself, surely one of the man-made wonders of the world, had to be put into place.

Some five million buckets of concrete were poured into the dam over a two-year period. When it was completed in 1935, Hoover Dam stood 656 feet (200 metres) wide at its base, 49 feet (15 metres) thick at its crest, 1,358 feet (414 metres) across and 794 feet (242 metres) tall. When the diversion tunnels were closed, it took another three years to fill Lake Mead. At 109 miles long, reaching a depth of 545 feet (166 metres) and containing 37.4 billion gallons (170 billion litres) of water, Lake Mead is the largest man-made lake in North America. The dam's legacy has been monumental, endowing Las Vegas with the power and water it needed to fulfil its promise.

THE NEW BOOM

Another event occurred in 1931 that was to have long-lasting implications for Las Vegas: the statewide legalisation of wide-open casino gambling. Backroom illegal gambling had long been the norm for the libertine frontier state of Nevada, but when the legislators gave it their blessing (along with easy divorces, no-wait marriages, legal prostitution and championship boxing matches), the transformation of Las Vegas from a railroad company town into a casino company town began.

Casino operators migrated in droves to the only state in the Union where they could ply their trade without risking arrest; vice-starved visitors streamed into town to partake in the naughtiness. The bars and casinos moved a block, from the shadows of Ogden Street to the cachet of Fremont Street, and though the ladies of the night stayed behind at Block 16, neon lights began to brighten the gambling joints along Las Vegas's main street, which was soon nicknamed 'Glitter Gulch'.

Las Vegas also enjoyed widespread publicity from the building of the dam. In 1935, 20,000 people attended the Hoover Dam dedication ceremony, led by President Franklin D Roosevelt. Word got around that this little

Viva Vegas Vic

'Still a Frontier Town!'

The tag line dreamed up in the 1940s by the J Walter Thompson Agency in Los Angeles, in order to promote a dusty little gambling town halfway between the City of Angels and the City of Saints (Salt Lake City), was an appealing one. The fact that Las Vegas had never actually been a frontier town – watering hole and railroad stop would be more accurate – was no bar to the creation of a quintessential cowpoke to go along with the Chamber of Commerce's PR campaign. Thus was born Vegas Vic, a long and lanky cartoon with a strong chin and a welcoming glint in his squinty eye. Decked out in dude-ranch finery, a cigarette dangling from his lips, Vic beckoned the weary traveller to fun and sun in the desert.

However, Vic would likely be forgotten if not for his incarnation as that most powerful of Vegas icons: the neon sign. Translated by the Young Electric Sign Company into 48 feet

(15 metres) of metal and glass, Vegas Vic became the unofficial mayor of Fremont Street when he was installed on the façade of the Pioneer Club in 1947 (the current version dates from 1951). Motors moved Vic's arm, his thumb out like some sort of demented hitchhiker, while a hidden loudspeaker boomed out, every few minutes or so, a welcome to the rubes: 'Howdy, Podner!'

Vic's monotonous greeting got on everyone's nerves after a few years, most famously actor Lee Marvin's. While in town working on a Western, Marvin leaned out of his hotel window, across the street at the Mint, and shot poor Vic full of arrows. It seems Vic's voice was interfering with a particularly heavy hangover. Vic was soon silenced; a few years later, when the mechanism in his arm gave out, the Pioneer Club's owners didn't bother to fix it.

They didn't need to. By then, Vic, in his gaudy wide-brimmed hat, yellow-checked shirt, red 'kerchief and blue jeans, was a signature part of Downtown. It's a measure of his fame that when the Fremont Street Experience canopy was built in 1995, he wasn't removed but merely lowered a few feet, giving him the appearance of a giant stuck in a low-ceilinged room. Long before then, though, he'd been joined on Glitter Gulch by Vegas Vicky, a neon cowgirl with entirely different assets.

Sadly, Vic and Vickie were doomed to enjoy each other only from afar: they literally work different sides of the street. Vic now presides over the Pioneer Club in name only, the casino having long since been replaced by a souvenir shop, while Vickie crowns the Topless Girls of Glitter Gulch strip joint. Vic and Vickie might not be remnants of an 'Old West' Vegas that never was, but they're cherished relics of the honky-tonk town of the last century, at the moment when the final frontier of glitz, glamour and gambling was about to be crossed forever.

Bugsy Siegel.

town by the dam was a slice of the authentic Wild West, with legal casinos, legal prostitution and legal everything else. Temptation led to prosperity, which in turn led to construction. Three new casinos were built at the start of the '40s: the El Cortez in Downtown, and the Last Frontier and El Rancho on the Los Angeles Highway, a stretch of road that would eventually come to be known as 'the Strip'.

With the nation preparing for World War II, the federal government took over a million acres north of Las Vegas for use as a training school for military pilots and gunners. Between 1940 and 1945, the Las Vegas Aerial Gunnery School trained thousands of pilots, navigators, bombers and gunners and shipped them to the front in Europe or the Pacific. The school eventually expanded to three million acres. And then, in 1942, Basic Magnesium, one of the largest metal-processing factories in the country, was built halfway between Las Vegas and Boulder City. At the peak of production, 10,000 workers were processing millions of tons of magnesium, a newly developed metal used in the manufacture of bomb casings, aeroplane components and flares. To house them, an entire town was built: Henderson, Las Vegas's first next-door neighbour. During the war years, its population doubled from 8,500 to 17,000.

THE MOB AND THE BOMB
As much as the war brought benefits to Las Vegas, it also gave a boost to organised crime throughout the US, with handsome profits made from the vast black market in scarce consumer goods. To the masters of the underworld, Las Vegas – where everything was legal – looked like the Promised Land. Gangsters from all over the country, flush with cash from bootlegging during Prohibition and black market trading during the war, stood poised to invade Nevada with money, management and muscle. All they needed was someone to raise a torch and show them the way. Enter Benjamin 'Bugsy' Siegel – tall, handsome, fearless and partnered by the most powerful criminal bosses in America.

Siegel elbowed into and bowed out of several casinos during the early 1940s, until he finally found the one he wanted: the Flamingo. He insinuated himself into the inner management (which, contrary to popular myth, already existed), then so terrorised the team that they fled for their lives, leaving him with the whole unfinished joint. Of course, Bugsy knew nothing about constructing a casino. The Flamingo eventually went $4 million over budget; what's more, Siegel, assassinated in his girlfriend's Beverly Hills mansion in June 1947, wasn't around long enough to enjoy it.

Thus began 20 years of the Italian-Jewish crime syndicate's presence in Las Vegas, and ten years of the biggest hotel-building boom the country had ever seen. Black money from the top bosses of the Mob, along with their fronts, pawns, soldiers and workers, poured in from the underworld power centres of New York, New England, Cleveland, Chicago, Kansas City, New Orleans, Miami and Havana. Between 1951 and 1958, 11 major hotel-casinos opened in Las Vegas, nine on the Strip and two Downtown. All but one was financed by dirty cash. Finally, a full 25 years after gambling was legalised in Nevada, the state and federal governments woke up to the questionable histories of the people – considered criminals in every other state in the country – who were in charge of the largest industry in Las Vegas. The war between the police and the gangsters began.

Something then happened that cast the town in a very strange light. The federal government needed a vast uninhabited tract of land to perfect its nuclear weapons, and found it at the Las Vegas Aerial Gunnery School. Just 70 miles north-west of the city, the Nevada Test Site hosted around 120 above-ground nuclear test explosions, about one a month for a decade. Thousands of guinea-pig soldiers were deployed near Ground Zero of the explosions, purposefully exposed to the shockwaves so that medical teams might measure the effects of the

Sammy, Frank, Dino and pals wisecrack for the masses at the Sands in 1960.

radiation. A few locals worried about which way the wind blew, but most of the 65,000 Las Vegans seemed to revel in the notoriety radiating from the tests. The boosters had a ball, marketing everything from atom burgers to pictures of Miss Atomic Blast. Indeed, the openings of several casinos were scheduled to coincide with blasts. People had picnics atop the tallest buildings in town, which afforded bird's-eye views of the mushroom clouds. The first Nuclear Test Ban treaty in 1962 drove the explosions underground, where 600 tests were held in the following three decades.

THE DIATRIBE

The Mob, the bombs, the gambling and the general naughtiness of Las Vegas attracted heat from the rest of the US, most of it magnified by the media. A steamroller of criticism levelled Las Vegas's reputation, turning the town into a national scandal. Known as 'the Diatribe', this systematic attack on Las Vegas remains the greatest public castigation of an American city in history. The assault coloured Las Vegas's image for another 30 years.

At the same time, though, people were flocking to the town, proving the rule that all publicity is good publicity. These pilgrims found that a strange thing happened at the

Nevada state line: criminals who crossed it were suddenly accorded the status of legitimate businessmen, while the good citizens of the rest of the country suddenly became naughty boys and girls. These were the glamour years, when you didn't go out in Las Vegas after dark if you weren't wearing a suit or a cocktail dress. Crap shooters rolled the bones elbow-to-elbow with hit men. Mafia pit bosses had the 'power of the pencil' (to hand out free rooms, food and beverages at their discretion), and the comps flowed as easily as the champagne.

> **'The $1-million-a-day profits with which the public greeted the Mirage galvanised the industry.'**

During this period, Frank Sinatra, Dean Martin and Sammy Davis Jr performed in the famous Copa Room at the Sands, then invaded lounges around town. Joining the likes of Shecky Greene, Buddy Hackett and Louis Prima on stage, the Rat Pack became iconic fixtures of the new, high-rollin' Vegas. Many locals and visitors who were around from the early 1950s to the mid 1960s still pine for these lost years.

The arrival of Howard Hughes in Las Vegas in 1966 (*see below* **Howard's way**), and the subsequent investment in the city from respected companies such as Hilton and Holiday Inn, marked the end of the Diatribe and the beginning of Las Vegas's coverage on the business pages. Of course, as anyone who's seen Martin Scorsese's movie *Casino* knows, in reality it took a little while longer for the various government task forces to hound the old gangsters into oblivion. One scandal after another erupted at the so-called 1950s casinos where the Mob was still entrenched. But finally, in the mid 1980s, experts were able to agree that Las Vegas casinos were free of any discernible Mob involvement.

Howard's way

He arrived, unannounced and unseen, in November 1966, the night before Thanksgiving. The train stopped five miles out of town, whereupon he was loaded into an ambulance and smuggled, under cloak of darkness, into his hotel room. When he left the city three years later, in similarly secretive circumstances, not a soul outside his inner circle had seen him, but his impact had been keenly felt.

The Aviator didn't attempt to tell the whole life story of Howard Hughes, and nor could it. By the time Hughes moved into the Desert Inn hotel-casino in Las Vegas, he had moved as far from the public eye as any man with his extraordinary levels of wealth and fame – he had spent the preceding four decades as a successful film producer, a record-breaking pilot, a successful aeroplane builder and an inexhaustible romancer of young Hollywood starlets – could conceivably have managed. His aviating days, though, were behind him, in more ways than one: earlier in 1966, Hughes sold his share of TWA for more than half a billion dollars, cash that came in very handy when he arrived in the city whose birth year, 1905, was the same as his own.

It's not known exactly what Hughes intended to do when he arrived in Las Vegas, or how long he originally intended to stay. However, he immediately made the place his own, converting the Desert Inn's ninth floor into an airtight, light-proof, armed command centre for his business operations and deeply eccentric personal life. By this time, the obsessive-compulsive Hughes was reputedly living an almost entirely nocturnal lifestyle, growing his hair down to his waist, storing his urine in bottles and developing a damaging addiction to codeine. When the hotel management, alarmed by his behaviour, threatened him with eviction, reputedly because they wanted to reserve Hughes's penthouse apartment for high-rolling gamblers, he bought the entire hotel for a little over $13 million.

He was, it turned out, just getting started. Over the next few years, Hughes went on to spend $300 million in the city, buying five casinos (including the Sands), an airport, an airline and assorted other incidentals. He even bought the KLAS TV channel: not for profit, but to control the all-night movie programming he absorbed every evening.

The publicity generated by Hughes's spending spree turned Las Vegas's reputation around: no longer was the town in the hands of the Mob. Between 1968 and 1973, another dozen hotel-casinos opened – several of them owned by respectable hotel chains which had previously been careful not to touch the town with a bargepole – and tens of thousands moved to the city. Hughes, though, lost interest in the place. He moved out of the Desert Inn in 1969, dying seven years later, but his Las Vegas legacy, preserved more by his land purchases than by his casino investments, is stronger than ever.

A rare shot of Hughes in the early 1970s, two years after he left Vegas.

Goodbye **Desert Inn**, hello Wynn Las Vegas.

THE NEW LAS VEGAS

In November 1989, a maverick 47-year-old businessman by the name of Steve Wynn opened a 3,000-room, $650-million pleasure palace in the heart of the Strip. The size, elegance and price tag of the Mirage stunned the old guard of the gambling business in Las Vegas, where a major resort hadn't been built in 16 years. But the phenomenal enthusiasm, not to mention the $1-million-a-day profits, with which the public greeted the Mirage galvanised the industry, and changed both the look and the culture of Las Vegas. The forlorn old casinos, with their scruffy buffets and dowdy lounges, were replaced by highly sophisticated resorts, with impressive restaurants, high-budget shows and plush new lounges. A new breed of vacationer, more moneyed than at any point since the 1960s, came to see them.

There was plenty to see. The Excalibur, a family-friendly, medieval-themed casino-resort, opened in June 1990, followed in 1993 by the great pyramid Luxor, the pirate-technic Treasure Island and the 5,005-room MGM Grand, the world's second largest hotel. The Hard Rock Hotel brought some glamour back to the town when it opened in 1995; the 1,257-foot

(383-metre) Stratosphere Tower, the opulent Monte Carlo and the pop art New York–New York all opened between April 1996 and January 1997. Another wave of construction crested in October 1998 with the grand opening of the $1.6-billion Bellagio, the most expensive hotel ever built. The $1-billion Mandalay Bay, all hipness and whimsy, followed six months later, with the $1.5-billion Venetian and the $760-million Paris Las Vegas also making their debuts in September 1999. And then, in August 2000, came the Aladdin.

While many major casinos went up, others came tumbling down. The building boom of the 1990s was accompanied by the spectacular implosion of a number of key Vegas casinos. Between October 1993 and April 1998, the Dunes, the Landmark, the Sands, the Hacienda and the old Aladdin were all blown sky-high (they've since been replaced by the Bellagio, a parking lot, the Venetian, Mandalay Bay and the new Aladdin). Implosions in 2001 and 2004 finally levelled the Desert Inn, on whose site stands Wynn Las Vegas, which in 2005 became the first major casino to arrive on the Strip in a half-decade. Locals and old-timers mourned the loss of these icons, but many turned up to watch them bite the dust.

21ST-CENTURY VEGAS

Despite the fact that the town already has over 130,000 hotel rooms and 16 of the 21 largest hotels on earth, Las Vegas looks set to grow further in future years. After a slight blip post-9/11, visitor numbers in Las Vegas have now reached record levels. An astonishing 37 million people, around ten per cent of them from abroad, visited the city in 2004, spending over $33 billion in the process. Many people check out Sin City once just to see what all the excitement is about, but millions more become regulars, attracted by the agreeable climate, the big-budget shows, the top-notch hotels, the increasingly excellent food and, of course, the chance of instant riches.

Indeed, many have relocated to the world's greatest boomtown. Las Vegas is the largest American city to have been founded in the 20th century, but has also been its fastest growing major metropolitan area for more than a decade. The city celebrated its 100th birthday in mid 2005, a century during which it developed from a desolate railroad town to the glitter and glamour capital of the world. Heaven only knows what the next ten decades will bring.

▶ For more on the Nevada Test Site and the **Atomic Testing Museum**, see p124.
▶ For more on the **Hoover Dam**, see p260.

Key events

c0 Anasazi civilisation begins to develop in the southern Nevada desert.
c1150 Semi-nomadic southern Paiute claim territory abandoned by the Anasazi.

MEXICANS AND MORMONS

1830 Rafael Rivera discovers a short cut via Big Spring while on the trading route from Santa Fe. He names the area Las Vegas (meaning 'the meadows').
1845 The surveyor John C Fremont visits the Las Vegas Valley. Big Spring has become a popular camping spot on the well-travelled Old Spanish Trail.
1855-8 Mormon missionaries from Salt Lake City establish a short-lived community at Las Vegas. Lead is discovered in the area.
c1858 Silver ore and gold are discovered, prompting the sudden growth of a mining boomtown around Big Spring and along the Colorado River.

OD GASS AND HELEN STEWART

1865 The old Mormon fort is appropriated by OD Gass and developed as Las Vegas Ranch.
mid 1870s Las Vegas Ranch is taken over by Archibald Stewart, who expands the property until his death in 1884.
1884-1903 The ranch is managed and developed by Stewart's widow Helen, who eventually sells most of it to the San Pedro, Los Angeles and Salt Lake Railroad.

LONG TRAIN COMING

1903 JT McWilliams claims 80 acres of land west of the Las Vegas Ranch. He sells them as lots of a planned town site, known as Ragtown.
January 1905 Completion of the Salt Lake City to Los Angeles railroad at Jean, Nevada.
15 May 1905 A subsidiary of the railroad company auctions off 1,000 lots for a new town site just across the tracks from Ragtown. Four months later, Ragtown burns to the ground.

SETTLING IN

1905 The new town of Las Vegas begins to develop with a nightlife district on Block 16 (the heart of today's Downtown).
1909 Las Vegas is made the seat of Clark County, prompting a mini-boom in the town.
c1915-30 Union Pacific buys up the San Pedro, Los Angeles and Salt Lake Railroad, leading to unemployment and economic decline in Las Vegas.

HOOVER DAM AND THE NEW BOOM

1924 Two canyons east of Las Vegas are chosen as the site of an ambitious new project to dam the Colorado River.
1931-5 Construction of the Hoover Dam. Boulder City is built to house the workers.
1931 Gambling is legalised in Nevada, prompting an influx of casino operators into Las Vegas, and the development of Fremont Street as the main nightlife area. It soon becomes known as Glitter Gulch.
1935 President Roosevelt and 20,000 others attend the Hoover Dam dedication ceremony.
1940 US government takes over a million acres of Nevada desert to the north-west of Las Vegas to train soldiers for World War II.
early 1940s Three major casinos are built: the El Cortez in Downtown, and El Rancho and the Last Frontier on the Los Angeles Highway.

THE MOB, THE BOMB AND BEYOND

1946 Construction of Benjamin 'Bugsy' Siegel's Flamingo casino.
1947 Bugsy Siegel is shot dead in Beverly Hills. For the next 20 years, the Mob dominates gambling in Las Vegas.
1951-8 Eleven major hotel-casinos open in Vegas; ten of them are funded by the Mob.
1951-62 Around 120 nuclear bombs are detonated above ground over the Nevada Test Site, north-west of Las Vegas.
1960-61 The legendary Rat Pack perform in the Copa Room at the Sands casino.
1962 First Limited Nuclear Test Ban Treaty prohibits atmospheric nuclear explosions.
1962-92 800 nuclear devices are detonated underground at the Nevada Test Site.
1966 Billionaire Howard Hughes takes up residence at the Desert Inn, buying up six casinos and stimulating a new boom. A dozen new casinos are built in the next seven years.

THE NEW LAS VEGAS

1989 Steve Wynn opens the Mirage, the first major hotel-casino to be built for 16 years.
1990-2000 Myriad new resorts are built on the Strip and beyond it, from the medieval-themed Excalibur in 1990 to the Aladdin in 2000. As the town undergoes a new lease of life, the population of Clark County almost doubles, from 770,280 in 1990 to 1,425,723 a decade later.
2005 As the town celebrates its centenary, Steve Wynn opens Wynn Las Vegas, the Strip's most luxurious property yet.

Las Vegas Today

It looks good for 100, but how healthy is centennial Vegas?

An unassuming woman sits on a stool in a Las Vegas coffee shop. Probably in her mid twenties, she has fair skin, short hair and a lip ring, and wears a T-shirt and jeans. She watches people as they walk in, or as they mind their own business. This is her regular hangout, her home from home. A place where she can get a bagel and answer her phone, which rings often.

'Hello?' She answers politely. 'Yes. Tonight after six.' A pause. 'Serenity is available, but not until after six.' She hangs up. The phone rings again. 'Hello?' Another pause. 'Yes, and she likes feet. She's into feet.' Ring ring. 'Hello?' She's less polite. 'Listen, you worm!' Still, despite the theatrics, it's clear she's enjoying herself. This is her escort service, after all, run not so clandestinely on any given day from a coffee house, and you get what you pay for.

With its matching stucco houses and beige gated suburban communities, Las Vegas looks like a girl-next-door kind of town. Until, of course, you reach that adult Disneyland of a Main Street, as shocking as a lip ring on a pretty face. Serving as an oasis in the most unexpected and unforgiving of places, the city sings a siren song that keeps bringing in the johns and taking them for the ride of their lives. It lures in more than 37 million fishbelly-white visitors a year, who come to hike up their fannypacks and get lucky in more ways than one.

But the city's fickle, too, known for illusions and sleight of hand. Las Vegas's boundless energy is mystifying, but there's a flip-side, specifically the city's mollifying inability to take care of its own. The city's speedy growth has boosted the economy, but has left the local authorities unable to cope in some areas: the city is among the worst in the country for education, teen pregnancy, aid to the homeless, pollution, addiction and suicide. Send along your weary masses and the city will entertain them, wine them and dine them. But leave them here too long and they're liable to become a statistic in one vice or another.

In a place where history is imploded into the future and the pace of development gives cause for a twice-annual reprinting of the phone book, it's easy to get lost. But despite the struggles against corruption, poor urban planning and the constant complaint that the city lacks culture, the world's eyes remain on it. Yesterday, it was proudly party-loving mayor Oscar Goodman telling a classroom of fourth-grade kids that if he were stranded alone on an island, the one thing he'd want with him would be a bottle of gin. Tomorrow, it could be discussion of whether to bring back prostitution within city limits or legalise marijuana. Whatever the attention, good or bad, the city always figures out a way to keep the business coming.

REALTY BITES

One of the most readily apparent themes of Las Vegas life is imitation. All it takes to see it is a walk along the Strip: past the half-size Eiffel Tower, the steaming sewers of New York–New York and the posters advertising celebrity impersonators. However, it doesn't end here. Look down from your plane window as you descend into the city, and you'll see swathes of Spanish tiled roofs and beige houses, each one looking as ordinary and indistinct as the next.

Within these master-planned communities, residents and visitors fear they'll get lost in a jungle of stucco, for each home looks exactly like the others. Even local realtors laugh about how they pull into the wrong driveway each night and only realise they're not home when the garage door fails to open when triggered. There's an eerie likeness to the suburbs that's hard to overcome. As a refreshing change of pace, more feisty residents speak in hushed tones about taking a can of spray paint to it all, just to wreak havoc and provide something interesting to look at. Perhaps a pink flamingo?

However, master-planned housing has lately been taking a different route: in what some have called the Manhattanisation of Las Vegas, buildings have begun moving up rather than out. Because most of the land surrounding Las Vegas is owned by the government, and is sold off to developers only in occasional chunks, there are just seven to ten years of developable land left here. The town has sprawled in every direction, and the infrastructure and planners have had little chance to keep up. The skyline is in constant metamorphosis as concrete slabs fill the air, escalating almost as quickly as land values. It's a mystery to locals, who wonder how many of the condos that have been approved will actually go up. And if they do sprout, is the town ready to handle it?

MULTIPLE PERSONALITIES

Then there are the small neuroses that pop up every so often, such as congestion. Solutions to the problem have been hard to find, but progress seemed on its way in 2003, when a peculiar sight appeared on the Strip. Bicycles! Actually, they were pedicabs (or rickshaws), pulled by human pedallers and carrying revellers from casino to casino for, in theory, the cost of a tip. Though they did sometimes obstruct cars and taxis, it was refreshing to see some green thoughts put into the transport issue, and equally good to have an option on busy nights that moved at greater than walking pace.

Predictably, the powers-that-be didn't like the new trend, crying about safety issues and the under-the-table fees some drivers were charging. But rather than regulating the industry, they outlawed it. Rickshaw drivers were stopped by police and endlessly ticketed until, eventually, they all pulled out. The bikes once more disappeared from the Strip, giving the place back to the taxis, buses and limos who add to the thick blanket of smog in the Valley.

Hot on the cyclists' heels came the Las Vegas Monorail. The $654-million monorail, funded entirely by the casinos, opened to much fanfare in July 2004, travelling its four-mile, seven-stop route from the Sahara to the MGM Grand. It looked good at the beginning, but then the inevitable early glitches got more and more worrying: doors opening on the wrong side of the train, doors not opening at all, debris toppling from the monorail on to a car passing it, even a wheel falling off one of the trains.

The monorail closed for 107 days for repairs, finally reopening – for good? – on Christmas Eve 2004. However, it was recently denied federal funding for a long-planned expansion to Downtown, thanks to lack of passengers and those pesky mechanical failures. The opinion that the monorail is just a folly bought by local juice found wider popularity when the public learned that it was built under the same kind of tax-exempt status that a charity would receive even though it's run by a private company. It makes those interloping rickshaws look like a better idea than ever.

And consider the drought that'd been further drying the desert for years. Local municipalities recently began harassing residents into saving water, even putting drought restrictions into place. However, it's a different story down on the Strip. Officials have suggested that some businesses actually depend on the use of water features, such as those at Bellagio, the Venetian and the Mirage. All three applied for and were granted exemptions to the drought restrictions. So as the water level in Lake Mead continues going down, the humidity on Las Vegas Boulevard is eternally on the rise.

Such stories only reiterate the power of the casinos, power that only seems to be increasing as the number of corporations in charge of them gradually decreases thanks to an array of major mergers and buyouts. In 2004, the MGM Mirage group, which already owns the MGM Grand, the Bellagio, the Mirage, Treasure Island and New York–New York, announced plans for a $7.9 billion buyout of Mandalay Resorts, which owns Mandalay Bay, the Luxor, the Excalibur and Circus Circus. As if it wasn't enough to have practically half of the Strip fall under one umbrella, Harrah's Entertainment, who run Harrah's and the Rio, then announced that they were paying $9.4-billion to slurp up the Caesars Entertainment properties on the Strip: Bally's, Caesars Palace, the Flamingo and Paris Las

Under the veil

In a run-down hotel on E Fremont Street, a tall, thin, African-American man is slamming cabinet doors, peeking under beds and glancing out of windows. He's wearing a grey T-shirt decorated with a smiling, decapitated M&M's candy. He calls himself a hitman, a two-time felon who's killed for money and will do it again for the right price. 'For $100,000, anyone can disappear,' he says. 'There's a lot of holes in the desert.' Then he comes clean, in a manner of speaking, about the latest scandal to hit the streets of Sin City.

The city's wedding chapels started throwing more than just rice in 2003: some began throwing punches. In a holy war with a Las Vegan twist, what began as a war of words escalated: one minister was allegedly beaten up, and two chapel owners got into a cat fight on the steps to the Clark County Marriage Bureau. According to the hitman, the industry was engrossed in more than a lovers' tiff: one chapel was apparently being framed.

It began when A Las Vegas Garden of Love Wedding Chapel opened about two miles from the courthouse and sent a fleet of limos to import business from the Marriage License Bureau, where more than 100,000 couples arrive annually. They also sent handbillers, armed with flyers. Neither of these practices were anything new at the courthouse, where scrums of men and women have long appealed to the thrifty sensibilities that often accompany a Vegas wedding. But, regardless, the hard sell got harder. When one hawker shouted '$35 wedding!', another countered '$20 wedding!'. Cries of 'Free photos!' were answered by offers of 'Free parking!'. Things weren't helped by the fact that A Las Vegas Garden of Love was throwing free limo rides into the mix. While most chapels are within a short distance of the courthouse, a limo is more appealing than even the shortest walk on a 115° desert day.

The competition on the steps became fierce, with representatives from the various chapels pushing, shoving and yelling in an attempt to get more business. Cliff Evarts, who owns the Vegas Wedding Chapel, filed for a protective order against Cheryl Luell, owner of A Las Vegas Garden of Love, and her employees. The minister husband of Sherrie Klute, the owner of the Stained Glass Chapel, claimed he was threatened in an alleyway by a homeless person, whom he alleged had been paid off by a rival chapel. An assortment of other accusations followed, from the dark (threatening phone calls, courthouse fights) to the darkly comic (nails placed under tyres, eggs thrown at limos). All pretty petty, until the man with the M&M's shirt surfaced.

Happily, no harm followed. No new holes were discovered in the desert. The main consequence – unsurprisingly, say the cynics – was that the chapels received masses of free local and national publicity. And all the while, brides continued blushing, Elvises continued officiating, and any shotgun weddings staged here remain, at least so far, shotgun weddings in a purely figurative sense.

Vegas. As if playing a giant game of Monopoly, it seems the casinos are in a race to pass go first and collect much, much more than $200.

GROWTH SPURTS

Still, there's movement, and improvement. For years, critics have predicted the city would self-cannibalise, but it hasn't done so yet. Sure, the Strip is lined with screaming tourists carrying footballs full of beer, but the city is no longer merely an adult theme park. The Venetian has a Guggenheim museum; Frank Gehry has signed on to design an Alzheimer's Research Center in Downtown. Chefs such as Alain Ducasse have reinvented Vegas as a fine-dining town, while entertainment has come miles from the lounge acts of the past. The new World Market Center should bring respect to the design community, just as Downtown's Arts District gains more

fans by the week. Shrimp cocktail and showgirls linger, but the forces of cultural influence have allowed such traditions to mingle with Kobe skirt steak and Cirque du Soleil.

The Las Vegas Convention and Visitors Authority hit the jackpot when they began marketing the town with the catchphrase, 'What happens in Vegas, stays in Vegas,' but there's no truth to it. From Britney Spears marrying Jason Alexander and then annulling the marriage 55 hours later, to Mayor Oscar Goodman suggesting that the homeless should be shipped to an abandoned prison 25 miles away, Las Vegas is a town that thrives on attention, good or bad. What happens in Vegas does anything but stay here. The siren song lures residents and visitors, but there's no promise for salvation, much less anonymity, in a town that sells itself any which way it can.

Lied Library. *See p28.*

Architecture

If you build it, they will come. And they have.

Architecturally, as in so many other ways, Las Vegas is a city more likely to tear down its laurels than rest on them. Along the Strip, it's survival not so much of the fittest, but of the tallest, the biggest and the boldest. There's invention here, but it's scale that defines the city's look, and specifically the desires of casino moguls to build structures more impressive than those of their competitors. As critic Alan Hess points out in his 2005 book *Architecture Las Vegas*, 'This kind of one-upmanship has been a part of Las Vegas architecture ever since the second neon sign, bigger and brighter than the first, went up on Fremont Street in the 1930s.' But whatever the reasons, one thing is for sure: nothing stays the same here for long.

The design emphasis in Las Vegas in recent years has been on three-dimensional forms, elaborate detailing and crowd-pulling attractions, where artistry lies in styrofoam statuary, precast mouldings, fake frescoes and faux marble. The casino moguls have become patrons of a new kind of arts and crafts, pouring millions into decorative effects. The town used to be seen as ex-urban and anti-architecture, a

linear amusement park of buildings as disposable as last year's Christmas cards. Now it consists of cheek-by-jowl complexes that are small cities in their own right.

In many ways, there's no better example of the town's constant reinvention, and of its movement from theme-park tackiness to more sophisticated design, than **Caesars Palace** (*see p65*), one of the oldest properties in the city. Its 40-year history is largely responsible for its bankable name, but Caesars is constantly updating. Over the last few years, the resort has boosted its marquee value by spending $95 million building the vast Colosseum theatre for Celine Dion; given its relatively new tower a brother, so as to not fall behind in the high-rise race for the skies; and expanded the landmark Forum Shops into a much-praised multi-level complex. Still recognisable as the Caesars of old, it's also now a very 21st-century resort; a gigantic hotchpotch, sure, but smarter and more calculated than it first appears.

However, the next big improvement to Caesars is surely only just around the corner, primarily because the next big thing is always right down the street. Most obviously, there's **Wynn Las Vegas** (*see p75*), a 2005 resort that forgoes theming in favour of simple sophistication inside a curvaceous 50-storey bronzed beauty. Before the doors of Wynn Las Vegas even opened, MGM Mirage announced its plans for **CityCenter**, a mini-metropolis to be built on the 66 acres where the Boardwalk currently stands. Phase one includes a big hotel, smaller boutique properties and high-rise condos, plus retail, dining and entertainment. At the same time, Donald Trump is building a 60-storey condo and hotel tower across from Wynn Las Vegas, while other residential high-rises are being thrown up within a chip's toss of the Strip (*see p28* **Looking up**).

Only time will tell what becomes of less 'corporate' resorts such as the ancient ruins of **Excalibur** (*see p86*), which date all the way back to 1990, and the positively prehistoric **Tropicana** (*see p90*), tipped by many to be the next major Strip casino to bite the desert dust. The future for them doesn't look bright. But in this town, nothing lasts forever; the end will come to all and sundry. Just as the hotels in which your parents may have stayed in the '60s have been bulldozed, so it follows that even the blockbuster resorts of the 1990s will come down sooner or later, to be replaced by something yet more extravagant, immense and ridiculous.

THE EARLY DAYS

Although Las Vegas has been a popular resort town for half a century, the way in which its resorts are built has altered immeasurably down the years. These shifts have been driven as much by social change as by any direct design imperative. The old Vegas was a Mafia-controlled *demi-monde*, a place in which men gambled wearing jackets and ties, watched by women clad in diamonds and ballgowns. Slot machines were for neophytes, and children were not welcome. Back then, though, gambling was illegal in much of the US; now that it's permitted in 48 of the 50 states and the industry is controlled not by the Mob but by big business, the town has again reinvented itself.

From World War II onwards, when the town's expansion began to take hold, Las Vegas developed its own casually distinctive style, a dazzlingly vulgar cocktail of expressionist modern architecture and monumental neon signs that illuminated stretches of otherwise empty desert on Las Vegas Boulevard. A key figure in this development was Wayne McAllister, a pioneering southern Californian architect whose influence over modern Vegas is greater than perhaps any other designer. It was McAllister who built the cowboy-flavoured **El Rancho**, the first ever themed resort on what's

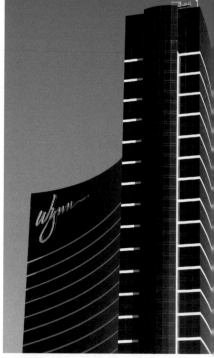

The cultured form of **Wynn Las Vegas**.

now known as the Strip, as early as 1941; a decade later, he built the original **Sands**, the Rat Pack's casino of choice, and he also had a hand in the design of the legendary **Desert Inn**.

> **'While the architecture of old Vegas was about vivid abstraction, the city's now hooked on replication.'**

The town's smaller hotels were, if anything, even more exotic, and in some cases positively space age; they were products of the automotive age, built to dazzle drivers and, went the theory, attract them. At the Mirage, underwater swimmers could be seen through portholes on the street-front side of the pool; indeed, the hotel is better known as the **Glass Pool Inn**, which it was rechristened more than three decades after its 1952 opening. Nine years later, Paul Revere Williams' famous **La Concha Motel** drew immediate attention for its zinging, free-form concrete lobby, the design of which aped the form of a shell. At the turn of the 21st century, it still looked strangely futuristic.

The new Vegas, however, has upped the scale and the sophistication of its hotel-casinos, adding shops and amusements to create huge themed entertainment complexes that replicate the kind of walk-through fantasies popularised by Disney. The kaleidoscope of neon that was once the city's trademark has been dwarfed by themed resorts approximating all kinds of cities, countries and (the key word here) experiences. As a result, there's little left on the Strip from the 1950s and '60s: all five of the properties mentioned in the preceding pair of paragraphs have been destroyed in the name of progress, as the town unsentimentally cuts ties with its past. And while the architecture of old Vegas was about vivid abstraction, the city' is now hooked on replication.

ENTERTAINMENT ARCHITECTURE

The earliest gambling joints on what became the Strip had a Western flavour. The El Rancho and the **Last Frontier**, which opened a year later in 1942, took as their themes nostalgia for the Old West. Benjamin 'Bugsy' Siegel, who showed up via LA's Sunset Strip, helped create the **Flamingo** (*see p77*) in 1946, an LA Moderne-style tropical paradise. With variations, this style reigned throughout the glamorous, adults-only, post-war years. But when Jay Sarno built his instantly sensational, cheeky, pseudo-Roman Caesars Palace in 1966, and followed it two years later with the camp **Circus Circus** (*see p85*), the die was cast.

The stakes in the theming game escalated in the late 1980s with the work of Steve Wynn, without whom modern Vegas would look very different. In 1989, Wynn opened the city's first 'mega'-resort: the South Seas-themed **Mirage** (*see p68*), which melded the upmarket stylings of Siegel's Flamingo with the fantasy of Caesars and the mass appeal of Circus Circus. Wynn's Caribbean-inspired **Treasure Island** (*see p71*) followed next door in 1993; the same period saw Excalibur (1990), a riotous, candy-coloured Camelot, the agreeably preposterous **Luxor** (1993; *see p80*), and the ugly but enormous **MGM Grand** (1993; *see p80*), it was Wynn's duo that really reversed the downward spiral of Las Vegas during the early 1980s.

Casino bosses have since gone for even more extravagant design. Where once the properties were signed by fizzing neon, the theming is now so wild that the buildings themselves are the signs. The Egyptian-themed Luxor is, from street level, a vast black glass pyramid guarded by a squatting sphinx; the hotel, casino and sign are integrated into one structure, so the building itself *is* the sign. With a mini-Grand Central Station, a 150-foot (46-metre) Statue of Liberty and 12 jaunty, 1:3-scale skyscrapers mimicking the Manhattan skyline, **New York–New York** (*see p83*) represented theming at its most fully realised when it opened in 1997.

City of lights

Reliant on electric light, Las Vegas was a queen of the night for years. Among the town's old neon favourites are the **Flamingo**'s blitzkrieg of blinking and running colours (by Paul Rodriguez for Heath & Company, 1976), the **Stardust**'s classic beacon (Paul Miller for Ad-Art, 1967) and the explosion of neon wattage in Downtown's **Glitter Gulch**. However, it wasn't just on the Strip and Fremont Street that the city shone: motels, restaurants and convenience stores all gleefully adopted neon flourishes to draw business.

The city's oldest sign-making company is the Young Electric Sign Company (YESCO), whose most celebrated designers can be credited with elevating neon signage to an art form. They produced some of the city's best-loved images, including Fremont Street's **Vegas Vic** and **Vegas Vickie** (Charles Barnard; *see p14* **Viva Vegas Vic**), and **Lucky the Clown** (Dan Edwards, 1976) at Circus Circus. Today, some famous old neon signs, including the Hacienda's **Horse & Rider** (Brian Leming for YESCO, 1967) and the **Red Barn**'s neon Martini (*pictured*; YESCO, 1960) have been renovated and put on display along Fremont Street as part of the city's Neon Museum project (www.neonmuseum.org).

It's also here that you can get a look at old Vegas dressed in new clothes. In a bid to stop Downtown's deterioration, the city fathers and casino moguls together formed an unprecedented partnership during the 1990s to create the Fremont Street Experience. The Jerde Partnership's design involved covering four blocks with a high ceiling vault and pedestrianising it. The sound and light extravaganza that's shown on the roof of the vault hourly after dusk is architecture at its most kinetic.

Summerlin: the American Dream in a Stepford style. *See p29.*

Two years later, **Paris Las Vegas** (*see p69*) dropped a half-size replica of the Eiffel Tower on to the Strip. It looks tongue-in-cheek, and it is, but the attempts at authenticity are touching. While the tower is welded together rather than riveted, cosmetic rivets have been positioned in appropriate places; paint chips from the original also ensured that the colour was copied as closely as possible.

Paris Las Vegas is just one of several recent resorts that have taken their cues from across the Atlantic. For the casino moguls – and, arguably, for the middle Americans who make up the greater part of Vegas's custom – Europe

equals sophistication; it's no surprise that two of the Strip's most luxurious and expensive resorts have carefully European themes. The $1.4 billion **Bellagio** (*see p63*), an Italianate theme park for high-rolling grown-ups built by Wynn in 1998, is fronted by an eight-acre imitation of a Lake Como villa; inside, marble is conspicuous in both the lobbies and the guestrooms. Never mind that the basic trefoil tower structure is hardly innovative; there are imaginative moments within, among them the glass anemones by sculptor Dale Chihuly on the lobby ceiling, the extravagant conservatory and the dancing fountains on the lake.

The Sands, meanwhile, was replaced in 1999 by the **Venetian** (*see p73*), which links the Rialto bridge to the Doge's Palace and piazza San Marco in painstakingly luxurious fashion. The resort opened a pair of Guggenheim museums in 2001, both designed by Dutch architect Rem Koolhaas. The larger museum, located outside the casino and nicknamed 'the Big Box', was a paean to minimalist design – a vertical container-like space with a six-storey entrance. It failed after one exhibit, and is soon to become home to a production of *The Phantom of the Opera*. However, the smaller Guggenheim Hermitage (aka 'the Jewel Box') remains popular, showcasing everything from priceless Renoirs to radical Rosenquists.

Other design developments in Vegas's casinos have come with the expansion of its shopping scene from negligible to extensive. For this, we have to credit the **Forum Shops** (1993; *see p177*) at Caesars Palace: one of Las Vegas's most stunning themed environments, it set the trend that's since been emulated at Paris Las Vegas, the Venetian and the Desert Passage shops at Aladdin/Planet Hollywood. This cod-Roman shopping street, complete with trompe l'oeil sky and lighting that simulates the transition from dawn to dusk, showed casino owners that malls could be money-spinners, and also introduced convincing aged walls and styrofoam sculptures to a city that had previously been quite happy with cheerfully silly evocation. The mall's latest expansion in 2004 brought yet another only-in-Vegas innovation: spiral escalators.

AFTER DARK

Aiming for younger, more upscale and more urbane customers, the gaming kings of Las Vegas have hired some of the world's top architects and designers to create swanky new restaurants, nightclubs and lounges inside their casinos. It's here that you'll find some of the city's more exciting design touches. Not all are original, granted; some restaurants have been described as 'New York-style', while other nightclubs are keen to play up their European origins or their keenly retro fittings. But there's vibrancy here, not to mention excess.

The **Palms** resort (*see p92*), which opened in 2001, has been at the forefront of the movement towards a cooler kind of ostentation. Three of its venues deliver it in spades: **Rain in the Desert** (*see p243*), a nightclub and concert venue with a 1950s or '60s vibe (lounge, elevated dancefloor and – the Vegas touch – light fixtures that shoot fire); **Ghostbar** (*see 170*), whose similarly deliberate retro edge (albeit with lighter colours) would make Austin Powers feel at home; and the **N9ne** steakhouse (*see p155*), where coloured lights wash the ceiling.

Other casinos are also getting in on the act. The **V Bar** (*see p168*) at the Venetian set the trend for 1950s-influenced design, but its dramatic curved wall of glass, with frosted bands separating the bar from the casino, have helped it hold its own against sundry imitators.

Not every ode to modernity sits on the Strip. The award-winning **Sedona Bar & Grill** (9580 W Flamingo Road) is way out west near the Red Rock National Recreation Area, which inspired the name and the look. The restaurant effectively mixes materials and shapes to mimic the red cliffs in their natural setting providing a stark, colourful contrast to the arid desert. **Panevino Ristorante** (246 Via Antonio, near Sunset Road), has a kidney shape and a curving wall of glass that offers a great view of the Strip and the airport. Downtown, the **Ice House Lounge** (*see p171*) reflects a bit of art deco Miami in creating a cool oasis in the desert.

NON-RESORT ARCHITECTURE

Away from the hospitality industry, things are also changing. Construction in Las Vegas used to be utterly utilitarian, unadorned metal frame and concrete block tract houses and industrial buildings catering to a low-income community (wartime military personnel stationed at Nellis Air Force Base, workers servicing the casino industry, retirees). Even the housing for the wealthy, seen over walls and through fences, was boring. But there are more exceptions than ever: Lonnie Hammargren's self-made palace of *objets trouvés* (**4318 Ridgecrest Drive**, East Las Vegas); Luxor architect Veldon Simpson's cartoonish Frank Lloyd Wright-style house (**6824 Tomiyasu Lane**, East Las Vegas); and Siegfried and Roy's eccentric white mansion (**1639 Vegas Drive**, Northwest Las Vegas).

'There is little evidence of planning, just an ugly checkerboard of "leapfrog" development.'

Las Vegas has also made faltering steps towards creating a public domain. The city first drew attention to itself architecturally in the late 1980s with Charles Hunsberger's ambitious and controversial library-building programme, using architects who would make each of the nine libraries (also vital loci for the performing arts) adventurous and unique. The programme reflected an attempt to create, without precedent, a Las Vegas 'high' architecture style. Characterised by earthen forms, variegated concrete and sandy stone, pyramids, cones and dry desert landscaping, it can be seen as an effort to reflect and adapt to the harsh

Looking up

As a town of the 'wild' west, Las Vegas has always been spoiled by space. Much like LA, it's a horizontal city. When Fitzgeralds casino opened Downtown as the Sundance in 1980, it was, at 34 stories, the tallest building in the state; it's still, for now, the tallest in the neighbourhood. The oft-cited statistic that Vegas has a similar population to San Francisco over ten times the area means that, just two minutes west of Downtown, 1950s era homes luxuriate on plots of up to 1.5 acres. Such single-family housing is the mark of western post-war development.

The pattern showed signs of change in the early 1990s, when suburban Summerlin began to offer high-priced, high(er)-density housing. But even cramming ten homes on to a single acre hardly foretold what would happen once Summerlin brushed against the western foothills. And when the federal government began to slow the sale of increasingly scarce (and, thus, increasingly expensive) open land to developers, a new movement gained favour seemingly overnight: high- and mid-rise condos.

Starting in 1998 with the unforeseen success of the four pricey towers at Turnberry Place just east of the Strip, so-called vertical development has gone, so to speak, through the roof. In the middle of 2005, Las Vegas had no fewer than 30 high-rise condo projects at various stages of development from dream to reality, reaching across the valley and ranging from 12 to 73 stories. On top of these are seven additional 'condotels', such as Trump International on the Strip, and eight timeshare projects , almost all of which came online since 2003. Every week, it seems, another plan is unveiled, as developers rush to capitalise on the trend by building upwards rather than outwards. Most come with sleek, modern design plans and websites promising

'urban-style' living, seemingly intent on realising what has come to be called the Manhattanisation of Vegas.

Still, anyone who has observed this upward rush finds more style than substance: even those eager to live in such developments admit it's unlikely even half the announced projects will be built. In early 2005, only two of the condo developments – Turnberry and the similarly upscale Park Towers – were occupied, and only a handful of others had poured any concrete. Downtown, Soho Lofts seems well on its way, while Panorama Towers, west of I-15, has made progress. But beyond that, it's still mostly talk, raising concerns of what may happen as homes, businesses and people are displaced for towers that never materialise. In March 2005, the 45-storey Krystal Sands development on the Strip, the establishment of which entailed the destruction of the historic Algiers Motel, was pronounced dead before ground had even been broken on the freshly cleared site.

Furthermore, there are greater concerns for the towers that may indeed be built, for residential Las Vegas is not yet prepared for the pressures placed upon the infrastructure by such high-density projects. As projects come before city and county governments seeking approval, protests are increasingly raised about a lack of schools, police, fire, medical and other services, and the demands that hundreds of people per acre will bring. Still, with the enthusiastic encouragement of the mayor behind them, and the continued reliance on the economic belief that growth fuels growth, few projects are denied when it comes to government muster. Only time will tell how many meet Vegas's ultimate test, that of financial success for the developer, and how many end up as cleverly designed adverts and little else.

environment of the Mojave desert. The best examples of this trend are the **Sahara West Library & Las Vegas Arts Museum** (9600 W Sahara Avenue), **West Charleston Library** (6301 W Charleston Boulevard) and the **Summerlin Library & Performing Arts Center** (1771 Inner Circle Drive). These tendencies can be seen at their most extreme in the 1995 red sandstone **Clark County Government Center** (500 S Grand Central Parkway, Downtown Las Vegas) by CW Fentress, JH Bradburn & Associates.

Other lively buildings in the city include the tech-savvy **Lied Library** on the UNLV campus, an inspiring concrete, steel and glass structure with towering east windows and a massive, inviting lobby. The valley's newest library, Henderson's **Palo Verde** by Holmes-Sabatini, has a contemporary feel, using native stone and metal as its material palette, with angles that mirror the nearby mountain range. However, one of the most visible of the more recent buildings in Vegas is downtown's **Lloyd D George Federal Courthouse** (333 Las

Clark County Government Center.

However, in recent years there has been a movement to create liveable dwellings Downtown, as well as low-income housing (of which there is very little in fervently free-market Las Vegas). The best example is Tom Hom Group's **Campaige Place**, an apartment complex east of Las Vegas Boulevard and Fremont Street. Designed by San Diego architect Rob Wellington Quigley, the colourful, art deco-flavoured building is a stark contrast to the drab motels and casinos that surround it. Another growing trend is reinhabiting historic Downtown areas, especially the **John S Park** neighbourhood near Las Vegas Boulevard South and Charleston Boulevard. Many of the 160 homes here, built in the 1930s, '40s and early '50s, retain their old-school charm.

As well as simply 'gated' neighbourhoods (walled housing compounds), Las Vegas has gone one step further – as usual – with 'master-planned' communities, town-sized swathes of privately owned land on which a management company creates an entire society, complete with housing in several price brackets, business and commercial districts, retirement complexes, schools, parks and hospitals. Residents contract into the community's rules and – in theory – settle back to enjoy their suburban utopia.

The most carefully planned community in Vegas is **Summerlin** (*see p134*). With its abundance of parks, sports fields, tennis courts and trails – not to mention its proximity to Red Rock Canyon – outdoorsy urbanites are hard-pressed to find a better place to settle. But it is not for those who thrive on an independent lifestyle. You want to paint your house green? Forget it. Park a car in the side yard? No way. But people are queuing up to buy in to what has become the new American Dream. Similar planned communities include **Seven Hills** and **Anthem**, both located in Henderson, and **Aliante** in north Las Vegas.

Of all the structures in and around Las Vegas, there's one you absolutely can't miss. The quirk? It's not a building, not in Las Vegas and not designed by an architect. Conceived by engineer John Savage and built, as part of Roosevelt's public works programme, the monumental **Hoover Dam** (*see p260*) on the Colorado River is a marvel of human ingenuity. Utterly utilitarian, with art deco touches, it has grandeur and permanence missing from most buildings in Vegas, and completed in 1935, it's older than almost anywhere else in the city.

Vegas Boulevard South). Designed by Dwarsky & Associates of LA with a keen emphasis on security in the wake of the 1995 Oklahoma City bombing the plaza is raised above street level and the building itself has a blast-resistant wall of windows facing Las Vegas Boulevard.

Despite growing aspirations, these buildings are still only a few bright points in what largely remains an architectural desert. Non-resort Las Vegas is defined by endless subdivisions of one- and two-storey stucco-and-Spanish-tile tract houses and monotonous shopping centres, convenience stores and fast-food restaurants. There is little evidence of planning, just an ugly checkerboard of 'leapfrog' development spreading in all directions.

Being close to the centre of town is seen as undesirable in a city whose roads have not yet become permanently gridlocked. Affluent and middle-class families are moving out in droves to the edges of the valley into residential enclaves built around golf courses and artificial lakes, while on the Strip, high-rise condos such as **Turnberry Place** at the north end and **Park Towers** at the south appeal largely to jetsetters here for six weeks a year. More than 80 building plans for similar behemoths have been submitted. Among them is the blueprint for **The Summit**, a 73-storey, contemporary-looking skyscraper full of luxury condos – including 16 floors' worth of 'Sky Homes' for permanent residents – that will anchor the north end of the Strip at Sahara Avenue.

► For more on **hotels**, *see pp60-108*.
► For more on **nightclubs**, *see pp241-244*.
► For more on the **Forum Shops**, *see p177*.

Casino. *See p31.*

Celluloid Vegas

Does Hollywood see more than neon and organised crime?

Using Las Vegas as a backdrop for television and film productions is a risky manoeuvre, owing to the city's proclivity for upstaging nearly every actor who tries to stand in front of it. Vegas is part of a small troupe of cities – New York, London, Paris and Tokyo among them – that demands billing on the marquee. Its presence in the title usually guarantees a respectable box-office showing, as evidenced by the likes of *Honeymoon in Vegas* (1992), *Leaving Las Vegas* (1995) and *Fear and Loathing in Las Vegas* (1998).

The city's profile is as distinctive as any movie star. Practically everyone on this planet knows what Las Vegas looks like, and what kind of story to expect when a movie opens with an aerial shot of the Strip. Viewers won't allow themselves to be cheated by a movie that takes place in Vegas, but isn't really about Vegas: if they wanted to see something along those lines, they'd watch a movie about New York that was actually filmed in Vancouver.

It is perhaps because of Vegas's star quality that the city's grand mythos is slowly being whittled down to a handful of tried-and-tested visual clichés. The aforementioned aerial shot of the Strip opens every Vegas movie now, even the good ones (of which, more later). Lines of showgirls are pictured in mid-kick; slot machines disgorge fountains of coins; disembodied hands sweep cards off blackjack

tables. So often are the images recycled, in fact, that one wonders why directors don't simply pull the needed footage from other films and adjourn to Canada, saving both time and money.

BIRTH OF THE COOL

The answer, of course, is **Ocean's 11**. The 1960 Rat Pack classic almost single-handedly defined Vegas as metonymic of a particular cultural epoch. Frank Sinatra, Dean Martin, Sammy Davis Jr, Peter Lawford and Joey Bishop are practically golden as they hustle their way through a five-casino heist without breaking a sweat or getting a wrinkle in their single-breasted suits.

Such a fuss is made of *Ocean's 11* that few recall that great stretches of it are deadly dull. The behind-the-scenes stories of the making of the film – the five stars performing at the Sands in the early evening, then filming all through the night – are more interesting than *Ocean's 11* itself, and you can catch a glimpse of the mayhem in the film's final, terrific scene, as the cast walks under the Sands marquee that bears all their real names. The effect that the film had on every heist movie that followed – as well as, some might argue, the James Bond franchise – is indisputable, and it couldn't have been made in any other city. Las Vegas is the sixth member of the Rat Pack; its energy infuses every frame of film shot within its city limits. Making a Vegas movie without Vegas is like trying to make a Sinatra movie using Harry Connick Jr.

Ocean's 11 started a long and fruitful cinematic streak for Vegas. Some were vehicles for Vegas performers, like Elvis Presley's **Viva Las Vegas** (1963); others placed unlikely characters in the Vegas mix, such as country singer Ferlin Husky in **Las Vegas Hillbillys** (1966), Ralph Bakshi's animated characters in **Cool World** (1992), superior stage actor and David Mamet acolyte Willam H Macy in **The Cooler** (2003) and Sean Connery's ageing James Bond in **Diamonds Are Forever** (1971).

Diamonds, a lesser chapter of Connery's Bond tenure but one of the best Vegas films, played fast and loose with Howard Hughes (named 'Willard Whyte' for the film and played by American sausage-king Jimmy Dean; Hughes offered the Bond crew his full cooperation), nodded to Nevada's military and aerospace industries, and presented the town in a glamorous light that hasn't dimmed in the three decades since. The Tropicana looks elegant ('Quite comfortable', says Bond), the Riviera looks vibrant (most casino interiors were shot there) and Circus Circus looks as demented as it was written in Hunter S Thompson's *Fear and Loathing in Las Vegas*, which would – naturally – receive its own cinematic treatment years later.

POWER, CORRUPTION & LIES
Another defining Vegas film, Martin Scorsese's **Casino** (1995), was also shot at the Riviera and manages to perfectly evoke the same period in Vegas's history as both *Diamonds* and *Fear and Loathing*: the start of the 1970s, when organised crime was slowly being pushed out of Vegas and the city's fate was uncertain. Though it didn't legalise casino gambling until 1978, Atlantic City was considered a threat, and the prevailing mood in Vegas was one of desperation.

Casino captures that paranoia and builds on it. Based on a book by *Goodfellas'* author Nicholas Pileggi, it's a fictionalised account of the life of Frank 'Lefty' Rosenthal (Sam 'Ace' Rothstein in the film), one of the most colourful Vegas figures alleged to have been involved in organised crime. This renowned oddsmaker fought loudly with the Nevada Gaming Control Board, hosted a talk show from the Stardust to evade state regulations, and suffered a failed execution attempt. *Casino* tells all these stories and, unlike the clichéd mob politics of *The Cooler*, nearly every last bit of them really happened.

Even more remarkable than the stories is the long-term, real-life effect *Casino* had on Vegas's power structure. Rosenthal's attorney, a man who also represented Tony 'The Ant' Spilotro, Nick Civella and Meyer Lansky, was asked by

Scorsese to reprise his real-life role in Vegas's history for the film. The attorney, one Oscar Goodman, readily agreed; five years on, he became Mayor Oscar Goodman, which he remains to this day.

FLEETING GLIMPSES
Las Vegas has a superstar's role in *Casino*, but the city has also enjoyed its share of bit parts, enlivening many films with brief bursts of neon. The Julia Roberts/Brad Pitt comedy **The Mexican** (2001) only comes alive when Roberts and James Gandolfini goof about to 'The Safety Dance' in their hotel room at the Plaza, the lights of Fremont Street twinkling behind them. **3000 Miles to Graceland** (2001) suffers a similar fate: shortly after Kurt Russell and Kevin Costner rob the Riviera in full Elvis garb, the movie sinks like a brick greased with pomade.

Honey, I Blew Up the Kid (1992) pits a 112-foot-tall (34-metre)baby against a pre-Experience Fremont Street. The climactic plane crash of **Con Air** (1997) takes out the façade of the late, lamented Sands (right after it snaps the Hard Rock's guitar sign in half). Burt Bacharach serenades Elizabeth Hurley and Mike Myers aboard a double-decker bus on the Strip in **Austin Powers: International Man of Mystery** (1997), **Rush Hour 2** (2001) finds Jackie Chan and Chris Tucker escaping an exploding Desert Inn, **Midnight Run** (1988) reaches its taut climax at McCarran International Airport, and Vegas even serves as a plot element in **The Godfather** (1971) and its sequels.

'If *Ocean's 11* is Vegas in a sharp suit, *Showgirls* is the town in a filthy raincoat.'

Often the Vegas movies we most enjoy aren't exactly great films. Doug Liman's **Go** (1999) is admittedly quite good, but it takes a silly turn when the action shifts to Vegas. A pair of 'weekend warriors', played by Desmond Askew and Taye Diggs, gets into ludicrous situations involving amorous bridesmaids, would-be mobsters and stolen sports cars. It's fun, but so stupid that there's little wonder many of the locations used were disguised (save the Riviera, which apparently doesn't care how it's perceived as long as the casino floor looks busy).

Tim Burton's **Mars Attacks!** (1996) treated Vegas as a shooting gallery, in both literal and narrative senses. Burton got some spectacular footage, including a chase through the Young Electric Sign Company's Neon Graveyard and the real-life destruction of the saucer-topped Landmark Hotel, with his Martians pretty much levelling the town, and most of Nevada with it, over the course of the film. It was mostly in good fun, although having Lake Mead stand in for a post-attack Lake Tahoe, with little cosmetic change to the former's shoreline, angered some Las Vegans.

Honeymoon in Vegas (1992), while only mildly funny, did give two boons to Vegas. One was Nicolas Cage, future star of **Leaving Las Vegas** (1995), in an Elvis costume, a match made in hillbilly heaven. The second was the Flying Elvis troupe, which performs a heroic parachute drop in front of Bally's at the end of the film. The troupe didn't exist when the movie was released; only later did Las Vegas producer Dick Feeney form an Elvis skydiving group, using costumes left over from a production show, to capitalise on the film's popularity.

Filmed at the nearby Lake Las Vegas resort, **America's Sweethearts** (2001) harks back to the golden age of the screwball comedy, the basic form of which was placing a man and two women in a confined area and showing the man's loyalties slowly shifting from one woman to the other. John Cusack traded Catherine Zeta-Jones for Julia Roberts, while a German shepherd dog molested Billy Crystal, and Christopher Walken evoked a tap-dancing Stanley Kubrick, and yet somehow the film wasn't any good. Go figure.

That brings us to Las Vegas's most famous cinematic wipeout, Paul Verhoeven's deathless **Showgirls** (1995). Cheetah's Topless Lounge,

one of the city's most popular strip clubs, achieved lifelong notoriety by allowing Verhoeven's gross misrepresentation of Vegas strip joints to be filmed in it (exteriors were shot here, interiors at the club's San Diego location). The movie is the anti-*Ocean's 11*; if the Sinatra film is Las Vegas in a sharp suit, *Showgirls* is the city in a filthy raincoat. That said, even the Vegas of *Showgirls* has a strange cinematic appeal: the film has developed a *Rocky Horror*-esque cult following, and new viewers are discovering the film in droves.

Showgirls may distort every fact with which it comes into contact – the film even places the club in front of the Stardust, when it's really off-Strip and blocks away – but at least it was shot in Las Vegas. A fair number of 'Vegas's films weren't shot in town at all. The aforementioned *Leaving Las Vegas* was filmed in Laughlin. The sets of **Bugsy** (1991) were built in California's Mojave Desert. Francis Ford Coppola's **One From the Heart** (1982), although set entirely in Vegas, was shot on a wildly expensive sound-stage replica in Hollywood. And Kevin Spacey's film biography of Bobby Darin, **Beyond the Sea** (2004), was shot largely in Europe, although Spacey did perform live (as Darin) at the Stardust for the film's Vegas debut.

Vegas suffers a similar disconnect on the small screen. The popular television drama **CSI: Crime Scene Investigation** (from 2000)

Quote, unquote

'You guys are pros. The best. I'm sure you can make it out of the casino. Of course, lest we forget, once you're out the front door, you're still in the middle of the fuckin' desert.'
Reuben Tishkoff (Elliott Gould) points out a flaw in the escape plan in *Ocean's Eleven*

'Trent, the beautiful babies don't work the midnight-to-six shift on a Wednesday. This is the skank shift.'
Mike Peters (Jon Favreau) fails to appreciate the late early-hours dealers in *Swingers*

'Who are these people, these faces? Where did they come from? They look like caricatures of used-car dealers from Dallas, and, sweet Jesus, there are a hell of a lot of them at 4.30 on a Sunday morning still humping the American dream.'
Raoul Duke (Johnny Depp) comes out the other end of a long Saturday night in *Fear and Loathing in Las Vegas*

'Running a casino is like robbing a bank with no cops around. For guys like me, Las Vegas washes away your sins. It's like a morality car wash.'
Sam 'Ace' Rothstein (Robert De Niro) comes clean in *Casino*

'What, you mean that Disneyland mookfest out there? Huh? C'mon, you know what that is? That's a fuckin' violation… Something that used to be beautiful, used to have class, like a gorgeous high-priced hooker with an exclusive clientele. Then along came that Steve Wynn cocksucker and knocks her up and puts her in the fuckin' family way. Now she's nothing but a cheap fat whore hiding behind too much fuckin' make-up.'
Shelly Kaplow (Alec Baldwin) waxes less than lyrical about the Strip in *The Cooler*

'First prize is a cheque for a million dollars. Does it have your name on it?'
Mike McDermott (Matt Damon) on his way to the World Series of Poker in *Rounders*

What's the betting he's found some crucial evidence? **CSI: Crime Scene Investigation**.

is mostly filmed in Hollywood studios, with an occasional exterior shot of the Strip dropped in to give the proceedings verisimilitude. The less-popular shows spawned in *CSI*'s wake, such as the plainly named **Las Vegas** (from 2003), may show more of the real town, but only fleetingly and without admiration. In the world of television, Vegas is just another place to work, whether your profession is solving crimes, playing tournament poker or folding towels. No one is trying to embrace Vegas's myth or really beat the house.

YOU'RE THE TOPS

The three best Las Vegas movies of recent years feature characters who are pursuing, each in his own way, the Rat Pack's libertine ideal. Doug Liman's breakthrough hit, **Swingers** (1996), almost single-handedly revived swing music and Vegas culture. While only the first segment of the picture takes place in the town, the attitude of Sin City colours the entire movie, with stars Vince Vaughn and Jon Favreau sipping Martinis and jiving *à la* Dean Martin. Even people who haven't seen the movie have been known to utter its rallying cry: 'Vegas, baby. Vegas!'

Terry Gilliam's funny, fever-dream interpretation of Hunter S Thompson's **Fear and Loathing in Las Vegas** (1998) has its own kind of swing, the kind one gets after chasing Elvis-sized fistfuls of painkillers with a swig of rum. As journalist Raoul Duke and Samoan attorney Dr Gonzo, Johnny Depp and Benicio Del Toro rip Vegas to shreds, pumping the town full of enough hallucinogenic drugs

to make it seem like rock 'n' roll itself: bright, loud and probably bad for your health if taken in excess.

Steven Soderbergh's 2001 remake of **Ocean's Eleven** (he elected to spell out the number to differentiate his picture from the original) has a kicking David Holmes soundtrack and gave Elvis Presley one last US hit in 'A Little Less Conversation', but its real music is in its settings, dialogue and style. Taking the Vegas heist and one character name from the original, Soderbergh recreated *Ocean's Eleven* as one of the best heist films you'll ever see.

Why? Well, for one thing, Soderbergh opens with the best ever aerial shots of Vegas, the last of which dives into the Bellagio's fountains. He filmed the city as a rich, colourful playground (Soderbergh is his own Director of Photography) begging to be picked clean by classy thieves. Even the unbelievable aspects of Las Vegas living – hotel implosions, the terrifyingly institutional aspect of casino backrooms, even those 'escort' flyers – are treated matter-of-factly and used to great effect.

But the best part of *Ocean's Eleven* is the one few fans outside of Vegas truly appreciate: for the first time, Las Vegas looks as beautiful and untouchable as it did in the Rat Pack original. The last few minutes of the film, a dialogue-free sequence set against the Bellagio's fountains to the lilting strains of Claude Debussy's 'Clair de lune', express the romance that Las Vegas effuses on its best days. You truly believe that somehow you could win your way into the kind of life you've seen in the movies.

The Riviera's **Crazy Girls**.

Sex & the City

Greed or lust: which is Las Vegas's deadlier sin?

The cat-and-mouse game is the same from San Diego to Southampton: a tussle of sex and sexuality, of tease and temptation, of offer and negotiation. Here in Las Vegas, though, the game is played out all day, every day, on a hyper-real playing field, a modern arena in which the unreal appears real and the real positively surreal. The whole playboy image is magnified by the expectations created by a sexual mythos that the city can neither live down nor live up to. While the San Fernando Valley's porn industry might beg to disagree, and while both San Francisco and New York City have their arguments, it's no exaggeration to say that Las Vegas is the sexual capital of the United States.

Though it's had a similar reputation for perhaps 50 years, the truth is that the city hasn't consistently lived up to it. In the 1960s, Las Vegas developed its burgeoning infamy as a sexy playground for adults, a place where made men escaped to smoke, swear and swagger up and down the Strip, pulling willing dolls into their arms as they strode from crap game to whisky bar. Anything went, or so the town's reputation suggested.

But by the late 1970s, the city seemed merely to be riding the last desert wind of a long since played-out glamour; during the '80s, the wind dropped to a barely discernible breeze. Watered-down, polyester-clad shadows of the Rat Pack clung desperately to the town's waning image. The bizarre postmodern Vegas of Hunter S Thompson had vanished, the city having declined into a poor caricature of a caricature. The most blatant sign of decline was appropriately sexual. Where ballgown-clad sophisticates once tipped winks to tuxedoed gentlemen over desert-dry Martinis, now streetwalking prostitutes prowled the Strip directly in front of the entrances to the casinos, brazen in both appearance and solicitation (while prostitution is famously legal in most of the state of Nevada, it's still a criminal offence within Clark County, in which the city of Las Vegas sits). Sex, so long the high-grade oil that drove the city's engine, was now the exhaust choking its dazzling core.

Meanwhile, the rest of the United States, always deeply suspicious of libertine Las Vegas, moved relentlessly into the stoic conservatism of the Reagan-Thatcher era.

No longer a small, isolated speakeasy, Vegas reluctantly found itself a growing modern city that, through an aggressive programme to bolster its convention trade, was catering more and more to Ronald Reagan's middle America. The smell of money never far from its nose, it could tolerate the Sin City image no more.

Following the lead of the nation – and a pair of politically motivated activist sheriffs, John McCarthy and John Moran Sr – Las Vegas cleaned up its act. McCarthy vowed to rid the town – again – of its Mob influence; Moran's main legacy is that he cleared the Strip of prostitutes (well, the most visible ones, anyway). Streetwalkers were swept away in well-publicised vice-squad activity as the city moved to rid itself of the image that had persisted since its founding. After all, what Midwestern wife would feel comfortable sending her conventioneering husband to spend a week working in the nation's moral cesspool?

COMING OUT

Most say the birth of modern Las Vegas began with the 1989 opening of Steve Wynn's Mirage, which launched a decade of new resort construction like the city had never seen. Old casinos were imploded and new themed resorts built in their stead, a process that can be likened to a spiritual reconstruction: rid the town of the old, Mob-controlled dens of sex and sin, and build – certainly not erect – a family-friendly collection of fantastical resorts loaded with attractions, theme parks and stage shows that made the Tropicana's tame-but-topless *Folies Bergere* look like *Deep Throat* in comparison.

'Many families evidently moved to the suburbs not realising that Las Vegas was just around the corner.'

The timing couldn't have been worse. Just as Las Vegas, much to the chagrin of the city's old timers, began to tout itself as sin-free and family-friendly, a romanticised vision of Sin City's lost excess began to capture the attention of young adults of just the right age to start visiting Las Vegas. The last thing this so-called 'new Rat Pack' wanted was Sin City stripped of all its sin.

Even more challenging was the fact that, despite an overlay of theme parks and adverts showing families enjoying themselves, this was still, in a nutshell, *Las Vegas*, and there can be never truthfully be any such thing as a 'wholesome' casino operation. Regardless of how elaborate the theming or how corporate the boardrooms, at the centre of Las Vegas resides

the greed-driven core of gambling and the riches it promises. Riches that, for the consumer who arrives in search of them, suggest unlimited access to all of the seven deadly sins, lust chief among them.

Sensing a shift in the morality of those visiting, and thus leading the charge back towards Sin City, the Hard Rock hotel and casino opened in 1995, directly courting that new Rat Pack: young, restless, monied and ready to play out the 24 hours of sex, sin and sun experienced by their grandparents but merely promised to their parents. The hotel was located away from the Strip – on, perhaps appropriately, Paradise Road – but its influence was immediate. In the early 1990s, resorts had been built with family-friendly themes, most notably the Excalibur and Treasure Island. But a new soon sophistication took over: the Venetian, the Bellagio and Mandalay Bay each packed their properties with lavish rooms, pricey restaurants, booming nightclubs, expensive boutiques and massive casinos. By the end of the 1990s, Las Vegas was openingly hawking every glorious excess possible, with the notable exception of sex.

And yet, everywhere one looked, there it was. It was on the dancefloors at the lavish nightclubs, where barely dressed punters, from spring breakers to swinging parents on a weekend away, were bumping and grinding like strippers in a lap dance contest. It was in the private dining rooms of celebrity-chef restaurants, from where sprang colourful rumours of high-profile guests taking the notion of afters a bit too far. And, most notably, it was on the backs of nearly every taxicab in town, where the just-off-the-Strip strip clubs boldly touted their greatest assets. The town may not have been selling sex, but its visitors were buying regardless.

OSCAR WINNER

Perhaps the single greatest signpost of the shift in Las Vegas's approach to sex was the landslide 1999 election of controversial former attorney Oscar Goodman (*see p128*) to the post of city mayor. While it's certainly true that the flashy phantasmagoria of the Strip, which is what most of what the world sees as Las Vegas, is not actually under his jurisdiction (it's administered by Clark County, not by the City of Las Vegas), the outspoken mayor has nevertheless asserted symbolic ownership of the entire Las Vegas valley, acting as a cheerleader to the hordes of visitors who again see Vegas as an adult playground.

Since being elected, Goodman has taken a pragmatic approach to the city's sinful image. When, in 2002, Clark County officials, apparently stunned by the lap dancing seen in undercover videos, adopted more restrictive ordinances covering dancers' behaviour, Goodman proclaimed that city-zoned clubs wouldn't be forced into any similar changes in rules. Along with courting businesses and national sports teams, as well as spearheading the revitalisation of Downtown, the gin-loving Goodman has also suggested – however briefly and off the cuff – the legalisation of prostitution and the creation of a 'Little Amsterdam' district of clubs and bars. Casino executives were quick to voice their disapproval.

Under Goodman's eager watch, the selling of sexuality is once again back in vogue. Just away from the Strip, some of the world's most elaborate strip clubs have been built in the past five years, swanky palaces that, despite their immense size, are filled to capacity every weekend and then some. Nor are these clubs shy about advertising themselves: witness the huge billboards that line Industrial Road. Back amid the neon and the glitz, Cirque du Soleil has been coaxed, perhaps by nothing more than the opportunity, to create *Zumanity*, an adult-themed circus of sexuality that plays

on the Strip alongside their other, more family-friendly shows. And casinos have edged ever closer to allowable limits, not only with the increased sexualisation of their nightclubs and with the introduction of ever naughtier showroom cabarets such as *La Femme* and *Bite*, but by taking burlesque – from bawdy to boring – right on site, at Forty Deuce, the Pussycat Dolls Lounge and others.

SEX SELLS

All this is entirely legitimate, but not all of Vegas's sex industry is quite so above board. Prostitution remains illegal in Clark County, but there's little doubt what all those flyers, cards and free papers thrust in the faces of visitors are truly soliciting, and it's not always just dancers direct to your room (*see below* **Rooms for manoeuvres**). Dancers at a couple of high-profile strip clubs have been busted in recent years for solicitation. Furthermore, while streetwalking has all but disappeared in the tourist sectors, the hookers have simply gone upmarket. The bartenders at more or less every major resort on the Strip can spot the working girls immediately.

Rooms for manoeuvres

From the ads atop taxicabs to the messages on the backs of the yellow jackets worn by greasy little men handing out flyers along Las Vegas Boulevard, there is an omnipresent aura of naughtiness about Las Vegas that haunts horny tourists like the ghosty siren song of a sexually fuelled ice-cream truck. The line between what's legal and illegal in Las Vegas is fairly clear, but that doesn't stop firms or individuals bending, twisting and sometimes just plain erasing it. While prostitution is illegal within Las Vegas, those ads you'll see all over town touting the services of 'entertainers', 'escorts', 'massage therapists' and other assorted code words are – make no mistake about it – selling sex.

Still, the businesses, wise to the letter of the law and to the potentially ruinous results if they cross it, are very good at maintaining the illusion of decency. The companies who offer Strip pedestrians 'dancers delivered to your room' are always keen to stress the legal limits when pressed, careful to avoid being pinned with pandering charges should anything… well, *unexpected* happen between the dancer and her client. Massage parlours are similarly cautious. And the town's strip clubs, terrified of losing their liquor licenses

(which essentially double as licenses to print money), have set extraordinary systems in place to guard against their employees soliciting customers. Though owners disguise them cleverly, there are cameras everywhere. You're never alone in a Vegas strip joint.

Couple the illegality of prostitution in Las Vegas with the high demand for it, and it becomes obvious that there's money to be made here. It's widely suspected, not least by the local vice squad (who rarely get involved), that a few of the aforementioned 'dancers delivered to your room' are delivering more than just a dance, but it's impossible to know how many, how often and for how much money. Which is, of course, the point. If they go further than advertised, the customer's not going to complain, but if they don't, and the customer finds himself stung for $500 or even $1,000, what's he going to do. Call the police? Phone the local consumer affairs office? At least, say the local tourist board ads, 'what happens here, stays here'. His lips duly sealed, it's straight down to the blackjack table to try and earn it all back. And so it goes that Las Vegas's shady prostitution industry remains, as a 2004 *Las Vegas Weekly* cover story called it, the town's 'dirty little secret'.

But there's been trouble amid the temptations. It's certainly a long way from Sheriff John McCarthy to Mayor Oscar Goodman, and in the intervening years, the local population of Las Vegas has exploded, much of it spreading out to the pancake-flat suburbs. Literally millions have moved to Las Vegas in the past two decades, most of them settling further and further away from its spiritual heart and thus shifting its moral heart as well. Goodman was easily reelected in 2003, but many postulate that it happened courtesy of a dying breed, longtime Las Vegans who either remember – or, in the case of the younger generation, pine for – the so-called good old days.

Many families evidently moved to the shiny, happy suburbs not realising that Las Vegas was just around the corner. Bewildered soccer moms have, in recent years, voiced concerns about sexually oriented businesses, suggestive billboards, and the promotion of the city using sex, increasingly stunned by the blatant nature of it all. Just look at the nightclub ads in *Las Vegas Weekly*, some of which could double as porn stills.

The local authorities, fearful of a backlash from voters, have been quick to react to the suburban outrage. Adult businesses have once again been targets of what many say are politically motivated crackdowns, while others have suffered federal investigations into political payoffs, corruption and persistent Mob ties. Even the Nevada Gaming Commission, which oversees the issue of lucrative casino licenses, has made its presence felt. In 2003 and 2004, the commission worked hard to punish the Hard Rock for a series of advertisements that provocatively put to paper the very same myths that are simultaneously being sold by the Las Vegas Convention & Visitors Authority in its notorious 'What happens here, stays here' advertising campaign. It seems that old Vegas lives on after all, as new Vegas tries desperately to reconcile the two.

What happens here may or may not stay here. But when you get right down to it, what's happening – increasingly open depiction and advertisement of sex, increasingly virulent reaction against it from middle-class families – is not much different from what's happening elsewhere in the US. Las Vegas simply provides a more atmospheric and encouraging setting for it. Certainly, while the country as a whole shows signs of a starting to follow a socially conservative agenda, you can bet the casino executives are watching closely. Nothing drives 21st-century Las Vegas harder than the pursuit of the tourist dollar, and if the tourists suddenly finds themselves turned off by adult-themed shows and nightclubs that fall a nick short of promising them a lucky night, they'll be gone just as quickly as they arrived.

▶ For more on **the local sex industry**, *see pp208-211*.

Gambling

How to make a fortune… or how to avoid losing one.

The old and often-told joke runs that no one ever got rich through gambling in Las Vegas except the owners of the casinos. For many people, it's a gag that's a lot funnier at the start of their trip than it is at the end. Gambling built Las Vegas, and the fact that the city is still expanding at record speed is proof enough that the novelty of this pastime is a long way from wearing off.

Sorry to shatter your dreams, then, but if you're hoping to walk away from Las Vegas set up for life, you'd best not let those hopes get too high. However, if all you're after is a little fun – the smart move is to file your gambling budget under 'entertainment', and prepare to chalk up reasonable losses but have a good time doing it – then you're definitely in the right place. And you'll probably have more fun if you know a little about the games you're playing. While these are not complicated games (though craps can take a bit of acclimatisation), a little knowledge will help your money last longer than it otherwise might. Indeed, play your cards right and you may even end up ahead. But don't bet on it.

HOW CASINOS MAKE MONEY

Before learning how to play the games, get acquainted with the casinos' angles on them. There are four ways for the casinos to generate gaming revenue: the *house edge*, favourable rules, commissions and dumb players.

● The *house edge* is the difference between the *true odds* of an event occurring and the odds used for payouts. For example, in double-zero roulette, there are 38 possible winning numbers. If the casino paid *true odds*, it would pay off a winning number at 37:1 (for a total of $38, including your $1 bet). Instead, the casino pays off a winning number at 35:1.

To calculate the *house edge*, imagine placing a $1 bet on every spot in double-zero roulette, a total wager of $38. Whichever number wins, you'll be given $36 ($35 plus your $1 bet). That's $2 less than the *true odds* payout; the two bucks went directly into the house's pocket. If you then divide the money kept by the house by the total it would have paid on *true odds*, in this case two divided by 38, you arrive at a *house edge* of 5.26 per cent, which means that the house expects to keep 5.26¢ of each dollar bet at roulette.

The *house edge* varies from game to game, and within each game. Casinos love it when gamblers keep playing for hour after hour, because the *house edge* grinds its little takeout from every dollar wagered.

● The rules for casino games are structured to favour the house. The best example is blackjack, where the dealer gets to play his hand last. Should a player *bust* beforehand, the dealer wins by default. Even if the dealer ends up *busting* later, the player loses and the house wins.

● Commissions are collected by the house in a few table games. In poker, the house serves as dealer, but doesn't play a hand. So to make money, the house takes a percentage of every pot, called the 'rake', or charges players a flat fee of $5 to $7 per half-hour of play. In baccarat, the house takes five per cent of all winnings from bank bets.

● Be they drunk, superstitious, careless or ill-informed, dumb gamblers are a boundless source of funds. Why else would casinos offer gamblers free drinks? Alcohol is not only wonderful for loosening inhibitions, such as the inhibition against losing next month's rent, but it also causes sensible players to make stupid mistakes. An example: although the *house edge* in blackjack has been calculated at around only two per cent, casinos expect a win (or 'hold') of 15 to 20 per cent of the total amount of money brought to the table (the *drop*), such is the general incompetence of the players.

BETTING LIMITS AND MINIMUMS

At every table game, there's a sign detailing the minimum (and often maximum) allowable bet. At blackjack, it might be $5 to $500. Casinos expect players to bet towards the low end of the limit. This separates players by class, so a big player seeking a speedy $500-a-hand game doesn't have to endure poky play from a piker betting five bucks a hand. *High rollers* can bet at higher-than-posted limits if the house is willing to 'fade' (cover) them. In roulette, the minimum means the sum total of all bets you place in one round. Hence, if the table has a $5 minimum, five $1 bets satisfies it. But in blackjack, if you play two hands at once, you must bet the minimum on each.

ETIQUETTE

Before you lay your money down, note the minimum-bet requirement, usually posted on a sign in the far left corner. If you don't want to embarrass yourself, don't toss out a red ($5) *chip* on a $100-minimum table. Likewise, don't put a quarter into a dollar slot or video poker machine; the coin will pass through the thing and clank into the hopper, alerting the other players that you're a novice.

Table games have strict rules about when players can touch *chips* or cards, rules that exist to discourage cheats. Many blackjack games are dealt face up and players never touch the cards. And once you make a bet, never touch the *chips* you've laid down (if you're 'splitting' or doubling down in blackjack, push out a new pile of *chips* but don't touch the original ones). This rule is to discourage 'past posting', a scam by which cheats sneak more *chips* on to their bet after peeking at their cards.

You should only handle dice with one hand. Everyone, from the players to the dealers and the bosses, will get very nervous if you touch them with two hands, or make a fist around them with one hand so they can't be seen. Blow on them, shake them and turn them so your favourite numbers are up, but don't hide them for a second. That's how dice cheats use sleight of hand to get loaded dice into a game of craps.

These are just a couple of examples. It's best if you stand back and watch the action initially; after a few minutes, you'll have the hang of the procedures. If you need to be corrected, the dealer will do so gently and unobtrusively. And don't worry. The other players at the tables have all been corrected at one time or another. They didn't step up to a crap table for the first time knowing everything about the game.

You must be 21 to gamble. If you're under 21 and start winning (or hit a jackpot that requires you to sign tax forms), not only will your *chips* or jackpot be confiscated, you'll be tossed out of the casino faster than you can say, 'But…'. You may even be turned over to a Gaming Control Board agent. The lower your age and the higher your bet, the bigger the trouble.

Most casinos subscribe to the old tradition that cameras are unwelcome. Generally, it's better to leave your SLRs and videocams in your room, car or backpack, but as long as you're discreet or ask permission, you can sometimes get away with taking photographs in casinos (particularly at the Excalibur and Harrah's). On the other hand, wherever you go in a casino (except the toilets), you'll be watched by *eye in the sky* cameras and taped by video. Nowhere on earth is Big Brother busier than in a casino; make sure you behave accordingly.

MONEY, MONEY, MONEY

To play table games, you'll need *chips*, though you can usually throw down a bill for your first plays (rules vary). In blackjack, cash can play, though any winnings will be paid as *chips*. You

---

▶ All terms in *italics* throughout this chapter are defined in **The gambler's lexicon**, for which *see p42*.

There's a poker player inside everyone.

Let yours out.

vc poker.com

Victor Chandler

can buy *chips* at the table in a process called a *buy in*; you can also buy *chips* at the *cage*. *Chips* can only be redeemed at the *cage*.

Chips are like currency in the casino from which they're issued, but due to counterfeiting and other problems, casinos rarely honour each others' *chips* for gambling (unless, as is the case with the MGM-operated Mirage and TI, they're under the same ownership). It's sometimes possible to exchange sub-$100 denominations from other casinos for house *chips* at the *cage*.

Most modern slot and video poker machines have bill acceptors that change greenbacks into credits. If you don't want to use the bill acceptor, or if you have a bill that's larger than is accepted by the machine, press the 'Change' button on the machine. This activates a light on top, which summons a roving change person. The larger casinos are converting to cashless machines (also known as 'ticket in/ticket out', or TITO). You play by putting a regular bill in the slot, but when you're ready to cash out, the machine prints a ticket that lists your credits, which is redeemable at the *cage* (though you can insert the ticket in another machine's bill acceptor for credits). Be very careful with the tickets; they're easier to lose than money. Be sure to redeem them before leaving the casino: some expire in 30 days. Also, don't leave a TITO machine for even a moment: someone will almost certainly press the Cash Out button, grab the ticket and run.

LEARNING TO GAMBLE

If you want to study before arriving, you'll find hundreds of books on everything from baccarat to video poker. For recommendations, *see p303*, though you're generally safe with anything published by Huntington Press. Numerous software programs have been developed over the past decade to teach you how to play most games, from blackjack to craps, roulette to slots. For catalogues, try the **Gamblers Book Club** (*see p183*), the **Gamblers General Store** (*see p196*) and **Huntington Press** (3687 S Procyon Avenue, Las Vegas, NV 89103, 1-800 244 2224, www.huntingtonpress.com).

Almost all the large casinos offer free hands-on lessons for most table games, taught by personable, informative and experienced instructors. They take you step by step through the playing procedures and etiquette, but don't expect them to warn you about sucker games and bets: after all, they're paid by the casino. Lessons are usually held in the late morning, when the casino is least busy, and some are followed by open low-minimum 'live' games for people who want to celebrate their new-found skills under casino conditions.

When you're ready to join a game, stand back, watch the action for a while and pick up the game's rhythms and routines (don't stand too long behind blackjack tables before you sit down, though; most bosses will suspect you of 'back counting' the deck in order to slip

Sucker bets

Just when you think you know the rules, Las Vegas changes the games. Take blackjack, for example. Many gamblers know that a blackjack game dealt from a single deck offers savvy players the best chance to win. Now, however, many casinos have made a seemingly minor change to the single-deck rules hoping players don't notice that it's no longer the best version of 21, but quite easily the worst.

A few years ago, single-deck blackjack was only available in the high-roller salons, with most of the low-limit games dealt from four or even six decks. In the last few years, however, single-deck tables have become more common than fake breasts at Mandalay Bay. This should be good news for gamblers. However, in the process, the payoff for *natural* 21s has been lowered in many casinos from 3:2 to 6:5; in other words, hitting a blackjack on a $10 bet will win you only $12 where it used to net $15. Doesn't sound much

of a difference? Think again. The rule change is so bad that the casino's profit is several times higher than at the city's worst six-deck shoe game, and up to eight times more than at a regular single-deck game.

Keen-eyed Europeans will also notice that the odds have been shifted out of their favour on the roulette wheel. In many European casinos, the wheel has only a single green '0'. However, in the US, there's also a double zero ('00') on the wheel; that one little extra green spot tips the *house edge* from 2.7 per cent to 5.26 per cent. Check before you play.

Finally, avoid almost anything called a 'side bet', extra betting opportunities beyond the basic wager at table games. They include jackpots for making certain hands at Let it Ride and three-card poker, or being dealt your first two cards of the same suit at blackjack. Don't waste your money: the casinos aren't charities, so there's no reason to give until it hurts.

The gambler's lexicon

ante a small bet that players must place into the *pot* before a hand of poker is dealt.

bankroll your total gambling budget.

Black Book a list, kept by the State Gaming Control Board, of people legally barred from casinos due to a history of cheating or a connection to organised crime.

boxman casino executive who acts as the umpire in a game of craps.

bust a blackjack hand exceeding 21.

buy in exchange cash for casino *chips*.

cage the cashier, where *chips* and tokens are converted into cash and credit is established.

carousel a group of slots that are often connected to a joint *progressive jackpot*.

change colour swapping *chips* for ones of a higher or lower denomination.

checks another word for *chips*.

chips tokens issued by casinos and used, instead of cash, for table games.

colour up exchange small denomination *chips* for larger denomination *chips* before leaving a table game.

comps 'complimentaries', anything from free cocktails to 'RFB' (room, food and beverage). Their value is calculated by the gambler's average bet, multiplied by the time spent playing, multiplied by the *house edge*. To qualify, you must be a *rated player* or belong to a *slot club*.

credit line amount of credit a gambler is allowed.

croupier casino employee who controls the action in games of baccarat and roulette.

drop total funds, including *chips*, cash and *markers*, brought to the gaming table.

European wheel a roulette wheel with a single '0' position, which gives players better odds. Most wheels in Vegas have '0' and '00'.

even money a bet that pays back an amount equal to the bet itself. In other words, if you win on a $5 bet, you receive back your $5 stake plus a $5 win.

eye in the sky the casino's in-house surveillance system.

face cards jacks, queens and kings.

funbook a magazine of vouchers (meal deals and the like) or match-play coupons (only valid in conjunction with hard cash).

George dealer-speak for a good tipper.

grind joint a casino with low table minimums and low-denomination slot machines.

high roller big-money gambler who bets a minimum of $100 per hand on a table game, and plays $5 slots.

hit in blackjack, to take another card.

hole card blackjack dealer's face-down card.

house advantage see *house edge*.

house edge the percentage difference (retained by the casino) between the true odds and the actual payout.

inside bet in roulette, betting on a single number or small combination of numbers.

juice power and influence; who you know.

layout diagram on the playing table that marks the area of the game.

loose used to describe a slot machine that pays out frequently. Casinos compete in claiming that their slots are the loosest.

low roller gambler who bets at low-minimum slot machines, usually in *grind joints*.

marker IOU signed by a rated player to obtain *chips* and paid off with *chips* or cash.

---

in a bet at the most advantageous time). Choose a table with the lowest minimum possible, so you're not risking $100, $25 or even $10 a hand at a game you're playing for the first time. Note that the locals' and Downtown casinos tend to have lower minimums than those on the Strip.

MAKING THE MOST OF IT

There are lots of ways to get the most of your money, many of them set up by casinos in an attempt to draw customers. Popular among them are the casino's *slot clubs* (*see p55*): they cost nothing to join, and the points you accrue can be redeemed for rooms, food and even cash.

Other freebies are slightly more obscure, but still very accessible. Always ask for *comps* when you play table games. As soon as you

make a bet, call over a floorman and ask: 'How long do I have to play to get a buffet *comp*?' He or she will look at your bet and tell you. Play for as long as he or she indicates, then collect your free buffet. And look for coupons in *funbooks*, free magazines handed out by hawkers in front of the casinos. Two-for-one, three-for-two and seven-for-five coupons on even-money bets give you a huge edge over the house at blackjack, craps and the like.

While the casinos can help you make your money last, you can also help yourself. Play slow, for one thing: you're better off exposing your *bankroll* to the *house edge* for 50 hands an hour at a busy table than 100 hands an hour playing one-on-one against the dealer, or pulling the handle on a slot machine for 400

natural in blackjack, a two-card hand totalling 21; in baccarat, a two-card total of eight or nine.

outside bet in roulette, betting outside the single-number layout: on black or red, on odds or evens, on the first, second or third 12 numbers as a group, etc.

pit area between the gaming tables reserved for casino employees.

pit boss casino executive who oversees the gambling action from inside the *pit*.

pot the bets accumulated while playing a hand of poker.

progressive jackpot a payout on a slot or video poker machine (or, often, a group of machines) that increases as each coin is played.

push in blackjack, where the dealer and player(s) have the same un-busted hand. No money changes hands.

rated player player whose gambling has been assessed by the casino and is thus eligible for *comps*.

shill casino employee who plays at empty tables (with house money) to encourage visitors to join the action.

shoe container for decks of cards from which card games are often dealt.

shooter the player who throws the dice in a game of craps.

slot clubs clubs for slots and video poker players where members accrue

points as they play; these can then later be redeemed against meals, gifts, cash and other perks.

stand in blackjack, to refuse another card.

stiff someone who doesn't tip; one of the worst insults in Las Vegas.

toke a tip for a casino employee, often given in the form of a bet on their behalf.

true odds real chances of winning on any game as opposed to the money actually paid out by the casino.

underlay a bet that's higher than strict probability suggests is wise.

up card the blackjack dealer's face-up card.

vigorish see *house edge*.

whale big-money gambler prepared to wager at least $5,000 a hand at high-stakes games.

spins an hour rather than running at double-time by hitting the spin button like a lunatic.

To ensure gambling funds for your whole trip, divide your money into 'session' portions. Lost one entire portion quickly? End of session. Don't dig into your remaining *bankroll* until it's time for the next session. And always keep an eagle eye on your coins, cash and *chips*. Always make sure back-to-back slot machines have a plastic or metal guard between them to prevent 'reach through' thievery. Watch for 'rail thieves' when you're at the crap table.

TIP TALK

From bellmen to doormen, Vegas is a town that runs on tips. It's the same for casino dealers, who are paid little more than the minimum wage. Every shift of dealers combines and divides their tips, which make up the bulk of their pay. Giving tips (or *tokes*, as dealers call them, short for 'tokens' of appreciation) is smart, as a happy dealer is your friend. Dealers can assist players in a number of ways: they can slow down the pace of the game (extremely useful when you're playing for *comps*), create a sociable atmosphere, and even deal a little deeper in the deck, critical for card counters.

You can *toke* the dealer as you leave the table, but while they appreciate this, it won't gain you any help while you're playing. A better method is to *toke* immediately after a big win; this way, the dealer knows you're thinking of him or her and could start to help you. Don't bother *toking* if the dealer is rude, creepy or uncooperative. In fact, don't even play there: just get up and move on to another table.

But the best way of all is to place a bet for the dealer alongside your wager. If you win, the *toke* is paid off at regular odds and the dealer takes it. If you lose, the house wins the *toke*, but the dealer will still appreciate the gesture. In blackjack, you can place a *chip* outside the line surrounding your wager circle, but if this *toke* bet wins, it has to be scooped up by the dealer right away. Alternatively, if you're riding a hot streak, place the dealer's *toke* next to your bet within your wager circle. If you win, you can let the *toke* ride (continue to the next deal): it's yours until you give it to the dealer. Just tell the dealer the extra bet is a *toke*. That said, some dealers resent it if you let their *tokes* ride, and have a take-the-money-and-run attitude.

The Games

Baccarat

Long viewed as an obscure, weirdly ritualised game for *high rollers*, baccarat ('bah-cah-rah') is a table game with a small *house edge*. Up to 15 players sit around the layout and bet on BANK, PLAYER or TIE. Dealers lay out two hands of two cards each, titled PLAYER and BANK. The object is for each hand to total as close to nine as possible. *Face cards* and tens count as zero and any total over nine is reduced by eliminating the first digit (for instance, 15 is valued as five). Players have no control over whether to 'draw' or 'stand'. Dealers follow a strict set of rules to determine if they must 'hit' either hand with a third card.

If PLAYER or BANK bets win, the house pays at *even money*. Since the rules determine that BANK wins slightly more often, the house retains a five per cent commission on all BANK winnings. Even with the commission, the house holds only a 1.17 per cent edge on BANK bets and 1.36 per cent on PLAYER bets. (The TIE bet should be avoided. It pays

The best Baccarat

If you can fade the minimums, the **Mirage** (*see p68*) has the most elegant baccarat pit in town, complete with a mini-buffet for the players. For mini-baccarat, try the **Gold Coast** (*see p102*), which has six tables with $10 minimums.

off at eight to one, but since the *true odds* are about 9.5:1, the *house edge* comes out at a whopping 14 per cent.)

The rhythm of baccarat is leisurely and the mood subdued. In fact, it's rarely necessary for players to speak, which might be why the game is popular with Asian gamblers. Baccarat pits are usually secluded behind velvet ropes or in high-limit rooms, which often come complete with small buffets to lend an air of exclusivity, but if you can handle the minimum – often $100 – you're welcome to join the action. Casinos catering to low-end gamblers tend to ignore baccarat, but high-end casinos hold it dear for good reason: it's very profitable. The Mirage has estimated that about ten per cent of its annual revenue comes from baccarat.

MINI BACCARAT
Mini baccarat is a low-stakes version of the game played in the main pit, usually near the blackjack tables. It's a good introduction: the rules are the same but the bets are lower. However, thanks to fewer players taking part, the pace of the game is faster.

Bingo

It might not be posh, but bingo is a gambling stalwart in Vegas, especially in neighbourhood casinos: the game's the same as in church basements all over the world. The *house edge* is slightly better than the similar keno (*see p48*), though it's hard to pin down since so much depends on the variety of the game and its payout. The one advantage bingo has over keno is that bingo numbers are called until a player wins. By contrast, a million keno games can go by without anyone hitting the big jackpot.

Blackjack (21)

Blackjack is by far the most popular table game in the casinos. The reasons are obvious: it's easy to play, the basic strategy slims the *house edge* to nearly zero, and dozens of books claim the house can be beaten with card counting.

THE BASICS
After putting up their bets, everyone at the table is dealt two cards. Single- and double-deck blackjack (games played with either one deck or two decks shuffled together) are dealt from the dealer's hand; for multiple-deck blackjack, the decks are combined and placed in a *shoe*, from which the dealer pulls cards. *Face cards* count as ten, and aces can count as one or 11. (A hand in which an ace is counted as 11 is known as a 'soft' hand; for example, an ace and a six is called 'soft 17.') Each player competes against the dealer's hand in trying

players never touch the cards, but instead indicate *hit* or *stand* with hand motions. This reduces the potential for misunderstandings between player and dealer, and makes it easier for disputed plays to be reviewed on security videos. For a *hit*, players hold one hand palm down and brush their fingers toward them. To *stand*, hold the hand the same way, but with fingers straight outward, and move it right and left.

Single- and double-deck games are almost always dealt face down, and players hold their own cards (hold them with one hand only; it makes the dealer and the *eye* nervous if you cup them with both). *Hitting* is indicated by scratching the cards towards you on the layout, while *standing* is indicated by sliding the cards face down under the *chips*.

Though blackjack sets each player's hand against the dealer's, most players view the game as everyone against the dealer. Their goal is to make the dealer *bust*, which means payoffs for all players still in the game. These folks don't take kindly to people playing stupidly ('splitting' tens or *hitting* a 14, say, against a dealer's six), especially if the offending party sits in the last seat on the left (known as 'third base'), since they feel those cards should have gone to the dealer. Don't sit at third base unless you have a good grasp of the game.

BETTING

There are four ways players can alter their bets once the cards have been dealt: 'doubling down', 'splitting', 'insurance' and 'surrender'. Splitting

to get as close as possible to a total of 21 without exceeding it (or *bust*). The game moves clockwise around the table, with the player sat on the right as he or she faces the dealer the first to play. The first of the dealer's cards is dealt face-up (the *up card*), with the second dealt face-down (the *hole card*).

First, check your cards. If you want an extra card, ask to *hit*; when satisfied with your total, you *stand*. After all players *stand* or *bust*, the dealer reveals his or her *hole card* and plays the hand, according to fixed rules: he or she must *hit* totals of 16 or less, and must stand on 17 or above. (The rules vary if the dealer has soft 17, with some casinos requiring dealers to *hit* and others to *stand*; the players' edge is increased by 0.2 per cent if it's the latter.)

Once the dealer has *stood* or *busted*, the hands are compared; players who beat the dealer are paid off at *even money*. Ties between the house and player are a *push* and no money changes hands; dealers indicate a *push* by knocking gently on the layout. If a player is dealt an ace and a ten-value card, it's considered a *natural* blackjack (also known as a 'snapper'); unless the dealer's *up card* is an ace or a ten, indicating a possible blackjack, the player is immediately paid at 3:2. Watch for single-deck games where *naturals* pay only 6:5; *see p41* **Sucker bets**.

ETIQUETTE

With the crucial exception of the dealer's *hole card*, almost all multi-deck blackjack games are dealt with the cards face up. In these games,

The best · Blackjack

More or less every casino on the Strip will claim to be the best place to play this most popular of table games. However, you're best off heading Downtown, where you'll find the best combination of good rules, low minimums, easy *comps* and tolerant dealers. (There's nothing worse than Strip dealers looking down their noses at you: they're minimum-wage card dealers, for cryin' out loud.)

If you just want to play on the cheap, you'll find $1-$3 blackjack on the Strip at **Slots-a-Fun** (2880 Las Vegas Boulevard South, 734 0410), and Downtown at the **Western** (899 E Fremont Street, 384 4620), just west of Las Vegas Boulevard. **El Cortez** (*see p97*) is among the few casinos that offer $5 minimum single-deck blackjack that pays 3:2 for a *natural*.

Blackjack strategy

Dealer's up card

If you have a total of	2	3	4	5	6	7	8	9	10	A
2-8	H	H	H	H	H	H	H	H	H	H
9	H	D	D	D	D	H	H	H	H	H
10	D	D	D	D	D	D	D	D	H	H
11	D	D	D	D	D	D	D	D	D	D
12	H	H	S	S	S	H	H	H	H	H
13-16	S	S	S	S	S	H	H	H	H	H
17-20	S	S	S	S	S	S	S	S	S	S

Dealer's up card

If you have an ace	2	3	4	5	6	7	8	9	10	A
A+2	H	H	D	D	D	H	H	H	H	H
A+3	H	H	D	D	D	H	H	H	H	H
A+4	H	H	D	D	D	H	H	H	H	H
A+5	H	H	D	D	D	H	H	H	H	H
A+6	D	D	D	D	D	H	H	H	H	H
A+7	S	D	D	D	D	S	S	H	H	S
A+8	S	S	S	S	S	S	S	S	S	S
A+9	S	S	S	S	S	S	S	S	S	S

Dealer's up card

If you have a pair	2	3	4	5	6	7	8	9	10	A
2s	Sp	Sp	Sp	Sp	Sp	Sp	H	H	H	H
3s	Sp	Sp	Sp	Sp	Sp	Sp	H	H	H	H
4s	H	H	H	H	H	H	H	H	H	H
5s	D	D	D	D	D	D	D	D	H	H
6s	Sp	Sp	Sp	Sp	Sp	H	H	H	H	H
7s	Sp	Sp	Sp	Sp	Sp	Sp	H	H	H	H
8s	Sp	Sp	Sp	Sp	Sp	Sp	Sp	Sp	Sp	Sp
9s	Sp	Sp	Sp	Sp	Sp	S	Sp	Sp	S	S
10s	S	S	S	S	S	S	S	S	S	S
As	Sp	Sp	Sp	Sp	Sp	Sp	Sp	Sp	Sp	Sp

H=hit; **S**=stand; **D**=double down; **Sp**=split

Players should consider 'surrendering':

● with hard 13-16 against dealer's A
● with hard 14-16 against dealer's 10
● with hard 15-16 against dealer's 9

But if all that's too much to memorise, at least remember the following five golden rules:

● stand on 17-21, but always hit soft 17
● stand on 12-16 against dealer's 2 to 6, but hit on 12-16 against dealer's 7 to A
● always split 8s and aces, but never split the 'F's, (4s, 5s and *face cards*)
● double down on 10s and 11s against the dealer's 2 to 9
● never take insurance

and doubling down aggressively is the secret to winning at basic strategy blackjack, as it gives players the chance to press their bets when they're holding a strong starting hand.
● When a player 'doubles down', he or she wagers another bet equal to the original and receives one (only one) more card. It's the choice move when you've got a total of nine, ten or 11 and the dealer shows a weak card such as a six; for full advice, *see opposite* **Blackjack strategy**. You can double down only if you haven't taken a hit.
● 'Splitting' is an option when players are dealt two cards of the same value. An additional bet equal to the original bet is put out and the cards are split, with each played as a separate hand. It's to the player's advantage to be able to double down or split each of the post-split hands, though some casinos limit what you can do. Check the chart (*opposite*) for more advice.
● 'Insurance' is a side bet offered when the dealer has a possible blackjack (the dealer is showing an ace or ten-value card). An insurance bet is limited to 50 per cent of the original bet and is lost if the dealer doesn't have blackjack. If he or she does, insurance pays at 2:1.

Despite the word's connotations, insurance is a sucker bet. Unless you're a card counter and can calculate the odds of a blackjack, there's no reason to take it, even if you're holding a *natural* 21. If you're holding a *natural* and the dealer is calling for insurance bets, you can take *even money* on your bet. If you don't take *even money* and the dealer has a two-card 21, it's a *push*. If the dealer doesn't have 21, your *natural* is paid at 3:2 (again, don't play 6:5 games; *see p41* **Sucker bets**).
● 'Surrender' is an obscure but useful rule that's not in effect everywhere. It permits players to fold and sacrifice half their bet as long as they haven't played their hand. This is an excellent way to drop out and minimise losses when dealt weak cards. If used correctly, it increases the player's edge by 0.2 per cent.

CARD COUNTING

Card counting is a technique whereby a player visually tracks exposed cards and mentally keeps a running total to determine if the deck is positive or negative. In the simplest count, the ten-value cards and aces are valued at −1, while cards numbered two to seven take a value of +1; the eights and nines have no value. If the running total is positive, players have an advantage and should raise their bets.

Does it work? Yes, but only if you devote weeks of practice, are cool under the pressures of casino play, and develop camouflage skills so that the house doesn't know you're counting;

though card counting is not against the law, casinos frown upon it, and 'back off' (bar them from playing blackjack) or 'bar' (kick them out of the casino for good) players they suspect of using the practice. Counting cards is a gruelling discipline at which most fail, but successful card counters, especially high-stakes players, are the few gamblers who beat the casinos at their own game.

The rest of us should stick to basic strategy. This involves memorising a chart that contains the answer to every decision in blackjack, based on your first two cards and the dealer's *up card*. You can usually bring the chart to the table and check it as you play, as long as you don't slow down the game. For the chart, *see p46*.

Craps

Fast, furious and enormously confusing, craps is an action-filled dice game that terrifies most novices. It can also be hugely exciting: if you hear a roar of excitement while wandering a casino, the chances are it's coming from a crap table. Players cheer, curse and scream, dice and *chips* fly across the table and everybody roots for different numbers. Fortunes can be won and lost in minutes, which is why craps is worshipped by a subculture. It's confounding, but by sticking to a few smart bets, players can enjoy a boisterous game with a *house edge* as low as one per cent, occasionally lower.

THE BASICS

Craps is played on a large table surrounded by a low, padded wall (there's a rail for *chips* on top and, outside, a shelf for the ever-present drinks). The game is staffed by one to four casino employees, and there's room for 12 to 14 players to belly up.

The layout is divided into three sections. The two at each end are identical, but in the centre is an area reserved for special wagers known as 'proposition bets'. A game of craps starts with dice being offered to a new *shooter* by the 'stickman' (the dealer located mid-table who's holding the stick). Each player will be offered the job at some point, though it's common to refuse. The *shooter* must throw two dice in such a way that they bounce off the table's far wall.

Basically, players bet on which numbers the *shooters* will throw and in what order. The *shooter* must lay a bet before his or her first throw, and traditionally chooses PASS. Those betting with the *shooter* are known as 'right' bettors, while those betting against the *shooter* are called 'wrong' bettors.

BETTING

There are four basic wagers known as 'line bets' marked on the layout: PASS, DON'T PASS, COME and DON'T COME (the DON'T bets are for wrong bettors). The *shooter*'s initial throw is called a 'come out roll'. Players bet on the PASS or DON'T PASS lines. If the dice show seven (statistically the most likely roll) or 11 on the come out roll, PASS bettors win at even odds and DON'T PASS bettors lose. If the shooter throws a two or three, DON'T PASS wins and PASS loses. If a 12 is tossed, PASS bettors lose and it's a 'push' (or tie) for DON'T PASS bettors. Rolling a two, three or 12 is known as 'crapping out'. If any other number is thrown (four, five, six, eight, nine, ten), that becomes the 'point'.

Once a point is established, the *shooter* keeps rolling, attempting to repeat the point before rolling a seven (known as 'sevening out'). Other numbers tossed don't count in this context. PASS and DON'T PASS bets ride until the

The best Craps

Don't bother heading to **Binion's** (*see p97*): after 50 years as the best crap joint in town, it's now just average. Instead, try **Main Street Station** (*see p96*), with its 20x odds, or the **California** (12 Ogden Street, 1-800 634 6255), which has five tables in a dedicated pit. If you hold the dice at the latter for at least an hour, you're inducted into the Golden Arm Hall of Fame and get your name on a plaque hanging on the wall on the pedestrian overpass.

On a budget? Head to **Slots-a-Fun** (2880 Las Vegas Boulevard South, 734 0410) for dollar craps with 3x odds. Downtown, **El Cortez** (*see p97*) offers $1 minimums; you can also find dollar-minimum tables with 10x odds at **Boulder Station** (*see p103*).

'point' is hit or the *shooter* 'sevens out'. If the *shooter* hits the 'point', PASS bettors win and DON'T PASS bettors lose. If the *shooter* tosses a seven, DON'T PASS bettors win, PASS bettors lose and the *shooter* relinquishes control of the dice. The shortest roll a *shooter* can have is two throws, by hitting a point on the come out roll followed by a seven (here, wrong bettors win). But if he or she avoids 'sevening out', the *shooter* can roll forever, and right bettors can rack up big bucks. Every time the 'point' is hit, the whole game is reset and the next throw is a fresh 'come out roll', although all the side bets – such as COME bets – remain in play.

COME and DON'T COME bets represent an optional second layer of betting that runs concurrently to the original layer. They are similar to PASS and DON'T PASS bets, with exactly the same set of outcomes – an immediate win, lose or 'push', or the establishment of a 'point' – but can only be made on throws subsequent to the come out roll. For instance, the *shooter* establishes a point of four; on the next roll you make a COME bet. (If you want, you can enter the game with a COME/DON'T COME bet at any time during a hand without having previously made a PASS or DON'T PASS bet.) The next roll is nine, so nine becomes your 'point'. Should that throw have yielded a seven or 11, you would have won immediately, and the DON'T COME bets would have lost. If the throw yielded a two, three or 12, your COME bet would have lost. If the *shooter* hits his number, the COME bets ride, awaiting a seven or a repeat of the come 'point'.

TAKING THE ODDS

If a player sticks to the four 'line' bets outlined above, the *house edge* is only about 1.4 per cent. But even that tiny amount can be reduced even further with the use of the 'odds' bet, a wager where the house holds an edge of, believe it or not, zero. Unsurprisingly, these are the only such wagers in the casino, which is doubtless the reason why the layout of a crap table doesn't even mention them at all.

Once a point is established, any player with a line bet can back up that wager with an 'odds' bet, placing the bet behind the original 'line' bet on the craps layout. This allows players to increase their bet midstream. In a game with single odds, the maximum odds bet equals the line bet. That alone slashes the *house edge* from about 1.4 per cent to 0.85 per cent. Some casinos offer double odds, triple odds, 10x or even 100x odds, all of which reduce the *house edge* even further. A few offer different odds on specified points. Anyone making line bets in craps should take, at the very least, single odds on every bet made. It's worth attending a lesson to learn how to make the most of this tactic.

THE REST OF THE TABLE

Smart players stick to line and odds bets, but action junkies need more. For them, the table offers another world of wagers, none of which is worthwhile. Granted, some bets offer an edge only slightly worse than line bets. But most of the one-roll proposition bets are simply horrific.

For instance, the ANY 7 proposition bet has a stunning *house edge* of 16.67 per cent, the worst edge of any game wager apart from keno and the Money Wheel. Don't waste time on it. Instead, stick to right and wrong betting with line bets pressed with odds and you'll get more than enough action. A straightforward odds-effective play is to bet the minimum stake on PASS, the same amount on two COME bets and take odds on both (double or triple, if they're offered and you can afford it).

Keno

This lottery offshoot is the worst bet in the casino, with an appalling *house edge* of 25 to 40 per cent. You might as well climb to the top of the Stratosphere Tower and throw your money into the wind. At least you'll have a nice view.

As with an old-style lottery or bingo, keno involves a ticket (or 'blank') containing 80 numbers, on which players circle as many as 15 or 20 numbers. When the game gets started, 20 numbers are selected at random (ping-pong balls are blown from a 'goose' into a pair of 'arms') and displayed on screens around the casino. If your numbers are picked, you win.

If not, you lose. (Get used to the second option.) The greater the proportion of your numbers picked, the higher the payback. Remember that, if by some remote chance you win at keno, you must claim your money before the next game begins or you will forfeit your winnings.

There are many variations for keno, but none makes the edge even remotely acceptable. Worst of all, payouts for keno in no way reflect the *true odds* of your bet, since they're capped at an arbitrary figure. For instance, your chances of selecting nine numbers and hitting all of them are about 1.38 million to 1. Your payout for such a feat? Usually no more than $250,000 on a $2 bet. Here's another fun fact: if two players hit the big jackpot at the same time, they have to split the cash. The only way to win at keno is never to play it.

Money Wheel or Big Six

You have to worry when a game is imported from the morally challenged world of carnivals. That's the case with the Money Wheel, aka Big Six, the grandchild of spin-the-wheel games loved by carnies everywhere. The game is simple. A large, ornate wheel is mounted vertically a few feet above the floor. On it are 54 evenly spaced slots. Two show joker or house symbols; the other 52 are divided into $1, $2, $5, $10 and $20 denominations. There are usually 24 $1 slots and only two $20 slots. A layout in front of the wheel has squares matching those denominations. Players put cash or *chips* on the squares of their choice, and the wheel spins. When it stops, bettors who selected the correct denomination win,

with the payoff determined by the dollar value of the winning slot. A $20 symbol pays off at 20 to 1; a $1 symbol pays off at *even money*. House or joker symbols pay off at 40 (sometimes 45) to 1. As you might guess, the casino holds a serious edge, ranging from 11 per cent on a bet on the $1 symbol to 25.9 per cent on the joker. Don't be a sucker.

Poker

From the casino's point of view, poker isn't a good bet. In poker, gamblers bet against each other, not the house. A casino employee merely deals and acts as the cashier, and the house's income is limited to a percentage taken from each pot, or a seat rental of $5 or $7 per half-hour. This small take is the main reason why many casinos opted out of the game in the '90s.

However, thanks to the explosion in popularity of the game over the past few years, many are getting right back into it. Almost every month, a casino either opens a new poker room, expands an old room or reopens a closed one. Nevada had 144 more poker tables in 2004

The best Keno

The least of all the keno evils might be the **Gold Coast** (*see p102*) or the **Silverton** (3333 Blue Diamond Road, 263 7777, www.silvertonhotel.com): the *house edge* on the eight-spot tickets is a 'mere' 25 per cent (it's 30 per cent at most other joints).

than it did in 2003 and posted a profit from the game of nearly $100 million, compared to $45 million the year before. Another telling statistic: in 2002, 631 players competed in the $10,000-buy in World Series of Poker at Binion's (now relocated to the Rio), the granddaddy of all gambling tournaments. The winner took down a first-place prize of $1.1 million. Two years later, the player pool had grown four-fold, as had the cash: tournament winner Greg Raymer won a cool $5 million.

Blame television, which has cottoned on to the camera-friendliness of the game to dramatic effect. Networks including ESPN, Fox and even NBC have started to televise poker tours and tournaments, celebrity matches, one-on-one showdowns and even dramas based on the game. Online poker is also growing hugely: a whole new generation of poker players are training on their computers for the big games and tournaments. However, while poker has arrived as a national pastime, it still has a way to go before overtaking blackjack (which netted casinos some $1.2 billion in 2004) as the biggest grossing table game in town.

PLAYING IN VEGAS

To join a poker game in a Las Vegas casino, just sit in an empty seat and *buy in* (which usually costs ten times the minimum or maximum bet, depending on the game) with *chips* or cash. If there's no space at any of the tables, put your name on a waiting list. The traditional rules everyone knows are in effect for poker in Las Vegas: the most popular games are Texas hold 'em and seven-card stud, but many casinos in town have recently been experimenting with variations that aren't uncommon outside the poker room.

In Texas hold 'em, each player is dealt two cards face down, while five common cards are pitched face up on to the layout for the table. Players calculate their best five-card hand from the seven cards available to them. In seven-card stud, players get two cards face down and one face up, followed by three cards face up and a final card face down. Again, they put together the best hand from their own seven cards.

Both of the above games have numerous rounds of betting and raising, so for all but the lowest-stakes games, a hefty *bankroll* is crucial. For games with betting limits, posted signs indicate the smallest and largest bet allowable (usually in the form '$5/$10'). In a limit game, you'll need a *bankroll* of at least 20 times the maximum bet. There are also pot-limit games, which means raises can go as high as the pot, and no-limit games, in which raises can go as high as the largest *bankroll* on the table. In all games, no matter the stakes, players are not allowed to bring more money to the table once a hand is dealt. If a player is 'all in' (meaning all his or her money is bet) and he or she can't match another player's raise, a side pot is formed for those who wish to continue betting. The player who is all in is limited to playing for the main pot.

Explaining poker strategy here is impossible. Besides the complexities of the game, much of poker is psychological. Reading other players and bluffing are a huge part of the process, which, if you didn't know it already, you'll learn the first time you sit down in a card room. If you're not a seasoned poker player, be very careful of high-stakes games, which can be populated by sharks (sometimes operating in teams). They've learned the primary casino secret: it's easy to take money from amateur gamblers. If you're a novice, stick to low-stakes games, which are straightforward and friendly.

CARIBBEAN STUD

Caribbean stud is a rather dumb game with a *house edge* of 5.27 per cent, just a hair worse than double-zero roulette. Sitting around a table with a layout similar to blackjack, players put out a single *ante* and receive five cards face down. The dealer also gets five cards, though one is dealt face up. At this point, players either fold (and lose their *ante*) or 'call' by adding a bet that's twice their *ante*. All players then reveal their cards. If the dealer doesn't 'qualify' with at least an ace and king in his or her hand, all players win *even money* for their *ante* and the call bets are returned. Should the dealer's hand qualify, each player's hand is compared against the dealer's. If the player wins, the *ante* is paid at *even money* and the call bet qualifies for a 'bonus' payout based on the hand. Bonus payouts range from *even money* for a pair to 100:1 for a royal flush (most of the payouts are lower than those found in Let it Ride; *see below*).

The maximum bonus payout in Caribbean stud is usually capped somewhere between $5,000 and $60,000, so make sure your bet is no higher than it needs to be to win that amount. For example, if the bonus payout is capped at $5,000, your ante should never be above $25: this would make your call bet $50 and so a 100:1 payout would hit the $5,000 ceiling exactly. The simple maths? Divide the maximum bonus payout by 200. Your *ante* should never exceed that figure.

The best Poker games

You might as well play pin the tail on the Caribbean stud donkey: most casinos in Las Vegas deal the game, with low minimums, *progressive jackpots* and bad odds. However, the **Golden Nugget** (*see p96*) in Downtown Vegas has had the fastest *progressive* meter for a couple of years. For Let it Ride, try **O'Shea's** (3355 Las Vegas Boulevard South, 697 2711): many see it as the best place to play this high-*house edge* game, due to the low minimums offered.

For a side bet of another dollar per hand, Caribbean stud poker also offers players the chance to hit a *progressive jackpot* with payoffs based on the quality of their hand. A royal flush wins 100 per cent of the jackpot, while a flush gets a mere $50. The fact that jackpots have been known to go up to $5 million tells you something about how often a royal flush occurs.

LET IT RIDE

Let it Ride offers the unusual feature of allowing players to take back two thirds of their wager. Players bet three equal amounts and are dealt three cards face down. Two common cards are then dealt, also face down. At this point, players can pull back one of their bets by signalling to the dealer (don't touch your *chips*). When the first common card is turned over, players can withdraw their second bet. The final common card is then shown and payouts are made according to a fixed schedule, ranging from *even money* for a pair of tens or better to 1,000:1 for a royal flush. As you might guess, the payouts are way below *true odds*. For instance, the odds against drawing a flush are 508:1, but the payout is eight to one. Overall, the house holds about a four per cent edge, if players make all the right decisions.

The biggest lure of Let it Ride is that players compete against the cards, not each other, so it's more appealing to amateurs. Also, there's that ability to withdraw two thirds of the bet, which gives the illusion your money is lasting longer than in other games. But don't be fooled. The *house edge* grinds down almost everyone in the end, and since it's basically five-card stud, it can be a long time between winning hands.

PAI GOW POKER

Pai gow poker – not to be confused with pai gow, a Chinese game that utilises tiles – is played with a 53-card deck, a standard deck plus a wild joker. Players get seven cards, which they assemble into a five-card hand and a two-card hand. The five-card hand must score higher than the two-card hand. The object is to beat both the banker's hands. The banker wins all hands that tie; if a player wins only one hand, it's a *push*. The house or any player can be the banker. Winning hands are paid at *even money*, minus a five per cent commission.

If it sounds intimidating, don't worry; the dealer will help you arrange your cards in such a way as to maximise your two hands. It only takes observing a few hands to get the hang of it. Pai gow poker is a lot slower – and friendlier – than blackjack or mini-baccarat, so it's a good game to play if you want to relax, socialise, or play as few hands as possible in a given period of time (more *comps*, less risk).

Roulette

Roulette doesn't have much of a fan club in the US. That's partly due to the calm nature of the game; Americans want action and speed when they gamble, and roulette gives them neither. Another reason is a subtle but crucial change in the US version. In Europe, roulette wheels typically have 36 numbered slots and one zero slot. On most American wheels, there are two zero slots (marked as zero and double zero). That change alone nearly doubles the *house edge* to 5.26 per cent, as compared to 2.7 per cent on single-zero wheels.

Roulette is simple to play. The wheel is mounted horizontally and a matching table layout serves as the betting area. All numbers are coloured red or black except for the zero and double zero, which are green. Players place their *chips* on the layout, the wheel is spun and a little ball is launched. Betting is halted, the ball comes to rest in a slot, and winners are paid off. To minimise confusion about who made which bet, each player receives specially coloured 'wheel' *chips* when they *buy in*; these *chips* can only be used at the roulette table.

The easiest wager is a straight-up bet, where the player drops a *chip* on a single number (17 is the most popular, supposedly due to its central location and the fact that James Bond bets it in the movies). If the number is the winner, it's paid off at 35 to 1. You can also make bets on groups of numbers; for example, on lines separating numbers, on rows

of numbers or in special areas denoting odd or even, red or black and so on. In this way, a single bet covers anywhere from two to 18 numbers. Needless to say, the more numbers the wager covers, the lower the payoff. For instance, betting odd or even pays *even money*.

The variety of wagers makes roulette an interesting game, especially if you like the languid pace. However, the odds are tough. Your best bet is to find a casino with a single-zero wheel – these come and go on occasion – and try to look elegant while losing.

Slot machines

Slot machines were once shunned by 'real' gamblers, patronised only by their bored wives and girlfriends or first-time casino-goers who knew nothing more about gambling than how to drop coins into a slot. How times have changed. These days, they're the most popular and profitable part of the entire casino industry, so much so that some (albeit smaller) casinos offer nothing but slots and video poker (*see p57*).

Novice gamblers prefer slots because there's little to learn and no pressure from dealers or other players. Put in money, pull the handle and in a few seconds, you're either a winner or a loser. Simple. Plus, jackpots can reach millions of dollars. But there is a downside, and a big one. Slots give the house an edge from two to 25 per cent, often making them one of the worst bets in the house. And your chance of hitting a million-dollar jackpot is… well, what's the tiniest unit of measurement you can imagine? Smaller than that. Way smaller.

The basic slot machine in Las Vegas accepts a maximum of either two or three coins; some take four or five, some just one, and a new breed of slots now is able to take hundreds of coins, including pennies. Each coin beyond the minimum increases the payout proportionally (twice as much for two coins, triple for three) should a winning combination appear. In most cases, the winnings on betting the maximum number of coins are exponentially higher; almost always, the posted jackpot can only be won by betting the maximum number of coins on the winning pull. Always check the pay tables at the top of the machine. Many machines have multiple pay lines. On these machines, an added pay line is activated each time another coin is wagered.

Modern slots usually have a coin counter that displays your credits. Instead of coins crashing into the stainless-steel bin, wins are registered as credits. Often, there's a bill changer attached: players can simply slide in a $20, and $20 of credits appear on the counter. Bets are made

The best Roulette

The **Stratosphere** (*see p90*) is the best place in Vegas to play roulette, thanks to its single-zero wheel. The **Monte Carlo** (*see p82*) also has one that's usually open. Several other casinos have single-zero wheels, but they're either often closed or have outrageous minimums.

Cheapskates unafraid of double-zero roulette should head for **El Cortez** (*see p97*) or the slightly tattier **Western** (899 Fremont Street, 384 4620), both Downtown, or **Casino Royale** (3419 Las Vegas Boulevard South, 1-800 854 7666) on the Strip, where tokens are a quarter. The biscuit, though, is taken by the **Klondike** (5191 Las Vegas Boulevard South, 739 9351), where you have to wager a total of 50¢ on each spin but with a minimum bet per number of just a dime.

by pulling a handle or pressing a 'Spin' button. When done, players hit the 'Cash Out' button, and one of two things happens. In older slots, coins equal to the unused credits drop into the bin; the casino provides plastic cups to carry coins to other machines or the cashier. Many of the newest slots, though, are 'coinless', and will instead print a voucher that can be redeemed at a change booth or the *cage*. You can tell a coinless slot machine at a glance: there's no coin slot.

Slots fall into two categories: non-progressive, aka regular, and *progressive*. Regular slots have fixed payouts, which are posted on the front of the machine. *Progressive slots* offer a fixed payout schedule, as well as the chance to hit a huge jackpot. This jackpot, funded by a percentage of every coin wagered, grows continuously until somebody wins it. A meter above the machines displays a running total of the current jackpot.

Many *progressive slots* are linked to form a system that feeds the jackpot. These machines might be from one *carousel* in a single casino (with a jackpot that resets at $1,000 and grows from there), or spread across casinos state-wide (with multi-million dollar jackpots). With literally hundreds of machines in the system, the jackpot can reach astronomical levels. The Megabucks linked *progressive*, for example, consists of more than 700 machines; the world record slot jackpot of nearly $40 million was hit in March 2003 at Excalibur (by a 25-year-old computer programmer). Though rare, these payouts are well publicised, not least because they make excellent bait.

NEW SLOTS
A few years ago, video machines with oversized screens, multiple games and other gimmicks were all the rage. Today, a whole new generation of slots is being developed. Slots are becoming more interactive and look a lot like video poker; on these slots, you'll be able to make choices about which symbols to hold or discard, based on a certain internal and intuitive logic. Slots are more fun to play today than they were even ten years ago, when they were still primarily 'one-armed bandits' (derisively referred to by table-game players as the 'idiot pull').

But they still won't line your pockets. Slot (and video poker) machines now account for upwards of 65 and even 70 per cent of total casino revenues, which means that gambling machines take in nearly twice as much revenue as all other casino games combined. Of the $10.6 billion won by Nevada casinos in 2004, $7.1 billion – just over 66 per cent – was from slots and video poker.

HOW SLOTS WORK
Modern slots are controlled by a computer chip called a random number generator, which churns out strings of numbers whether the game is being played or not. Pulling the handle of a machine (or pressing the spin button) releases the reels and selects one of these numbers. Each number corresponds to a certain set of symbols on the reels, which is how the outcome is determined. The force of the pull has nothing to do with where the reels stop.

Since this is computer technology, regulating the payout is a science. By adjusting the random number generator, a slot technician

can make a machine 'tighter' (pays out less money) or 'looser' (pays out more money). In the old days, slots often had a built-in edge of 20 to 30 per cent. But players flocked to machines with the higher returns. Casinos did the sums and realised it was better to get five per cent of a lot than 30 per cent of nothing; hence, most Vegas slots now return between 92 and 95 per cent of the drop (less on nickel machines), leaving the *house edge* at five to eight per cent.

Certain casinos boldly advertise 98 or 99 per cent payouts, but read the small print. It's usually 'up to 99 per cent': that means one machine on the floor might be set at 98 or 99 per cent, if that. Short of running 2,000 to 5,000 plays through similar machines and comparing payouts, there's no way to find out which slots are set tight or *loose*. Payout percentages are supposedly verified by the state Gaming Control Board, but it rarely checks unless a casino advertises something absurd.

The real advantage for the house comes with the constant repetition of slot plays. For instance, a player with $50 starts betting $1 per pull on a quarter machine (via four 25¢ bets per pull). Sometimes the player wins and those winnings are reinvested: the *drop* might only be $50, but if they're playing at a reasonable speed, they could end up giving the casino $240 of action per hour. The five per cent edge is enough for a slot machine to retain about $12 an hour (five per cent of $240), a hold equal to nearly a quarter of the original *bankroll*. With a little less luck, that money could vanish even faster. Over time, even an edge of half of one per cent grinds down players, which is why so many of them stumble away from machines empty-handed. That and the fact that the payout percentage factors in the big (and seldom won) jackpots.

The best Slots

You'll find slots in every corner of Vegas. Reliable statistics on whose slots are the *loosest* are notoriously rare. However, a groundbreaking survey of the city's nickel slots carried out by Michael Shackleford for the *Las Vegas Advisor* in 2002 ranked the **Palms** (93.42 per cent payback; *see p92*), the **Gold Coast** (92.84 per cent; *see p102*) and the **Sahara** (92.81 per cent; *see p88*) as the top three casinos, and **Mandalay Bay** (87.51 per cent; *see p67*), the **Bellagio** (87.42 per cent; *see p63*) and the **Venetian** (86.66 per cent; *see p73*) as the three worst.

SLOT TIPS

Slot jockeys say non-*progressive* machines are *looser* (the technical term for this is 'hit frequency') than *progressive* machines, though payouts are smaller (again, the technical term is 'average payback'). Non-*progressive* machines that give smaller top payouts are reportedly *looser* than those that give large top payouts. Similarly, among *progressive* machines, those with smaller jackpots hit more often. In fact, the amount of your bet that goes to the *progressive jackpot* is an indication of payout frequency. According to one executive, if the amount is less than one per cent, the *progressive* machine is likely to have more non-jackpot winners. If three to five per cent of every bet goes towards the *progressive jackpot*, that game is seriously weighted toward fewer large payouts.

It gets more complicated. Machines with high hit frequencies (meaning they return coins frequently) pay out small amounts. Those with low hit frequencies pay out less frequently overall, but when they do, each return is higher. And there's no correlation between hit frequency and average payback; hit frequency can be high while average payback is low and vice versa, or both can be low or high. Of course, none of this is posted or known, so you're mostly flying blind. As such, rumours abound. Some believe that slots placed near doorways and aisles are *looser* than others: the constant sound of coins dropping is supposed to lure folks into betting a few bucks. One casino executive has said that the house machines – those with the casino's name and logo on them – are more generous than non-house brand slots.

The only recommendation that makes any sense is that if you're going to play the slots for big money, bet the maximum number of coins on each pull. This way, if lightning strikes and you're a winner, you'll get the biggest payout possible. If you want to lay out a dollar per pull, play four coins in a quarter machine (even though $1 and higher machines tend to have higher average paybacks). Avoid pumping cash into slots in non-casino locations such as the airport and convenience stores, which have a *house edge* one step below thievery. And, of course, never put a nickel into a slot machine without having inserted your *slot club* card into the reader. As long as you're playing the house's favourite game, you might just as well get a bit of your play returned in the form of cashback or *comps*.

Slots can only pay out so many coins at any one time, so if you hit a monster jackpot, stay put and wait for an attendant to arrive. If you walk away, someone might claim your prize. The attendant will inform you of your

Viva Jean Scott

Jean Scott grew up in Indiana in the 1940s and 1950s, the daughter of an evangelical Christian minister. Cards and dice were considered sinful, so it wasn't until she was in her late thirties, as a high-school English teacher who'd repudiated the fundamentalist environment, that she learned to recognise the four suits of playing cards. In her forties, she began playing gin rummy with a friend, betting a penny a point to add excitement to the game. She was hooked.

Scott only played slot machines at first, but she had so much fun that she immediately started plotting her second trip, plans that included learning to play basic-strategy blackjack. From there, she gave herself a crash course in card counting, but found she had to move her lips to keep up with the count, a dead giveaway. In desperation, Jean turned to video poker. And a star was born.

After Scott and her husband retired in the late 1980s, their trips to Las Vegas grew more and more frequent. With a minister for a father, Scott had been thrifty her entire life, and Las Vegas, at least in those days, was frugal heaven: she had soon discovered coupons, slot clubs, comps and promotions. Playing quarter video poker and working the casino low-roller comp system, Scott piled up the freebie food, shows and hotel rooms, until she was featured in a 1994 issue of the *Las Vegas Advisor* for spending 50 nights in casino hotel rooms and paying for only one. The *Advisor* dubbed her the 'Queen of KuPon'.

From there, Scott's fame spread far and wide as her fortune grew from successful low-rolling. TV shows *48 Hours* (where Dan Rather renicknamed her the 'Queen of Comps') and

Dateline NBC have both profiled her in the past; today, she's a regular on gambling programmes on cable TV, especially on the Travel Channel, and has written two best-selling books: *The Frugal Gambler* and *More Frugal Gambling* (both Huntington Press). The Gambling Gramma is proof that, with the proper attitude and a little study and practice, anyone can get a big bang for their buck in casinos in Las Vegas and around the world.

"Jean Scott is the Queen of Casino Comps."
—CBS' '48 Hours'

The

FRUGAL GAMBLER

Jean Scott

Second Edition

COMPLIMENTARY

tax obligations. (US citizens need to fill out IRS paperwork on slot wins of more than $1,200; the tax situation varies for non-nationals.)

SLOT CLUBS

Virtually every casino has a *slot club*, whose main aims are to keep track of a customer's slot and video poker play, and to retain customer loyalty by providing rewards in the form of points that can be redeemed for hard cash or merchandise. Many clubs offer introductory gifts such as free buffets, bonus points or other perks to get your name on the dotted line.

All *slot clubs* issue members with an ID card, which should then be inserted into the slot or video poker machine to allow the machine's

computer to track the amount of play. Points awarded by the computer are then redeemable for cash or for *comps* in the casino's restaurants and shows. Members also qualify for discounts in the resort's shops, reduced room rates, free meals and tickets to parties, barbecues and special tournaments.

Slot club benefits change frequently; you can get an idea of what the clubs are offering by checking out the *Las Vegas Advisor*, or the 'Best Bets' section of the Friday edition of the *Las Vegas Review-Journal* newspaper. All it takes to join a *slot club* is a picture ID and a few minutes at the casino's slot booth. Some casinos even have roving recruiters who will sign you up at the machine. Membership is always free.

Sports betting

Thanks in no small part to Frank 'Lefty' Rosenthal, the casino executive whose life was dramatized in the movie *Casino*, betting on sports in Vegas is now a cult all of its own. Almost every casino has a sports book, where money is gambled on countless aspects of the outcomes of pro sports and college games. They're lively and passionate places on big game days, such as Sundays during the football season; even if you're not betting, they're often good places to watch the action. Whatever sports wagers you make and wherever you make them, remember that cellphones and two-way communicators are prohibited in or near the sports books, a policy that's strictly and universally enforced.

Glance up at the vast boards, and you might think that sports betting here was tough to understand. It's not: but it is hard to beat the system and come away rich. Below we list some of the common sports bets.

THE MONEY LINE

Most of the sports on which you can bet (baseball, boxing, football, hockey, college basketball) offer 'money lines', where you lay the odds on the favourite or take the odds on the underdog. Take the following baseball-related example:

| Boston Red Sox | +145 |
| New York Yankees | −160 |

This means that you must bet $16 on the Yankees to win $10 (plus your stake back). However, you need bet only $10 on the Red Sox to win $14.50. The favourite team is always the one with the '−' prefix, with the underdog denoted by '+'. (Also, unlike in European sports, the home team is always listed second.)

OTHER BETS

There's a large variety of bets in the Vegas sports books. Here, though, are two of the more common ones. Both even the odds so punters can make a 'straight bet', which here means putting up $11 to win $10 (plus your $11 stake back). In team games, one very popular bet is on the margin of victory, or the 'point spread'. Take, for example, these odds for the 2005 Super Bowl:

| New England Patriots | −7 |
| Philadelphia Eagles | |

This means that the Patriots were favoured to beat the Philadelphia Eagles by seven points. Everyone favouring the Patriots on the point spread were betting on them to win by more than seven points, while everyone favouring the Eagles were betting on either an Eagles victory *or* a Patriots win by fewer than seven points. The game ended Patriots 24, Eagles 21. So, while the Patriots won the game, they didn't cover the point spread, and everyone who bet on them lost. (Indeed, the books raked in a record $16 million thanks to the Eagles's late touchdown, which closed the gap from ten to three points.)

Betting on the total number of points scored in the game is another popular bet. The casino advertises the total number of points they think will be scored in the game, and punters decide if they think the number that will actually be scored will be higher or lower than this total. This is known as the 'over/under'. Like the point spread, this pays off at 10:11 odds.

Note that, for both of these bets, if the outcome of a game matches the casino's prediction – for example, if the Patriots had beaten the Eagles by exactly seven points – it's a *push*, and all money is refunded.

Video poker

This electronic cousin of live poker enjoys a huge following in Las Vegas, much of it made up of hardcore local gamblers. Although a video poker machine resembles a slot machine and is typically located on the slot floor, it is an entirely different beast. Make no mistake about it: video poker is a game not of chance but of skill. If played perfectly, the *house edge* can often be flattened to zero or even pushed into the negative, which means a return to players of over 100 per cent. Casinos can only afford to operate their machines in this way because perfect play is the province of the merest handful of experts, those people who use powerful computer programs to work out strategies that are accurate to within ten thousandths of a percentage point.

Instead of a slot machine's spinning reels, a video poker screen displays a five-card hand of draw poker. Every deal comes from a freshly shuffled 52-card deck. Buttons allow the player to hold or replace the dealt cards. After the draw, the game pays off according to a payout schedule listed on the screen. A pair of aces might pay *even money*, while a royal flush almost always pays out at a rate of 4,000:1. Most basic poker rules are in effect as far as hand rankings go (minus 'kickers', or unpaired or unsuited high cards, on all but one or two variations), but the psychological angle is jettisoned. You're playing against a machine that doesn't respond to bluffing, so the quality of your hand is everything.

There's no way to summarise basic strategy for video poker, partly because it's extremely complex and partly because the game comes in so many different varieties. Each variety of video poker has its own unique characteristics such as wild cards and bonus options, giving rise to different pay tables and different strategies. You can buy video poker strategy cards (Huntington Press produces a good set), which allow you to make the right decision on every hand; in essence, you'll be playing computer-perfect strategy.

The most basic variation of video poker is 'Jacks or Better' (JoB), which plays most like five-card stud (no wild cards) and pays out on pairs of jacks or better. The strategies for JoB are pretty much intuitive for anyone who already knows how to play poker, but some rules have to be learned: for example, you never hold a kicker (a high-value card to be held along with a pair); you never draw to a four-card inside straight (for example, you're holding 3, 4, 6, 7 and you're looking for a 5); and you always go for the royal flush if you hold four of the cards required for it, even if it's going to mean sacrificing a pair, a flush or a straight in the process.

The best Sports betting

The 'super books' in the giant Strip casinos are the most popular in town, especially those at **Caesars Palace** (*see p65*), the **Mirage** (*see p68*) and the **Bellagio** (*see p63*). Some, the Mirage included, have individual TV monitors on the seats; the book at the **Imperial Palace** (*see p79*) has individual monitors and tiered seating for the big screens.

Two books stand out. The **Las Vegas Hilton** (*see p92*) has the original 'Super Book', and

leagues of diehard gamblers to go with it. The manager is a proposition-bet freak; he puts up wild prop bets year-long, and posted 250 of them for the 2005 Super Bowl. The sports book at the **Stardust** (*see p89*), meanwhile, is immensely popular for its 'handicappers' library of stats, live talk-radio sports programming and the 'early line' on football betting, broadcast on Monday morning on KDWN (720 AM).

As with slots, play the maximum number of coins, as this greatly increases the top payout for a royal flush. Another tip: be sure to play 'full-pay' games as opposed to their 'short-pay' brethren. The same style of game might pay the same hand differently in different casinos. For instance, in JoB, the full-pay version returns 9:1 on a full house and 6:1 on a flush; it's called a '9/6 machine. On the short-pay version, it's sliced to 8/5, 7/5 or even 6/5. The only reason to play a short-pay version of JoB would be if it was connected to a *progressive jackpot* or paid off on a pair of tens or better. However, 8/5 Bonus, with extra payouts for four-of-a-kind, is a different animal. So are Double Bonus, Double Double Bonus, Triple Bonus and Double Triple Bonus variations. Then there's Joker Poker, plus many different varieties of Deuces Wild.

Video poker players should consult the books and reports on the market that detail proper play for sample video poker hands. There are excellent computer programs available that tutor players in strategies. Casinos don't mind if you refer to strategy charts while playing, but they draw the line at laptops. Since it's impossible to absorb the tactics for all the possible variations at once, we recommend you study and master strategy for JoB, then, as you feel more comfortable, move on to the more complex – and rewarding – games such as full-pay Deuces Wild and Double Bonus varieties.

The latest varieties of machine to become all the rage in Las Vegas are multi-play

The best Video poker

machines, such as Triple-Play, Five-Play, Ten-Play, 50-Play and even 100-Play. Here, three, five, ten, 50 and 100 hands of video poker are dealt at the same time from the equivalent number of decks, requiring three, five, ten, 50, and 100 times the bet. The twist is that only the cards in the bottom hand are displayed on the deal. When you hold cards from the hand, the held cards appear in all the upper hands; when you draw, all the hands' cards are filled in around the held cards.

In Spin Poker, when you discard cards, the open spots spin like slot reels. Heads Up Poker, meanwhile, combines live poker with video poker. You're dealt five cards and you bet the hand. The machine responds by calling, raising or folding (and sometimes bluffing). You play out the video poker hand, but you still have the live hand to be resolved.

Casinos & Hotels

Casinos & Hotels   60

Casinos & Hotels

Choose carefully: this is where you'll be spending most of your time.

And still it changes, and grows, and improves. Six decades ago, Vegas was framed around Downtown, a raffish cluster of buildings that provided little more than lairy gaming arenas and a few scruffy bedrooms. In the 1940s, a number of large resorts opened several miles away on deserted highway, spurring a boom that saw the city reinvent itself as a swanky resort town. In 1989, Steve Wynn opened the **Mirage** (*see p68*) and inspired an eight-year regeneration of Las Vegas Boulevard, during which period a dozen casinos were built from scratch. And in 2005, after a spell when work was limited to expansion of existing casinos rather than the construction of new operations, Wynn returned with **Wynn Las Vegas** (*see p75*), raising the bar once again for aspiring casino operators and prompting yet more improvement works among his rivals.

The industry is always building something new: a 1,000-room tower, a 4,000-seat theatre, a 100-unit shopping mall (the latest trend). And hotel-casinos that don't expand are quick to change; it's a case of adapt or die. If you've not been to Vegas for four or five years, the changes will be noticeable. But even if you were here six months ago, you'll still see something new.

Staying in Las Vegas

Though you could plump for an alternative – a motel, a hostel, even an RV park – the majority of visitors to Las Vegas stay where the action is: a hotel-casino. These often vast complexes, which line the Strip and clutter Downtown, are where most tourists spend upwards of 90 per cent of their time. All have gambling arenas, a range of restaurants and bars, assorted entertainments, and other amenities that range from the predictable (pools, malls) to the eye-catching (galleries, zoos, rollercoasters). All, of course, have guestrooms, from the 100 or so offered at the **Golden Gate** (*see p98*) to the 5,000-plus at the **MGM Grand** (*see p80*).

Visitors to Las Vegas were once expected to spend very little time in their gaming-subsidised guestroom, so rooms in hotel-casinos built pre-1989 are small-ish. But during the 1990s, casino moguls realised the value of providing guests with a nice place to sleep: rooms in newer hotel-casinos are brighter and more capacious. Phones, TVs (with cable) and air-conditioning are standard in Las Vegas hotel-casino guestrooms, which all also offer free parking. Beyond that, it's a crapshoot.

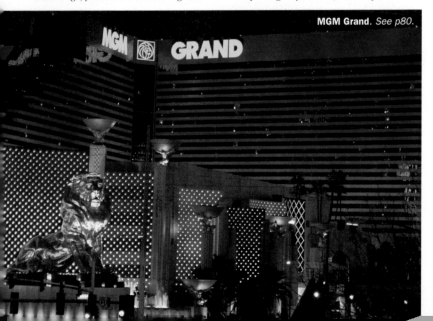

MGM Grand. *See p80.*

WHERE TO STAY

The vast majority of visitors to Las Vegas stay on the three-mile stretch of Las Vegas Boulevard South that runs from the Mandalay Bay resort north to the Sahara, aka **the Strip**. Most never leave it. The Strip is where you'll find almost all of the city's most glamorous, upscale and eye-catching resorts, as well as a number of its best bargains. If you want to stay on the Strip, remember it's a long (and, in summer, debilitating) 3.2-mile hike from one end to the other. It's not enough simply to stay at a property with a Las Vegas Boulevard South address; the street number is also crucial.

The range of properties on the Strip is not as immense as it was a half-decade ago: most of its cheaper historic motels have been imploded in the name of progress. However, there's still plenty of variety. The older (pre-1989) resorts tend to have smaller guestrooms than newer properties such as the Venetian, and fewer facilities. However, while a good deal of hotel amenities are off-limits to non-guests (pools, in particular, are usually reserved for residents), many are open to everyone (bars, restaurants, clubs, shows). Access to spas, for which *see p194* **Star spas**, varies by hotel; most are open to the public, albeit at a price, but a few limit their access to guests.

There are, of course, hotels in other parts of town. **Downtown** was the hub of Las Vegas until the resort-building boom on the Strip in the 1950s and '60s; its hotels can't compete with the Strip in the glamour stakes, but you'll find bargains galore. **East of the Strip**, near the Convention Center, are hotels aimed squarely at the business traveller. Several hotels, such as the **JW Marriott Las Vegas/Rampart Casino** (*see p100*) in Summerlin and the new **Renaissance Las Vegas** (*see p106*), cater for visitors who want pure luxury. And though the Station casinos are chiefly aimed at locals and are best approached as gambling destinations, a couple – **Sunset Station** (*see p105*) and **Green Valley Ranch** (*see p104*) – offer fine guestrooms away from the bustle of the Strip.

Hotel-casinos generally offer such good value that the budget accommodation sector is relatively small. Any number of fading 1950s motels clutter up the more unfashionable stretches of Las Vegas Boulevard; their modern counterparts, the chain cheapies (*see* **The chain gang**), spread to all corners of the valley.

RATES AND RESERVATIONS

Las Vegas may have more hotel rooms that anywhere else in the world (over 130,000; nowhere else is even into six figures), but with 37 million visitors a year, it needs them. Some weeks, bargains abound in even the poshest properties; at other times, you'll need to book way in advance if you want to avoid being forced to sleep in your car.

The prices in this chapter are meant as guidelines only. Rates fluctuate wildly above and below the published rate depending on the date: always call ahead to check. If price is your main motivation, you'll often find exceptional bargains midweek and/or during off-season, when $200 rooms can go for as little as a third of their rack rate. Always ask about discounts. The flipside to this coin are weekends and major holidays, when prices can skyrocket. Steer clear of major conventions, too; we've listed the major ones on *pp293-294*, but for a full list, check the Las Vegas Convention & Visitors Authority's Convention Calendar, online at www.lvcva.com.

For one night in a double room, expect to pay $40-$70 in a budget hotel-casino, $70-$150 in a mid-range operation, and $150-$300 in a first-class property. In addition to these basic rates, rooms are subject to hotel tax (11 per cent Downtown, nine per cent elsewhere). You can book with the vast majority of hotel-casinos either by phone or online. For more information, try the **Las Vegas Convention & Visitors Authority** (*see p301*).

Playing in Las Vegas

The hotel parts draw the visitors, but it's the casino elements of their operations that make the moguls the bulk of their money. Depending on the time and location, the action on Vegas's

The chain gang

The following hotel chains have branches in Las Vegas, many near the Strip.

Moderate

Holiday Inn 1-800 465 4329/
www.holiday-inn.com.
Howard Johnson 1-800 446 4656/
www.hojo.com.
La Quinta 1-866 725 1661/www.lq.com.

Budget

Best Western 1-800 780 7234/
www.bestwestern.com.
Comfort Inn 1-877 424 6423/
www.comfortinn.com.
Motel 6 1-800 466 8356/
www.motel6.com.
Super 8 1-800 800 8000/
www.super8.com.

casino floors can be fast and furious, as slot players hammer 'spin' buttons, blackjack players celebrate 21s and crap players whoop it up in the dice pit. The scene is played out to the soundtrack of clinking glasses, rattling chips, tinkling coins and the electronic arpeggios of slot machines. It's overwhelming.

Still, with the nationwide spread of gambling, the experience has been dumbed down from the high-rolling James Bond image, and there's little casino etiquette to worry about. Common sense and common courtesy should see you through. Any outfit will do, from shorts to a dinner jacket, though you may want to carry a watch (clocks are conspicuous by their absence) and a sweater (the air-con is always cranked up to dissuade gamblers from leaving; Vegas casinos in summer would please a polar bear).

But playing in Las Vegas is no longer just about casino games: casino attractions have evolved with the times. There are still the circus acts at **Circus Circus** (*see p85*), the fake volcano at the Mirage and the beautiful dancing fountains at the **Bellagio** (*see p63*), but in recent years resorts have embraced adulthood. Nightclubs are all the rage, though given the open arms with which this city welcomes change, it can't be long until another fad or fashion shows up to replace them.

About this chapter

This chapter is divided into three sections.

MAJOR HOTEL-CASINOS
Las Vegas's hotel-casinos provide the bulk of the city's guestrooms. Most are stretched along the Strip, with a handful of similarly themed operations a few blocks from it (Off-Strip). The hotel-casinos Downtown are smaller, less Disneyfied and cheaper than those on the Strip.

LOCALS' CASINOS
In addition to the tourist-tilted casinos on or near the Strip and Downtown, Las Vegas has a number of casinos whose appeal is greater among locals. Typically, they don't offer much in the way of accommodation or splashy entertainment, but compensate with a full array of gambling and good-value eating options.

NON-CASINO ACCOMMODATION
In this section you'll find the pick of the town's casino-free hotels, motels, hostels and long-stay complexes. Rates in non-casino lodgings can be a lot cheaper than in Strip casinos.

Listings information

The address we've given for each casino is its main entrance, the place to arrive whether you're on foot or in a car. Here you'll find valet parking and directions to self-parking: some casinos have additional entrances at the side or back, useful if you don't want to be constantly driving up and down the traffic-choked Strip.

Each review in the 'Major Hotel-Casinos' section has four headings: **Accommodation**, a survey of the guestrooms; **Eating & drinking**, where you'll find details on each hotel's bars and restaurants (many are reviewed elsewhere; follow the cross-references for fuller critiques); **Entertainment**, a rundown of the main shows and lounges (again, many are detailed in other chapters); and **Games**, which provides an overview of the gaming facilities. Reviews in the 'Locals' Casinos' and 'Non-Casino Accommodation' sections are shorter, for an obvious reason: there's generally less to review.

At the end of each hotel-casino review, we have detailed the property's key **Amenities** and the range of **Gambling** it offers. Bear in mind that minimums can rise at night.

Major Hotel-Casinos

The Strip

Most hotels and resorts are on Las Vegas Boulevard South, between Russell Road and Sahara Avenue – aka the Strip. Furthest south are **Mandalay Bay** (plus the adjoining **Four Seasons Las Vegas** and **THEhotel at Mandalay Bay**) and the **Luxor**; a little north of here, at the junction of Tropicana Avenue, sit four large casinos: the **Tropicana**, **Excalibur**, **New York–New York** and the **MGM Grand**.

The centre of the Strip has the biggest cluster of hotel-casinos: the **Monte Carlo**, the **Aladdin/Planet Hollywood** and **Paris Las Vegas** are followed to the north by **Bally's** (adjoining Paris), the **Bellagio**, **Barbary Coast** and **Caesars Palace**, all of which occupy the junction with Flamingo Road; it's the liveliest corner of the city. Slightly further north, past the **Flamingo**, the **Imperial Palace**, **Harrah's** and the **Venetian**, is the intersection with Spring Mountain/Sands Avenue, home to the Fashion Show Mall and **Wynn Las Vegas**. North of here is the **Stardust**, **Circus Circus**, the **Riviera** and, a long block north, the **Sahara**.

Expensive

Bellagio

3600 Las Vegas Boulevard South, at W Flamingo Road, Las Vegas, NV 89109 (reservations 1-888 987 6667/front desk & casino 693 7111/fax 693 8559/www.bellagio.com). Bus 202, 301, 302/self-parking Las Vegas Boulevard South/valet parking Las Vegas Boulevard South or E Flamingo Road. **Rates** $159-$799 single/double; $350-$6,000 suite. **Credit** AmEx, DC, Disc, MC, V. **Map** p320 A7.

Built by Steve Wynn on the site of the old Dunes and immortalised in the recycled crime caper *Ocean's Eleven*, the Bellagio (now owned by MGM Mirage) has always been the lap of luxury. With the recent opening of a new Spa Tower, which added 928 rooms and spearheaded an ongoing 'soft' remodel that's replacing the gaudy bright reds and yellows with a more sophisticated palette of muted neutrals, it's only grown posher. Of course, the bosses haven't tampered too much with a winning formula, and so the hotel still evokes the ambience of a Lake Como villa (albeit supersized), complete with an eight-acre lake fronting the Strip, a lush garden conservatory that changes with the holidays and an elegant pool area imagined as a formal Old World Italian garden.

The resort is the archetypal playground for well-heeled adults, and not only because unaccompanied under-18s aren't allowed on site. The Bellagio is wholly geared for high-minded, grown-up entertainment, whether in the form of posh restaurants, a tiny but tony promenade of boutiques (**Via Bellagio**; *see p178*), Cirque du Soleil's most sophisticated show, Via Fiore, a new walkway between the conservatory and the Spa Tower that's dotted with shops and informal eateries. The freshly expanded spa (*see p194* **Star spas**), salon and fitness centre is a lavish perk available only to guests, as is access to the renowned **Shadow Creek** golf course. And then there's the hotel's signature fountain ballet (*see p117*), which, in the afternoons and evenings, shoots water into the air. The sidewalk on the Strip in front of the hotel offers superb vantage points, as do the Bellagio's many lakefront restaurants and bars.

Accommodation

Bellagio's 3,933 rooms are large, beautifully furnished and recently remodelled to the tune of $110 million. The beds all have Serta mattresses, and the spacious, marble-floored bathrooms come with deep-soaking tubs and private-label amenities. Flat-screen TVs (27-inchers), electronic drapes and well stocked minibars are standard. The resort's nine luxury villas – outfitted with gold fixtures, Lalique

Bellagio.

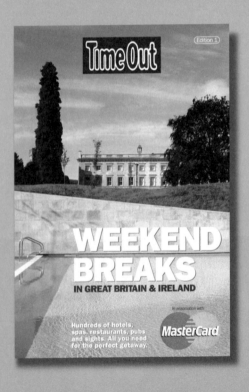

crystal accents, butler service, gyms, steam rooms, kitchens and private pools – are open to anyone willing to fork out up to $6,000 a night, not just to high rollers. The Presidential suites atop the Spa Tower are ultra-modern. Regardless of which tower you choose, the hotel's TV channel simulcasts the fountain show music, so you can listen in your room.

Eating & drinking

The Bellagio almost single-handedly raised the city's culinary profile. The pick of the restaurants is Julian Serrano's French/Mediterranean **Picasso** (*see p145*), hung with the artist's paintings; lovers of steak head for **Prime** (*see p143*), Jean-Georges Vongerichten's superior chophouse; for pan-Asian, try **Noodles** (*see p151*); while those after seafood seek out **Michael Mina** (*see p150*). For Italian, try Todd English's **Olives** (*see p148*) or the circus-themed **Osteria del Circo** (*see p148*); it's overseen by Sirio Maccioni, who also owns the more formal **Le Cirque** (*see p144*) next door. In the Spa Tower, you'll find **Sensi** (*see p147*), where Asian, Italian, grilled and seafood delicacies are served in a serene room, and the **Jean-Philippe Patisserie**, whose tri-coloured chocolate fountain (milk, white and dark) hints at the sweet sensations held within. The glitterati enjoy the upscale comfort food at **Fix** (*see p142*), while those looking for casual fare can check out the 24-hour **Café Bellagio**. Seasonally, dine at the **Pool Café**.

Entertainment

An international cast of dancers, musicians, clowns, acrobats, divers, swimmers and aerialists takes to the watery stage in **O** (*see p221*), the stunning spectacle from Cirque du Soleil. Evenings, catch covers bands at the **Fontana Bar** (*see p175*), a lounge with great cocktails and superb views of the fountains. For late-night fun, check out the pretty crowds sipping pricey Martinis at **Caramel** (*see p166*) or gyrating at upstairs nightclub **Light** (*see p242*).

Gambling

The casino is luxurious if vulgar: the upholstery, carpets and striped canopies above the tables are a clash of colours and patterns. Still, it offers all the usual games. Celebs such as Drew Barrymore (playing $5 blackjack) and Dennis Rodman have been known to gamble here. As you might expect, table limits are higher than at most Strip properties: minimums are often $25-$50 and it's difficult to find a $5 blackjack game (maybe they opened one just for Drew). The race and sports book is one of the most comfortable in town, and the poker room has replaced Binion's as the mecca for the pros, sharks and big-time players.

Amenities *Bars (8). Business centre. Concierge. Disabled-adapted rooms. Gym. High-speed internet (ADSL). No-smoking floors. Pools (outdoor). Restaurants (19). Spa.* **Games** *Baccarat ($100-$15,000); mini baccarat ($25-$15,000); Big Six; blackjack ($10-$10,000); Caribbean stud; craps (3x, 4x, 5x); casino war; Let it Ride; pai gow poker; pai gow tiles; poker; roulette (single & double zero); three-card poker.*

Caesars Palace

3570 Las Vegas Boulevard South, at W Flamingo Road, Las Vegas, NV 89109 (reservations 1-800 634 6661/front desk & casino 731 7110/fax 967 3890/www.caesarspalace.com). Bus 202, 301, 302/ self-parking & valet parking Las Vegas Boulevard South or S Industrial Road. **Rates** $129-$500 single/double; $500-$3,000 suite. **Credit** AmEx, DC, Disc, MC, V. **Map** p320 A7.

Caesars Palace just keeps growing, often in a manner that appears motivated by available acreage rather than any coherent design plan. Yet, even as the resort continues its steroidal growth spurt, it at least strives for elegance rather than camp. While the Bellagio is the epitome of new Vegas luxury, Caesars is an icon of classic Sin City decadence, a meld of affluence, kitsch and glamour. Since opening in 1966, it's been the quintessential pleasure-dome, the backdrop for countless films, and the site of many sports events, among them Evel Knievel's near-fatal motorcycle jump in 1967 (and a successful follow-up by his son Robbie 22 years later).

Though Caesars' craziest kitsch has been toned down, the resort remains a monument to ancient Greece and Rome, with miles of gold decor, marble columns, arches and colonnades, manicured gardens, costumed centurions, and copies of Greek and Roman statuary. A five-acre outdoor Roman Plaza Amphitheatre has recently opened, and in late 2005, the resort is scheduled to open the all-suites, 949-room Augustus Tower, which cost $289 million and will increase the room count to 3,370.

Key to Caesars' continuing allure is the 4.5 acre Garden of the Gods pool area (a section of which is set aside for topless sunbathing), a San Simeon-like masterpiece with four mosaic pools, marble statuary, fountains and mini-throne lifeguard stands. And when it comes to retail, the ever-expanding **Forum Shops** (*see p177*), fashioned after an ancient Roman streetscape, is unmatched. The resort also has a spa and a wedding chapel; guests have access to **Cascata**, the resort's golf course in Boulder City.

Accommodation

Caesars' standard rooms are expansive, with king-size beds, marble bathrooms and jacuzzi tubs, high-speed internet and wireless keyboards. The suites are fancier: some have circular beds, in-room saunas, bathrobes, wet bars, living/dining rooms, home theatres, wine grottos, saunas, steam and workout rooms. The highest of high rollers – and celebs like Oprah and Michael Jordan – are comped into the luxurious Pool Villas, with private pools, an indoor driving range, a cigar den and a games room.

Eating & drinking

Top of the tree are **Bradley Ogden**'s chic regional American eaterie (*see p141*) and Jean-Marie Josselin's Euro-Asian-Pacific Rim restaurant **808**. Continuing to build its roster of top toques, Caesars recently welcomed the Vegas edition of Bobby Flay's NYC hot spot **Mesa Grill**, serving Southwestern fare; in late 2005, **Guy Savoy** will bring a branch of his eponymous Parisian restaurant to the Augustus Tower. Other options include **Terrazza**, which overlooks the pool; trattoria **Viale**, by the Roman Plaza Amphitheatre; the **Empress Court** for upscale Chinese; and **Café Lago**, the prettiest (and priciest) coffee shop on the Strip.

There are also a number of excellent eateries in the Forum Shops, among them Florida's **Joe's Stone Crab** (*see p150*), Santa Monica's **Boa Steakhouse** and Manhattan's ridiculously pricey **Il Mulino**. Other options include the new **Sushi Roku**, Italian trattoria **Bertolini's**, and two Wolfgang Puck spots, Asian restaurant **Chinois** and trend-setting **Spago** (*see p147*). For casual fare, there's a **Stage Deli**, where portions and prices are huge.

Entertainment

The biggest name here, and one of the biggest in town, is **Celine Dion** (*see p219*), who performs her show *A New Day* in the custom-built, $95-million, 4,100-seat Colosseum. When she's off, Elton John deps with his *Red Piano* show; other semi-regular headliners include comic Jerry Seinfeld, always a popular choice with visitors. The newest nightlife choice is **Pure** (*see p242*), a SoBe-meets-Manhattan spot owned by Dion, Shaquille O'Neal, Andre Agassi and Steffi Graf; included in it is the burlesque-oriented **Pussycat Dolls Lounge** (*see p244* **A nudge and a wink**). The **Shadow Bar** (*see p168*) boasts flair bartenders and silhouetted beauties bumping and grinding behind backlit scrims; for

The biggest *and* the best?

Las Vegas has a reputation for a lot of things. It even has a reputation for having a reputation. And that's not even the end of it: Las Vegas is constantly associated with possessing the biggest, the best, the most and the greatest of this, or for being the capital of that. But does the truth match up?

MOST GAMBLING? Who's arguing? In terms of gambling seats, Moscow is a distant second.

MOST HOTEL ROOMS? There are over 130,000 here. Las Vegas is home to 18 of the 20 largest hotels in the US, including the top 13, and even the big ones are getting bigger: the Venetian is building a sister hotel that'll give the entire complex 7,000 rooms.

MOST CIRQUE DU SOLEIL PRODUCTIONS? Easily. With *O*, *Mystère*, *Zumanity* and now *Kà* all resident in town, Las Vegas may also boast more French-Canadian trapezists than anywhere else in the world. In 2006, the Mirage will open a fifth Cirque show.

MOST CHURCHES PER CAPITA? Sorry: that's just urban legend, even counting the wedding chapels. Speaking of which…

MOST WEDDINGS? Certainly: the city ties as many as 120,000 knots per year.

MOST DIVORCES? Surprisingly not. Reno holds a slim lead in untying knots: 15 per cent of its population, compared with 'just' 14 per cent in Vegas.

COUNTRY'S LOWEST WELFARE EXPENDITURE? No. Ranking spending by capita, Nevada is 'only' 49th of 50 states.

BRIGHTEST SPOT ON EARTH? Intellectually, perhaps not, but the Luxor's beam is actually visible from the moon.

MOST SUCCESSFUL MALL? Easily. Even after the J-Lo and Ben Affleck split, the Forum Shops still takes in $1,300 per square foot, $970 more than the national average.

FASTEST-GROWING METROPOLITAN AREA IN THE US? Nobody produces driver's licences like Nevada. Most of them are for Las Vegas's 10,000 monthly newcomers.

MOST STRIP CLUBS PER CAPITA? Sorry: that's Portland, Oregon. Though Vegas does have the largest strip club in the US, if that makes you feel any better.

TALLEST STRUCTURE WEST OF THE MISSISSIPPI? The Stratosphere has been king for a decade, at 1,149 feet (350 metres). It has also been nominated as the ugliest.

HIGHEST WATER USE PER CAPITA? The average drought-stricken Las Vegan uses 307 gallons of water a day, compared to the national average of 190. Evidently not all royal flushes happen in the casinos.

WORLD'S LARGEST NEON COWBOY? Vegas Vic (*see p14* **Viva Vegas Vic**) went up in 1951 at a cost of $25,000. It is still among the largest mechanical neon signs on earth.

MOST ELECTIVE PLASTIC SURGERIES PER PERSON? Close, but Las Vegas is just behind Washington, DC. Then again, it's sometimes hard to tell which statistics are real.

WORLD'S MOST EXPENSIVE RESORT? Wynn Las Vegas, though to have cost $2.7 billion.

HIGHEST ALCOHOL CONSUMPTION? According to a survey by *Men's Fitness* magazine in 2005, Nevadans consume 3.67 gallons of ethanol per person per year, the highest of any state in the union.

Fit for an emperor: **Caesar's Palace**. *See p65.*

old-time Caesars Palace kitsch, there's the enduring **Cleopatra's Barge** (*see p166*). Also here are the **Seahorse Lounge**, serving Martinis, champagne and, at midday, tea amid a giant aquarium stocked with Australian potbelly seahorses; and the fine **Terrazza Lounge** and **Galleria Bar**, both of which have live music. Above Chinois, in the Forum Shops, there's **OPM** (*see p242*).

Gambling

Few casinos offer the limits or the atmosphere of Caesars; when there's a big fight in town, limits on the main floor can go through the roof. The sports book is one of the highest-energy spots to watch big-screen TVs and accepts some of the biggest bets. You get a good view of the baccarat pit, an intimate nook where huge wagers per hand are not uncommon. And for the boldest of slot players, the $500 machine – with a $1 million jackpot – uses gold-plated tokens. (The machine itself pays a winning spin of only two $500 coins; for every other payback, the machine locks and an attendant hand-pays the gambler.) The high-limit slots are in the Palace Casino near the main entrance; blackjack pits and slots in the Forum Casino offer slightly lower limits.

Amenities *Bars (7). Business centre. Concierge. Disabled-adapted rooms. Gym. High-speed internet (ADSL, web TV). No-smoking floors. Pools (outdoor). Restaurants (10). Spa.* **Games** *Baccarat ($100-$15,000); mini baccarat ($20-$10,000); Big Six; blackjack ($5-$10,000); Caribbean stud; casino war; craps (3x 4&10, 4x 5&9, 5x 6&8); keno; Let it Ride; pai gow poker; pai gow tiles; poker; roulette (single zero & double zero); Spanish 21; three-card poker. Gambling lessons. Games designed for sight- & hearing-impaired players.*

Mandalay Bay

3950 Las Vegas Boulevard South, at E Hacienda Avenue, Las Vegas, NV 89119 (reservations 1-877 632 7000/front desk & casino 632 7777/fax 632 7234/www.mandalaybay.com). Bus 105, 301/ self-parking & valet parking E Hacienda Avenue. **Rates** *$109-$599 single/double; $199-$2,999 suite.* **Credit** *AmEx, DC, Disc, MC, V.* **Map** *p320 A9.*

The South Seas island-themed Mandalay Bay is one of the Strip's most luxurious resorts and the flagship property of the Mandalay Bay group, which currently also includes the Luxor, the Excalibur and Circus Circus. At its heart is an 11-acre water park with a sandy beach, a wave pool, a lazy river, two additional pools and a jogging track set in lush green foliage. There's also the newly opened **Moorea Bay Beach Club**, a limited-access beach retreat by day where topless sunbathing is permitted (a small fee gets you in); it becomes a sultry hotspot on warm-weather weekend nights.

The interior is just as impressive. An understated oasis of water features, lush foliage, huge aquariums and island architecture, it encompasses a sensuous spa, a classy collection of restaurants, a pair of wedding chapels, several theatres and the truly splendid, kid-friendly **Shark Reef** aquarium (*see p115*). **Mandalay Place**, a nice sky-bridge mall that connects the hotel with the Luxor, contains a number of upscale boutiques and restaurants, a chic barber and even Forty Deuce, a 'back-alley strip-tease lounge'. Some 1.8 million sq ft (170,000sq m) of top-class convention space opened in 2003.

If all this doesn't work for you, then there are also two other hotels accessible from Mandalay Bay. A corridor off the lobby leads to the **Four Seasons Las Vegas** (*see p105*), which has its rooms on floors 35 to 39 but is run as a separate operation, while **THEhotel at Mandalay Bay** (*see p106*) is an all-suites, casino-free tower that eschews the island theme entirely.

Accommodation

Guestrooms at Mandalay Bay proper are elegant, and are decorated with the same serene sophistication brought to the rest of the hotel. Bathrooms come with giant soaking tubs, separate showers and bathrobes. Larger suites command excellent views of the Strip or the surrounding mountains and come with wet bars, robes, large TVs and brand-name spa products. A neat perk: all guests can tune in to Shark TV, an in-house channel that lets you spy on the fish swimming in the aquariums at Shark Reef.

Casinos & Hotels

Eating & drinking

Mandalay Bay is unusual among the major resorts on the Strip in that it locates many of its eateries in a 'restaurant row' away from the casino, so you can dine without seeing – or, just as crucially, hearing – so much as a single slot machine. The new boîte on the block is an outpost of San Francisco's **Fleur de Lys** (*see p144*), helmed by chef Hubert Keller. Also noteworthy are Charlie Palmer's **Aureole** (*see p141*); Wolfgang Puck's **Trattoria del Lupo** (*see p148*); **Border Grill** (*see p148*), serving nouveau Mexican and couture tequila; and **3950** (Mandalay Bay's address, in case you were wondering), an intimate and suitably pricey steak-and-seafood place. Other options: **China Grill** (*see p143*) and **Shanghai Lily** for Asian fare; **Rumjungle**, a Brazilian *rodizio* and rum bar/nightclub (*see p168*); **Red Square** (*see p168*), a communist theme bar; and **Red, White & Blue**, a decent but way-too-pricey café.

You'll have to venture into the casino to sample the Cajun cooking at **House of Blues** (*see p142*), upstairs from the nightclub/concert venue. The venue's super-exclusive **Foundation Room** serves dinner to members and VIPs amid luxe furnishings on Mandalay Bay's top floor. Ringing the casino are the nice 24-hour **Raffles Café**, the **Noodle Shop** and the **Coral Reef Lounge**, where dancing to live music and supping on sushi are the order of the evening. Over at Mandalay Place, carnivores can have theirs with lettuce and tomato at **Burger Bar** (*see p141*); also here are **RM Seafood** (with two dining rooms, **R-Bar-Café** and the more intimate restaurant **RM**) and **Chocolate Swan**.

Entertainment

The 12,000-seat **Mandalay Bay Events Center** (*see p237*) always has a full schedule of boxing events and concerts, but a better choice is the more acoustically enjoyable **House of Blues** (*see p237*), which features the best concert schedule in town – though fans of the Joint at the Hard Rock might argue the point – and hosts post-show retro dance parties on weekends. When the weather's warm, the hotel produces the Bay Rock Concert series on Mandalay Beach. The hotel's resident show, imported from London but tweaked for Vegas, is featherweight Abba-fest **Mamma Mia!** (*see p221*).

Bar- and clubwise, Hollywood's **Forty Deuce** (*see p244* **A nudge and a wink**) in Mandalay Place is all the rage, while **Rumjungle** (*see p243*) continues to draw a young, pretty crowd with pounding Latin/Caribbean beats. Late on Mondays, the aforementioned Foundation Room opens to host **Godspeed** (*see p241*), a night of house music for the scenesters. Looking for a quieter vibe? There's piano music in the casino's **Orchid Lounge** and, on weekends (6-8pm), at Charlie Palmer Steak.

Gambling

The 135,000sq ft (12,500sq m) casino is airier than many, with 2,400 machines (including nickel video slots that take up to 45 or 90 coins), but you have to hunt for the better video poker machines. Table games (122 of them) include blackjack, roulette, craps, Let it Ride, Caribbean stud, pai gow poker and mini baccarat. You'll also find a poker room where you can get your fix of seven-card stud and Texas or Omaha hold 'em. The race and sports book has 17 large screens, enough seating for some 300 sports fans, and a good deli.

Amenities *Bars (3). Business centre. Disabled-adapted rooms. Gym. High-speed internet (web TV, wireless). No-smoking floors. Pool (outdoor). Restaurants (21). Spa.* **Games** *Baccarat ($100-$15,000); mini baccarat ($15-$15,000); blackjack ($10-$15,000); Caribbean stud; craps (3x, 4x, 5x); keno; Let it Ride; pai gow poker; pai gow tiles; poker; roulette (single zero & double zero); three-card poker. Gambling lessons.*

Mirage

3400 Las Vegas Boulevard South, between Spring Mountain Road & W Flamingo Road, Las Vegas, NV 89109 (reservations 1-800 627 6667/front desk & casino 791 7111/fax 791 7414/www.the mirage.com). Bus 203, 213, 301, 302/self-parking Spring Mountain Road/valet parking Las Vegas Boulevard South. **Rates** *$109-$599 single/double; $275-$5,000 suite.* **Credit** *AmEx, DC, Disc, MC, V.* **Map** *p320 A6.*

This $650 million tropical island hotel, with its Polynesian village decor, lush landscaping, lagoon-like pool, waterfalls and marine-life fixation, set the industry standard for modern megaresorts when it was opened by Steve Wynn in 1989. Now owned by MGM Mirage, it's looking a little dated: not shabby by any means (it's extremely well maintained), just a bit naff and decidedly ten-years-ago. Despite its history, it seems not to notice the trends that sweep the Strip almost constantly: unlike most of its direct rivals, there's virtually no shopping to speak of here, and the nightlife is designed largely for early birds. However, despite all this, the Mirage is still a draw among high rollers who appreciate both the excellent service and the absence of pesky young people, as well as passers-by who've stopped by purely to enjoy the exploding volcano (recently overhauled to make it more realistic: it's not, but it's a good show nonetheless), the 90-foot-high rainforest atrium filled with fresh and faux palm trees and orchids, the much-imitated 20,000-gallon aquarium behind the registration desk, and the **Secret Garden & Dolphin Habitat** (*see p119*). And do make time to stop by the pool, perhaps the corner of the hotel where the theme is rendered most convincingly of all.

Accommodation

The redecoration of the Mirage in 2002 freshened the colour scheme from pale pastels to deeper cranberry, green and yellow, with island-like cane furnishings, crown mouldings and floor-to-ceiling headboards with louvred panels. Sadly, it couldn't make the rooms any bigger: next to some of its recent competitors, the rooms here aren't huge. An in-house TV network features films on demand,

and there's now high-speed internet access in the rooms (albeit at a price). The gorgeous pool area comprises a series of blue lagoons, inlets and waterfalls, plus two islands exotically landscaped with various palms and tropical flowers.

Eating & drinking

Renoir, formerly the hotel's keystone restaurant, unexpectedly closed in 2004; its chef, Alessandro Stratta, has since adjourned to open a new eaterie at Wynn Las Vegas. The restaurant has yet to be replaced, leaving the hotel with a rather unexciting range of eateries. One good, reliable spot is the long-standing **Samba Grill**, which features impressive Carmen-Miranda-on-steroids decor and a hearty all-you-can-eat rodizio where the meats, fish and fowl keep coming until you eat yourself sick or waddle away, replete, into the sunset. **Onda** serves Italian food; **Kokomo's** is the hotel's classic steakhouse; Oriental food is covered with the theatrical **Moongate** (Chinese) and **Mikado** (Japanese). The best bets, though, may be a pair of low-price chains from opposite coasts: the **California Pizza Kitchen** and, an unlikely arrival from New York City in 2005, the **Carnegie Deli**.

Entertainment

Siegfried & Roy having been forced to cancel their show after Roy had an on-stage disagreement with one of his tigers, the Mirage has been left in the unenviable position of having to bet all its chips on desperately mediocre singer/impressionist **Danny Gans** (*see p214*). Gans's show is supplemented by a roster of irregular headliners (the likes of **Dana Carvey** and **Jay Leno**), but the 2006 arrival of a **Cirque du Soleil** show themed around the music of the Beatles can't come soon enough. Reflecting the affluent but not exactly stylish nature of its clientele, there's no nightclub here: you'll have to make do with uptempo covers bands in the **Ava** lounge, and too-smooth jazz in the **Onda Lounge** outside (yes, you guessed it) the Onda restaurant.

Gambling

The Mirage has nearly 100 blackjack tables, most dealt from six-deck shoes. Minimums are high: $10 for 21, craps and roulette, $25 for mini baccarat, $100 for baccarat. You can find a good game of poker at any hour of the day, and since many players are tourists, the action, both on the low- and high-limit tables, is good. You'll also find some alternative table games, such as Let it Ride and casino war. For a break, check out the high-limit slots. If you're polite, and it's not too busy, an attendant will show you around, and perhaps offer you some fresh, sliced fruit, normally reserved for players who insert $100 tokens five at a time (their generosity truly knows no bounds). The Red, White & Blue slot offers a $1 million jackpot.

Amenities *Bars (3). Business centre. Disabled-adapted rooms. Gym. High-speed internet (ADSL). No-smoking floors. Pool (outdoor). Restaurants (13). Spa.* **Games** *Baccarat ($100-$15,000); mini baccarat ($25-$15,000); Big Six; blackjack ($10-$10,000); Caribbean stud; casino war; craps (3x 6&8); keno; Let it Ride; pai gow poker; pai gow tiles; poker; roulette (single zero & double zero); Spanish 21; three-card poker.*

Paris Las Vegas

3655 Las Vegas Boulevard South, at E Flamingo Road, Las Vegas, NV 89109 (reservations 1-877 796 2096/front desk & casino 946 7000/fax 946 4405/www.parislasvegas.com). Bus 202, 301, 302/ self-parking & valet parking Las Vegas Boulevard South or Audrie Street. **Rates** *$99-$599 single/double; $350-$2,500 suite.* **Credit** *AmEx, DC, Disc, MC, V.* **Map** *p320 A7.*

What happens when the City of Lights collides with the City of Light? Versions of Paris's greatest monuments cut down to size, all-you-can-eat crêpes at the buffet, reasonably polite waiters, ancient Rome across the street... and, of course, the lights never go out. If only the real Paris could be so accommodating. Even the French love Las Vegas.

Casinos & Hotels

Mirage.

To say that this huge resort in the heart of the Strip is one of the town's most eye-catching is to do its effervescent absurdity a rank injustice. Its reproductions of Parisian landmarks start with the 34-storey tower of 2,916 rooms modelled after the Hôtel de Ville, and also take in the Louvre, the Paris Opéra, the Arc de Triomphe and, of course, the half-scale replica of the Eiffel Tower, built using Gustav Eiffel's original plans, that plunges into the casino. The theming continues within, with French-themed restaurants, shops and even, though you'll need to look closely, the casino. It may seem rather sub-Disney at first glance, but it's by no means all haw-hee-haw cliché: you can also lose yourself in a cocktail at a 'Beverly Hillbillies' slot machine, get a massage in a mock-Balinese spa or relive your parents' youth to the music of Queen.

Accommodation
The smallish guestrooms are comfortable and somewhat stately, decorated in rich Regency style and furnished with charming canopied beds and armoires. The spacious marble bathrooms are outfitted with vanities, a make-up mirror and soaking tubs.

Eating & drinking
Paris Las Vegas doesn't do too badly at living up to its theme city's culinary reputation, albeit without the breadth of styles you'll find at the Venetian, the Bellagio or the MGM Grand. Along with **JJ's** Boulangerie and **La Creperie**, serving sandwiches and delicious sweet and savoury crêpes, and the quaint **Le Village Buffet** (*see p164*), which features regional cuisine from five French provinces, the hotel has the **Eiffel Tower Restaurant** (*see p144*), located on the tower's 11th floor, and the bustling **Mon Ami Gabi** (*see p145*), a streetside brasserie serving classics such as steak-frites. **Les Artistes Steakhouse** has a menu of rotisserie-style meats, fish and poultry, while **Ah Sin** is a chic place with patio dining that serves Thai and Chinese dishes along with Korean barbecue and sushi. **Ortanique** offers island twists on French classics, among them jerk foie gras.

Entertainment
If Paris Las Vegas's strolling mimes leave you unenthusiastic, there's a variety of ways to spend the night wisely (or otherwise). The big show here is **We Will Rock You** (*see p221*), a senseless London import that manages the almost impossible feat of debasing the music of Queen. A rather better bet is **Risqué** (*see p243*), a nightclub where old-world France meets contemporary Asian-tilted ultralounge, complete with house music and dessert bar. Downstairs there's dance music under sparkly lights among the shady faux trees of **Le Cabaret**. And for a bit o' bubbly you can't beat **Napoleon's** (*see p167*), a champagne and cigar bar where jazz combos play nightly.

Paris Las Vegas. *See p69*.

Gambling

Three of the Eiffel Tower's four legs plunge into the casino, which is smaller, noisier and more energetically crowded than most. The 100 table games and 2,000-plus slot machines are not as budget-friendly as they used to be, meaning you'll have a harder time finding $5 blackjack and crap tables, though there are still plenty of 25¢ slots. The race and sports book has big TVs and 'pari-mutuel' betting on horse racing. Theming is rampant, from Monet-style floral carpets and Metro-like wrought-iron canopies above the table games to security guards in gendarme uniforms. Check out the LeRoy Neiman paintings in the classy high-limit pit.

Amenities *Bars (6). Business centre. Concierge. Disabled-adapted rooms. Gym. High-speed internet (ADSL). No-smoking floors. Pool (outdoor). Restaurants (11). Spa.* **Games** *Baccarat ($100-$15,000); mini baccarat ($15-$5,000); Big Six; blackjack ($5-$10,000); Caribbean stud; casino war; craps (3x, 4x, 5x); Let it Ride; pai gow poker; roulette (single zero & double zero); Spanish 21; three-card poker.*

TI (Treasure Island)

3300 Las Vegas Boulevard South, at Spring Mountain Road, Las Vegas, NV 89109 (reservations 1-800 944 7444/front desk & casino 894 7111/fax 894 7414/www.treasureisland.com). Bus 203, 213, 301, 302/self-parking or valet parking Las Vegas

Boulevard South or Spring Mountain Road. **Rates** $79-$399 single/double; $159-$2,500 suite. **Credit** AmEx, DC, Disc, MC, V. **Map** p320 A6.

An object lesson in what happens when you slavishly follow focus groups rather than your own commercial instincts. Treasure Island has struggled with an identity crisis in recent years – We're Pirates of the Caribbean! No, we're Robinson Crusoe! We're for families! No, adults! – and is only now beginning to emerge from it, freshly plum-coloured, as a comfortable resort for the mid-price traveller. But it's not quite there yet. Much of the campy pirate paraphernalia that lingered around the casino, leftovers from its original incarnation as a family resort, has finally been buried. But the general design of the place doesn't live up to the fine assortment of adult-oriented shows, nightclubs and restaurants that the hotel has brought in to try and reposition itself in the market. Worse still, the pyrotechnic pirate battle in the lagoon out front remains, but in line with changes throughout the hotel, it's dropped the kid-friendly content, employed some scantily clad women and rebranded itself **Sirens of TI**. It might be the most embarrassing and undignified spectacle in North America.

Still, though its identity is a mess, there's a good deal here to like. The new line-up of restaurants is worlds better than what came before, and though TI has little shopping to speak of on its own property, a new pedestrian bridge (due to open in mid 2005) will provide easy access to **Fashion Show Mall** (*see p178*) across the street.

Accommodation

The 2,885 rooms in TI's 36-storey Y-shaped tower are average, decorated in light woods and soft pastels, with high-speed internet (for a daily fee). Many have good views of the Mirage volcano and the Sirens show below. The 220 suites are spacious, with living rooms, wet bars, two baths, jacuzzis and impressive TVs and stereos: a good deal if you feel like splashing out but not breaking the bank. The spa is disappointing; the pool has recently been remodelled in an attempt to make it more lush, though few pools can compete with the island oasis at the Mirage next door. In a bid to further distance itself from its kid-friendly past, TI has added to it the Party Tub, an oversized hot tub that seats 50.

Eating & drinking

The second-floor **Buccaneer Bay Club** remains the hotel's top restaurant, offering continental cuisine in a fortress-style dining room with a decent view of (but, praise the Lord, no sound from) the Sirens below. There's northern Italian fare at **Francesco's** and the **Steak House** serves, well, you can guess. All three restaurants now offer special packages that combine tickets for Cirque du Soleil's *Mystère* with dinner before or after the show. However, three new-ish restaurants (all opened in 2004) have revived the previously slumbering culinary scene: Richard Sandoval's buzzing Mexican spot **Isla** (*see p150*), the Jeffrey Beers-designed

Dishes buffet, and **Canter's Deli** (*see p162* **Hold the pickle!**), an offshoot of the famous LA enterprise. For casual fare, there's TI's 24-hour **Terrace Café**; the chain restaurant **Kahunaville**, which has dependable sandwiches and salads, as well as duelling pianos nightly; plus **Starbucks, Ben & Jerry's** and **Krispy Kreme**.

Entertainment

Though the captivating pitch and tumble of Cirque du Soleil's **Mystère** (*see p221*) is still good G-rated fun, the rest of TI's offerings run to more lascivious tastes. Along with the Sirens of TI, the hotel has jumped on the American burlesque bandwagon with **Tangerine** (*see p244* **A nudge and a wink**), where would-be exotic dancers do a tame bump and grind to live music and shimmy down to decorative undies; the outdoor deck opens at 11am, while the lounge opens at 5pm. The Martini crowd shakes things up among the leather couches at **Mist** (*see p167*), the small, clubby lounge brought to you by the folks behind the Bellagio's Light, Caramel and

Fix. For those who think not of gimlets but of golf when they hear the word 'club', the hotel offers access to the exclusive **Shadow Creek** golf course, a perk reserved for guests of MGM Mirage resorts.

Gambling

In the always-crowded casino, you'll find all the usual games, as well as a race and sports book, but you're the one who's likely to be plundered. As at the Mirage, the table limits are high and six-deck shoes are the rule, but the video poker – and, by association, the slots – are known to have good payback percentages.

Amenities *Bars (4). Business centre. Disabled-adapted rooms. Gym. High-speed internet (ADSL). No-smoking rooms. Pool (outdoor). Restaurants (11). Spa.* **Games** *Baccarat ($100-$15,000); mini baccarat ($25-$10,000); blackjack ($10-$15,000); Caribbean stud; casino war; craps (2x 4&10, 5&9; 3x 6&8); keno; Let it Ride; pai gow poker; pai gow tiles; roulette (double zero); Spanish 21; three-card poker.*

All through the night

It's been said that New York is the city that never sleeps, but the nickname has always had more to do with a healthy nightlife and a snappy lyric than the ability to get pizza as the sun comes up. Certainly, Frank Sinatra, king of the wee small hours, would have agreed: Las Vegas is the original 24-hour city. When the Rat Pack finished performing, they could head over to the chuckwagon buffet and pile up on some vittles, or stroll back to the bar and start the party over.

That was when the clockless Strip pervaded the city's lifestyle, but look at Vegas today, sprawled out to the hills and full of everyday folk (doctors, lawyers, master illusionists) orbiting in their own little worlds, far from the action. The city still has plenty of things that go bump (not to mention grind) through the night, but many of its residents now live nine-to-five lives, getting up and getting down when the sun does. Could it be the case that, having turned 100, Sin City is slowing down?

The term '24/7' is relatively new in pop culture, but it seems to have exploded over the last few years when everyone and their book publisher is referring to the Western world's '24-hour society'. While Vegas has long been the chief proponent of the round-the-clock lifestyle, from 5am weddings to the first all-hours 7-11, the whole world's gone nocturnal. Anyone can work out after midnight or get a prescription at 3am. Heck, Long Island's got its own 24-hour hardware store.

But surely when it comes to the wackier stuff, Las Vegas would still be in the front seat, right? So how come it fell to a little town in Colorado (Littleton, Colorado, in fact) to invent all-night indoor golf? Here in Lost Wages, meanwhile, a daytime call to the 24-Hour Income Tax Service went unanswered, and a subsequent phone call to 24-Hour Realty's number only served to further debunk the myth. 'It's just a name,' said the lady on the other end of the line, confessing to regular office hours.

But in case you think Vegas is sleeping on the job, it's worth considering that the concept of 24/7 living isn't pop culture here: it's the real deal. It isn't about globalisation, endless internet access, bosses expecting you to answer your cellphone in the middle of the night, or the FedEx mentality that makes us absolutely have to have something right now. In Vegas, it's business.

And what about that rumour about the city diluting its famous graveyard workforce with thousands of work-a-day transplants? The census shows that from 1990 to 2000, the years of Las Vegas's most seismic growth activity, the percentage of drivers who went to work between 6am and 9am in the morning changed not one bit. They still account for a steady 64 per cent of the population. Rest assured, then: this is still the same 24/7 town, and the only place on Earth that really needs pizza at dawn.

Venetian

3355 Las Vegas Boulevard South, at Sands Avenue, Las Vegas, NV 89109 (reservations 1-877 883 6423/front desk & casino 733 0201/fax 414 1100/ www.venetian.com). Bus 203, 213, 301, 302/self-parking & valet parking Las Vegas Boulevard South or E Harmon Avenue. **Rates** $169-$1,299 suite. **Credit** AmEx, DC, Disc, MC, V. **Map** p320 A6.

On the site of the Sands, this reproduction of Venice is, in places, curiously convincing, due in no small part to the historians who supervised the project. Owner Sheldon Adelson tried to recreate the real city of canals with accurate, to-scale replicas of many of its landmarks – the Rialto Bridge, the Doge's Palace, the Campanile – along with indoor and outdoor chlorinated canals traversed by singing gondoliers and itinerant 'street' performers who entertain the crowds in St Mark's Square. The exterior is a show-stopper – largely because the verisimilitude stops short of importing Venice's pigeons – but the ornate interior is also impressive, with beautiful marble floors, plush furniture and hand-painted frescoes.

Cultural attractions are a mixed bunch. The Guggenheim Las Vegas, designed by Rem Koolhaas, closed after only one show – the space will be taken over by *The Phantom of the Opera* in 2006 – but his 'jewel box' **Guggenheim Hermitage Museum** (*see p231*) remains. **Madame Tussaud's** (*see p119*) pitches at a rather different audience. The **Grand Canal Shoppes** (*see p177*) is a meandering mall with flowing canals and faux façades that curve around to St Mark's Square, from where it's possible to catch a gondola. Another key draw is **Canyon Ranch SpaClub** (*see p194* **Star spas**), which offers a full range of spa services along with movement and wellness classes, a climbing wall and a café. The resort connects to the **Sands Expo** (*see p293*); indeed, the Venetian pulls in much of its business, especially midweek, from the growing convention market. Those looking to tie the knot can now do so in the resort's new wedding chapel.

Accommodation

At 700sq ft (65sq m), standard guest suites (there are no regular suites) are far larger than the Vegas norm. Sumptuously appointed in rich blues and yellows, the suites have Italian marble foyers, crown mouldings, canopied beds, oversized marble bathrooms, minibars, multiple TVs and laptop safes. Nothing's been forgotten: even the bathroom phone has a dataport. In June 2003, the Venetian added 1,013 non-smoking rooms in the 12-storey **Venezia Tower**, built atop the resort's parking structure. Though the rooms are similar to those in the original Venetian tower, some extra amenities – private elevator, separate check-in, complimentary newspaper delivery, access to the secluded Italian-style pool garden and arboretum – make the upgrade worthwhile. For a little more exclusivity, there's the concierge level: the tower's top three floors where an Old World drawing room-style lounge and speciality baths, drawn per your request, are among the extra perks. But the Venetian isn't stopping with all

this lot: in February 2005, construction began on the Palazzo Resort-Hotel-Casino, a separate resort that will add 3,000 suites to the Venetian family.

Eating & drinking

Where to begin? The Venetian's restaurant roster reads like a *Who's Who* of top chefs. Thomas Keller (of French Laundry fame) runs stellar brasserie **Bouchon** (*see p144*); David Feau's contemporary French **Lutèce** (*see p144*) remains in Vegas after the 2004 closing of the NYC original; Wolfgang Puck and Emeril Lagasse respectively run Mediterranean café **Postrio** (*see p147*) and Cajun **Delmonico Steakhouse** (*see p142*); both Joachim Splichal's **Pinot Brasserie** (*see p145*) and Tom Moloney's **AquaKnox** serve California cuisine; and Kevin Wu's **Royal Star** (*see p143*) specialises in Cantonese and Mandarin dishes. This being ersatz Venice, there's plenty of Italian food: Piero Selvaggio's dual rooms **Valentino** and **The Grill at Valentino**; **Zeffirino** (*see p148*), a Genoan-style seafood restaurant with a fan club that includes Pavarotti; and **Canaletto** (*see p148*). Coming late in 2005 is **Tao Asian Bistro**, sibling to the fashionable New York City restaurant-nightclub. Less pricey options (it's all relative) include **Tsunami Asian Bar and Grill** for sushi, Chinese, Korean and Thai; the excellent 24-hour **Grand Lux Café**; and **Taqueria Cañonita**.

Entertainment

The Venetian has improved its night-time entertainment options, ditching *V: The Ultimate Variety Show* and the tiresome *Lord of the Dance* in favour of the **Blue Man Group** (*see p220*), lured from the Luxor to open in the renovated **C2K** nightclub/showroom in September 2005. There's also Andrew Lloyd Webber's **Phantom of the Opera**, which will move into the old Guggenheim Las Vegas space in the spring of 2006. Meanwhile, the Venetian, which never had much luck with C2K as a nightclub, has rolled the dice again with **Vivid** (*see p244*). A branch of **Tao**, the chic New York City pan-Asian boîte and über-cool nightclub, has joined sizzling minimalist lounge **V Bar** (*see p169*).

Gambling

In the casino, the 109 table games include blackjack, craps, Caribbean stud, Let it Ride and pai gow, as well as a James Bond-friendly, single-zero roulette wheel, of which there aren't many in Vegas. The casino's 2,655 slots are weighted toward reel games, with a large mix of $1 machines. For the player with pull, there are some high-denomination machines – $5, $25 and $100 – in the casino's high-limit salon, which also includes a baccarat pit and 12 table games (blackjack for $50,000 a hand).

Amenities Bars (3). Business centre. Concierge. Disabled-adapted rooms. Gym. High-speed internet (ADSL). No-smoking floors. Pool (outdoor). Restaurants (18). Spa. **Games** *Baccarat ($50-$15,000); mini baccarat ($25-$10,000); Big Six; blackjack ($10-$50,000); Caribbean stud; casino war; craps (3x, 4x, 5x); keno; Let it Ride; pai gow poker; pai gow tiles; poker; roulette (single & double zero).*

Wynn Las Vegas

*3131 Las Vegas Boulevard South, at Spring
Mountain Road, Las Vegas, NV 89109 (reservations
1-888 320 9966/front desk 770 7100/fax 770
1571/www.wynnlasvegas.com). Bus 203, 213, 301,
302/self-parking & valet parking Las Vegas
Boulevard South or (Tower Suites only) Spring
Mountain Road.* **Rates** $250-$450 single/double;
$400-$1,700 suite. **Credit** AmEx, DC, Disc, MC, V.
Map p319 B6.

Sit on the patio at Ra Sushi, directly across Las
Vegas Boulevard from Steve Wynn's new megaresort, and what springs to mind is Flagstaff, Arizona:
all pine trees and mountainous terrain, save for the
bronze and concrete curved structure rising out of
the mountain with the Strip baron's name scrawled
in neon across the top. Only the view from Spring
Mountain Road alludes to the grandeur that awaits
inside. Once known as the man who brought Vegas
entertainment curbside, Wynn has gone against
his own convention and designed this luxury resort,
the only one to which he's signed his name, from the
inside out.

Luxury is everywhere, as you'd expect from a
casino that cost somewhere in the region of $2.7 bil-
lion to build. The 35,000sq ft (3,300 sq m), garden-
themed spa houses 45 treatment rooms, a beauty
salon, a barber and a state-of-the-art fitness centre.
It's the only spa in the country to offer Crème de la
Mer facials and body treatments. The 18-hole championship golf course was designed by Tom Fazio;
the 18th hole contains a 35-foot waterfall, and is
overlooked by 36 fairway villas. Luxury boutiques
present at the **Wynn Esplanade** (*see p178*) include
Louis Vuitton, Christian Dior, Oscar de la Renta and
Brioni, as well as such signature shops as La Flirt,
a upscale beauty store with all of the Estée Lauder
brands under one roof, and Penske Wynn Ferrari
Maserati, Nevada's only factory-authorised Ferrari
and Maserati dealership. The Gallery features paintings from Steve and Elaine Wynn's personal collection; among them are Picasso's *Le Rêve*, the original
inspiration for, and name of, Wynn Las Vegas.

Accommodation

The lavish (naturally) 640sq ft guestrooms offer an
'ultimate retreat', with floor-to-ceiling windows, pil-
low-top signature Wynn beds with 320-thread-count
European linens, a seating area with a sofa and
ottomans, a dining table and chairs, flat-screen LCD
TVs in the living rooms, spacious bath areas and
bedside drapery controls. The suites promise to set
a new Vegas standard: some have their own private
massage rooms, VIP check-in areas, private pools
and dining rooms.

Eating & drinking

Though Steve Wynn has been partly responsible for
the onslaught in Vegas of absentee celebrity chefs
who slap their names on the marquees but leave the
cooking to others, the restaurants at Wynn Las
Vegas will be run directly by their name chefs. The
signature spot is **Alex**: run by Alessandro Stratta

of Renoir fame, it promises to be one of the best
dining additions to the Strip in 2005. Other much-
anticipated hotspots here include Daniel Boulud's
Brasserie, Eric Klein's **SW Steakhouse**, Takashi
Yagihashi's **Okada**, Mark LoRusso's **Tableau**
and Paul Bartolotta's **Bartolotta Ristorante di
Mare**. Bring a credit card. *See p142* **Every one's
a Wynner** and *p155* **Viva Elizabeth Blau**.

Entertainment

Creator of Cirque du Soleil's *O* and *Mystère*, both of
which are still performed at former Wynn properties, Franco Dragone has been called on to design
the debut production in Wynn Las Vegas's domed
theatre. **Le Rêve** (*see p221*) is named after the
Picasso masterpiece, initially the inspiration for the
hotel itself, and promises to be an aquatic wonder
with a unique set-up. In late 2005, Tony-winning
musical **Avenue Q** will open in a $40 million, 1,200-
seat theatre designed specifically for it.

Gambling

As with the rest of the resort, the action at Wynn
Las Vegas seems likely to be both sophisticated and
decidedly spendy. The casino's minimums and maximum bets were not finalised as we went to press,
but they're unlikely to favour the low-roller. Expect
blackjack to start at $10 and baccarat at $50. There'll
be around 2,000 slots on site, plus a sports book.

Amenities *Bars (6). Business centre. Concierge.
Disabled-adapted rooms. Gym. High-speed internet
(ADSL). No-smoking floors. Pool (outdoor).
Restaurants (18). Spa.* **Games** *Baccarat; mini
baccarat; Big Six; blackjack; Caribbean stud; casino
war; craps; Let it Ride; pai gow poker; pai gow
tiles; poker; roulette (single & double zero); Spanish
21; three-card poker.*

Wynn Las Vegas.

Moderate

Aladdin/Planet Hollywood

3667 Las Vegas Boulevard South, at E Harmon Avenue, Las Vegas, NV 89109 (reservations 1-877 333 9474/front desk 785 5555/fax 785 9600/www. aladdincasino.com). Bus 301/self-parking & valet parking E Harmon Avenue. **Rates** *$59-$499 single/double; $199-$2,000 suite.* **Credit** *AmEx, DC, Disc, MC, V.* **Map** *p320 A7.*

The Aladdin, where Elvis and Priscilla tied the knot, was built in the mid 1960s and imploded back in 1998, before rising phoenix-like in 2000 with an updated 1,001 Nights theme. When it descended into bankruptcy in 2002, it was put up for sale and later acquired by Starwood and Planet Hollywood International founder and CEO Robert Earl. Until plans to transform it into a Planet Hollywood resort finally take place (Aladdin is scheduled to rub his magic lamp one last time in late 2006 or maybe early 2007), it still holds its own as a destination resort. Amenities include the Elemis Spa, fashioned after a Moroccan retreat; **Desert Passage** (*see p177*), a galleria of shops and eateries that loops through a Middle Eastern-style market (complete with hourly indoor rainstorm); and the historic Aladdin Theatre for the Performing Arts, which will undergo a 'modernisation' when the renovations take place. The new Planet Hollywood promises to offer 'a real taste of Hollywood' and plans to compete for the hipsters that now flock to the Palms and the Hard Rock.

Accommodation

The Aladdin's 2,567 rooms aren't knockouts by any means, but they are new, comfortable and decorated in soft pastels with dark-wood furnishings. The marble bathrooms have separate showers, extra-deep soaking tubs and button-cute sink fixtures that resemble Aladdin's lamp and wisps of genie smoke. Bonus: all rooms are equipped with flat-screen computers. Now a member of Starwood Preferred Guest, guests can earn and redeem Starpoints at more than 750 Westin, Sheraton, W, St Regis and Luxury Collection Hotels.

Eating & drinking

The **Spice Market Buffet** is one of the best in town, serving a variety of ethnic dishes (including many options for vegetarians). There's good steak and seafood at **Elements**, decent Italian grub at **Tremezzo** and, amazingly, the city's only 24-hour **Starbucks**. The branch here of contemporary Asian chain **PF Chang**'s is said to be one of the nation's busiest. The adjoining Desert Passage includes **Commander's Palace** (*see p143*), outpost of the famous New Orleans Garden District eatery; **Cheeseburger at the Oasis**, a beach-themed burger joint; and the 2003-vintage **Prana**, operated by the An family of **Crustacean** fame (*see p147*). More recent additions to the resort include the trendy **Bonsai Sushi and Sashimi Bar** for dinner and late-night dining, and **Flights**, with its 600-bottle wine list served by the flight, glass or bottle.

Entertainment

The main headliner is mega-illusionist Steve Wyrick (*see p218*). Also here is the **Aladdin Theatre**, the only building left from the original Aladdin. Inside Desert Passage, Crustacean morphs into a nightclub after hours, Prana. Tucked into Aladdin's London Club is the mansion-like 'hyper-lounge' **Curve**. **Sinbad**, a mezzanine lounge overlooking the casino, also has live pop, jazz and R&B.

Gambling

The 100,000sq ft (9,300sq m) multi-tiered casino is one of the most impressive on the Strip. There are 87 table games, 2,800 slot machines, a live keno lounge and a race and sports book. Well-heeled players frequent the high-limit pit on the second floor. The salon features 30 high-limit tables including blackjack, roulette and baccarat and 100 high-denomination slot machines. The entrance to the Curve nightclub is at the rear of the salon.

Amenities Bars (3). Business centre. Concierge. Disabled-adapted rooms. Gym. High-speed internet (ADSL). No-smoking floors. Pool (outdoor). Restaurants (4). Spa. **Games** *Baccarat ($100-$15,000); mini baccarat ($10-$15,000); Big Six; blackjack ($5-$5,000); Caribbean stud; casino war; craps (3x, 4x, 5x); keno; Let it Ride; pai gow poker; poker; roulette (single zero & double zero).*

Bally's

3645 Las Vegas Boulevard South, at E Flamingo Road, Las Vegas, NV 89109 (reservations 1-888 742 9248/front desk & casino 967 4111/fax 967 4405/www.caesars.com/ballys/lasvegas). Bus 202, 301, 302/self-parking & valet parking Las Vegas Boulevard South or E Flamingo Road. **Rates** *$89-$399 single/double.* **Credit** *AmEx, DC, Disc, MC, V.* **Map** *p320 A7.*

Rather than resorting to Vegas gimmickry, this grand dame of the Strip's Famous Four Corners has stayed true to its Hollywood roots since opening as the MGM Grand in 1973; for the most part, at least. Don't let the eight miles of ostentatious looping neon – part of a multimillion-dollar 'grand entry' that supposedly entices tourists strolling the Strip to hop aboard the 200ft-long people-movers – dissuade you from taking the short trip from the Strip to the elegant porte cochère: once inside, you'll find Bally's has retained its classic appeal. The tasteful, Euro-style casino conjures up images of James Bond (albeit à la Roger Moore), while Donn Arden's *Jubilee!* pays tribute to the old-school showgirl.

Amenities include an oversized, heated pool with private cabañas; eight floodlit tennis courts next to a pro shop where you can sign up for lessons (this is one of the last hotels on the Strip with tennis courts); a full-service health club; and access to the Caesars Entertainment-owned **Cascata** golf course. The **Bally Avenue Shoppes** houses one-off boutiques.

Accommodation

Standard rooms at Bally's are a good-sized 450sq ft (40sq m), decorated with a West Coast casual elegance of bright velvet couches offset by muted earth

Flamingo.

the Jubilee Theater. Enjoy jazz and swing music performed by a rotating line-up of local acts in the **Indigo Lounge** (*see p175*).

Gambling

The casino is one large, rectangular space, an inviting atmosphere of soft lighting and art deco accents with 65 table games and 2,100 slot machines. Among them are the town's first $1,000 slots, with a top payout of a cool mil. Not surprisingly, the machine selection includes all the latest creations from machine-maker Bally, including laserdisc versions of craps, roulette and blackjack; all are excellent practice tools before heading to the actual tables. The buy-ins at the tables are lower than you might expect, though the majority of Bally's players wager far more than the minimum. The sports book, located on the lower level, is as classy and technically advanced as those in the Bellagio and the Las Vegas Hilton, but it's rarely crowded.

Amenities *Bars (5). Business centre. Concierge. Disabled-adapted rooms. Gym. High-speed internet (ADSL). No-smoking floors. Pool (outdoor). Restaurants (5). Spa.* **Games** *Baccarat ($100-$15,000); mini baccarat ($15-$5,000); blackjack ($5-$3,000); Caribbean stud; casino war; craps (3x 4&10, 4x 5&9, 5x 6&8); keno; Let it Ride; pai gow poker; poker; roulette (double zero); Spanish 21; three-card poker. Gambling lessons.*

Flamingo

3555 Las Vegas Boulevard South, at E Flamingo Road, Las Vegas, NV 89109 (reservations 1-808 308 8899/front desk & casino 733 3111/www. flamingolasvegas.com). Bus 202, 301, 302/self-parking & valet parking Las Vegas Boulevard South or Audrie Street. **Rates** *$65-$400 single/double; $350-$1,000 suite.* **Credit** *AmEx, DC, Disc, MC, V.* **Map** *p320 A7.*

Its fame was guaranteed for all eternity from the moment Benjamin 'Bugsy' Siegel, one of the driving forces behind its construction and a classic Mob figure, was shot dead in 1947. These days, the Flamingo lacks the glamour it must have had back in its early years, and is little more than a middlebrow resort whose chief attraction is its central Strip location.

Behind the signature pink neon sign, the resort is huge, with six guestroom towers. Hidden between them is the resort's centrepiece, a lush 15-acre tropical pool area with waterslides, waterfalls and jungle-like foliage enveloping four distinct pools – including Bugsy's oval-shaped original – where 300 tropical birds vie for attention. The interior of the Flamingo is less impressive, all white marble, mirrors and ersatz plants. An assortment of boutiques beckon, as do a hair salon, a small spa and a fitness centre. There are four tennis courts, and guests have access to the **Cascata** golf course.

Accommodation

Good news: the rooms at the Flamingo received a long-overdue renovation in recent years, and are now respectable, if hardly thrilling. The standard rooms are 350sq ft (33sq m) – smaller than many in

tones. Of 2,814 rooms, 185 are suites: the one- or two-bedroom Grand Suites are slightly more contemporary, and each has a huge jetted tub and wet bar; there are Honeymoon and Penthouse suites, too. The 22nd Club offers special guests access to private concierge services, free breakfast and evening cocktails with gorgeous views of the Strip.

Eating & drinking

Bally's restaurant selection is like the rest of the resort: a throwback to old-school subtlety. It should come as no surprise that the best place to eat is an all-you-can-scoff affair: the **Sterling Brunch** (*see p163*), a truly spectacular linen-and-champers buffet staged only on Sundays for which booking is necessary. **Al Dente** offers contemporary Italian food, and the New England-style **Steakhouse** does grilled beef and seafood right. **Chang's** spreads Singapore- and Hong Kong-style cuisine about in a contemporary atmosphere. Along with the **Big Kitchen Buffet** (*see p163*), there's a host of casual spots for sushi, ice-cream, sandwiches and Italian fast food, plus cocktails at three lounges: the sport-and-slots bar **Sully's**, the intimate **Indigo Lounge** and the Mexican-slanted **Tequila Bar**.

Entertainment

For a true Vegas show experience, **Jubilee!** (*see p220*) is the ticket: beautiful showgirls reprising world-famous production numbers with lavish sets and spectacular choreography (topless on the late run). Lani Misalucha headlines the **Society of Seven** Hawaiian-style variety show afternoons in

Auto Collection at
Imperial Palace. *See p79*.

Vegas, but they are trimmed in pleasant earth tones. The slightly more cultured mini suites are more than twice as big, with a bedroom separated off by a curtain; some have wet bars. At 1,700sq ft (160sq m), the luxury suites are bigger than many homes: some have walk-in showers and jetted tubs.

Eating & drinking
The Flamingo could really do with a signature eaterie, but a recent reworking of their restaurant roster didn't provide one. Instead, choose from Asian (**Pink Ginger**), Italian (the good-value **Ventuno**), steaks and seafood (**Conrad's**) or sushi and teppan (reliably popular chain **Hamada of Japan**). The serviceable buffet and 24-hour coffee shop have been joined by the reliably, wildly ridiculous **Jimmy Buffet's Margaritaville** (*see p167*), a theme bar-restaurant decorated in colours loud enough to blind from 50 paces.

Entertainment
The main act here is a good one: Grammy-winning singer **Gladys Knight** (*see p220*), who performs a very decent show here (without the Pips) five nights a week for much of the year. **Frankie Valli** takes audiences back to December 1963 with semi-regular week-long runs in the Showroom; the 10pm slot is held down by **George Wallace** (the comedian, not the segregationist former governor of Alabama; *see p217*). Also popular is **Second City** (*see p223*), a satellite branch of the Chicagoan improv troupe who inspired much modern comedy.

Gambling
The casino area, accented by bright pinks, yellows and tangerines, offers you a real chance to survive: craps and blackjack minimums are a reasonable $5 (during non-prime time). It's tougher to come out ahead in the slot area: none of the 2,100 machines are considered loose (the last renovation cost $130 million, after all). You'll also find a lively card room, a keno parlour, and a race and sports book.

Amenities *Bars (6). Business centre. Disabled-adapted rooms. Gym. High-speed internet (ADSL, web TV). No-smoking floors. Pool (outdoor). Restaurants (7).* **Spa.** **Games** *Mini baccarat ($10-$3,000); Big Six; blackjack ($3-$2,000); Caribbean stud; craps (3x 4&10, 4x 5&9, 5x 6&8); keno; Let it Ride; pai gow poker; poker; roulette (double zero); three-card poker. Gambling lessons.*

Harrah's
3475 Las Vegas Boulevard South, between Sands Avenue & E Flamingo Road, Las Vegas, NV 89109 (reservations 1-800 427 7247/front desk 369 5000/ www.harrahs.com). Bus 301/self-parking & valet parking Koval Road. **Rates** *$65-$450 single/double.* **Credit** *AmEx, DC, Disc, MC, V.* **Map** *p320 A6.*
Decent room rates and a great location – right in the heart of the Strip – compensate for Harrah's not keeping up with the Wynns. The 32-year-old resort, once known as the Holiday Casino, plays the tired Mardi Gras theme card, perhaps a tribute to its casino cousin in New Orleans (which, ironically, has a Vegas theme – if you count slots).

But a good party is a good party in Vegas, and Harrah's succeeds at nothing if not as an entertaining host. All of the credit goes to the talented Clint Holmes and Mac King, who put on two of the best shows on the whole Strip. And besides, appearances can be deceptive. Harrah's might look a bit feeble, but its parent company are among the most powerful in town: already the owners of the Rio, the group bought Binion's in 2004 and later announced plans to take over the Caesars group of casinos.

Accommodation
The 2,579 rooms in Harrah's three towers are comfortable and festive, with bright accent colours over blonde woods. Many have minibars, some have jet-ted tubs. Overall? Mid-range satisfaction.

Eating & drinking
There are no celeb chefs or brand-name chains here (though, at last count, there were three **Starbucks**), and all the restaurants are suitable for casual or smart-casual diners. If you're all dressed up, you'll feel most at home at the **Range Steakhouse**, with its nice view of the Strip. Your next best bets are **Andreotti** (Italian) and the gourmet restaurant formerly known as Asia, which is due to be renovated and renamed for summer 2005. Casual diners have the large but relatively expensive **Fresh Market Square Buffet** (see p164) or café-styled **Club Cappuccino**, which continues to survive the Starbucks onslaught.

Entertainment
Veteran Strip headliner **Clint Holmes** (see p219) rules Harrah's showroom with a golden voice and a great 12-piece band of musicians' musicians. **Mac King** (see p218) has a great deal going in the afternoons, with a comedy magic show the whole family will love. Budd Friedman's famous **Improv** comedy club (see p222) brings in three fresh comedians each week, and the late, late revue **Skintight** is nice but not naughty enough.

Gambling
Harrah's has a wide selection of table games, including Caribbean stud, Let it Ride and casino war. Most blackjack games are dealt from the shoe, but higher limits – at least $25 minimum – are dealt from hand-held decks. Beware the single decks, which have lower limits but pay a measly 6:5 for naturals. Occasionally, gracious pit bosses will bring in the European single-zero roulette wheel for high rollers. For lively action, take a seat in the cosily compact poker room, while the race and sports book offers booths and table seating. The casino area has been expanded by a third, but the 'Party Pit', once located at the north Strip entrance, has gone.

Amenities *Bars (2). Business centre. Disabled-adapted rooms. Gym. No-smoking floors. Pool (outdoor). Restaurants (6). Spa.* **Games** *Baccarat ($25-$10,000); mini baccarat ($10-$5,000); blackjack ($5-$5,000); Caribbean stud; craps (3x, 4x, 5x); keno; Let it Ride; pai gow poker; poker; roulette (double zero); three-card poker. Gambling lessons.*

Imperial Palace
3535 Las Vegas Boulevard South, between Sands Avenue & E Flamingo Road, Las Vegas, NV 89109 (reservations 1-800 634 6441/front desk & casino 731 3311/fax 735 8328/www.imperialpalace.com). Bus 301/self-parking & valet parking Las Vegas Boulevard South. **Rates** $69-$219 single/double; $119-$249 suite. **Credit** AmEx, DC, Disc, MC, V. **Map** p320 A6.

'Palace' is pushing it, especially as the Imperial is across from the more glamorous Caesars, but its proximity to such good company on the centre of the Strip keeps this Oriental-themed hotel hopping. That, and you don't have to be royalty to stay here.

Escaping is easy, with the newly expanded monorail station on site, but the resort offers a few reasons of its own for you to stay put. The main Imperial Palace attraction is the **Auto Collection** (see p118), which has more than 200 antique, classic and special-interest vehicles on display and for sale. If you can't afford to buy one, take advantage of one the best deals in Vegas: get your photo taken with an old car for free. Only in Vegas. Speaking of which, the IP's venerable Legends in Concert is still thriving. Indeed, it's spilling over into the casino, where, at the new 'Dealertainers Pit', the guy or gal behind the blackjack table may be Michael Jackson or Dolly Parton, primed to belt out a song any second. The hotel, which is remodelling all of its rooms and suites, offers a variety of services for its guests: shopping promenade, video arcade, wireless internet access, wedding chapel, fitness centre, spa, and golf and business centres.

Accommodation
All guestroom decor, from the small standard room through to the King suite, is getting a much-needed facelift. The best penthouse suites have one or two bedrooms, a Luv Tub with jacuzzi jets, an unstocked bar and an extra-large living room.

Eating & drinking
There are ten restaurants to satisfy most cravings, from the **Burger Palace** to the **Pizza Palace**, plus a couple of decent buffets in between. Head to the Fifth Floor Dining Plaza for fancier places: **Embers** steakhouse, the **Seahouse**, the **Rib House**, and **Ming Terrace**, the obligatory Asian spot. **Tequila Joe's** has a mean daiquiri bar and regular karaoke.

Entertainment
The long-running **Legends in Concert** tribute/impersonator show (see p215) features a variety of good-to-excellent tributes to a variety of modern artists (Madonna, Shania Twain) and classic Vegas performers (Liberace, Elvis). From April to October, the pool area outside transforms into a luau scene, with traditional food and a Polynesian revue, while inside at Tequila Joe's guests dance to DJs nightly.

Gambling
Thanks to its high-traffic location, the casino action is always busy, though that doesn't necessarily mean it's particularly favourable: typical central-Strip blackjack rules and video poker paybacks gouge the

Casinos & Hotels

first-time tourist; the rest of the games gouge the sucker no matter where you are. 'Dealertainers' in the IP's party pit impersonate Madonna, the Blues Brothers, Elvis and other pop stars while pitching cards and rockin' out to the loud music.

Amenities *Bars (10). Business centre. Concierge. Disabled-adapted rooms. Gym. High-speed internet (wireless). No-smoking floors. Pool (outdoor). Restaurants (10). Spa.* **Games** *Baccarat ($25-$5,000); mini baccarat ($10-$100); Big Six; blackjack ($5-$1,000); Caribbean stud; casino war; craps (3x, 4x, 5x); keno; Let it Ride; pai gow poker; poker; roulette (double zero); three-card poker.*

Luxor

3900 Las Vegas Boulevard South, between W Tropicana Avenue & Russell Road, Las Vegas, NV 89109 (reservations 1-800 288 1000/front desk 262 4000/fax 262 4405/www.luxor.com). Bus 105, 301/ self-parking & valet parking Reno Avenue. **Rates** $79-$399 single/double; $179-$699 suite. **Credit** AmEx, DC, Disc, MC, V. **Map** p320 A9.

The Luxor impresses on scale long before you've set foot within it. While many casinos limit their theming to their interiors, leaving the buildings in which they're housed as smart but not altogether memorable towerblocks, the 30-storey glass pyramid housing much of the Luxor, and guarded by a massive sphinx, makes one hell of a first impression when you pass it on the Strip. At night, a high-intensity light shoots skywards from the top; visible in space, it's also a beacon to a swarm of insects and bats during warm months.

The homage to ancient Egypt continues inside, in faintly ridiculous but effective and likeable fashion. Hieroglyphics and other Egyptiana line the walls. Although the campiest elements have been tidied up, the recreation of Tutankhamun's tomb (*see p115*) impresses: two Egyptologists were drafted in to keep things authentic. The lovely cerulean pools are surrounded by Egyptian temple architecture; happily, the 24-hour spa doesn't milk the theme. The Pharaoh's Pavilion offers some neat attractions – a games arcade, an IMAX theatre, a silly but enjoyable motion simulator – but it's badly situated and impossible to simply stumble across, which is why it's rarely busy. Another demerit is that superstitious Asian gamblers reportedly dislike the resort for being, basically, a tomb. However, the Luxor manages to please both families and funseeking adults better than almost every other hotel on the Strip, which goes some way towards explaining why, despite being the second largest hotel in town, it's rarely less than busy.

Accommodation

Only around half of the hotel's 4,408 guestrooms are actually located in the pyramid: the Strip-fronted rooms offer great views and are accessed by special elevators called 'inclinators', which rise, like enclosed ski lifts, at an angle of 39°. However, there are compensations if you don't get hooked up with a room in it: the guestrooms in the tower, just behind the pyramid, are actually larger, and all have bathtubs. Decor throughout is tasteful and cultured; the Egyptian theming is never invasive.

Eating & drinking

Pharaoh's Pheast gets the gold star for the most inventive buffet decor in town: it serves all the typical fare, but does so in the midst of an archaeological dig, complete with ropes, pulleys, sand and ladders. More upscale are the clubby, colonial-style **Luxor Steakhouse**, seafood spot the **Sacred Sea Room**, the excellent Polynesian and Asian fare at **Papyrus** and, best of all, the continental **Isis**. Less pricey are popular chain **Hamada of Japan** and the Mexican **La Salsa**.

Entertainment

In a slightly surprising movie, the Luxor have let Blue Man Group, for years their signature show, move across to the Venetian. Its replacement is a production of Broadway hit **Hairspray**, slightly abbreviated from the original run to a Vegas-standard 90 minutes and scheduled to open in late 2005. The **Midnight Fantasy** (*see p214*) adult revue is very new Vegas and not especially sexy; the **Luxor IMAX Theatre** (*see p229*) screens documentaries and pop features. If you want to dial it down, there's live music in **Nefertiti's Lounge**, but club-hoppers will want to check out the silvery, *Stargate*-like **Ra** (*see p243*).

Gambling

The massive casino, decorated with hieroglyphics and ancient artefacts, is filled with the latest high-tech slot and video poker machines. The norm is $5 minimums at blackjack and crap tables. For poker players the card room offers weekend action so lively Cleopatra herself would have appreciated it. Take a few minutes to walk the perimeter of the casino and get your bearings; since the casino is round, if you can't identify landmarks, you'll wind up going around in circles.

Amenities *Bars (4). Business centre. Concierge. Disabled-adapted rooms. Gym. High-speed internet (ADSL). No-smoking floors. Pool (outdoor). Restaurants (7). Spa.* **Games** *Baccarat ($100-$15,000); mini baccarat ($5-$3,000); Big Six; blackjack ($5-$3,000); Caribbean stud; casino war; craps (3x, 4x, 5x); keno; Let it Ride; pai gow poker; poker; roulette (single zero & double zero); three-card poker. Gambling lessons.*

MGM Grand

3799 Las Vegas Boulevard South, at E Tropicana Avenue, Las Vegas, NV 89109 (reservations 1-800 929 1111/front desk 891 7777/fax 891 1003/www.mgmgrand.com). Bus 201, 301, 302/ self-parking Las Vegas Boulevard South or Koval Avenue/valet parking E Tropicana Avenue. **Rates** $109-$499 single/double; $199-$15,000 suite. **Credit** AmEx, DC, Disc, MC, V. **Map** p320 A8.

Until recently the largest hotel on earth, the MGM Grand went all *Wizard of Oz* in 1993, trying to grab the family market with a cartoony lion's-mouth entrance (which spooked superstitious Asian gamblers) and an outdoor Grand Adventures theme park. All that remains now is the glowing emerald exterior. Along with the other family- oriented Strip resorts, the MGM reconsidered its focus and remade itself into the elegant City of Entertainment, with glam shots of MGM film stars, expensive dining, chic lounges, three theatres, an Asian-inspired spa, an expansive, palm-lined pool area and enormous convention facilities. That said, a huge bronze lion now sits at the Tropicana/Strip intersection, and you can see descendants of the original MGM lion, Metro, in the popular **Lion Habitat** (*see p115*).

Accommodation

The resort's 5,034 rooms (including 751 suites) were decorated a few years ago with art deco-styled furnishings, designed to evoke backlot bungalows from Hollywood's glamour age. They manage it pretty well, too, though you suspect Clark Gable and Louise Brooks would sooner be down the street at the Bellagio. A fourth-floor guest services desk functions as an additional concierge, a real plus in this huge hotel. High rollers can cosy up in 29 ultra-private, opulent villas in the Mansion. The villas were joined at the top end of the price scale in 2005 by 51 Skylofts, chic two-storey accommodations designed by Tony Chi that are among the town's more fashionable temporary addresses.

Eating & drinking

The MGM's gradual reinvention of its dining in recent years has been a spectacular success, mixing name-brand chefs with low-key eats to excellent, inclusive effect: this is among the best dining resorts on the Strip. Among the high-end options are Tom Colicchio's **Craftsteak** (*see p141*), where the focus is on meat, fish and fowl from small farms; **Fiamma** (*see p148*), an Italian trattoria imported from New York; Japanese eaterie **Shibuya**; and **Nobhill** (*see p150*), Michael Mina's Californian eaterie. Mina is also behind the highly regarded **Seablue** (*see p150*), a posh new seafood spot; other celeb chefs in attendance (in name only: other people do the cooking) are Emeril Lagasse (at **Emeril Lagasse's New Orleans Fish House**; *see p143*) and Wolfgang Puck (at the laid-back **Wolfgang Puck Bar & Grill**; *see p145*). There's slightly more casual fare at the **Rainforest Café**, **'Wichcraft** (*see p143*) and the **Grand Wok & Sushi Bar**, which shares a kitchen with the 24-hour coffee shop.

Entertainment

If in doubt in Vegas, opt for Cirque du Soleil. The fourth Cirque production opened at the MGM Grand in late 2004, and what a production: **Kà** (*see p220*) is the most outlandish show yet staged on the Strip. The other resident piece here is **La Femme** (*see p214*), oxymoronically billed as a classy topless revue but perhaps the best tits-and-shadows show on the Strip. The 740-seat Hollywood Theatre hosts perhaps half a dozen acts on regular rotation for runs of anywhere from a week to a month, among them the always impressive David Copperfield, the perennially camp Tom Jones and the utterly punchable Carrot Top. The 16,000-seat **MGM Grand Garden Arena** (*see p237*) is one of the top places

Ancient Egypt comes to Vegas – sort of – in the distinctive shape of the **Luxor**. *See p80.*

in town to see big-name concerts – from the likes of Rod Stewart, U2, Jimmy Buffett and Matchbox 20 – as well as big sports events.

The nightlife here is strong and relentlessly fashionable. Nightclub **Studio 54** (*see p243*) lacks the cocaine, celebrities and gay hookers that defined the New York original, but it's still a popular spot. **Tabú**, a sleek lounge, has lately been upstaged by **Teatro**, an even sleeker one (for both, *see p244*).

Gambling

The MGM has four gaming areas – Entertainment, Hollywood, Monte Carlo and Sports – where you'll find all the games, including Spanish 21. Table minimums can go down to $10 on weekdays, but most are higher; in the pit you'll find $25 minimums and $15,000 maximums. There's also a large race and sports book with floor-to-ceiling screens, one of the best poker rooms in town, and 3,700 slots, from a nickel to $500.

Amenities *Bars (7). Business centre. Disabled-adapted rooms. Gym. High-speed internet (ADSL). No-smoking floors. Pool (outdoor). Restaurants (22). Spa.* **Games** *Baccarat ($100-$15,000); mini baccarat ($25-$15,000); Big Six; blackjack ($10-$15,000); Caribbean stud; casino war; craps (3x, 4x, 5x); keno; Let it Ride; pai gow poker; pai gow tiles; roulette (single zero & double zero); Spanish 21; three-card poker. Gambling lessons.*

Monte Carlo

3770 Las Vegas Boulevard South, at Rue de Monte Carlo, between W Harmon Avenue & W Tropicana Avenue, Las Vegas, NV 89109 (reservations 1-888 529 4828/front desk & casino 730 7777/fax 739 7275/www.monte-carlo.com). Bus 201, 301, 302/ self-parking & valet parking Rue de Monte Carlo. **Rates** $69-$299 single/double; $139-$4,000 suite. **Credit** AmEx, DC, Disc, MC, V. **Map** p320 A8.

Modelled after the Place du Casino in (of course) Monte Carlo, this handsome but low-key resort will either be an appealing, value-packed mid-range place to stay or, like the hotel's star magician Lance Burton, a master of deception, depending on your point of view. The many attractive features, not least of which is the impressive exterior architecture (twin archway entrances, a big streetside fountain), suggest this $344 million resort might be on the same page as, say, the $1.4 billion Bellagio. The truth is that the Monte Carlo, a joint venture of what were then Mirage Resorts (the Bellagio) and Circus Circus Enterprises (Excalibur), successfully appeals to those after an approximation of high style at low prices.

To some extent, the resort is a Bellagio for families, boasting restaurants ranging from spartan to splendiferous, family-friendly entertainment, and a waterfall-filled pool area that kids love (there's even a special enclosed pool reserved for tinies). Adults can escape to the full-service spa and salon, or perhaps the tennis courts: a rarity on the Strip, and lit for night-time use. The front desk's picture windows look over the verdant water park, giving the best lobby view in town.

Accommodation

The Monte Carlo's tri-tower set-up contains 3,002 rooms, including 259 suites. The standard rooms and Monaco suites exhibit a comfortable if slightly garish style, decorated with cherry furniture and

Wanna wake up in the city that never sleeps? **New York–New York**. *See p83.*

fin-de-siècle brass fixtures, Italian marble and polished granite. The top-shelf Spa suites, complete with wet bar, sauna and jetted tub, are surprisingly contemporary and stylish.

Eating & drinking
The Monte Carlo's signature eaterie is an excellent choice for dinner: **André's** (*see p156*), the Strip location of André Rochat's venerable Downtown establishment. The pleasing **Monte Carlo Pub & Brewery** (*see p167*) is an industrial-styled space showcasing beers brewed on site, while the **Dragon Noodle Company** features a speciality tea bar to complement its Cantonese and Sichuan cuisine. There's also a steakhouse (**Blackstone's**), a casual Italian trattoria (**Market City Caffè**), and the requisite 24-hour coffee shop (**Café**) and buffet.

Entertainment
The family-friendly nature of the resort is only emphasised by the nightly presence of wholly traditional, entirely unthreatening and disturbingly charisma-free magician **Lance Burton** (*see p218*), The Pub & Brewery has DJs and a live covers band nightly, while the relaxing **Houdini Lounge** offers a pianist at the weekend and a roving close-up magic specialist during the week.

Gambling
There's an abundant selection of $5 blackjack tables in the Monte Carlo's casino, plenty of 5¢ opportunities among the 2,200 slots, and a bright and casual atmosphere. Players appreciate the details, such as stools with backs at every machine, wider walkways through the casino and the single-zero roulette. The Monte Carlo attracts brisk traffic from neighbouring casinos, but the tables never seem crowded. Players stand a better chance of landing a one-on-one blackjack game with the dealer here than at most Strip resorts.

Amenities *Bars (4). Business centre. Disabled-adapted rooms. Gym. High-speed internet (ADSL). No-smoking floors. Pool (outdoor). Restaurants (7). Spa.* **Games** *Baccarat ($25-$15,000); mini baccarat ($10-$5,000); Big Six; blackjack ($5-$5,000); Caribbean stud; craps (3x, 4x, 5x); keno; Let it Ride; pai gow poker; pai gow tiles; poker; roulette (single & double zero); three-card poker. Gambling lessons (poker).*

New York–New York

3790 Las Vegas Boulevard South, at W Tropicana Avenue, Las Vegas, NV 89109 (reservations 1-888 693 6763/front desk & casino 740 6969/fax 740 6700/www.nynyhotelcasino.com). Bus 201, 301, 302/self-parking Las Vegas Boulevard South or W Tropicana Avenue/valet parking W Tropicana Avenue. **Rates** *$99-$249 single/double; $599-$2,500 suite.* **Credit** *AmEx, DC, Disc, MC, V.* **Map** *p320 A8.*
So good they named it twice? Well, yes, as it goes. The most audacious, preposterous example of hotel theming in Las Vegas – and, for that matter, perhaps even the world – is a thrilling success. Built for $460 million and opened in 1997, it's been called the largest piece of pop art in the world.

You absolutely can't miss it. Along with a mini New York Harbor, complete with tugboats, a scaled-down Brooklyn Bridge and a giant Statue of Liberty looming over the Tropicana/Strip intersection, the resort's skyline includes a dozen of the Big Apple's most famous landmarks, among them the Empire State Building, the Chrysler Building and the New Yorker Hotel (but, happily for the owners, no World Trade Center; the hotel was themed after 1950s New York, long before the twin towers were built). Inside, along with representations of Times Square, Central Park, Greenwich Village and Wall Street, you'll find every New York cliché in the book: a Broadway subway station, graffitied mailboxes, steam rising from the manhole covers… It's tremendous fun, and seems to inspire visitors to act like they were out on the East Coast: it's got energy like no other casino floor in town.

Just like the original, New York–New York is as interested in keeping the kids happy as in pleasing the adults. The **Coney Island Emporium** (*see p114*) is nirvana for kids and wanna-be-kids-again, a mix of old-fashioned midway games, hi-tech interactive videos and virtual-reality rollercoasters. The entrance to the hotel's real rollercoaster, the Manhattan Express, which twists, turns and rolls around the property. The pool and spa are, alas, real letdowns: a replica of the famous Vertical Club would have been fitting. Or, perhaps, the Central Park Reservoir.

Accommodation
New York–New York's 2,024 rooms are concealed behind an assortment of towers and skyscrapers. The rooms are pretty standardised – mainly art deco wood with black accents – and, in another stab at authenticity, as small as New York studios. Check when you make your booking that the Manhattan Express doesn't rumble by your window, or you'll be continually disturbed not so much by the rumble of wheels, but by the squeals of riders.

Eating & drinking
It's amazing that they didn't think of it before, but New York–New York finally got a proper Irish pub-restaurant in 2004, with the arrival of the inevitably rather hokey **Nine Fine Irishmen** (*see p148*). The other eating options are surprisingly standard: given the number of top-notch Manhattan restaurants that have recently been imported to the Strip, it's surprising that New York–New York has chosen to content itself with **Gallagher's** steakhouse, the Chinese restaurant **Chin-Chin**, competent Italian at **Il Fornaio** and Mexican café **Gonzalez y Gonzalez**. Sports fanatics plant themselves in souped-up La-Z-Boys at the **ESPN Zone** (*see p142*) by the sports book. The coffee shop **America** is a must-see, if only for the enormous floor-to-ceiling pop art sculpture-map of the US. A food court fashioned after Greenwich Village (cobblestone streets, a subway station, apartment buildings) contains burgers, pizzas and fried fish, though – disappointingly – no knishes.

Entertainment

New York–New York's leading show is the Cirque du Soleil **Zumanity** (*see p214*), an intriguing but only partly successful attempt at mixing Cirque's ever-dazzling acrobatics with the sexiness of the Strip-standard adult revue. The squeaky-voiced stand-up of always enjoyable **Rita Rudner** is a rather better bet (*see p217*). The other entertainments are all participatory: duelling piano players lead boozy singalongathons all night, every night at the **Bar At Times Square** (*see p166*), while **Coyote Ugly** (*see p167*) is a loud, lairy nightclub modelled on the film (which was, in turn, modelled on a New York City bar) of the same name. The **Big Apple Lounge**, inspired by the supper clubs of the '30s, is a tad more sophisticated.

Gambling

The 84,000sq ft (7,800sq m) casino area is modelled on Central Park, only without the muggers. But everything's pricier in NYC, and the tuxedo-backed chairs at the tables set the right tone. Minimums for blackjack (practically all six-deck shoes) are $10; it's $1 for roulette. The range of slots is one of the best on the Strip. A new touch is the Dragon Pit, with its Asian games and flair; dim sum hors-d'oeuvres are served, with saké, plum wine, Asian beer and teas.

Amenities *Bars (6). Business centre. Disabled-adapted rooms. Gym. High-speed internet (ADSL). No-smoking floors. Pool (outdoor). Restaurants (16). Spa.* **Games** *Blackjack ($10-$2,000); Caribbean stud; casino war; craps (3x, 4x, 5x); Let it Ride; pai gow poker; roulette (double zero); three-card poker. Gambling lessons.*

Fame makes a man take things over

Las Vegas has always drawn more than its share of stars, either for playing or for performing. These days, though, it seems half of Hollywood is here, along with goodly portions of the sports world, the music industry and the mysterious category of fame inhabited by Anna Nicole Smith and Paris Hilton. What happened?

Robin Leach, Vegas-resident host of *Lifestyles of the Rich and Famous*, recalls the big bang happening in the late 20th century, when the alignment of certain planets – the Venetian, the Bellagio – fed a growing nucleus of star chefs 'who were', he says, 'integral in making Vegas the dining capital of the world.' TV followed, flooding cable with food and travel documentaries; the nightclub era blasted off, the awards shows moved in and, in 2001, George Maloof opened the Palms and let MTV film *The Real World* on one of his hotel floors.

That's when the floodgates opened and the bold-faced names poured in. The city that once had nary a single gossip columnist suddenly had three. Even the *National Enquirer* opened a Vegas bureau. Jessica Simpson

and Nick Lachey arguing in public, Nicky Hilton and Todd Meister annulling their 85-day marriage, Michael Douglas and Brent Musburger lunching at the same place: that was just a half-column's worth of Vegas scoops on a single day for Norm Clarke. 'I could write seven days a week and still have left-over stuff,' says the *Las Vegas Review-Journal*'s 'Vegas Confidential' columnist, who does indeed write daily and still had enough left-over stuff to write a book, *1,000 Naked Truths* (Stephens Press, $9.95).

The parade continues, he says, because 'the Vegas vibe is unequalled. It is truly all here: it's in a compact area and you can go all night.' That doesn't quite explain why you'll see Paris Hilton dancing on a table

Budget

Barbary Coast

3595 Las Vegas Boulevard South, at E Flamingo Road, Las Vegas, NV 89109 (reservations 1-888 227 2279/front desk & casino 737 7111/fax 894 9954/www.barbarycoastcasino.com). Bus 202, 301, 302/self-parking & valet parking Las Vegas Boulevard South. **Rates** $53-$259 single/double. **Credit** AmEx, DC, Disc, MC, V. **Map** p320 A7.
In case you missed it (thanks to the blinding lights of its next-door neighbour), there's a cosy little slice of *fin-de-siècle* San Francisco tucked in behind the more demonstrative Flamingo. Inside there are deluxe displays of stained glass and chandeliers throughout, but what really draws a crowd to the

Barbary Coast, an anomaly among Strip casinos, is its prime location on the Fabulous Four Corners, and some terrific dining.

Accommodation
You'll be pleasantly surprised by the Victorian wallpaper and paintings, etched mirrors and white lace curtains in this boutique-style hotel's 200 guestrooms, some of which have four-poster brass beds, minibars and whirlpools.

Eating & drinking
Michael's (*see p145*) intimate gourmet room (seats only 50) gushes Victorian-style luxury, with red velvet and mahogany furnishings, lace tablecloths, wingback chairs and a 40-panel stained-glass domed ceiling. **Drai's** (*see p144*) offers a more contemporary dining flavour, but equally serious cuisine: 'seven-hour leg of lamb', Chilean sea bass and sensuous hot chocolate soufflé. After midnight on Wednesday through Sunday, stick around for some clubby action and hot dining specials during **Drai's After Hours** (*see p241*).

Entertainment
There's live music in Drai's 'living room-style' lounge on weekends, and **Pete Vallee as Big Elvis** – you won't believe how big – plays Tuesday through Friday in the lounge.

Gambling
This little Strip casino doesn't look like much, but it packs a pretty big wallop. Though it's a mere thin tomato in a megaresort sandwich (between the big Flamingo and Bally's), the Barbary Coast has a halfway-locals' flavour. The video poker is decent, especially if you take advantage of the good slot club. The 21 pit, however, has been the scene of many ugly incidents over the years, as anyone even suspected of card counting is shown the door. Otherwise, the casino often has lower minimums than its giant neighbours and a good gambling promotion or two going on; ask.

Amenities *Bars (1). Disabled-adapted rooms. High-speed internet (dataport). No-smoking rooms. Restaurants (3).* **Games** *Baccarat ($100-$10,000); mini baccarat ($10-$2,000); blackjack ($5-$2,000); Caribbean stud; casino war; craps (3x, 4x, 5x); keno; pai gow poker; roulette (double zero); three-card poker.*

Circus Circus

2880 Las Vegas Boulevard South, at Circus Circus Drive, between Desert Inn Road & W Sahara Avenue, Las Vegas, NV 89109 (reservations 1-877 224 7287/front desk & casino 734 0410/fax 734 5897/www.circuscircus-lasvegas.com). Bus 301/self-parking S Industrial Road/valet parking Las Vegas Boulevard South or S Industrial Road. **Rates** $39-$249 single/double. **Credit** AmEx, DC, Disc, MC, V. **Map** p319 B5.
If you think Vegas is a circus, wait until you step inside this Big Top. Lucky the Laughing Clown has greeted tourists since 1968, inviting them to enter his garish casino and stumble from gaming table to slot machine surrounded by Russian aerialists and

or Britney Spears having what Clarke calls her 'wedding annulment dinner' in Vegas, and not in Hollywood or New York City. Clarke's theory: 'They're counting on the masses, that they can blend in here and after three shots of Cuervo they're invisible. They really do think it's "Vegas, baby". It's almost like they think they're getting a free pass here.' The celebrities not only drop their guards in Vegas, but they often drop their entourages, leaving them more accessible to average humans who, for some reason, tend to viva and let viva in Vegas. Especially locals, whom Leach says aren't easily star-struck. 'They see celebrities all the time. They're like neighbours.' As for the tourists: 'This is a pounding, pulsing, non-stop night city, and everybody's too busy to crowd them.' Hotel security and the casinos' no-cameras policy also deters mobs and 'pesky paparazzi parasites' from forming, according to Leach.

However, hot stars will draw a crowd no matter what. And these days, that club includes Britney Spears, Paris Hilton, Anna Nicole Smith ('Maybe because we like seeing a train wreck,' says Clarke) and, though his star has been fading of late, Ben Affleck (*pictured*). Leach, a fan of the Vegas lifestyle in general and its cuisine in particular, has also somehow managed to keep himself on the Vegas A-list. 'If I could figure out why and bottle it, I could have appeared on *Rich and Famous* as a guest,' he laughs. 'It's nice, though, at age 63 to still get asked for autographs by young and old alike. But it still amazes me.'

waitresses juggling trays of fruity cocktails. Trapeze artists, acrobats and clowns perform on the Midway Stage above the casino, and there's a huge carnie-style midway where the young-at-heart squirt water into a clown's mouth to win stuffed animals.

Accommodation

After several expansions, there are now 3,773 spartan rooms, including 135 parlour and jacuzzi suites, mainly decorated with soft-blue carpeting, pastel bedspreads and upholstery, and light wood furniture. The West tower is the newest (built in 1997), while the cheapest (and oldest) rooms are in the motel-like Manor section. Ask for a south-facing room in the Skyrise tower for the best view of the Strip. Other amenities include pools and the 399-space **Circusland RV Park**, with such conveniences as a 24-hour store and pet runs.

Eating & drinking

The **Steak House** (*see p143*) is a surprisingly high-quality dining room, while **Stivali** serves good Italian and the cantina-like **Blue Iguana** does Mexican. Little-known fact: when *Comedy Central* wanted Chef from the animated series *South Park* to have worked in a Las Vegas buffet, they chose the mediocre **Circus Buffet** (*see p164*), famous for feeding more than 8,000 hungry souls a day. The **Horse-a-Round Bar** (*see p167*) is a big draw.

Entertainment

Circus Circus never had a showroom; it no longer even has the pony girls, who used to ride plastic ponies on a ceiling-hung track, tossing balloons at the kiddies. The carnival midway and circus acts remain: acrobats, trapeze artists and magicians perform every 30mins, 11am-midnight. The **Adventuredome** (*see p121*) features 21 rides and attractions, including the world's only double-loop, double-corkscrew roller-coaster, as well as a carousel and bumper cars for the younger set.

Gambling

The three casinos are connected by walkways and a monorail; each offers the same gaming options. The race book is located near the back of the resort, in the Skyways Tower area. No more than $5 is enough to get you started at most tables; it might take all day to find someone risking more than $10.

Amenities *Bars (3). Business centre. Disabled-adapted rooms. Gym. No-smoking floors. Pool (outdoor). Restaurants (7). Spa.* **Games** *Mini baccarat ($5-$5,000); Big Six; blackjack ($5-$5,000); Caribbean stud; casino war; craps (2x); keno; Let it Ride; pai gow poker; poker; roulette (double zero); three-card poker. Gambling lessons.*

Excalibur

3850 Las Vegas Boulevard South, at W Tropicana Avenue, Las Vegas, NV 89109 (reservations 1-800 937 7777/front desk 597 7777/fax 597 7009/www.excalibur.com). Bus 201, 301, 302/self-parking & valet parking W Tropicana Avenue. **Rates** *$49-$499 single/double/suite.* **Credit** *AmEx, DC, Disc, MC, V.* **Map** *p320 A8.*

During those years of which Las Vegas PR hacks do not speak, when the Suits attempted to transform this adult playground into a family affair, castles and pyramids and pirate ships sprouted up along the Strip. Some have retooled their image, but not much has changed at the Excalibur, one of few places still geared toward families. There's a kid-friendly pool, gift shops hawking not designer handbags but magic tricks, and free shows by puppeteers, jugglers and magicians in the Medieval Village. The interior is still very King Arthur's Court; a moving sidewalk still transports you from the street through Sherwood Forest and over the moat via a drawbridge, where you're greeted by – what else? – big purple dragons. And couples can still tie the knot in the **Canterbury Wedding Chapel**, replete with cathedral-style vaulted ceilings and stained-glass windows.

Still, it's surely only a matter of time before Merlin goes medieval on the asses of the knights, wenches and mandolin players roaming the castle halls, now that MGM Mirage has bought the Mandalay Resort Group. The trick will be transforming this caricature of a castle into a modern Vegas experience. If not, it'll simply become the next generation's Circus Circus.

Accommodation

These small rooms – nearly 4,000 in all, housed in two towers behind the castle façade – have none of the elegance of Excalibur's sister resorts, the Luxor and Mandalay Bay. But there are a handful of spacious Parlor Suites with guest bathrooms, dining and living areas; with bold colours, dark wood furniture and wrought-iron fixtures, they're nowhere near as shabby as those at Circus Circus.

Eating & drinking

Tops among the restaurants is **Sir Galahad's Prime Rib House**, where you'll find generous portions of prime rib and yorkshire pudding. The **Steakhouse at Camelot** serves decent cuts, while **Regale Italian Eatery** dishes out pastas. There's also a kids' menu at the 24-hour **Sherwood Forest Café** and an extensive **Round Table Buffet**.

Entertainment

The family orientation extends into the night with the kid-friendly **Tournament of Kings** (*see p218*), which features jousting, pyrotechnics and a decent game-hen dinner, while the **Court Jester's Stage**, has variety acts at regular intervals all day. The only exception is the hilarious male revue **Thunder from Down Under** (*see p213*).

Gambling

Neon knights slay neon dragons in the 100,000sq ft (9,300sq m) casino, one of the few in town where photography is allowed. Visitors are surrounded by images of playing-card kings and queens, but the table games are affordable for any commoner; there are 10¢ slot and video poker machines – hard to find in Las Vegas – alongside the more common 5¢, 25¢ and $1 varieties. When you're done throwing coins in machines, toss a few in the moat for good luck: they'll be donated to local charities.

Amenities *Bars (7). Disabled-adapted rooms. Gym. High-speed internet (web TV). No-smoking floors. Pool (outdoor). Restaurants (12). Spa.* **Games** *Mini baccarat ($10-$100); blackjack ($5-$2,000); Caribbean stud; casino war; craps (3x, 4x, 5x); keno; Let it Ride; pai gow poker; poker; roulette (double zero); Spanish 21; three-card poker. Gambling lessons.*

Riviera

2901 Las Vegas Boulevard South, at Riviera Boulevard, Las Vegas, NV 89109 (reservations 1-800 634 6753/front desk & casino 734 5110/ fax 794 9451/www.rivierahotel.com). Bus 301/ self-parking Riviera Boulevard or Paradise Road/ valet parking Las Vegas Boulevard South. **Rates** $79-$149 single/double. **Credit** AmEx, DC, Disc, MC, V. **Map** p319 B5.

When the Riviera opened in 1955, Liberace headlined in its showroom. Though Liberace is long gone, the entertainment offerings at the Riv a half-century later are just as camp. The first high-rise hotel on the Strip continues to thumb its nose at family-style entertainment, staying true to its roots as an adult playground. Other Riv throwbacks to a bygone era in Sin City include two lighted tennis courts, an old-school pool, surrounded on all sides by hotel towers, and the Goodfellas Shoeshine service. While the neon doesn't shine as brightly now, there are still plenty of reasons to visit this undervalued spot.

Accommodation

There are five levels of 2,075 rooms at the Riviera, two of them suites. The standard rooms are all in the original tower, while the deluxe rooms (better

Excalibur. *See p86.*

views) and suites are in the two newer towers. The newer tower rooms are smallish but not cramped, and decorated with dark wood furniture. Half the rooms have views over the swimming pool; the rest face the surrounding mountains. The two-bed suites are just larger versions of the standard rooms, but the penthouse suites have marble floors, pianos and huge windows.

Eating & drinking

As at most middlebrow resorts, there are a couple of nice restaurants and a handful of casual, low-end ones. At the top, there's **Ristorante Italiano** and **Kristofer's Steak House**, though the specials at **Kady's** coffee shop are better bargains. The **World's Fare Buffet** offers a fine selection of international food: some special deals combine the buffet with the Riviera's shows. Among the **Mardi Gras** food court's seven fast-food joints, **La Salsa** and **Panda Express** are pretty good. So are the **Krispy Kreme** doughnuts.

Entertainment

Splash (*see p221*), once the most recognisable production show in town, trots out the Vegas clichés twice nightly, while **Crazy Girls** (*see p213*), once the city's most sexed-up topless show, now appears dated. **An Evening at La Cage** (*see p214*) offers cross-dressing action, while the **Comedy Club** (*see p223*) presents the bluest comics in town. A more recent addition is the madcap illusionist comedy of **The Amazing Johnathan** (*see p218*) and his wacky assistant, Psychic Tanya. Formerly home to the Lon Bronson All-Stars, the once-swinging **Le Bistro Lounge** now features Jay White as Neil Diamond, comedy hypnotist Scott Lewis and the SynCity Night Club with bevertainers and house-spinning DJs, proving progress isn't always positive.

Gambling

The gaming area is an L-shaped expanse of red and gold with an elevated lounge and bar in the centre (your best bet for a meeting place that everyone can find). Minimums at the tables are not as low as the surroundings would suggest: $5 blackjack in a $2 setting. The lowest limits and nickel slots are found in a part of the casino dubbed Nickel Town, these days a decent nickname for the whole resort.

Amenities *Bars (3). Business centre. Disabled-adapted rooms. High-speed internet (ADSL). No-smoking floors. Pool (outdoor). Restaurants (4).* **Games** *Mini baccarat ($10-$2,000); blackjack ($5-$2,000); Caribbean stud; craps (2x); keno; Let it Ride; pai gow poker; roulette (double zero); Spanish 21; three-card poker. Gambling lessons.*

Sahara

2535 Las Vegas Boulevard South, at E Sahara Avenue, Las Vegas, NV 89109 (reservations 1-888 696 2121/front desk & casino 737 2111/fax 791 2027/www.saharahotel.com). Bus 204, 301, 302/ self-parking or valet parking Las Vegas Boulevard South or Paradise Road. **Rates** *$49-$249 single/ double; $159-$500 suite.* **Credit** *AmEx, DC, Disc, MC, V.* **Map** *p319 C4.*

When the Sahara opened in 1952, its then-exotic African theme – from the famed camels perched outside to the Congo Showroom – seemed right at home on the barren Strip. It's a niche that has kept the hotel viable on a Strip filled with resorts bustling with more enticing entertainment options and attractions. Unless, of course, you prefer motor racing: the NASCAR Café, the **Las Vegas Cyber Speedway** and **Speed: The Ride** (for both, *see p122*) all attract the attention of racing fans.

Accommodation

The 1,720 guestrooms range from standard through three different sizes of suite, up to a smallish 786sq ft (75sq m). All rooms are decorated in simple but comfortable style, featuring earth tones accented by jewel-toned chairs. Most non-smoking rooms are in the deluxe range, with wet bars and balconies, and located in the Alexandria tower.

Eating & drinking

The Sahara recently resurrected a classic: its **House of Lords** steakhouse had been lost in the renovations to the more generic Sahara Steakhouse. There's decent Mexican food at **Paco's Hideaway**, a 24-hour coffee shop and a buffet. The car-themed **NASCAR Café** (*see p225*) is a popular gathering spot and proof of the resort's mid-America appeal.

Entertainment

Comedy hypnotist **Justin Tranz** plays the late show in the **Congo Room**, while the **Platters, Cornell Gunter's Coasters and Beary Hobbs' Drifters** (original members are few and far between) deliver hits nightly at 7.30pm. The legendary **Casbar Lounge** is where Louis Prima made a splash in the 1950s; today's performers have less potential. You won't escape without checking the **Las Vegas Cyber Speedway** (*see p122*), an entertaining $15-million indoor racing-car simulation that uses cars that are 7/8 the size of authentic stock and Indy cars to offer the thrill of driving a high-performance motor without the risk. Nor can you miss **Speed: The Ride** (*see p122*), a roller-coaster that zips around the front entrance.

Gambling

Alas, the days of $1 blackjack at the Sahara have passed into the mists of history. But you can still find single-deck, double-deck and shoe blackjack games with $5 minimums, among the Strip's lowest. Minimum craps bets are also $5. Low-limit Texas hold 'em and seven-card stud games are spread daily in the card room, and $22 tournaments are held at 7pm on weekdays. The slots include the latest high-tech machines and are touted as the 'loosest on the Strip'; not that this really means anything.

Amenities *Bars (3). Business centre. Disabled-adapted rooms. High-speed internet (ADSL, web TV). No-smoking rooms. Pool (outdoor). Restaurants (5). Spa.* **Games** *Blackjack ($5-$500); Caribbean stud; craps (2x, 3x, 5x); keno; Let it Ride; pai gow poker; poker; roulette (double zero); Spanish 21; three-card poker. Gambling lessons.*

Stardust

3000 Las Vegas Boulevard South, at Stardust Drive, between W Sahara Avenue & Desert Inn Road, Las Vegas, NV 89109 (reservations 1-866 642 3120/ front desk & casino 732 6111/fax 732 6257/ www.stardustlv.com). Bus 301/self-parking & valet parking Las Vegas Boulevard South or Industrial Road. **Rates** *$65-$300 single/double; $115-$400 suites.* **Credit** *AmEx, Disc, DC, MC, V.* **Map** *p319 B5.*

When other hotels were trying to attract families to the Strip, the 1958 Stardust was having none of it, and a relatively inexpensive $100 million renovation in 1991 did little to alter the atmosphere. For better or for worse, the Stardust has remained true to the heritage of its signature sign: there's comfortable accommodation and adult action. But though *Casino* was based on activities at the Stardust and parts of *Showgirls* were filmed here, you're more likely to run into Wayne Newton than Elizabeth Berkley.

Accommodation

The original low-slung motor inn building contains the Stardust's 431 cheapest rooms but the 2,000 tower rooms and suites are tastefully done up and among the best buys on the Strip. The suites – at 700sq ft (65sq m), 'mini-suites' is more accurate – have fine marble bathrooms and whirlpool baths.

Eating & drinking

The Stardust is old fashioned in a number of ways, not least in its aversion to the celebrity-chef cult. The resort's range of restaurants are uncomplicated; the list is headed by **William B's** (steaks and seafood), with barbecue chain **Tony Roma's** just below it. There's also the 24-hour **Island Paradise** coffee shop (whose broad menu includes Chinese), the **Coco Palms** buffet, the self-describing **Sushi King**, and espresso and ice-cream joints.

Entertainment

The Stardust has a history of traditional stage spectaculars (*Lido de Paris* featured the city's first showgirls) but, though it certainly considers itself a throwback, they recently allowed longtime headline act Wayne Newton to seek other challenges in the entertainment industry. His main replacement, in the theatre that currently still bears his name, is vibrant Latino dance show **Havana Night Club** (*see p220*), though there's also a rota of occasional guest stars, headlined by the agreeably grumpy, foul-mouthed comic **George Carlin**. Veteran magician **Rick Thomas** has recently taken over the afternoon shift. At the **Stardust Ballroom**, the wooden dancefloor eases the ankles of those who gather for dancing to swing orchestras. Bands play in the old-style **Starlight Lounge** (*see p175*).

Gambling

There are 35 blackjack tables offering double-deck or shoe action. Crap players like the modest minimums and spirited action, while baccarat players gamble thousands a hand. The 'Peace Pit' has the music and the fun dealers. The card room is a stalwart, offering sprightly and friendly low-limit action. There are nearly 2,000 slots of all varieties, and the slot club offers straightforward cash instead of prizes or gimmicks. The sports book is a mecca for sports fans, hosting sports-oriented radio shows on weekdays, setting the early line, and displaying stats in the 'handicappers' library'.

Amenities *Bars (7). Business centre. Disabled-adapted rooms. Gym. No-smoking floors. Pool (outdoor). Restaurants (8).* **Games** *Baccarat ($25-$100,000); mini baccarat ($10-$2,000); blackjack ($5-$2,000); Caribbean stud; craps (3x, 4x, 5x); keno; Let it Ride; pai gow poker; poker; roulette (double zero); three-card poker. Gambling lessons.*

Stardust. See p89.

Stratosphere

2000 Las Vegas Boulevard South, at St Louis Avenue, between Oakey Boulevard & E Sahara Avenue, Las Vegas, NV 89104 (reservations 1-888 236 7495/front desk & casino 380 7777/fax 383 5334/www.stratospherehotel.com). Bus 301/self-parking & valet parking Las Vegas Boulevard South. **Rates** *$39-$300 single/double; $139-$369 suite.* **Credit** *AmEx, DC, Disc, MC, V.* **Map** *p319 C3/4.*

The Stratosphere entices thrill-seekers with rides atop its 1,149-foot (107-metre) pinnacle, the highest free-standing observation tower in the US. **The Tower** features indoor and outdoor observation decks, a revolving restaurant, and such mental diversions that they actually titled the newest one Insanity – The Ride. Guests are whisked from the ground floor to the observation decks in less than 35 seconds via double-decker elevators travelling at three floors a second. Once there, climb aboard the bottle rocket Big Shot or the world's highest rollercoaster. The newest addition to the Tower Shops is the **Trick Art Museum**, which features Japanese art techniques to transform flat paintings into 'living' 3D artwork.

Accommodation

Guestrooms in the tower would be interesting, but all the Stratosphere's sleeping quarters are in separate buildings. Some are in the original Vegas World mid-rise; a more recent tower brought the total to 2,444 rooms and suites. There are an overwhelming 13 different types of room, from the smallish 340sq ft (32sq m) standard room to the massive 2,165sq ft (200sq m) Premier Suite, with the pricier rooms generally having lighter decor.

Eating & drinking

Eating options run from the pricey **Top of the World** (*see p151*), which rotates once every 90mins, to **McDonald's**. Among those in the middle are the **Crazy Armadillo** oyster and tequila bar. **Lucky's** is a 24-hour café that brazenly rips off Mr Lucky's 24/7 in the Hard Rock.

Entertainment

As impersonator shows go, the Strat's **American Superstars** is pretty good. On the tower, there's an indoor/outdoor observation deck, plus the **High Roller** rollercoaster (tame coaster, scary location) and the ass-clenching **Big Shot**. You'd have to be certifiable to take the **X Scream**, a teeter-totter ride that tilts passengers 30 feet over the edge of the tower, or **Insanity – The Ride** (*see p122*), which dangles and spins riders over the edge at 40 mph.

Gambling

The casino area is spacious and comfortable, if a bit generic. The layout approximates a series of circles, which looks good but complicates any attempt to get straight from one end to the other. The emphasis is on liberal machines and table-game gimmicks to improve players' odds. The Stratosphere advertises a 98% return on more than 150 dollar slots, a 100% return on some video poker machines and 10x odds on craps, as well as single-zero roulette, double-exposure blackjack and crapless craps (with a bunch of cockamamie rules that aren't player-friendly).

Amenities *Bars (3). Business centre. Concierge. Disabled-adapted rooms. Gym. High-speed internet (wireless). No-smoking floors. Pool (outdoor). Restaurants (7). Spa.* **Games** *Mini baccarat ($5-$1,000); Big Six; blackjack ($5-$2,000); Caribbean stud; craps (10x); Let it Ride; pai gow poker; roulette (single & double zero); three-card poker. Gambling lessons.*

Tropicana

3801 Las Vegas Boulevard South, at E Tropicana Avenue, Las Vegas, NV 89109 (reservations 1-888 826 8767/front desk & casino 739 2222/fax 739 2469/www.tropicanalv.com). Bus 201, 301, 302/self-parking & valet parking Las Vegas Boulevard South, E Tropicana Avenue or Reno Avenue. **Rates** *$49-$399 single/double; $199-$699 suite.* **Credit** *AmEx, DC, Disc, MC, V.* **Map** *p320 A8.*

Rumours continue to swirl around the fate of this former 'Tiffany of the Strip', including a possible buyout by MGM Mirage. But plans to raze the Polynesian-themed hotel have been put on hold, even though new blueprints have already been drawn up that would transform the Trop into a contemporary Vegas adult playground. Most areas of the casino are fairly generic, not very attractive and, in the worst examples, altogether incongruous (a huge canopy ceiling made of leaded stained-glass and mirrors). That said, if you want a decent room and a nice pool – between the hotel's two towers lie five acres of tropical landscaping with pools, lagoons, waterfalls and swim-up blackjack tables – at a good price, the Tropicana is still worth considering. The **Casino Legends Hall of Fame** (*see p114*), featuring historical Vegas gambling artefacts, is also worth a look.

Accommodation
The original two-storey motor inn buildings surround the pool and are thus conveniently close to it; although they're the oldest at the resort, they can be comfortable if you get one with a balcony and pool view. The newer tower rooms are generally better. The 1,878 rooms and super, theme and jacuzzi suites are all done out with colorful prints, and wood and bamboo furnishings.

Eating & drinking
The intimate **Pietro's** offers service and French-inspired cooking good enough to have won awards. The Japanese-style teppan room and steakhouse **Mizuno's**, where they cook your food (steaks, Gulf shrimp and Australian lobster) at your table, is one of the resort's best eateries. The traditional **Savanna Steakhouse** serves steaks and seafood, while other recently revamped rooms include **Tuscany** (Italian) and the **Island Buffet**.

Entertainment
The Trop is home to old-fashioned feathers-and-sequins spectacular **Folies Bergere** (*see p220*): the longest-running production show in America, it opened here in 1959. The **Comedy Stop** (*see p222*) has a weekly rotation of stand-ups. The **Tropicana Bird Show** presents chatty, stunt-performing birds three times daily in the Tropics Lounge.

Gambling
The swim-up blackjack is the Tropicana's one special gaming pull. Otherwise, there's the usual variety of games, with a bit less video poker than at other places and some of the slots showing their age. A tiny, dingy sports book is at the bottom of a stairway at the back of the casino, apparently hidden as if the hotel were embarrassed by it. It should be.

Amenities Bars (3). Business centre. Disabled-adapted rooms. Gym. No-smoking floors. Pool (indoor/outdoor). Restaurants (7). Spa. **Games** *Blackjack ($5-$1,000); Caribbean stud; craps (3x, 4x, 5x); keno; Let it Ride; pai gow poker; roulette (double zero); three-card poker. Gambling lessons.*

Off-Strip

Expensive

Hard Rock
4455 Paradise Road, at Harmon Avenue, Las Vegas, NV 89109 (reservations 1-800 473 7625/front desk & casino 693 5000/fax 693 5010/www.hardrock hotel.com). Bus 108/self-parking Paradise Road/valet parking E Harmon Avenue. **Rates** $99-$599 single/double; $250-$1,000 suite. **Credit** AmEx, DC, Disc, MC, V. **Map** p320 C7.

The exact point at which rock 'n' roll sold its soul to commerce is a mystery, but you can bet the Hard Rock took a cut of the proceeds. The image of Sid Vicious adorns slot machines, Bob Dylan's lyrics line the elevators, and a notice on the wall reminds guests that smart dress is required, a rule that would bar more or less every icon the casino idolises. Still, despite its blazingly middle-American appropriation of once-potent rock imagery, the hotel has been an unqualified success since its 1995 opening. The golf-shooting, Dockers-wearing baby-boomer brigade is here in force during the week, but at night the hotel draws a crowd of boisterous funseekers, A-list glitterati and local hipsters, especially on weekends.

Though other casinos cater to the Gen-X crowd, most notably the Palms, the Hard Rock remains the city's premier party place. The casino design (circular, with a bar in the middle) is a beauty, and means the place always feels buzzing even when it's not. Out back, the pool scene's even hotter: sandy beaches, waterfalls, swim-up blackjack and craps. Amenities include the RockSpa (hey, don't shoot the messenger), electric purple limos and SUVs for guests, some terrific restaurants and the coolest sundries boutique: selling everything from liquor to lube, it embodies the concept of the convenience store.

Accommodation
The casino itself may be like a zoo, but the upstairs guestrooms are remarkably peaceful and minimalist – if not, perhaps, stunningly luxurious – with mod space-agey furnishings that are sort of *Jetsons* meets the I-Ching. Most rooms are decorated with museum-quality photos of rock stars. Try to get digs overlooking the pool.

Eating & drinking
You'll find the hippest eateries at the Hard Rock, from sublime sushi at **Nobu** (*see p153*) to upscale comfort food at **Simon Kitchen & Bar** (*see p152*) and prime cuts of beef at the 1950s-retro **AJ's Steakhouse** (*see p152*). **Pink Taco** (*see p154*) serves excellent Mexican, while **Mr Lucky's 24/7** (*see p152*) ranks as the city's coolest coffee shop (with a great-value $7.77 steak-and-shrimp special that's not on the menu). For celebrity and general gorgeous people-watching, nowhere beats the **Center Bar** (in the middle of the circular casino) and **Viva Las Vegas Lounge** (*see p170*).

Entertainment
Inaugurated by Sheryl Crow in 1994, the 3,000-capacity **Joint** (*see p237*) helped bust any lingering stigma about playing Vegas. After-hours, the party continues in **Body English** (*see p241*), a fantastically fashionable nightclub full of women who are way out of your league.

Gambling
A mid-1990s beast it may be, but this is still a hip and popular gambling den. The casino remains small by Vegas standards: only 800 slots and video poker machines and 76 tables. The main floor is one big circle, with an outer hardwood walkway and an

elevated bar in the centre. Dealers are encouraged to be friendly and enthusiastic; some will give you a high-five if you a natural blackjack, a stunt that would give the pit boss a heart attack anywhere else.

Amenities Bars (6). Business centre. Concierge. Disabled-adapted rooms. Gym. High-speed internet (ADSL). No-smoking floors. Pool (outdoor). Restaurants (5). Spa. **Games** *Baccarat ($100-$5,000); mini baccarat ($10-$3,000); blackjack ($5-$2,000); Caribbean stud; craps (3x, 4x, 5x); Let it Ride; pai gow poker; roulette (double zero); three-card poker.*

Moderate

Las Vegas Hilton

3000 Paradise Road, between Karen Avenue & Desert Inn Road, Las Vegas, NV 89109 (reservations 1-800 732 7117/front desk & casino 732 5111/fax 732 5805/www.lvhilton.com). Bus 108, 112/self-parking Paradise Road or Joe W Brown Drive/valet parking Paradise Road. **Rates** $69-$299 single/double; $299-$9,999 suite. **Credit** AmEx, DC, Disc, MC, V. **Map** p319 C5.

Everything at this, the former International built by Kirk Kerkorian on what was to be the 'Paradise Strip', comes on a grand scale. There are 3,000 rooms, 200,000sq ft (18,600sq m) of convention space, a smörgåsbord of fine restaurants and the Super Book, which lives up to its heavyweight title as the most popular sports book in town. The Hilton also is known for its headliners, dating back to Elvis and his 837 straight sold-out performances in the 1970s. The star of the show these days? Barry Manilow. Don't come here expecting to find heiresses Paris and Nicky dancing on the tables: they'll probably be at the Palms.

Accommodation

Sited just east of the Strip, the Hilton is perfect for those who want to be close to, but not in the middle of, the bustle. The seven room 'levels' each have their own decor, not just increasingly plush renditions of the standard decor. The Park Avenue, for instance, is classic Manhattan style, while the Classic goes for 1920s Hollywood. Some standard rooms are dark and claustrophobic. In addition to the standard ('deluxe') room, there are six 'levels' of suites.

Eating & drinking

With André Rochat's classy **Mistral**, the Hilton finally landed a chef with a name. The rest of the stable are quiet winners. Disney-esque teppan-yaki chain **Benihana** has an impressive $2 million 'Japanese village' setting, though the food is costly. Three other Asian eateries (**Robata**, **Garden of the Dragon**, **Teru Sushi**) complement **Andiamo** (Italian) and the **Hilton Steakhouse**. Good fun for lunch is the *Star Trek*-themed **Quark's Bar & Restaurant** (*see p170*).

Entertainment

The bill at the 1,600-seat **Hilton Theater** is led by **Barry Manilow**, whose regular engagement is called *Music and Passion (see p219)*. In the Shimmer Cabaret is stand-up comic **David Brenner** (*see p217*) and the sexy (and sometimes topless) **Aussie Angels** dancers.

Gambling

Aside from the kitschy Space Quest Casino, which has $5 tables and sci-fi slots that offer the singular experience of starting the game by passing your hand though a laser beam, this is a high-roller haven, where class divisions are more conspicuous than at most casinos. The baccarat pit and high-limit tables are detached from the main gaming area, and the Platinum Plus slot machines, $5 and up per pull, have their own space. High limits dominate the main floor: $5 is the minimum at any table, and the $100 tables are jumping year-round. They'll bring out a single-zero roulette wheel if you agree to bet $25-plus per spin. Sports bettors still flock to the 400-seat Super Book, where explanations on how to bet on various sports have been posted to help novices.

Amenities Bars (8). Business centre. Concierge. Disabled-adapted rooms. Gym. High-speed internet (web TV). No-smoking floors. Pool (outdoor). Restaurants (11). Spa. **Games** *Baccarat ($100-$15,000); mini baccarat ($15-$5,000); Big Six; blackjack ($5-$10,000); Caribbean stud; casino war; craps (3x, 4x, 5x); keno; Let it Ride; pai gow poker; roulette (double zero; single zero on request); three-card poker. Gambling lessons.*

Palms

4321 W Flamingo Road, at S Valley View Boulevard, Las Vegas, NV 89103 (reservations 1-866 725 6773/front desk & casino 942 7777/fax 942 6999/www.palms.com). Bus 104, 202/self-parking W Flamingo Road, Arville Street or S Valley View Boulevard/valet parking W Flamingo Road. **Rates** $89-$499 single/double; $139-$10,000 suite. **Credit** AmEx, DC, Disc, MC, V. **Map** p317 X3.

Ever since MTV's *Real World* took over a floor in the aquamarine tower, owner George Maloof has shown a Midas touch for being in touch with everybody from twentysomething hipsters to blue-rinse daytime gamblers. At night, the Palms attracts a *Who's Who* of Hollywood players and sports stars with two nightclubs, some chic restaurants, a tattoo parlour, a tarot-card reader, 'bachelor suites' replete with dancer poles and even some rooms with giant beds (Maloof and his brother own the Sacramento Kings basketball team). But the magic also works on locals, with a movie theatre, a food court, a slots-driven casino that's often voted the best in town and, most of all, quality service. A dramatic expansion is due to be completed in January 2006.

Accommodation

The 470 rooms aren't giant, but many have great views and you get to curl up on the same beds as in Four Seasons, right down to the Egyptian cotton linens. Pop-culture fans can check into the Real World Suite. Don't forget the aforementioned bachelor suites for an *Austin Powers*-style good time, and the Sacramento Kings-sized suites with special fixtures and furnishings for the vertically blessed.

Eating & drinking

Up in the penthouse is André Rochat's third French restaurant, **Alizé** (*see p155*). Downstairs, there's **Little Buddha** (*see p155*), where you can dine on Asian dishes with a French twist or nosh with the beautiful people at the sushi bar. From Chicago comes **N9ne** (*see p155*), a steakhouse, champagne/ caviar bar and celebrity hangout. **Garduño's** offers tasty Tex-Mex, the **Sunrise Café** is a serviceable 24-hour diner, and there's a buffet and food court.

Entertainment

Rain in the Desert (*see p243*) gives the House of Blues and the Joint some competition for live music, but the three-storey spot shines as a proper night-club. High above it all (and with an equally lofty attitude) is the white-on-white **Ghostbar** (*see p170*), kind of LA East. When the weather heats up, so does **Skin**, a twice-weekly stripped-down pool party complete with cavorting 'mermaids'. When the lines at Ghostbar and Rain are too long (and they will be, they will be), hipsters head for the bar scene at N9ne. There's also the **Lounge** (*see p222*) or the **Roller Lounge**, a quieter corner behind the high-stakes gaming area, where you'll find soft leather chairs and hand-rolled cigars; everyone is welcome.

Gambling

The 95,000sq ft (8,800sq m) casino includes 2,400 slot machines, 55 table games, and a race and sports book. A survey recently conducted by gambling Bible the *Las Vegas Advisor* found the slots here to be the loosest in Las Vegas; let's hope that this relative generosity wasn't limited to the casino's opening few years.

Amenities *Bars (11). Beauty salon. Business centre. Concierge. Disabled-adapted rooms. Gym. High-speed internet (ADSL). No-smoking floors. Pool (outdoor). Restaurants (7). Spa.* **Games** *Baccarat ($100-$10,000); mini baccarat ($5-$10,000); blackjack ($10-$5,000); Caribbean stud; casino war; craps (3x); Let it Ride; pai gow poker; roulette (double zero); three-card poker.*

Rio

3700 W Flamingo Road, at Valley View Boulevard, Las Vegas, NV 89103 (reservations 1-800 752 9746/front desk & casino 252 7777/fax 252 8909/ www.playrio.com). Bus 104, 202/self-parking & valet parking W Flamingo Road, S Valley View Boulevard or Viking Street. **Rates** *$89-$399 suite.* **Credit** AmEx, DC, Disc, MC, V. **Map** p317 X3.

The carnival party never ends here. Or, at least, that's the idea. The theme is reinforced seven times a day by a free fantasy parade of overhead floats called the **Masquerade Show in the Sky**, backed by some wildly enthusiastic musicians and dancers. It's all part of the hyperactive Masquerade Village, which features, as well as the requisite gaming machines, two storeys of dining, a variety of drinking (from an Irish pub to a wine cellar), dancing, shopping and shows. And that's just one wing of the Harrah's-owned Rio, located off the Strip but with a truly garish sign that dominates the landscape for drivers heading west on Flamingo.

The 15-year-old casino works hard to keep up with the times, mixing new entertainment efforts (the minimalist yet over-the-top I-Bar) in with proven successes (the razor-sharp Penn & Teller). All of the 2,563 guestrooms are suites; amenities include four

Hard Rock. *See p91.*

waterfall-filled pools complete with a sandy beach and volleyball courts, three wedding chapels and a floor of honeymoon suites, the top-of-the-line Michael's Salon, a spa, and access to the **Rio Secco** golf course.

Accommodation
The comfortable 600sq ft (60sq m) mini-suites (not quite as big as at the Venetian) are the basic accommodation. Rooms feature floor-to-ceiling windows, big (32in/81cm) televisions and fridges. Top of the line are the 1,600sq ft (150sq m) suites, with better sound systems and wet bars.

Eating & drinking
The range of options here is wide and appealing: the **All-American Bar & Grille**, San Francisco's award-winning Indian **Gaylord's** (see *p155*), wildly popular local chain **Hamada of Japan**, serviceable Italian at **Antonio's**, **Buzio's** seafood, **Fiore's Steakhouse** and **Bamboleo** for Mexican. The **Carnival World Buffet** (see *p164*), one of the first in the city to feature live cooking stations, is a longtime favourite.

Entertainment
The **Scintas** (pronounced 'shin-tas'; see *p215*) moved from lounge shows to a permanent spot in the Copacabana and show no signs of letting up; the postmodern comedic magic of **Penn & Teller** (see *p218*) holds the fort in the Samba Theatre; the revamped **Chippendales** (see *p213*) do exactly what you'd expect. For something different, try the live interactive comedy theatre of **Tony 'n' Tina's Wedding**, or the vocal trickery of **Ronn Lucas** (for both, see *p217*).

While **Bikinis** seems tired (despite the scantily clad servers), **I-Bar** has enlivened the Rio's nightlife of late, combining natural elements of design (rock, water and light) with natural elements of Vegas nightlife (dancing bartendresses in flesh-coloured costumes). **Club Rio** is popular with ageing party people and conventioneers; the formerly fashionable **VooDoo Lounge** offers ghastly decor, ordinary service and – the key – great views.

Gambling
The casino is huge, sprawling for two blocks, and the predominant colours are green ($25) and black ($100): at weekends, it's hard to find $10-minimum blackjack. Smaller-stakes gamblers should aim for the lower-limit tables in the outlying areas of the casino; or better yet, walk across the street to the Gold Coast. Poker is offered – the Rio is the new home of the **World Series of Poker** (see *p202*) – but it's a tough room filled with locals. A shuttle bus runs between the Rio and the Strip (9am-1am daily).

Amenities *Bars (3). Business centre. Concierge. Disabled-adapted rooms. Gym. High-speed internet (ADSL). No-smoking floors. Pool (outdoor). Restaurants (12). Spa.* **Games** *Baccarat ($100-$10,000); mini baccarat ($25-$5,000); Big Six; blackjack ($10-$10,000); Caribbean stud; casino war; craps (3x, 4x, 5x); keno; Let it Ride; pai gow poker; pai gow tiles; roulette (double zero).*

Westin Casuarina
160 E Flamingo Road, at Koval Lane, Las Vegas, NV 89109 (reservations 1-888 625 5144/front desk & casino 836 9775/fax 836 9776/www.starwood hotels.com). Bus 102, 105/self-parking & valet parking E Flamingo Road. **Rates** $149-$329 single/double; $299-$779 suite. **Credit** AmEx, DC, Disc, MC, V. **Map** p320 B8.

Westin's first hotel in Las Vegas is a low-key resort, which is just how the majority of its guests like it. There is a small casino here, and even (though you'll need to look to find it) a cosy little showroom, but the Casuarina is aimed not at holidaymakers but at the business traveller who wants to get some work done and also wants the bright lights of the Strip within easy reach should he or she fancy a drink or three. There's a good deal of meeting space, and rooms contain all the amenities a laptop-toting workaholic could want. But it's also a comfortable place to stop a while: the service is solid, the pool area is relaxing, and the Hibiscus spa has 15 treatment rooms and a full-service salon.

Accommodation
The rooms here are everything you'd expect from a Westin, which is to say that they're comfortable, handsome (in a discreet way) and well equipped for the business traveller. The 'Heavenly Beds' live up to their names.

Eating & drinking
The **Silver Peak Grill** offers comfort food 24/7; there's also a **Starbucks** here.

Entertainment
New in 2005, **Forbidden Vegas** (see *p220*) is a musical that spoofs the Strip headliners against whom it purports to compete.

Gambling
The gambling is low-key, almost an afterthought. There are just ten table games; the rest is slots.

Amenities *Bars (1). Business centre. Concierge. Disabled-adapted rooms. Gym. High-speed internet (ADSL). No-smoking floors. Pool (outdoor). Restaurants (1). Spa.* **Games** *Blackjack ($5-$500); craps (3x, 4x, 5x); roulette (double zero); three-card poker.*

Downtown

In 1906, people were gambling in what is now Downtown. Sawdust joints – casinos with wooden boardwalks and floors – attracted railroad workers, ranchers and the like. For classic Vegas, you should still head Downtown, where old neon turns night into day and casinos offer fewer sideshows (read: unreconstructed dining, no spas, few shows) to distract from serious gambling. The house rules at Downtown casinos are often more liberal than on the Strip and minimum bets also tend to be lower, making casinos here a good place for beginners or low rollers to polish their skills.

Games without frontiers

The no-limit hold 'em poker craze isn't quite dead yet, but it's certainly gasping for air. Sure, there are still a few TV addicts who think Phil Helmuth's temper tantrums are hysterically scandalous, and remain amused and amazed that Chris Moneymaker and Greg 'Fossilman' Raymer, World Series of Poker champions in 2003 and 2004 respectively and weighing in at a combined total of about 550 pounds, are considered athletes. However, most of the rest of us have put our barely used sets of clay chips in the closet and have moved on to other televised entertainment.

However, hotshot studio executives aren't about to go quietly. Among Hollywood players, at least those who have already given up trying to wring the last drop of excitement out of televised poker, the desire runs strong to be the next... uh, guy who thought to put the World Series of Poker on TV. To save them the time and effort of actually learning a thing or two about casino games, we've eliminated some of the possibilities.

GAME	WHAT THEY'RE HOPING	THE AWFUL TRUTH
Baccarat	If it's good enough for James Bond, it's good enough for cable TV.	The only game more boring to watch than slot machines.
Craps	Flying red dice always look great on casino promotional videos. It must be exciting, right?	Turns out Jerry, the toothless crazy guy who's been tracking dice rolls for 35 years for patterns, is 'colourful', but not in a Doyle Brunson kind of way. More in an everyday toothless crazy guy kind of way.
Roulette	Perhaps the most iconic game of chance on the casino floor. The spinning wheel and bouncing marble contain a built-in, jaw-dropping sense of anticipation.	Viewers will quickly tire of teasers announcing, 'Tonight on *World Roulette Showdown*, the casino wins again. By a lot.'
Slots	By far the casino's biggest moneymaker. There's some reason these machines are so popular.	Highly addictive to play, slightly more boring to watch than a security tape loop of a bank vault.
Video poker	Predetermined pay tables and truly random card selection make this game's potentially beatable probabilities genuinely fascinating to mathematicians.	Mathematicians are too busy watching hot librarian porn to tune in to anything else.

Moderate

Golden Nugget

*129 E Fremont Street, at Casino Center Boulevard,
Las Vegas, NV 89101 (reservations 1-800 846
5336/front desk & casino 385 7111/www.golden
nugget.com). Bus 107, 108, 207, 301, 302/self-
parking 1st Street/valet parking Casino Center
Boulevard.* **Rates** *$79-$229 single/double; $350-$750
suite.* **Credit** *AmEx, DC, Disc, MC, V.* **Map** *p318 C1.*

Considered the slightly faded jewel in the sparkling
Downtown crown, the 49-year-old Golden Nugget
remains the classiest place to stay in the immediate
vicinity, and one in which gambling is still the main
attraction. However, no one knows exactly what the
future holds for this grand old stager. The hotel was
bought in 2003 by Tim Poster and Tom Breitling,
who promised to give the place a *Swingers*-type
makeover and bring some of the old vibrancy back
to Downtown. They did, too… and then sold it in
early 2005 to Landry's Restaurants. One to watch.

Accommodation

Tim and Tom put more than $30 million into reno-
vations and upgrades during their brief spell in
charge of the Nugget. Surrounding the elegantly
revamped pool area are three hotel towers containing about 1,900 remodelled rooms; there are also 27
luxury apartments and six penthouse suites. The
pampering continues with a state-of-the-art spa,
beauty salon and fitness centre.

Eating & drinking

Zax, a contemporary restaurant with continental
cuisine, has done a reasonable job in raising the chic
stakes. The **Buffet** *(see p164)* beats its more upscale
Strip competitors hands down for value, but its
upscale seating area is small, which both makes it
feel like a clubby Sunday brunch and forces people
to queue. Other options include some Italian (with
singing waiters) at **Stefano's**; Cantonese cuisine
and mesquite-grilled steaks at **Lillie Langtry's'**
and the 24-hour **Carson Street Café** *(see p156)*.

Entertainment

Poster and Breitling's masterplan included a dramatic reviving of the hotel's entertainment, mixing
vintage stars such as Tony Bennett with the
younger likes of Staind's Aaron Lewis. When they're
not drawing crowds to the 400-seat Theatre
Ballroom, it's home to musical comic and impressionist **'Downtown' Gordie Brown** *(see p214)*.

Gambling

The Nugget's elegant marble lobby may seem
out of place on Fremont Street, but the low table
minimums are appropriate. You'll find $5 blackjack
and craps, and a good selection of nickel machines.
There's a segregated pit for players with larger
bankrolls who want to play baccarat and blackjack
without being bugged by the hoi polloi; it's the
only high-limit pit downtown. The sports book is
more of a sports boutique: small but plush and thoroughly comfortable.

Dig it! Downtown's **Golden Nugget**.

Amenities *Bars (3). Business centre. Disabled-
adapted rooms. Gym. No-smoking rooms. Pool
(outdoor). Restaurants (5). Spa.* **Games** *Blackjack
($5-$5,000); Caribbean stud; casino war; craps (10x);
keno; Let it Ride; pai gow poker; poker; roulette
(double-zero); Spanish 21; three-card poker.*

Main Street Station

*200 N Main Street, at Stewart Avenue, Las Vegas,
NV 89101 (reservations 1-800 465 0711/front desk
& casino 387 1896/fax 386 4421/www.mainstreet
casino.com). Bus 107, 108, 207, 301, 302/self-
parking & valet parking Main Street.* **Rates** *$50-
$150 single/double.* **Credit** *AmEx, DC, Disc, MC, V.*
Map *p318 C3.*

Main Street was purchased in 1996 by Boyd Gaming
(Stardust, Sam's Town), since when the place has
come into its own as the nicest Downtown casino not
called the Golden Nugget. Themed as a *fin-de-siècle*
delight – check out the gas street-lamps that front
the property – the casino is filled with antiques of all
kinds, not all of them Victorian. Teddy Roosevelt's
Pullman car is here, now a chic smoking lounge; a
carved oak fireplace from Prestwick Castle in
Scotland and a set of doors from an old London bank
are also on display; and chunks of the Berlin Wall sit
in the men's room. Unlike the Nugget, which can feel
a bit hoity-toity, Main Street has an accessible,
upscale-yet-fun feel all too rare in Downtown.

Accommodation

The 430 guestrooms are comfortable if rather basic.

Eating & drinking

The choice might be small, but it's all good stuff.
The **Pullman Grille** sells delicious steaks and
seafood, while the **Triple 7 Brew Pub** *(see p172)*,
on the other hand, runs at everyone's speed: aside
from five beers, the pub offers excellent wood-fired

pizza and decent sushi. Finally, many locals swear by the **Garden Court Buffet** (*see p164*): the room is beautiful, the selections are excellent and the price is most definitely right.

Entertainment
Live entertainment is limited to sporadic live music (swing, jazz, rock) in the Triple 7 Brewpub.

Gambling
Main Street offers a good selection of slots and video poker, three-card poker and low limits at the tables; $5 blackjack dominates and the crap tables offer 20x odds. An illuminated sign over the roulette area depicts a single-zero wheel, though the actual wheel contains both the single zero and the double zero.

Amenities *Bars (1). Disabled-adapted rooms. No-smoking rooms. Pool (outdoor). Restaurants (3).* **Games** *Blackjack ($5-$1,000); craps (20x); keno; Let it Ride; pai gow poker (with a progressive); roulette (double zero); three-card poker.*

Budget

Binion's

128 Fremont Street, at Casino Center Boulevard, Las Vegas, NV 89101 (reservations 1-800 937 6537/front desk & casino 382 1600/fax 384 1574/www.binions.com). Bus 107, 108, 207, 301, 302/self-parking Casino Center Boulevard, Ogden Avenue or Stewart Avenue/valet parking Casino Center Boulevard or Ogden Avenue. **Rates** $39-$95 single/double. **Credit** AmEx, DC, Disc, MC, V. **Map** p318 D1.

One school of thought has it that for Downtown to truly regenerate itself, the old casinos that have long defined it need to be swept away. The opposite opinion holds that these vintage gambling halls are where you'll find the area's true character, and as such should be treasured.

Chalk this one up as a victory for the former camp. Once a gloriously vibrant and atmospheric old staging post under legendary owner Benny Binion, the casino is a shadow of its former self. The serious gambling, once the centrepiece of the whole operation, has been gutted in recent years, and the rooms left to rot. Harrah's have recently taken on ownership of the property, and it's not out of the question that things will improve. But the hotel's glory days have gone, much like the 'Horseshoe' that was dropped from its name in 2005.

Accommodation
Eighty of the rooms are from the original casino; the other 286 were added when the hotel acquired the Mint. The vast majority of them could use some fairly serious regeneration.

Entertainment
Comic **Vinnie Favorito** plays ten shows a week.

Eating & drinking
The **Coffee Shop** is still pretty decent, and the 24th-floor **Binion's Ranch Steakhouse** offers excellent views, but there's otherwise not much here.

Gambling
When the Binions owned Binion's, you found savvy, renegade dealers, some of the best in town. But the casino has gone through dramatic changes since the change in ownership. Only four crap tables remain from what was once the centre of the dice universe. The blackjack pits have also shrunk, replaced by some newfangled poker derivatives like Crazy 4 Poker and 3-5-7 Poker, which would've rendered Benny Binion apoplectic. Still, you'll find some good slot-club promotions – the video poker isn't half bad, and the poker room is one of the largest in town. The race book occupies a former lounge in the West Horseshoe; the sports book is in a separate part of the casino.

Amenities *Bars (2). Disabled-adapted rooms. No-smoking rooms. Pool (outdoor). Restaurants (3).* **Games** *Mini baccarat ($10-$1,000); blackjack ($5-$1,000); craps (3x, 4x, 5x); keno; Let it Ride; poker; roulette (double zero); three-card poker.*

El Cortez

600 Fremont Street, at 6th Street, Las Vegas, NV 89101 (reservations 1-800 634 6703/front desk & casino 385 5200/fax 385 1554/www.elcortez.net). Bus 107, 301, 302/self-parking Ogden Avenue/valet parking 6th Street. **Rates** $25-$99 single/double; $99-$169 suite. **Credit** AmEx, DC, Disc, MC, V. **Map** p318 D2.

The old-timey El Cortez keeps the spirit of post-war Downtown alive, which comes with the good, bad and ugly. Built in 1941, the historic building's Spanish-style architecture is good to see, and so is another relic: Jackie Gaughan, who bought the property way back in 1963, still walks the floors daily. Jackie's mission statement – 'Give the customer a good deal and he'll come back' – is nice to hear in the age of resorts run by corporations. Still, while people do come back for such deals as low-stakes slots in the city's oldest operating casino, cheap rooms and bargain meals, or for such quaint old-school touches as the barbershop (nine bucks a haircut!), you have to like slumming it.

Accommodation
The rooms are spartan to say the least (what do you expect for 30 bucks?), but they all are being remodelled. The 'suites' are slightly larger, slightly newer rooms. History buffs on a budget might want to consider staying in the original adobe brick building, with wooden floors and tile baths.

Entertainment
You make your own fun here.

Eating & drinking
If you fancy yourself as a character from *Fear and Loathing in Las Vegas*, there is a great deal of kitsch value to dining at the El Cortez. **Roberta's** circular booths and kelly-green and hot-pink decor scream Tarantino, and the Porterhouse steak special is a local favourite. **Careful Kitty's** 24-hour coffee shop is unrivalled for local colour and its myriad late-night specials.

Gambling

The El Cortez is the place to go if you're short on cash and high on hope: there are plenty of penny and nickel video poker machines, and some of the last remaining $3 blackjack tables in town. Craps and roulette, both with $1 minimums, also offer cheap entertainment, as does the 40¢-ticket keno. The casino hosts a twice-yearly social security number lottery: if your nine-digit number is drawn, you win $50,000.

Amenities Bars (3). Disabled-adapted rooms. No-smoking rooms. Restaurants (2). **Games** *Mini baccarat ($5-$1,000); blackjack ($3-$500); craps (2x); keno; Let it Ride; poker; roulette (double zero).*

Fremont

200 E Fremont Street, at Casino Center Boulevard, Las Vegas, NV 89101 (reservations 1-800 634 6182/front desk & casino 385 6244/fax 385 6270/ www.fremontcasino.com). Bus 107, 108, 207, 301, 302/self-parking & valet parking Casino Center Boulevard or Ogden Avenue. **Rates** $50-$120 single/double. **Credit** AmEx, DC, Disc, MC, V. **Map** p318 D1.

The Fremont celebrates its 50th birthday in 2006, and a lot has changed since it was Las Vegas's first high-rise. Most of the old 1950s charm is gone and a tropical island motif has moved in, which may have something to do with the large Hawaiian clientele that's been aggressively – and successfully – courted by management. The famous block-long neon sign still holds its own, except when outglared by the Fremont Street Experience that canopies it.

Accommodation

The hotel's 447 guestrooms (including 23 suites) are modern and comfortable and feature floral patterns in hues of emerald and burgundy.

Eating & drinking

The Fremont courts visitors from the Pacific Rim, hence the surprising **Second Street Grill** (*see p157*): an unexpectedly upscale and risk-taking fusion-focused dining room, it delights discerning visitors with *mahi mahi* and *ono*. The **Paradise Café** coffee shop offers American and Chinese specialities, and **Lanai Express** is an Asian fast-food joint. There's also a **Tony Roma's** – of the chain's 150 restaurants, the most successful branch is right here. At night, the Paradise rolls out a buffet.

Entertainment

Nothing doing here.

Gambling

A nondescript grind joint in the middle of Grind Central, with nothing much to recommend it and nothing much to warn against. There's usually a slot or slot-club promotion going on; if you're in the neighbourhood, enquire at the slot-club booth.

Amenities Bars (4). Disabled-adapted rooms. No-smoking rooms. Restaurants (4). **Games** *Blackjack ($5-$1,000); Caribbean stud; craps (2x); Let it Ride; keno; pai gow poker; roulette (double zero); Spanish 21; three-card poker.*

Golden Gate

1 Fremont Street, at Main Street, Las Vegas, NV 89101 (reservations 1-800 426 1906/front desk 385 1906/fax 382 5349/www.goldengatecasino.net). Bus 107, 108, 207, 301, 302/self-parking & valet parking Main Street. **Rates** $39-$89 single/double. **Credit** AmEx, DC, Disc, MC, V. **Map** p318 C1.

Being the oldest and smallest of anything aren't normally qualities about which a Vegas property brags, but the Gate pulls it off. Celebrating its 100th birthday in 2006, this 106-room hotel is positively quaint alongside the flashy Golden Nugget and the garish Fremont Street Experience. While the casino is pleasantly intimate and its piano player an unexpected touch of class, the marquee attraction remains the 99¢ shrimp cocktail in the deli.

Accommodation

Many of the original 10ft-by-10ft bedrooms remain, though they've been updated with air-conditioning, private baths, cable TV, voicemail and even ADSL. Weekend rates have been bumped up, but the mahogany doors, plaster walls and tiled bathroom floors are a reminder of the joint's more basic past.

Eating & drinking

In 50 years, the 24-hour **San Francisco Deli** has served 25 million shrimp cocktails, tangy treats in tulip-shaped glasses that never fail to make the *Las Vegas Advisor's* list of best bargains in the city. For a classically Las Vegan dining experience, there's the **Bay City Diner** (*see p156*).

Entertainment

Save for the occasional ivory-tinkling pianist, there's nothing special laid on here.

Gambling

An old-time, no-frills, family-owned casino. The carpet's worn, the tables and machines packed like sardines, and the bosses brook no nonsense. There's live piano music and, from the far dice-table closest to the deli, you can make a dash for the famous 99¢ shrimp cocktail between rolls.

Amenities Bars (1). No-smoking rooms. Restaurants (2). **Games** *Blackjack ($5-$1,000); Caribbean stud; craps (5x); pai gow poker; roulette (double zero).*

Las Vegas Club

18 E Fremont Street, at Main Street, Las Vegas, NV 89101 (reservations 1-800 634 6532/385 1664/ www.vegasclubcasino.net). Bus 107, 108, 207, 301, 302/self-parking & valet parking Main Street. **Rates** $29-$69 single/double. **Credit** AmEx, MC, V. **Map** p318 C1.

This old stager was bought in recent years by the Barrick Gaming group, who've attempted to inject it – and their other three properties in the area – with a little Downtown cool. They've not yet managed it: the sports-themed decor and bright lighting are worlds apart from the casinos of yore. But while it's not enormously characterful, the Vegas Club is still a very decent option if you're on a budget, thanks to the recently spruced-up rooms and the casino's proximity to the other Downtown attractions.

Main Street Station. See p96.

Casinos & Hotels

As well as the Vegas Club and the **Plaza** (*see below*), Barrick also operate the very basic 110-room **Gold Spike** (400 E Ogden Avenue, 1-877 467 7453, 384 8444, www.goldspikehotelcasino.com) and, west of Las Vegas Boulevard, the extremely spartan **Western** (899 E Fremont Street, 1-800 634 6703, 384 4620, www.westernhotelcasino.com).

Accommodation
The guestrooms here got a refit relatively recently, and while they're not dazzling by any means, they're airy and comfortable. The guestrooms in the North Tower are in the best shape, something usually reflected in the prices.

Eating & drinking
The **Great Moments** restaurant aims for a vintage Vegas vibe, and sometimes gets away with it. Two baseball-themed joints offer snacks: the **Upper Deck** and the 24-hour **Seventh Inning Scoop**.

Entertainment
Nothing to speak of.

Gambling
The casino here is bigger than it first appears, stretching around the ground floor. In line with the rest of the hotel, it's in pretty good shape following the recent clean-up, though there's not much in the way of atmosphere about the place.

Amenities Bars (2). Disabled-adapted rooms. No-smoking rooms. Restaurants (4). **Games** *Mini baccarat ($5-$3,500); Big Six; bingo; blackjack ($5-$2,500); craps (5x); keno; Let it Ride; pai gow poker; poker; roulette (double zero); three-card poker.*

Plaza
1 Main Street, at Fremont Street, Las Vegas, NV 89101 (reservations 1-800 634 6575/front desk 386 2440/casino 386 2110/fax 382 8281/www.plaza hotelcasino.com). Bus 107, 108, 207, 301, 302/self-parking & valet parking Main Street. **Rates** $39-$169 single/double. **Credit** AmEx, DC, Disc, MC, V. **Map** p318 C1.

This was formerly Jackie Gaughan's Plaza, but Jackie is long Gaughan and the Barrick Gaming Corporation has taken over ownership and operation of the place. The ambitious company has set out to be a major player in reshaping Downtown, starting here with a seven-figure renovation and a finger-snappin' logo inspired by the retro-Vegas movement. An expansion plan features 1,200 new rooms, which would make the Plaza Downtown's biggest hotel. Already you get a lot of destination for the money: amenities include an outdoor sports deck with pool, four tennis courts, private cabañas, a gym, a chapel and a beauty salon.

Accommodation
Home to 1,037 rooms and suites, in two towers and in four configurations, each accommodation at the Plaza is basic and comfortable, but with some much-needed remodelling under way.

Eating & drinking
New with the takeover is **Manetti's**, a family-style Italian restaurant replete with singing waiters. For an upscale menu and a better view, there's the **Center Stage** (*see p156*), a glass-topped restaurant and bar overlooking Fremont Street. On Sundays,

the **Celebrity Champagne Brunch** takes over the Stage, hosted by *Magnum PI*'s Larry Manetti. For breakfast, go **Backstage**, a buffet restaurant where you'll be fed for less than $6.

Entertainment
The **Comedy Zone Showroom** (*see p222*) showcases a selection of nationally known stand-ups. The afternoon show, which only costs one drink, is **Stars of the Strip**, starring Robbie Howard. At 6pm, find out if Larry G Jones lives up to his billing as 'The Man of 1,002 Voices'.

Gambling
The casino teems with 1,200 slot machines. In the pit, gamblers can play $1 craps or $5 blackjack. Seven-card stud, Texas hold 'em and Omaha hold 'em poker are played in the card room, where limits are low and the players more gentlemanly than on the Strip. But if you really want to gamble on the cheap, the keno lounge is your best bet. The Plaza is the only place in the US that offers double keno (simultaneous action on two boards) with games starting at 40¢ – a bargain, despite the ridiculous odds. The bingo room is on the third floor.

Amenities *Bars (5). Disabled-adapted rooms. Gym. No-smoking rooms. Pool (outdoor). Restaurants (4).* **Gambling** *Mini baccarat ($5-$3,000); Big Six; bingo; blackjack ($5-$2,000); craps (10x); keno; Let it Ride; pai gow poker; poker; roulette (double zero); three-card poker.*

The rest of the city

Expensive

Hyatt Regency Lake Las Vegas
1600 Lake Las Vegas Parkway, Henderson, NV 89109 (reservations 1-800 554 9288/front desk 567 1234/fax 567 6103/www.lakelasvegas.hyatt. com). No bus/self-parking & valet parking Lake Las Vegas Parkway. **Rates** $249-$429 single/double; $499-$1,999 suite. **Credit** AmEx, DC, Disc, MC, V.
The romantic comedy *America's Sweethearts* was like one long commercial for this Moroccan-themed resort, the first in this $4.4 billion, 2,242-acre resort community about 17 miles south-east of the Strip. Along with hiking, biking and bird-watching, the major attractions are watersports on a 320-acre private man-made lake (sailing, canoeing, kayaking, windsurfing and fishing), and three golf courses (two designed by Jack Nicklaus, the other by Tom Weiskopf). The spa is average, though guests aren't charged fees to use it. And there's a pretty white-sand beach, fortified annually with eight tons of sand, as well as a sports area with a small putting green, basketball, volleyball and tennis, and the chain's renowned daycare programme for kids.

Accommodation
The 493 rooms all have mini-fridges, bathrobes and Portico bath products. There are also private two- and three-bedroom 'casbahs' with butler service.

Eating & drinking
Japengo serves Pacific Rim cuisine and sushi prepared by Nevada's only master sushi chef, Osamu Fujita, while **Café Tajine** serves breakfast, lunch and dinner in a bright, laid-back atmosphere. For outdoor dining there's **SandsaBar Grill**. For pre- or post-dinner cocktails, the **Arabesque Lounge** has beautiful views of the lake and mountains, and live music nightly.

Entertainment
Though the Hyatt's options are limited – even the casino shuts down at 2am – you can wander over to **MonteLago Village** and stroll its cobblestone streets, enjoying its restaurants, shops and casino as well as gondola rides on Lake Las Vegas.

Gambling
The Hyatt's casino seems more of an afterthought than a main attraction, which is just fine with the hoity-toity golfers and upscale vacationers who frequent Hyatts in general and this one in particular. In fact, the casino is open only 10am to 2am, one of the few casinos in Nevada that ever closes. Still, this is a comfortable and roomy gambling hall and the limits aren't too bad for such a top-shelf resort.

Amenities *Bars (2). Business centre. Concierge. Disabled-adapted rooms. Gym. High-speed internet (ADSL). No-smoking floors. Pool (outdoor). Restaurants (4). Spa.* **Games** *Blackjack ($5-$5,000); craps (3x, 4x, 5x); pai gow poker; roulette (double zero).*

JW Marriott Las Vegas/ Rampart Casino
221 N Rampart Boulevard, at Summerlin Parkway, Northwest Las Vegas, NV 89145 (reservations 1-877 869 8777/front desk & casino 507 5900/fax 869 7771/www.rampartcasino.com). Bus 207/self-parking & valet parking N Rampart Boulevard. **Rates** $189-$599 single/double. **Credit** AmEx, DC, Disc, MC, V.
This expansive Spanish-style spa and golf resort is not your typical Marriott. The resort sits on some 54 acres in the heart of Summerlin, Howard Hughes' upscale planned community about 30 minutes from the Strip, and boasts spectacular views of the Red Rock Conservation Area and access – via the hotel's new executive golf desk – to eight of the area's most sought-after golf courses. There's also a beautiful waterfall pool, the splendid 40,000sq ft (3,700sq m) Aquae Sulis spa (*see p194* **Star spas**), a new full-service beauty salon, a fully equipped fitness centre, several restaurants and clubs, and a few shops. A complimentary shuttle provides access to the Strip.

Accommodation
Divvied between two towers, the resort's 541 spacious rooms, elegantly furnished with antiques bought at auctions and from estate sales, are more luxurious than anything you'd usually encounter at a Marriott. You'll find triple sheeting on the beds along with plush robes and supersized towels in the large marble bathrooms. All rooms feature oversized raindrop showers and separate whirlpool baths.

Celebrate Mardi Gras 365 days a year at the **Orleans**. *See p102.*

Eating & drinking

Local celebrity chef Gustav Mauler has carved a very neat niche for himself out here with the Italian trattoria **Spiedini** and his classy, eponymous cigar/Martini bar. Those in the mood for *tekka maki* can indulge at **Shizen**, a sushi bar/teppanyaki room, while a lively standing-room crowd enjoys bangers 'n' mash and top-shelf Irish whisky at **JC Woolloughan's Irish Pub**. The resort's fine-dining options include **Ceres**, which serves breakfast, lunch and dinner amid gorgeous views of the resort's lush grounds and waterfalls; and the Rampart's elegantly intimate **Carmel Room**, which features fine continental cuisine served with Mediterranean flair. In season, you'll find light fare poolside at the **Waterside Grill**.

Entertainment

In 2004, the folks behind West Hollywood's Key Club opened **Plush** (*see p242*), a mod nightclub that caters to a pretty Summerlin crowd with dance music, speciality drinks and a light bar menu crafted by Mauler. There's Celtic folk and rock in JC Woolloughan's.

Gambling

This is one of the most beautiful casinos in Las Vegas: expansive, luxurious, multi-level, with a stunning palm-painted backlit dome over the pit. Originally targeted at affluent visitors – but a $50 cab ride from where visitors tend to stay – it quickly went bankrupt. The new owners hired a veteran management group that went after affluent Summerlin locals with playable machines and decent slot-club benefits.

Amenities Bars (4). Business centre. Concierge. Disabled-adapted rooms. Gym. High-speed internet (ADSL). No-smoking floors. Pool (outdoor). Restaurants (6). Spa. Games Baccarat ($100-$5,000); mini baccarat ($5-$500); blackjack ($5-$5,000); Caribbean stud; casino war; craps (5x); keno; pai gow poker; roulette (double zero); Spanish 21; three-card poker.

Locals' Casinos

Many Las Vegas residents don't gamble, but there are enough so-called 'locals' casinos' to suggest that those who do, play hard. Locals' casinos have become the social focal point of many neighbourhoods, providing cinemas, bowling alleys and other amenities for residents looking for a sense of community. Combined with good-value restaurants and generous slot clubs, they're a good bet for visitors who fancy a breather from the bustle of the Strip. Most offer pretty basic accommodation.

Arizona Charlie's

740 S Decatur Boulevard, at Alta Drive, Southwest Las Vegas (reservations 1-800 827 1518/front desk & casino 258 5111/www.arizonacharliesdecatur. com). Bus 103, 207/self-parking & valet parking S Decatur Boulevard.

A no-frills bunkhouse for serious players, the majority of them locals, Arizona Charlie's is long on action and short on atmosphere. The theme is the Yukon gold rush, though you won't notice: the interior design is little more than a floor, a ceiling and rows of machines. The **Yukon Grille** is a good steak house, and the **Sourdough Café**'s steak-and-eggs special will set you back just $2.99. There's also a buffet. The **Naughty Ladies Saloon** plays host to a range of lounge acts.

Arizona Charlie's opened a second branch on the Boulder Strip in 2000 (4575 S Boulder Highway, East Las Vegas, 1-877 951 0002, www.arizonacharlies boulder.com), with basically the same restaurants and a slightly larger casino. The **Palace Grand Lounge** offers live music, heavy on the country. *Games Bingo; blackjack ($5-$2,000); craps (3x); Caribbean stud; keno; Let it Ride; pai gow poker; roulette (double zero); three-card poker (Decatur branch only).*

Gold Coast

*4000 W Flamingo Road, at S Valley View Boulevard,
West of Strip (reservations 1-888 402 6278/front
desk & casino 367 7111/www.goldcoastcasino.com).
Bus 104, 202/self-parking & valet parking S Valley
View Boulevard, W Flamingo Road or Wynn Road.*
Map p317 X3.

The Barbary Coast took its act off the Strip in 1984
and begat the Gold Coast. Like most sequels, it's bigger, but relies on the same formula for success.
Locals love the machines and the slot-club, both of
which usually take top honours in the *Las Vegas
Review-Journal*'s 'Best of Vegas' survey. Banks of
non-smoking machines were a good idea; putting
them next to the smoking machines was not. There's
plenty of $5 blackjack and $1 roulette for low rollers,
one of the city's bigger bingo rooms (eight sessions
daily) and a 70-lane bowling alley.

For food, choose between the **Cortez Room**, a
mid-priced steakhouse; **Arriva**, which serves bargain seafood and Italian cuisine; the all-Asian **Ping
Pang Pong**; the **Monterey Room** coffee shop; or
the buffet, rated highly by locals. In early 2005, the
Gold Coast's renovated showroom took on a production of 1950s musical **Forever Plaid** (*see p220*).
Games *Mini baccarat ($10-$1,000); bingo; blackjack
($5-$1,000); Caribbean stud; craps (2x); keno; pai
gow poker; poker; roulette (double zero); Spanish 21;
three-card poker.*

Orleans

*4500 W Tropicana Avenue, at Arville Street,
Southwest Las Vegas (reservations 1-800 675 3267/
front desk & casino 365 7111/www.orleanscasino.
com). Bus 104, 201/self-parking & valet parking W
Tropicana Avenue, Cameron Street or Arville Street.*
Despite the painstaking attention to detail – French
Quarter-style latticework, hand-carved door frames
and ceiling trim – the overall feel of the Orleans is
closer to an aircraft hangar than the jazz-soused intimacy of Bourbon Street. Still, the high ceilings do
make an airy (and less smoky) change from the
oppressive, chandeliered norm, and there's no doubt
the place is a real locals' favourite. The casino offers
lively, low-limit action: the poker room is one of the
best in town, with 'bad-beat jackpots' (awarded to
the player who loses with a very big hand) that
sometimes top $40,000, and regular tournaments.

You might find fine jazz in the 999-seat **Orleans
Showroom**, but country and nostalgic rock are the
usual fare. The intimate feel gives ageing performers (Bobby Vinton, Neil Sedaka) a perfect setting in
which to recapture a bit of their magic. There's
lounge music in the **Bourbon Street Cabaret**,
though you may be better off catching a blockbuster
at the **Century Orleans 18** cinema (*see p229*).
Eight eateries prepare everything from shrimp
parmigiana to Las Vegas-style jambalaya, and
there's even a hilariously inauthentic Irish pub.
Games *Mini baccarat ($5-$1,000); bingo; blackjack
($5-$2,000); Caribbean stud; craps (2x); keno; Let it
Ride; pai gow poker; poker; roulette (double zero);
Spanish 21; three-card poker.*

Green Valley Ranch. *See p104.*

Sam's Town

5111 Boulder Highway, at E Flamingo Road, East Las Vegas (reservations 1-800 634 6371/front desk & casino 456 7777/www.samstownlv.com). Bus 107, 115, 202/self-parking & valet parking Boulder Highway, E Flamingo Road or Nellis Boulevard.

Opened in 1979, Sam's Town remained a low-key, Western-themed gambling hall for 15 years, until several expansions and makeovers transformed it into a cowboy theme park. The casino has the same low-limit tables and machines as before, but it's big enough to drive cattle through. Take the escalator downstairs for 24-hour bowling.

An enclosed atrium houses shops, restaurants and the **Sunset Stampede** water and laser show, presented four times daily. Each December, the holiday lights display in the courtyard is the most beautiful in Las Vegas. The most recent renovation added a new buffet and an 18-screen movie theatre. The 1,100-seater **Sam's Town Live!** showcases pop, country and rock.

Games *Bingo; blackjack ($5-$2,000); craps (10x); keno; Let it Ride; pai gow poker; poker; roulette (double zero).*

Suncoast

9090 Alta Drive, at N Rampart Boulevard, Northwest Las Vegas (reservations 1-877 677 7111/front desk & casino 636 7111/www.suncoastcasino.com). Bus 207/self-parking & valet parking Alta Drive & Rampart Avenue.

As is the case at the other Coast properties (the Gold Coast, the Barbary Coast and the Orleans), the Suncoast's casino floor is large and player-friendly, with plenty of machines, bingo, a race and sports book, and a progressive slot-club that plies regular players with comps. It's a Mediterranean-style, low-rise building with a red tile roof and adobe-like walls. The 440 good-sized rooms and suites are contained in a ten-storey tower.

Entertainment at the Suncoast is focused on the **Showroom**, which stages an eclectic mix of oldie rock bands and individual singers (Debbie Reynolds was even seen here in 2005). There's also a 64-lane bowling alley, plus, as is the case at many locals' joints, a movie theatre, and a very good one at that. Foodwise, there's a standard all-you-can-eat buffet and coffee shop, but you'd be better off with the steaks, seafood and lamb at **Primo's** or **Señor Miguel's** tasty Mexican specialities. The **Kid's Tyme** childcare centre is open seven days a week.

Games *Baccarat ($15-$2,500); bingo; blackjack ($5-$2,000); Caribbean stud; craps (2x); keno; Let it Ride; pai gow poker; poker; roulette (double zero); Spanish 21; three-card poker.*

Station Casinos

It all began with the success of **Palace Station**, a just-off-the-Strip hotel-casino that catered to both tourists and locals. Now the Las Vegas community – everywhere, in fact, but the Strip and Downtown – is virtually a Monopoly board of Station casinos (this version of the game features only railroad properties). With the scheduled 2006 opening of the $450 million **Red Rock Station** in the posh Summerlin area (near the junction of I-215 and W Charleston Boulevard), this local gaming empire will have a collection of 11 hotel-casinos. All are beloved by Las Vegans for their slot-clubs: you can earn points in one of its casinos and redeem them in any other, a perk no other local chain can claim. For information on all Station casinos, see www.stationcasinos.com.

Boulder Station

4111 Boulder Highway, at E Desert Inn Road, East Las Vegas (reservations 1-800 683 7777/front desk & casino 432 7777/www.boulderstation.com). Bus 107, 112/self-parking & valet parking Boulder Highway.

This Victorian-styled Station, located along the Boulder Strip which heads out towards Henderson (about 15 miles from that other Strip), lures locals with solid entertainment from a good stable of B-list headliners (Toto, Foreigner, Diane Schuur) in an intimate showroom called the **Railhead**, family-friendly amenities (including an 11-screen movie theatre and a **Kids Quest** childcare and entertainment centre, *see p227*) and some decent dining options: the **Feast Gourmet Buffet** is popular, and the **Broiler's** Sunday champagne brunch is one of the best in Vegas. The 300 rooms in the 15-storey hotel tower have been recently remodelled.

Games *Mini baccarat ($5-$50); bingo; blackjack ($3-$1,000); Caribbean stud; craps (10x); keno; Let it Ride; pai gow poker; pai gow tiles; poker; roulette (double zero); three-card poker.*

Fiesta Rancho

2400 N Rancho Drive, between Lake Mead Boulevard & Carey Avenue, North Las Vegas (reservations 1-888-889 7770/front desk 631 7000/http://rancho.fiestacasino.com). Bus 103, 106, 210, 211/self-parking Rancho Drive, Lake Mead Boulevard or Carey Avenue/valet parking Lake Mead Boulevard.

Acquired by Station in 2001, Fiesta Rancho bills itself as 'the Royal Flush Capital of the World'. Though some claim the machines have tightened up since Station took over, the casino still offers some of the best video poker on the planet. The slot-club is known for weekly triple-point days and no-hassle food comps. The Fiesta also has a drive-up sports-betting window, where you don't even have to get out of the car to bet on an upcoming game.

However, it's the party-style atmosphere with a yen for old Mexico that draws visitors to the northwest part of the city. A variety of country and rock 'n' roll legends – David Allan Coe, Molly Hatchet, Nazareth – headline **Club Tequila**, followed by the late-evening Saturday Night Fiesta. The Fiesta Rancho does Mexican food too: at **Garduno's** restaurant (with 300 flavours of Margarita) and the **Blue Agave Steakhouse**. The newly renovated, five-storey hotel tower offers 100 rooms and suites

at affordable rates. Escape the desert heat in the outdoor swimming pool or the NHL-size ice arena.
Games *Bingo; blackjack ($5-$1,000); casino war; Caribbean stud; craps (10x); keno; Let it Ride; pai gow poker; poker; roulette (double zero); three-card poker.*

Green Valley Ranch
2300 Paseo Verde Parkway, at S Green Valley Parkway, Henderson (reservations 1-888 782 9487/front desk & casino 617 7777/www.greenvalley ranchresort.com). No bus/self-parking & valet parking S Green Valley Parkway or Paseo Verde Parkway.

Business hotels

Several national hotel and motel chains have set up shop in the general vicinity of the Las Vegas Convention Center, the majority of them on Paradise Road. They're tilted at the business traveller: none have casinos, and all claim, to a greater or lesser degree, to offer facilities suitable for a travelling conventioneer. There's not much to choose between them. All are decorated in familiar, inoffensive fashion; all have outdoor pools and gyms (or, in a couple of cases, access to a nearby health centre); all offer high-speed internet connections; and all are quiet places to stay. Expect to pay around $70-$130 for a double room, $50 more for a suite.

Among the largest of the bunch are **Candlewood Suites** (4034 Paradise Road, 1-888 226 3539, 836 3660, www.candlewoodsuites.com), a nicely appointed 276-suite property about half a mile from the Convention Center; the Vegas outpost of the **Embassy Suites** chain (3600 Paradise Road, 893 8000, http://embassysuiteslasvegas.com), which boasts ten more suites than the Candlewood; and the 192-suite, Marriott-operated **Residence Inn** (3225 Paradise Road, 1-800 331 3131, 796 9300, www.residenceinn.com/lasnv). All are good both for short-term travellers and those here for a longer spell on business. Just next door to the Residence is another, slightly cheaper Marriott property, the **Courtyard by Marriott** (3275 Paradise Road, 1-800 661 1064, 791 3600, www.courtyard.com/lasch). And not far from here is a branch of **La Quinta** (3970 Paradise Road, 1-800 531 59800, 796 9000, www.laquinta.com), which is as much vacation spot as business hotel but merits mention for its clean rooms, wireless internet access and good rates.

Much of Green Valley feels like a South American hacienda, albeit one owned by a rancher with good taste and a lot of money: the rooms are elegant with Old World style, the decor is handsome with Spanish flair, and there's even a vineyard out back. The rest is pure Palm Beach: there's an upscale Euro-style spa, the futuristic **Drop Bar** and the ultra chic **Whiskey** nightclub, where the party spills out on to a patio that features lounging (with TVs, music and drinks service) and great views of the Strip. Perhaps owing to its starring role on the Discovery Channel's *American Casino* series, the hotel recently expanded to 490 rooms and 80 suites.

The gaming area is lined with dining options, including the sports-themed **Trophy's** (a great lunch spot), a couple of Asian options in the shape of **China Spice** and **Sushi + Sake**, upscale Italian at **Il Fornaio**, Irish fusion pub grub at **Fado**, and contemporary American at stylish **BullShrimp**. Still hungry? You need the **Feast Around the World Buffet**.
Games *Baccarat ($25-$2,500); blackjack ($5-$2,000); Caribbean stud; craps (10x); Let it Ride; pai gow poker; poker; roulette (double zero).*

Palace Station
2411 W Sahara Avenue, at N Rancho Drive, West of Strip (reservations 1-800 634 3101/front desk & casino 367 2411/www.palacestation.com). Bus 106, 204/self-parking & valet parking W Sahara Avenue, N Rancho Drive or Teddy Drive. **Map** *p317 X2.*

The original Station casino has been a locals' favourite for more than 25 years, thanks largely to the popular gaming promotions. You'll find 1,900 slot and video poker machines here, along with 50 gaming tables, a 600-seat bingo room, a nine-table poker room, a keno lounge, and a race and sports book. While the plainish interiors and air quality – blue-haired little old ladies with a cigarette in one hand and a players' card in the other – could be improved, several of the restaurants offer fine neighbourhood fare, including the **Gourmet Feast** buffet, Mexican dishes in the **Guadalajara Bar & Grille**, and steaks and seafood in the **Broiler**. Seasoned touring acts and young comedians entertain audiences in **Laugh Trax** (*see p222*); bands play often at **Sound Trax**. And like all other locals' casinos, there's an Irish pub, **Jack's**, featuring music by the still wildly popular **Wild Celtics**. The 1,000-plus rooms and suites range from economy courtyard rooms to luxury deluxe tower rooms.
Games *Baccarat ($10-$5,000); bingo; blackjack ($5-$1,000); Caribbean stud; craps (10x); keno; Let it Ride; pai gow poker; pai gow tiles; poker; roulette (double zero).*

Santa Fe Station
4949 N Rancho Drive, at US 95 (junction 90A), Northwest Las Vegas (reservations 1-866 767 7771/front desk & casino 658 4900/www.santafe.station casinos.com). Bus 101, 102, 104, 106, 219/self-parking & valet parking N Rancho Drive or Lone Mountain Road.

One of the earliest locals' casinos, the Southwest-inspired Santa Fe Station has undergone a renaissance of late. The popular ice arena has now gone (moved to the nearby Fiesta Rancho) but the small-ish room has low-limit table games, low-hold video poker, a 450-seat bingo room and a wide variety of slots. Additions include a 650-seat entertainment venue, the trendy **Charcoal Room** steakhouse, new lanes and scoring inside the bowling centre and a state-of-the-art Century cinema. There's a **Memphis Championship Barbecue** (see p158) on site, but locals flock to Station's north-west outpost for great Mexican fare at **Cabo**, where flair bartenders blend equally entertaining Margaritas. Remodelled guestrooms start at $39 per night. Santa Fe also operates a **Kids Quest** childcare and entertainment centre (see p227).

Games Blackjack ($5-$1,000); craps (3x); Let it Ride; pai gow poker; roulette (double zero); three-card poker.

Sunset Station

1301 W Sunset Road, at Stephanie Street, Henderson (reservations 1-888 786 7389/front desk & casino 547 7777/www.sunsetstation.com). Bus 212, 217/self-parking & valet parking Stephanie Street, W Sunset Road, Marks Street or Warm Springs Road.

Slot-clubbing locals keep every inch of the 100,000sq ft (9,300sq m) Sunset Station casino buzzing, and there are enough amusements and eating options to keep the rest of this workhorse entertaining. The hotel has more than 450 newly renovated rooms that follow the Sunset's Spanish motif. During swimming season, big-name entertainers perform at the 5,000-seat amphitheatre by the Mediterranean-style pool; a smallish showroom hosts lesser known acts, such as lounge-rock parodist Richard Cheese.

The restaurants range from chicks and wings at **Hooters** to the relatively upscale **Sonoma Cellar Steakhouse**. In between, there's the worth-the-wait **Feast Around the World Buffet**; **Costa Del Sol**, which features fresh seafood and an oyster bar; and the **Guadalajara Bar & Grille**, with a sweet tequila collection and a saucy salsa bar. Don't miss the gaudy **Gaudí Bar** in the centre of the action. In back, there's a 13-screen **Regal Cinema** (see p229) and a **Kids Quest** childcare centre (see p227).

Games Mini baccarat ($5-$1,000); bingo; blackjack ($5-$1,000); craps (10x); keno; Let it Ride; pai gow poker; poker; roulette (double zero); three-card poker.

Texas Station

2101 Texas Star Lane, at N Rancho Drive, between Lake Mead Boulevard & Vegas Drive, North Las Vegas (reservations 1-800 654 8888/front desk 631 1000/www.texasstation.com). Bus 106, 210/self-parking N Rancho Drive/valet parking Lake Mead Boulevard or N Rancho Drive. **Map** p317 X1.

Size matters here, but what did you expect from a Texas-themed casino? There's a 60-lane bowling centre, an 18-screen movie theatre, a 5,000sq ft (470sq m) arcade, and 2,400 very popular slot and video poker machines in a sprawling 91,000sq ft (8,500sq m) casino. In the poker room, the game of

choice is, inevitably, Texas hold 'em. And where would Texas be without a steakhouse? The award-winning **Austins** is a fine example of what a steakhouse should be: prime steaks dry-aged for 21 days, hand-cut on the premises and then marinated in Austins' secret sauce. Texas-style entertainment can be found in **Club Armadillo** and the **Dallas Events Center** with the likes of the Oak Ridge Boys. Surprisingly, Texas Station only offers 200 rooms, making the hotel side of this casino almost boutique. Texas also has a **Kids Quest** childcare and entertainment centre (see p227).

Games Bingo; blackjack ($5-$1,000); craps (10x); keno; Let it Ride; pai gow poker; poker; roulette (double zero); three-card poker.

Non-Casino Accommodation

The Strip

First class

Four Seasons Las Vegas

3960 Las Vegas Boulevard South, at E Hacienda Avenue, Las Vegas, NV 89119 (reservations 1-877 632 5000/front desk 632 5100/fax 632 5195/www. fourseasons.com/lasvegas). Bus 301/no self-parking/valet parking Las Vegas Boulevard South. **Rates** $250-$520 single/double; $435-$3,500 suite. **Credit** AmEx, DC, Disc, MC, V. **Map** p320 A9.

Though (surprise!) not the only hotel on the Strip without a casino, the Four Seasons is one of the most sumptuous. Furnished with antiques and expensive artwork, the Four Seasons is often mistaken for an elegant wing of **Mandalay Bay** (see p67) next door. Its 424 rooms, accessed only by private elevators, are sequestered on the top five floors of Mandalay's original tower but the Four Seasons has its own entrance, valet and crack concierge staff (eight are Les Clefs d'Or members), as well as an award-winning spa, a secluded pool and wireless internet access in public areas. However, guests have access to Mandalay Bay's facilities, as well as those within **THEhotel at Mandalay Bay** (see p106).

Guestrooms are spacious and luxurious, if a bit understated compared to the splashy digs at the Venetian or Bellagio. However, the extras are fabulous: thick, comfy robes in the closets, Frette sheets on the beds, L'Occitane products in the bathrooms. Extra points are garnered for superior service – repeat guests will find their room keys waiting for them at valet, while families will find their rooms child-proofed and stocked with age-appropriate amenities (nappies for babies, Playstations for older kids). Joggers get chilled water and towels after exercising; sunbathers are misted with Evian water and given cucumber slices for their eyes. Dining options include **Charlie Palmer Steak** (see p141); the new

Bar and Lounge, which serves a menu of tasty appetisers; and the freshly renovated **Verandah Café** (*see p147*), which features Italian-influenced American fare.
Amenities Bars (2). Concierge. Disabled-adapted rooms. Gym. High-speed internet (ADSL). No-smoking rooms. Pool (outdoor). Restaurants (2). Spa.

THEhotel at Mandalay Bay

3950 Las Vegas Boulevard South, at E Hacienda Avenue, Las Vegas, NV 89119 (reservations 1-877 632 7800/front desk 632 7777/fax 632 7234/www. mandalaybay.com). Bus 105, 301/self-parking & valet parking E Hacienda Avenue. **Rates** $169-$10,000 suite. **Credit** AmEx, DC, Disc, MC, V. **Map** p320 A9.
The rather clumsy name of this property has reputedly caused cab drivers no end of confusion, to the point where a change has been rumoured. The hotel itself, though, needs no such alterations. Located around the back of Mandalay Bay (follow the signs carefully, or you'll end up in entirely the wrong car park), THEhotel has filled a gap in the market that most major cities have plugged with a W Hotel, which is to say that it's chic without being too fashionable, and a big hit with hipsters in their late 20s while being careful not to exclude everyone else.

The rooms here are all suites, decorated in rich colours and furnished with chairs and beds that manage to be both stylish and extremely comfortable. Most suites have an ADSL connection and/or a web TV facility, a nod to the business travellers who choose the hotel for its proximity to the Strip but its absence of gambling. The restaurants, shows and gaming at Mandalay Bay itself only a corridor away, but the handsome hotel lobby is slot-free. Atop the rooms tower is Alain Ducasse's ultra-posh restaurant **Mix** (*see p147*), and its in-the-moment attached lounge (*see p167*). The whole place doesn't feel like Vegas, which, for many guests, is a good part of the appeal. Recommended.
Amenities Bars (1). Business centre. Disabled-adapted rooms. Gym. High-speed internet (ADSL, web TV). No-smoking rooms. Pool (outdoor). Restaurants (2). Spa.

Off-Strip

Expensive

Renaissance Las Vegas

3400 Paradise Road, between Desert Inn Road & Sands Avenue, Las Vegas, NV 89109 (reservations 1-866 352 3434/front desk 733 6533/fax 735 3130/ www.marriotts.com). Bus 108/self-parking & valet parking Paradise Road. **Rates** $179-$309 single/double; $550-$1,200 suite. **Credit** AmEx, Disc, MC, V. **Map** p319 A6.
This brand-new 14-storey, 550-room Marriott hotel just south of the Las Vegas Convention Center seems all business, with a list of high-tech amenities that features wireless internet access, ergonomic desk chairs and specially designed 'Exhibitor Suites'. The cool and confident hotel pulls off a clubby little vibe

with handsome contemporary design and a VIP atmosphere. There's no mention of a nightclub or casino for good reason: the Renaissance is the city's largest non-gaming property. Still, there is one type of sin on the premises: **Envy**, chef Richard Chamberlain's restaurant, which serves a variety of comfort foods from a kobe filet mignon to wild mushroom mac and cheese. There's also a swanky little lounge area where you can sip a Flirtini. The hotel has a hip executive level with a lounge, a pool area, spa service, comfy beds with high-end linens and piles of pillows, and flat-screen televisions in every room. Escaping work is easy, with a monorail station nearby and the Strip a block away.
Amenities Bars (2). Concierge. Disabled-adapted rooms. Gym. High-speed internet (ADSL). Pool (outdoor). Restaurants (2). Spa.

Moderate

Alexis Resort & Villas

375 E Harmon Avenue, between Koval Lane & Paradise Road, Las Vegas, NV 89109 (reservations 1-800 582 2228/front desk 796 3300/fax 796 3354/ www.alexispark.com). Bus 108, 213/self-parking E Harmon Avenue. **Rates** $139-$400 suite. **Credit** AmEx, DC, Disc, MC, V. **Map** p320 C8.
Originally constructed as an apartment complex and later transformed into an all-suites hotel (where local teenagers often booked suites on prom night, until the resort wised up and required guests to be 21), the non-gaming, Mediterranean-style Alexis offers a relaxing oasis not far from the Strip. The two-storey white stucco buildings, nestled along winding pathways, house 500 well-appointed guest suites, each of which features a European wet bar and refrigerator. The Regal, Majestic, Crown and Monarch suites – which range in size from 450sq ft to 1,275sq ft (42sq m to 120sq m) – offer a host of unexpected accoutrements: gas fireplaces, two-and-a-half baths and upstairs lofts. The other main advantage? It's right across from the **Hard Rock** (*see p71*).
Amenities Bars (1). Business centre. Disabled-adapted rooms. Gym. High-speed internet (ADSL). Pool (outdoor). Restaurants (1).

Carriage House

105 E Harmon Avenue, between Las Vegas Boulevard South & Audrie Lane, Las Vegas, NV 89109 (reservations 1-800 221 2301, ext 65/front desk 798 1020/fax 798 1020 ext 112/www.carriage houselasvegas.com). Bus 213/self-parking E Harmon Avenue or Audrie Street/no valet parking. **Rates** $79-$165 single/double; $109-$225 suite. **Credit** AmEx, DC, Disc, MC, V. **Map** p320 B8.
Tucked between the monolithic MGM Grand and Aladdin resorts, and next door to the soon-to-open Grand Chateau by Marriott, the Carriage House is often overlooked by visitors. But the tasteful, moderately priced rooms are some of the best buys in town, with plush carpeting, grass-paper wall coverings, overstuffed sofas and love seats, and fully-equipped kitchens in the suites (kitchenettes in

standard rooms). On the 9th floor, **Joey's Bistro & Bar** boasts a wall of fame with 'celebrity' photos of folk such as Regis Philbin. Outside, there's an attached tennis court, heated swimming pool and sun deck with simple landscaping.

Amenities *Bars (1). Business centre. Disabled-adapted rooms. Gym. No-smoking floors. Restaurants (1).*

Budget

Artisan

1501 W Sahara Avenue, at Highland Drive, between Western Avenue & the I-15, West of Strip, Las Vegas NV 89102 (reservations 1-800 554 4092/ front desk 214 4000/fax 733 1571/www.theartisan hotel.com). Bus 204/self-parking W Sahara Avenue/ no valet parking. **Rates** $65-$99 single/double; $400 suite. **Credit** AmEx, DC, Disc, MC, V. **Map** p319 B4.

This off-Strip boutique hotel shares a Vegas trait with most Strip resorts: it has a theme. The charming old-world European decor is inspired by art and artists; paintings cover every inch of wall space, including the ceilings. The art deco-stylings are combined with a massive collection of pieces by local artists, as well as reproductions of iconic works by such greats as Chagall, Rembrandt, Renoir and Van Gogh. Guests gather in the lobby in the late afternoons for complimentary wine receptions. The 64 individually decorated guestrooms and suites – with names such as 'Masterpiece' and 'Artist' – offer all the usual accoutrements including WiFi internet access. Downstairs, you'll find the **Artisan Lounge** (*see p170*), a late-night hotspot frequented by local hipsters; the **Artisan Café**, serving American cuisine; and **Palette**, a gourmet room featuring the food of Executive Chef Franco Spinelli. The staff of the spa perform a different form of art: treatments such as the Artist's Mud Palette Facial or Mud Paint Body Wrap. Quietly, in its own gentle and cultured way, this is one of the most fashionable spots to stay in Las Vegas.

Amenities *Bars (1). Disabled-adapted rooms. High-speed internet (wireless). No-smoking (all rooms). Pool (outdoor). Restaurants (2). Spa.*

Budget Suites

3684 Paradise Road, at E Twain Avenue, East of Strip, Las Vegas, NV 89109 (reservations 1-866 877 2000/front desk 699 7000/fax 792 2611/www. budgetsuites.com). Bus 108, 203, 213/self-parking Paradise Road/no valet parking. **Rates** $79-$99 daily; $199 weekly; $749 monthly. **Credit** AmEx, MC, V. **Map** p320 C6.

With branches all over the Valley (though most are near the Strip), Budget Suites are perfect for long-term visitors; daily rates are nothing special, but stay for a week or a month and the savings can be vast. Each safe, secure 220- to 300-unit complex is made up of basic mini-suites complete with kitchen, ranging from studio spaces to two-bed apartments. Maid service is available, but you can save on the expense by bringing your own linen and towels. Family-friendly branches have barbecue pits, good-sized pools, free phone calls and plenty of parking.

Amenities *Pool (outdoor).*

THEhotel at Mandalay Bay. See p106.

Raising the bar in the luxury stakes: **Ritz-Carlton, Lake Las Vegas**.

Other locations closest to the Strip: 3655 W Tropicana Avenue, West of Strip (739 1000); 4205 W Tropicana Avenue, West of Strip (889 1700); 1500 Stardust Road, West of Strip (732 1500).

Sin City Hostel

1208 Las Vegas Boulevard South, at E Charleston Boulevard (868 0222). Bus 206, 301/self-parking Las Vegas Boulevard South/no valet parking. **Rates** $18.50 dorm; $37 room. **Credit** AmEx, Disc, MC, V.
The lack of hostels in Vegas is easily explained by the fact that you can get a reasonable room in a Downtown casino for $30 or so. The Sin City Hostel closed for a year fairly recently, and few missed it. But renovations improved the place no end: it's now a tidy little operation, offering good-value accommodation to travellers and backpackers. Dorms have only four beds, a welcome change from the usual free-for-all. There's an internet terminal on site, and a payphone; the downside is the location, on a not very attractive stretch of Las Vegas Boulevard South. All guests must produce a passport or an international drivers' licence on check-in.
Amenities *No-smoking rooms.*

The rest of the city

First class

Ritz-Carlton, Lake Las Vegas

1610 Lake Las Vegas Parkway, at Lake Mead Boulevard, Henderson, NV 89011 (reservations 1-800 241 3333/front desk 567 4700/casino 939 8888/fax 567 4777/www.ritzcarlton.com). No bus/ *self-parking & valet parking Lake Las Vegas Parkway.* **Rates** $179-$229 single/double; $349-$579 suite. **Credit** AmEx, DC, Disc, MC, V.
This Mediterranean-style lakeside resort within the Lake Las Vegas community – and the only Ritz-Carlton in Nevada – has raised the bar for Vegas hoteliers since opening in 2003. Among the amenities: Frette bed linens and oversized marble bathrooms in the guestrooms (many of which come with balconies); afternoon tea served at 1pm and 3pm in the lobby lounge; a 30,000sq ft (2,800sq m) spa (*see p194* **Star spas**) and manicured meditation garden; a tiny white sand beach; and access to myriad outdoor activities such as hiking, kayaking and guided stargazing, and golf at two locally renowned courses. The resort is also just steps away from **MonteLago Village** and its meandering cobblestone streets, chic shops and restaurants, gondola rides on Lake Las Vegas, a 24-hour boutique casino and a floating stage that morphs into an ice rink in winter. For even more pampering, upgrade to the Club Level, which gets you lodgings on the Pontevecchio Bridge, as well as access to the well-stocked **Club Lounge**.
Dining options include the pan-Mediterranean **Medici Café & Terrace** and the open-air **Vita di Lago Pool & Garden** café, serving up healthy cuisine poolside. Two lobby lounges, the elegant drawing room-style **Firenze** and the clubby **Galileo**, both of which have terrace seating, complete the picture.
Amenities *Bars (1). Business centre. Concierge. Disabled-adapted rooms. Gym. High-speed internet (ADSL). No-smoking floors. Pool (indoor). Restaurants (3). Spa.*

Sightseeing

Introduction

Come out and play.

Las Vegas, as you might have gathered, is not a regular city in many ways, but it's particularly off-kilter in regard to its sightseeing. There are but a handful of museums here, virtually no tangible history and precious little natural beauty (until you get out of town, for which *see p258*). The galleries here are relatively slight, and the parks barely there at all. And this being a young western American city, the neighbourhoods, at least away from the pedestrian-friendly central Vegas action, are best explored not on foot but by car, and yield little of aesthetic or intellectual interest.

When pondering the sights and attractions of Las Vegas, then, it's possible to draw only one conclusion: Las Vegas is its own main attraction. Sure, while you're here, you can look at a Renoir before riding a rollercoaster, climb the Eiffel Tower to watch a water fountain erupt below you and see a stunning show after, well, after throwing the kids' college fund into a gold-plated slot machine. But the leading light among all these diversions is the sheer sensory overload, the inimitable ridiculousness, of the city itself, and specifically of Las Vegas Boulevard South, aka the Strip. Certainly, its wild visual excess will be the most vivid memory – and certainly the most photographed – with which you return home.

For full details of the city's hotel-casino resorts, *see pp60-108*: our **Casinos & Hotels**

section covers every major casino in Vegas, from its entertainment to its eating options, its guestrooms to its golf courses. The following Sightseeing chapters should be taken more as a primer to the city, a brief guide to what it has to offer. Follow the cross-references around the book to find full reviews of galleries, nightclubs and restaurants mentioned only in passing here.

The one mistake made by many visitors is not leaving the Strip; understandable, given the hypnotic, wow-inducing glitz of the place. But there is a whole city beyond it, low on sights but with plenty of bars, restaurants and points of local interest worthy of your attention. Try to get out and see a couple.

ORIENTATION

The Las Vegas valley is divided into quarters by two freeways that cross each other: I-15 coursing north–south through the centre of town on its way from Los Angeles all the way to Salt Lake City, and US 95 (aka I-515), a north–south Canada–Mexico freeway that makes an east–west jink across Las Vegas. On a map, these two approximate a twisted pinwheel shape, with its pivot just north-west of Downtown Las Vegas.

The 'centre' of Las Vegas, where street numbering starts, is at the junction of Fremont and Main Streets in Downtown. From the Plaza hotel-casino at 1 S Main Street, numbers increase as you travel out in any direction. Main Street ends at its intersection with Las Vegas Boulevard South at the base of the Stratosphere, and everything either east or west of the Main Street/Las Vegas Boulevard artery is tagged accordingly. North/south street delineations are based on an imaginary line running from the eastern reaches of Charleston Boulevard, along Fremont Street in Downtown as far as Main Street, and then on to US 95 to the west.

Metropolitan Las Vegas is made up of four jurisdictions: Las Vegas, North Las Vegas, Henderson and unincorporated Clark County. Within and overlapping these jurisdictions are a number of 'areas', some with commonly used names, many others without. Area names as used in this guide are shown and defined on the map on page 312. **The Strip** (*see p113*) is the nickname for the stretch of Las Vegas Boulevard South between Russell Road in the south and Sahara Avenue in the north; **Off-Strip** (*see p123*) loosely covers the streets immediately surrounding it; and **Downtown** (*see p126*) is centred around the junction of Fremont Street and Las Vegas Boulevard. Surrounding areas fall into the chapter entitled **The Rest of the City** (*see p132*).

Trips & tours

Adventure Photo Tours
1-888 363 8687/889 8687/www.adventurephoto tours.com. **Credit** AmEx, Disc, MC, V.
Guided full- or half-day SUV trips to nearby spots such as Red Rock Canyon (4.5hrs, $89), Valley of Fire State Park (5hrs, $119) and Area 51 (8hrs, $185), as well as a variety of trips to the Grand Canyon.

Casino Travel & Tours
1-888 444 9928/946 5075/www.casinotravel.com. **Credit** AmEx, Disc, MC, V.
Among the innumerable tours offered here are plane trips to Bryce Canyon in Utah (11hrs, $368), jeep expeditions to Death Valley (11hrs, $195) and helicopter rides down the Strip (45mins, $80).

Desert Eco-Tours
647 4685/www.lasvegaszoo.org. **Credit** AmEx, MC, V.
These naturalist-led tours, conducted in four-wheel drive vehicles by the non-profit Nevada Zoological Foundation, are themed: take in ghost towns, Area 51 or old mining districts. Half-day tours are $129, full-day tours $179.

Drive-Yourself Tours
565 8761/www.drive-yourselftours.com. **Rates** *City tour map & tape* $14.95. **Credit** AmEx, Disc, MC, V.
A nice idea, this: for $14.95, you get a 90-minute cassette and map, with which you can direct yourself around Las Vegas, Mount Charleston and Red Rock Canyon, among other areas. The catch: most rental cars now come only with CD players.

Gray Line Tours
1-800 634 6579/www.grayline.com. **Credit** AmEx, Disc, MC, V.
Gray Line offers a handful of Vegas-based bus tours, including an evening city tour (6hrs, $40), a trip to the Grand Canyon (10hrs, $150), and a half-day jag to Lake Mead and the Hoover Dam (7hrs, $65).

Sundance Helicopters
1-800 653 1881/736 0606/www.helicoptour.com. **Credit** AmEx, Disc, MC, V.
If you care to disregard the concerns of Vegas locals and Grand Canyon environmentalists, then Sundance is southern Nevada's best regarded helicopter tour operator. City tours run from $80, with trips to the Grand Canyon (they offer quite a variety) coming in at around $303. Other by-air Grand Canyon options include Scenic Airlines (1-800 634 6801, www.scenic airlines.com) and Papillon (*see p271*).

The best Attractions

For starters
A walk down Las Vegas Boulevard South from Russell to Sahara, the length of the **Strip**. *See p113*.

For old Vegas redux
The **Liberace Museum** (*see p133*), Downtown's **Neon Museum** (*see p129*) and the impersonators at **Elvis-a-Rama** (*see p124*).

For new Vegas redux
The **Bellagio Fountains** at the Bellagio (*see p63*), the gallery at **Wynn Las Vegas** (*see p75*), and **King Tut Museum** (*see p115*) at the Luxor.

For a little history
The **Old Las Vegas Mormon Fort Historic Park** (*see p130*) and the new **Atomic Testing Museum** (*see p124*).

For the ride of your life
Speed: The Ride at the Sahara and **Insanity: The Ride** at the Stratosphere (for both, *see p122*).

For the kids
Shark Reef at Mandalay Bay (*see p67*), the **GameWorks** arcade (*see p116*) and the **Adventuredome** at Circus Circus (*see p85*).

For escaping the madness
Nevada State Museum & Historical Society (*see p135*), **Red Rock Canyon** (*see p263* and **UNLV Barrick Museum** (*see p133*).

Sightseeing

THESE BOOKS ARE MADE FOR WALKING

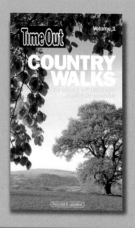

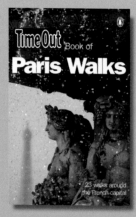

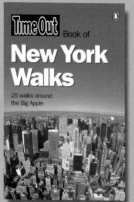

The Strip

Las Vegas Boulevard: the most fabulous street in the world?

The Strip at night.

When Steve Wynn built the tropical-themed, volcano-fronted **Mirage** on Las Vegas Boulevard back in 1989, he lit the fuse on a renaissance that continued with large pirate ships moored outside **Treasure Island** and elaborate dancing fountains at the entrance to the **Bellagio**. Populist attractions started to spring up all along the four-mile stretch of Las Vegas Boulevard South that runs from the welcome sign up to Sahara Avenue. Hotels were fashioned after pyramids, castles and even entire cities. Resorts were being themed to the nth degree.

On the eve of the city's centennial in 2005, a new era dawned. Wynn took his second act indoors by designing **Wynn Las Vegas** from the inside out and shielding it from view behind a man-made mountain. Resorts such as **Mandalay Bay**, the **Venetian** and **Caesars Palace** had either already built additional boutique environs or were getting ready to do so, upping the upmarket ante. Will Trump towers and glitzy high-rises overrun old Vegas? Only time will tell. But Steve Wynn has already announced **Encore**, a lavish annexe to Wynn Las Vegas, on the site of the Desert Inn.

Russell Road to Tropicana Avenue

Map p320 A9-A8

Very few of the tiny motor courts of the 1950s and '60s remain near Russell Road, and even they might be gone by the time you read this. In this city of tomorrow, even the classic **Welcome to Fabulous Las Vegas** sign was threatened not long ago, before the voices of reason spoke up and saved the icon. Good thing, too: first-timers still brave the traffic to get a snap under this iconic landmark. You can purchase a mini version, complete with flashing lights, at various gift shops along Las Vegas Boulevard. Facing the sign, the old Howard Hughes air terminal is behind you to the east (right), while the **Panevino** restaurant lies beyond the runways on Sunset Road. Miles beyond that are Henderson and Boulder City. At your back, 300 miles away, is Los Angeles; in front of you lies the Strip, Las Vegas's *raison d'être*.

To the east is the **Little Chapel of the West** (*see p256*). Dating to 1942, it's the oldest building on the Strip, though with the caveat

Into the jaws of **Shark Reef**. *See p115*.

that it's been moved several times, most recently from the front lawn of the old Hacienda casino (imploded in 1996) to its new site just south of where the classic Glass Pool Inn stood until developers trashed it in 2004.

Across the Boulevard is the **Bali Hai Golf Club** (*see p248*), one of only two golf courses on the Strip (the other is the guests-only facility at **Wynn Las Vegas**; *see p75*). Just north, where the Hacienda once stood, is the South Seas-themed **Mandalay Bay** (*see p67*); the tranquil, non-gaming **Four Seasons** (*see p105*); and the ultra-chic **THEhotel at Mandalay Bay** (*see p106*). Mandalay Bay's **Shark Reef** aquarium (*see p115*) is perhaps the best of the many animal-focused attractions in the city, but the casino is also home to a broad range of excellent eateries, the **House of Blues** (*see p237*) and its collection of folk art, retro-styled burlesque joint **Forty Deuce** (*see p244*), and one of the Strip's newest shopping attractions, **Mandalay Place** (*see p178*). Next to Mandalay Bay is the unmistakeable onyx pyramid of the **Luxor** (*see p80*), lights racing up its angles and exploding in a dramatic sky-bound beacon. Inside is an **IMAX Theatre** (*see p229*), a games arcade, **In Search of the Obelisk** motion-simulator ride and an impressive recreation of Tutankhamun's burial chamber (for both, *see p115*).

Where the Strip meets Tropicana Avenue, you'll be within easy walking distance of more hotel rooms than you'll find in the whole of San Francisco. All around the intersection, crowds spill on to street corners and squeeze through pedestrian overpasses. On the south-east corner are the white towers of the **Tropicana** (*see p90*): it was built in 1957 and looks its age, but the **Casino Legends Hall of Fame** (*see below*), a homage to past entertainers and casino moguls, is worth a peek. Until 31 October 2005, you can also see **Titanic – The Artefacts**

Exhibition, more than 300 bits and pieces discovered 12,500 feet beneath the sea. Across Tropicana to the north is the **MGM Grand** (*see p80*), its signature lion guarding the entrance is the nation's largest bronze sculpture, though the 5,005-room resort is now only the second largest on the planet. There are more felines inside the resort, lurking in the **Lion Habitat** (*see p115*), the **La Femme** cabaret and new nightclub **Teatro** (*see p244*).

To the north-west, opposite the MGM Grand, is **New York–New York** (*see p83*), where the Statue of Liberty replica is hosed down by mock fire boats. The scene inspired emotion after 9/11, and a grassroots memorial sprang up; many items have now been donated to the Smithsonian. Overhead is the **Manhattan Express** rollercoaster (*see p115*); inside, kids will enjoy the **Coney Island Emporium** (*see below*), while adults sweat at Cirque du Soleil's sexy **Zumanity** (*see p214*). Across a walkway to the south, completing the circle of casinos, looms the medieval-themed **Excalibur** (*see p86*).

Casino Legends Hall of Fame

Tropicana *3801 Las Vegas Boulevard South, at E Tropicana Avenue (739 5444/www.tropicanalv.com). Bus 201, 301, 302.* **Open** 9am-9pm daily. **Admission** $6.95; $5.95 seniors; under-18s must be accompanied by an adult. **Hotel** p90. **Map** p320 A9.

At the Hall of Fame there are hundreds of photos and documents, and audio and video displays covering the Mob's involvement in Vegas, old-time stage acts and hotel implosions. You can often find free admission coupons in tourist magazines or inside the Tropicana casino.

Coney Island Emporium

New York–New York *3790 Las Vegas Boulevard South, at W Tropicana Avenue (736 4100/www. nynyhotelcasino.com). Bus 201, 301, 302.* **Open** 8am-midnight Mon-Thur, Sun; 8am-2am Fri, Sat. **Admission** free. **Hotel** p83. **Map** p320 A8.

This arcade and family amusement centre recreates the atmosphere of the original Coney Island with more than 200 video and midway games, Bumper Cabs, a prize counter and lots of sticky candyfloss.

In Search of the Obelisk
Luxor *3900 Las Vegas Boulevard South, between W Tropicana Avenue & W Russell Road (262 4000/ www.luxor.com).* **Bus** *201, 301, 302.* **Open** 9am-11pm daily. **Tickets** $7.50. **Credit** AmEx, Disc, MC, V. **Hotel** p80. **Map** p320 A9.
One of Vegas's better motion-simulators takes the audience on a *Raiders of the Lost Ark*-style action adventure through the Luxor archaeological dig.

King Tut Museum
Luxor *3900 Las Vegas Boulevard South, between W Tropicana Avenue & W Russell Road (262 4000/ www.luxor.com).* **Bus** *201, 301, 302.* **Open** 9am-11pm Mon-Thur, Sun; 9am-midnight Fri, Sat. **Admission** $5. **Credit** AmEx, DC, Disc, MC, V. **Hotel** p80. **Map** p320 A9.
This flagship attraction is a full-size re-creation of Tutankhamun's burial chamber and his golden throne and sarcophagus, hand-crafted by Egyptian artisans from historically correct materials.

Lion Habitat
MGM Grand *3799 Las Vegas Boulevard South, at E Tropicana Avenue (891 7777/www.mgmgrand. com).* **Bus** *201, 301, 302.* **Open** 11am-10pm daily. **Admission** free. **Hotel** p80. **Map** p320 A8.
Not to be outdone by the Mirage's tigers, the MGM has its own pride of 'display' lions. The habitat is distressingly small, but the glass walls mean you can get a close-up view of cubs and adult lions.

Manhattan Express
New York–New York *3790 Las Vegas Boulevard South, at W Tropicana Avenue (740 6969/www. nyny.hotelcasino.com).* **Bus** *201, 301, 302.* **Open** 11am-11pm Mon-Thur, Sun; 10am-midnight Fri, Sat. **Tickets** $12.50; re-rides $6; all-day Scream Pass $25. **Hotel** p83. **Map** p320 A8.
Gotham never saw anything like it: a rollercoaster soaring around skyscrapers and Miss Liberty. The Express twists, loops and dives at breakneck speeds,

and features the first ever 'heartline roll', which creates the sensation a pilot feels when going through a barrel roll in an aeroplane. Try hard to smile in the last section: this is where the photos are taken.

Shark Reef
Mandalay Bay *3950 Las Vegas Boulevard South, at W Russell Road (632 4555/www.mandalaybay. com).* **Bus** *201, 301.* **Open** 10am-11pm daily (last entry 10pm). **Admission** $15.95; $9.95 concessions; free under-5s. **Credit** AmEx, Disc, MC, V. **Hotel** p67. **Map** p320 A9.
A 'walk-through' aquarium, the AZA-accredited Shark Reef is filled with 100 species of underwater life, including rays, jellyfish, eels and, of course, 11 varieties of shark. A perfect complement to the South Seas-themed Mandalay Bay, the Shark Reef is an unexpected gem in a city lacking in the educational entertainment department.

Tropicana Avenue to Harmon Avenue

Map p320 A8

A pleasant pedestrian boardwalk that morphs into a replica Brooklyn Bridge leads north on the eastern side of New York–New York as far as the **ESPN Zone** restaurant and sports bar (*see p142*). As you stroll, note the classic Pepsi and Pete sign on the wall of a replica brownstone building, challenging the Times Square-style giant neon Coke bottle on the **Showcase Mall** across the street. (Coke reportedly pays the MGM $1 million a year for sponsorship rights and exclusivity at the hotel, while Pepsi has undertaken a similar arrangement with New York–New York; both, of course, are owned by MGM Mirage.) Also in the Showcase Mall are the only cinema on the Strip, the **UA Showcase 8** (*see p229*), **M&M World** and **GameWorks** (for both, *see p116*), a huge arcade with the world's tallest indoor climbing wall, and the occasional all-ages rock gig.

Sightseeing

Taxi, madam?

Further on, you'll find tasty burgers and shakes at **Fatburger** (No.3763, 736 4733); just beyond here is the pink-and-mauve **Polo Towers** timeshare, unremarkable except for its top-floor **Sky Lounge** (*see p168*). The **Hawaiian Marketplace** is a jumble of souvenir shops, restaurants and a bird show. Due west are the fountains and arches of the aspiringly glam **Monte Carlo** (*see p82*), flanked on the south by in-progress condo-resort casino the **Cosmopolitan** and on the north by the hokey, soon-to-be-imploded fairground façade of the **Boardwalk** casino, which will become the site of MGM Mirage's ambitious hotel-casino-condo-retail-dining development **CityCenter** (*see p24*).

GameWorks

Showcase Mall, 3785 Las Vegas Boulevard South, between E Tropicana Avenue & E Harmon Avenue (432 4263/www.gameworks.com). Bus 301, 302. **Open** 10am-midnight Mon-Thur, Sun; 10am-2am Fri, Sat. **Admission** free. **Credit** AmEx, Disc, MC, V. **Map** p320 A8.

If you'd rather shove quarters into a video game than a slot machine, this place is for you. The creation of Steven Spielberg, this huge madhouse is a great place in which to try out the latest games: you can save money if you pay by the hour. There are over 250 games, a billiards lounge, two restaurants, a coffee bar and a 75ft (23m) indoor climbing wall.

M&M World

Showcase Mall, 3785 Las Vegas Boulevard South, between E Tropicana Avenue & E Harmon Avenue (736 7611/www.m-ms.com). Bus 301, 302. **Open** 9am-11pm Mon-Thur, Sun; 9am-midnight Fri, Sat. **Admission** free. **Credit** MC, V. **Map** p320 A8.

This is a four-level chocolate lover's paradise. Check out M&M Academy, an interactive entertainment attraction showing visitors how these chocolate candies earn their trademark. The attraction includes a 3-D movie, and 'graduates' get a diploma. Yes, it's a bit overmarketed. But at least it's free.

Harmon Avenue to Flamingo Road

Map p320 A7

The rebuilt **Aladdin** (*see p76*), which opened in 2000, stands to the east of the Harmon Avenue intersection, engulfing the original **Aladdin Theatre** (*see p236*) with new construction. It's

Walk this way

Las Vegas is clearly home to some amazingly influential environmentalists. How else can you explain the fact that just about every major tourist attraction – from Madame Tussaud's wax museum, to the 'skyline' of New York–New York casino, to the Cirque du Soleil shows on every corner – is in some way recycled? No idea seems safe from the 'us too' spirit of Vegas developers, as illustrated by the city's latest bit of cultural thievery.

The **Las Vegas Walk of Stars** sounds a lot like the Hollywood Walk of Fame for one good reason: it *is* a lot like the Hollywood Walk of Fame. As is the case with its Angeleno equivalent, the Walk of Stars aims to honour the entertainers and visionaries who helped shape the town by embedding three-foot sparkly granite stars into the sidewalk of its most famous street. Also following the LA example, the non-profit company behind the Walk are charging celebrities – or their sponsors – $15,000 for the privilege of being stepped on daily by several thousand tourists.

The Walk of Stars and the Motion Picture Hall of Fame Foundation together compiled a list of the first 100 people to be honoured. The first star – naturally enough, Wayne Newton – was put in place on 26 October 2004 in front of the New Frontier. Other big names on the list include Elvis, Ann-Margret, Howard Hughes, Charo, Steve Wynn, Jerry Lewis and, of course, Frank Sinatra and the rest of the Rat Pack (minus Peter Lawford). Along with these obvious choices, though, were some rather more obscure selections, among them treacly variety act the Scintas and wild-eyed country star Roy Clark. At the same time, the Walk of Star's criterion that 'honorees must have worked or lived in the Greater County of Clark, for periods of considerable regularity' hardly seems to square with the nominations of Johnny Carson and the Beatles. The Walk of Stars' website (www.lasvegaswalkofstars.com) suggests that some 3,000 stars could eventually be fitted along the four miles of the Strip. That's a mighty big barrel to scrape.

Thus far, very few actual stars have been set into the sidewalk: after Newton, the next in line were Liberace and Frank Marino, both of whom have been honoured in front of the Riviera, and impressionist Rich Little, whose memento rests outside the Flamingo. In other words, you might be walking a long way before you see any Hollywood-style glitz and glamour.

Watch the water at the **Bellagio**.

never been one of the Strip's more popular casinos, though new owners Starwood hope things will change in 2006, when it's made over as **Planet Hollywood**. The most prominent feature is the front façade that leads directly into the **Desert Passage** mall (*see p177*), also due to get a facelift (along with some new shops) by 2006. In the adjoining mall wing are restaurant **Crustacean Las Vegas** (*see p147*) and nightlife hotspot **Prana Lounge**. The west side of this section of the Strip is uncharacteristically blasé: a helipad for airborne city tours, a strip mall of T-shirt shops and exotic car hire desks, scooter rental shops and the timeshare Jockey Club, which looks even more out of place now it's dwarfed between the Monte Carlo and the Cosmopolitan. Expect a massive redevelopment in the future.

To the north of the Aladdin is the spectacular (but small, in Vegas terms) **Paris Las Vegas** (*see p69*), with its half-scale **Eiffel Tower** (*see below*), architectural replicas, grand fountains and chi-chi sidewalk café **Mon Ami Gabi** (*see p145*). From here, it's a pleasant skip north to the original 'Four Corners', where the Strip meets Flamingo Road. On the south-west corner of the street, at **Bally's** (*see p76*), a blazing video screen competes with the bizarre light-and-water tunnel entrance. To the north sits the

wedged-in **Barbary Coast** (*see p85*), the unexpected home of restaurants **Drai's** (*see p144*) and spendy **Michael's** (*see p145*).

At the southwest corner is the drama of the **Bellagio** (*see p63*), whose large replica of Lake Como is the site of one of the best loved attractions in Las Vegas. Every 30 minutes during the day (3-7pm weekdays, noon-7pm weekends) and every 15 minutes in the evening (7pm-midnight daily), the eight-acre lake throws up entrancing fountain displays choreographed to music from Pavarotti to Sinatra. The 1,200 water cannons, arranged in lines and circles, shoot water that dances and sways to the music, reaching as high as 240 feet (73 metres). The best seats are in the Bellagio restaurants, but you get a good view from the pavements out front, and from the top of the Eiffel Tower at Paris Las Vegas. Inside Bellagio, don't miss the **Gallery of Fine Art** (*see p231*) or the glass-domed **Conservatory & Botanical Gardens**, which lie beyond the lobby and are home to thousands of exotic plants and flowers. The hotel's Spa Tower features a newly expanded spa, the dramatic **Sensi** restaurant (*see p147*) and the decadent **Jean-Philippe Patisserie** (*see p66*).

With its striking blue-white lighting and huge fountains, the opulent and ever-expanding **Caesars Palace** (*see p65*) commands attention as perhaps the sole classic casino to successfully mate the past with 21st-century Vegas. Just to the north of the main fountain (the one Evel Knievel's son vaulted with his motorcycle in 1989) is a small Brahma shrine, where visitors worship and leave offerings of fruit and flowers in exchange for good luck. Near where Caesars meets the **Mirage**, pedestrians can board one-way conveyors to the **Forum Shops** (*see p177*). On the southern corner, there's now an open-air **Roman Plaza** that's home to Italian trattoria **Vialé** (650 5915), an outdoor amphitheatre and, flanked by the expanded **Forum Shops**, a three-storey atrium served by the country's only spiral escalator and filled with luxury designer boutiques such as Pucci, Harry Winston and Thomas Pink.

Eiffel Tower Experience

Paris Las Vegas *3655 Las Vegas Boulevard South, at E Flamingo Road (946 7000/www.caesars. com/Paris/LasVegas). Bus 202, 301, 302.* **Open** 10am-midnight Mon-Thur, Sun; 10am-1am Fri, Sat. **Tickets** $9; $7 concessions. **Credit** AmEx, Disc, MC, V. **Hotel** p69. **Map** p320 A7.
OK, so it's only half the size of the original, but the Vegas Eiffel Tower gives visitors a great view of the Strip and the surrounding mountains, something you won't find in Paris. You take a lift to the 46th-floor observation deck; go at dusk to watch the Strip suddenly light up as if someone's flicked a switch.

Flamingo Road to Spring Mountain Road

Map p320 A7-A6

Wedged against the Barbary Coast, the **Flamingo** (*see p77*) features some of the Strip's best remaining neon. The casino is the same spot as Bugsy Siegel's original, although nothing of it remains. In its place are lush grounds and winding pathways that take you past penguins, Chilean flamingos, Mandarin ducks and koi fish swimming in ponds under three-storey-high waterfalls. If it weren't for the tennis courts, pool and spa, it could be a wildlife habitat, albeit the only one in the world with a plaque honouring a mobster. **O'Sheas** (No.3355, 697 2711), a casino-only operation that's part of the Flamingo, and the right-up-to-the-asphalt oriental-looking **Imperial Palace** (*see p79*) follow. The latter's **Auto Collections** (*see below*) is tucked behind the hotel.

Near the Roman-themed **Forum Shops** (*see p177*) at Caesars Palace – where, under an ever-changing 'sky', animated statues come to life every hour for a bizarre seven-minute revel with dancing water and laser lights – is the **Atlantis** attraction atop an aquarium near Dolce e Gabbana, which offers an unintentionally hilarious (and too loud) lights and effects drama every hour on the hour.

North of Caesars begins a block-long tropical paradise created by the **Mirage** (*see p68*) and **TI (Treasure Island)** (*see p71*). In 1989, the Mirage introduced the first large-scale free spectacle to Las Vegas: an erupting 54-foot (16-metre) volcano, next door to the Strip. Even though the revamped volcano is small, lacks a cinder dome and looks more like a granite wall, the ten-minute spectacle (every 15 minutes; 7pm-midnight daily), spewing fire and a piña colada scent into the palm trees, waterfalls and lagoon, is worth a look. Inside the resort, pygmy sharks swim about in a large aquarium behind the registration desk, while, a short walk away, Siegfried & Roy's white tigers look bored inside a glass-enclosed compound. For a closer look at the illusionists' pets, visit the not-so-**Secret Garden & Dolphin Habitat** (*see p119*).

TI (Treasure Island) fronts the Strip with a replica of an 18th-century sea village set on a lagoon, surrounded by cliffs, palm trees and nautical artefacts. The focus of attention, however, are the two fully rigged ships on which the **Sirens of TI** clash with a band of renegade pirates (every 90 minutes, 7-11.30pm daily). The show was formerly a family-friendly pantomime, but received a recent – and, to be honest, horribly crass – revamp in line with the hotel's general rebranding as a more adult

resort. Regardless, it fills the pavement to capacity, as onlookers stare slack-jawed at the cannons blazing, masts toppling, powder kegs exploding, chests heaving and actors leaping into the lagoon. The view from the outdoor deck of **Tangerine** (*see p244*) is even better.

The abysmal Vegas of the 1980s is too much in evidence back on the east side at **Harrah's** (*see p78*), whose tired carnival look disappears into the surrounding overkill. Further on, inside the small **Casino Royale** (No.3411, 854 7666), a 24-hour parade of hungry characters scoff food at Denny's, an excellent stop if you're slumming for Hunter S Thompson's Vegas. Past here, on the site of the famed Sands casino, ghosts of the Rat Pack wander another imposing Euro-mimic, the **Venetian** (*see p73*). Once the king of Las Vegas nightlife – only **V Bar** (*see p169*) and **Vivid** (*see p244*) remain, though New York's Tao is headed here in late 2005 – the Venetian also has the **Grand Canal Shoppes** (*see p177*) and singing gondoliers (*see below*), who transport embarrassed tourists along the resort's canals.

The Venetian is also home to the high-art **Guggenheim Hermitage Museum** (*see p231*), which opened in autumn 2001. Designed by architect Rem Koolhaas, the original two museums were supposed to signify Vegas's new cultural credibility. Comically, the larger Guggenheim Las Vegas closed in 2003 after just one exhibition, and while the remaining 'Jewel Box' continues to stage temporary shows, the Venetian's typically feeble branch of **Madame Tussaud's** (*see p119*) draws the larger crowds.

Gondola rides

Venetian *Grand Canal Shoppes, 3355 Las Vegas Boulevard South, at Sands Avenue (414 1000/ www.venetian.com). Bus 203, 213, 301, 302.* **Open** 10am-11pm Mon-Thur, Sun; 10am-midnight Fri, Sat. **Tickets** *Indoor ride* $15; $7.50 under-12s; $60 private, 2-passenger gondola. *Outdoor ride* $12.50; $5 under-12s; $50 private, 2-passenger gondola. **No credit cards. Hotel** p73. **Map** p320 A6.
Purchase your tickets at St Mark's Square, then take a gondola ride along canals that weave through replica Venetian architecture. The wooden gondolas are authentic and the singing gondoliers are tuneful, but despite the number of newly married couples that take the ride, the backdrop of gawking tourists will dampen any hopes of a romantic moment.

Imperial Palace Auto Collections

Imperial Palace *3535 Las Vegas Boulevard South, between Sands Avenue & E Flamingo Road (731 3311/www.imperialpalace.com). Bus 301, 302.* **Open** 9.30am-9.30pm daily. **Admission** $6.95; $3 concessions. **Hotel** p79. **Map** p320 A6.
If you can find the place (it's in the parking garage), you'll discover about 200 rare and speciality cars (part of a fine rotating collection of 750, all for sale).

Among them are Hitler's 1936 Mercedes, JFK's 1962 Lincoln, vehicles that once belonged to Al Capone, WC Fields and Howard Hughes, and a room full of Duesenbergs. This latter room was where former casino owner Ralph Engelstad held secretive 'Hitler birthday parties', before being fined by the Nevada Gaming Control Board for the activity.

Madame Tussaud's

Venetian *3355 Las Vegas Boulevard South, at Sands Avenue (367 1847/www.venetian.com).* Bus 203, 213, 301, 302. **Open** 10am-11pm daily. **Admission** $20.95; $9.95-$14.95 concessions; free under-5s. **Credit** AmEx, Disc, MC, V. **Hotel** p73. **Map** p320 A6.
The first US incarnation of London's cheesy attraction, with more than 100 wax celebs in various settings. The most notorious figure of recent times? Saddam Hussein has been getting plenty of photo attention from guests pretending to strangle, kick and stab the deposed Iraqi dictator's likeness.

Secret Garden & Dolphin Habitat

Mirage *3400 Las Vegas Boulevard South, between W Spring Mountain & Flamingo Roads (791 7111/ www.themirage.com).* Bus 203, 213, 301, 302. **Open** *Spring/autumn: Secret Garden & Dolphin Habitat* 11am-5.30pm Mon-Fri; 10am-5.30pm Sat, Sun. *Summer: Secret Garden & Dolphin Habitat* 11am-7pm Mon-Fri; 10am-7pm Sat, Sun. *Winter: Secret Garden* 11am-4pm Mon-Fri; 10am-4pm Sat, Sun. *Dolphin Habitat* 11am-5.30pm Mon-Fri; 10am-5.30pm Sat, Sun. **Admission** *Joint ticket* $12; free under-10s. **Credit** AmEx, DC, Disc, MC, V. **Hotel** p68. **Map** p320 A6.

Not even marine mammals in the desert seems far-fetched in Las Vegas. Here, bottle-nosed dolphins frolic in a special habitat behind the Mirage. Adjacent to the Dolphin Habitat is the Secret Garden, a small but attractive zoo with Asian-themed architecture and some big-ticket animals: white tigers, white lions, Bengal tigers, an Indian elephant, a panther and a snow leopard.

Spring Mountain Road to Convention Center Drive

Map p319 B6-B5

This is the corner that is defining the face of 21st-century Las Vegas. Glance south and see new Las Vegas: themed resorts, neon-free façades and celebrity chefs dominating the scene. Look north and witness old Vegas: smoky casinos, garish neon and cheap eats. In a nutshell, it's the difference between Sinatra's *Ocean's 11* and Soderbergh's *Ocean's Eleven*.

It's at this symbolic confluence that Steve Wynn has just built the 5.5-million-square-foot, $2.7 billion **Wynn Las Vegas** (*see p75*), a hyperreal return to the 'intimacy' of old Las Vegas. In a reversal of the philosophy of streetside spectacle pioneered by Wynn at the Mirage, the development will be hidden from the Strip by a massive mountain, which visitors can walk around, revealing a golf course, a lavish spa, top-end shops, a Ferrari dealership and the **Gallery** (*see p231*), where paintings on

Elephants never forget to take a break at the **Secret Garden & Dolphin Habitat**. *See p118.*

Sightseeing

show from Wynn's personal collection will no doubt include Picasso's *Le Rêve*, after which the hotel was initially named.

Accelerating the redefinition of Vegas is the **Fashion Show Mall** (*see p178*) across the road: the city's first purveyor of high(er) fashion, it now dominates the Strip's west side with its massive 'cloud', a 479-foot metal oval suspended between two 13-storey towers. It serves as an outdoor projection screen, but also provides much needed shade for the *de facto* piazza and two rare outdoor restaurants facing Wynn Las Vegas: get rock 'n' roll sushi at **RA Sushi** and tasty tapas at **Café Ba Ba Reeba** (*see p144*). The cloud is the visual centrepiece to the recent $1 billion expansion doubling the size of the mall and introducing the city's first **Nordstrom** (*see p181*). In coincidental synergy with Wynn Las Vegas, the Fashion Show is a theme-free shopping centre. Soon enough, themed resorts will seem as dated as the old Vegas resorts did in 1989.

Just north of the Fashion Show is the **New Frontier** (No.3120, 794 8200), the site of the longest labour strike in US history. A pathetic shell of the once-bustling gambling den where Elvis first played Vegas, the Frontier's only draw is **Gilley's**, a country and western bar where two-stepping babes in their bikinis sometimes straddle a mechanical bull to the hollers of cowboy wannabes. Plans to raze and rebuild this dowdy property will likely coincide with the arrival of the adjacent Trump International Hotel & Tower, a joint venture between the New York real-estate mogul and New Frontier owner Phil Ruffin that's expected to open in autumn 2006.

North of here, you pass almost unknowingly over the Desert Inn Super Arterial, an east–west expressway that avoids both the Strip (by tunnelling under) and I-15 (by flying over). To the east is the **Catholic Guardian Angel Cathedral** (336 Guardian Angel Way, 735 5241). The themed stained-glass windows here are one of the few places where you can still see old Vegas icons such as the Landmark Hotel. Across from the Cathedral is the **Stardust** (*see p89*), whose dramatic neon and fibre-optic sign may be the most impressive in the city.

Convention Center Drive to Sahara Avenue

Map p319 B5-C4

A cluster of development sits north-east of here, with a new drugstore replacing much of what was once a tacky shopping centre. Further along is **Peppermill's Fireside Lounge** (*see p168*): once one of the best places in the city for

Cop an Eiffel at **Paris Las Vegas**. *See p117*.

romantic relaxation, the lounge recently ruined its cosy, *Playboy*-like atmosphere by bolting flat-panel TVs on every surface. Next door, on the site once home to the delightfully Googie-style La Concha Motel, will be the Majestic Resort and Residences, a $250 million art deco project featuring a Conrad hotel and condo tower, and **Majestic Court & Marketplace**.

It's back to blazing neon at the 50-year-old **Riviera** (*see p87*), whose façade and sign very nearly constitute overkill even by Vegas standards. Don't miss the life-sized bronze statues of the **Crazy Girls** (*see p214*) just in front of the casino; punters rub their butts for a boozy photo-op. Across the street are the neon umbrellas of **Westward Ho!** (No.2900, 731 2900) and, next door, **Slots-o-Fun** (No.2880, 734 0410). Back in the early 1990s, this was where Vegas's New Year's Eve crowds first grew so large they spilled into the street. Since then, New Year has become such a mob party that the whole Strip is closed to traffic.

The Lucky the Clown sign of **Circus Circus** (*see p85*), the original family-fun palace, still leers cheerfully over the Strip, though it's been upgraded with a fibre-optic reader board. The casino under the pink concrete big top has free circus acts every 25 minutes (11am-midnight daily) high above the casino floor. The **Horse-a-Round Bar** (*see p167*), immortalised in Hunter S Thompson's *Fear and Loathing in Las Vegas*, is open on Friday and Saturday nights only. Although the cramped space and shabby decor lessen the spectacle, it's an odd experience watching a spangly trapeze artist fly overhead. While mom and pop gamble away the rent, kids whoop it up at **Adventuredome**, a popular theme park (*see below*).

North of here, things are less engaging. On the east side, the classic Algiers motor court was levelled in 2004 to make room for a proposed skyscraper that will, after the developers pulled out, now never be built (the neighbouring **Turnberry** development has reportedly bought the land). Across on the west side is a somewhat low-rent Travelodge motel, followed by the **Hilton Grand Vacations Club** timeshare, originally stalled by the 9/11 attacks. Also planned here is the 43-storey, blue-glass façade of **Sky Las Vegas**, which will, if completed, house over 300 luxe condos. At ths Strip's southwest corner with Sahara Avenue is empty, fenced wasteland. The site of the original **El Rancho** (*see p15*), built in 1941 and once regarded as the most expensive piece of undeveloped property in Nevada, the land has been on and off the market for some time.

The east side finishes brightly, however. The decaying eyesore of the second El Rancho was bought and cleared by Turnberry Associates, who are almost finished building four towers of rapidly selling condos. The site that once held the Wet 'n Wild water park may yet be home to the Archon Corporation's **Palace by the Sea** resort, which will putatively contain a giant observation wheel and 80 hotel suites on boats moored in a man-made lake, but signs of activity on the site are currently conspicuous by their absence. Nearby is the **Sahara** (*see p88*), where animated camels on a fibre-optic sign usher value-conscious customers into the resort's bright porte cochère, and thrill-seekers flock to the virtual racing at the **Las Vegas Cyber Speedway** and to **Speed: The Ride** (for both, *see p122*). According to most of the area's residents, the Strip begins and ends right here, Stratosphere or none.

Adventuredome

Circus Circus *2880 Las Vegas Boulevard South, at Circus Circus Drive, between W Sahara Avenue & Stardust Road (794 3939/www.adventuredome.com).* Bus 301. **Open** 10am-6pm Mon-Thur; 10am-midnight Fri, Sat; 10am-8pm Sun. **Admission** *Unlimited rides* $22.95; $14.95 concessions. *Individual rides* $4-$6. **Credit** AmEx, DC, Disc, MC, V. **Hotel** p85. **Map** p319 B5.

The five-acre park, climate-controlled under a pink plastic dome, is a scene Fred Flintstone would love: waterfalls, faux mountains and animated spitting dinosaurs stuck in fake tar pits. The rides here are good, though hardly white-knuckle; the best is the double-loop, double-corkscrew rollercoaster ($5), but it is a little disappointing in that it lasts only 90

Sightseeing

Harry, can you hear us?

Ignite the candles, dim the lights and let the summons begin. Harry? Mr Houdini? Great escape artist who's been dead about 80 years: can you hear us?

Nothing. No rattling chains. No moaning. *Wait!* Was that a sniffle? Hmm. Flu season.

And so it's gone for the past 20-odd years during the annual **Harry Houdini Seance**, held on Hallowe'en at the **Riviera** (*see p87*) and led by Las Vegas escape artist and Houdini fan Dixie Dooley. This isn't the Official Houdini Seance, mind you: the rights to that are held by Sid Radner, who, until he auctioned them off on Hallowe'en 2004, also owned many of Houdini's tricks and tortures. The city's attempts to conjure up some sort of ectoplasm are unofficial and, like so much of Vegas, something of a knock-off. But it's certainly no less entertaining for that, and is open to the public for all to enjoy. In any case, who's to say Houdini would discriminate between official and unofficial, were he actually to make contact with us? Though the Houdini Museum is all the way over in

Scranton, Pennsylvania, and the Houdini Historical Center is in Appleton, Wisconsin, the magic is undeniably in Vegas.

Though Houdini, much as Dooley does now, spent parts of his career debunking séances, he thought that if anyone could make contact from the afterlife he'd be the one to find the way. Since the master's death from an infection on 31 October 1926, scads of fans, followers and psychic sidekicks have been trying to reach him. It's said that Houdini's wife, Bess, attempted to contact him for ten years before giving up. These days, escape artists like Dooley are left to pick up the slack.

But of course Las Vegas doesn't limit itself to contacting just Houdini in the afterlife. Attempts in recent years have also been made to channel Elvis Presley and casino heir Ted Binion, who died in mysterious circumstances in September 1998. And while the mediums never fail to garner a bit of press and notoriety, they've yet to scrounge up evidence of paranormal activity or solve any of the world's mysteries.

Go loopy on **Speed: The Ride**.

At the corner of Sahara Avenue and the Strip, you can hear screams. Glance north, and you'll see why: at the top of the **Stratosphere** (*see p90*), the tallest building in Nevada, are the **Big Shot**, a ride that propels the daring vertically; the **High Roller**, a rollercoaster that circles above the observation deck in twists and rolls; the **X Scream**, which dangles passengers over the edge of the tower; and **Insanity – The Ride**, an inverted centrifuge that spins passengers over the edge of the observation deck at a 70° angle (for all, *see below*). It's enough to make anyone scream… including Bob Stupak, the Stratosphere's former owner, who suffered a series of financial and construction setbacks when trying to complete the tower.

North from Sahara is the site of another high-rise development, the 21-storey **Liberty Tower Las Vegas**. Across from here is the must-stop **Bonanza Gifts** (*see p195*), which claims to be the world's largest gift shop and sells a vast array of souvenirs. Behind it is **Allure**, yet another high-rise. Approaching the Stratosphere, the east side has the **Holiday House Motel** (No.2211, 732 2468), a hangover from the old days, notable for its wacky animated neon sign and Palm Springs-like motor court design.

The Stratosphere sits where Main Street and Paradise Road cross Las Vegas Boulevard and turn into each other by way of St Louis Avenue. Beyond here, at the intersection with Oakey Boulevard, is the **White Cross Drugstore** (*see p199*); in it is **Tiffany's** (*see p151*), one of the few drugstore food counters left in town.

seconds. Tots will like the bumper cars, Ferris wheel and other small rides, as well as an obstacle course for creative crawling. New to the Adventuredome are the tilt-a-whirl-esque Chaos and the rocket-launching slingshot. In October, the park transforms into the pleasantly creepy FrightDome.

Las Vegas Cyber Speedway

Sahara *2535 Las Vegas Boulevard South, at W Sahara Avenue (737 7223/www.saharavegas.com).* Bus 204, 301, 302. **Open** noon-9pm Mon-Thur; noon-10pm Fri; 11am-10pm Sat; 11am-9pm Sun. **Admission** $10 1 ride; $16 2 rides. *Joint ticket with Speed: The Ride* $15. **Credit** AmEx, Disc, MC, V. **Hotel** p88. **Map** p319 C4.

This high-tech virtual reality racing simulator teams effectively with the neighbouring NASCAR Café (*see p226*): you should see this place on race weekends. It's a fun schtick and frighteningly realistic, but at these prices, it should be.

Speed: The Ride

Sahara *2535 Las Vegas Boulevard South, at W Sahara Avenue (737 2111/www.saharavegas.com).* Bus 204, 301, 302. **Open** 10am-10pm Mon-Thur, Sun; 10am-midnight Fri, Sat. **Admission** $10 all-day pass. *Joint all-day pass with Las Vegas Cyber Speedway* $19.95. **Credit** AmEx, Disc, MC, V. **Hotel** p88. **Map** p319 C4.

Although it may look like one, Speed is not, according to the strict definition, a rollercoaster: it doesn't have a lift hill, nor does it run by gravity. Instead, it's driven by the force of magnetic impellers that rush it from zero to soil-your-pants in three seconds. Riders shoot out from the Sahara into a tunnel drop, only to re-emerge directly into a vertical loop and up a 23-storey tower at 70mph. And then they do it all over again… backwards. Twice.

High Roller, Big Shot, X Scream & Insanity – The Ride

Stratosphere *2000 Las Vegas Boulevard South, at St Louis Avenue, between W Oakey Boulevard & W Sahara Avenue (380 7777/www.stratospherehotel. com).* Bus 301. **Open** 10am-1am Mon-Thur, Sun; 10am-2am Fri, Sat. **Tickets** *All-day ride pass* $24.95. *Individual tickets* $8 ($4 High Roller); $6 hotel guests, 4-12s. **Credit** AmEx, DC, Disc, MC, V. **Hotel** p90. **Map** p319 C3/4.

If you're afraid of heights, stay away from the 1,150ft (350m) Stratosphere Tower. Those with cast-iron stomachs can try the High Roller. Because of space limitations, don't expect high speeds; you may, however, experience vertigo. More invigorating is the Big Shot, which rockets you 160ft (49m) up the tower's spindle under a force of 4Gs; at the top you experience a moment of weightlessness before free-falling back to the launch pad. X Scream propels riders headfirst, 27ft (8m) over the edge of the Tower, where they dangle. Insanity: an arm extends 64ft (19.5m) over the edge of the Tower and spins passengers at suffient speed to pull up to 3Gs.

Off-Strip

How to boldly go where few tourists have gone before.

East of Strip

Paradise Road, also known as the Convention Corridor, is the busiest area east of the Strip, especially now the **Las Vegas Monorail** (*see p291*) is finally on track. Running parallel to the Strip, it's been the site of development since 1969, when the Landmark and International casinos opened south of Sahara Avenue. The Landmark was erased a while ago (see *Mars Attacks!* to witness its real-life destruction), while the International has long been the **Las Vegas Hilton** (*see p92*), which appeared as the Whyte House Hotel in the James Bond film *Diamonds Are Forever*. The showroom here has history, having staged Elvis Presley's record-breaking run of 837 straight sell-outs in the 1970s; it's recently hired Barry Manilow in the hope of recapturing its former entertainment glory. Also here is the unstoppable **Star Trek: The Experience** (*see p124*).

West of the Hilton is **Turnberry Place**, a swanky four-tower, high-rise condominium development. Behind the Hilton to the east is the exclusive **Las Vegas Country Club**. West on Desert Inn Road, across from the Las Vegas Convention Center, is one of several high-rises going up on and around the Strip, the art deco-style Metropolis. From the south end of the Hilton, stretching across Desert Inn Road, is the **Las Vegas Convention Center**, the largest convention facility in the world (*see p293*). If you aren't attending a convention, stop by the **Las Vegas Convention & Visitors Authority** (*see p301*) at the top of the main entrance drive, for of brochures and magazines. Fronting the building is a monorail station.

South of here is the **Beach** (*see p241*), a huge club that's a big favourite with conventioneers, followed by a few comfortable business hotels, including the swanky new **Renaissance Las Vegas** (*see p106*). Just past Twain Avenue begins a high-density collection of restaurants known as Restaurant Row; it really takes shape where Paradise meets Flamingo, with branches of (among others) **PF Chang's** (4165 Paradise Road, 792 2207), **Bahama Breeze** (375 Hughes Center Drive, 731 3252) and **Cozymel's** (355 Hughes Center Drive, 732 4833).

Further south, the junction of Harmon Avenue is an epicentre of hipster attractions. The giant guitar sign of the **Hard Rock Café** may be striking, but you should head for the **Hard Rock** hotel-casino to the north-west (*see p91*). The collection of memorabilia includes stuff from legends such as Elvis and the Beatles, plus pieces from more contemporary icons such as the Paul Oakenfold, Madonna and Michael Hutchence, who donated his guitar to the Hard Rock after playing at the **Joint** (*see p237*) a couple of months before his death. Despite competition from Palms, the Hard Rock is holding its own as the top overall resort for the young and restless. Also here is Germany's own **Hofbrauhaus** (*see p153*), as well as the site of a branch of LA's famed Rainbow Room.

Star Trek: The Experience. *See p124*.

Beckoning further south is the Fruit Loop (aka the Gay Triangle), home to gay-oriented bars, clubs, cafés and shops (see p232), followed by the vast expanse of **McCarran International Airport** (see p290); to the east, meanwhile, are the delights of the **University District** (see p132). Before you get there, though you'll pass the **Atomic Testing Museum**: located on the Desert Research Institute campus.

Atomic Testing Museum

755 E Flamingo Road, between Swenson Street & Paradise Road (794 5151/www.atomictesting museum.org). Bus 202. **Open** 9am-5pm Mon-Sat; 1-5pm Sun. **Admission** $10; $7 concessions; free under-6s. **Credit** AmEx, Disc, MC, V. **Map** p317 Y3.
From the city that used to trot out atomic pin-up girls in mushroom-cloud swimsuits for cheesy publicity stills comes a one-of-a-kind insight into the Nevada Test Site, which served as the US's principal 'on-continent' nuclear weapons testing facility from 1951 to 1992. The 8,000sq ft (2,500sq m) permanent exhibit hall, on the first floor of the Frank H Rogers Science and Technology Building, includes artefacts on loan from personal collections, the Smithsonian and the Lawrence Livermore Laboratory, and pieces of the Berlin Wall and the World Trade Center. Next to the museum is the Nuclear Testing Archives, a collection of more than 310,000 documents related to radioactive fallout from US testing of nuclear devices. All in all, it's a blast. (Sorry.)

Flyaway

200 Convention Center Drive, between Las Vegas Boulevard South & Paradise Road (1-877 545 8093/731 4768/www.flyawayindoorskydiving.com). Bus 301, 302. **Open** 10am-6pm daily. **Rates** $50. **Credit** AmEx, MC, V. **Map** p319 B5.
Skydiving without an airplane? Well, sort of: you can free-fall in one of only three skydiving simulators in the world, an indoor 21ft vertical wind tunnel that generates air speeds of up to 130mph. After an hour of instruction, you get 15 minutes of flying time shared with five others. An additional $25 will double your flying time.

Star Trek: The Experience

Las Vegas Hilton 3000 Paradise Road, between Karen Avenue & E Desert Inn Road (732 5111/ www.startrekexp.com). Bus 108, 112. **Open** 11am-11pm daily. **Admission** $34.99. **Credit** AmEx, DC, Disc, MC, V. **Hotel** p92. **Map** p319 C5.
This space-age attraction promises to 'boldly go where no entertainment experience has gone before'. There are now two different immersive 'experiences' to be had: although your trip includes a stunning 'beaming' to the bridge of the *Starship Enterprise* and a ride in a virtual shuttle, most of your time is spent looking at costumes, props and weaponry from every Trek incarnation. Unusually tall Ferengi and unusually friendly Klingons roam around, happy to pose for photos and chat you up about their last trip through the Gamma Quadrant. There's also

the Space Quest Casino, which uses dozens of TV monitors disguised as portholes in order to create the illusion that you're orbiting Earth. If you're not interested in throwing your money away on 24th-century slot machines, at least step into Quark's Bar & Restaurant (see p170). You may not be surprised to learn that the management found room to squeeze in a couple of souvenir shops.

West of Strip

Between Las Vegas Boulevard and Valley View Boulevard, the west of Strip corridor is bisected by the roaring thrust of the I-15. Wedged next to it and running parallel, Frank Sinatra Drive offers quicker, back-door access to many Strip hotels from Russell to Industrial Roads. Industrial itself is a good, low-traffic alternative to the Strip, with many access roads along the way. However, it's a mistake to use this road *only* as a useful short cut, since among the industrial businesses and strip clubs, you'll also find the **Elvis-a-Rama Museum** (see p125) which has a jam-packed gift shop and regular tribute shows by Elvis impersonators.

Overpasses at Tropicana, Flamingo or Sahara take you across I-15 to Valley View Boulevard, but note that Valley View isn't continuous between Tropicana and Flamingo. The Valley View intersections with Flamingo Road and Sahara Avenue are the focus of development in this area of town. At Flamingo Road, you'll find a trio of casino-hotels. You can go bowling at the **Gold Coast** (see p102), or pop into the flamboyant **Rio** (see p93) for the

Elvis-a-Rama. See p125.

Only in Vegas?

It was an ordinary October day inside Treasures on Industrial Road (*see p210*). The women were dancing, while the men either ogled or helped themselves to crab legs from the strip club's buffet. But outside, things were different: Coolio was talking or rapping or simply commenting on the passing dancers as a man named Jimmy Luv lowered himself into a long, plastic box, near the club's parking lot. Here, he would remain for 10 days, with no food or water, and resurface on Hallowe'en, a few pounds (and a few kidney stones) lighter. Why? To Luv, the answer lies in the challenge.

The same week, a man calling himself Masochisto had planned to wow the masses. Masochisto's talent is dangling from his own flesh while hooks protrude from it. On Hallowe'en, he was due to dangle from AJ Hackett's bungee-jumping centre, 80 feet (24 metres) above Las Vegas, for two whole hours. Though they'd never heard of one another, Masochisto and Luv were brought together a few days before Hallowe'en by an ambitious reporter who couldn't hide her own curiosity at a potential meeting of minds. The met minds were not impressed. Luv had been in the box for about four days. He'd had his catheter removed because he was too

dehydrated to urinate; though he had few other places to look, he could hardly make eye contact with Masochisto out of sheer disgust. Masochisto, for his part, had few good things to say about the abuse Luv was putting his body through, as well as the lack of preparation for such an event. Luv drank a lot of Ensure in the days leading up to the entombment; Masochisto said he would have eaten only fruits and nuts.

A few days later, on Hallowe'en, Masochisto was hoisted into the air on giant hooks. He glanced down at the crowd of roughly 20 people who'd come to watch him, but they soon sought warmer shelter and wandered off. Meanwhile, a few blocks away, the lid to Luv's tomb was lifted in front of a similarly sparse crowd made up mostly of Treasures dancers and members of the media, and Luv was lifted by paramedics to an IV tube of fluid. Crowd or no crowd, both seemed satisfied. The events may have drawn more spectators in a city with fewer oddities than Las Vegas. But here, where contortionists are practically passé, sirens lure pirates to their deaths and volcanoes burst along the busiest streets, a couple of men with the lofty goals of attracting attention and pushing their own bodily limits is nothing out of the ordinary.

free Masquerade Show, which takes place in the casino's Masquerade Village four times a day. It's a kind of Mardi Gras parade in the sky, during which floats glide high above the floor to an orchestration of music and dance.

More likely, though, you'll end up at the **Palms** (*see p92*), the closest competitor to the Hard Rock in terms of attracting the beautiful people that make up the MTV set (the Real World Suite is often the site of celebrity bashes). The nightlife here is energising, ranging from great views from the celeb-friendly **Ghostbar** (*see p170*), via the nightclub **Rain in the Desert** (*see p243*), and on to numerous trend-setting spots such as **Little Buddha** (*see p170*) and **N9ne** (*see p155*). One of the top cinemas in town, the nightclub-esque **Brenden Las Vegas 14** (*see p229*), complements the fun (it even has a disco ball spinning in the lobby, but the casino action isn't as energetic as at the Hard Rock (the Maloofs remembered to cater to their loyal slot players, and smartly split the hotel into two identities), and the lack of a proper concert venue keeps the **Joint** (the Hard Rock's music hall; *see p237*) jumping.

Beyond the Rio, the Gold Coast and the Palms, Valley View continues north through a semi-residential, semi-industrial district. An easterly turn at Sahara leads past small strip malls *ad infinitum* until the train-themed casino **Palace Station** (*see p104*) just before I-15. Families may also want to check out the **Scandia Family Fun Centre** (*see p226*), a sports and games complex south of Palace Station on Rancho Drive.

Elvis-a-Rama Museum

3401 S Industrial Road, between E Desert Inn Road & Spring Mountain Road (309 7200/www.elvis arama.com). Bus 203, 301, 302. **Open** 10am-6pm daily. **Admission** $12.95. **Credit** Disc, MC, V. **Map** p319 A5.

Does Las Vegas idolise Elvis, or did Elvis idolise Vegas? Investigate for yourself at this shrine to one of the city's most enduring icons. The museum has the largest collection of Elvisabilia this side of Graceland: $5 million worth, claim the owners, including the 1955 Cadillac touring limo, a racy handwritten letter, a boat, the King's army uniform, a gold lamé suit and the obligatory blue suede shoes. You can even get married here.

Downtown

What's the future for Las Vegas past?

Bellowing powerfully from his mighty-bully pulpit, iconoclast Mayor Oscar Goodman (*see p128* **Viva Oscar Goodman**) has decreed the revival of the Downtown area is upon us, and so it shall be. In truth, the Las Vegas City Council and its colourful leader have no real authority to do much beyond creating incentives for development and (dread word) gentrification. Still, after years of pretence and wishful thinking, there's been a genuine resurgence of interest and investment in Downtown Las Vegas.

The revival is about the vision that has sprung from the Mayor's recurring and oft-recited 'dream'; like any dream, while it may be distorted and fuzzy at the edges, it still contains ample intrigue and curiosity. Part of this fuzziness is simple geography: ask ten Las Vegans for their definition of Downtown's borders, and you'll get at least that many different answers.

A HUNDRED YEARS OF HISTORY

Regardless of where its borders now lie, the centre of Downtown is where the city began. In May 1905, land-hungry settlers and speculators gathered in front of a wooden railroad platform (on the site of the **Plaza**, *see p99*) to auction off the 1,200 lots that constituted the Clark town site. In the 1930s and 1940s, hotels and casinos dotted **Fremont Street**, the area's main commercial drag for a century, along with the city's main department stores and a host of other businesses. But the rise of the Strip saw a drain of trade away from Downtown, whose casinos didn't have the luxury of space for expansion, and the area grew dowdy.

The construction of the **Fremont Street Experience** in 1995, which turned a five-block section of the road into a pedestrian-friendly gambling mall and covered it with a dazzling canopy that screened electronic light and sound shows, succeeded in luring some tourists back to Glitter Gulch, but many residents complain that it destroyed much of Fremont Street's character in the process: what was once a public street is now a private 'park', owned indirectly by the participating hotels.

Perhaps because of this oppressive domination, many tourists think Downtown begins and ends here. It doesn't, though it is the best starting and finishing point for an exploration of the area on the grounds of both safety and convenience. The trite canopy light

show and the bare-bones gambling halls yield few surprises (save for the occasional arrest of a homeless person, in order to make the pedestrian walkway 'blight-free'), but beyond Fremont Street lie plenty more interesting corridors of culture and history.

It used to be the case that anything north of Fremont Street signalled the beginning of 'scary' North Las Vegas, while anything south was debilitated and uninteresting. Neither cliché is really true any more, both in terms of area (the boundaries of Downtown are only as limited as your sense of adventure) and ambience (it's debilitated only in places, and never uninteresting). When folks simply choose not to look outside the obvious, the obvious conclusion is all they draw. But if they looked around the corner from the Fremont Street Experience, they'd see progress looming overhead. Construction crews are building vertically to the heavens all around the area; soon, Downtown will be filled with high-rise condos and more high-end drinking experiments than you can shake a Martini at. Some are all-local endeavours, but the imminent arrival of Hogs & Heifers and the **Beauty Bar** (*see p171*), two New York transplants, validates the notion that there's real estate afoot.

Regardless, Downtown still manages to retain an old-school Vegas appeal that even the high-tech razzle-dazzle cannot dispel. While much of Vegas has gone upmarket, Downtown retains the spirit of what Las Vegas used to be: Sin City, a playground for adults to drink and dice until they drop. As this style of Las Vegas play comes back in vogue, perhaps Downtown will experience its own renaissance as an area of Vegas originality, untouched by themes and almost, though not quite, devoid of attractions.

During the **First Friday** (*see p204* **Viva Cindy Funkhouser**) of each month, as many as 10,000 people walk – that's right, walk – the oft-knocked 'dangerous' streets of Downtown to catch art, music and a lively and festive street scene. At night during the rest of the month, common-sense rules governing personal safety should be carefully observed. Nonetheless, there's never been a better time to discover the area. No guidebook can keep up with the ever-changing face of Downtown; like the Mayor himself, it can only push you in the right direction. Consider yourself pushed.

Fremont Street.

GETTING THERE

If you're using public transport, you can reach Downtown from the Strip by catching bus 301. Alternatively, if you're driving, head north on the I-15, then east on US 93/95, taking the Casino Center Exit (which is the faster route); otherwise, drive north on the Strip and 4th Street (which is the more interesting route). The public and casino parking garages are safe places to park your car, and they are also free with validation (you must stamp your parking ticket in a machine inside the casino). Validation for the public garage beneath the lacklustre Neonopolis mall is also available from some businesses.

Fremont Street & around

Fremont Street, once the cultural and commercial centre of Las Vegas, is now completely dominated by the **Fremont Street Experience** (*see p129*). At night camera-toting tourists are disgorged by the bus load to stand, heads back, mouths agape, watching the hourly light-and-sound spectacle. For years a slightly pathetic, dated sight, the FSE has recently undergone a complete technological upgrade: get there while it's still state-of-the-art.

Standing at the entrance to the FSE canopy at the intersection with 4th Street, surrounded by the incomparable glare of 50 miles of neon

Viva Mayor Oscar Goodman

Always careful to point out that he was a lawyer to suspected criminals and not a mobster himself, Goodman cast himself as the defender of businessmen who were being harassed by the FBI, at times claiming there was no such thing as organised crime in the US (but later taking in a cameo role as himself in Martin Scorsese's gangster-romanticising 1995 film *Casino*). Such a past would spell disaster for political candidates in every other city in the United States, but during Goodman's first run for the mayoralty in 1999, he was seen as the kind of tough-talking, tell-it-like-it-is iconoclast that dyed-in-the-wool Las Vegans seem to love.

In 2003, Oscar Goodman won a second term as mayor of Las Vegas with a massive 86 per cent of the vote. Although only a small number of those eligible voted (turnout was just 18 per cent), the landslide is indicative of the extraordinary popularity Goodman enjoys in his adopted home town. Indeed, there was next to no competition for Goodman in the election, in part because nobody wanted to embarrass themselves by taking on such a well liked mayor.

Goodman was born in Philadelphia in 1939, earning a degree from Haverford College before attending law school at the University of Pennsylvania. Upon arriving in Las Vegas in 1965, he took a job as a public defender, but by 1967 he had gone into private practice. After winning a few cases defending minor mafia figures, Goodman began to build a client roster that reads like a who's who of the most notorious Vegas mobsters. Among them: Frank 'Lefty' Rosenthal, Meyer Lansky, Nick Civella and, most infamously, Tony 'the Ant' Spilotro, suspected of 22 murders before his own body, and that of his brother, was discovered in an Indiana cornfield, apparently a victim of the Chicago mob.

Goodman ran on a platform of revitalising Downtown and quickly made progress; having acquired a 61-acre plot of land just west of Downtown, he plans to fill it with high-rise housing, a performing arts centre and an academic medical centre. Already built are an Internal Revenue Service and the beginnings of the World Market Center (*see p176*). Other endeavours have been less successful, most notably his efforts to bring a Major League Baseball team to town. For years, Goodman had his eyes on the Montreal Expos, who were searching for a new home. They chose Washington, DC, instead; Goodman's next target, the Florida Marlins, seem set to stay put. Still, even though turning Vegas into a major-league city may be unlikely, only a fool would bet against this brash but likeable character getting his way in the end.

tubing, the visitor is within easy walking distance of all the major casinos in Downtown (assuming, of course, that the word 'major' can even be applied). Once upon a time, the former Binion's Horseshoe was the Wild West home of outlaw gaming and odds, the World Series of Poker and true no-frills, no-nonsense gambling. Sadly, scandal and debts gave rise to a sequence of ownership shuffles that resulted in both its name – having dropped the 'Horseshoe', it's now just **Binion's** (*see p97*) – and its charm diminishing. The **Golden Nugget** (*see p96*) has also changed hands: the symphony of white and gold was bought by two youngster internet millionaires who promised a return to the old school. They lasted a year before selling it in early 2005, and the casino's future is uncertain.

Happily unchanged down the years is the **Golden Gate** (*see p98*), the city's oldest hotel (and site of its first telephone). Built in 1906 as the Hotel Nevada, the Golden Gate was known as the Sal Sagev (try reading it backwards) for decades; the **Bay City Diner** still serves a 99 cent shrimp cocktail in a classic tulip glass. Similarly old-school, albeit slightly posher, is the throwback restaurant elegance and overwrought decor of **Hugo's Cellar** at the **Four Queens** (*see p156*). True to postcard fame, **Vegas Vic**, the neon cowboy, still waves atop the long-closed Pioneer Club, though he no longer calls out 'Howdy, podner!' from a hidden speaker (*see p14* **Viva Vegas Vic**). Across the street, his female counterpart **Vegas Vickie** kicks up her heels over the **Girls of Glitter Gulch** strip club (*see p209*).

On the east side of 4th Street, just across the way from the FSE, is **Neonopolis** (No.450), a three-storey mall anchored by a fine, multiplex cinema, the **Crown Neonopolis 14** (*see p229*). Also here are **Jillian's** (759 0450, *see p171*), a two-storey recreation spot with billiards, a bowling alley, an arcade and a sports bar, and the **Saloon** (*see p171*), a handsome bar whose appeal to the local community has ebbed and flowed down the years but, these days, seems to be doing more ebbing than flowing.

In the mall's open-air courtyard, the central elevator tower is adorned with a dozen restored neon signs from around the US. They make a nice counterpoint to the open-air **Neon Museum** (387 6366, www.neonmuseum.org), a small but growing collection of classic Las Vegas neon signs, restored and placed on poles along the pedestrian mall between Neonopolis and the FSE parking garage. The Hacienda Horse and Rider sign is the centrepiece of the museum, but the smaller Aladdin's Lamp, Flame Restaurant, Chief Hotel Court and Andy Anderson Dairy signs are all beautiful examples of neon art. Several more restored signs can be found on 3rd Street between Fremont and Ogden. *See p25* **City of Lights**.

Continue east past the small, somewhat seedy souvenir shops on Fremont to the **El Cortez** casino (*see p97*), the only hotel-casino Downtown that retains its original 1940s façade (though a modern hotel tower rises behind it). Further east, far beyond the controlling influence of the FSE, Fremont becomes decrepit, littered with low-rent hotels and drug dealers – though

there is the interesting dive **Atomic Liquor** and the stylish **Beauty Bar** (for both, *see p171*). It makes a great night drive (just remember to make sure to lock your car doors): you can see the vintage neon signs of many old motels, giving a glimpse of the era when east Fremont resembled the Strip. On the north side at 7th Street, look for the 1960s-mod **City Center Motel**, followed by the **Fergusons Motel** and the kitschy red-and-yellow-trimmed motor court of the **Gables**.

Back to Las Vegas Boulevard and heading north from Fremont takes you to Stewart Avenue and the recently expanded **City Hall** (400 Stewart Avenue, 229 6011). Heading west on Stewart will take you past **City Park**, the site of free pop and jazz concerts. Next to it is the original federal courthouse building, which formerly housed the Downtown Post Office. There's been talk of someday making this example of neo-classic architecture into a so-called 'Mob museum'; until a decision is made, the City is running the space as an attraction with rotating exhibits and surprises set for the near future. Watch this space.

Further along, Stewart Avenue leads straight into the Victorian-styled **Main Street Station** (*see p96*), which is an unpretentious gem of a hotel-casino that's full of impressive antiques and fronted by restored railroad carriages once owned by Buffalo Bill, Annie Oakley and Theodore Roosevelt. Left down Main, you'll head right past the **Plaza** (*see p99*), whose handsome upstairs restaurant offers perhaps the best views of the Fremont Street Experience, before reaching the **Greyhound bus depot** (*see p290*) right next door.

Fremont Street Experience

Fremont Street, between Las Vegas Boulevard South & Main Street (www.vegasexperience.com). Bus 107, 301. **Shows** *hourly, dusk-midnight daily.* **Map** *p318 C/D1.*

This five-block pedestrian mall, which is covered by a 90ft-high (27m) white metal lattice space frame, was supposed to become Downtown's saviour by attracting tourists who had forsaken Vegas's roots in favour of the glitzy Strip resorts. Unfortunately, it dated in a hurry. But in 2004 a major, $17 million technical upgrade of the canopy has definitely improved things. Five different seven-minute shows play in rotation on the 12.5 million synchronised LED modules, with the soundtrack booming out over a 550,000-watt sound system. Undoubtedly an amazing experience, although it can be a bit awkward to watch as the images are directly overhead; the best position is to stand right in the middle, outside the entrance to Binion's. Free concerts are held here semi-regularly; special events, from Mardi Gras parties to NASCAR celebrations, periodically take over the place.

Sightseeing

From Fremont Street north to Washington Avenue

To the north along Las Vegas Boulevard sit more remnants of the city's past. Run by the people behind the Neon Museum (see p129), the three-acre **Neon Boneyard** is a kind of purgatory where all cool Vegas signs go to be restored or destroyed. Further up the road are a series of low-key attractions designated, slightly optimistically, the Cultural Corridor: the usually above-par **City of Las Vegas Galleries** (see p230) in the Reed Whipple Cultural Center, the **Las Vegas Natural History Museum** and the smart **Lied Discovery Children's Museum** (for both, see below).

To the east is **Cashman Field**, where the Las Vegas 51s (see p247), the Los Angeles Dodgers' AAA team, play baseball through the overpowering heat of summer; the venue also hosts numerous arts and crafts shows, plus touring productions featuring great talents such as Morgan Fairchild and Joe Piscopo. Also in the general area is the fascinating **Old Las Vegas Mormon Fort Historic Park** (see below). Those into old architecture should check the **Biltmore Bungalows** (which aren't really bungalows), just a block off Las Vegas Boulevard to the west on Bonanza Road: created to house all the civilian workers stationed in Las Vegas to aid in the war effort, they're a great representation of a circa mid-1940s master-planned community.

Las Vegas Natural History Museum

900 Las Vegas Boulevard North, at E Washington Avenue (384 3466/www.lvnhm.org). Bus 113, 208. **Open** 9am-4pm daily. **Admission** $6; $3-$5 concessions; free under-2s. **Credit** AmEx, Disc, MC, V. **Map** p318 E1.
This small, enthusiastically run museum doesn't offer much in the way of bells and whistles, but the Marine Life Room features small sharks in a large tank, the Wild Nevada Room has exhibits on the flora and fauna of Nevada and the Young Scientist Center has some interactive displays. But the big draw is five roaring, robotic dinosaurs, including a vast Tyrannosaurus rex. Combine a visit with a trip to the nearby Lied Discovery Children's Museum.

Lied Discovery Children's Museum

Las Vegas Library, 833 Las Vegas Boulevard North, between W Washington Avenue & Bonanza Road (382 5437/www.ldcm.org). Bus 113. **Open** 10am-5pm Tue-Sun. **Admission** $7; $5-$6 concessions. **Credit** MC, V. **Map** p318 D1.
A stimulating museum similar to (though much smaller than) the Exploratorium in San Francisco, the Lied features dozens of scientific exhibits that involve the viewer as a part of the demonstration. Don't be put off by the name: this is the sort of place many adults would visit by themselves if they

thought they could. It's all good fun, and rather more edifying than Circus Circus's Adventuredome. Creative exhibits include a tin can telephone, which the kids will be entertained by for hours.

Old Las Vegas Mormon Fort Historic Park

500 E Washington Avenue, at Las Vegas Boulevard North (486 3511/www.parks.nv.gov/olvmf.htm). Bus 403. **Open** 8am-4.30pm daily. **Admission** $2; free under-6s. **No credit cards. Map** p317 Y2.
Built by a group of Mormon missionaries in 1855, then abandoned to become part of the Las Vegas Ranch, this is Vegas's pioneer settlement site, the oldest Euro-American structure in the state, and an example of what the area was like before the railroad. Though only remnants of the original structure remain, restoration and reconstruction have brought the compound back to life, and guides are on hand to answer any questions you may have.

From Fremont Street south to Oakey Boulevard

The walk south from Fremont Street down Las Vegas Boulevard grows less pleasant the further from Fremont you travel. It begins with several points of interest: the **Lloyd George Federal Courthouse** (333 Las Vegas Boulevard South) is a handsome building; nearby on Lewis Avenue stand **André's** (see p156), the best French restaurant in the state of Nevada, and **Poets Bridge**, with quotes from 20 Nevadan poets.

There's history here, too, not to mention some unexpected buildings. Although most of residential Las Vegas is unimaginatively cast in the same faux-Mediterranean stucco, the area around 6th, 7th, 8th and 9th Streets, south from Bridger Avenue to Oakey Boulevard, is an example of architectural diversity and small-town comfort: well-kept single-storey homes with large yards and wide driveways are typical.

The list of 1940s and '50s buildings in the area is headlined by the **Las Vegas Academy of International Studies & Performing Arts** (315 S 7th Street; see p251 for details of the theatre) – the only example of 1930s Art Deco architecture in the city. Further south, on S 7th Street just before Charleston Boulevard, are a cluster of attractive, early-20th-century bungalows with plaster walls and wooden floors; it's an area now known as 'Lawyer's Row', after the punk attorneys who've taken over the locale. And a little further down towards the Strip – just south of Charleston Boulevard, in fact – is the **John S Park** neighbourhood, which became the city's first official Historic District a few years ago: it's filled with 1940s bungalows, along with swanky '50s and '60s dwellings.

However, back on Las Vegas Boulevard, the scene soon degenerates south of Fremont, the street lined with shady-looking storefronts and vintage motels that do most of their business either by the hour or by the month. Among the various buildings offering quickie marriages, the angels-on-crack ceiling of the 24-hour drive-thru **Little White Wedding Chapel** (*see p256*) is worth a look. Otherwise, while the street isn't as dangerous as it looks, nor is it an especially salubrious neighbourhood.

The stretch of **Main Street** that leads south from Fremont Street all the way to Oakey Boulevard is similarly sketchy on occasion, but does offer all sorts of intriguing diversions, few of which have much in common. Pricey modern boozehouse the **Ice House** (*see p171*) sits steps away from scruffily old-fashioned Mexican eaterie **El Sombrero** (*see p157*); the low-end thrifting at **Opportunity Village** (No.921, 383 1082) sits within a stone's throw of the high-end retro duds offered at the **Attic** (*see p186*) and the card-playing, chip-tossing paraphernalia of the **Gamblers General Store** (*see p195*).

When you reach Charleston Boulevard, you'll be on the edge of the **Arts District**, loosely bordered by Charleston Boulevard, Las Vegas Boulevard, Carson Avenue and Main Street. The focal point of the area is the **Arts Factory** (www.theartsfactory.com), a block-long, two-storey 1940s building filled with galleries, artists' studios, photography studios, graphic design firms and other creative businesses. It was set up by photographer Wes Isbutt in 1997, his aim being to establish a community of creative forces, both commercial and non-profit, that would energise each other and centralise the incipient arts scene. After several false dawns, it seems to be working.

The area's at its best on **First Friday** (*see p204* **Viva Cindy Funkhouser**), when the roads around here come alive with festive cheer. Galleries and shops open into the evening and theatre groups stage special productions, while out on the streets, bands play, leather-clad terrors juggle fire and an array of street food is served to crowds that have numbered in the region of 10,000. On the other 30-odd days of the month, the scene is infinitely quieter, but there are signs of life. New galleries such as **Dust** and **Godt-Cleary Projects** (for both, *see p231*) have joined the long-standing likes of the **Funk House** (*see p182*) in bringing culture and edge to this once-downtrodden area, with some of their exhibits created by artists based in the area. Also in the area are antique and vintage stores such as **Gypsy Caravan** (1302 S 3rd Street, 868 3302), **Yana's Junk** (1229 S Casino Center Drive, 388 0051) and the **Red Rooster Antique Mall** (*see p182*). Next to the

The up-and-coming **Arts District**.

Red Rooster is Holsum Lofts, a repurposing of a loved old commercial bakery into numerous galleries, artists studios, and similarly aligned creative operations, readying for occupancy (it's almost entirely leased) in Spring 2005.

Main Street eventually curves around and meets Las Vegas Boulevard, to which it otherwise runs parallel, at the east–west Oakey Boulevard. Chow on an omelette at **Tiffany's** (*see p141*), a classically shambolic greasy spoon inside the White Cross Drugstore; try the city's greatest dessert at **Luv-It Frozen Custard** (*see p151*); and then wash it all down with a beer at venerable old bar **Dino's** (*see p169*). When you're sufficiently lubricated, two nearby adult businesses are waiting to take the dollars you didn't donate to Dino's video poker machines: the relatively high-end **Olympic Garden Cabaret** (*see p209*), which has barely clothed offerings for both men and women, and the **Talk of the Town** (*see p210* **Dirty secrets**), which caters to a rather more down-at-heel clientele.

The Rest of the City

Beyond the neon.

UNLV Barrick Museum.
See p133.

Like Los Angeles, off-Strip Las Vegas is a sprawling, unwalkable suburb made up of still-mushrooming residential developments, along with the institutions and infrastructures of a large city. Its interest to visitors lies not in any great beauty but as a reassuringly banal refuge from neon overload and a starting point for addressing the question that Vegas raises: what kind of town lies behind the neon façade? Notoriously devoid of any non-confected sense of neighbourhood or coherent town-planning, Vegas nonetheless contains trailing wisps of history, small pockets of character and defiant markers of civic identity.

Buses ply most of the suburban arteries and will usefully get you to single destinations, but are not a practical way to explore. A car is a must. Factor in time for the delays caused by the new construction work taking place in the valley, and be reassured that it's hard to get lost in a flat city that has at its centre the tallest observation tower west of the Mississippi.

The areas in this chapter are arranged clockwise, starting closest to the Strip with the University District, and finishing with the city of Henderson, further out to the south-east.

University District

Bounded roughly by Flamingo Road, Paradise Road, Tropicana Avenue and Eastern Avenue, the University District is an enclave of normality and casual academia-induced sophistication a skip from the Strip. Businesses stick mostly to Maryland Parkway, while the rest of the area is filled with apartments.

The **University of Las Vegas**, aka UNLV (4505 S Maryland Parkway, 895 3011), runs along S Maryland Parkway, where the stunning **Lied Library** (895 3531) and a beautiful desert garden (open to visitors) compete for attention. Art-lovers should check out the **UNLV Barrick Museum** (*see p133*) and the **Donna Beam Fine Arts Gallery** (*see p231*) on campus, both of which have shows by student and professional artists; the Barrick also houses a permanent natural history exhibition. A mile north of the university, sample Vegas's only Peruvian restaurant, **Inka Si Señor** (*see p161*).

Though the focus is on the university, the entire area has plenty to offer. On the south-west corner of Flamingo and Maryland you'll find the **Paymon's Mediterranean Café**

& Market (*see p163*), a local lunch favourite. Adjacent is the **Hookah Lounge** (*see p173*), an intimate, Bedouin-styled cocktail bar and one of the city's nightlife gems; across the way is the used-clothing superstore **Buffalo Exchange** (*see p186*). The striking **Clark County Library** (*see p297*) is to the east.

Along Maryland Parkway are two shopping centres filled with pizza joints, coffee houses such as **Coffee Bean & Tea Leaf** (No.4550, 944 5029), bars (**Freakin' Frog** has the best selection of beers in town, hands down; *see p170*), music stores – check out **Big B's** (*see p198*) – and tattoo and piercing studios (**Pussykat Tattoo Parlor** is one of the best; *see p198*). Any one of these places provides a great opportunity to tune into the youth culture of Las Vegas: you'll find nightclubs, poetry readings, live music and friendly natives. This is particularly true at the **Double Down Saloon** (*see p169*), easily the hippest dive in Nevada. And, in case you forgot you're in Vegas, nearby on Tropicana is the **Liberace Museum** (*see below*), as if you could have mistaken the neon-piano topped, giant-keyboard wrapped ark for anything else.

Liberace Museum

Liberace Plaza, 1775 E Tropicana Avenue, at Spencer Street (798 5595/www.liberace.org). Bus 201. Free shuttle service to Strip hotels Mon-Sat; 335 3530. **Open** 10am-5pm Mon-Sat; 1-5pm Sun. **Admission** $12.50; $8.50 seniors, students; free under-10s. **Credit** AmEx, Disc, MC, V. **Map** p317 Y3.

Unless you have a pathological aversion to camp, don't miss this place. A testament to Las Vegas's dedication to the ersatz, it's like a costume-jewellery shop run wild. On display are Mr Showmanship's rhinestones, stage jewellery, sequinned jackets, hot pants and a genuine mirrored Rolls-Royce. About 15 of his finest antique pianos are also on show, while on selected afternoons, Wes Winters' extraordinary tribute offers a taste of Liberace's music. As Las Vegas rediscovers what it once meant to be 'Vegas, baby!', this shrine to excess and bad taste is a kitschy storehouse of the city's heritage.

UNLV Barrick Museum

4505 S Maryland Parkway, between E Flamingo Road & E Tropicana Avenue (895 3381/www.unlv. edu). Bus 109, 201, 202. **Open** 8am-4.45pm Mon-Fri; 10am-2pm Sat. **Admission** free. **Map** p317 Y3.

Technically UNLV's natural history museum, the Barrick has fine permanent displays on ancient and modern Vegas, including a wonderful collection of folk-art masks. But it's also one of the city's finest art exhibition spaces: a number of excellent shows have graced its front rooms, drawing from UNLV's art faculty and regional sources. A must for any gallery crawl; call or check local listings magazines for details of current exhibitions.

Southwest Las Vegas

Southwest Las Vegas is one of the city's older, more established suburbs, and easily accessible by travelling west on Tropicana Avenue. Most of the area is unremarkable in the sense that, like much of Vegas, it consists of middle-class suburban homes surrounded by strip malls. Along Tropicana beyond I-15 is the **Orleans** (*see p102*), a locals' joint notable for its Century movie theatres (*see p229*). Further west, halfway to the mountains, are the ultra-posh custom residential developments of **Spanish Trail** and **Spanish Hills**. Many of Las Vegas's notable residents live behind the walls of these pricey, immaculate communities and, though you can't get inside, you can gaze longingly at the dramatic elevations and landscaping provided for the city's elite. Heading south at Durango leads to the stucco lookalikes in new yuppie enclave **Southern Highlands**; go north at Rainbow and you'll head through **Spring Valley**, one of the older Vegas locales. You won't see much unless you turn off, and frankly there's little point.

Northwest Las Vegas

Sahara Avenue

A couple of miles west of the Strip, Sahara hits Decatur Boulevard, and the **Sahara-Decatur Pavilions**. Here, four corners of development offer locals an afternoon's eating and shopping. Most notable is the north-east side, with food ranging from tasty Mexican at **Baja Fresh** (No.4760, 878 7772) to Persian at **Habib's** (No.4750, 870 0860). A short hop north on Decatur leads past **Trader Joe's** (*see p192*) to Westland Fair shopping centre, where you'll find the ever fashionable **Globe Salon** (*see p197*). Continuing on, you'll pass countless car dealerships and chain eateries, eventually reaching Rainbow Boulevard. This intersection was dark and nearly empty in the mid 1980s, but today it's surrounded by residential and heavy commercial development.

Further west, you'll pass **Rosemary's Restaurant** (*see p159*), consistently voted one of the best restaurants in the city, before coming to Durango Drive. This marks the beginning of the Lakes neighbourhood, where you'll find the **Mermaid Café** (2910 Lake East Drive, 240 6002), **Marché Bacchus** (*see p191*) – a perfect lunch stop on the lake – and lakeside homes with boating and fishing. Lake East Drive features a walking trail that twists through the surrounding parks, eventually dumping you out at Twain Avenue.

Sightseeing

Sahara's western reaches are home to the beautiful **Sahara West Library** (507 3630) and the adjoining **Las Vegas Art Museum** (*see p231*). The neighbouring **Village Square** has some pleasant shopping and dining outlets, and its cinema (*see p229*) is known for the art-house selections it regularly screens. At the far-western end of Sahara Avenue, nestled at the base of the mountains, lies the **Red Rock Country Club** (2466 Grassy Spring Place, 360 3100), a desert golf community a galaxy away from the Strip.

Charleston Boulevard

Charleston cuts a broad line through the city, extending westwards right out to the foothills of the mountain from which it takes its name. Along the way, it defines the southern edge of the clean and somewhat snobby enclave of Summerlin. The community incorporates housing (ranging from $100,000 condos to multimillion-dollar homes), schools, parks, churches and businesses to create a regular prefab life. The infrastructure is magnificent, but the *Truman Show* effect is disconcerting.

At **Rampart Boulevard**, development has transformed what were empty acres in the late 1990s into a bustling commercial area, including **Boca Park Fashion Village** (*see p178*), an upscale 'lifestyle center' of shops (**Ligne Roset**, **Von Dutch**) and restaurants (**Kona Grill**, **Melting Pot**) and **Rampart Commons** (*see p178*) for **Chico's**, **Banana Republic** and **Pottery Barn**. A skip north are the dual resorts of **Suncoast** (*see p103*) and the **JW Marriott Las Vegas/Rampart Casino** (*see p100*), surrounded by the green, manicured fairways of several major golf courses.

Further west, at Charleston's intersection with Town Center Drive, the Summerlin Town Center features a massive Borders, a Best Buy and a Costco across from the site of the **Red Rock Station** casino, due to open in 2006. Just east is hip salon **Moxie Studios** (*see p197*). If you head further west yet, beyond all the housing developments and across the Beltway, you'll enter open country. Past the entrance of **Red Rock Canyon** (*see p263*), you'll find an agreeable taste of the Wild West over at **Bonnie Springs/Old Nevada** (*see p264*), a 115-acre ranch that was actually an honest-to-goodness mining town back in the 1800s. For just $7-$10, a carful of visitors can mosey through the re-created town, visit a petting zoo and watch re-enactments of shootouts and public hangings. Back at Charleston's urban end, the Charleston Heights Arts Center houses one of the **City of Las Vegas Galleries** (*see p230*).

Rancho Drive

Rancho Drive offers you a different taste of old Vegas. Bordered by Oakey and Charleston Boulevards, Rancho Drive and I-15, the **Scotch 80s** are a swanky neighbourhood of large-lot homes built mostly in the 1950s and '60s. This is where Mayor Oscar Goodman resides; entertainer Shecky Greene once lived here, as did Nevada's first African-American neurosurgeon, Dr Frederick Boulware. The 80-acre enclave is only a dice throw from Downtown, yet its quiet labyrinth of tree-lined streets hides ranch-style estates and one-acre home sites with tennis courts. The gardens are beautifully tended and surprisingly lush: in the old days underground water meant the area was almost swampy.

Nearby are several notable neighbourhoods, representing more sides of old-school Las Vegas. To the south are the **Glen Heather Estates**, smallish homes with a modernist bent. West are the **McNeil Estates**, a reviving locale where young professionals are joining more established residents in a bid to restore the charming 1950s ranch-style homes.

If you continue north, you'll reach the corner of Rancho and Alta Drive. To the west is **Rancho Nevada** and just north is **Rancho Circle**, perhaps the city's most exclusive old district; BB King lived here, Bob Stupak and Phyllis McGuire still do. Continuing north on Rancho and cutting under US 95 will bring you into some of the city's oldest districts. On your way, you'll pass the 180-acre **Las Vegas Springs Preserve** (www.lvspringspreserve. org). Loosely bordered by US 95, Valley View Boulevard and Alta Drive, this is the largest area of undeveloped land in the central city. Also known as Big Springs, this is where legendary Old West explorers Kit Carson and John Fremont parked their horses in the mid 1800s. Huge cottonwoods and natural scrub fill the area, surrounding an early 19th-century well house, and wild animals – including coyotes and foxes – roam behind the freeway fencing. The land has survived both fire and the threat of being paved over in the name of freeway expansion; it's now been restored for a 2005 opening as the **Central Park of Las Vegas**, for the city's centennial.

The primarily African-American area of **West Las Vegas** spreads out north-east from Bonanza Road. Here you'll find the long-closed **Moulin Rouge** (900 W Bonanza Road), Las Vegas's first interracial casino. In the bad old days, when Las Vegas was disparagingly called 'the Mississippi of the West', hotels forced African-American entertainers to flee the Strip after showtime. Performers including Nat King Cole and Sammy Davis Jr sought refuge at the

Moulin Rouge, generating a short-lived but legendary stint of after-hours performances that drew Frank Sinatra and other white Strip players to the hotel-casino. It was at the Rouge in 1960 that casino bosses signed an agreement ending the city's racial segregation. Many plans to revive this historic landmark have been derailed; most recently, in June 2003, the casino, nearly restored, was gutted by a suspicious fire. Bone up more on the history of black Las Vegas at the **West Las Vegas Library** (951 W Lake Mead Boulevard, 507 3980), where collections highlight the achievements of African-American Nevadans.

Also here, east of Rancho Drive at Tonopah Drive, is **Binion Ranch**, the property of the legendary gambling family who launched – and, until recently, owned – **Binion's** (*see p97*). Family patriarch Benny Binion once lived in this long-boarded-up two-storey block-and-timber ranch house and, as recently as the 1990s, horses and cattle were still kept on the property. Although it didn't occur here, the murder in 1998 of Lonnie 'Ted' Binion has invested the ranch with even greater historical significance.

To the west of Rancho Drive are Twin Lakes and **Lorenzi Park**. The park has sports facilities and is the site of the **Nevada State Museum & Historical Society** (*see below*), with good displays on the history of the region. Further north, a turn west at Vegas Drive leads you past the **Southern Nevada Zoological Park** (*see below*) to the palatial home of master illusionists Siegfried & Roy. It's on the north side and certainly quite gracious, though you can't see much. Look for the white adobe walls and the wrought-iron gate bearing the initials S and R. Tiger Woods-wannabes can try out their skills at the good-value **Las Vegas Golf Club** (*see p248*) just across the road, while budding Schumachers might want to try the **Las Vegas Mini Gran Prix** (*see p226*).

Rancho Drive continues in a north-westerly direction past North Las Vegas Airport and the **Texas Station** (*see p105*), **Fiesta Rancho** (*see p103*) and **Santa Fe Station** casinos (*see p105*), en route to the outdoor attractions of **Floyd Lamb State Park** and **Mount Charleston** (*see pp264-265*). Five years ago much of this area was empty desert; today, the relentless stucco has engulfed everything from the State Park to the old Vegas restaurant **Bob Taylor's Ranch House** (*see p157*).

Nevada State Museum & Historical Society

Lorenzi Park, 700 Twin Lakes Drive, at Washington Avenue (486 5205/http://dmla.clan.lib.nv.us/docs/museums/lv/vegas.htm). Bus 108, 204. **Open** 9am-5pm daily. **Admission** $2; free under-18s. **No credit cards. Map** p317 X1.

The Nevada State Museum has permanent exhibits on the natural and anthropological history of the region, from ancient Paiute Indians to 19th-century pioneers and the men and women of the Nellis Gunnery School in World War II. The standout exhibit tells the story of Bugsy Siegel's Flamingo, complete with interactive recordings of Bugsy (played by an actor) threatening business partners.

Southern Nevada Zoological Park

1775 N Rancho Drive, between Vegas Drive & Lake Mead Boulevard (648 5955/www.lasvegaszoo.org). Bus 106, 208, 209. **Open** 9am-5pm daily. **Admission** $6.50; $4.50-$6 concessions; free under-2s. **Credit** AmEx, MC, V. **Map** p317 X1.

This will never be confused with the Bronx or San Diego zoos, but it contains an interesting collection of reptiles and birds indigenous to the state of Nevada, as well as a variety of endangered cats and the last family of Barbary apes in the US. The park also has a coati exhibit (it's a racoon-like animal), botanical displays of endangered palms and rare bamboos, and a children's petting zoo.

North Las Vegas

After suffering years of disrespect, North Las Vegas, a city unto itself, has experienced a limited renaissance, a result of the tremendous growth in the valley as a whole. African-American, Asian and Mexican residents have moved in as Anglos have moved out, turning the area into a melting pot of ethnicities. It is also the main campus of the **Community College of Southern Nevada** (which has a great planetarium; *see p136*).

New homes and shops have sprung up to fill previously undeveloped land north of Craig Road (between Rancho Drive and I-15), creating an area of new development known as the **Golden Triangle** that's on a par with pricier Northwest Las Vegas. In reality, the shiny new Golden Triangle seems somewhat removed from most of North Las Vegas, a working-class city that grew from the Nellis Air Force Base to the north-east; indeed, the areas are physically separated from one another by the interstate.

The older area, largely untouched by redevelopment, carries more of the historical and urban flavour of a modern city than does the city of Las Vegas proper. A good way to reach these parts is to turn off either US 95 or Rancho Drive at Craig Road, heading east. A southward turn at Las Vegas Boulevard North, leading back towards Downtown, will take you past **Jerry's Nugget** casino (No.1821, 399 3000), famous for the freshly baked cakes and pies available 24 hours a day in its coffee shop, plus numerous ethnic eateries (**El Sombrero Café**, *see p157*, is one of the city's best places for Mexican food), the historic public **Forest**

Get rich, quick: it's **Lake Las Vegas**.

Lawn Cemetery, the only one of its kind in the city, and the **Las Vegas Paiute Indian Reservation** (1 Paiute Drive, 386 3926). Now surrounded by metropolitan Las Vegas, this small reservation with its smoke shop represents the original ten acres deeded to the Paiute by Helen Stewart back in the 1900s. A much larger reservation at Snow Mountain, north-west of Vegas, incorporates the **Las Vegas Paiute Golf Club** (10325 Nu-Wav Kaiv Boulevard, 658 1400).

Planetarium

Community College of Southern Nevada, 3200 E Cheyenne Avenue, between Las Vegas Boulevard North & Van Der Meer Street (651 4759/www.ccsn. nevada.edu/planetarium). Bus 110. **Shows** 6pm, 7.30pm Fri; 3.30pm, 7.30pm Sat. **Admission** $4; $2.50 concessions. **Credit** AmEx, Disc, MC, V.
Stargazers will enjoy the presentations in this small cinema with its 360° screen. After the day's last performance, you can also scan the sky through the planetarium's telescopes (weather permitting).

East Las Vegas

East Las Vegas is a large and slightly older section of town, once characterised by ugly quick-build housing tracts and trailer parks, but unable – and, in all likelihood, unwilling – to avoid the incursion of new development. At the far eastern end of the valley is Frenchman's Mountain, commonly known as **Sunrise Mountain**. Here, in the 1960s and '70s, the independently minded rich who had declined spots in the Scotch 80s built modern desert homes with pools and panoramic views of the

city. Following their lead, most new housing development in this area has been focused on and around Sunrise Mountain.

Closer to town, south of Sahara Avenue, is the **John S Park Historic District**, the only neighbourhood in the city to boast such a designation. At Maryland Parkway, you're within walking distance of the old **Commercial Center**, which has numerous ethnic restaurants and groceries, plus some boutiques, gay bars and swingers' clubs. Go south at Maryland to see historic **Bishop Gorman Catholic High School** (No.1801, 732 1945), a central Las Vegas landmark that's planning to abandon the city for Summerlin, a remarkably unpleasant example of 'white flight'. Further south is the popular **Boulevard Mall** (*see p178*), behind which is the modernist **Paradise Palms**, another old neighbourhood at the earliest stages of revival.

Following Fremont Street away from Downtown to the south-east eventually leads to **Boulder City** (*see p261*). At No.2504 is the long-closed (despite being listed on the National Register of Historic Places) **Green Shack** restaurant. In continuous operation from the 1930s until July 1999, the Green Shack evokes decades of memories: construction workers building Hoover Dam stopped by here; politicos lunched within its walls; even Bugsy Siegel ate here. But history is yesterday and, in Vegas, yesterday is long gone. The building is a sad and empty shell awaiting an unknown future.

South of Sahara, Fremont Street becomes Boulder Highway, along which you'll find a handful of locals' casinos, including **Arizona**

Charlie's (*see p101*). Catch a movie at **Boulder Station** (*see p103*) and, if you're in town in December, don't miss the Christmas lights at **Sam's Town** (*see p103*). Shortly after, a turn down Tropicana Avenue (or an interstate ride from town) takes you east to the **Acacia Desert Demonstration Gardens** (50 Casa Del Fuego Street, 267 4265), where you can explore gardens and wetlands dedicated to animal habitats.

Green Valley & Henderson

The history of Henderson and Green Valley is a tale of two cities within two cities. Founded in 1941 as a company town housing employees of the then-new Basic Magnesium Plant, **Henderson** developed a reputation as an industrial town. Today, some manufacturing continues, notably at **Ethel M Chocolates** (*see p138*), which offers tours. The city also boasts its original downtown area, urban community centres and one of Southern Nevada's newest and most dynamic suburban developments.

Lake Las Vegas is a high-dollar resort community with hotels, residential properties and golf courses surrounding a vast man-made lake that empties into Lake Mead. Set in a desert environment of various elevations, homes start at a chilly half-million dollars; opulent but somewhat obscene, for environmentalists at least. The **Hyatt Regency** (*see p100*) and **Ritz-Carlton** (*see p108*) hotels offer the Strip's **Four Seasons** (*see p105*) some serious competition in the ultra-luxe casino-free lodgings sector. The **MonteLago Village** is a nicely done village walk with tiny boutiques,

restaurants and a wine bar dotting the way down to the lake. In the summer, bring a blanket and watch as musicians take to the floating marina. At the eastern end, **Casino MonteLago** (8 Strada di Villaggio, 1-877 553 3555) and its winery theme beckon.

Inside Henderson proper, just west of Boulder Highway at Lake Mead Boulevard, the historic Water Street was, in better times, the city's main thoroughfare. It's now mostly utility offices, banks and a few bars, with the **City of Lights Gallery** (No.26, 260 0300) one of the few gems. Made up of members of a local artists' collective, the gallery's collection includes watercolours, sculpture and original prints and is the first step in Henderson Redevelopment Agency's push for a downtown arts district. Whether or not the **Ron Lee Gallery** (7665 Commercial Way, Suite A, 1-800 829 3928, www.ronlee.com) would make the artistic cut is a moot point, but as 'the 'world's largest collection of limited edition clown scuptures' it is certainly an institution. The clowns are made here in town to the tune of 50,000 a year. Also worth a look if you're in Henderson is the **Clark County Heritage Museum** (*see p138*). It's a long way from town, but handy for combining with an excursion to the Hoover Dam and Boulder City further to the south-east.

Green Valley, north-west of Henderson and separated from it by US 95 (though technically still a part of the city), was the valley's first master-planned community. Like Summerlin, it's home to a massive corporate development of homes in all price ranges, plus shops, schools, parks and more. So many Green Valley dwellers hail from Southern California that it's often referred to as 'Little LA'; some have even taken to wearing shirts emblazoned 'Green Valley 89014', a take on TV series *Beverly Hills 90210* (although expansion has been so rapid that it's taken over 89074 as well). Locals here participate in and provide financial support for numerous cultural activities in their neighbourhood. Ethnic eateries, creative businesses and community cultural events survive and thrive here, creating a sense of community synergy of which others in the metropolis are undoubtedly envious.

The stylish, high-tone **Green Valley Ranch** (*see p104*) is the subdivision's best accomplishment, with bars, a day spa and a comfortable casino. In the summertime, the resort's outdoor pool area – which flaunts bocce courts and a design by Michael Czyz, also credited with Lenny Kravitz's home – hosts headliner and local jazz band concerts at its amphitheatre. The **District** strip mall is filled with scads of restaurants and shops. Across from here is the new **Henderson Pavilion**, an outdoor performing arts facility that hosts **Shakespeare in the Park** and the **Vegas Valley Book Festival** (for both, *see p206*). South on Green Valley Parkway is **Anthem**, an over-the-top country club community that introduces the absurdist notion of gated neighbourhoods within gated neighbourhoods.

In the older section of Green Valley, visit the **Green Valley Town Center**, a mall and plaza in the north-west corner of Sunset at Green Valley Parkway, for a perfect example of the area's community focus. The north-east side is home to **Café Sensations** (456 7803), a great mom-and-pop coffeeshop, pub and restaurant that serves up meatloaf sandwiches. Behind it is **Barley's** (458 2739), a micro brewery and casino with plenty of plasma TVs ready for sports viewing. The **Galleria Mall** (434 0202) lies east on Sunset Road, and across the street is **Sunset Station** (*see p105*), a neighbourhood casino with a fabulous, Gaudi-inspired bar. Heading west on Sunset leads past the newish **Ambiance Bistro** (*see p159*), Wayne Newton's home (at the south-west corner of Russell Road) and the huge **Sunset Park** (at Eastern Avenue, 455 8200), with picnic sites, grills and games courts.

Clark County Heritage Museum

1830 S Boulder Highway, between Horizon Drive & Wagon Wheel Avenue (455 7955/www.co.clark.nv.us/ Parks/Clark_County_Museum.htm). Bus 107. **Open** 9am-4.30pm daily. **Admission** $1.50; $1 concessions; free under-3s. **Credit** MC, V.
Long before Las Vegas was a resort mecca, it was just another Western railroad town. Here you'll find an assortment of exhibits relating to Southern Nevada's past: a recreated city street featuring historic area homes with period furnishings, a 'timeline' mural and a 1918 Union Pacific steam engine.

Ethel M Chocolates

2 Cactus Garden Drive, at Sunset Way & Mountain Vista Street (458 8864/www.ethelm.com). Bus 217. **Open** 8.30am-7pm daily. **Admission** free.
Major chocolate-producer Ethel M offers self-guided factory tours complete with samples. To offset any feelings of overindulgence, it also has an environmentally aware cactus garden and a fascinating 'living machine', showing how plants can recycle wastewater. Here at the holidays? Check out the gardens, bedecked in millions of lights (*see p207*).

Ethel M Chocolates.

Eat, Drink, Shop

Restaurants & Buffets

Lose dollars in the casino. Put on pounds at the dinner table.

Eat, Drink, Shop

Las Vegas's unfailing talent for self-publicity doesn't always work in the city's favour, but when it has something with which to back up its relentless hype machine, it's a force few can resist. There's no greater example of this than the change in Las Vegas's eating scene over the last decade or so, and the town's ceaseless but justifiable boasting about its improvement.

For decades, dining in Las Vegas consisted of steakhouses, coffee shops and – most famously – the all-you-can-eat buffets, vast filling stations at which Midwestern vacation-makers could trick themselves into believing they were getting great value for money before wandering off and dropping $200 at the blackjack table. But with the arrival of the Mirage in 1989, and the subsequent regeneration of the Strip, came a sea-change in the way Las Vegas ate. Star chefs, most notably Wolfgang Puck and Emeril Lagasse, came from all over the world to launch their own restaurants, courted by casino moguls desperate to impress both customers and business rivals. The increased international presence in Vegas was reflected in a far wider array of cuisines. But the greatest change was not in image but in quality: for the first time, dining became an exciting part of a trip to Vegas, rather than just something one did to line the stomach before gorging on Martinis.

Of course, the circuit isn't perfect. Many of the star chefs who've lent their names and/or reputations to restaurants in the city don't cook here; this isn't to say the food in such eateries is necessarily bad (it rarely is), more that it'll often cost a little more than it should. A few places on the Strip seem to have expended all their creative energies on interior design and saved none for the kitchen, but such places rarely survive: fashion changes with the wind, and restaurants that come to the table with style but no substance will be found out. And while the resorts on the Strip do now contain a huge number of restaurants high in both class and quality, there's still a good deal of mediocrity: overpriced steakhouses, inauthentic Chinese eateries, dreary breakfast bars.

But on the whole, the quality of food on the Strip is remarkably high. In most cities, restaurateurs are generally content to keep up with the Joneses. In Vegas, a town that offers the purest distillations of both capitalism and showmanship on Earth, the casino moguls demand that they not only edge ahead of the Joneses, but knock them into submission. The scene here changes weekly; with the arrival of **Wynn Las Vegas** (*see p142* **Every one's a Wynner**), things are sure to improve further.

Away from the bright lights of the Strip, things are less consistent but, if you know where to look, often impressive. Carnivores are well served by a fine array of steakhouses and barbecue joints; a handful of excellent low-key, high-value Asian restaurants sit tucked away in unlikely strip-mall locations; and there's even a plethora of Middle Eastern eateries. Follow the recommendations in this chapter, and you can't go far wrong.

Burger Bar.
See p141.

PRACTICALITIES

The ebb and flow of visitors in and out of Las Vegas is so unpredictable that reservations, while not always necessary, are nonetheless recommended for all major Strip restaurants listed here. Weekends are inevitably busy, but many eateries also do a brisk trade during the week, thanks mainly to the regular influx of conventioneers. Away from the Strip, you'd do well to book for Friday and Saturday nights. Aside from some special Sunday feeds (such as the **Sterling Brunch** at Bally's, *see p163*), the casino buffets don't accept reservations; prepare to queue at busy times.

Vegas is a casual town, and few restaurants enforce a dress code that moves much beyond an insistence on shoes and a shirt. You should be all right if you employ common sense: you can get away with almost any uniform at the **Burger Bar** (*see p141*), but men would do well to wear a jacket when dining at **Picasso** (*see p145*). If in doubt, ask when you make your reservation, or check online.

The Strip

American & steakhouses

Aureole
Mandalay Bay *3950 Las Vegas Boulevard South, at E Hacienda Avenue (632 7401/www.aureolelas vegas.com).* Bus 105, 301. **Open** 6-11pm daily. **Set menu** $69-$85. **Credit** AmEx, Disc, MC, V. **Hotel** p67. **Map** p320 A9.
Vegas is full of dramatic restaurants, but nowhere else can you dine overlooking a swan-filled lagoon or within sight of a four-storey, 4,500-bottle wine tower, up and down which float harnessed wine angels. The food, orchestrated by Charlie Palmer and overseen by Vincent Pouessel, is also a delight, with seasonal American dishes including roasted rack of venison and pan-seared John Dory filet. Executive Pastry Chef Megan Romano's ethereal sweets – milk chocolate hazelnut parfait and cinnamon doughnuts with apple strudel – are worth the calories.

Bradley Ogden
Caesars Palace *3750 Las Vegas Boulevard South, at W Flamingo Road (731 7410/www.caesars.com).* Bus 202, 301, 302. **Open** 5-11pm daily. **Main courses** $33-$175. **Credit** AmEx, DC, Disc, MC, V. **Hotel** p65. **Map** p320 A7.
Ogden's cultivated close relationships with region-al suppliers and boutique growers in the US, with everything from Utah salt to Oregon seafood is purchased from special suppliers. The result is a distinctly American cuisine that doesn't come cheap, but if melt-in-your-mouth Sonoma lamb shanks or butter-braised lobster with sweetbreads ring your bell, consider this an essential stop. The best part of all? Ogden sticks around to cook it.

Burger Bar
Mandalay Bay (Mandalay Place) *3950 Las Vegas Boulevard South, at E Hacienda Avenue (632 9364/www.mandalaybay.com).* Bus 105, 301. **Open** 10.30am-11pm Mon-Thur, Sun; 10am-1am Fri, Sat. **Main courses** $8-$60. **Credit** AmEx, DC, Disc, MC, V. **Hotel** p67. **Map** p320 A9.
This restaurant, which reinvents the eponymous American classic in terms of both food and design, gets expensive in a hurry: by the time you've added a couple of toppings, you're looking at ten bucks, and that's before you've even thought about the fries or the (stellar) milkshakes. Still, it's worth it: the meat is immaculate, the service is quick (but not suspiciously so) and the process of stuffing yourself in such a chic environment is an enjoyable novelty.

Charlie Palmer Steak
Four Seasons Las Vegas *3960 Las Vegas Boulevard South, at E Hacienda Avenue (632 5120/www.charliepalmersteak.com).* Bus 105, 301. **Open** 5.30-10.30pm daily. **Main courses** $24-$42. **Credit** AmEx, DC, Disc, MC, V. **Hotel** p105. **Map** p320 A9.
Every upscale steakhouse chain in America has an outpost in Vegas, but Charlie Palmer stays a couple of cuts above by offering unique twists on the steak-spuds-seafood genre, thanks to resident Executive Chef Joe Romano. Entrées such as shell steak, veal porterhouse, Kansas City ribeye and truffled chicken please even jaded palates; Romano's wife Megan is a whiz with desserts.

Craftsteak
MGM Grand *3799 Las Vegas Boulevard South, at E Tropicana Avenue (891 7318/www.mgmgrand.com).* Bus 201, 301, 302. **Open** 5.30-10.30pm daily. **Main courses** $28-$200. **Credit** AmEx, DC, Disc, MC, V. **Hotel** p80. **Map** p320 A8.
You'll come once for the fine selection of meats (grass-fed veal, lamb shank, filet mignon), but you'll return for the sides (charcuterie sampler with pretzel bread-sticks and gourmet mustards, roasted chanterelles, white truffle-purée potatoes and butternut squash

The best Restaurants

For a sensual breakfast
Bouchon. *See p144*.

For a decadent brunch
Sterling Brunch at Bally's. *See p163*.

For a hearty lunch
Burger Bar. *See p141*.

For a high-class dinner
Picasso. *See p145*.

For the 4am munchies
Mr Lucky's 24/7. *See p152*.

Eat, Drink, Shop

agnolotti). Tom Colicchio and Chef de Cuisine Chris Albrecht, who also oversees 'Wichcraft (*see p143*), use only ingredients from 'small family farms, artisanal producers and day-boat fishermen'.

Delmonico Steakhouse

Venetian *3355 Las Vegas Boulevard South, at Sands Avenue (414 3737/www.emerils.com). Bus 203, 213, 301, 302.* **Open** 11.30am-2pm, 5.30-10.30pm Mon-Thur, Sun; 11.30am-2pm, 5.30-11pm Fri, Sat. **Main courses** $14-$44 lunch; $27-$80 dinner. **Credit** AmEx, Disc, MC, V. **Hotel** p73. **Map** p320 A6.
Emeril Lagasse's Cajun take on the steakhouse is a gem: the simple but exquisite steaks aren't easily topped, and neither is the elegantly detailed room or the heralded wine list. Of course, with Lagasse in charge, there's more here than beef: though it's hard to take your eyes off the bone-in ribeye, other favourites include sauté of Gulf shrimp with fresh pasta, and grilled pork chops with bacon-wrapped shrimp, which come with bourbon-smashed sweet potatoes and Emeril's own Worcestershire sauce.

ESPN Zone

New York–New York *3790 Las Vegas Boulevard South, at W Tropicana Avenue (933 3776/www.espnzone.com/lasvegas). Bus 201, 301, 302.* **Open** 11.30am-12.30am Mon-Thur; 11.30am-1.30am Fri; 11am-1.30am Sat; 11am-12.30am Sun; last seating 90mins before closing. **Main courses** $6-$9. **Credit** AmEx, Disc, MC, V. **Hotel** p83. **Map** p320 A8.
The sports-themed ESPN Zone is rapidly becoming the most popular themed entertainment chain in the US. A family-friendly, hyper-sized combination of a restaurant, sports bar and games arcade, the Zone is a Middle American wet dream: a non-challenging menu of big bar-food portions, big-screen sports, big glasses of beer and a big games room. It's madness on college football Saturdays and NFL Sundays.

Fix

Bellagio *3600 Las Vegas Boulevard South, at W Flamingo Road (693 8400/www.bellagio.com). Bus 202, 301, 302.* **Open** 5pm-midnight Mon-Thur, Sun; 5pm-2am Fri, Sat. **Main courses** $30-$60. **Credit** AmEx, DC, Disc, MC, V. **Hotel** p63. **Map** p320 A7.
Representing a new trend among scene eateries, Fix – operated by Light, *see p242* – opens its dark, modern interior to the casino floor rather than secluding itself or its cast of primping diners, who would be just as much at home at Simon or N9ne. An upscale, wood-fired surf 'n' turf menu features some too-rich variations of pasta, but everyone should try the 'forks': smoked salmon and caviar appetisers.

House of Blues

Mandalay Bay *3950 Las Vegas Boulevard South, at E Hacienda Avenue (632 7600/www.hob.com). Bus 105, 301.* **Open** 7.30am-midnight Mon-Thur, Sun; 7.30am-1am Fri, Sat. **Main courses** $9-$28. **Credit** AmEx, DC, Disc, MC, V. **Hotel** p67. **Map** p320 A9.
Quite apart from its role as one of the premier music venues in the city, this chain operates a successful restaurant. The menu's a curious and sometimes rather directionless mix of cuisines: the expected burgers and steaks are supplemented by some more distinctive Nawleens-inflected dishes (gumbo, catfish) and even a little barbecue. Sundays, there's a terrific gospel brunch buffet. Hallelujah!

Olives

Bellagio *3600 Las Vegas Boulevard South, at W Flamingo Road (693 8181/www.bellagio.com). Bus 202, 301, 302.* **Open** 11am-2.30pm, 5-10.30pm daily. **Main courses** $15-$22 lunch; $20-$38 dinner. **Credit** AmEx, DC, Disc, MC, V. **Hotel** p63. **Map** p320 A7.
A recent remodel to something more clubby and a menu revamp away from a Mediterranean influence and towards new American cuisine has made this

Every one's a Wynner

As this guide went to press, **Wynn Las Vegas** (*see p75*) opened. As with the rest of the operation, little if any expense has been spared on its dining options, with Wynn calling in some of the biggest names in American cuisine to run his eateries. What you see is what you get: all the names attached to the resort's restaurants will be cooking in them. For all Wynn Las Vegas venues, reservations can be made on 1-888 320 7110 or 770 9966. *See also p155* **Viva Elizabeth Blau**. A few of the potential culinary highlights:

Alex: Alessandro Stratta, who formerly worked with Wynn as the Executive Chef at the Mirage's now-defunct Renoir, has been lured back to Vegas by his former boss to provide a menu of treats from the French Riviera.

Bartolotta Ristorante di Mare: Only his location – he's been based in the Midwest for most of his career – has prevented Paul Bartolotta from achieving celebrity. His arrival in Vegas to open this seafood-heavy Italian restaurant may change things.

Chocolat: Much-garlanded pâtissier Frédéric Robert promises a devilishly tempting array of sweet treats.

Daniel Boulud Brasserie: New York City's favourite chef heads to Vegas for the first time to open a traditional French eathouse.

SW Steakhouse: Hot-shot young French-born chef Eric Klein anchors this eatery, fusing a traditional steakhouse experience (every casino must have one) with flavours from his home country.

Bellagio brother to Todd English's Boston eateries slightly less accessible. The crispy flatbreads stayed, but new entrées include Alaskan halibut over fava beans, crab-stuffed trout, and oven-roasted chicken.

Prime

Bellagio *3600 Las Vegas Boulevard South, at W Flamingo Road (693 7223/www.bellagio.com).* *Bus 202, 301, 302.* **Open** 5.30-10pm daily. **Main courses** $25-$48. **Credit** AmEx, DC, Disc, MC, V. **Hotel** p63. **Map** p320 A7.

Prime indeed. In fact, one could go further: first class, superior and pre-eminent pretty much sum up Jean-Georges Vongerichten's steakhouse, whose striking setting comes with a perfect view of the Bellagio's fountains. There's magic on the plate, too: prime steak is the highlight, but don't overlook the free-range chicken, seared ahi tuna, wood-grilled veal chop and a choice of 11 sauces and seven mustards.

Smith & Wollensky

3767 Las Vegas Boulevard South, between E Tropicana Avenue & E Harmon Avenue (862 4100/ www.smithandwollensky.com). Bus 201, 301, 302. **Open** 5pm-midnight daily. *Grill* 11.30am-3am daily. **Main courses** $30-$45. **Credit** AmEx, DC, Disc, MC, V. **Map** p320 A8.

Another New York City steakhouse clone: steer and spuds rule in this 500-seat, three-storey restaurant next to the MGM Grand. The crowds that pack the place nightly don't seem to mind the noise, but locals prefer the outdoor patio in the downstairs café for a lunch that's more sedate but just as meaty.

Steak House

Circus Circus *2880 Las Vegas Boulevard South, between W Sahara Avenue & Stardust Road (794 3767/www.circuscircus.com). Bus 301.* **Open** 5-10pm Mon-Fri, Sun; 5-11pm Sat. **Main courses** $28-$38. **Credit** AmEx, DC, Disc, MC, V. **Hotel** p85. **Map** p319 B5.

The casino in which it's housed neuters some of the sophistication, but this is still a fine choice if you've a yen for a large lump of dead cow. The steaks here are aged for 21 days and then mesquite-grilled (more so than usual, order rare or miss out on some of the flavour), all at prices well below those of other beef emporia along the Strip.

'Wichcraft

MGM Grand *3799 Las Vegas Boulevard South, at E Tropicana Avenue (891 3166/www.mgmgrand. com). Bus 201, 301, 302.* **Open** 10am-6pm daily. **Main courses** $6-$9. **Credit** AmEx, DC, Disc, MC, V. **Hotel** p80. **Map** p320 A8.

Tom Colicchio's over-excited little sibling to Craftsteak (*see p141*) succeeds at giving credibility to both boring old sandwiches and the idea of (faster) food. Walk up to the counter for sophisticated and pricey variations on the theme, from the meatloaf sandwich with cheddar, bacon and tomato relish on ciabatta roll, to grilled broccoli rabe, roasted peppers, black olives, caramelised onions and mozzarella on baguette. Breakfast is served all day.

Cajun & creole

Commander's Palace

Aladdin/Planet Hollywood (Desert Passage) *3663 Las Vegas Boulevard South, at E Harmon Avenue (892 8272/www.commanderspalace.com). Bus 301.* **Open** 9am-10pm daily. **Main courses** $16-$25 lunch; $25-$39 dinner. **Credit** AmEx, DC, Disc, MC, V. **Hotel** p76. **Map** p320 A7.

The seafood-heavy Creole menu of New Orleans' Brennan family travelled well to this comfortable desert room. Big Easy favourites such as Louisiana pecan-crusted fish are slightly toned down, but without compromising on flavour. Don't deny yourself dessert: the Brennans invented bananas Foster, and the Creole bread-pudding soufflé is ridiculously good.

Emeril Lagasse's New Orleans Fish House

MGM Grand *3799 Las Vegas Boulevard South, at E Tropicana Avenue (891 7374/www.emerils.com). Bus 201, 301, 302.* **Open** 11.30am-2.30pm, 5.30-10.30pm daily. **Main courses** $22-$40 lunch; $27-$60 dinner. **Credit** AmEx, DC, Disc, MC, V. **Hotel** p80. **Map** p320 A8.

In honour of his signature Vegas restaurant's 10th birthday, Food Network superstar Emeril Lagasse kicked the place up a notch: more sophisticated decor, a new wine tower and an oyster bar. The menu has a few added attractions, but you can still get the New Orleans chef's greatest seafood hits, including pecan-crusted Texas redfish. Whatever you pick for an entrée, save room for one of the best desserts on the Strip: Emeril's banana cream pie.

Chinese

China Grill

Mandalay Bay *3950 Las Vegas Boulevard South, at E Hacienda Avenue (632 7404/www.mandalay bay.com). Bus 105, 301.* **Open** 5-11pm Mon-Thur, Sun; 5pm-midnight Fri, Sat. **Main courses** $25-$35. **Credit** AmEx, DC, MC, V. **Hotel** p67. **Map** p320 A9.

The ultra-mod decor makes this restaurant worth a looksee. Even if you just drop by for a pre- or post-dinner cocktail in the chic lounge, be sure to check out the washrooms: see-through, unisex, igloo-esque pods, each with its own small TV screen. Stay for dinner and feast family-style on such appetisers as lamb spare ribs and crackling calamares salad, entrées including Shanghai lobster, barbecued salmon and grilled, dry-aged Sichuan beef, and sides such as wasabi mashed potatoes and duck fried rice.

Royal Star

Venetian *3355 Las Vegas Boulevard South, at Sands Avenue (414 1888/www.venetian.com). Bus 203, 213, 301, 302.* **Open** 11am-3pm, 5-11pm daily. **Main courses** $3-$7 lunch; $15-$38 dinner. **Credit** AmEx, DC, Disc, MC, V. **Hotel** p73. **Map** p320 A6.

Californian restaurateur Kevin Wu brought his distinctive, upmarket Chinese cuisine to the Venetian in 1999. Open for lunch, tea and dinner, the Royal

Eat, Drink, Shop

Star will satisfy those who want an exquisite dim sum snack as well as flash hosts spending an entire evening in the ornate private dining rooms. Live lobster, shrimp, scallops and crab are kept in tanks on site until the chefs turn them into classic Cantonese and Mandarin dishes.

French & Mediterranean

Bouchon

Venetian *3355 Las Vegas Boulevard South, at Sands Avenue (414 6200/www.venetian.com). Bus 105, 203, 213, 301, 302.* **Open** 7am-11pm daily. **Main courses** $8-$22 breakfast; $17-$33 lunch/dinner. **Credit** AmEx, Disc, MC, V. **Hotel** p73. **Map** p320 A6.
Inside this bistro and oyster bar in the Venezia Tower, much-garlanded chef Thomas Keller serves authentic French country fare modelled after the original Bouchons of Lyon. The restaurant also has poolside seating in the gardens, where you can indulge in Bouchon French toast served bread-pudding style with warm layers of brioche, custard and fresh fruit topped with maple syrup for breakfast, or the truite aux amandes, pan-roasted trout with almonds, brown butter and haricots verts for dinner. Either way, get the three-piece cheese tasting with honeycomb for dessert.

Café Ba Ba Reeba

Fashion Show Mall, 3200 Las Vegas Boulevard South, at W Spring Mountain Road (258 1211/www.cafebabareeba.com). Bus 203, 301. **Open** 11.30am-11pm Mon-Thur, Sun; 11.30am-midnight Fri, Sat. **Main courses** $5-$33. **Credit** AmEx, DC, Disc, MC, V. **Map** p320 A/B6.
The menu suggests that this might not be the quietest spot on the Strip, and so it proves: as is the case with its Chicago sibling, Café Ba Ba Reeba is a lively spot, especially if you're in a group. It's run by the people behind Mon Ami Gabi (*see p145*); the Spanish theming here, in terms of both food and design, is similarly inauthentic but just as enjoyable. Great Spanish restaurants are hard to find in the US. This isn't one, but it's pretty good.

Le Cirque

Bellagio *3600 Las Vegas Boulevard South, at W Flamingo Road (693 7223/www.bellagio.com). Bus 202, 301, 302.* **Open** 5.30-10pm daily. **Set menu** $95 5 courses. **Credit** AmEx, DC, Disc, MC, V. **Hotel** p63. **Map** p320 A7.
This Vegas version of restaurateur Sirio Maccioni's famed New York establishment serves the same classic French fare with contemporary influences as the original: 'Le Cirque' lobster salad with black truffle dressing, braised beef short ribs and grilled monkfish tournedos, here delivered by talented, young chef Jeremy Lieb. Both are housed in fine hotels, the Bellagio in Vegas and the Palace Hotel in New York. Both were designed by Adam Tihany. But only one offers views of dancing waters on a man-made lake choreographed to Sinatra's 'Luck Be a Lady'.

Drai's

Barbary Coast *3595 Las Vegas Boulevard South, at E Flamingo Road (737 0555/www.draislasvegas. com). Bus 202, 301, 302.* **Open** 5.30-10pm daily. **Main courses** $18-$37. **Credit** AmEx, MC, V. **Hotel** p85. **Map** p320 A7.
Victor Drai's restaurant offers a sophisticated four-section dining area and some serious Mediterranean cuisine. The menu features such gourmet treasures as seven-hour leg of lamb, baked Maine salmon with lobster mousse in puff pastry, and a sensuous hot chocolate soufflé. After midnight from Wednesday to Sunday, stop for dancing, music, mingling and some extraordinary dining specials during Drai's After Hours, which lasts until the sun comes up.

Eiffel Tower Restaurant

Paris Las Vegas *3655 Las Vegas Boulevard South, at E Flamingo Road (948 6937/www.paris-lv.com). Bus 202, 301, 302.* **Open** 5-10pm Mon-Thur, Sun; 5-11pm Fri, Sat. **Main courses** $30-$51. **Credit** AmEx, DC, Disc, MC, V. **Hotel** p69. **Map** p320 A7.
The food – lamb, foie gras, braised quail, which is to say high-class French dishes with subtle twists – doesn't live up to the location, but then how could it? Eleven floors above the Strip in the Eiffel Tower (with great views of the Bellagio's fountains) and designed with a beautifully modern sophistication, it's a stunner. The prices reflect this state of affairs, with lobster thermidor at an outrageous $51. But then this is more about occasion than cuisine.

Fleur de Lys

Mandalay Bay *3950 Las Vegas Boulevard South, at E Hacienda Avenue (632 9400/www.mandalay bay.com). Bus 105, 301.* **Open** 5.30-10.30pm daily. **Set menus** $68 3 courses; $76 4 courses; $88 5 courses. **Credit** AmEx, DC, Disc, MC, V. **Hotel** p67. **Map** p320 A9.
San Franciscan Stanlee Gatti designed every aspect of this restaurant, whose key features are 30-foot walls of cultured stone and a live floral sculpture of more than 3,000 fresh-cut roses. Hubert Keller's contemporary French cuisine is just as impressive. The signature Blackjack appetiser of cod brandade, osetra caviar and tomato on cucumber jelly shaped into two playing cards is a winner. Other sure bets include Alaskan king salmon, Colorado lamb loin and sweetbreads, and a spread of artisanal French cheeses. Add $5 for the Grand Marnier soufflé.

Lutèce

Venetian *3355 Las Vegas Boulevard South, at Sands Avenue (414 2220/www.arkvegas.com). Bus 203, 213, 301, 302.* **Open** 5.30-11pm daily. **Main courses** $27-$49. **Credit** AmEx, DC, Disc, MC, V. **Hotel** p73. **Map** p320 A6.
On and around the Strip, competition is fierce among fine French restaurants – **Alizé** at the Palms (*see p155*), **Bouchon** at the Venetian (*see p144*), **Le Cirque** at Bellagio (*see p144*) – but Lutèce holds its own. The decor is striking, albeit in a *Beetlejuice* kind of way; the food is traditional French with a modern twist. The red-wine braised short ribs,

An artist at work: Julian Serrano at **Picasso**.

Dover sole meunière and Grand Marnier soufflés are best enjoyed overlooking the Grand Canal with its opera-singing gondoliers.

Mariposa

Neiman Marcus, Fashion Show Mall, 3200 Las Vegas Boulevard South, at Spring Mountain Road (697 7330). Bus 203, 213, 301, 302. **Open** 11.30am-3pm Mon-Sat. **Main courses** $9-$23. **Credit** AmEx, DC, MC, V. **Map** p320 B6.
On the second floor of this city's temple of chic, you'll find a jewel box of a dining room where food is also in fashion. The perfect spot for a chichi lunch before or after a luxe shopping spree, Chef de Cuisine David Glass prepares yummy treats that are as pretty as the designer frocks sold just outside the door, including a green apple and smoked salmon salad, a miso-glazed ahi tuna burger, and a truffle and asiago macaroni and cheese casserole and gratinée.

Michael's

Barbary Coast 3595 Las Vegas Boulevard South, at E Flamingo Road (737 7111/www.barbarycoast casino.com). Bus 202, 301, 302. **Open** 6pm-midnight daily. **Main courses** $45-$88. **Credit** AmEx, DC, Disc, MC, V. **Hotel** p85. **Map** p320 A7.
An old-school gourmet room, perhaps the best in town. Attentive wait staff fawn over 50 diners beneath Victorian-style decor that features red velvet, deep mahogany and white lace, and a pricey menu that sticks with surefire Vegas winners: rack of lamb,

Dover sole, flaming cherries jubilee and, of course, the most impressive shrimp cocktail in town, a $24 beaut that comes in a lit-up, star-shaped ice tower.

Mon Ami Gabi

Paris Las Vegas 3655 Las Vegas Boulevard South, at E Flamingo Road (944 4224/www.monami gabi.com). Bus 202, 301, 302. **Open** 11.30am-3.30pm, 5-11pm Mon-Thur, Sun; 11.30am-3.30pm, 5pm-midnight Fri, Sat. **Main courses** $8-$32 lunch; $16-$32 dinner. **Credit** AmEx, DC, Disc, MC, V. **Hotel** p69. **Map** p320 A7.
Lettuce Entertain You Enterprises (ouch!) runs some of Chicago's most innovative eateries; in Las Vegas, it's responsible for, among others, the Eiffel Tower Restaurant (*see p144*) and this spot on the ground floor. While the Eiffel is decidedly upscale, Mon Ami Gabi wears its French theming more casually. As such, it's an enjoyable place, and if the food (steak frites or go home) sometimes fails to live up to its reputation, the people-watching's always excellent.

Picasso

Bellagio 3600 Las Vegas Boulevard South, at W Flamingo Road (693 8105/www.bellagio.com). Bus 202, 301, 302. **Open** 6-9.30pm Mon, Wed-Sun. **Set menu** $90 4 courses; $100 5 courses. **Credit** AmEx, DC, Disc, MC, V. **Hotel** p63. **Map** p320 A7.
When your room is lined with $20 million of Picasso paintings, you have to work pretty hard to make an impression. But Julian Serrano manages it, and in spectacular fashion. Make no mistake: Serrano is the key here. Unlike a lot of celebrity chefs with high-profile restaurants in Vegas, he actually cooks at Picasso, building two crisp, daisy-fresh and wonderfully uncomplicated French-slanted menus nightly. Service is a treat and the wine list is stellar, especially if you rely on the sommelier to make your choices.

Pinot Brasserie

Venetian 3355 Las Vegas Boulevard South, at Sands Avenue (414 8888/www.venetian.com). Bus 203, 213, 301, 302. **Open** 11.30am-3pm, 5.30-10pm daily. **Main courses** $10-$15 lunch; $25-$33 dinner. **Credit** AmEx, DC, Disc, MC, V. **Hotel** p73. **Map** p320 A6.
Joachim Splichal gives his French cuisine a lighter touch, with pastas, seafood, steak and wild game. The Franco-Californian entrées range from apricot brandy-glazed pulled pork sandwiches to baby lamb with miniature vegetables. The six-course tasting menu with wine ($90) or without ($65) is worth every penny. The homey decor is *très rustique*, with copper pots, leather club chairs and paintings depicting wildlife frolicking in the French countryside. The bistro also has a large rotisserie and oyster bar.

Wolfgang Puck Bar & Grill

MGM Grand 3799 Las Vegas Boulevard South, at E Tropicana Avenue (891 7777/www.mgmgrand. com). Bus 201, 301, 302. **Open** 11.30am-11pm Mon-Thur, Sun; 11.30am-11.30pm Fri; 10am-11.30pm Sat; 10am-11pm Sun. **Main courses** $17-$28. **Credit** AmEx, DC, Disc, MC, V. **Hotel** p80. **Map** p320 A8.

Wolfgang Puck Bar & Grill. *See p145.*

Eat, Drink, Shop

Puck spreads himself so thin these days – he's the town's culinary equivalent of Cirque du Soleil – that it's hard to get excited when he opens yet another restaurant. However, this one's a true winner, well worthy of his name. Essentially, it's a Mediterranean-influenced California grill shoved across the Nevadan border, with a slightly smarter but still very affordable menu. If you can resist ordering the truffled potato chips with blue cheese for starter, main and dessert, you'll find an appetising entrées menu that includes some thin and crispy pizzas but also runs to steak and calf's liver.

Fusion

Crustacean Las Vegas
Aladdin/Planet Hollywood (Desert Passage) *3663 Las Vegas Boulevard South, at E Harmon Avenue (650 0507). Bus 301.* **Open** 5.30-8.30pm Mon-Thur, Sun; 5.30-10pm Fri, Sat. **Main courses** $25-$45. **Credit** AmEx, DC, Disc, MC, V. **Hotel** p76. **Map** p320 A7.
This sexy restaurant and lounge, perhaps the most stylish thing in the Desert Passage layout, manages to capture the energy of the legendary Metropole of French Colonial Vietnam with decor that's as exotic as the fare. Nibble on Dungeness crab puffs or coconut prawns while lying supine in one of the converted-opium-bed dining tables. Executive Chef Hélène An makes magic with peppercorn-crusted filet of beef and tamarind-glazed lobster. Save room for poached pear Napoleon, strawberry consommé or white chocolate macadamia nut and banana mousse cake.

Mix
THEhotel at Mandalay Bay *3950 Las Vegas Boulevard South, at E Hacienda Avenue (632 7800/www.mandalaybay.com). Bus 105, 301.* **Open** 6-10.30pm daily. **Main courses** $30-$75. **Credit** AmEx, DC, Disc, MC, V. **Hotel** p106. **Map** p320 A9.
French designer Patrick Jouin has created an ethereal space worthy of Alain Ducasse, the world's most Michelin-starred chef. Underneath a halo of glass spheres, 43 floors up, you'll find a suspended silver-leaf 'pearl' platform that houses a VIP dining area, where contemporary and classic American and French dishes such as tender potato gnocchi, roasted Maine lobster and guinea hen are served to equally stunning guests. The restaurant is attached to an equally attractive modern cave lounge, where cocktails are served on a terrace overlooking the Strip.

Postrio
Venetian (Grand Canal Shoppes) *3355 Las Vegas Boulevard South, at Sands Avenue (796 1110/www.wolfgangpuck.com). Bus 203, 213, 301, 302.* **Open** 11.30am-11pm Mon-Thur, Sun; 11.30am-midnight Fri, Sat. **Main courses** $9-$28 lunch; $9-$41 dinner. **Credit** AmEx, DC, Disc, MC, V. **Hotel** p73. **Map** p320 A6.

The most intimate – and, some say, best – restaurant in Wolfgang Puck's Vegas collection, Postrio blends San Francisco and Venice to achieve a romantic atmosphere. Food fuses Mediterranean and Asian influences; specials include grilled quail with spinach and soft egg ravioli, and Chinese-style duck with mango sauce and crispy fried scallion. The desserts are a must: try the warm chocolate tart with crumbled toffee ice-cream and fresh raspberries.

Sensi
Bellagio *3600 Las Vegas Boulevard South, at W Flamingo Road (693 7223/www.bellagio.com). Bus 202, 301, 302.* **Open** 11am-2.30pm, 5.30-10pm daily. **Main courses** $14-$22 lunch; $22-$42 dinner. **Credit** AmEx, DC, Disc, MC, V. **Hotel** p63. **Map** p320 A7.
Martin Heierling hit the melon out of the park his first time at the plate with this new restaurant in the Bellagio's Spa Tower. Japanese firm Super Potato designed this culinary theatre to complement Heierling's world cuisine, a combination of Italian, Asian, grilled dishes and seafood classics. Four glass-enclosed kitchens in the middle of the dining room provide an interactive stage: watch curries plunge into a red-hot tandoori oven on the Asian stage; spot focaccias with vacherin cheese and black truffles slipped into a wood-fire oven in the Italian corner; see blue point oysters shucked in the raw section; and spy a New York steak broiled on the grill.

Spago
Caesars Palace (Forum Shops) *3500 Las Vegas Boulevard South, at W Flamingo Road (369 6300/www.wolfgangpuck.com). Bus 202, 301, 302.* **Open** *Café* 11am-11pm Mon-Thur, Sun; 11am-midnight Fri, Sat. *Restaurant* 5.30-10pm daily. **Main courses** $10-$21 lunch; $12-$43 dinner. **Credit** AmEx, DC, Disc, MC, V. **Hotel** p65. **Map** p320 A7.
The restaurant that changed Vegas? Not quite. But if the culinary revolution that's swept the city in the last decade or so can be traced back to any one opening, then it's arguably this Wolfgang Puck-owned success story in the Forum Shops, which opened in 1992. The menu – an airy, California-slanted Pacific Rim-influenced selection – no longer seems as innovative, but that's due more to Puck's influence on others than anything else. A great lunch spot.

Verandah Café
Four Seasons Las Vegas *3960 Las Vegas Boulevard South, at E Hacienda Avenue (632 5121/www.fourseasons.com/lasvegas). Bus 105, 301.* **Open** 6.30am-10pm Mon-Fri; 7am-10pm Sat, Sun. **Main courses** $8-$14 breakfast; $14-$27 lunch; $16-$34 dinner. **Credit** AmEx, DC, Disc, MC, V. **Hotel** p105. **Map** p320 A9.
The epitome of the California country club (Brooks Brothers to Lacoste), this impressive eaterie suffered from its recent, rather stuffy remodel. The poolside seating increased, however, so we suggest dining there (specify when booking). The menu remains delicious, particularly for breakfast and weekend brunch: an all-you-can-savour taste treat, it puts buffets to shame at a price that says it should.

Italian

Canaletto

Venetian *3355 Las Vegas Boulevard South, at Sands Avenue (733 0070/www.venetian.com).* Bus 203, 213, 301, 302. **Open** 11.30am-11pm Mon-Thur, Sun; 11.30am-midnight Fri, Sat. **Main courses** $15-$32. **Credit** AmEx, DC, Disc, MC, V. **Hotel** p73. **Map** p320 A6.

On the edge of the Grand Canal Shoppes in St Mark's Square, you'll find an Italian eatery created by the founders of Il Fornaio restaurants at New York–New York and Green Valley Ranch. Here, Chef Luigi Bomparola culls from a long list of regional recipes his Northern Italian-inspired fresh seafood, beef, game and poultry dishes, prepared in wood-fired rotisseries and grills. The food isn't especially adventurous, but that hardly matters: it's also rarely less than excellent

Fiamma

MGM Grand *3799 Las Vegas Boulevard South, at E Tropicana Avenue (891 7600/www.mgmgrand. com).* Bus 201, 301, 302. **Open** 5.30-10.30pm Mon-Thur, Sun; 5.30-11pm Fri, Sat. **Main courses** $24-$36. **Credit** AmEx, DC, Disc, MC, V. **Hotel** p80. **Map** p320 A8.

New York's Stephen Hanson remodelled the once-proud Olio into MGM's beautiful (if oversized) trattoria, a sister to his Fiamma Osteria in SoHo. The bar scene makes this a favourite stop among those heading to the Grand Garden Arena: we can't decide if the joint's affinity for playing only the music of the night's featured performer is inspired or annoying. Munch on an ever-changing selection of Italian faves, but save room for the freshly fried doughnut dessert.

Osteria del Circo

Bellagio *3600 Las Vegas Boulevard South, at W Flamingo Road (693 8150/www.bellagio.com).* Bus 202, 301, 302. **Open** 11.30am-2.30pm Wed-Sun; 5.30-10.30pm daily. **Main courses** $14-$28 lunch; $21-$44 dinner. **Credit** AmEx, DC, Disc, MC, V. **Hotel** p63. **Map** p320 A7.

Sirio Maccioni and his talented sons came west from New York in 1998 and brought their talent for running ultra-fabulous restaurants with them. This colourful circus, designed by Adam Tihany, looks out at Bellagio's lake and inwards for authentic but imaginative Italian eats. The upscale Tuscan fare, inspired by Maccioni matriarch Egidiana, includes poached jumbo shrimp, hand-rolled spaghetti with bolognese sauce and a Tuscan stew of calamares, clams, mussel, shrimp and monkfish.

Trattoria del Lupo

Mandalay Bay *3950 Las Vegas Boulevard South, at E Hacienda Avenue (740 5522/www.wolfgang puck.com).* Bus 105, 301. **Open** 5.30-10pm Mon-Fri; 11.30am-3pm, 5.30-11pm Sat, Sun. **Main courses** $9-$12 lunch; $10-$34 dinner. **Credit** AmEx, DC, Disc, MC, V. **Hotel** p67. **Map** p320 A9.

With an array of ever-changing northern Italian menus (wood-fired pizza, risotto), a location on Mandalay Bay's restaurant row and an open, high-ceilinged room, Wolfgang Puck's Lupo is popular with the thirtysomething culturati, but we can't quite figure out why. Everything tastes good and the service is attentive, but it's just not enough. Perhaps it's the noise level, the too-high prices or the fact that, by Vegas standards, it's getting a little dated.

Zeffirino

Venetian (Grand Canal Shoppes) *3355 Las Vegas Boulevard South, at Sands Avenue (414 3500/www.venetian.com).* Bus 203, 213, 301, 302. **Open** 11.30am-midnight daily. **Main courses** $17-$65 lunch; $26-$65 dinner. **Credit** AmEx, DC, Disc, MC, V. **Hotel** p73. **Map** p320 A6.

Chef Gian Paulo 'Zeffirino' Belloni specialises in Italian seafood dishes inside his canalside bistro. Cold appetisers include the classic caprese or prosciutto and melon salads; hot ones include sautéed sea scallops, and chickpea and shrimp bisque. There's a fine selections of pastas and risottos, but the pan-seared filet of Mediterranean bass and grilled tuna steak with black olives and sun-dried tomato purée are the most enticing.

Irish

Nine Fine Irishmen

New York–New York *3790 Las Vegas Boulevard South, at W Tropicana Avenue (740 6969/www. ninefineirishmen.com).* Bus 201, 301, 302. **Open** 9am-3am daily. **Main courses** $10-$25. **Credit** AmEx, DC, Disc, MC, V. **Hotel** p83. **Map** p320 A8.

This two-storey pub was imported from Ireland; the whiskies and the beer followed soon after. But the rest of the experience is a combination of new country and old: a lively, humorous house band that can cover everything from Christy Moore to U2; views of the Strip from cosy, wooden pub booths; and a chef so cool he named a dish 'salmon of knowledge' yet carries on serving chips in a newspaper cone.

Latin American & Southwestern

Border Grill

Mandalay Bay *3950 Las Vegas Boulevard South, at E Hacienda Avenue (632 7403/www.bordergrill. com).* Bus 105, 301. **Open** 11.30am-10pm Mon-Thur, Sun; 11am-11pm Fri, Sat. **Main courses** $12-$20 lunch; $19-$30 dinner. **Credit** AmEx, DC, Disc, MC, V. **Hotel** p67. **Map** p320 A9.

Imported from Santa Monica, this lively Angeleno take on Mexican food is not especially authentic, but works a treat regardless. Mary Sue Milliken and Susan Feniger, frontwomen of popular show *Too Hot Tamales*, have given some classic dishes a twist (the quesadillas are a great call), but also look to their home state for inspiration: witness the deep-fried snapper, served over refried beans. There's a take-out taqueria if your budget doesn't run to a full feed.

Isla. *See p150.*

Eat, Drink, Shop

Isla

TI (Treasure Island) *3300 Las Vegas Boulevard South, at W Spring Mountain Road (894 7111).* Bus 203, 301. **Open** 4-11pm daily. **Main courses** $10-$30. **Credit** AmEx, DC, Disc, MC, V. **Hotel** p71. **Map** p320 A6.

While Treasure Island's ongoing rebranding from family resort to adult pleasure palace hasn't been wholly successful, the dining is certainly a vast improvement on what was here a few years ago. The reinvention has been led by Richard Sandoval's Isla, which really adds a spark to some old Mexican favourites (burritos, chicken mole, a lengthy menu of Margaritas) while also adding a slightly Californian angle to some less familiar dishes. If you like your Mexican food but aren't precious about tradition, you'll have a great meal.

Seafood

Joe's Stone Crab

Caesars Palace (Forum Shops) *3570 Las Vegas Boulevard South, at W Flamingo Road (792 9222).* Bus 202, 301, 302. **Open** 11.30am-11pm Mon-Thur, Sun; 11.30-midnight Fri, Sat. **Main courses** $19-$47. **Credit** AmEx, DC, Disc, MC, V. **Hotel** p65. **Map** p320 A7.

Even middlebrow seafood places now boast of fresh fish flown in daily, so what makes Joe's, affiliated with the Miami legend, so special? Simple: even though it's pricey, the impeccable service, glamorous environs and taste of the signature fresh stone crab, regional specialities (salmon, scallops, mahi mahi) and bone-in steaks leaves you willing to pay much more. A rarity of upscale value, and one of the gems of the Forum Shops expansion.

Michael Mina

Bellagio *3600 Las Vegas Boulevard South, at W Flamingo Road (693 7223/www.bellagio.com).* Bus 202, 301, 302. **Open** 5.30-10pm daily. **Main courses** $36-$72. **Set menus** $85-$110. **Credit** AmEx, DC, Disc, MC, V. **Hotel** p63. **Map** p320 A7.

Michael Mina's flagship restaurant may have changed its name (it was formerly known as Aqua), but it still delivers, along with Mina's SeaBlue restaurant (*see below*) at the MGM Grand, the best seafood anywhere on the Strip. His caviar parfait is legendary here, but the always-changing menu also features such deep-sea delights as truffle-crusted turbot, a savoury black mussel soufflé and a miso-glazed Chilean sea bass.

Nobhill

MGM Grand *3799 Las Vegas Boulevard South, at E Tropicana Avenue (891 7337/www.mgmgrand. com).* Bus 201, 301, 302. **Open** 5.30-10.30pm daily. **Main courses** $30-$75. **Credit** AmEx, Disc, MC, V. **Hotel** p80. **Map** p320 A8.

Top-notch products from the Bay Area – fresh abalone, clams, oysters and king salmon, to name but a few – become spectacular creations in the hands of celebrity chef Michael Mina. His menu, inspired by traditional neighbourhood restaurants found throughout San Francisco, has a decidedly gourmet twist: black truffle cheese fondue with toasted brioche is an example. Must-orders include a sugar-rimmed cable car, North Beach cioppino and lobster pot pie.

SeaBlue

MGM Grand *3799 Las Vegas Boulevard South, at E Tropicana Avenue (891 3486/www.mgmgrand. com).* Bus 201, 301, 302. **Open** 5.30-10pm Mon-Thur, Sun; 5.30-10.30 Fri, Sat. **Main courses** $27-$75. **Credit** AmEx, DC, Disc, MC, V. **Hotel** p80. **Map** p320 A8.

Following on from Nobhill at the MGM Grand and his eponymous seafooder at Bellagio (for both, *see above*), Michael Mina's third Las Vegas venture is intimate and well designed, but aren't they all? Fish entrées grilled over wood and/or baked in clay are tasty, but what makes this place stand out is its big raw bar. For a desert venue, the selection of fresh seafood is almost embarrassing, and even the gimmicky lobster corndog is worth a bite.

Thai, Vietnamese & Pan-Asian

Noodles

Bellagio *3600 Las Vegas Boulevard South, at W Flamingo Road (693 8131/www.bellagio.com). Bus 202, 301, 302.* **Open** 11am-2am Mon-Thur; 11am-3am Fri-Sun. **Main courses** $12-$30. **Credit** AmEx, DC, Disc, MC, V. **Hotel** p63. **Map** p320 A7.

Once a gem showcasing the subtle, modern elegance of Tony Chi's pan-Asian dishes, Noodles has somewhat declined of late, in regards to the quality of both food and service. You'll still enjoy the urban diner feel, the late hours, and the selection of dim sum (lunch), Hong Kong barbecue and, of course, the hot and chilled noodle dishes from across Asia. Hopefully, they'll sort out the rest.

Stratosphere Area

American & steakhouses

Luv-It Frozen Custard

505 E Oakey Boulevard, at Las Vegas Boulevard South (384 6452/www.luvitfrozencustard.com). Bus 301. **Open** 1-10pm Tue-Thur; 1-11pm Fri, Sat. **Main courses** $3-$6. **No credit cards. Map** p319 C3.

While most of Vegas sweeps through the sweet life in a Häagen daze, those in the know head to this tiny little walk-up window yards from Las Vegas Boulevard for a taste of days gone by. Frozen custard looks like ice-cream and even tastes a bit like ice-cream, but it's better: richer (made from eggs and cream), smoother and more moreish than anything either Ben or Jerry could conjure. A Western sundae's a good place to start, but you really can't go wrong with any of it. Heroic, in its way.

Tiffany's

White Cross Drugstore, 1700 Las Vegas Boulevard South, at E Oakey Boulevard (444 4459). Bus 301. **Open** 24hrs daily. **Main courses** $5-$15. **No credit cards. Map** p319 C3.

Your archetypal diner-in-a-drugstore, but there aren't many left these days, itself reason enough to cherish this agreeably charmless operation. Breakfasts are greasy, lunches are greasy and your fellow diners will be greasy, but no matter. If your night runs into day, there's no better spot to soak up the alcohol.

French & Mediterranean

Top of the World

Stratosphere *2000 Las Vegas Boulevard South, between W Oakey Boulevard & W Sahara Avenue (380 7711/www.topoftheworldlv.com). Bus 301.* **Open** 11am-3pm, 5.30-10.30pm Mon-Thur, Sun; 11am-3pm, 5.30pm-11pm Fri, Sat. **Main courses** $27-$60 ($30 min). **Credit** AmEx, DC, Disc, MC, V. **Hotel** p90. **Map** p319 C4.

The Stratosphere's answer to the gourmet room is quite a ride: the restaurant rotates a full 360° every hour and a half. Despite the ever-changing view, the well-trained staff will have you paying attention to what's on your plate: continental cuisine that includes gourmet dishes such as Colorado rack of lamb and Chilean sea bass. *USA Today* named it one of their 'ten great places to pop the question'.

Thai, Vietnamese & Pan-Asian

Thai BBQ

1424 S 3rd Street, at Las Vegas Boulevard South (383 1128). Bus 301. **Open** 11am-10pm daily. **Main courses** $7-$18. **Credit** AmEx, Disc, MC, V. **Map** p319 C3.

Despite its gritty locale, Thai BBQ remains one of the best Thai eateries in town. The friendly and helpful service makes choosing from the large menu of Thai specialities simple; the hearty portions of such classics as pad Thai are worth the trip. Highlights include papaya salad, excellent satay, and rich and spicy beef noodle soup.

Other locations: 4180 S Jones Boulevard, Southwest Las Vegas (222 0375).

SeaBlue. *See p150.*

East of Strip

American & steakhouses

AJ's Steakhouse

Hard Rock *4455 Paradise Road, at E Harmon Avenue (693 5500/www.hardrockhotel.com). Bus 108.* **Open** 6-11pm Tue-Sat. **Main courses** $23-$37. **Credit** AmEx, DC, Disc, MC, V. **Hotel** p91. **Map** p320 C7.

Attracting probably the 'oldest' crowd at the eternally young Hard Rock hotel, this swingin' retro-Vegas room has for ten years held its own, feeling almost authentically as though it's from the Rat Pack era. Powerful Martinis at the bar, a pianist crooning standards, well-prepared slabs of meat, fish served with the appropriate starches... Hey: is that Danny Ocean over there?

Del Frisco's

Hughes Center, 3925 Paradise Road, between Sands Avenue & E Flamingo Road (796 0063/www.del friscos.com). Bus 108, 202, 203, 213. **Open** 5-11pm Mon-Sat; 5-10pm Sun. **Main courses** $25-$50. **Credit** AmEx, DC, Disc, MC, V. **Map** p320 C6.

'Big and beefy' best describes this steak emporium: a high-end offshoot of the Lonestar chain, it serves a simple menu – prime sirloins, bone-in ribeyes, simple seafood and even simpler salads – in a south-ern-style country club setting. Highlights include Australian cold-water rock lobster tails, turtle soup and salad wedge with chunky blue-cheese dressing. The deep wine cellar includes some 8,000 bottles.

Mr Lucky's 24/7

Hard Rock *4455 Paradise Road, at E Harmon Avenue (693 5592/www.hardrockhotel.com). Bus 108.* **Open** 24hrs daily. **Main courses** $8-$16. **Credit** AmEx, DC, Disc, MC, V. **Hotel** p91. **Map** p320 C7.

So distracting is the stream of underdressed hotties and wannabe rock stars (along with a few genuine ones) that your eyes might well end up diverted from the fresh diner fare served at Vegas's hippest 24-hour hangout. Breakfast is good enough; at other times, in-the-know types order the $7.77 steak and shrimp special that's not on the menu. Beyond cool.

Simon Kitchen & Bar

Hard Rock *4455 Paradise Road, at E Harmon Avenue (693 4440/www.hardrockhotel.com). Bus 108.* **Open** 6-10.30pm Mon-Fri; 6.30-11pm Sat, Sun. **Main courses** $22-$44. **Credit** AmEx, DC, Disc, MC, V. **Hotel** p91. **Map** p320 C7.

Rock 'n' roll chef Kerry Simon and Wynn-presario Elizabeth Blau are the consummate hosts to the hip at this Palm Springs-styled eatery inside – where else? – the Hard Rock, in which groovy lounge music and top-shelf retro-comfort food (massive shrimp cocktail, meatloaf, giant bowls of cotton candy) are served to celebs every weekend. No matter if your album hasn't hit platinum: the hosts do a great job of making everyone a star.

Chinese

PF Chang's China Bistro

4165 Paradise Road, at E Flamingo Road (792 2207/www.pfchangs.com). Bus 108, 202. **Open** 11am-11pm Mon-Thur, Sun; 11am-midnight Fri, Sat. **Main courses** $7-$18. **Credit** AmEx, DC, Disc, MC, V. **Map** p320 C7.

Noodles and rice served a hundred ways and layered over a bustling bar scene that's itself dumbed down a bit as nearby competition has increased. It's still more popular than it deserves to be, but that cute accountant or the divorced real-estate agent might help you forget about the indifferently seasoned pseudo-Sichuan dishes.
Other locations: throughout the city.

French & Mediterranean

Firefly

3900 Paradise Road, between E Flamingo Road & Sands Avenue (369 3971/www.fireflylv.com). Bus 108. **Open** 11.30am-2pm, 5pm-2am Mon-Thur; 11.30am-2pm, 5pm-3am Fri; 5pm-3am Sat; 5pm-2am Sun.* **Main courses** $10-$20. *Tapas* $3-$10. **Credit** AmEx, DC, Disc, MC, V. **Map** p320 C6.

It can be hard to get a seat at the city's first – but, since the opening of Café Ba Ba Reeba (*see p144*), no longer only – tapas restaurant, operated by alumni of Mon Ami Gabi (*see p145*). The small plates menu (mushroom tarts, ahi skewers) is very good, the atmosphere (dining room, lounge, patio, DJs) is comfortably hip and the prices are reason-able, all of which conspires to make for a loungey scene that lets you spend as little or as much as you'd like.

Pamplemousse

400 E Sahara Avenue, at Paradise Road (733 2066/www.pamplemousserestaurant.com). Bus 108, 204. **Open** 5.30-10pm Tue-Sun. **Main courses** $18-$29. **Credit** AmEx, DC, Disc, MC, V. **Map** p319 C4.

Along with André's (*see p156*) and the Bootlegger (*see p160*), Pamplemousse is one of a very few non-casino old Vegas classics. Owned by local Georges LaForge, it's been serving country-style French fare to such regulars as Wayne Newton, Bob Goulet and Robin Leach for years. The menu-less tradition con-tinues to this day: the wait staff recite the specialities – chateaubriand, veal sweetbreads and French onion soup gratinée – so be sure to pay attention.

German

Café Heidelberg

610 E Sahara Avenue, at S 6th Street (731 5310). Bus 204. **Open** 11am-10pm daily. **Main courses** $7-$10 lunch; $18-$29 dinner. **Credit** AmEx, DC, Disc, MC, V. **Map** p317 Y2.

This charming Bavarian eaterie features such German delicacies as sauerkraut schweinebraten (pork roast), sausage platters with German potato salad, spatzle and a good selection of German beers, which go down very nicely on a hot day. You can even build your own schnitzel.

Hofbrauhaus

4510 Paradise Road, at E Harmon Avenue (853 2337/www.hofbrauhauslasvegas.com). Bus 108. **Open** 11am-11pm Mon-Thur, Sun; 11am-midnight Fri, Sat. **Main courses** $9-$25. **Credit** AmEx, DC, Disc, MC, V. **Map** p320 C7/8.

Planting this near-identical replica of the famous Munich brewhouse across from the Hard Rock was a great idea, but the results are hot and cold. To wit: pretzel girls, hot; the rest of the menu, not. While the authentic German grub is mostly bland, the beer makes up for it. Where you drink it is another matter: the *schwemme* can be a good time, if you like long tables and oompah bands (we'd prefer a quartet of jackhammers). Unlike the Munich version, the *biergarten* here has a roof, which dilutes the experience to the level of a glorified cafeteria.

Indian

Gandhi

4080 Paradise Road, at E Flamingo Road (734 0094/www.gandhicuisine.com). Bus 108, 202. **Open** 11am-2.30pm, 5-10.30pm daily. **Main courses** $9.95 lunch buffet; $10-$23 dinner. **Credit** AmEx, DC, Disc, MC, V. **Map** p320 C7.

Good Northern Indian and Southern Indian cuisine, along with a fine selection of vegetarian dishes, combine to make Gandhi the best Indian restaurant in Vegas. Cherished recipes include lamb and chicken curries, tandoori prawns, samosa fritters and garlic

naan bread. The all-you-can-eat lunch buffet is nice and spicy, and stars such dishes as chicken pakora, keema naan (stuffed bread with minced lamb) and chicken tikka masala for just $9.95.

Japanese

Nobu

Hard Rock *4455 Paradise Road, at E Harmon Avenue (693 5090/www.hardrockhotel.com). Bus 108.* **Open** 6-11pm daily. **Main courses** $17-$55. **Credit** AmEx, DC, Disc, MC, V. **Hotel** p91. **Map** p320 C7.

Forget the best Japanese meals town: Nobu is said by some to serve the finest food in Vegas of any kind. World-renowned Japanese chef Nobu Matsuhisa's Asian/South American fusion room expects its diners to be both well heeled and sushi-experienced. Looking like a star is optional. Big prices and little slices follow the leads of its New York and London brethren; if you can cover it, unleash the chef's omikase tasting menu.

Togoshi Ramen

Twain Center, 855 E Twain Avenue, at Swenson Street (737 7003). Bus 203, 208, 213. **Open** 11.30am-9.30pm daily. **Main courses** $7-$12. **No credit cards. Map** p317 Y3.

If the only ramen you've tried is the bulk, packaged, grocery-store ramen with powdered flavouring, hike here and try the real stuff. Known for its Japanese comfort-food fare, such as tonkatsu, gyoza and curry rice, this place specialises in much more than noodle soup. The menus are in English, but the specials are listed on the walls in Japanese and appeal to the true Japanese palate. Food is inexpensive, soothing and unassuming, and goes great with a Sapporo.

Trust us: it's never, ever this quiet: **Simon Kitchen & Bar**. *See p152.*

Eat, Drink, Shop

Latin American & Southwestern

Pink Taco

Hard Rock *4455 Paradise Road, at E Harmon Avenue (693 5000/www.hardrockhotel.com). Bus 108.* **Open** 11am-10pm Mon-Thur, Sun; 11am-midnight Fri, Sat. **Main courses** $8-$14. **Credit** AmEx, DC, Disc, MC, V. **Hotel** p91. **Map** p320 C7.

While other Mexican restaurants in Vegas casinos aim for a degree of sophistication, this spot – like everything in the Hard Rock, a hugely fashionable place to eat and be seen to eat – is a lot more casual and affordable. The burritos are good; the carne asada is better. Wash it down with Negra Modelo.

Middle Eastern

Marrakech

Citibank Park, 3900 Paradise Road, between E Twain Avenue & E Flamingo Road (737 5611/www. marrakech-vegas.com). Bus 108, 203, 213. **Open** 5.30-11pm daily. **Set meal** $28 6 courses. **Credit** AmEx, DC, Disc, MC, V. **Map** p320 C6.

The plain-as-day strip mall location doesn't inspire confidence, but once you're inside, Marrakech makes a brave attempt at authentic North African food. None of the six courses are overwhelmingly subtle, but they're fun, especially with the waiters explaining what you're about to enjoy. Did we mention there's belly dancing?

Seafood

McCormick & Schmick's Seafood

335 Hughes Center Drive, between Howard Hughes Parkway & Paradise Road (836 9000/www. mccormickandschmick.com). Bus 108, 202. **Open** 11am-11pm Mon-Fri; 5-11pm Sat; 5-10pm Sun. **Main courses** $5-$20 lunch; $7-$35 dinner. **Credit** AmEx, DC, Disc, MC, V. **Map** p320 C7.

This upmarket national seafood chain has a popular link a few miles off the Strip. The handsome restaurant has a large menu, but the star is always conveniently at the top of the page: the lengthy 'fresh list' of catches, which changes daily. The oysters are so fresh and briny you'll swear you're eating on the coast. The especially good happy hour features huge platters of top-shelf crab, quesadillas and fish tacos, sinfully cheap and shrimply delicious.

Thai, Vietnamese & Pan-Asian

Komol

Commercial Center, 953 E Sahara Avenue, between S 6th Street & S Maryland Parkway (731 6542). Bus 109, 204. **Open** 11am-10pm Mon-Sat; noon-10pm Sun. **Main courses** $8-$18. **Credit** AmEx, Disc, MC, V. **Map** p317 Y2.

Despite its location in a run-down mall, Komol remains hugely popular with locals for its authentic rendering of Thai cuisine, a huge vegetarian menu,

plus 1950s Americana such as egg foo yung, all at bargain prices. Specify the degree of heat you'd like, and the kitchen will try to comply.

Lotus of Siam

Commercial Center, 953 E Sahara Avenue, between S 6th Street & S Maryland Parkway (735 3033). Bus 109, 204. **Open** 11.30am-2pm, 5.30-9pm daily. **Main courses** $9.95 lunch buffet; $7-$18 dinner. **Credit** AmEx, Disc, MC, V. **Map** p317 Y2.

The knowledgeable folks at *Gourmet* magazine have rated this the best Thai restaurant in the US; we might not quite go that far, but Lotus of Siam is certainly a rare and unexpected treat in this unprepossessing strip mall otherwise dominated by gay bars and swingers' clubs. Saipin Chutima puts her specialities on the easy-to-read menu, though many opt for the excellent lunch buffet, which'll leave you with change from a $10 bill.

West of Strip

American & steakhouses

Coffee Pub

2800 W Sahara Avenue, between S Rancho Drive & S Valley View Boulevard (367 1913). Bus 204. **Open** 7am-3pm daily. **Main courses** $5-$9. **Credit** AmEx, Disc, MC, V. **Map** p317 X2.

The service has grown a little blasé in recent times at this longtime favourite, as if the staff have suddenly grown aware of the Coffee Pub's role as Vegas's best spot for a discreet, casual power breakfast. Still, if you can catch the staff in a good mood, happiness is assured: the food, all breakfast and brunch staples (you can't beat the stuffed French toast), is as good as ever.

Golden Steer Steak House

308 W Sahara Avenue, between Las Vegas Boulevard South & S Industrial Road (384 4470). Bus 105, 204. **Open** 11am-10pm Mon-Thur; 11am-11pm Fri; 4.30-10pm Sat, Sun. **Main courses** $24-$85. **Credit** AmEx, DC, Disc, MC, V. **Map** p319 B4.

The enormous (and, yes, golden) steer that sign posts this old-school steak place on Sahara also advertises its decor. Discreet it certainly is not: think updated bordello crossed with an Old West saloon and you're almost there. But the steaks are classic: large, juicy and perfectly grilled, albeit served at prices that could stun a cow at 20 paces.

Omelet House

2160 W Charleston Boulevard, at S Rancho Drive (384 6868). Bus 206. **Open** 7am-3pm daily. **Main courses** $6-$9. **Credit** MC, V. **Map** p319 A3.

It's not just the speciality: it's more or less the only thing on the menu. Sure, they make 'em in around 60 varieties, but eggs is eggs is eggs, and they do 'em as well as anyone at this unassuming little diner. Making lunch plans is foolhardy: each omelette is made with six eggs, and will have you napping at the table until the heartburn wakes you up.

Viva Elizabeth Blau

Others nick the limelight: star chefs, chic designers. However, though Elizabeth Blau is no headline-seeker, the thirtysomething former model is one of the most influential names behind Las Vegas's dining renaissance.

It's been a long haul from her teen job slinging fast food in West Hartford, Connecticut, to her new role as Executive VP of Restaurant Marketing and Development for Wynn Las Vegas. But to close observers of the local dining scene, it's not unexpected: after all, it was Blau who was the driving force behind the line-up of eateries and celeb-chef imports that launched Steve Wynn's Bellagio in 1998. Combining her East Coast cuisine connections (she wrote a business plan for New York's original Le Cirque as a grad student at Cornell, and later worked for Sirio Maccioni) with the socio-analytical mind of a potential attorney (Government & International Relations at Georgetown) and

the grace and composure of a perfect party host (watch her work a room), Blau carved Bellagio into the epicentre of the Vegas restaurant world. Six years later, again cooking concepts with Wynn and Kevin Stuessi, Blau has changed the recipe.

Many knock Vegas for housing mere name-brand imitations of world-famous originals. Not at Wynn Las Vegas. The plan is to add lesser known names (Eric Klein, Stephen Kalt, Takashi Yagihashi) to the starry likes of Alessandro Stratta and Daniel Boulud, and give them a sympathetic environment in which to work on all-new concepts. Indeed, in time, perhaps their concepts will be exported to other cities, rather than the reverse; Las Vegas, long the imitator, will at last become the initiator. So when the Boulud Brasserie makes a play for your hometown, you'll know who to thank, though it's likely she'll defer the spotlight to others. It's just her way.

N9ne

Palms *4321 W Flamingo Road, at S Valley View Boulevard (933 9900/www.n9nesteaks.com). Bus 104, 202.* **Open** 5-11pm Mon-Thur, Sun; 5-11.30 Fri, Sat. **Main courses** $20-$38. **Credit** AmEx, Disc, MC, V. **Hotel** p92. **Map** p317 X3.

The seafood at this ever-popular Palms eaterie is excellent, but it takes a backseat to the spectacle: a busy bar scene, circus-like lighting, and acoustics seemingly designed to force diners to yell, just like in a nightclub. A decent Saturday reservation requires an A-list name or weeks of planning. The signature steaks are good and the appetisers and side dishes a cut above, but if quiet romance is on the cards, go elsewhere.

French

Alizé

Palms *4321 W Flamingo Road, at S Valley View Boulevard (951 7000/www.palms.com). Bus 104, 202.* **Open** 5.30-10pm daily. **Main courses** $40-$60. **Credit** AmEx, DC, Disc, MC, V. **Hotel** p92. **Map** p317 X3.

Up on the 56th floor, venerated local André Rochat has teamed up with rising star Jacques van Staden for some classic and fresh takes on French cuisine. Many dishes – pan-seared Muscovy duck breast and duck rillette in puff pastry with sautéed spinach, almonds and raspberry sauce – taste as great as they sound. It comes at a price, but Rochat, who's been cooking foie gras in Vegas since Dan Tana was still around, knows how to give good bang for your buck. The cognac list is one of the best in America.

Fusion

Little Buddha

Palms *4321 W Flamingo Road, at S Valley View Boulevard (942 7778/www.littlebuddha lasvegas.com). Bus 104, 202.* **Open** 5.30-11pm Mon-Thur, Sun; 5.30-midnight Fri, Sat. **Main courses** $15-$38. **Credit** AmEx, DC, Disc, MC, V. **Hotel** p92. **Map** p317 X3.

Buddha Bar's sexy baby sister serves decent fusion in a dramatic setting, with prices to match. Go for the scene, the sounds and the sushi, and be sure to look as fabulous as possible, but leave the Asian cooking to the restaurants a mile to the west (around Chinatown Plaza), where the same fare can be had for a third of the price.

Indian

Gaylord's

Rio *3700 W Flamingo Road, at S Valley View Boulevard (777 2277). Bus 104, 202.* **Open** 11.30am-2.30pm, 5-10pm daily. **Main courses** $14-$28. **Credit** AmEx, DC, Disc, MC, V. **Hotel** p93. **Map** p317 X3.

Northern Indian cuisine at its best, at least in Las Vegas terms, featuring authentic tandoori and mughlai-style dishes, fresh-baked breads, meat dishes and an array of vegetarian delights. There's nothing *faux* about the rich, warm dining area, which, when combined with the food, adds up to a deliciously exotic experience. A nice find amid the usual Vegas fare.

Eat, Drink, Shop

Thai, Vietnamese & Pan-Asian

Pho So 1
*4745 W Spring Mountain Road, at S Decatur
Boulevard (252 3934). Bus 103, 203.* **Open** 9am-
10pm daily. **Main courses** $7-$22. **No credit cards.**
Granted, there's not an awful lot of competition, but
this is the best Vietnamese in town. The place is
always busy, with helpful, trilingual staff guiding
neophytes through the menu of pho (beef noodle
soups), com (rice dishes) and anything made with
beef. The spring rolls are to die for and prices are
predictably cheap.

Downtown

American & steakhouses

Bay City Diner
Golden Gate *1 E Fremont Street, at Main Street
(385 1906). Bus 108, 207.* **Open** 6am-1am Mon-Thur,
Sun; 6am-2am Fri, Sat. **Main courses** $5-$12. **Credit**
AmEx, DC, Disc, MC, V. **Hotel** p98. **Map** p318 C1.
Like the casino in which it's housed, this is a classic icon of Old Vegas. There's nothing fussy or
upscale about the Bay City Diner: it's just a small
room serving basic food for 20 hours a day. But
it oozes history, from the grainy decor via the
predictable menu to the ageing, no-nonsense waitresses. Anyone interested in the city's past should
eat here at least once.

Carson Street Café
Golden Nugget *129 E Fremont Street, at Casino
Center Boulevard (385 7111). Bus 107.* **Open** 24hrs
daily. **Main courses** $10-$24. **Credit** AmEx, DC,
Disc, MC, V. **Hotel** p96. **Map** p318 C1.
The Golden Nugget's requisite 24/7 coffee shop is
an oasis of comfort in the bustling grit of Downtown.
If the neighbouring Bay City Diner (*see above*) is 'LV
Confidential', then this is 'LV Law': a parade of attor-
neys, barristers and other suits enjoy big breakfasts,
flaky croissant sandwiches, salads and hearty
entrées. No pretence, all value.

Center Stage
Plaza *1 Main Street, at Fremont Street, Las Vegas,
NV 89101 (386 2440/www.plazahotelcasino.com).
Bus 107, 108, 207, 301, 302.* **Main courses** $20-
$60. **Credit** AmEx, DC, Disc, MC, V. **Map** p318 C1.
A pianist twiddles away in the corner, subservient
waiters waft through carrying wine glasses and
hearty platters of meat… and outside, the lights of
the Fremont Street Experience – the window seats
here offer the best views of it in town – blaze away.
Still, if you keep your eyes away from the canopy,
this is a true, almost mythic slice of Old Vegas.

Hugo's Cellar
Four Queens *202 E Fremont Street, between E
Ogden Avenue & N Main Street (385 4011). Bus 108,
207.* **Open** 5.30-10.30pm daily. **Main courses** $38-
$60. **Credit** AmEx, DC, Disc, MC, V. **Map** p318 C1.

One of Vegas's original fine-dining establishments.
Hugo's old traditions are still good ones: a pampering wait staff, a tableside visit from the famous salad
cart, a solid wine list and a rose for the lady. The
menu is vintage Vegas gourmet room, heavy on the
meat and seafood (steak and lobster are the stars),
and just what you'd expect for dessert (cherries
jubilee and bananas Foster). If you're looking for
fusion, you're in the wrong place.

French & Mediterranean

André's
*401 S 6th Street, at Lewis Avenue (385 5016/www.
andresfrenchrest.com). Bus 301.* **Open** 6-9pm Mon-
Sat. Closed July. **Main courses** $28-$55. **Credit**
AmEx, DC, MC, V. **Map** p318 D2.
Check out the expense-account crowd at this
Downtown institution, with patio dining that's
oh-so-New York. Chef/owner André Rochat (of Alizé,
see p255), a local legend of sorts, serves French
haute cuisine accompanied by a world-class cellar
(though with few bargains). The Monte Carlo branch
has a plush cigar and cognac bar.
Other locations: Monte Carlo, 3770 Las Vegas
Boulevard South (730 7955).

Italian

Chicago Joe's
*820 S 4th Street, between Gass Avenue & Hoover
Avenue (382 5637/www.chicagojoesrestaurant.com).
Bus 206, 301.* **Open** 11am-10pm Mon-Fri; 5-10pm
Sat. **Main courses** $5-$25. **Credit** AmEx, DC, Disc,
MC, V. **Map** p318 C2/3.
Housed in a tiny 1932 brick house, locals' fave CJ's
has lasted a quarter of a century thanks to the solid
southern Italian cooking produced by its kitchen. No
frills, fair prices and quirky service make Joe's a fantastic bargain if you're looking for comfort pasta and
regional specialities (Chicago spicy lobster) in a
homey, authentic but still slightly quirky setting.

Tinoco's Bistro
*103 E Charleston Boulevard, at Main Street (464
5008). Bus 206.* **Open** 5-10pm Mon-Sat. **Main
courses** $16-$25. **Credit** AmEx, DC, Disc, MC, V.
Map p315 C3.
Slip into chef Enrique Tinoco's urban bistro inside
the Arts Factory and you'll hardly believe you're in
Vegas, whatever that means. Intimate is an under-
statement, but the tiny, artsy, industrial space serves
delicious own-made soups and salads, lobster ravioli, Chilean seabass and more besides. The service
is well meaning but slow, so plan accordingly.

Latin American & Southwestern

Casa Don Juan
*1202 S Main Street, at W California Street (384
8070). Bus 108, 206.* **Open** 7am-10pm daily. **Main
courses** $6-$12. **Credit** MC, V. **Map** p319 C3.

El Sombrero Café.

In the fifty-something years it's been open, housed in a small hut-like structure that looks like a Mexican prison, El Sombrero has had only two different people in charge of the kitchen. If you want exotic updates of Mexican staples, try Isla (*see p150*). But if you're just after some basic, hearty and straightforward South American peasant food in quiet and authentic surroundings, this place'll do it.

Seafood

Second Street Grill

Fremont *200 E Fremont Street, at S Casino Center Boulevard (385 6277/www.fremontcasino. com). Bus 107, 108, 109, 207, 315.* **Open** 6-10pm Mon, Thur, Sun; 6-11pm Fri, Sat. **Main courses** $20-$30. **Credit** AmEx, Disc, MC, V. **Hotel** p98. **Map** p318 D1.
It claims to be 'Vegas's best-kept secret', but that's the double-edged sword of being Downtown: if you're a decent restaurant, who's going to know? Just those savvy Hawaiian tourists, and they're obviously not talking. They have taste, though: this grill is an upscale, attractive place for innovative Pacific Rim cuisine, including a whole fried Thai red snapper that manages to be both art and architecture.

The rest of the city

American & steakhouses

Big Mama's Rib Shack

2230 W Bonanza Road, at N Rancho Drive, North Las Vegas (597 1616/www.bigmamasribs.com). Bus 106, 215. **Open** 11am-9pm Mon-Thur; 11am-10pm Fri, Sat; noon-8pm Sun. **Main courses** $3-$18. **Credit** AmEx, Disc, MC, V. **Map** p317 X1.
Memphis Championship Barbecue (*see p158*) has its fans, but, at least for our money, this spartan place on a sketchy stretch of Bonanza Road is the best barbecue joint in Las Vegas. Eat here two or three times a week, and you'll figure out why Mama got to be Big: this stuff is rich, hefty and irresistible. Try the BBQ combo – ribs, chicken, sliced pork and a sausage link, with bread and two sides – for a survey of the menu. Then have a lie down.

Bob Taylor's Ranch House

6250 Rio Vista Street, at Azure Drive, North Las Vegas (645 1399/www.bobtaylorsranchhouse.com). No bus. **Open** 4-10pm Mon-Thur, Sun; 4-11pm Fri, Sat. **Main courses** $7-$19 lunch; $14-$43 dinner. **Credit** AmEx, Disc, MC, V.
Fans of spurs – the pointed cowboy boot-heel things, not the perennially sub-standard English football team – should head for Bob Taylor's, where a huge collection is displayed on the walls. When BT's opened in the 1950s it was surrounded by desert and a few ranches, but now the suburbs have closed in. Mesquite-grilled steaks, cooked almost inside the ranch-styled dining room, are the speciality. An old-school classic.

This recently renovated Mexican restaurant in the Arts District offers a large menu that thankfully goes well beyond the typical blasé combo plate with seafood specialities (try the fish or shrimp tacos), tender and flavoursome chilli rellenos, and tasty ranchero breakfasts. On First Friday, this place gets overwhelmed, proving just how small the kitchen is compared to the dining room.

Doña Maria's

910 Las Vegas Boulevard South, at Hoover Avenue (382 6538). Bus 206, 301. **Open** 8am-10pm daily. **Main courses** $7-$10 lunch; $9-$16 dinner. **Credit** AmEx, DC, Disc, MC, V. **Map** p318 C3.
The prices are good and the location is central, but Doña Maria's is very popular with the city's large Mexican community for one reason above all others: this loud and boisterous place serves some of Vegas's best Mexican food. The tamales (spicy chopped meat and ground corn, served in a corn husk) are the real draw, but the tortas (sandwiches) and fiery salsas also help keep the place packed.

El Sombrero Café

807 S Main Street, at Gass Avenue (382 9234). Bus 108, 207, 301. **Open** 11am-9pm Mon-Sat. **Main courses** $7-$12. **Credit** AmEx, MC, V. **Map** p318 C2.

Eat, Drink, Shop

Hot Rod Grille

1231 American Pacific Drive, between Stephanie Street & Gibson Road, Henderson (567 5659). Bus 107. **Open** *Bar* 24hrs daily. *Restaurant* 7am-11pm daily. **Main courses** $9-$16. **Credit** AmEx, DC, Disc, MC, V.

Those people who remember George Lucas's 1973 classic *American Graffiti* for what they wanted to be (a piece of dreamy, soft-focus rock 'n' roll nostalgia) rather than what it actually was (an edgy, almost nihilistic drama about the iniquities of youth and the dreariness of the adulthood that waits) will love this heavily themed retro diner. However, even those who paid attention will find it hard to resist the cracking burgers and worthwhile pizzas.

M&M's Soul Food

4485 S Jones Boulevard, between W Flamingo Road & W Tropicana Avenue, Southwest Las Vegas (795 3663). Bus 102. **Open** 11am-11pm daily. **Main courses** $10-$18. **Credit** AmEx, Disc, MC, V.

The location's a little curious, wedged upstairs in a small strip mall and hard to find if you don't know where you're looking. But the food is a treat: soul food the way it was meant to be served, which is to say very fresh and in immense portions. If you only have one thing, make it the smothered chicken, fried chicken left to drown in delectable gravy. There's a full bar menu, but you're best off washing it down with sweet tea.

Memphis Championship Barbecue

2250 E Warm Springs Road, at S Eastern Avenue, Southeast Las Vegas (260 6909/www.memphis-bbq.com). Bus 217. **Open** 11am-10pm Mon-Thur, Sun; 11am-10.30pm Fri, Sat. **Main courses** $7-$20. **Credit** AmEx, Disc, MC, V.

The appellation arouses suspicion: usually, restaurants that take in vain the name of a foreign city don't last five minutes in the place to which they're meant to be paying tribute. However, if that's the rule, then this is the exception: this is a terrific place, and one that manages to maintain its high quality between all of its four locations. The ribs are the best in the city and the brisket's not far behind. If you're not a vegetarian, you'll eat very well here indeed. **Other locations**: 1401 S Rainbow Boulevard, Southwest Las Vegas (254 0520); 4949 N Rancho Drive, North Las Vegas (396 6223); 4379 Las Vegas Boulevard, North Las Vegas (644 0000).

Sweet Georgia Brown

2600 E Flamingo Road, at S Eastern Avenue, East Las Vegas (369 0245). Bus 202. **Open** 10am-10.30pm daily. **Main courses** $8-$13 lunch; $16-$20 dinner. **Credit** AmEx, DC, Disc, MC, V.

The swanky 1980s decor is very curious, not at all what you'd expect from a glance at the southern-style menu. But the food is just what you'd hoped for when you made the effort to head out east for some fill-me-up home cookin'. The ribs are a real winner, but you pretty much can't go wrong with anything chicken-based.

Hot Rod Grille.

Table 34

600 E Warm Springs Road, between Bermuda Road & Paradise Road, Southeast Las Vegas (263 0034).
Bus 217. **Open** 11am-3pm Mon; 11am-3pm, 5-10pm Tue-Fri; 5-10pm Sat. **Main courses** $14-$29. **Credit** AmEx, MC, V.

New American eaterie Wild Sage was once one of the best locally owned restaurants. It didn't last: the place crashed financially. But good comes of bad, and the sibling Kendricks (including Puck-protégé Wes) have returned with this place, Wild Sage reborn bigger and stronger. The comfortably modern decor serves as a palate cleanser for Puckish pizza, own-made soups and entrées such as braised pot roast.

Chinese

Sam Woo BBQ

Chinatown Plaza, 4215 W Spring Mountain Road, at Wynn Road, Southwest Las Vegas (368 7628).
Bus 203. **Open** 10am-11pm Mon-Thur, Sun; 10am-midnight Fri, Sat. **Main courses** $7-$20. **No credit cards.**

Grumpy service and an atmosphere that can be charitably called authentic filters out those who would better be served at a chain, leaving the BBQ (try the must-share combi: sweet pork, caramelised duck breast and a whole chicken), noodles and seafood for those who dare to live a little. Vegetarians run from the pigs and drained poultry that are displayed as a carnivorous shopfront collage.

Shanghai Noon

3943 Spring Mountain Road, at S Valley View Boulevard, Southwest Las Vegas (257 1628). Bus 104, 203. **Open** 11am-11pm daily. **Main courses** $7-$14. **Credit** MC, V.

The best Chinese in Vegas, but unless you have the stomach for adventure, you'll be relegated to raving about the incredible northern noodles. This immensely popular hole-in-the-wall cockily struts out one gorgeous, low-priced plate after another of exotic, otherworldly sounding delights (seafood, hot pots; all translated on the specials menu) to giddy patrons who know their way around.

Fondue

Melting Pot

8704 W Charleston Boulevard, between S Durango Drive & S Fort Apache Road, Northwest Las Vegas (384 6358). Bus 206. **Open** 5-10pm Mon-Thur; 5-11pm Fri; 4-11pm Sat; 3-9pm Sun. **Main courses** $16-$60 2 sharing; $39 4 courses. **Credit** AmEx, Disc, MC, V.

This stylish national chain takes the 1970s fondue phenomenon out of the Yahtzee party and into the 21st-century restaurant. It's very expensive to cook your own food, but you'll have enough fun doing it, and the ingredients are so tasty, that it won't matter much when you get the bill. You can have a romantic meal here if you want, but it's more fun to

get together a (small or large) group of adventurous friends who don't mind the intimacy of a lengthy, shared meal.

French & Mediterranean

Ambiance Bistro

3980 E Sunset Road, at Annie Oakley Drive, Henderson (454 3020/www.ambianceusa.com). Bus 212. **Open** 7.30am-9pm Mon-Fri; 8.30am-10pm Sat. **Main courses** $17-$30. **Credit** AmEx, Disc, MC, V.

Speaking French helps you get by at this place, one of a clutch of expat-owned eateries to open in Vegas in 2004. The pleasant family-run bistro/bakery is a secret fave among Green Valley's sizeable French community (thank Cirque du Soleil for that). Secure a patio table for lunch and enjoy extraordinarily fresh sandwiches on fresh-baked baguettes, or come back for dinner and the upscale bistro menu.

Bonjour Casual French Restaurant

Suite 100, 8878 S Eastern Avenue, at E Pebble Road, Henderson (270 2102). Bus 111. **Open** 11am-2pm, 5.30-10pm Tue-Fri; 5.30-10pm Sat, Sun. **Main courses** $8-$15 lunch; $17-$25 dinner. **Credit** AmEx, DC, Disc, MC, V.

Expat natives of Cannes operate this cheerful Green Valley bistro where the service (surprise!) and the food justify the expense, even if the plain decor doesn't. A well-chosen – albeit brief – selection of wines complements a lengthy list of French Riviera traditions in appetisers (frogs' legs, onion soup), salads (roquefort and pear) and entrées (seafood, steak au poivre). Plan to finish with dessert crêpes.

Marche Bacchus

2620 Regatta Drive, at Breakwater Drive, Desert Shores (804 8008). **Open** 10am-10pm Mon-Sat; 10am-3pm Sun. **Main courses** $10-$15 lunch; $15-$30 dinner. **Credit** AmEx, MC, V.

Owners Gregoire and Agathe Verge couldn't have chosen a better spot – next to a lake stocked with ducks, fish and turtles – to open this French bistro. The lakeside wine shop and dining terrace in the northwest Las Vegas community of Desert Shores has an authentic European feel, with crated wines sold at bargain prices and a menu that features such delicacies as French onion soup, roasted chicken and the *l'assiette composée*, a selection of French cheeses, grainy country pâté and salamis.

Rosemary's Restaurant

West Sahara Promenade, 8125 W Sahara Avenue, at S Cimmaron Road, Southwest Las Vegas (869 2251/www.rosemarysrestaurant.com). Bus 204. **Open** 11.30am-2.30pm, 5.30-10.30pm Mon-Fri; 5.30-10.30pm Sat, Sun. **Main courses** $20 3-course lunch; $20-$40 dinner. **Credit** AmEx, DC, Disc, MC, V.

Michael and Wendy Jordan have made this neighbourhood haunt an alluring place, an a source of Las Vegas pride. Though nestled in a strip mall, the interior is comfortable and classy, and the menu is tantalisingly innovative: Hugo's Texas barbecued shrimp with Maytag blue cheese 'slaw, roasted chestnut soup, and roasted rack of lamb with kalamata-olive-mashed potatoes. The wine list is among the best in the city.

Italian

Anthony & Mario's Broadway Pizzeria

850 S Rancho Drive, at E Charleston Boulevard, Northwest Las Vegas (259 9002). Bus 106, 206, 215. **Open** 11am-11pm daily. **Main courses** $8-$15. **Credit** AmEx, Disc, MC, V. **Map** p319 A3.
It's small, brightly lit and 'decorated' with two sports-oriented TVs and much 9/11 memorabilia. But there's a reason why so many BMWs from the nearby Scotch 80s development are parked here: A&M's serves quite possibly the best take-out NYC-style pizza in town, but at prices to suit the budget traveller. The baked ziti, spaghetti and meatballs, and huge, hot grinders (sandwiches) aren't bad at all, and the garlic knots are addictive.

Bleu Gourmet

8751 W Charleston Boulevard, between S Rampart Boulevard & S Durango Drive (363 2538). Bus 206. **Open** 7am-9pm daily. **Main courses** $7-$20. **Credit** AmEx, Disc, MC, V.
Is it a wine store? A café? A bistro? Nowhere else but here can you enjoy retail wine (with no corkage fee), delicious pizza, salads and sandwiches on baked-to-order bread: try the scrambled egg, asparagus and fontina cheese). Urban, friendly and different, and with free wireless internet to boot.

Bootlegger Bistro

7700 Las Vegas Boulevard South, at Blue Diamond Road, South of Strip (736 4939/www.bootleggerlas vegas.com). **Open** 24hrs daily. **Main courses** $13-$35. **Credit** AmEx, DC, Disc, MC, V.
This extraordinary operation south of the Strip comes with a flamboyance that's two parts Italian, one part Las Vegan and three parts pure show business. There's a full menu here, Italian staples sold at prices several dollars in excess of their actual worth. But the entertainment is the key: old-school lounge acts crooning the evenings away, with patter as old as the city itself and just as irresistible. The fact that the owner is the Lieutenant Governor of Nevada, a lounge artist in her own right who'll happily do a turn when prompted, somehow makes perfect sense. A classic.

Casa di Amore

2850 E Tropicana Avenue, at S Eastern Avenue, Southeast Las Vegas (433 4967). Bus 201. **Open** 24hrs. **Main courses** $8-$10 lunch; $11-$30 dinner. **Credit** AmEx, DC, Disc, MC, V. **Map** p317 Z3.
Recently opened (in a former pizza joint) but implying classic Vegas in a 1960s way, this cosy, clubby Amer-Italian restaurant offers a selection of throw-back dishes (red sauce pasta, chicken Angelo), delish pizza, authentic recipes (baked clams, chicken pasta soup) and seafood. The Rat Packmosphere draws old-school Las Vegans 24/7, but after-hours weekends, when the place has live music, are especially busy.

Fellini's

5555 W Charleston Boulevard, between S Decatur Boulevard & S Jones Boulevard, Northwest Las Vegas (870 9999). Bus 206. **Open** 5-10pm Mon-Thur, Sun; 5-11pm Fri, Sat. **Main courses** $10-$30. **Credit** AmEx, Disc, MC, V.
Searching for that elusive old Vegas feel? Find it here, at this 1998 conversion of one of the city's oldest pizza parlours. At this upscale southern Italian (forget the red sauce) restaurant out west, politicos, aging Strip stars and up-and-comers in the gold jewellery set enjoy excellent antipasti and entrées (linguini pescatore, veal, chicken) washed down by a wide selection of quality scotches.

Montesano's Deli & Restaurant

3441 W Sahara Avenue, between S Valley View Boulevard & Arville Street, Southwest Las Vegas (876 0348). Bus 104, 204. **Open** 10am-9pm Mon-Sat. **Main courses** $7-$18. **Credit** AmEx, Disc, MC, V. **Map** p317 X2.
If bread's your thing, you'll want to pop this family-run establishment, which operates as a successful wholesale Italian bakery but bakes a mean pizza too. Of these, the five-cheese and fresh tomato are favourites, but you can't go wrong with the gnocchi with pink cream sauce. The fresh-baked tiramisu, cannoli and Italian cheesecakes are superb.

Nora's Cuisine

Flamingo Verde, 6020 W Flamingo Road, at S Jones Boulevard, Southwest Las Vegas (873 8990/www. norascuisine.com). Bus 102, 202. **Open** 11am-2.30pm, 4.30-10pm Mon-Fri; 4.30-10pm Sat, Sun. **Main courses** $6-$16. **Credit** AmEx, Disc, MC, V.
A classic family-run Italian restaurant, almost to the point of cliché. There are pizzas and there are mains, but the smart browser orders chicken Mount Etna, a cheese-topped chicken breast served over fried angel hair that's an absolute blast. Whatever you order, you won't need a starter: the bread is moreish and the portions are enormous.

La Scala

Mark I Tower, 1020 E Desert Inn Road, between S Maryland Parkway & Swenson Street, East Las Vegas (699 9980). Bus 112. **Open** 11.30am-2pm, 5-10pm Mon-Fri; 5-10pm Sat, Sun. **Main courses** $12-$34. **Credit** AmEx, Disc, MC, V. **Map** p317 Y3.
Located on the site of the now-departed Vesuvio's and sadly saddled with its unimpressive decor, La Scala pops out some outstanding northern Italian dishes that compete for quality with similar Strip offerings, but at almost half the price. You can tell from the superior bread that you're in for something special; if that doesn't do it for you, then the cool artichoke salad (big enough for two) or prosciutto with figs will.

Japanese

Osaka

4205 W Sahara Avenue, between S Valley View Boulevard & Arville Street, East Las Vegas (876 4988/www.lasvegas-sushi.com). Bus 204. **Open** 11.30am-midnight daily. **Main courses** $8-$50. **Credit** AmEx, DC, Disc, MC, V.

Sushi, hibachi cooking and traditional Japanese fare are all done very well at Las Vegas's oldest Japanese restaurant. There's a teppan (hibachi) grill area in addition to the main space; both are great for groups. The spotlight is on sushi, with everything from the expected (yellowtail) to the exotic (flying fish eggs). There's a discernible fusion twist to the menu, and the bilingual staff are very helpful.

Latin American & Southwestern

Chipotle

10251 S Eastern Avenue, at Coronado Center Drive, Henderson (361 6438). Bus 110. **Open** 11am-10pm daily. **Main courses** $5-$8. **Credit** AmEx, MC, V.

Get plenty of bang for your buck at this joint, via massive customised fast-food burritos (share one if you eat light) and beef or chicken tacos served in a stylish raw-urban environment through which blasts a pleasantly eclectic music mix. Not quite the spicy Tex-Mex taste treat of Baja Fresh (*see p133*), Chipotle relies on more traditional, lime-heavy flavours, and makes for a pleasant change. Popular with the college crowd.

Inka Si Señor Peruvian Grill

2797 S Maryland Parkway, at Koval Lane, East Las Vegas (731 0826). Bus 109. **Open** 11am-9.30pm Mon-Thur; 11am-10.30pm Fri, Sat; 11am-9pm Sun. **Main courses** $11-$15. **Credit** AmEx, DC, Disc, MC, V.

Diners at this laid-back eaterie are surrounded by colourful Peruvian tapestries and art depicting the sacred condor and Peruvian Incas, and there's live Peruvian music on Saturdays to complete the experience. Try ceviche with onions and peppers or fried yucca dipped in a spicy cream sauce and green onions to start, before delving into the chicken breast in pisco, a Peruvian brandy made from green grapes. Wash it down with a Peruvian beer or the Inka Kola.

Lindo Michoacan

2655 E Desert Inn Road, between S Eastern Avenue & S Pecos Road, East Las Vegas (735 6828/www. lindomichoacan.com). Bus 112. **Open** 11am-10pm Mon-Wed; 11am-11pm Thur, Fri; 9.30am-11pm Sat, Sun. **Main courses** $6-$8 lunch; $5-$17 dinner. **Credit** AmEx, Disc, MC, V. **Map** p317 Z3.

After suffering a debilitating kitchen fire that almost finished the business, this spot happily reopened in 2004; it may not be better than ever, but nor has it gotten worse. Uniquely Michoacan dishes made with shrimp, chicken and steak supplement the burritos, and it's all fresh, tasty and excellent value.

Quinta Belina

8665 W Flamingo Road, at S Durango Drive, Southwest Las Vegas (227 9191). Bus 201, 203. **Open** 11am-10pm Mon-Sat. **Main courses** $6-$10 lunch; $10-$14 dinner. **Credit** AmEx, Disc, MC, V.

Memphis Championship Barbecue. *See p158.*

Belina Garcia's authentic Mexican features recipes heavy on traditional mole sauces, which seem to scare away the combo-plate crowd. Foodies, however, chat about it like it's the undiscovered country: squash blossom quesadillas, Swiss enchiladas and shrimp Jalisco, all cooked with no concession to Texas tastes.

Rigo's Tacos #8

2737 Las Vegas Boulevard North, at N Pecos Road, North Las Vegas (399 1160). Bus 111, 113. **Open** 24hrs daily. **Main courses** $1-$6. **No credit cards.**
A small SoCal chain that sells fast Mexican food done right, Rigo's gives North Las Vegas's Hispanic community, and anyone smart enough to forgo the horrible countrywide chains, a range of excellent tortillas, tacos and fried pork burritos. There's a fantastic salsa bar for fresh tomato, smoked chilli and green chilli sauces. Gringos are thin on the ground.

Z Tejas

9560 W Sahara Avenue, at S Fort Apache Road, Summerlin (638 0610/www.ztejas.com). Bus 204. **Open** 11am-10pm Mon-Thur; 11am-11pm Fri; 9-11pm Sat; 9am-9pm Sun. **Main courses** $9-$18. **Credit** AmEx, DC, Disc, MC, V.
Cajun influence touches upon this Southwestern chain, which is way better than it could be. A revamped and tightened menu focuses on a few favourites (wild mushroom enchiladas) alongside strong new items such as horseradish-encrusted salmon. Margaritas, especially the potent and delicious Big Stick, help you forget the suburban brood running amok in the booth next to you.

Zaba's Burritos

3318 E Flamingo Road, at S Pecos Road, East Las Vegas (435 9222). Bus 202. **Open** 11am-10pm Mon-Sat; 11am-8pm Sun. **Main courses** $5-$8. **Credit** Disc, MC, V. **Map** p317 Z3.
Aye-aye-aye! Part of the ever-growing trend of burrito and taco chains, Zaba's is as fresh as salsa fresca, with tender grilled meats and delectable guacamole. The decor is stark but the selections are miles away from fast food, despite the speed with which they're prepared. *Muy delicioso!*

Middle Eastern

Hedary's

7365 W Sahara Avenue, at S Buffalo Drive, West Las Vegas (873 9041). **Open** 11am-10pm Mon-Thur; 11am-11pm Fri, Sat. **Main courses** $9-$17 lunch; $11-$22 dinner. **Credit** AmEx, DC, Disc, MC, V.
Only the third outpost of a family-run favourite (opened in Texas in 1976), this Lebanese eatery offers fabulous, fresh renditions of the expected falafel, houmous, tabouleh and kibbeh, plus plenty of speciality items (maniq, lamb kebabs). Order the tasting meze for a never-ending supply of incredibly good small plates.

Hold the pickle!

Las Vegas has plenty of breakfast and dinner options, but a quick, decent lunch can be harder to find. One solution is to gorge yourself at a buffet and then sleepwalk through the afternoon; another is to grab a hot dog from the stand by the nickel slots and then find yourself dyspeptic long before evening. Happily, a handful of good delis have recently migrated to Las Vegas to serve quality, overstuffed sandwiches. The catch? Similarly oversized prices.

The **Stage Deli** was the first to arrive from New York, and now has outlets at Bally's (650 2922), the Forum Shops at Caesars Palace (893 4045) and the MGM Grand (891 7777). In Manhattan, the Stage is renowned for dishes named for celebrities, such as the 'Martha Stewart Chef's Salad'. The menu is similar here, with the expensive but expansive sandwiches named after Las Vegas stars, but also includes some full cooked meals. The Stage Delis are walk-ups with small seating areas, so customers don't get much 'Big Apple' ambience beyond a few murals and the possibility of a rude cashier.

The Mirage has recently gotten into the act, adding a branch of Manhattan's **Carnegie Deli** (791 7111). It's primarily a sit-down restaurant, open from breakfast through to the early hours and offering a shorter version of the original menu at full-strength prices: a pastrami sandwich with a pickle garnish costs more than many lunch buffets. Take-out costs extra, as does sharing one of their oversized meals. Perhaps high prices are a way of giving visitors a real New York experience. Still, the matzoh ball soup, herring and cheesecake are all great.

Another recent arrival, this time from the West Coast, is TI's **Canter's Deli** (894 7370). The original is a 75-year-old LA institution, and it looks like the Naugahyde decor and some of the waitresses have been there from the start. Las Vegas's branch looks rather more modern, and the younger servers aren't as likely to mother and scold you, but you'll still get the same hearty sandwiches on Canter's own sourdough-rye bread, and great soups, including the best matzoh ball on the Strip.

Paymon's Mediterranean Café & Market

Tiffany Square, 4147 S Maryland Parkway, at E Flamingo Road, University District (731 6030/www. paymons.com). Bus 108, 202. **Open** *Café* 11am-1am Mon-Thur; 11am-3am Fri, Sat; 11am-5pm Sun. *Market* 9am-8pm Mon-Fri; 10am-5pm Sat. **Main courses** $7-$15. **Credit** AmEx, Disc, MC, V. **Map** p317 Y3.

Long before the idea caught on, Paymon Raouf was serving the kind of ethnic food that the college crowd adores. Even now, when so many Middle Eastern restaurants have opened up here, the Med – decent for dinner but best for lunch – still wins out, simply because its falafel and kebabs are better than anyone else's. Next door's Hookah Lounge (*see p173*) makes a curious but effective companion.

Pita Place

3429 S Jones Boulevard, at W Desert Inn Road, Southeast Las Vegas (221 9955). **Open** 11am-8pm daily. **Main courses** $10-$14. **Credit** MC, V.

Finding a quality restaurant in a redesigned Taco Bell is like a karmic Easter Egg balancing out the cuisine world. The variety is astounding: falafel, top chicken shawarma, and grape leaves meet malhwa, jahnoon and other tastes from the Middle East. The salad bar is excellent. A largely undiscovered gem.

Thai, Vietnamese & Pan-Asian

Thai Spice

4433 W Flamingo Road, at S Arville Street, Southwest Las Vegas (362 5308). Bus 104, 202. **Open** 11am-10pm Mon-Sat. **Main courses** $7-$17. **Credit** AmEx, Disc, MC, V.

Escape the glitz to this clean, big, bright and modern restaurant, an anomaly among the local Asian eateries. A short drive or cab ride west of the Strip hotels (or a stroll from the Palms) is justified by the excellent, pocket-friendly versions of favourites such as Thai beef salad, pad Thai, tom kha gai (hot and sour chicken soup) and fish cakes.

Buffets

The idea of the buffet started in the 1940s at the original El Rancho. Looking to keep customers in his casino after the show, Beldon Katleman dreamed up the Midnight Chuckwagon Buffet, promising 'all you can eat for a dollar'. His idea of treating all guests to a feast for a small price was soon copied and expanded by other hotels: why not offer it all day round? Thus was born the cult of the value-packed Las Vegas buffet.

Casino buffets typically serve breakfast, lunch and dinner, often scrapping breakfast and lunch at weekends in favour of an all-day brunch (many including a glass of champagne). At most major resorts, buffets cost $8-$15 for breakfast, $10-$17 for lunch and $15-$25 for dinner. Prices are lower in locals' casinos away from the Strip; kids often eat for less (generally half-price, with under-4s sometimes eating for free). But whatever the price and time, all Vegas buffets work in the same way: you pay your money at the start and then stuff yourself silly.

Modern buffets barely resemble the old chuckwagon smörgåsbords. Featuring a variety of carving and cooking stations, plus steam tables or kiosks, the average dinner buffet has at least 50 food selections, from salads to cakes. Most buffets offer a fairly standard selection of American favourites, but the more adventurous ones supplement them with foreign dishes. Some offer theme buffets featuring a 'guest' cuisine on different nights of the week; call for details.

Buffet etiquette is simple: you can eat as much as you want while you're there, but don't take anything away. Health codes oblige you to take a new plate every time you return; leave your used plates and a small tip on the table, to be picked up by the buffet staff. If you don't like to wait in line, a time-tested rule of thumb goes something like this: early for breakfast, late for lunch and early for dinner. It seems to work.

All the buffets listed below are in casinos. However, a handful of local restaurants also offer good buffet deals: among them are the Indian lunch buffet at **Gandhi** (*see p153*) and the sushi buffet at **Makino** (3965 S Decatur Boulevard, Southwest Las Vegas, 889 4477). For the town's best kept buffet secret, head to the **Verandah Café** (*see p147*) for weekend brunch.

Bay Side Buffet

Mandalay Bay *3950 Las Vegas Boulevard South, at E Hacienda Avenue (632 7777/www.mandalaybay. com). Bus 105, 301.* **Buffets** *Breakfast* 7-11am daily. *Lunch* 11am-2.45pm daily. *Dinner* 2.45-10pm daily. **Prices** $9.25-$12.75 breakfast; $11.50-$15.50 lunch; $19.75-$22.75 brunch/dinner. **Credit** AmEx, Disc, MC, V. **Hotel** p67. **Map** p320 A9.

Flexing their marketing muscle in the direction of the sophisticated, moneyed traveller, Mandalay Bay doesn't make any big deal about its buffet. A pity: while the selection isn't anything remarkable, it's very well executed and decent value to boot.

Big Kitchen Buffet/Sterling Brunch

Bally's *3645 Las Vegas Boulevard South, at E Flamingo Road (967 7999/www.caesars.com/ballys/ lasvegas). Bus 202, 301, 302.* **Buffets** Big Kitchen Buffet: *Brunch* 7am-4pm daily. *Dinner* 4-10pm daily. Sterling Brunch: 9.30am-2pm Sun. **Prices** *Big Kitchen Buffet* $12.95 brunch; $18.95 dinner. *Sterling Brunch* $58. **Credit** AmEx, Disc, MC, V. **Hotel** p76. **Map** p320 A7.

The daily Big Kitchen Buffet at Bally's is one of the town's best. However, Sunday's swanky Sterling Brunch takes the biscuit, plus the caviar, the lobster, the beef tenderloin and the champagne cocktail. It really is a class apart.

Eat, Drink, Shop

Buffet at Bellagio

Bellagio *3600 Las Vegas Boulevard South, at W Flamingo Road (693 7111/www.bellagio.com). Bus 202, 301, 302.* **Buffets** *Breakfast* 8-10.30am Mon-Fri. *Brunch* 8am-3.30pm Sat, Sun. *Lunch* 11am-3.30pm daily. *Dinner* 4-10pm Mon-Thur, Sun; 4-11pm Fri, Sat. **Prices** $13.95 breakfast; $21.95 brunch; $17.95 lunch; $25.95-$33.95 dinner. **Credit** AmEx, Disc, MC, V. **Hotel** p63. **Map** p320 A7.

The Buffet at Bellagio is – much like the rest of the hotel – smart yet approachable, stylish yet undemonstrative, expensive yet probably just about worth it. Usual buffet fare gets upgraded with extras such as venison, steamed clams and crab legs.

Carnival World Buffet

Rio *3700 W Flamingo Road, at S Valley View Boulevard, West of Strip (252 7777/www.playrio. com). Bus 104, 202.* **Buffets** Carnival World Buffet: *Breakfast* 7-11am Mon-Fri; 7.30am-10.30am Sat, Sun. *Brunch* 10.30am-3.30pm Sat, Sun. *Lunch* 11.30am-3.30pm Mon-Fri. *Dinner* 3.30-10pm daily. Village Seafood Buffet: *Dinner* 4-10pm Mon-Thur, Sun; 3-11pm Fri, Sat. **Prices** *Carnival World Buffet* $12.99 breakfast; $22.99 brunch; $14.99 lunch; $22.99 dinner. *Village Seafood Buffet* $34.99. **Credit** AmEx, Disc, MC, V. **Hotel** p93. **Map** p317 X3.

A favourite among locals, the pioneering Carnival World Buffet journeys the planet for its food. It's an idea that several other casinos have since copied, but no one has yet topped the Rio's international spreads, which take in everything from lasagne to Peking duck, sushi to cheesecake. The expensive Seafood Buffet offers sushi, oysters and lobster as well as a range of meat dishes.

Fresh Market Square Buffet

Harrah's *3475 Las Vegas Boulevard South, between Sands Avenue & E Flamingo Road (369 5000/www. harrahs.com). Bus 301.* **Buffets** *Breakfast* 7-11am Mon-Fri; 7-10am Sat, Sun. *Brunch* 10am-4pm Sat, Sun. *Lunch* 11am-4pm Mon-Fri. *Dinner* 4-10pm daily. *Late night* 10pm-5am daily. **Prices** $10.99 breakfast; $16.99 brunch; $12.99 lunch; $16.99 dinner. **Credit** AmEx, Disc, MC, V. **Hotel** p78. **Map** p320 A6.

The buffet at Harrah's is one of several in the city that tries to cover the planet, from Japan to South America via Italy and France. However, the real USP are the hours: the Harrah's buffet keeps the food coming until five in the morning. A worthwhile mid-Strip choice.

Golden Nugget Buffet

Golden Nugget *129 Fremont Street, at Casino Center Boulevard, Downtown (385 7111/www.golden nugget.com). Bus 107, 108, 207, 301, 302.* **Buffets** *Breakfast* 7-10.30am Mon-Sat. *Brunch* 8am-10pm Sun. *Lunch* 10.30am-3pm Mon-Sat. *Dinner* 4-10pm Mon-Sat. **Prices** $6.99 breakfast; $13.99 brunch; $7.99 lunch; $12.99 dinner. **Credit** Disc, MC, V. **Hotel** p96. **Map** p318 C1.

Downtown's smartest buffet more than delivers the goods that its reputation demands of it. The offerings are near the top of the Vegas food chain, especially the carvery, typically serving turkey and prime rib. Excellent desserts, too.

Le Village Buffet

Paris Las Vegas *3555 Las Vegas Boulevard South, at E Flamingo Road (946 7000/www.parislasvegas. com). Bus 202, 301.* **Buffets** *Breakfast* 7-11.30am daily. *Lunch* 11.30am-5.30pm Mon-Sat. *Brunch* 11.30am-4pm Sun. *Dinner* 5.30-10pm Mon-Thur, Sun; 5.30-11pm Fri, Sat. **Prices** $12.95 breakfast; $24.95 brunch; $17.95 lunch; $24.95 dinner. **Credit** AmEx, DC, Disc, MC, V. **Hotel** p69. **Map** p320 A7.

You'd hope the one French-themed casino in town would offer a good buffet, and so it goes. The 400-seat Le Village Buffet has stations representing five French provinces, dishing up a variety of surprisingly fine foods (it's especially good for meat-lovers). Save room for the fresh pastries and desserts.

Other buffets

Almost every casino in the city has a buffet of some description. The ones reviewed above are the city's best; those below are decent alternatives, notable either by dint of size (**Circus Circus** serves up to 10,000 diners a day), price (of the cheaper buffets, **Palace Station** is among the best) or food (the **Mirage**, **Main Street Station** and **Caesars Palace** all offer very decent spreads). Other locals' casinos, such as the **Suncoast** and **Sunset Station**, offer fairly ordinary food, but at ridiculously cheap prices.

Caesars Palace *3570 Las Vegas Boulevard South, at W Flamingo Road (731 7110/www.caesarspalace. com). Bus 202, 301.* **Buffets** *Breakfast* 7-11.30am daily. *Lunch* 11.30am-3pm Mon-Fri. *Brunch* 11am-5pm Sat, Sun. *Dinner* 5-10pm daily. **Prices** $14 breakfast; $21.99 brunch; $16 lunch; $21.99 dinner. **Credit** AmEx, Disc, MC, V. **Hotel** p65. **Map** p320 A7.

Circus Circus *2880 Las Vegas Boulevard South, between Stardust Road & W Sahara Avenue (734 0410/www.circuscircus.com). Bus 301.* **Buffets** *Breakfast* 7am-2pm Mon-Fri. *Brunch* 7am-4pm Sat, Sun. *Dinner* 4.30-10pm daily. **Prices** $8.49 breakfast; $9.49 brunch; $10.49 dinner. **Credit** AmEx, Disc, MC, V. **Map** p319 B5.

Main Street Station *200 N Main Street, at Stewart Avenue, Downtown (387 1896/www.main streetcasino.com). Bus 107, 108, 207, 301, 302.* **Buffets** *Breakfast* 7-10.30am Mon-Fri. *Brunch* 7am-3pm Sat, Sun. *Lunch* 11am-3pm Mon-Fri. *Dinner* 4-10pm daily. **Prices** $5.75 breakfast; $9.95 brunch; $7.75 lunch; $10.79-$15.98 dinner. **Credit** AmEx, Disc, MC, V. **Map** p320 A6.

Mirage *3400 Las Vegas Boulevard South, between Spring Mountain Road & W Flamingo Road (791 7111/www.themirage.com). Bus 203, 213, 301, 302.* **Buffets** *Breakfast* 7-11am Mon-Fri. *Brunch* 8am-3pm Sat, Sun. *Lunch* 11am-3pm Mon-Fri. *Dinner* 3-10pm daily. **Prices** $12.50 breakfast; $20.50 brunch; $17.50 lunch; $22.50 dinner. **Credit** AmEx, Disc, MC, V. **Map** p320 A6.

Palace Station *2411 W Sahara Avenue, at Rancho Drive, West of Strip (367 2411). Bus 204, 401.* **Buffets** *Breakfast* 7-11am Mon-Fri. *Brunch* 7am-3pm Sat, Sun. *Lunch* 11am-3.30pm Mon-Fri. *Dinner* 4-10pm daily. **Prices** $4.99 breakfast; $8.99 brunch; $6.99 lunch; $6.99 dinner. **Credit** AmEx, Disc, MC, V. **Map** p319 A4.

Bars & Lounges

Last call? Who needs last call?

Locals and tourists might argue that civilisation stops somewhere in the Mojave Desert. But when it comes to bar culture, Las Vegas can drink your town under the table. With no requisite last call, there's something particularly Vegas about walking out of a dark bar and emerging, blinking, into the morning light. Look around, shading your eyes from the assault of a Nevadan sun that, while never what you might call gentle, seems to pay particular attention to barflies emerging from the pupal pub stage. And don't worry should anyone point a finger and make quips about alcoholics: this is liquid research into *aqua vitae*, a journey into America's beer-stained heart and whiskey-strained soul. Still, keep in mind that if you become too unruly, the bartender can and will cut you off at any time.

Many of the bars in town, including at least one in every casino, are open 24 hours a day, and if there's gambling, drinks are free with a minimal deposit into your closest video poker machine (usually $10 to $20, depending on the establishment). Besides the subsidised drinking, the sheer variety of bars in Las Vegas is impressive. The hallucinatory creativity that built a neon oasis in the middle of the desert, complete with manufactured mountains, an imitation Eiffel Tower and too many Statues of Liberty to count, offers you mermaids (and mermen) swimming for your pleasure, Lenin's head in deep freeze and the chance to piss on the Berlin Wall. Should these fail to inculcate a sense of wonder in even the

The best Bars

For a cocktail
V Bar. *See p169.*

For a beer
Crown & Anchor Pub. *See p172.*

For a binge
Double Down Saloon. *See p169.*

For a flirt
Viva Las Vegas Lounge. *See p170.*

For a snog
Peppermill's Fireside Lounge. *See p168.*

most jaded tourist, then we can only suggest you deserve to be introduced to a bacon Martini (*see p172* **Viva Moss**).

In a city where yesterday is already out of date, even the local karaoke bar has to work hard to stand out from the competition. If you're looking for a plastic football full of beer, head to the **Fremont Street Experience** (*see p129*). Want a Trekkie-tinny, smoking with dry ice? **Quark's Bar & Restaurant** in the Las Vegas Hilton (*see p170*). And for a classic Blue Hawaiian, zip along to **Peppermill's Fireside Lounge** (*see p168*), and sip your beverage by the matching blue fire pit.

Eat, Drink, Shop

Atomic Liquors. *See p171.*

Lenin goes off his head at **Red Square**. *See p168.*

BOOZE AND THE LAW

You have to be 21 to consume or buy alcohol in Nevada. If you look less than 40, you'll regularly be required to produce some photo identification, such as a driver's licence or passport, even in off-Strip establishments.

Las Vegas's drink-driving laws are as harsh and uncompromising as those in any major US city, and the cops don't let too many woozy fish swim by. So leave the car behind: you can easily walk back and forth between bars on the Strip and Fremont Street, and a taxi ride to and from most of the more distant joints is cheap. Cabs are plentiful around the Strip and the bartender will be happy to call one for you.

The Strip

Bar at Times Square

New York–New York *3790 Las Vegas Boulevard South, at W Tropicana Avenue (740 6969/www.nyny hotelcasino.com). Bus 201, 301, 302.* **Open** 8pm-2am Mon-Thur, Sun; 8pm-3am Fri, Sat. **Credit** AmEx, Disc, V, MC. **Hotel** p83. **Map** p320 A8.

Upbeat energy and off-key voices pour from this bar at New York–New York, where duelling pianos and warbling punters provide the entertainment. The musicians can and will play anything if you've got the money to tip 'em; booties both large and small shake themselves to the tunes. If you're not in a good mood, don't even think about it.

Caramel

Bellagio *3600 Las Vegas Boulevard South, at W Flamingo Road (693 8300/www.caramelbar.com). Bus 202, 301, 302.* **Open** 5pm-4am daily. **Credit** AmEx, Disc, MC, V. **Hotel** p63. **Map** p320 A7.

Caramel is as refined and urbane as the hotel in which it's housed. With opaque marble tables, one-way windows on to the casino floor and a sophisticated, ultra-modern atmosphere, it seems less like a lounge than a private club. The drinks menu is deep, the liquor selection is broad and the prices are high ($15 Martinis are the norm), but so is the quality of the experience. Collared shirts are required and jeans are a definite no-no.

Cleopatra's Barge

Caesars Palace *3570 Las Vegas Boulevard South, at E Flamingo Road (731 7110/www.caesars.com). Bus 202, 301, 302.* **Open** 10am-4am daily. *Lounge* 8pm-3am daily. **Credit** AmEx, Disc, MC, V. **Hotel** p65. **Map** p320 A7.

Yes, that really is a pool in the middle of Caesars Palace, and that really is a boat on it: if ever a bar could claim to really rock, this is the one. It's supposed to be a replica of the boat that transported Egyptian royalty back in Julius Caesar's time. It's certainly a testament to times past, but back to the days when kitsch and imitation were the siren songs luring the tourists. The crowd is less haughty here than at some other bars, allowing Cleopatra's to continue making waves on Las Vegas's very own little Nile.

Coyote Ugly

New York–New York *3790 Las Vegas Boulevard South, at W Tropicana Avenue (740 6969/www. coyoteuglysaloon.com/vegas).* Bus 201, 301, 302. **Open** 6pm-4am daily. **Credit** AmEx, Disc, MC, V. **Hotel** p83. **Map** p320 A8.

The waitresses are the coyotes, but they're not dogs; if they were, they certainly wouldn't be working at this joint, based on a New York bar that was the subject of a ghastly Jerry Bruckheimer movie. During the lairy proceedings, the girls invite boozed-up revellers to join them on a stage; the brave ones are rewarded with shots of liquor poured down their throats. There's nowhere to sit, and it takes a lot of expensive liquor to make standing and watching super-sized tourists gyrate with svelte dancers an enjoyable experience. A *lot.*

Fix

Bellagio *3600 Las Vegas Boulevard South, at E Flamingo Road (693 8400/www.caramelbar.com).* Bus 202, 301, 302. **Open** 5pm-midnight Mon-Thur, Sun; 5pm-2am Fri, Sat. **Credit** AmEx, Disc, MC, V. **Hotel** p63. **Map** p320 A7.

A fresh celebrity hotspot, this bar and restaurant is known for comfort food with contemporary flair. The place manages to be upmarket, sleek and comfortable. There are tasty appetisers and tantalising beverages; inevitably, the waiting staff seem to have been selected from a genetic pool that counts attractiveness as the main determinant of survival. A good spot in which to drink and drift away.

Horse-a-Round Bar

Circus Circus *2880 Las Vegas Boulevard South, between Desert Inn Road & W Sahara Avenue (734 0410/www.circuscircus.com).* Bus 301. **Open** 5pm-midnight Fri, Sat. **Credit** AmEx, Disc, MC, V. **Hotel** p85. **Map** p319 B5.

Even to someone fully in possession of their faculties, Circus Circus is bizarre. Imagine what it must have seemed like to a drug-addled journalist bingeing his talent away in search of the dream that had deserted him (*requiescat in pace*, Hunter S Thompson). There are few more extraordinary places in Las Vegas for a drink than this reopened merry-go-round, surrounded by screaming children, carousel horses, jugglers and the slightly sinister (ever read *It*?) clowns.

Jimmy Buffet's Margaritaville

Flamingo *3555 Las Vegas Boulevard South, at E Flamingo Road (733 3302/www.margaritaville.com).* Bus 202, 301, 302. **Open** 10am-2am Mon-Thur, Sun; 10am-3am Fri, Sat. **Credit** AmEx, DC, Disc, MC, V. **Hotel** p77. **Map** p320 A7.

You've heard of Deadheads, right? Well, here you'll find their ornithological equivalent: Parrotheads. Men dressed in khaki shorts and floral shirts, with parrots perched on their heads, united in their devotion to the 'gulf and western' music of Jimmy Buffet. The theme is tropical, musical, fruitical, cocktailical. The ambience is not for the faint of heart or the sophisticated of taste.

Mist

TI (Treasure Island) *3300 Las Vegas Boulevard South, at Spring Mountain Road (894 7330/www. mistbar.com).* Bus 203, 213, 301, 302. **Open** 5pm-4am daily. **Credit** AmEx, Disc, MC, V. **Hotel** p71. **Map** p320 A6.

Built into the Treasure Island casino's eastern wall, Mist is a handsomely appointed but largely soulless bar with a typically sleek design, a few plasma-screen TVs and some decidedly lackadaisical staff. Perhaps because of this, it's a quiet place to get a drink. They serve a Bugsy Siegel Martini, but there's little else to recommend the joint. The dress code is business-casual.

Mix

THEhotel at Mandalay Bay *3950 Las Vegas Boulevard South, at E Hacienda Avenue (632 7777/ www.mandalaybay.com).* Bus 105, 301. **Open** 5pm-3am Mon-Thur, Sun; 5pm-4am Fri, Sat. **Credit** AmEx, Disc, MC, V. **Hotel** p106. **Map** p320 A9.

Don't wait to wee. Get yourself straight to the restroom and marvel at the size of each cubicle, sufficient to raise a family in some countries. But don't stop there. This water closet of wonder has some of the best views in town, looking out from the 64th floor. Should you ever leave the lavs, you'll find a swank-incarnate lounge, done out in black leather and red lighting. The drinks are pricey and early arrival is required to avoid queues, but Mix is worth it just for the ride up in the glass elevator. Be sure to check out the restaurant next door and its $500,000, 13,000-glass-bulb chandelier.

Monte Carlo Pub & Brewery

Monte Carlo *3770 Las Vegas Boulevard South, between E Harmon Avenue & W Tropicana Avenue (730 7777/www.monte-carlo.com).* Bus 201, 301, 302. **Open** 11am-2am daily. **Credit** AmEx, DC, Disc, MC, V. **Hotel** p82. **Map** p320 A8.

Even if you're not a beer drinker, you'll like the surroundings: huge copper barrels (if you're interested, you can roam the catwalk and gaze down on the brewing process), antique furnishings and an outdoor patio overlooking a lavish pool. Six beers are produced, including an IPA, an unfiltered wheat ale, a stout and a rich amber. Soak it up with brick-oven pizzas, salads and sandwiches, then drink more to blot out the risible bar bands.

Napoleon's

Paris Las Vegas *3655 Las Vegas Boulevard South, at E Flamingo Road (946 7000/www. caesars.com).* Bus 202, 301, 302. **Open** 4pm-2am Mon-Thur, Sun; 2pm-3am Fri, Sat. **Credit** AmEx, Disc, MC, V. **Hotel** p69. **Map** p320 A7.

Name a French city? Paris. Name a Frenchman? Napoleon. Name a French drink? Champagne. And here they are, all present and correct, in Las Vegas, where you can travel the world without leaving the desert. In a manner of speaking, there are 100 varieties of champers from which to choose; study the menu while enjoying the jazz that bubbles through the booze and goes straight to your head.

Peppermill's Fireside Lounge

*Peppermill Inn Restaurant, 2985 Las Vegas
Boulevard South, at Convention Center Drive
(735 7635). Bus 112, 301.* **Open** 24hrs daily.
Credit AmEx, DC, Disc, MC, V. **Map** p319 B5.
One of the last surviving embodiments of Old
Vegas. Known for its romantic seats around the fire
pit (for which it was rated one of 'America's 10 Best
Make-Out Bars' in *Nerve Magazine*), this place is
Vegas at its best. Or, at least, it was, until they put
flat-screen TVs on every available surface and
ruined the vintage feel. Still, the drinks here are
impressive: try a Scorpion, which will arrive in a
glass bigger than your head.

Red Square

Mandalay Bay *3950 Las Vegas Boulevard South,
at E Hacienda Avenue (632 7407/www.mandalay
bay.com). Bus 105, 301.* **Open** 5pm-2am Mon-Thur,
Sun; 5pm-4am Fri, Sat. **Credit** AmEx, DC, MC, V.
Hotel p67. **Map** p320 A9.
The vodkas here are so good they made Lenin lose
his head: an enormous decapitated statue of the
father of the Soviet Union looms over the entrance.
Once you make it through the door, try asking the
barman, over a Martini, just what happened to
Lenin's missing body part. (It's in the freezer, on ice.)
Good food, strong drinks and enough Commie pro-
paganda to make you forget the 110 million people
they killed during the 20th century.

Rumjungle

Mandalay Bay *3950 Las Vegas Boulevard South,
at E Hacienda Avenue (632 7408/www.mandalay
bay.com). Bus 201, 301.* **Open** noon-2am Tue-Thur,
Sun; noon-4am Mon, Fri, Sat. **Credit** AmEx, DC,
MC, V. **Hotel** p67. **Map** p320 A9.

Cowneck, Kill-Devil or Nelson's Blood: it all amounts
to the same thing. At Rumjungle, the signature beverage is the main attraction, no small feat in a room
with walls made of fire and water. A hundred different varieties are served in countless ways; they
bubble, seethe and… well, you'll just have to show
up to find out more. Later on, it becomes a nightclub
(admission $20-$25; *see p243*). Dress smart-casual.

Shadow Bar

Caesars Palace *3750 Las Vegas Boulevard South,
at E Flamingo Road (731 7110/www.caesars.com).
Bus 202, 301, 302.* **Open** 11am-2am Mon-Thur,
Sun; 24hrs Fri, Sat. **Credit** AmEx, DC, Disc, MC,
V. **Hotel** p65. **Map** p320 A7.
Question: how do you get naked women to shake,
writhe and strut their voluptuous stuff without
showing any flesh? Answer: shadow play. The
Shadow Bar continues Las Vegas's hesitating
shimmy towards bringing strip clubs to the Strip
without actually having any stripping. The ladies
concerned, silhouetted on screens, play up what
comes naturally (or, possibly, surgically), while the
expensive drinks bring a haughty air to the proceedings. The dress code is smart-casual.

Sky Lounge

*Polo Towers, 3745 Las Vegas Boulevard South, at E
Harmon Avenue (261 1000). Bus 301.* **Open** 8.30am-
1am daily. **Credit** AmEx, Disc, MC, V. **Map** p320 A8.
Some 19 floors up in a timeshare property, this is
one of the Strip's hidden gems. The lounge is old
school Vegas rendered in millennial style: fuzzy
chairs, a beige interior and a fabulous view of the
Strip, including the fountain show at Bellagio. It's
a soothing place to watch the lights of the suburbs
dim and the city brighten.

V Bar

Venetian 3355 Las Vegas Boulevard South, at Sands Avenue (414 3200/www.venetian.com). Bus 105, 203, 213, 301, 302. **Open** 5pm-4am daily. **Credit** AmEx, DC, Disc, MC, V. **Hotel** p73. **Map** p320 A6.

Brought to you by the creators of the Big Apple's Lotus and LA's Sunset Room, V Bar is as basic, simple and understated as its name. The young, attractive and affluent clientele put on a show for lesser mortals peeking in through small slits in the wall-length frosted glass windows. Dress code smart-casual unless you want to be on the outside.

Stratosphere Area

Dino's

1516 Las Vegas Boulevard South, at W Utah Avenue (382 3894/www.dinoslv.com). Bus 301. **Open** 24hrs daily. **No credit cards. Map** p319 C3.

Located near the burgeoning Arts District, Dino's dubs itself 'The Last Neighborhood Bar in Las Vegas'; that's a slight exaggeration, but a good one. The scene wavers between dark, bespectacled hipsters, local artists – particularly during First Friday – and barflies. The pally bartenders are on first-name terms with many regulars; karaoke nights, hosted by Elton John doppelgänger Danny G (Thursday through Saturday) are among the best off-key moments in town.

Huntridge Tavern

Huntridge Shopping Center, 1116 E Charleston Boulevard, at S Maryland Parkway (384 7377). Bus 109, 206. **Open** 24hrs daily. **No credit cards. Map** p318 D3.

For over 35 years, this hangout has been everything a dive bar should be: low-estate without being seedy, intriguing without being dangerous, careworn without being ugly. Presumably, the fiftysomethings who warm the stools here do go home to their families for an hour or two every once in a while. Still, with brews this cheap, you couldn't really blame them if they just stayed where they are.

East of Strip

Champagnes Café

3557 S Maryland Parkway, between E Desert Inn Road & E Twain Avenue (737 1699/www.champagnecafe.com). Bus 109, 112, 203. **Open** 24hrs daily. **No credit cards. Map** p317 Y3.

In a word: vintage. Dark, velvety wallpaper, Frank and Dino on the jukebox, and even a shrine – consisting of a Martini, a coffee cup and a cigarette – dedicated to Marty, a former manager. The drinks are cheap, and Pat, the shorts-clad bartender, is self-contained entertainment. Hipsters, barflies and regular, discerning Las Vegas locals head here at all hours, and find it hard to leave. A Dom Pérignon '53 among Las Vegas bars.

Double Down Saloon

Paradise Plaza, 4640 Paradise Road, between E Harmon Avenue & E Tropicana Avenue (791 5775/www.doubledownsaloon.com). Bus 108. **Open** 24hrs daily. **No credit cards. Map** p320 C8.

No head for drink? Then hand over $20 for puke insurance; if you barf, they'll clean up. Otherwise, you're on your own at this darkly chaotic bar; 'The Happiest Place on Earth', they bill it, and with good reason. The music is loud, whether from the

Eat, Drink, Shop

Champagnes Café.

impeccably punkish jukebox or the regular bands (see p239), and the vibe is welcoming. House specialities include Ass Juice and bacon Martinis. Beers are a better bet. See also p172 **Viva Moss**.

Freakin' Frog

4700 S Maryland Parkway, near Tropicana (597 9702/www.freakinfrog.com). Bus 109, 201, 213. **Open** 11am-3am daily. **Credit** AmEx, DC, Disc, MC, V. **Map** p317 Y3.

Despite its irritatin' name, this bar is a locals' favourite, and not just because of the 400-strong beer selection. The Frog is across the road from UNLV, and draws students, professors and a variety of professionals. The decor is fairly basic, with hints of froggy green everywhere; there's a slight diner feel to it. But with good food and cult-classic movies showing in the background, no one's grumbling.

Gordon Biersch

3987 Paradise Road, at E Flamingo Road (312 5247/www.gordonbiersch.com). Bus 108, 202. **Open** 11am-midnight Mon-Thur, Sun; 11am-1am Fri, Sat. **Credit** AmEx, Disc, MC, V. **Map** p320 C7.

If you're looking to meet someone in a suit, head to Gordon Biersch for happy hour; or, indeed, any time it's open. There's tasty beer (it's a brewpub, part of a chain based in San Francisco) and good food, but this is chiefly a singles hop for thirtysomethings with close-cropped hair, Banana Republic threads and more money than you.

Quark's Bar & Restaurant

Las Vegas Hilton 3000 Paradise Road, between E Sahara Avenue & E Desert Inn Road (697 8725/ www.startrekexp.com). Bus 108, 112. **Open** 11.30am-11pm daily. **Credit** AmEx, Disc, MC, V. **Hotel** p92. **Map** p319 C5.

We won't speak for the quality of the food at this establishment, which is named after the alien-run watering hole of *Deep Space Nine*. However, you'll be able to accompany your Harry Mudd Martini or rum-based, dry-iced Warp Core Breach with Glop on a Stick (that's a corn dog to you) or the Holy Rings of Betazed (onion rings). It's a fun coda to a visit to the Las Vegas Hilton's Star Trek: The Experience (see p124), and the drinks pack a punch you won't find in most theme park bars.

Viva Las Vegas Lounge

Hard Rock 4455 Paradise Road, at E Harmon Avenue (693 5000/www.hardrockhotel.com). Bus 108. **Open** 24hrs daily. **Credit** AmEx, DC, Disc, MC, V. **Hotel** p91. **Map** p320 C7.

Known as the Side Bar, owing to its location on the edge of the bustling casino, Viva Las Vegas is pretty lively through the week, but really jumps on Friday and Saturday nights, when young singles pack the area to overflowing. The drinks are expensive, but the people-watching makes it worth the cash. Look out for the lightbulb suits worn by the Red Hot Chili Peppers at Woodstock '99 and now reverently displayed behind the bar. Despite this, there's no live music.

West of Strip

Artisan Lounge

Artisan Hotel 1501 W Sahara Avenue, at Highland Drive, West of Strip (214 4000/www. theartisanhotel.com). Bus 204. **Open** 24hrs daily. **Credit** AmEx, MC, V. **Hotel** p107. **Map** p319 B4.

The lobby bar at the Artisan was, until early 2005, one of the best-kept secrets in town. Now the word is getting out, and those in the know are chattering in whispers: they'd really rather not share this place with the masses. This is one of the most impressive and intimate lounges in town, but also one of the quietest: there's no gambling here. Paintings line the walls and ceiling; statues and busts are interspersed with comfort-chic chairs and couches. A unique amalgam of lodge, bar and art house, it's fast becoming arty Vegas's living room away from home.

Ghostbar

Palms 4321 W Flamingo Road, at S Valley View Boulevard (942 7777/www.palms.com). Bus 202. **Open** 8pm-1am Mon-Thur, Sun; 8pm-3am Fri, Sat. **Credit** AmEx, Disc, MC, V. **Hotel** p92. **Map** p317 X3.

After they stopped at this space-aged bar, Britney Spears and Jason Alexander headed to the marriage license bureau. Par for the course in a hotel made infamous by MTV's *The Real World*. Ghostbar has its own private elevator and its own private cover charge ($10-$20); if you deign to pay it, you'll find a cool blue interior, draped with clubbers sipping expensive drinks and bobbing their heads to whatever the DJ is spinning (hip hop, usually). The patio outside has a see-through area where you can look all the way to the ground, 51 floors below.

Little Buddha

Palms 4321 W Flamingo Road, at S Valley View Boulevard (942 7778/www.littlebuddhalasvegas.com). Bus 202. **Open** 5.30-11pm Mon-Thur, Sun; 5.30pm-midnight Fri, Sat. **Credit** AmEx, DC, Disc, MC, V. **Hotel** p92. **Map** p317 X3.

This restaurant and bar, a smaller version of Paris's famed Buddha Bar (and operated by the same folks), has a low-key and sophisticated air, as smooth and relaxing as the popular ambient DJ compilations created in its name. The bar area is small and crowded, but it's still worth checking out for the Asian decor. The drinks and sushi aren't half bad, either.

Tilted Kilt

Rio 3700 W Flamingo Road, at S Valley View Boulevard (777 2463/www.tiltedkilt.com). Bus 202. **Open** 4pm-2am Mon-Thur, Sun; noon-2am Fri, Sat. **Credit** AmEx, Disc, MC, V. **Hotel** p93. **Map** p317 X3.

The Tilted Kilt has its own special play on the Oirish theme, combining blarney with English, Scottish and American themes, and dressing its cocktail waitresses in a Scots-meets-schoolgirl style (short kilts, matching bras, lots of skin). The bar has a brewpub feel, due in part to the 24 premium beers on tap. If the kilts don't do it for you, there are also billiards, darts and tasty pub fare.

Downtown

Atomic Liquors

*917 Fremont Street, at S 9th Street (384 7371).
Bus 107, 109.* **Open** 6am-10pm daily. **No credit
cards**. **Map** p318 D2.

Founded in 1935 and located at the sketchy end of
Fremont Street, this is an absolute gem, from its
cut-to-the-chase sign – 'Liquor' in huge white neon
lights – to the cast of crims, bums, chancers and
Bukowskis who sup here. This is the dive bar to end
all dive bars: shady yet friendly, kooky to outsiders
yet normal to its regulars. If you're looking for trouble, you came to the right place, but most of the
barflies are harmless enough.

Beauty Bar

*517 Fremont Street, at Las Vegas Boulevard South
(598 1965/www.beautybar.com). Bus 301.* **Open** call
for hours. **Credit** AmEx, Disc, MC, V. **Map** p318 D2.

Beauty Bar opened in the spring of 2005, and is one
of the new tenants of what Mayor Oscar Goodman
has proclaimed the 'Entertainment District'; the idea,
not yet realised, is to transform a few Downtown
blocks previously overrun with drug dealers and
hookers into an area holding – gasp! – non-gambling
bars and entertainment. It's part of a national chain:
the New York version often featured in *Sex and the
City* as a place where you could drink a Martini while
getting a manicure.

Ice House Lounge

*650 S Main Street, at E Bonneville Avenue (315
2570). Bus 105, 108, 207.* **Open** 8am-1am daily.
Credit AmEx, DC, Disc, MC, V. **Map** p318 C2.

To locals hoping for a Downtown renaissance, the
Ice House seemed like a mirage: a $5-million free-
standing art deco-style building across the way from

a weekly-rental motel and a porn shop. Located near
the site of Las Vegas's original ice house, it was a
primary player in the development of the town, but
burned down in the 1990s. The lounge sports a retro-
mod '60s interior festooned with photos of old Vegas.
Two ice-topped bars keep your Martinis fresh.
There's happy hour nightly, but on Fridays, it's silly
with downtown hipsters and off-duty barristers.

Jillian's

*Neopolis, 450 Fremont Street, at Las Vegas
Boulevard South (388 4116/www.jillians.com). Bus
301.* **Open** 11am-midnight Mon-Thur, Sun; 11am-1am
Fri, Sat. **Credit** AmEx, Disc, MC, V. **Map** p318 D1.

Jillian's provides 42,000sq ft (3,900sq m) of manufactured fun, drink and food. You can drink and play
video games, drink and bowl, drink and dine, drink
and dance, or, this being Vegas, just drink. Still, the
place hasn't lured as many people to Neopolis as
the mayor would like, perhaps because its offerings
(it's a chain) aren't as unusual here as they would be
in other towns.

Saloon

*Neopolis, 450 Fremont Street, at Las Vegas
Boulevard South (388 4116/www.arkvegas.com/
saloon). Bus 301.* **Open** 11am-10pm Mon-Thur, Sun;
11am-midnight Fri, Sat. **Credit** AmEx, DC, Disc,
MC, V. **Map** p318 D1.

Its thunder has been thieved by the Ice House
(*see above*), where the crowd is usually livelier and
(crucially) the parking is free. However, some locals
love the slots-free Saloon for its friendly staff and
fine location (you can watch the hordes overwhelm
Fremont Street without having to battle through
them), while tourists get to drink in a bar favoured
by Mayor Oscar Goodman (he has his own Martini
glass). Finding a seat is rarely a challenge.

The happy **Hookah Lounge**. *See p173.*

Eat, Drink, Shop

Viva Moss

Las Vegas only has one **Double Down Saloon** (*see p169*). For that matter, the world has only one Double Down Saloon, a bar that has hosted 'all-girl pony rodeos', extends 'special consideration' to bands that include midgets, is powered by one of the planet's greatest jukeboxes and serves a now-infamous bacon Martini (be assured, you probably won't get around to ordering a second). The crowd is equal parts lawyers, strippers, winos and millionaires, and the joint hasn't locked its doors once in a decade. Even the United Nations, with a similar crowd (except, perhaps, the strippers), closes for the occasional holiday.

One would expect such a place to be operated by someone of rare calibre, and Moss – *pictured left*; that's his entire name – is as rare as the Double Down itself. You couldn't pick him out in a crowd if your life depended on it: not because he doesn't have style – he's the only man in Vegas who can get away with wearing vintage shirts and smoking cigars – but because Moss would

Triple 7 Brew Pub

Main Street Station *200 N Main Street, at Stewart Avenue (387 1896/www.mainstreetcasino. com). Bus 106, 108, 207.* **Open** 11am-7am daily. **Credit** AmEx, DC, Disc, MC, V. **Hotel** p96. **Map** p318 C1.

The Triple 7 serves decent beer and bar food – the garlic and herb fries are among the best in town – but the real reason to visit this microbrewery is to gawk at Main Street's multimillion-dollar collection of antiques and collectibles, which even extends to the restroom: gentlemen can express their opinion of communism by relieving themselves on a portion of the Berlin Wall.

The rest of the city

Crown & Anchor Pub

1350 E Tropicana Avenue, at S Maryland Parkway, University District (739 8676/www.crownand anchorlv.com). Bus 109, 201. **Open** 24hrs daily. **Credit** AmEx, DC, Disc, MC, V. **Map** p317 Y3.

The British-themed Crown & Anchor manages the feat, difficult in this town, of being a freestanding, independent pub, separated from a casino or a strip mall. Collegiate types and football-shirted expats head here to down pints of Boddingtons, tuck into fish 'n' chips and bash away hopefully at Thursday's quiz night. Inevitably, it gets packed out during the football matches.

Dispensary Lounge

2451 E Tropicana Avenue, at S Eastern Avenue, East Las Vegas (458 6343). Bus 110, 201. **Open** 24hrs daily. **Credit** MC, V. **Map** p317 Z3.

You can look at the waterwheel. You can listen to the waterwheel. But you certainly can't touch it. Sort of like the waitresses. The Dispensary is a throwback to old Vegas, complete with shag carpeting, fake plants and leotard-clad serving staff who become more boisterous and less balanced as the night wears on (well, you try wearing high heels on a shag carpet). A dark and quiet answer to a bright and frenetic city, particularly early in the evening.

rather you didn't see him at all. He's a true connoisseur of characters; hell, that's why he owns the joint. 'My favourite thing about running it is that I get to hang out here, under the guise of working,' he says. 'If I weren't running the bar, I would still be sitting there drinking, and writing a novel about the crazy characters that inhabit the place.'

He's too modest to mention the occasions that he's crossed that line himself. His easygoing manner coexists with an acerbic wit, a combination that allows him to say and do things that most people simply can't. He christened the bar's signature drink 'Ass Juice', once offered free beers to anyone missing two teeth in a row ('Toothless Tuesday'), lets loose the most astonishing exclamations ('Piss on my brain!') and has politely inquired of at least one couple out on a first date if the evening was going to end in intercourse. In other words, Moss embodies the classic Vegas attitude: he lives defiantly in a bygone era, when, as he says wistfully, 'all that mattered were cards and dice, booze and broads. Back when no one tried to regulate your fun.'

Since he can't travel back in time, Moss has brought the old spirit of Vegas into the present day, in the form of a glorious punk-rock bar. He runs the Double Down because Vegas, and the world at large, needs it. And Vegas needs a few more guys like Moss.

Drop Bar

Green Valley Ranch *2300 Paseo Verde Parkway, at S Green Valley Parkway, Henderson (221 6560/ www.greenvalleyranchresort.com). Bus 114.* **Open** 24hrs daily. **Credit** AmEx, Disc, MC, V. **Hotel** p103.
The Drop Bar's clientele is a mixed-bag: not all that friendly and with varying levels of attractiveness. Set in the middle of the Green Valley Ranch, this casino bar has white leather couches and matching cocktail slingers. If you come out here, bring some cash: credit card charges require a $20 minimum, and you'll often have to stand while trying to drink enough to cover the investment.

Fado Irish Pub

Green Valley Ranch *2300 Paseo Verde Parkway, at S Green Valley Parkway, Henderson (407 8691/ www.fadoirishpub.com). Bus 114.* **Open** 11am-2am Mon-Thur, Sun; 11am-3am Fri, Sat. **Credit** AmEx, DC, Disc, MC, V. **Hotel** p103.
Irish bars tend to act as a frat-boy magnet, but Fado seems more balanced than many of the others around. It's part of a chain (there are nine

sister locations throughout the country), but this branch draws some good Irish bands and serves a surprising selection of decent beers (Smithwick's, Blackthorn Cider, Boddingtons and, of course, Guinness) in 20-ounce glasses. The dark furniture, ceiling and bar, all imported from Ireland, serve to keep the casino feel at bay.

Hookah Lounge

Paymon's Mediterranean Café & Market, Tiffany Square, 4147 S Maryland Parkway, at E Flamingo Road, University District (731 6030/www.hookah lounge.com). Bus 109, 112, 202, 203. **Open** 5pm-midnight Tue-Thur; 5pm-2am Fri, Sat. **Credit** AmEx, Disc, MC, V. **Map** p317 Y3.
No, you can't sneak your own private stash in; yes, they have been asked that question before. Voted best lounge by *Las Vegas Life* in 2004, this dark, ornate bar adjoins Paymon's Mediterranean Café & Market (*see p163*). Sitting at low tables, you'll be served by both a cocktail waitress (wonderful Martinis) and a hookah jockey. The latter will list the tobacco flavours for you (pistachio and Turkish

are both excellent) and then arrange it on the hookah, pass around mouthpieces and instruct you in the art of smoking. And, yes, you will inhale.

Kennedy Tavern

2235 Village Walk Drive, at Paseo Verde & Green Valley Ranch, Henderson (320 8100/www.kennedy tavern.com). Bus 111. **Open** 24hrs daily. **Credit** AmEx, Disc, V.

'Tavern' is a misnomer. It's a bar. An impressive, chic bar, with a relaxed but classy ambience, a creative menu and fairly priced drinks, but a bar nonetheless. There's a large circular bar anchoring the centre, and short and raised tables off to either side. Large pieces of glass adorn the ceiling, splattered with what looks like a tasty merlot, and aquariums separate the restrooms from the bar. But don't bother squinting. You won't catch a glimpse of anything no matter how hard you look.

Mermaid Bar & Lounge

Silverton Casino, 3333 Blue Diamond Road, at Industrial Road, West of Strip (263 7777). Bus 117. **Open** 11am-3am Mon-Thur, Sun; 24hrs Fri, Sat. **Credit** AmEx, DC, Disc, MC, V.

While you're sitting and sipping your Shark Attack and gazing into the 117,000-gallon aquarium, it might occur to you to wonder: where are the mermaids? Don't fret: they, and their companion mermen, will be along in a while, diving in on the hour in the evenings (except Tue) and performing underwater versions of *Swan Lake* and other shows. Coming complete with a lively atmosphere, cheap drinks, flat-screen TVs and large tanks of live jellyfish above the bar, this is an eccentric gem.

Moose's Beach House

4770 S Maryland Parkway, at E Tropicana Avenue, University District (798 0441). Bus 109, 201. **Open** 10am-midnight Mon, Tue, Thur, Sun; 10am-4am Wed, Fri, Sat. **Credit** AmEx, Disc, MC, V. **Map** p317 Y3.

The most wildly successful college bar in Sin City, and you can read into that whatever you like. Stay past 8pm and you'll be buried in waves of clueless hotel management majors, howling jocks and every blonde airhead within a ten-mile radius. If you're looking to hook up with someone who won't remember you tomorrow – or, for that matter, ever – this is the place to come.

Boulder City

Backstop Bar

533 Avenue B, at Nevada Highway & Wyoming Street (294 8445). Bus 116. **Open** 8am-1am Mon-Thur; 8am-3am Fri, Sat. **No credit cards**.

By virtue of its Boulder City location, the Backstop offers one bonus that very few other bars in the area can claim: there's no gambling. That diversion removed, you can enjoy the rustic ambience, the Old West bar (taken from an Arizona saloon), and a few drinks with the friendly citizens of the town that built the Hoover Dam. Your first drink is free on any

day that the sun doesn't shine here, which happens perhaps once every eight years. Our advice? Best make it a large one.

Matteo's Underground Lounge

Boulder Dam Hotel, 1305 Arizona Street, Boul;der City (293 0098/www.matteodining.com). Bus 116. **Open** 4-8pm Mon-Thur, Sun; 4-10pm Fri, Sat. **Credit** AmEx, Disc, MC, V.

Matteo's is in the basement of Boulder City's historic and reportedly haunted hotel, built during the construction of the Hoover Dam. It's now a hotspot on the local music scene; Las Vegans, usually known for their aversion to driving, regularly make the half-hour trek. Though it can be reminiscent of an angst-filled high school concert on the punkish nights, the music ranges from rock and R&B to jazz and Latin.

Lounges

There's an argument that Las Vegas's lounges belong not in the Bars section of this guidebook, but in the chapter titled Casino Entertainment (for which, *see pp212-223*). Those making the argument have a rather more liberal definition of 'entertainment' than we do. However, while many of the too-smooth jazzers, wedding bands and *American Idol* wannabes who play the town's lounges are better overheard than heard, you might strike it lucky with some cosy jazz. And hell, even the most obnoxious covers bands will sound great after half-a-dozen beers.

Armadillo Lounge

Texas Station 2101 Texas Star Lane, at N Rancho Drive, between Lake Mead Boulevard & Vegas Drive, North Las Vegas (1-800 654 8888/631 1000/ www.texasstation.com). Bus 106. **Open** 10pm-2am Fri, Sat; 4pm-8pm Sun. **Credit** AmEx, DC, Disc, MC, V. **Hotel** p105. **Map** p317 X1.

Fridays and Saturdays, this red-tin-roofed lounge hosts bands playing rock, pop and top-40 hits from 10pm 'til the crowd says 'uncle!' Sundays, sample a little swing music with Jerry Tiffe and his band.

Big Apple Bar

New York–New York 3790 Las Vegas Boulevard South, at W Tropicana Avenue (740 6969/www.nyny hotelcasino.com). Bus 201, 301, 302. **Open** 24hrs daily. **Credit** AmEx, Disc, V, MC. **Hotel** p83. **Map** p320 A8.

Reminiscent of a '40s supper club, this art deco-esque lounge in New York–New York features a heady drinks menu and reminiscent live music nightly from 8pm to 3am. If you can make it here, you'll make it – bam! bam! – anywhere.

Le Bistro Lounge

Riviera 2901 Las Vegas Boulevard South, at Riviera Boulevard (734 5110/www.theriviera.com). Bus 301. **Open** hrs vary. **Credit** AmEx, DC, Disc, MC, V. **Hotel** p87. **Map** p319 B5.

Vegas's first skyscraper, the Riv is a real piece of vintage Vegas. Appropriate, then, that it's now home to throwback entertainer Art Vargas, the swingin'-est cat in town.

Bourbon Street Cabaret

Orleans *4500 W Tropicana Avenue, at Arville Street, Southwest Las Vegas (1-800 675 3267/365 7111/www.orleanscasino.com). Bus 104, 201.* **Open** 24hrs daily. **Admission** 2-drink minimum. **Credit** AmEx, DC, Disc, MC, V. **Hotel** p102.

Local bands play a mix of rock, pop, Latin and disco in this small lounge every night, but Monday. It's styled like a French Quarter courtyard, adorned with wrought iron decorations and grand pianos suspended overhead.

Le Cabaret

Paris Las Vegas *3655 Las Vegas Boulevard South, at E Flamingo Road (946 000/www.caesars.com). Bus 202, 301, 302.* **Open** 2pm-3am daily. **Credit** AmEx, Disc, MC, V. **Hotel** p69. **Map** p320 A7.

Le Cabaret has more character than most antiseptic casino lounges. With its *faux* shady trees and sparkling lights, you almost feel like you're doin' the *Neutron Dance* in gay Paree. Or, at least, you will after the eighth drink of the evening.

Carnaval Court

Harrah's *3475 Las Vegas Boulevard South, between E Flamingo Road & Sands Avenue (369 5000/www.harrahs.com). Bus 202, 301, 302.* **Open** noon-2am Mon-Thur, Sun; noon-3am Fri, Sat. **Credit** AmEx, Disc, MC, V. **Hotel** p78. **Map** p320 A6.

Essentially, a large outdoor stage area. The bar carries on the theatrical theme: it's not uncommon to see a bartender pouring shots into the upturned mouths of waiting patrons, like baby birds begging to be fed. On a hot summer's afternoon, this oasis can be as entertaining as it is refreshing.

Celebration Lounge

Tropicana *3801 Las Vegas Boulevard South, at E Tropicana Avenue (739 2222/www.tropicanalv.com). Bus 201, 301, 302.* **Open** 5pm-3am daily. **Credit** AmEx, DC, Disc, MC, V. **Hotel** p90. **Map** p320 A8.

House band TKO's 'hip' billing on the hotel's website is a trifle optimistic, but they get the loungers out of their seats from Tuesdays through Saturdays from 8pm until late. If you think you can do better, the hotel's Tropics Lounge hosts regular karaoke.

Chrome

Santa Fe Station *4949 N Rancho Drive, at US 95 (junction 90A), Northwest Las Vegas (658 4900/www.santafecasino.com). Bus 101, 102, 106.* **Open** 7pm-1am Wed, Thur; 9pm-3am Fri, Sat. **Credit** AmEx, Disc, V, MC. **Hotel** p105.

If '80s music is your guilty pleasure, moonwalk over to this sleek new club/showroom, where accomplished covers band Loveshack play your faves from the Big Hair Era on Fridays and Saturdays. Wednesdays, Boulder Station's Yellow Brick Road entertain the late-night crowd.

Coral Reef Lounge

Mandalay Bay *3950 Las Vegas Boulevard South, at E Hacienda Avenue (632 7407/www.mandalaybay.com). Bus 105, 301.* **Open** 9.30pm-2am daily. **Credit** AmEx, DC, MC, V. **Hotel** p67. **Map** p320 A9.

Dance bands play at Mandalay Bay's largest music lounge and sushi bar, just beyond the resort's restaurant row. There are mellower vibes in the Island Lounge and the Orchid Lounge.

Fontana Bar

Bellagio *3600 Las Vegas Boulevard South, at W Flamingo Road (1-800 963 9634/693 7722/www.bellagio.com). Bus 202, 301, 302.* **Open** 5pm-1am Mon-Thur, Sun; 5pm-2am Fri, Sat. **Credit** AmEx, Disc, MC, V. **Hotel** p63. **Map** p320 A7.

The sophistication to which this lounge aspires is rather wrecked by the function-band fluff who currently perform in it. Still, the views are great and the drinks are good; if the noise is too ghastly, adjourn to the balcony to watch the water fountains.

Indigo Lounge

Bally's *3645 Las Vegas Boulevard South, at E Flamingo Road (739 4111/www.ballyscasino.com). Bus 202, 301, 302.* **Open** 7pm-4am daily. **Credit** AmEx, Disc, MC, V. **Hotel** p76. **Map** p320 A7.

Right next to the Bally's/Paris Las Vegas walkway, this casual, enjoyable lounge features a scattering of pop, dance, Motown and R&B.

Piano Bar

Harrah's *3475 Las Vegas Boulevard South, between Sands Avenue & E Flamingo Road (369 5000/www.harrahsvegas.com). Bus 301.* **Open** 6pm-2am daily. **Credit** AmEx, DC, Disc, MC, V. **Hotel** p78. **Map** p320 A6.

Would-be songbirds can make their *American Idol* (or *Nashville Star*) dreams come true at TJ's All-Star Karaoke Party, from 6pm to 9pm nightly. Hey, it's one way to play Vegas. Afterwards, the duelling pianos come out, though New York–New York's take on the theme (*see p166*) is far more fun.

Railhead

Boulder Station *4111 Boulder Highway, at E Desert Inn Road, East Las Vegas (432 7777/www.boulderstation.com). Bus 107, 112.* **Open** hrs vary. **Credit** AmEx, Disc, MC, V. **Hotel** p103.

A wide selection of rock, pop, jazz, country and blues headliners feature at this cabaret-style lounge, which hosts a mix of ticketed events and free shows. Fridays and Saturdays, house band Yellow Brick Road bang out '80s rock tunes from 11pm.

Starlight Lounge

Stardust *3000 Las Vegas Boulevard South, at Stardust Road (1-866 642 3120/732 6213/www.stardustlv.com). Bus 301.* **Open** hrs vary. **Credit** AmEx, Disc, MC, V. **Hotel** p89. **Map** p320 B5.

A throwback to old Vegas, the Stardust's dark and smoky cabaret has a small dancefloor where you can dance every night except Monday. Fridays, release your inner pop star with karaoke (6-10pm). There's sometimes a cover charge (never more than $10).

Shops & Services

Playing cards, snow globes and dice clocks are all still available, but Las Vegas's shopping scene now offers far more than mere tacky souvenirs.

In Las Vegas's dusty, ancient past – the 1960s or thereabouts – the casino's big cheeses thought of shopping not as a money-maker or kudos-booster, but simply as something with which they could pacify the wives and girlfriends of big gamblers. They thought pretty much the same thing about slot machines, too. Now, of course, slots rake in the greater part of every casino's gambling revenue, and a number of resorts have made new names for themselves – and brought in thousands of extra visitors a year – by expanding their shopping options. According to the latest statistics available from the Las Vegas Convention & Visitors Authority, visitors are spending over $5 billion a year in the shops of Las Vegas, and it's not all going on dice clocks and shot glasses.

The story of how Las Vegas's shopping scene changed beyond all recognition is told elsewhere in this chapter (*see p186* **Come the revolution**) and further changes are afoot. After the opening of the cool, urban **Mandalay Place**, the completion of the dramatic **Fashion Show Mall** renovations and the christening of a new wing at the **Forum Shops**, all within a few months during 2004, the next year saw the curtain finally lifted on **Wynn Las Vegas** and its hand-picked selection of super-smart, *haute*

couture establishments. However, not all the activity is confined to malls or the Strip: 2004 saw the openings of **REI** (*see p200*), **Tweeter** (*see p183*) and **Bass Pro Shops Outdoor World** (*see p200*), all now local favourites.

One development sure to have an impact on the scene is the **World Market Center**, a 1.3-million-square-foot wholesale furnishings and accessories centre due to open in 2005. Located at 495 S Grand Central Parkway, close to Downtown and the **Las Vegas Premium Outlets**, it'll hold two wholesale events a year (in July and January) for around 100,000 credentialled interior designers and retail buyers. Though it's closed to the general public, its presence is yet another confirmation that Vegas is fast becoming one of the West Coast's commercial powerhouses. Nearby, the **Holsum Lofts**, a redevelopment of a landmark Las Vegas bakery, was getting ready to open in 2005, full of galleries, home furnishing and decorating merchants plus the requisite café.

However, lest all this sound too serious, rest assured that good taste hasn't completely taken over Las Vegas just yet. You'll still be able to find all the kitsch you want in the town's many souvenir stores: certainly, **Bonanza Gifts** (*see p195*), the self-proclaimed 'World's Largest Gift Store', isn't getting any smaller.

Caesars' fabulous **Forum Shops**.
See p177.

WHERE TO SHOP
Most visitors remain confined to the Strip, and not without good reason: the majority of the town's more interesting and popular malls are found on it. However, there are many other major malls throughout the city, albeit offering rather more prosaic goods than you'll find in the casinos. The majority of Las Vegas's best independent stores, meanwhile, are in strip malls or stand-alone buildings all around the city. So it does pay to travel.

SERVICE WITH A SMILE?
It may come as a surprise, but service is not always Las Vegas's strong suit. Shopkeepers can veer from wonderfully helpful to downright rude in a matter of seconds; it might seem rather odd in a city so completely based on pleasuring its visitors, until you work out that this is just about the only major service industry in town where the professionals stand no chance of being tipped handsomely for their work. No wonder a fair few of them seem more than a little grumpy.

Note that a 7.5 per cent sales tax will be added to your purchases at the till.

One-Stop Shopping

Casino malls

Le Boulevard
Paris Las Vegas *3655 Las Vegas Boulevard South, at E Flamingo Road (946 7000/www.parislasvegas.com). Bus 202, 301, 302, 807.* **Open** 10am-11pm daily. **Hotel** p69. **Map** p320 A7.
Just about every shop in this small but divine mall comes with a heavy and largely delightful French influence. **Les Enfants** has a great collection of Eloise, Babar the Elephant and Madeline toys and dolls, as well as the casino's signature pink-ribboned poodle named Fifi and her counterpart, Jacques the bulldog. **La Cave** has cheeses, pâtés and wine, while **Lenôtre** is known for its bread and pastries.

Desert Passage
Aladdin/Planet Hollywood *3663 Las Vegas Boulevard South, at E Harmon Avenue (1-888 800 8284/www.desertpassage.com). Bus 301.* **Open** 10am-11pm Mon-Thur, Sun; 10am-midnight Fri, Sat. **Hotel** p76. **Map** p320 A7.
Located in a 1.2-mile ring around the Aladdin/Planet Hollywood resort, Desert Passage offers a fair to middling selection of largely mainstream shops (clothes are a speciality; the city's sole **FCUK** is here) and restaurants: should you get peckish, get a **Cheeseburger at the Oasis** or head to **Crustacean** for Euro-Asian fare. The other main selling point are the gimmicky but rather enjoyable indoor rainstorms.

Forum Shops
Caesars Palace *3500 Las Vegas Boulevard South, at W Flamingo Road (1-877 427 7243/ 893 4800/www.caesars.com). Bus 202, 301, 302.* **Open** 10am-11pm Mon-Thur, Sun; 10am-midnight Fri, Sat. **Hotel** p65. **Map** p320 A7.
The *faux* pillars, the constantly changing skies, the huge fountains, the lush lighting… Sure, it's not going to convince anyone they're in ancient Rome, but you'll likely be too drawn in by the shops to notice. Far and away the best of the casino malls, the Forum Shops is a must-visit for anyone with a shopping jones to fulfil. In the main mall, mid-range chains such as **Gap**, **Abercrombie & Fitch** and **Diesel** punctuate the serious designer line-up, with gift shops (including **FAO Schwarz**) adding further colour. But the real jewel are the new and extremely refined shops that front directly on to the Strip. Circular escalators and quality marble help create a swanky setting for fabulous new tenants such as jewellers **Harry Winston**, fashion house **Kate Spade** and British hairdressers **Truefitt & Hill**, to name but a few. There are attractions at either end of the mall: statues come to life at one extremity, with Atlantis rising from the waves at the other.

Grand Canal Shoppes
Venetian *3355 Las Vegas Boulevard South, at Sands Avenue (414 4500/www.venetian.com/shoppe). Bus 203, 213, 301, 302.* **Open** 10am-11pm Mon-Thur, Sun; 10am-midnight Fri, Sat. **Map** p320 A6.

The best Shops

For kitsch
Bonanza Gifts. *See p195.*

For art and antiques
Funk House. *See p182.*

For luck, or news on when to expect some
Worton's Palmistry Studios. *See p196.*

For cheap chic
Las Vegas Premium Outlets or Buffalo Exchange. *See p181 & p186.*

For expensive cars
Wynn Esplanade. *See p178.*

For chips
Gamblers General Store. *See p195.*

For chips
Gamblers General Store. *See p183.*

For a full day's shopping
Forum Shops or the Fashion Show Mall. *See pp177-178.*

It felt like a second-rate Forum Shops when it opened in 1999, and still resembles one in places (especially with recent improvements to the Forum Shops), but the Grand Canal Shoppes has gradually found its place in Las Vegas. The walkways are narrow and cramped, but the smaller space does give a reasonable impression of an intimate city streetscape. **Lladró**, **Movado**, **Jimmy Choo** and **Burberry** are among the best of the generally high-end retailers; there's pleasant 'patio' dining to be enjoyed at **Postrio** (see p147) and **Zeffirino** (see p148).

Mandalay Place

Mandalay Bay *3930 Las Vegas Boulevard South, at E Hacienda Avenue (632 9333/www.mandalay bay.com)*. Bus 105, 301. **Open** 10am-11pm Mon-Thur, Sun; 10am-midnight Fri, Sat. **Hotel** p67. **Map** p320 A9.

What separates this smallish retail experience from other Strip malls is its vow to 'break the chains': it leases its stores only to companies otherwise absent from Vegas. It's a savvy move, and one that has brought the mall **Urban Outfitters**, the world's first **Samantha Chang** lingerie boutique and the **Reading Room**, the city's best bookstore. Beauty services come from **Skinklinic**, the **Art of Shaving** and the **Robert Cromeans Salon**; when hunger nibbles, try the **Burger Bar** (see p141). The mall is located on a bridge that connects Mandalay Bay to the Luxor, and is accessible from either resort.

Via Bellagio

Bellagio *3600 Las Vegas Boulevard South, at W Flamingo Road (693 7111/www.bellagio.com)*. Bus 202, 301, 302, 807. **Open** 10am-midnight daily. **Hotel** p63. **Map** p320 A7.

In line with its upmarket image, the Bellagio's small mall contains ten of the smartest designer names this side of New York with **Tiffany**, **Prada**, **Chanel** and **Hermès**. If your wallet can't cope, at least head over there to enjoy the location: the venue is a shrine to materialism, with daylight streaming in through the vaulted glass ceilings on to opulent walkways and tidy storefronts. The food is hardly mall fodder, either: try **Olives** (see p145), a Mediterranean bistro overlooking the lake.

Wynn Esplanade

Wynn Las Vegas *3131 Las Vegas Boulevard South, at Sands Avenue (770 7000/www.wynnlas vegas.com)*. Bus 203, 213, 301, 302. **Open** call for details. **Hotel** p75. **Map** p319 B6.

Steve Wynn took Oscar de la Renta on a personal tour of a then under-construction Wynn Las Vegas, in an attempt to convince the couture tsar that it would be the finest resort in town. It worked. **De la Renta** decided to locate a signature shop inside the Wynn Esplanade, as have **Jean-Paul Gaultier**, **Chanel**, **Louis Vuitton**, **Manolo Blahnik** (the second signature store in the US) and **Jo Malone** perfumers, to name but a few. Peppered throughout the rest of the resort are other interesting spots, such as **Shoe In**, **w.ink** and **La Flirt**.

Non-casino malls

In addition to the usual malls, Las Vegas now has its very own 'lifestyle centre', an open-air shopping complex which 'serves as a multi-purpose leisure-time destination' (according to the International Council of Shopping Centers). **Rampart Commons** (S Rampart Boulevard, at Alta Drive) has been well received by the locals out in Summerlin, who no longer have to journey to the city to fulfil their chain-shopping needs at the likes of **Chico's**, **Banana Republic** and homewares emporium **Pottery Barn**. Across the way, **Boca Park Fashion Village** gathers some of the more interesting local shops, including **Talulah G** (see p185) and **Girard's Boutique** (see p193). When hunger strikes, there's **Kona Grill**, **Melting Pot** and a **Cheesecake Factory**.

On the other side of the city, Green Valley is home to the **District** (Green Valley Parkway, just south of the I-215), another 'lifestyle centre' with two blocks of shops and restaurants topped off by condos. Shopping highlights include **REI**, **Along Came a Spider** and **Fitigues**, an ultra-spendy leisurewear boutique for ladies who lounge. Eateries, among them **Lucille's Barbecue**, **Kennedy's** and **King's Fish House**, are also a big part of the mix.

Boulevard Mall

3528 S Maryland Parkway, at W Desert Inn Road, East Las Vegas (732 8949/www.blvdmall.com). Bus 109, 112, 203, 213. **Open** 10am-9pm Mon-Sat; 11am-6pm Sun. **Map** p317 Y3.

This is a bastion of the Las Vegas shopping scene and the first mall of its type to open in the city: centrally located, reasonably priced and loaded with stores such as **Sears**, **Dillard's**, **Macy's** and **JC Penney**. When you're weighed down with bags and nearing collapse, check out the **Panorama Café**'s food court for cheap international cuisine.

Fashion Show Mall

3200 Las Vegas Boulevard South, at W Spring Mountain Road (369 8382/www.thefashionshow. com). Bus 105, 203, 213, 301, 302. **Open** 10am-9pm Mon-Fri; 10am-8pm Sat; 11am-6pm Sun. **Map** p320 B6.

A $1 billion expansion of the Fashion Show Mall included the addition of the Cloud, an amazing 300ft (90m) image projection screen/sunshade that hovers over the front of the shopping centre broadcasting to the Strip. The mall's nearly doubled in size; its new anchor tenants include the likes of **Nordstrom**, **Bloomingdale's Home** and **Zara**, plus restaurants including the hip **Ra Sushi**, **Café Ba Ba Reeba** and **Capitol Grille**. The original line-up was nothing to sneer at (try **Macy's**, **Neiman Marcus**, **Saks Fifth Avenue** and **Robinsons-May** for starters), but new arrivals such as **Cole Haan**, **Apple** and **Cinnamon Girl** add some spice.

Four malls: (from top) Fashion Show Mall, Desert Passage, Mandalay Place and the Grand Canal Shoppes.

Check out swap meets, where new and used goods are hawked at bargain rates: both the **Broadacres Open Air Swap Meet** (2930 N Las Vegas Boulevard, North Las Vegas, 642 3777) and the **Fantastic Indoor Swap Meet**

(1717 S Decatur Boulevard, Southwest Las Vegas, 877 0087) are open Friday to Sunday.

Las Vegas Outlet Center
7400 Las Vegas Boulevard South, at E Warm Springs Road, Southwest Las Vegas (896 5599/ www.premiumoutlets.com). Bus 117, 217, 303. **Open** 10am-9pm Mon-Sat; 10am-8pm Sun.

Casino malls at a glance

THE MALL	AMBIENCE	GOOD FOR	BAD FOR	KEY STORES
Le Boulevard, Paris Las Vegas (15 shops)	The streets of Paris, only without the dogshit.	*Marchandise avec une saveur française*: food to bags, shades to souvenirs.	All those American high-street names you know and love.	Kids' kit at Les Enfants; specs at L'Oasis; souvenirs at Eiffel Tower.
Desert Passage, Aladdin/Planet Hollywood (140 shops)	Quasi-exotic Africana – *Marrakech: The Theme Park*.	Cheery clothes from familiar names; gifts both stylish and tasteless.	Cutting-edge fashion; uniquely Vegas shopping outlets.	Dreary gear at Tommy Bahama; catwalk copyists Bebe; art chain Thomas Kinkade.
Forum Shops, Caesars Palace (150 shops)	A Midwesterner's idea of ancient Greece; ie, the set of *Cleopatra: The Musical*.	More or less anything, but it's especially strong on fashion.	The health and beauty selection could be a little better, but that's about it.	Classic Italian threads at Bernini; classic British scents at Penhaligon's; classic American sneakers at Niketown.
Grand Canal Shoppes, Venetian (60 shops)	Venice on the nicest day of the year. Or Desert Passage with gondolas.	Chain fashions sold at above-average but still affordable prices; jewellery.	Health and beauty products; gifts you don't wear.	Simayof (jewels); Banana Republic (jeans); In Celebration of Golf (balls).
Mandalay Place, Mandalay Bay (25 shops)	Like a mall, only with wider walkways. Or fewer people.	Tokens to aid affluent urban living, whether shirts, chocolate or novels.	Basic high-street fashions and tacky gifts.	55° Wine + Design; Botox injections at Skinklinic; Urban Outfitters.
Via Bellagio, Bellagio (10 shops)	Like the rest of the hotel: casually ostentatious.	Fashion. If you need to check the price, you can't afford it.	Anyone who hasn't just won very big at the roulette table.	The holy trinity of Eurofashion: Armani, Dior and Gucci.
Wynn Esplanade, Wynn Las Vegas (30 shops)	Put it this way: it lives up to its reputation.	Living in the lap of luxury, chiefly by way of some of the world's most exclusive designers.	Daily necessities, main street chains, poor people.	Cartier, a girl's best friend; shoes by Manolo Blahnik; Penske Wynn Ferrari Maserati, for the ride home.

Though they're now owned by the same company, the long-established Las Vegas Outlet Center has rather had its thunder stolen in recent years by the new Las Vegas Premium Outlets. Still, there's a decent amount of bargains on offer here. Among the highlights: **Calvin Klein**, **Off 5th** (the Saks Fifth Avenue discount outlet), **Nike**, **Vans**, **Liz Claiborne** and **Bose**. The giant carousel should keep the kids content.

Las Vegas Premium Outlets

875 S Grand Central Parkway, at W Charleston Boulevard, Downtown (474 7500/www.lasvegas premiumoutlets.com). Bus 105, 106, 108. **Open** 10am-9pm Mon-Sat; 10am-8pm Sun. **Map** p319 C2.
As the name suggests, this excellent outdoor outlet mall, which opened in late 2003, is geared to the higher end of the fashion market, featuring labels such as **Armani**, **Dolce e Gabbana**, **Lacoste**, **Coach**, **Banana Republic** and **Ralph Lauren**, to name but a few. The complex is close to Downtown, though not quite close enough to walk if you're without a car: it gets absolutely baking in the summer.

Department stores

For a more mundane one-stop shop experience, **Wal-Mart** (www.walmart.com) has numerous branches here, all open 24 hours.

Dillard's

Fashion Show Mall, 3200 Las Vegas Boulevard South, at W Spring Mountain Road (733 2008/ www.dillards.com). Bus 105, 203, 213, 301, 302. **Open** 10am-9pm Mon-Sat; 11am-6pm Sun. **Credit** AmEx, DC, Disc, MC, V. **Map** p320 B6.
The American West's equivalent of Marks and Spencer has excellent beauty aisles, a good selection of women's shoes, and a great range of men's suits at decent prices. By the same token, though, there's not much to quicken the pulse.
Other locations: Boulevard Mall, 3528 S Maryland Parkway, East Las Vegas (734 2111); Galleria at Sunset Mall, 1300 W Sunset Road, Green Valley (435 6300); Meadows Mall, 4300 Meadows Lane, Northwest Las Vegas (870 2039).

JC Penney

Boulevard Mall, 3528 S Maryland Parkway, at Sierra Vista Drive, East Las Vegas (735 5131/www. jcpenney.com). Bus 109, 112, 203, 213. **Open** 10am-9pm Mon-Sat; 11am-6pm Sun. **Credit** AmEx, Disc, MC, V. **Map** p317 Y3.
JC Penney is as American as apple pie. You'll find updated classic staples for both men and women, of good quality and at down to earth prices (check the seasonal sales). The Boulevard Mall branch has an extensive housewares and home decor section, and reasonable ranges of watches and jewellery.
Other locations: Galleria at Sunset Mall, 1300 W Sunset Road, Green Valley (451 4545); Home Store, 771 S Rainbow Road, Southwest Las Vegas (870 7727); Meadows Mall, 4300 Meadows Lane, Northwest Las Vegas (870 9182).

Macy's

Fashion Show Mall, 3200 Las Vegas Boulevard South, at W Spring Mountain Road (731 5111/ www.macys.com). Bus 105, 203, 213, 301, 302. **Open** 10am-9pm Mon-Sat; 11am-8pm Sun. **Credit** AmEx, MC, V. **Map** p320 B6.
The king of department stores in the US, Macy's offers a variety of quality merchandise at competitive prices. Clothing, strong on mens lines, ranges from the classic (Ralph Lauren) to the hip (Ben Sherman) to the utilitarian. The Spring Mountain Road homewares-only branch has frequent sales.
Other locations: Home Store, 4450 W Spring Mountain Road, Southwest Las Vegas (731 5111); Meadows Mall, 4300 Meadows Lane, Northwest Las Vegas (258 2100).

Neiman Marcus

Fashion Show Mall, 3200 Las Vegas Boulevard South, at W Spring Mountain Road (731 3636/www. neimanmarcus.com). Bus 105, 203, 213, 301, 302. **Open** 10am-8pm Mon-Fri; 10am-7pm Sat; noon-6pm Sun. **Credit** AmEx, DC, MC, V. **Map** p320 B6.
The world's best designers are on display at this upmarket department store: among them are the catwalk-friendly likes of Prada, Manolo Blahnik, Escada, Missoni and Chanel. It also has a good range of accessories, make-up, lingerie and perfumes, and a fantastic houseware selection. It's nicknamed 'Needless Mark-Up' for a reason, but there are discounted goods at the store's discount outlet.
Other locations: Last Call at Neiman Marcus, 32100 Las Vegas Boulevard South, Primm (874 2100).

Nordstrom

Fashion Show Mall, 3200 Las Vegas Boulevard South, at W Spring Mountain Road (862 2525/ www.nordstrom.com). Bus 105, 203, 213, 301, 302. **Open** 10am-9pm Mon-Fri; 10am-8pm Sat; 11am-6pm Sun. **Credit** AmEx, DC, Disc, MC, V. **Map** p320 B6.
Those who swear by Nordstrom agree that it's a good place for style-conscious people of any age to find great stuff at reasonable prices. (Both the men's and women's shoe departments are worth checking out.) Harking back to the days when shopping used to be an 'experience', Nordy's even treats its customers to piano music and a very good café. Those of straitened means should try the Henderson outlet.
Other locations: Nordstrom Rack, Silverado Ranch Plaza, 9851 S Eastern Avenue, Henderson (948 2121).

Saks Fifth Avenue

Fashion Show Mall, 3200 Las Vegas Boulevard South, at W Spring Mountain Road (733 8300/ www.saksfifthavenue.com). Bus 105, 203, 213, 301, 302. **Open** 10am-8pm Mon-Wed; 10am-9pm Thur, Fri; 10am-7pm Sat; noon-6pm Sun. **Credit** AmEx, DC, Disc, MC, V. **Map** p320 B6.
For those with discriminating taste and a heavyweight bank account, a trip to Saks is like a visit to church: you have to go once a week to pay homage, get grounded and hear the word. The men's and women's apparel sections are especially strong (Marc Jacobs, Dolce e Gabbana, Hugo Boss). If you've got

Las Vegas Premium Outlets. *See p181.*

the taste but not the money – and if so, you're not alone – check out Off 5th, Saks's discount shop in the Las Vegas Outlet Center.
Other locations: Off 5th, Las Vegas Outlet Center, 7400 Las Vegas Boulevard South, Southwest Las Vegas (896 5599/www.saksincorporated.com).

Individual Stores

Antiques

Charleston Antique Shops
2014-2040 E Charleston Boulevard, at S Eastern Avenue, East Las Vegas (386 0238). Bus 107, 110, 206. **Open** varies. **Credit** varies. **Map** p317 Y2.
Even some locals don't know that there are more than two dozen tiny antiques shops in converted old houses at the east end of Charleston. The dealers are knowledgeable and approachable, and sell all kinds of stuff: fine china, dolls, postcards, Tiffany lamps, telephones, perfume bottles, train sets, clocks…

Funk House
1228 S Casino Center Boulevard, at E Colorado Avenue, Downtown (678 6278/www.thefunkhouselasvegas.com). Bus 108, 206, 301. **Open** 10am-5pm Mon-Sat; noon-5pm Sun. **Credit** AmEx, MC, V. **Map** p319 C3.
Cindy Funkhouser's ever-growing collection is especially strong in late 1950s and early '60s pieces, and there's a wide variety of glass, jewellery and toys. Her store, one of the best antiques stores in Las Vegas, is also one of the focal points of Downtown's First Fridays (*see p204* **Viva Cindy Funkhouser**).

Gypsy Caravan
1302 S 3rd Street, at W Colorado Avenue, Downtown (868 3302). Bus 108, 206, 301. **Open** 10am-5pm Mon-Sat; noon-5pm Sun. **Credit** Disc, MC, V. **Map** p319 C3.
This colourful antiques avenue comprises several historic bungalows. There are particularly strong selections of Victorian light fixtures, furnishings and typewriters, plus whatever else the owner has gathered. Be sure to investigate the courtyard and its medley of patio furnishings.

Red Rooster Antique Mall
1109 Western Avenue, at W Charleston Boulevard, Downtown (382 5253). Bus 106, 108, 206. **Open** 10am-6pm Mon-Sat; 11am-5pm Sun. **Credit** AmEx, MC, V. **Map** p319 B3.
A labyrinth of cluttered rooms and individually run stalls, with racks of dusty magazines holding shelf space next to $100 antique bottles. Look carefully and you'll find some fabulous casino memorabilia: ashtrays, gaming chips, matchbooks, postcards and more. If you like the look of that tiki bar, snap it up: the good stuff goes fast.

Showcase Slots & Antiquities
4305 S Industrial Road, at W Flamingo Road, West of Strip (740 5722/www.showcaseslots.com). Bus 202. **Open** *Summer* 9am-5pm Mon-Sat; 10am-3pm Sun. *Winter* 9am-5pm Mon-Sat. **Credit** AmEx, DC, Disc, MC, V. **Map** p320 A7.
What could be more appropriate as a souvenir of Las Vegas than an old slot machine? This store behind the Bellagio has reconditioned machines from the 1930s and '40s.

Victorian Casino Antique Auction
4631 S Industrial Road, at W Tropicana Avenue (382 2466/www.vcaauction.com). Bus 201. **Open** auctions in Apr & Oct. **No credit cards**. **Map** p320 A8.
Slots rule the roost here, but there's far more than mere one-armed bandits in this huge warehouse filled with vintage advertising, old fashioned craps tables, posters and heaven knows what else. Auctions are held twice a year; check the website to browse the catalogue.

Books

There are branches of both the big book chains in Las Vegas. The nearest **Barnes & Noble** to the Strip is at 3860 Maryland Parkway (734 2900), while the closest **Borders** is at 2323 S Decatur Boulevard (258 0999).

Albion Book Company
2466 E Desert Inn Road, at S Eastern Avenue, East Las Vegas (792 9554). Bus 110, 112. **Open** 10am-6pm daily. **Credit** AmEx, Disc, MC, V. **Map** p317 Z3.
Just about the quintessential used bookstore, with obscure first editions crammed alongside well-thumbed tomes by Dickens and Tolstoy. Prices are low and there's an air of comfortable chaos both on the shelves and behind the counter.

Dead Poet Books

937 S Rainbow Boulevard, between W Charleston Boulevard & Alta Drive, East Las Vegas (227 4070). Bus 101, 206. **Open** 10am-6pm daily. **Credit** AmEx, Disc, MC, V. **Map** p317 X2.

You'll find a charming hotchpotch of antiquarian books here; specialities include metaphysical cookbooks, military histories and first editions.

Gamblers Book Club

630 S 11th Street, at E Bonneville Avenue, Downtown (382 7555/www.gamblersbook.com). Bus 109, 206. **Open** 9am-5pm Mon-Sat. **Credit** Disc, MC, V. **Map** p318 D3.

The Gamblers Book Club is supposedly the world's largest distributor of gambling books, whether industry histories or tips on beating the system. If you don't just want to read, there are also cards, chips and gambling-related software for sale.

Reading Room

Mandalay Bay (Mandalay Place) *3930 Las Vegas Boulevard South, at E Hacienda Avenue (632 9374).* Bus 105, 301. **Open** 8am-11pm Mon-Thur, Sun; 8am-midnight Fri, Sat. **Credit** AmEx, Disc, MC, V. **Hotel** p67. **Map** p320 A9.

The first bookshop in a Vegas casino has become a favourite with Las Vegans: not only does it have a strong local interest selection, but it also stocks many well-regarded and obscure books from around the globe. The staff picks are always on the mark.

Cameras & film processing

The most affordable film processing in town is offered at the myriad branches of chain drugstores **Walgreens** (*see p198*) or **Sav-On**.

Sahara Camera Centre

Albertson's Shopping Center, 2305 E Sahara Avenue, at S Eastern Avenue, East Las Vegas (457 3333). Bus 110, 204. **Open** 9am-6pm Mon-Fri; 9am-5pm Sat. **Credit** AmEx, Disc, MC, V. **Map** p317 Z2.

Claiming to be 'Nevada's largest full-service camera store', the Sahara Camera Centre pretty much has – and does – it all, with rentals and repairs, quality new and used equipment, knowledgeable staff and one-hour photo processing. Prices are fair.

Wolf Camera

Sahara Pavilion, 2580 S Decatur Boulevard, at Sahara Avenue, Southwest Las Vegas (889 1998/ www.wolfcamera.com). Bus 103. **Open** 10am-7pm Mon-Sat; 11am-5pm Sun. **Credit** AmEx, Disc, MC, V.

This nationwide chain sells all manner of image equipment and the necessary accessories, and also develops film (APS is processed in an hour). **Other locations**: throughout the city.

Electronics

Best Buy (3820 S Maryland Parkway, 732 8283), **Circuit City** (4860 S Eastern Avenue, 898 0500) and **Good Guys** (4580 E Sahara

Avenue, 364 2500), national chains dealing in audio, visual and computing kit of every stripe, have stores throughout the city. For more specialist needs, the Fashion Show Mall (*see p178*) houses branches of audio/visual high-flyer **Bang & Olufsen** (731 9200) and the wonderful **Apple Store** (650 9550).

Fry's Electronics

6845 Las Vegas Boulevard South, at I-215, East of Strip (932 1400/www.outpost.com). Bus 105, 301, 302. **Open** 8am-9pm Mon-Fri; 9am-9pm Sat; 9am-7pm Sun. **Credit** Disc, MC, V.

This San Jose-based retailer is best known for outfitting Silicon Valley's dotcommers during the boom. This branch stays true to Fry's not-so-humble roots, but also caters for those who merely want quality in computing, audio and video. The DVDs include a fine selection of adult-orientated Japanimation.

Tweeter

Boca Park Shopping Center, 8950 W Charleston Boulevard, at S Fort Apache Road, Summerlin (940 0900/www.tweeter.com). Bus 206. **Open** 10am-9pm Mon-Sat; noon-6pm Sun. **Credit** AmEx, Disc, MC, V.

Tweeter have created a totally interactive store that shows visitors what their world would be like if it were completely computerised: home theatre, lights, security and so on. It also sells stand-alone plasma screens, computers, satellite radios and the like.

Fashion

General

Las Vegas's wild and unexpected growth as a shopping mecca has benefitted one industry above all others: fashion. Every major chain is here now, and a good many designer labels have also shown up to make their pitch. Some savvy Europeans have started to use the town much as they previously used New York: as a chance to restock their wardrobe. However, while chains both upscale and low-rent are much in evidence here, Vegas does still lack its own fashion scene – there aren't really many local designers here, leaving even the most style-conscious of local residents to be dressed by outsiders.

The casino malls are the best places to start. **Via Bellagio** (*see p178*) is where you'll find the high-end stuff: **Prada** (866 6886), **Gucci** (732 9300) and **Chanel** (693 7995) are all in residence there. **Mandalay Place** (*see p178*) also has a few stores that you won't find elsewhere in town, chiefly hipster-house **Urban Outfitters** (650 2199). The range of fashion stores at **Desert Passage** (*see p177*) is middlebrow: among the stores are super-polite **Eddie Bauer** (697 0670) and **Tommy Bahama** (731 3988), though there is also a **Bebe** (892 0406) and an **FCUK** (733 6420). And the stores at the **Grand**

Eat, Drink, Shop

Canal Shoppes (*see p177*) generally reflect the affluence of the casino in which it's situated: among the retailers here are **Kenneth Cole** (836 1916), **Ann Taylor** (731 0655) and **Burberry** (735 2600).

However, as in so many categories, the **Forum Shops** (*see p177*) comes out tops by a long way. The shops here include the pick of the nationwide chains, among them casual **Abercrombie & Fitch** (731 0712), preppy **Express** (892 0421) and perennial favourite **Banana Republic** (650 5623), alongside chic but accessible designer labels such as **DKNY** (650 9670) and **Dolce e Gabbana** (892 0880) and rarely seen imports such as classic London shirtmaker **Thomas Pink** (696 1713) and **Ted Baker** (*see below*).

Non-casino malls (*see p178*) are also worth a look. The best of them, conveniently, is located right on the Strip: the **Fashion Show Mall** (*see p178*) mixes upscale fashions with casual workaday togs in a similar way to, and with almost as much success as, the Forum Shops. Among those present are surf shack **Quiksilver** (734 1313) and femme favourite **Betsey Johnson** (735 3338). And don't forget about the **Las Vegas Premium Outlets** (*see p181*): among the 120 companies offering cut-price (but not cut-quality) fashions at factory or outlet shops here are **Banana Republic** (383 6117), the ever-popular **Calvin Klein** (366 9898), **Timberland** (386 3045) and **Tommy Hilfiger** (383 8660).

Obviously, there's a lot more to the scene than just the stores mentioned above and below. However, there's help at hand. Every mall website contains a comprehensive list of the shops contained within it: a little pre-trip browsing will help you get the best out of your limited shopping time.

Men

Men's fashion has come a long way in the past few years, and so has Las Vegas's selection of stores. The Forum Shops offers both **Brooks Brothers** (369 0705) and **Ralph Lauren** (650 5656), along with the more cutting-edge clothes of **Roberto Cavalli** (893 0369).

Lacoste

Caesars Palace (Forum Shops) *3500 Las Vegas Boulevard South, at W Flamingo Road (791 7616). Bus 202, 301, 302.* **Open** 10am-11pm Mon-Thur, Sun; 10am-midnight Fri, Sat. **Credit** AmEx, MC, V. **Hotel** p65. **Map** p320 A7.

In the transitory world of fashion, the crocodile shirt, created by French tennis champion René Lacoste in the 1930s, is a true survivor, and chic once again. The logo comes from his nickname, gained when he won some luggage on a tennis bet.

Suite 160

Aladdin/Planet Hollywood (Desert Passage) *3663 Las Vegas Boulevard South, at E Harmon Avenue (734 0399). Bus 301.* **Open** 10am-11pm Mon-Thur, Sun; 10am-midnight Fri, Sat. **Credit** AmEx, Disc, MC, V. **Hotel** p76. **Map** p320 A7.

Enter the realm of street chic at Suite 160, the brain-child of Jeffrey Brown, a former skateboarder who now sells the stuff style is made from. Look for lots of old-school favourites from Adidas Originals and Lacoste, alongside new urban favourites by (among others) Elwood.

Other locations: 9350 W Sahara Avenue, West Las Vegas (562 6136).

Ted Baker

Caesars Palace (Forum Shops) *3500 Las Vegas Boulevard South, at W Flamingo Road (369 4755/ www.tedbaker.co.uk). Bus 202, 301, 302.* **Open** 10am-11pm Mon-Thur, Sun; 10am-midnight Fri, Sat. **Credit** AmEx, Disc, MC, V. **Hotel** p76. **Map** p320 A7.

This London-based label – there is no 'Ted Baker' *per se* – has brought the button-down shirt back to the forefront of men's fashion by producing colourful, well-cut and (above all) fun apparel.

Women

Bellies & Blossoms

10271 S Eastern Avenue, at Coronado Center Drive, Henderson (255 1100/www.belliesandblossoms.com). Bus 110. **Open** 10am-6pm Mon-Sat; noon-3pm Sun. **Credit** AmEx, MC, V.

Many a mum-to-be thanks her lucky stars for this store, which sells fun and funky maternity wear for label queens. Look for real denim jeans from Citizens of Humanity and Seven for All Mankind, Naissance on Melrose blouses and Chiarakruza dresses.

Deetour

Fashion Show Mall, 3200 Las Vegas Boulevard South, at W Spring Mountain Road (894 9898/ www.deetourlv.com). Bus 105, 203, 213, 301, 302. **Open** 10am-9pm Mon-Fri; 10am-8pm Sat; 11am-6pm Sun. **Credit** AmEx, DC, Disc, MC, V. **Map** p320 B6.

Deetour offers fun fashions for the Hollywood star-let copycat. Prices are as hefty as the attitude of the staff, which itself can hardly squeeze through the door, but there's a great selection from the hippest street designers.

Musette

Village Square Shopping Center, 9420 W Sahara Avenue, at S Fort Apache Road, Southwest Las Vegas (309 6873). Bus 204, 213. **Open** 10am-7pm Mon-Thur; 10am-8pm Fri, Sat; noon-6pm Sun. **Credit** AmEx, Disc, MC, V.

Owner Gary Ghonik – along with Molly, his trusty canine companion – suggests that you 'explore your inner princess'. Follow this directive with the latest creations from Citizens of Humanity, Diane Von Furstenberg, Dolce e Gabbana, Earl Jean and plenty of other hip designers.

Scoop

Caesars Palace (Forum Shops) *3500 Las Vegas Boulevard South, at W Flamingo Road (734 0026/ www.scoopnyc.com). Bus 202, 301, 302.* **Open** 10am-11pm Mon-Thur, Sun; 10am-midnight Fri, Sat. **Credit** AmEx, DC, Disc, MC, V. **Hotel** p76. **Map** p320 A7.
This NY-based boutique chain has been hugely successful with its 'ultimate closet' concept, allowing tragically hip shoppers to find everything they need under one roof. Clothes, accessories and shoes from the likes of James Perse, Marc Jacobs and Lolita Jaca.

Still

Fashion Show Mall, 3200 Las Vegas Boulevard South, at W Spring Mountain Road (696 1209). Bus 105, 203, 213, 301, 302. **Open** 10am-9pm Mon-Fri; 10am-8pm Sat; 11am-6pm Sun. **Credit** AmEx, DC, Disc, MC, V. **Map** p320 B6.
Todd Burden and Tamara Knechtel have struck the fashion motherlode with this urban hipster boutique that sells super clothing by metro-magnets such as Rachel Polly, Nike White Label and Diesel Style Lab.

Talulah G

Fashion Show Mall, 3200 Las Vegas Boulevard South, at W Spring Mountain Road (737 6000/ www.talulahg.com). Bus 105, 203, 213, 301, 302. **Open** 10am-9pm Mon-Fri; 10am-8pm Sat; 11am-6pm Sun. **Credit** AmEx, MC, V. **Map** p320 B6.
Owner Meital Grantz is a New York expat with a fantastic eye. Her strong selection includes pieces by Sonia Rykiel, Matthew Williamson, Havaianas and Citizens of Humanity, and her Vegas success has led to a branch in Newport Beach's Fashion Island. **Other locations**: Boca Park Fashion Village, 750 S Rampart Boulevard, Summerlin (932 7000).

Children

Gap Kids and BabyGap can both be found in the **Desert Passage** mall (862 4042); check the phone book or www.gap.com for other locations. **Las Vegas Premium Outlets** (*see p188*) also has a whole slew of children's stores, among them **OshKosh B'Gosh** (221 1400), **Strasburg Children** (676 1459), **Hartstrings** (386 5033) and **Stride Rite Keds Sperry** (388 2055).

Along Came a Spider

Fashion Show Mall, 3200 Las Vegas Boulevard South, at W Spring Mountain Road (735 2728). Bus 105, 203, 213, 301, 302. **Open** 10am-9pm Mon-Fri; 10am-8pm Sat; 11am-6pm Sun. **Credit** AmEx, DC, Disc, MC, V. **Map** p320 B6.
This boutique stocks brands such as Hollywood Babe and Sarah Sarah, as well as a host of toys, accessories, furniture, bedding and children's gifts. Sizes are from infant to age 14.

Oilily

Mandalay Bay (Mandalay Place) *3930 Las Vegas Boulevard South, at E Hacienda Avenue (736 6587/www.oilily-world.com). Bus 105, 301.* **Open** 10am-11pm Mon-Thur, Sun; 10am-midnight Fri, Sat. **Credit** AmEx, Disc, MC, V. **Hotel** p67. **Map** p320 A9.
Quilted clothes in vivid colours and a variety of patterns make the Oilily brand totally recognisable in the world of children's fashion. Sizes range from infant to adult size 14, so, should she want to, a mother can match her babe.

Buffalo Exchange. *See p186.*

Vintage & second-hand

Attic

1018 S Main Street, at E Charleston Boulevard, Downtown (388 4088/www.atticvintage.com). Bus 108, 206, 301. **Open** 10am-5pm Mon-Thur; 10am-6pm Fri; 11am-6pm Sat. **Credit** AmEx, Disc, MC, V. **Map** p319 C3.

Its claim to be the largest vintage store in the world is as silly as the $1 admission (refundable on purchase, but that's not the point). Despite this, and its often high prices, the Attic is still the best vintage store in Vegas. The ground floor has custom-made clothing and vintage homewares; shoes and accessories are upstairs.

Buffalo Exchange

Pioneer Center, 4110 S Maryland Parkway, at E Flamingo Road, University District (791 3960/www. buffaloexchange.com). Bus 109, 202, 213. **Open** 10am-8pm Mon-Sat; 11am-7pm Sun. **Credit** MC, V. **Map** p317 Y3.

Although it's just celebrated its 30th birthday, this countrywide vintage chain is more popular than ever, especially with students at nearby UNLV. Its prices range between budget and middling; the clothing is mainly second-hand or from shop clearances. As we went to press, there were plans to remodel and expand the store to include 2,000 square feet of additional floor space.

Come the revolution

In recent years, the influx of celebrity chefs and Broadway-style shows has knocked gambling down a notch or two on the list of reasons people visit Las Vegas. Shopping is gaining fast. While most men prefer to sit for hours in the casino, their fashion-savvy wives are taking full advantage of their luck at the tables. Just a coin's toss away from many casino floors sit a collection of boutiques that rival those in New York, Rome, Paris... even the choicest global shopping cities.

Designers are now beginning to view Las Vegas Boulevard as one big runway on which to display their dazzling creations.

It wasn't always so. In the 1980s, at least until retail powerhouses such as Neiman Marcus and Saks Fifth Avenue gambled on the **Fashion Show Mall** (*see p178*), shopping on the Strip consisted largely of souvenir shops and hat emporiums. It wasn't until Caesars Palace opened the **Forum Shops** (*see p177*) in 1992 that savvy entrepreneurs began to see the commercial possibilities in the town. This pioneering mall, whose range of shops was generally high-end but by no means exclusive, adjoined the casino and was themed to fit the Caesars aesthetic; some guests went looking for it, but many more stumbled upon it.

Thus was a revolution born. When Steve Wynn opened the **Bellagio** in 1998, he brought with him such elite labels as Chanel, Gucci and Giorgio Armani, their names only adding to the hotel's kudos. The Venetian and the Aladdin hotel-casino resorts followed the Caesars example, pitching a selection of aspirational shops into a heavily themed setting close to the casino action, thus creating the **Grand Canal Shoppes** (*see p176*) and the **Desert Passage** (*see p176*). The fabric of Las Vegas consumerism changed beyond all recognition.

It didn't stop there, however. The transformation has extended into the suburbs: in the north-west, the Fashion Village at **Boca Park** hosts a slew of hip boutiques, while to the south-east, the **District** at Green Valley Ranch offers a select group of stores in an outdoor setting not dissimilar to Santa Monica's 3rd Street Promenade. Back on the Strip, **Mandalay**

D'Loe's House of Style
220 E Charleston Boulevard, at S 3rd Street, Downtown (382 5688). Bus 105, 108, 206, 301. **Open** 11.30am-6.30pm Mon-Sat. **Credit** AmEx, Disc, MC, V. **Map** p318 C3.
Mario D'Loe cut his teeth as a costume designer for several Las Vegas shows before going on to fill his store with great finds from the 1950s, '60s and '70s. Great menswear and accessories, in particular.

Valentino's Zoot Suit Connection
906 S 6th Street, at E Charleston Boulevard, Downtown (383 9555). Bus 206, 301. **Open** 11am-5pm Mon-Sat. **Credit** AmEx, MC, V. **Map** p318 C3.

Place (*see p178*) opened with a unique collection of speciality shops – **Fornarina**, **Max & Co**, **GF Ferre** – in the sky bridge between Mandalay Bay and Luxor, while the Fashion Show Mall recently completed a $1 billion expansion that attracted such fresh faces as **Paul Frank**, **Zara** and Cuban designer **Eddie Rodriguez**. Most dramatically, the Forum Shops at Caesars completed its third phase in October 2004, landing even more Vegas firsts – **Juicy Couture**, **Kate Spade**, **Thomas Pink**, **Carolina Herrera**, **Ted Baker**, **Pucci** and **Giuseppe Zanotti**, to name but a few – in a dazzling makeover.

And there's more to come. Look out for the renaming and re-theming of Desert Passage in late 2005 or early 2006; related in no small part to the Aladdin's rebranding as Planet Hollywood, the switch will no doubt also see a little juggling of the store line-up. There's also likely to be change at the Grand Canal Shoppes, since its recent acquisition by General Growth Property. If all goes according to schedule, expect **Town Square Las Vegas** to open in early 2006. A family-friendly development, it'll feature a cinema, offices, a number of restaurants, a 200-room hotel and, of course, a hand-picked collection of shops.

However, it'll have to go some in order to match the array of outlets at the new Wynn Las Vegas. When Steve Wynn said that he wanted his new project to be the most luxurious in town, he meant it: the **Wynn Esplanade** features fashion VIPs Jean-Paul Gaultier, Oscar de la Renta, Jo Malone, Graff jewellers, Manolo Blahnik and Brioni, plus the city's only authorised Ferrari dealership.

Go retrospectively wild at this well-stocked vintage shop, where you'll find Lilli Ann suits, handpainted neckties, great wing-tips and fancy cocktail dresses. Prices can be high, but so, mostly, is the quality.

Jewellery & accessories
Hit the jackpot? Celebrate at **Via Bellagio** by picking up a **Tiffany & Co** tiara (697 5400) or some **Fred Leighton** baubles (693 7050). Alternatively, trip the light fantastic at **Harry Winston** (933 7370) or **Cartier** (733 6652) inside the **Forum Shops**, or check out the rocks at Mandalay Bay's **Paradise Jewels** (632 6133) and the Venetian's **Simayof** (731 1037). Smaller spenders might prefer the pirate's treasures of **Jewelers of Las Vegas** (2400 Western Avenue, 382 7411, www.thejewelers.com).

Chrome Hearts
Caesars Palace (Forum Shops) *3500 Las Vegas Boulevard South, at W Flamingo Road (893 9949/www.chromehearts.com). Bus 202, 301, 302.* **Open** 10am-11pm Mon-Thur, Sun; 10am-midnight Fri, Sat. **Credit** AmEx, DC, Disc, MC, V. **Hotel** p76. **Map** p320 A7.
Free your rock 'n' roll wild child at this fine silver and leather shop. Its signature handcrafted heavy silver jewellery is adorned with plenty of skulls and crossbones, crucifixes and flames, but the store also sells some of the softest and most stylish leather jackets, trousers and coats money can buy. Steven Tyler just *loves* this place.

Hahn's World of Surplus
2908 E Lake Mead Boulevard, at Belmont Street, North Las Vegas (649 6819). Bus 210. **Open** 9am-6pm Mon-Fri; 9am-5pm Sat; 10am-4pm Sun. **Credit** MC, V.
Prepare for Armageddon at this warehouse that carries everything you might need should the world threaten to implode. Look for tents, fatigues, boots, canteens, knives, parachutes and other supplies.

Hat Company
Las Vegas Outlet Center, 7400 Las Vegas Boulevard South, at E Warm Springs Road (897 1666/www.thehatco.com). Bus 117, 217, 303. **Open** 10am-9pm Mon-Sat; 10am-8pm Sun. **Credit** AmEx, Disc, MC, V.
The variety here is overwhelming. Plumes, flowers and ribbons take their place alongside the sober felt, cloth and straw of classic panamas and stetsons. A selection of 'novelty' hats is also stocked.

Jacqueline Jarrot
Aladdin/Planet Hollywood (Desert Passage) *3663 Las Vegas Boulevard South, at E Harmon Avenue (731 3200/www.jacquelinejarrot.com). Bus 301.* **Open** 10am-11pm Mon-Thur, Sun; 10am-midnight Fri, Sat. **Credit** AmEx, DC, MC, V. **Hotel** p76. **Map** p320 A7.
Probably the best place for casual accessories, from handbags to toe rings, this shop gathers some 300 trendy designers in one convenient location.

Rainbow Feather Dyeing Company

1036 S Main Street, at E Charleston Boulevard, Downtown (598 0988/www.rainbowfeatherco.com). Bus 206. **Open** 8am-4pm Mon-Fri; 8am-noon Sat. **Credit** AmEx, MC, V. **Map** p319 C2.

Master feather-crafter Bill Girard sells big, beautiful, colourful, handmade boas at his unassuming store in the emerging Arts District. The customers include Cirque du Soleil and many a Las Vegas showgirl. Go on, give a boa a whirl.

Serge's Showgirl Wigs

Commercial Center, 953 E Sahara Avenue, between Paradise Road & S Maryland Parkway, East Las Vegas (732 1015/www.showgirlwigs.com). Bus 109, 204. **Open** 10am-5.30pm Mon-Sat. **Credit** AmEx, Disc, MC, V. **Map** p317 Y2.

In Las Vegas, wigs never went out of style. Serge's is the world's largest wig retailer, offering thousands of natural and synthetic hairpieces in hundreds of styles and colours. You don't have to be a showgirl to shop here. But it helps.

Lingerie

Agent Provocateur

Caesars Palace (Forum Shops) *3500 Las Vegas Boulevard South, at W Flamingo Road (696 7174). Bus 202, 301, 302.* **Open** 10am-11pm Mon-Thur, Sun; 10am-midnight Fri, Sat. **Credit** AmEx, MC, V. **Hotel** p76. **Map** p320 A7.

The smarties behind Agent Provocateur know that there's something rather empowering about wearing fine lingerie, whether you share it or not. Look for some of the most titillating and trashy yet tasteful creations currently on the market.

Bare Essentials Fantasy Fashions

4029 W Sahara Avenue, at S Valley View Boulevard, West of Strip (247 4711/www.bareessentialsvegas. com). Bus 104, 204. **Open** 10am-7pm Mon-Sat; noon-5pm Sun. **Credit** AmEx, Disc, MC, V. **Map** p317 X2.

Whatever your fantasy (or, crucially, gender) Bare Essentials will do you right. The camp-as-cowboys owners are correct in their claim that they make women feel at ease while shopping in LV's largest 'intimate apparel' store, but there are also men's essentials, costumes and 'accessories'.

Frederick's of Hollywood

3680 S Maryland Parkway, at E Twain Avenue, East of Strip (735 5065/www.fredericks.com). Bus 109, 112, 203, 213. **Open** 10am-9pm Mon-Sat; 11am-6pm Sun. **Credit** AmEx, Disc, MC, V. **Map** p317 Y3.

The lingerie at this old standby used to be wild but now seems a tad mild, with the Frederick's chain having made an effort to reposition itself as more couple-friendly in recent years. But there's still some raunch in there, and some decent day-styles. **Other locations**: 4300 Meadows Lane, Southwest Las Vegas (870 8129).

Love Jones

Hard Rock *4455 Paradise Road, at Harmon Avenue, East of Strip (693 5007/www.lovejones. com). Bus 108.* **Open** 10am-11pm Mon-Thur, Sun; 10am-1am Fri, Sat. **Credit** AmEx, DC, Disc, MC, V. **Map** p320 C7.

Fur-lined handcuffs, paddles, silk stockings, garter belts, lacy underalls, panties, bras, collars and corsets from the likes of Honey Dew and Christie's make this a truly mentionable unmentionables

Fancy dress Vegas-style at **Williams Costume Company**. *See p190.*

boutique. It also sells a few flavoured lotions, potions and toys (but nothing electric). Hotel guests have access to 24-hour room service: order in.

Shoes

There are plenty of brand-name shoe stores scattered around the Strip, whether your taste runs to slingbacks or sneakers. The selection at the **Grand Canal Shoppes** is led by super-chic **Jimmy Choo** (733 1802) and the more casual **Rockport** (735 5082), while the **Fashion Show Mall** has smart-casual Euro-import **Clarks** (732 1801), sports label **Puma** (892 9988) and the all-conquering, quietly stylish **Skechers** (969 9905). Over at the **Forum Shops**, you can find the high-class **Salvatore Ferragamo** (933 9333), the very Californian footwear of **Donald J Pliner** (796 0900) and **Niketown** (650 8888).

Arteffects

Fashion Show Mall, 3200 Las Vegas Boulevard South, at W Spring Mountain Road (796 7463/www. sharparteffects.com). Bus 105, 203, 213, 301, 302. **Open** 10am-9pm Mon-Fri; 10am-8pm Sat; 11am-6pm Sun. **Credit** AmEx, DC, Disc, MC, V. **Map** p320 B6.
Las Vegas has the distinction of being the venue for this former wholesaler's first signature shop. Among the stock are pixie-like clogs, sandals, wedges, heels high and low, and handbags made from a range of amazing fabrics and stamped leather.

Bellagio Collection Shoes

Bellagio *Via Bellagio, 3600 Las Vegas Boulevard South, at W Flamingo Avenue (693 7921). Bus 202, 301, 302.* **Open** 10am-midnight daily. **Credit** AmEx, DC, Disc, MC, V. **Hotel** p63. **Map** p320 A7.
Head here for fine footwear from the likes of Christian Dior, Salvatore Ferragamo, Pucci, Stuart Weitzman and Giuseppe Zanotti. In a word? Well-heeled. (OK, two words.)

David's Western Wear

3441 W Sahara Avenue, at S Valley View Boulevard, West of Strip (871 0350). Bus 104, 204. **Open** 10am-8pm Mon-Sat; 11am-4pm Sun. **Credit** AmEx, Disc, MC, V. **Map** p317 X2.
Nothing says pure cowboy like a pair of custom-made Teju Lizard boots, complete with matching belt. David's Western Wear, Nevada's only custom cowboy boot shop, can help you say whatever you want in every hide imaginable. There's also a great selection of hats.

Designer Shoe Warehouse

Best in the West Shopping Center, 2100 N Rainbow Boulevard, at W Lake Mead Boulevard, Northwest Las Vegas (636 2060/www.dswshoe.com). Bus 101, 210. **Open** 10am-9pm Mon-Sat; 11am-7pm Sun. **Credit** AmEx, Disc, Visa.
Shoehounds can help themselves to the finest selection of discounted designer cobbling in town: footwear is stacked from floor to ceiling here.

While the shoes may be trailing a season or two behind the current fashions, they're still fabulous. Accessories are available in the form of handbags, scarves and wraps.
Other location: Sun Mark Plaza, 671 Marks Street, Henderson (547 0620).

New Rock Boots

804 Las Vegas Boulevard South, at E Gass Avenue, Downtown (614 9464). Bus 301. **Open** 11am-7.30pm Mon-Sat. **Credit** AmEx, Disc, MC, V. **Map** p318 C3.
Combine John Fluevog's sinister style with the Doc Martens aesthetic, stir into the mix the 1970s rock 'n' roll stylings of Kiss, and lo: New Rock Boots. Decorative touches such as buckles, straps, flames, skulls and crossbones make the boots here popular with punks, bikers and muscled-up bouncer types, but there's also a wide selection of dominatrix-worthy stilettos. Down boy!

Stiletto

Fashion Show Mall, 3200 Las Vegas Boulevard South, at W Spring Mountain Road (791 0505). Bus 105, 203, 213, 301, 302. **Open** 10am-9pm Mon-Fri; 10am-8pm Sat; 11am-6pm Sun. **Credit** AmEx, DC, Disc, MC, V. **Map** p320 B6.
Stiletto's combination is a winning one: hot shoes in a cool location at the centre of the Fashion Show Mall. You'll find a similarly strong selection of footwear – Guess, Charles David, Natalie M, Via Spiga, Donald J Pliner and Aquatella – at **Shoooz** in the Forum Shops (734 7600).

Spectacles

Frame Fixer (3961 W Charleston Boulevard, Northwest Las Vegas, 735 7879) does fast, friendly and gentle repairs.

Lunettes

Fashion Show Mall, 3200 Las Vegas Boulevard South, at W Spring Mountain Road (733 7624). Bus 105, 203, 213, 301, 302. **Open** 10am-9pm Mon-Fri; 10am-8pm Sat; 11am-6pm Sun. **Credit** AmEx, DC, Disc, MC, V. **Map** p320 B6.
In a city that sees an average of 320 days of sunshine per year, sunglasses are a must. Lunettes sells shades by designers including Gucci, Oliver Peoples, Cartier and Kia Yomoto. **Sunshades** (731 3598), also in the Fashion Show Mall, has a similarly strong selection, including sportier shades from Oakley and fancier specs from Kate Spade.

Nu Vision Cyclery/Sport Optics

8447 W Lake Mead Boulevard, at N Rampart Boulevard, Summerlin (228 1333). Bus 210. **Open** 10am-6pm Mon-Fri. **Credit** MC, V.
Mike Hileman, a licensed optician and avid cyclist, runs this one-stop shop where sportspeople can find cool prescription eyewear that stays on the head, no matter how rough the play. Also in stock are sport goggles for swimming and skiing. Hileman sells and services Oakley Rx, Adidas, Rudy Project and Dragon Optical, as well as a peloton of bikes.

Eat, Drink, Shop

Oculus

Caesars Palace (Forum Shops) *3570 Las Vegas Boulevard South, at W Flamingo Road (731 4850).* Bus 202, 301, 302. **Open** 10am-8pm Mon-Thur, Sun; 10am-9pm Fri, Sat. **Credit** AmEx, Disc, MC, V. **Hotel** p76. **Map** p320 A7.

This Strip-convenient outpost of Dr Ed Malik's stylish Eyes & Optics boutique offers an excellent selection of frames from designers such as Oliver Peoples and Alain Mikli, plus eye examinations and specs repairs. The doctor is also available for prescription emergencies.

Cleaning & repairs

Al Phillips (www.alphillips-thecleaner.com) has locations all over Vegas, the most central at 4130 Koval Lane (733 1043). All branches provide dry-cleaning, laundry, alterations and repairs, and rent out men's formal wear.

Cora's Coin Laundry

1097 E Tropicana Avenue, at S Maryland Parkway, University District (736 6181). Bus 109, 201. **Open** 8am-8pm daily. **No credit cards. Map** p317 Y3.

Just two miles off the Strip, Cora's is popular with UNLV folk, offering self-service or drop-off laundry, dry-cleaning and – you betcha – video poker.

Shoe Lab

3900 Paradise Road, between Sands Avenue & E Flamingo Road, East of Strip (791 2004). Bus 108. **Open** 8am-6pm Mon-Fri; 9am-4pm Sat. **Credit** AmEx, Disc, MC, V. **Map** p319 C5.

The Shoe Lab can work miracles on any busted shoe or damaged handbag. It also sells leather care accessories such as polish, brushes and shoe trees.

Wedding outfits & costume hire

For the gen on Vegas weddings, *see p253.*

I&A Formalwear

3345 S Decatur Boulevard, between W Desert Inn & W Spring Mountain Roads, Southwest Las Vegas (364 5777/www.iaformalwear.com). Bus 103, 213. **Open** 9am-6pm Mon-Fri; 9am-5pm Sat; 11am-2pm Sun. **Credit** MC, V.

The biggest range of designer-name wedding gowns and dresses (Cardin, de la Renta, Dior) in Las Vegas. Tuxedo rentals start at $77 and gowns from $149.

Tuxedo Palace

Renaissance Center West, 4001 S Decatur Boulevard, at W Flamingo Road, Southwest Las Vegas (367 4433). Bus 103, 202. **Open** 9am-6pm Mon-Thur; 9am-7pm Fri; 9am-5pm Sat; 11am-4pm Sun. **Credit** AmEx, Disc, MC, V.

There's a huge selection of tuxedos available here, with suits costing $59.95-$114.95 for a two-day rental (shoes are an extra $10-$25). The Bridal Salon has wedding dresses from $225 to $525.

Williams Costume Company

1226 S 3rd Street, at W Colorado Avenue, Downtown (384 1384). Bus 105, 108, 206, 301. **Open** 10am-5.30pm Mon-Sat. **Credit** AmEx, Disc, MC, V. **Map** p319 C3.

The only place in town that carries enough ancient Egyptians, Renaissance gentry, Elvises and pioneers to dress the bride, groom and guests too. Nightly rental is $50 to $100, plus a hefty deposit.

Food & drink

Bakeries & pâtisseries

Freeds Bakery

4780 S Eastern Avenue, at E Tropicana Avenue, University District (456 7762/www.freedsbakery. com). Bus 110, 201. **Open** 9am-6.30pm Mon-Sat; 9am-3pm Sun. **Credit** AmEx, Disc, MC, V. **Map** p317 Z3.

For more than 40 years, Freeds has been baking rye breads, chollah breads and all kinds of cakes and cookies for Las Vegas's most discerning eaters. They also make speciality, themed and traditional wedding cakes. It gets busy, so be patient.

Krispy Kreme Doughnuts

Excalibur *3850 Las Vegas Boulevard South, at W Tropicana Avenue (736 5235/www.krispykreme. com). Bus 201, 301, 302.* **Open** 24hrs daily. **Credit** AmEx, MC, V. **Hotel** p86. **Map** p320 A8.

Discover the doughnut that took the US by storm. Wait around for the neon 'Hot Doughnuts Now' sign to light up, then indulge in a fresh-cooked, tasty treat – and see what all the fuss is about. **Other locations:** throughout the city.

Lenôtre

Paris Las Vegas *Le Boulevard, 3655 Las Vegas Boulevard South, at E Flamingo Road (946 4341).* Bus 202, 301, 302. **Open** 6.30am-11pm daily. **Credit** AmEx, DC, Disc, MC, V. **Hotel** p69. **Map** p320 A7.

Lenôtre is loaded to the gunwales with the most luscious eclairs, pains au chocolat, cookies and croissants. You have to order cafeteria-style, but the premises are bright and spacious, and there's plenty to keep the eyes happy while you wait.

Nothing Bundt Cake

9711 S Eastern Avenue, at E Silverado Ranch Boulevard, Southeast Las Vegas (1-877 238 6223/314 0520/www.nothingbundtcakes.com). Bus 110. **Open** 9am-6pm Mon-Fri; 9am-4pm Sat. **Credit** AmEx, MC, V.

Bundt cake? Think *My Big Fat Greek Wedding.* The chocolate-chocolate-chip is a big crowd pleaser, but carrot cake is the real show-stopper. Other flavours include lemon, spice, pineapple-upside-down, and plain, regular chocolate. Decorated cakes start at $6 for a bundtlet (serves two). **Other locations:** 8512 W Sahara Avenue, Southwest Las Vegas (871 6301).

Beer, liquor & wine

55° Wine + Design

Mandalay Bay (Mandalay Place) *3930 Las Vegas Boulevard South, at E Hacienda Avenue (632 9355). Bus 105, 301.* **Open** 10am-11pm Mon-Thur, Sun; 10am-midnight Fri, Sat. **Credit** AmEx, DC, Disc, MC, V. **Map** p320 A9.

Brought to you by the people behind the four-storey wine tower at the Aureole restaurant (*see p141*), 55° offers a comprehensive wine selection, a tasting bar offering wine by the glass and interactive PCs enabling customers to select wines. The shop also features all the wine accoutrements you'll need.

Lee's Discount Liquor

3480 E Flamingo Road, at S Pecos Road, East Las Vegas (458 5700). Bus 111, 202. **Open** 9am-10pm Mon-Thur; 9am-11pm Fri, Sat; 9am-9pm Sun. **Credit** AmEx, Disc, MC, V. **Map** p317 Z3.

Old favourites, hard-to-find European wines and dirt-cheap prices make Lee's the best liquor store in town. There's a surprisingly good range of beers from around the planet, and a few ciders as well. Further discounts apply if you pay cash.
Other locations: throughout the city.

Marché Bacchus

2620 Regatta Drive, at Mariner Way, West Las Vegas (804 8008). Bus 210. **Open** 10am-10pm Mon-Sat; 10am-4pm Sun. **Credit** AmEx, MC, V.

This fabulous little French store all the way out in Desert Shores sells fine wines, champagnes, pâtés, cheeses, some sandwiches and salads, and tasting kits. There are also monthly wine-tasting sessions, and outdoor seating on a terrace by the lake where you can enjoy an à la carte Sunday brunch (10am-4pm). The similar **Bleu Gourmet** opened in Summerlin in early 2005.

Chocolate

True chocolate fiends should make sure they don't miss the **Ethel M Chocolates** factory in Henderson (*see p138*), but in central Las Vegas there are only three real choices for your chocofix. The most distinctive is Chicago-based chocolatier **Vosges Haut-Chocolat** (at the Forum Shops, 836 9866), whose selection is highlighted by some glorious truffle concoctions. The other two are global chains: Belgian confectioner **Godiva** (with branches at Caesars, Desert Passage, Grand Canal Shoppes and the Fashion Show Mall) and Swiss chocolatier **Teuscher** (at Desert Passage, 866 6624).

Ethnic

For **Paymon's Mediterranean Café & Market**, *see p162*.

Everything's '-free' at **Trader Joe's**. *See p192*.

Gee's Oriental Market
4109 W Sahara Avenue, at Arville Street, West of Strip (362 5287). Bus 104, 204. **Open** 7.30am-8pm daily. **Credit** AmEx, Disc, MC, V. **Map** p317 X2.
The place for Chinese, Thai, Vietnamese and Filipino groceries, with first-rate fresh produce and seafood. Plenty of other Asian shops have opened up around here but this is, should you have developed a craving, the only place in Las Vegas that sells the delicacy *meang da na* (a cockroach-like insect).

International Marketplace
5000 S Decatur Boulevard, between W Reno & W Tropicana Avenues, Southwest Las Vegas (889 2888). Bus 103, 201. **Open** 9am-6pm Mon-Sat. **Credit** AmEx, Disc, MC, V.
This huge building is basically a warehouse containing every kind of imported edible, goodie and gadget, with prices on the better side of cheap.

Italcream
3871 S Valley View Boulevard, between W Spring Mountain & W Flamingo Roads, West of Strip (873 2214). Bus 104, 202. **Open** 8am-4pm Mon-Fri. **No credit cards.** **Map** p317 X3.
Magnifico! Giovanni Parente and his family have a secret recipe for the best *gelato* in town.

Siena Deli
Renaissance Plaza, 2250 E Tropicana Avenue, at S Eastern Avenue, University District (736 8424). Bus 110, 201. **Open** 8.30am-6.30pm Mon-Sat. **Credit** AmEx, Disc, MC, V. **Map** p317 Z3.
Siena hasn't changed in decades, and its Italian owner continues to bring the best of his homeland's cuisine to Vegas. Prices can be steep (119-year-old balsamic vinegar at $149.95) but the quality and authenticity are beyond doubt. Siena also carries Italian cooking hardware, such as pasta machines.

Health food & vitamins

Rainbow's End Natural Foods
1100 E Sahara Avenue, at S Maryland Parkway, East Las Vegas (737 1338). Bus 109, 204. **Open** 9am-8pm Mon-Sat. **Credit** AmEx, Disc, MC, V. **Map** p317 Y2.
A broad range of herbs, vitamins and bodycare items, but limited produce and food. Never mind: there's also a café that's full of veggie delights.

Wild Oats Natural Marketplace
7250 W Lake Mead Boulevard, between N Buffalo Drive & N Rainbow Boulevard, Summerlin (942 1500/www.wildoats.com). Bus 210. **Open** 7am-10pm daily. **Credit** AmEx, Disc, MC, V.
Wild Oats dominates the Vegas health food industry, and for good reason. Prices are a bit steep, but its stock of organic produce, health foods, natural bodycare products, homeopathic medicines and macrobiotic supplies is exemplary. The adjacent café offers fab juices and healthy snacks.
Other locations: 517 N Stephanie Street, Henderson (458 9427).

Supermarkets & grocery shops
There are four main chains in Vegas – **Vons**, **Albertson's**, **Smith's** and **Raley's** – but all off-Strip. Check the *Yellow Pages* for locations.

British Foods
Pioneer Square, 3375 S Decatur Boulevard, at W Desert Inn Road, Southwest Las Vegas (579 7777/ www.britishgrocers.com). Bus 103, 213. **Open** 10am-6pm daily. **Credit** AmEx, Disc, MC, V.
Offering 40,000 resident Brits a taste of home: HP sauce, kippers, marmalade, teas and so on. Pip pip!

Trader Joe's
2101 S Decatur Boulevard, at W Sahara Avenue, Northwest Las Vegas (367 0227/www.traderjoes. com). Bus 103, 204. **Open** 9am-9pm daily. **Credit** DC, Disc, MC, V.
An old-style grocery store with a twist: all products are tested to ensure that they are 'the best' (it claims). You can find gluten-, sodium- and GM-free produce as well as chocolate and cookies, and party foods.
Other locations: 2716 N Green Valley Parkway, Henderson (433 6773); 7575 W Washington Drive, Summerlin (242 8240).

Whole Foods
8855 W Charleston Boulevard, at S Fort Apache Road, Summerlin (254 8655/www.wholefoods market.com). Bus 206. **Open** 8am-10pm daily. **Credit** AmEx, Disc, MC, V.

Gamblers General Store. *See p195.*

Foodies and fans of natural food celebrated when the world's leading natural and organic grocer opened in Summerlin in 2004. The produce and meat sections are enough to write home about, but check out the seafood case, and the deli for wonderful cheeses and breads, before visiting the impressive prepared food/café section. Yum.

Brits abroad

Most visitors arrive in Vegas in the hope of escaping their everyday drudgery for a while. But what happens when a little everyday drudgery is what you need? Worry not, at least if you're British: there are a variety of places here that may remind you of home.

The gents should start with a trip to **Truefitt & Hill** in the Forum Shops (see p198). Barbers to the British aristocracy since the 18th century, the company has secured itself a plum site on the edge of the mall, away from the bustle but handy for cab traffic. While the guys are having an immaculate short, back and sides and a cut-throat shave, the ladies can adjourn around the corner to **Penhaligon's** (796 6100), the wonderfully olde-worlde London perfumiers who've also just opened their first Vegas store at the Forum Shops.

By then, it'll be time for lunch, which you can prepare yourself with the help of **British Foods** (see p192). Sausage rolls, kippers, biscuits, curry sauce, crisps… if you have a craving for it, they'll likely have it. You'll pay fairly handsomely for the privilege, mind, but then there are times when only HP Sauce will do.

It isn't just the casinos that are themed in Vegas, as an afternoon round at the **Royal Links** golf course (5995 E Vegas Valley Drive, 1-888 427 6678) will reveal. The course designers have magpied a number of holes from famous British courses – among them the Road Hole from St Andrew's – and compiled them into a highly curious desert links.

After all this adventure and adventure, you'll likely deserve a drink, which you ought to get at the **Crown & Anchor Pub** (see p172). The British theming in this boozer is a little inauthentic, not least the lack of a bell and shouts of 'Time at the bar!' when 11pm rolls around. Still, its popularity with the local expat community, who come here to slouch about by the dartboard and watch televised football, means it must be doing something right.

Gifts & collectibles

Amen Wardy Home Store

Caesars Palace (Forum Shops) *3500 Las Vegas Boulevard South, at W Flamingo Road (734 0480/ www.amenwardy.com). Bus 202, 301, 302.* **Open** 10am-11pm daily. **Credit** AmEx, DC, Disc, MC, V. **Hotel** p76. **Map** p320 A7.
This successful boutique has great home accessories including fine china, Diptyque candles, and hand-blown glass, and features most of Wardy's eclectic furniture as well as some McKenzie Child pieces. Gourmet sweets include chocolate body paint. **Other location**: Grand Canal Shops, Venetian, 3377 Las Vegas Boulevard South (696 9005).

Ca' d'Oro

Venetian (Grand Canal Shoppes) *3355 Las Vegas Boulevard South, at Sands Avenue (696 0080/www.thecadoro.com). Bus 105, 203, 213, 301, 302.* **Open** 10am-11pm Mon-Thur, Sun; 10am-midnight Fri, Sat. **Credit** AmEx, DC, Disc, MC, V. **Hotel** p73. **Map** p320 A6.
This gorgeous gallery is named after one of the finest façades in Venice, the House of Gold on the Grand Canal. From the delicate hand-blown Murano glass light fittings to the beautiful handmade custom tiles, it's a real gem.

Chihuly Store

Bellagio (Via Bellagio) *3600 Las Vegas Boulevard South, at W Flamingo Road (693 7995). Bus 202, 301, 302.* **Open** 9am-midnight daily. **Credit** AmEx, Disc, MC, V. **Hotel** p63. **Map** p320 A7.
It seems fitting that respected glass sculptor Dale Chihuly should open his first signature gallery inside the Bellagio, since his largest sculpture – with more than 2,000 pieces of glass – hangs from the ceiling of the hotel lobby. Mainly focusing on affordable Chihuly glass editions – which sell like hot cakes – the store also has some more elaborate (and more expensive) pieces.

Entertainment Galleries

Venetian (Grand Canal Shoppes) *3355 Las Vegas Boulevard South, at Sands Avenue (866 6813). Bus 105, 203, 213, 301, 302.* **Open** 10am-11pm Mon-Thur, Sun; 10am-midnight Fri, Sat. **Credit** AmEx, DC, Disc, MC, V. **Hotel** p73. **Map** p320 A6.
This amazing lithograph shop specialises in limited editions of Hollywood movie posters and classic French posters, all of which it produces on 130-year-old printing presses in the Downtown Arts District (at the S^2 Art Group Atelier, see p231). **Other locations**: Jack Gallery, Mandalay Bay, 3950 Las Vegas Boulevard South (632 4770); Galleries America, Fashion Show Mall, 3200 Las Vegas Boulevard South (731 0074).

Girard's Boutique

740 S Rampart Boulevard, at W Charleston Boulevard, Summerlin (953 8888). Bus 206. **Open** 11.30am-7pm Mon-Sat. **Credit** AmEx, Disc, MC, V.

Eat, Drink, Shop

Specialising in beautiful handmade knick-knacks, lovely picture frames, and places to store fancy baubles, Girard's is an extremely hip shop. Among its stock is an amazing selection of Domsky Glass and fine work by local jewellers. There's also a branch in Boca Park.

Unica Home
7540 S Industrial Road, between W Warm Springs & Blue Diamond Roads, Southwest Las Vegas (1-888 898 6422/616 9280/www.unicahome.com). **Bus** 117. **Open** 10am-6pm Mon-Sat; noon-4pm Sun. **Credit** AmEx, Disc, MC, V.

A modernist oasis in a neo-classical desert, Unica sells mouth-watering designs (from flatware to bedroom sets to jewellery and books) by Tom Dixon, Castiglioni, Tord Boontje and Ivan Baj.

Vegas souvenirs

The cash-burdened hordes schlep through the upmarket resort malls, spending money on stuff you can pick up in any global city. However, it's not hard to find souvenirs that really scream 'Las Vegas'. The Strip is dotted with tatty little

Star spas

If all you want is a basic massage, a facial or a french manicure or pedicure, then just about any old spa will do. But if you want an *experience*, a memory that you can bring out to see-through the gloom of some cold, grey February morning, then you want a spa with some style.

In the new Vegas, where the emphasis is as much on entertainment and pampering as it is on gaming, spas have become as essential to the luxury resort experience as designer shopping and restaurants helmed by celebrity chefs. Many are worthy, but the five we list below are a cut above the rest, by virtue of their serene ambience, their vast range of treatments from many different cultures and their extra amenities (wellness consultants, restaurants and so on).

Aquae Sulis
JW Marriott Resort & Spa *221 N Rampart Boulevard, at Summerlin Parkway, Northwest Las Vegas (869 7807/www.marriott.com).* **Open** 5.30am-8pm daily. **Daily pass** $20 guests; $50 non-guests. Free with spa services. **Hotel** p100.
Marriott's 40,000sq ft (3,700sq m) spa Aquae Sulis, the name of which pays homage to the Roman town of Bath, more than lives up to its name, offering a host of water-based treatments and features. Even better, some are free: the outdoor hydrocircuit pool (six water massage pods with varying jet frequencies), hot and cold plunges, and torrential waterfall showers are 'DIY', so you don't need an appointment to enjoy them. The interior baths are single-sex, but the outdoor patio is mixed and has its own separate sauna, steam room and jacuzzi. The fitness centre is super-modern, and includes an airy glassed-in studio for yoga,

Pilates and aerobics, with a great view of the gardens. Recently, Aquae Sulis added a full-service salon.

Canyon Ranch SpaClub
Venetian *3355 Las Vegas Boulevard South, at Sands Avenue (414 3600/ café 414 3633/www.canyonranch.com).* **Open** 5.30am-10pm daily. *Café* 7am-6pm daily. **Daily pass** $35. $15 with spa services. **Hotel** p73.
While Canyon Ranch's 65,000sq ft (6,000sq m) Vegas outpost at the Venetian has none of the charm of the spa's Berkshire and Tucson locales, the somewhat sterile surroundings hardly matter once you get a glimpse of the sheer range of treatments and services available. For starters, there's the well-stocked gym, the yoga/Pilates studio, the 40ft (12m) climbing wall, the splendid Canyon Ranch Café and the staff of health professionals available for consultations. On the body beautiful side, Canyon Ranch has a salon and an enviable menu of 120-plus massages, facials, wraps and scrubs. But there are helpful extras, too, such as programmable combination lockers (so there's no key to lose in the jacuzzi) and exquisitely soft robes from Robeworks. Any downside? The highest facility-use fees on the Strip. And unlike most places, where the fees are waived with spa services, Canyon Ranch still insists on charging $15 to access the gym and take classes. The sauna, steam room and whirlpool are, however, complimentary.

Spa & Salon Bellagio
Bellagio *3600 Las Vegas Boulevard South, at W Flamingo Road (693 7472/www.bellagio. com).* **Open** 6am-8pm daily. **Daily pass** $25. Free with spa services. **Hotel** p63.

gift shops selling everything from snow domes (it's the desert, folks!) to dice clocks, and more gambling mementoes than you could shake a croupier's rake at. For that extra-special someone, many of Vegas's major shows have their own souvenir shops. Few can top Celine Dion's (at Caesars Palace) for sheer tackiness.

Bonanza Gifts

2460 Las Vegas Boulevard South, at W Sahara Avenue (385 7359). Bus 204, 301, 302. **Open** 8am-midnight daily. **Credit** AmEx, Disc, MC, V. **Map** p319 C4.

Bonanza's huge sign declares it to be the 'World's Largest Gift Store'. It's certainly hard to imagine one much bigger. The store sells everything from postcards to place mats, dice clocks to Elvis shot glasses, playing cards to earrings. Harkening back to the days of Route 66 gift shops, there's also plenty of American Indian turquoise and silver jewellery.

Gamblers General Store

800 S Main Street, at E Gass Avenue, Downtown (382 9903/www.gamblersgeneralstore.com). Bus 105, 108, 207, 301. **Open** 9am-5pm daily. **Credit** AmEx, Disc, MC, V. **Map** p318 C2.

Although non-guests are welcome to avail themselves of Bellagio's first-floor salon services (including couples' pedicures and straight-razor shaves in a traditional barber setting), the upstairs spa, which reopened in late 2004, remains a lavish perk available only to those bedding down at the hotel. A major expansion/renovation more than doubled the spa's size to 65,000sq ft (6,000sq m) putting it, at least size-wise, on a par with the Canyon Ranch SpaClub. And along with spanking new decor (wide hallways, stone and glass accents, reflecting pools and water walls), the new spa now includes a 6,000sq ft (600sq m) state-of-the-art fitness centre staffed with trainers who can be booked for private sessions, an exercise studio, a watsu pool, a meditation room, several relaxation lounges (some mixed), a full kitchen and 56 treatment rooms, many of which are thoughtfully fitted out with showers so guests don't have to traipse the halls in search of a post-treatment rinse-off. A cool perk? Disposable swimsuits, in case you left yours at home.

Spa Mandalay

Mandalay Bay *3950 Las Vegas Boulevard South, at E Hacienda Avenue (632 7300/ www.mandalaybay.com).* **Open** 6am-10pm daily. **Daily pass** $27 guests; $30 non-guests. Free with spa services. **Hotel** p67. Mandalay Bay's fees may seem steep but, for sheer beauty alone, nothing comes close to rivalling the spacious Roman-style baths at this 30,000sq ft spa (2,800sq m), with their saunas, eucalyptus steam rooms and beautiful mosaic whirlpools. It's possible to feel utterly pampered simply by spending all day lounging on a cushioned chaise without ever splurging on spa treatments,

though the services are worth the indulgence. A nice touch: apart from the reception lounge, where you can take coffee and peruse the papers, there's another, quieter area where you can relax and unwind before having your treatment. Spa Mandalay also has a well-equipped fitness centre (with complimentary headsets and workout clothes if you didn't bring your own). Personal trainers are on hand for private sessions. From March to September, there's a daily yoga session on Mandalay Beach (at 7am).

Spa Vita di Lago

Ritz-Carlton, Lake Las Vegas *1610 Lake Las Vegas Parkway, at Lake Mead Boulevard, Henderson (567 4600/www.ritzcarlton.com).* **Open** 6am-8pm daily. **Daily pass** free with $20 daily 'resort fee'. **Hotel** p108. Like a guesthouse set apart from the main building, the Ritz-Carlton's stately 30,000sq ft (2,800sq m) spa is a world away even from the gracious accommodations at the hotel. Along with a fitness centre, an exercise studio, 'healing waters' showers, steam rooms, jacuzzis, a full-service salon and a restaurant (with 'pool' and 'healthy' menus), the spa has 24 treatment rooms, two of which – the only ones in the US – feature La Culla, an Italian speciality that's essentially four continuous treatments (exfoliation, wrap, massage, facial) carried out in a 'multi-sensory' environment. But what really sets Spa Vita di Lago apart is its manicured meditation garden, in which you can lose yourself among hedgerows for an hour or an afternoon, as well as enjoy outdoor massages against the backdrop of a rushing waterfall, guided meditation hikes and stargazing. Personal trainers and other health pros can be tapped for private consultations.

Eat, Drink, Shop

This well-stocked shop in Downtown Vegas is packed with gift ideas for that special gambler in your life. There's something to suit all prices, from a single casino chip costing a couple of coins to vintage video poker machines. Along with the collectibles are pretty much everything you need to play any of the casino games, along with a veritable library of 'how to' gaming books.

Health & beauty

Many casinos have lavish full-service spas and beauty salons; for the best pampering on the Strip, *see p194* **Star spas**. For health food and vitamins, *see p192*.

Complementary therapies

Body Works Massage Therapy

5025 S Eastern Avenue, between E Tropicana & E Hacienda Avenues, East Las Vegas (736 8887). Bus 110, 201. **Open** by appointment. **Credit** MC, V. **Map** p317 Z4.

For almost ten years, Body Works' masseurs and masseuses have been kneading, prodding and pounding, with treatments including Swedish deep tissue and Chinese mix, as well as muds and salts.

T&T Ginseng

Chinatown Mall, 4115 W Spring Mountain Road, between Arville Street & Wynn Road, Southwest Las Vegas (368 3898). Bus 104, 203, 213. **Open** 10am-8.30pm daily. **Credit** Disc, MC, V.

A fascinating store and Chinese herbal pharmacy, where diagnosis and treatment are handled with ancient wisdom and extreme care. An oriental medical doctor and herbalist are on duty every day.

Worton's Palmistry Studios

1441 Las Vegas Boulevard South, between E Charleston Boulevard & E Oakey Avenue, Stratosphere Area (386 0121). Bus 301. **Open** by appointment only. **No credit cards**. **Map** p319 B5.

The first licensed psychic in Las Vegas, Worton's has been offering professional palmistry and astrology readings since 1958. The owners have recently been on the look out for new premises, so it's advisable to check the address when making your appointment.

Cosmetics & perfume shops

Fresh

Caesars Palace (Forum Shops) *3500 Las Vegas Boulevard South, at W Flamingo Road (631 5000/ www.fresh.com). Bus 202, 301, 302.* **Open** 10am-11pm Mon-Thur, Sun; 10am-midnight Fri, Sat. **Credit** AmEx, MC, V. **Hotel** p76. **Map** p320 A7.

Clean gets tasty with Fresh bath products, made with sugar, milk, soya, and now saké. The line also includes some great perfumes and basic cosmetics in natural-looking hues for all skin tones.

Kiehl's

Caesars Palace (Forum Shops) *3500 Las Vegas Boulevard South, at W Flamingo Road (784 0025/ www.kiehls.com). Bus 202, 301, 302.* **Open** 10am-11pm Mon-Thur, Sun; 10am-midnight Fri, Sat. **Credit** AmEx, MC, V. **Hotel** p76. **Map** p320 A7.

The simplicity of the skin and hair care products sold at Kiehl's is part of its appeal, along with its total commitment to never test on animals. It sells lotions, sunscreens, scrubs, cleansers and conditioners for all skin and hair types, created with the entire family in mind.

MAC Cosmetics

Caesars Palace (Forum Shops) *3500 Las Vegas Boulevard South, at W Flamingo Road (369 8770/ www.maccosmetics.com). Bus 202, 301, 302.* **Open** 10am-11pm Mon-Fri; 10am-midnight Sat, Sun. **Credit** AmEx, DC, Disc, MC, V. **Hotel** p76. **Map** p320 A7.

Though you'll find MAC counters in many department stores, this retail centre is the only one of its kind in Vegas. The high-profile cosmetics line is most popular with celebrities and the city's many professional make-up artists. The store includes an upstairs area for make-up lessons and makeovers.

Sephora

Venetian (Grand Canal Shoppes) *3355 Las Vegas Boulevard South, at Sands Avenue (735 3896/www.sephora.com). Bus 105, 203, 213, 301, 302.* **Open** 10am-11pm Mon-Thur, Sun; 10am-midnight Fri, Sat. **Credit** AmEx, Disc, MC, V. **Hotel** p73. **Map** p320 A6.

The largest and most comprehensive cosmetics emporium in town contains stock from Dior and Yves Saint Laurent, along with the latest hip offerings from Smashbox, Nars, Paul & Joe, plus an impressive and good-value own-brand range. Test out the goods in the application areas or let a pro get to work on you. There's even an opportunity to create your own scent.
Other locations: Desert Passage, 3663 Las Vegas Boulevard South (737 0550).

Hair & beauty salons

Cristophe of Beverly Hills

MGM Grand *3799 Las Vegas Boulevard South, at E Tropicana Avenue (891 3339). Bus 201, 301, 302.* **Open** 9am-7pm daily. **Credit** AmEx, Disc, MC, V. **Hotel** p80. **Map** p320 A8.

Rumour has it that the venerable Cristophe himself shows up to service his Las Vegas-based regulars at this super-swanky salon. If he's not around to cut your locks, rest assured that his staff is chock-full of other talented stylists.

Dolphin Court

Coronade Square Center, 7581 W Lake Mead Boulevard, at N Buffalo Drive, Northwest Las Vegas (432 9772). Bus 210. **Open** 9am-8pm Mon-Sat; 9am-6pm Sun. **Credit** AmEx, DC, Disc, MC, V.

One of numerous 'day spa' operations in Vegas, Dolphin Court is also one of the popular in town. Hair care is offered, but the spa services are the real strength at these locations.
Other locations: 3455 S Durango Drive, Southwest Las Vegas (949 9999).

Globe Salon

Westland Fair Center, 1121 S Decatur Boulevard, at W Charleston Boulevard, Northwest Las Vegas (938 4247/www.globesalon.com). Bus 103, 206. **Open** 11am-6pm Tue; 10am-7pm Wed, Thur; 9am-5pm Fri, Sat. **Credit** AmEx, MC, V.

This award-winning hair- and skin-care boutique is run by Vegas native and 'Hairstylist to the Hip' Staci Linklater, who oversees a talented team of professionals in a mod style space just west of the Strip.

Moxie Hair Studios

10247 W Charleston Boulevard, between Town Center Drive & Hualapai Way, Northwest Las Vegas (254 9000/www.moxiehairstudios.com). Bus 206. **Open** 9am-7pm Tue-Fri; 9am-5pm Sat. **Credit** AmEx, Disc, MC, V.

The top team of hairstylists at Moxie, headed by talented master designer Tonia Fike, creates some of the best hairdos in the Las Vegas area. Located in the far western Valley, but the trip's worth the effort.

Big B's CDs & Records.
See p198.

ARCS: A Robert Cromeans Salon

Mandalay Bay (Mandalay Place) *3930 Las Vegas Boulevard South, at E Hacienda Avenue (632 6130). Bus 105, 301.* **Open** 9am-7pm Mon-Fri, 8am-8pm Sat, 10am-7pm Sun. **Credit** AmEx, Disc, MC, V. **Hotel** p67. **Map** p320 A9.

Crazy coiffeur Robert Cromean has opened an outlet within Mandalay Bay. The prices are about the same as his California salons: in other words, eye-watering. You'd better believe you're worth it.

Men's barbers

Art of Shaving

Mandalay Bay (Mandalay Place) *3930 Las Vegas Boulevard South, at E Hacienda Avenue (632 9356). Bus 105, 301.* **Credit** AmEx, Disc, MC, V. **Hotel** p67. **Map** p320 A9.

The warm scent of sandalwood permeates the air in this handsome shaving boutique. You can get trimmed on the premises, but there's also an array of gear for sale: lotions, potions and full shaving sets, which run from $99 to $3,000.

Truefitt & Hill

Caesars Palace (Forum Shops) *3500 Las Vegas Boulevard South, at W Flamingo Road (735 7428/www.truefittandhill.com). Bus 202, 301, 302.* **Open** 9am-11pm Mon-Thur, Sun; 9am-midnight Fri, Sat. **Credit** AmEx, Disc, MC, V. **Hotel** p65. **Map** p320 A7.

Gents have been getting cropped and shaved at Truefitt & Hill in London since 1805, and in Las Vegas since late 2004. The look of the store – mahogany woods, navy accents – reflects the company's rich history, and so do the classic cuts offered. Other services include straight-razor shaves, manicures, pedicures and shoe shines. *See p194* **Star spas**.

Tattoos

Absolute Ink

1141 Las Vegas Boulevard South, at E Charleston Boulevard, Stratosphere Area (383 8282). Bus 206, 301, 302. **Open** 10am-midnight Mon-Thur, Sun; 10am-2am Fri, Sat. **No credit cards**. **Map** p319 C3.

If you'd like your souvenir of the city to be permanent, come here. Piercings start at $20 and tattoo prices are claimed to be the lowest in town. The attitude-free staff are serious about their art, and so should you be: it'll still be there in the morning.

Hart & Huntington Tattoo Company

Palms *4321 W Flamingo Road, at Arville Street, Off-Strip (942 7777/http://hartandhuntingtontattoo.com). Bus 202.* **Open** 11am-2am daily. **Credit** AmEx, Disc, MC, V. **Hotel** p92. **Map** p317 X3.

Freestyle motocross legend Carey Hart and nightclub promoter John Huntington (the man behind the original Pimp 'n' Ho Costume Ball) have set up this hip tattoo parlour inside the Palms; guests can book tattoo time at the same time as they make their hotel reservations.

Pussykat Tattoo Parlor

4972 S Maryland Parkway, at E Tropicana Avenue, University District (597 1549). Bus 109, 201. **Open** varies. **Credit** AmEx, Disc, MC, V. **Map** p317 Y3.

Owner/artist Dirk Vermin is a local legend who has dedicated his life to bettering the local subculture. His tattoo work is well known among aficionados, but be sure also to check out his Gallery au Go-Go (*see p231*) where his non-flesh-based art is on show.

Music & video

Blockbuster is everywhere; to find a branch, use the store locator at www.blockbuster.com. Alternatively, try the lower-key **Hollywood Video** (www.hollywoodvideo.com). New-release CDs are often sold at huge discounts at **Best Buy** (*see p183*). Look out for two arrivals, due in 2005 or '06: a new **Virgin Megastore**, to replace the branch in the Forum Shops that closed in late 2004 and, perhaps, a branch of venerable Arizona chain **Zia**, to give Big B's some competition.

Big B's CDs & Records

4761 S Maryland Parkway, at E Tropicana Avenue, University District (732 4433). Bus 109, 201. **Open** 10am-9.30pm Mon-Sat; 11am-7.30pm Sun. **Credit** AmEx, Disc, MC, V. **Map** p317 Y4.

If you want to buy a CD in Vegas, this is where you head. There's a decent and clued-in selection of new music here, but also a high turnover of used CDs, many of them at very keen prices. The best music store in town by a mile.

Tower Records

4580 W Sahara Avenue, at S Decatur Boulevard, Southwest Las Vegas (364 2500/www.towerrecords.com). Bus 103, 204. **Open** 10am-midnight daily. **Credit** AmEx, Disc, MC, V.

Tower offers the biggest range of CDs in town, not to mention a healthy stock of DVDs, magazines and books, but prices are prohibitively expensive.

Wax Trax Records

2909 S Decatur Boulevard, between W Sahara Avenue & W Desert Inn Road, Southwest Las Vegas (362 4300). Bus 103, 204, 213. **Open** 10am-5pm Mon-Sat; 10am-2pm Sun. **Credit** AmEx, Disc, DC, MC, V.

Two storeys of vinyl and memorabilia – bins bursting with old soul and R&B, jazz and doo-wop – plus a mixed selection of used CDs and walls covered with signed photos. Be prepared for some boisterous East Coast conversation, owner Rich Rosen's friendly house pup, Bobo, and an earful of music.

Pharmacies

You'll find drugstores that offer pharmacy services all over Las Vegas. On the Strip, try **Walgreens** (1101 Las Vegas Boulevard South, at E Charleston Boulevard, 471 6844,

Bass Pro Shops Outdoor World.
See p200.

www.walgreens.com) and **White Cross Drugs** (1700 Las Vegas Boulevard South, at E Oakey Boulevard, 382 1733). Both are open 24 hours a day, although the White Cross pharmacist is only available 8am-9pm Monday to Friday, 9am-6pm Saturday and Sunday.

Sex & erotica

The best of the small adult bookstores, the **Rancho Adult Entertainment Center** (4820 N Rancho Drive, Northwest Las Vegas, 645 6104), is open all day, every day. The friendly staff, including several women, makes for a comfortable atmosphere whatever your gender. For the more seedy **Showgirl Video** store, *see p210* **Dirty secrets**.

Adult Superstore
3850 W Tropicana Avenue, at S Valley View Boulevard, West of Strip (798 0144). Bus 104, 201. **Open** 24hrs daily. **Credit** AmEx, Disc, MC, V. **Map** p317 X3.
There are four branches of this locals' favourite, but the 'mega-superstore' here is the one to visit. The magazine and video sections are devoted to every fetish and fantasy that's legal in Nevada, and there's an unequalled selection of toys, fetish gear and sexy food items. Good movie selection, too. **Other locations**: 1147 Las Vegas Boulevard South, Stratosphere Area (383 8326); 3226 W Spring Mountain Road, West of Strip (247 1101); 601 S Main Street, Downtown (383 0601).

Paradise Electro Stimulations
1509 W Oakey Boulevard, at S Western Avenue, Stratosphere Area (474 2991/www.peselectro.com). Bus 105, 108. **Open** 10am-7pm Mon-Fri; noon-5pm Sat. **Credit** AmEx, Disc, MC, V. **Map** p319 B3.

PES (aka 'the Studio') is known for electric muscle-stimulation devices: dildos, plugs and sheaths, all composed of crystal-clear plastic and attachable to an electrical impulse control unit that purportedly stimulates the user from the inside out, 'harmonising with the body's own electrical impulses'.

Smoking

Davidoff
Venetian (Grand Canal Shoppes) *3355 Las Vegas Boulevard South, at Sands Avenue (733 5999/www.davidoff.com). Bus 105, 203, 213, 301, 302.* **Open** 10am-11pm Mon-Thur; Sun; 10am-midnight Fri, Sat. **Credit** AmEx, DC, Disc, MC, V. **Hotel** p73. **Map** p320 A6.
Cigar smokers rejoiced when this Swiss tobacco purveyor arrived on the Strip. Some say Davidoff cigarettes are as terrific as its premium cigars.

Havana Cigar Bar
3900 Paradise Road, between E Flamingo Road & Sands Avenue, Off-Strip (892 9555/www.havana smoke.com). Bus 108, 202. **Open** 9am-11pm Mon-Thur; 9am-midnight Fri, Sat; 2-10pm Sun. **Credit** AmEx, Disc, MC, V. **Map** p320 C7.
Aficionados swear this cigar and wine bar is the best place in town to take time, sit down and enjoy the nuances of a fine cigar and a good glass of wine. Its range of accessories is as strong as that of its cigars.

Las Vegas Cigar Co
3750 Las Vegas Boulevard South, between E Tropicana & E Harmon Avenues (262 6140/www. lvcc.com). Bus 301. **Open** 8am-11pm Mon-Sat; 8.30am-11pm Sun. **Credit** AmEx, Disc, MC, V. **Map** p320 A8.
Their 12 established varieties of cigars are hand-rolled daily, in-house, using Cuban-seed tobacco imported from Ecuador and Dominican Republic.

Sport & outdoor

The two best general sports stores are chains: **Copeland's Sports** (Best in the West Shopping Center, 2178 N Rainbow Boulevard, Northwest Las Vegas, 631 7497, www.copelandsports.com) and the **Sports Authority** (Sahara Pavilion, 2620 S Decatur Boulevard, Southwest Las Vegas, 368 3335, www.thesportsauthority.com). Both have branches. The two biggest names in sports have shops here, too: the Forum Shops is home to a **Niketown** (650 8888), while the Showcase Mall has **Adidas Sports Performance Store**, the first in the US (597 1652).

Bass Pro Shops Outdoor World

8200 S Industrial Road, at Blue Diamond Road, Silverton (730 5200). Bus 117. **Open** 9am-10pm Mon-Sat; 10am-7pm Sun. **Credit** AmEx, Disc, MC, V.
With a firing range, a gunsmith, an archery range and a custom tie shop (for anglers), this massive store is a lesson in retail as entertainment. The displays include a host of animals from around the world: a stuffed giraffe, a pride of lions and Nevada's own state animal, the Bighorn Sheep.

Desert Rock Sports

8221 W Charleston Boulevard, between S Buffalo & S Durango Drives, West Las Vegas (254 1143). Bus 206. **Open** 9am-7pm Mon-Fri; 9am-6pm Sat; 10am-6pm Sun. **Credit** AmEx, Disc, MC, V.
Desert Rock carries super-cool climbing, hiking, camping and backpacking gear for the outdoor enthusiast, as well as stuff for children and dogs. The prices are fairly high, but the staff are well informed. You can rent equipment at next door's Powerhouse Rock Climbing Centre (254 5604).

McGhie's

4503 W Sahara Avenue, between Arville Street & S Decatur Boulevard, Southwest Las Vegas (252 8077/www.mcghies.com). Bus 204. **Open** 10am-7pm Mon-Fri; 10am-6pm Sat; 10am-5pm Sun. **Credit** AmEx, Disc, MC, V.
In business for 40 years, McGhie's embraced the snowboarding craze in the early 1990s, and later added mountain biking to its ski (both water and snow) goods. Rentals, plus advice on the area's better recreation areas, are also available.

Pro Cyclery

7034 W Charleston Boulevard, at Antelope Way, Northwest Las Vegas (228 9460/www.procyclery.com). Bus 206. **Open** 10am-7pm Mon-Fri; 10am-5pm Sat. **Credit** AmEx, Disc, MC, V.
This long-term fixture on the Vegas cycling scene is a great source of gear for both hire and purchase.

REI

Green Valley Ranch *The District, 2220 Village Walk Drive, at S Green Valley Parkway, Henderson (896 7111/www.rei.com). Bus 114.* **Open** 10am-9pm Mon-Sat; 11am-6pm Sun. **Credit** AmEx, Disc, MC, V. **Hotel** p104.
In 1938, 20 mountain climbers banded together to form a co-operative, so they could purchase some of the better equipment available in Europe. Recreation Equipment Inc now has over 2 million members worldwide, and some 70 store locations. This shop is great for backpacking, biking, mountain climbing and kayaking gear, and also sells apparel and accessories by the likes of North Face and Patagonia.

St Andrews Golf Shop

Callaway Golf Center, 6730 Las Vegas Boulevard South, between Sunset Road & I-215 (896 4100). Bus 105, 301. **Open** 8am-7pm Mon-Sat; 8am-6pm Sun. **Credit** AmEx, DC, Disc, MC, V. **Map** p317 X4.
St Andrews sells top-flight golf gear, and the Callaway offers a nine-hole par–27 course if you're itching to try out your acquisitions (book ahead).

Subskates

840 N Rainbow Boulevard, at Washington Avenue, Northwest Las Vegas (258 3635/www.subskates.com). Bus 101, 208. **Open** 11am-6.30pm Mon-Fri; 10am-6.30pm Sat; noon-5pm Sun. **Credit** AmEx, Disc, MC, V.
Anyone with a fetish for balancing on a board heads here to buy their equipment. Stock includes everything from boards to bearings, plus plenty of clothes. Shoes come from the likes of Fallen and Etnies.
Other locations: 9151 W Sahara Avenue, Summerlin (233 3842).

Toys

Build-A-Bear Workshop

Aladdin/Planet Hollywood (Desert Passage) *3663 Las Vegas Boulevard South, at E Harmon Avenue (836 0899/www.buildabear.com). Bus 301.* **Open** 10am-11pm Mon-Thur, Sun; 10am-midnight Fri, Sat. **Credit** AmEx, Disc, MC, V. **Map** p320 A7.
Create an individual stuffed bear for the one you love, or take the children here for a treat. Pick fur colour, eye colour, costume (the range is huge) and stuffing type, and watch as the bear is assembled.

FAO Schwarz

Caesars Palace (Forum Shops) *3500 Las Vegas Boulevard South, at W Flamingo Road (796 6500/www.fao.com). Bus 202, 301, 302.* **Open** 10am-11pm Mon-Thur, Sun; 10am-midnight Fri, Sat. **Credit** AmEx, Disc, MC, V. **Hotel** p76. **Map** p320 A7.
For kids, FAO Schwarz is right up there with Willie Wonka's Chocolate Factory: three storeys of playthings make it one of the largest toy shops in the US. There's also a private room for serious collectors.

Toys of Yesteryear

2028 E Charleston Boulevard, at S Eastern Avenue, East Las Vegas (598 4030). Bus 110, 206. **Open** 11am-4pm Mon-Sat. **Credit** AmEx, Disc, MC, V. **Map** p317 Z2.
Forget the dice clocks and gambling chips: this tiny shop has old-fashioned toys and collectibles for adults as well as children, including Kewpie dolls, *Star Wars* figures, books and cast-metal toys.

Eat, Drink, Shop

Arts & Entertainment

Festivals & Events

Every day's a party in Sin City. Here's where you'll find the biggest in town.

New York got in first with its claim to be the city that never sleeps. Las Vegas, however, is the city that never rests, a state of affairs that's nowhere more apparent than on its calendar. While much here remains static, the rapid turnover of visitors is reflected in – and, to a large extent, driven by – the massive turnover of special events. While many travel to Vegas without glancing at the calendar, a good portion of each week's influx are here for a specific event, whether a business convention, a NASCAR race or a rockabilly concert. There's always something going on to draw the crowds.

However, alongside myriad huge-scale events, drawing thousands of like-minded souls to town for a four-day gallop on their favourite hobby horse, are an increasing array of festivals aimed mainly at the expanding local population. There are food and wine festivals, balloon rallies and Renaissance fairs, fun runs and skateboard showdowns. Best of all, there's **First Friday**, a monthly arts event featuring visual art, theatre, music and other performances, all of it free, plus a tidy selection of food and a lot of drink. For more details, *see p204* **Viva Cindy Funkhouser**. And Vegas being Vegas, the regular holidays are celebrated here with enthusiasm, notably **Valentine's Day** (weddings around the clock) and the two weeks surrounding **Christmas** and **New Year's Eve**, when the city starts the holiday season busy and closes it with utter madness.

The best Events

For making a million on the turn of a card
The **World Series of Poker**. *See right*.

For ridin' 'em, cowboy
National Finals Rodeo. *See p207*.

For getting your motor running
Four wheels: the **Vegas Cruise**. *See p204*.
Two wheels: the **Las Vegas Bikefest**. *See p206*.

For sheer bloody chaos
New Year's Eve. *See p207*.

For information about what's on while you're here, check the *Las Vegas Weekly* or *CityLife*, or look online (*see p303* for a list of useful websites). For details of major conventions and tips on when to visit, *see p293 and p301*.

Spring

NASCAR/Nextel Cup
Las Vegas Motor Speedway, 7000 N Las Vegas Boulevard, at Speedway Boulevard, North Las Vegas (information 644 4444/tickets 1-800 644 4444/ www.lvms.com). Bus 113A. **Tickets** $40-$150. **Credit** AmEx, Disc, MC, V. **Date** early Mar.
Race fans get their fill of excitement during this stop on the NASCAR circuit. The Sam's Town 300 Busch Series Grand National Division race precedes the big event. Book tickets and rooms as early as possible.

Monster Jam World Finals
Sam Boyd Stadium, 7000 E Russell Road, at Boulder Highway, Southeast Las Vegas (739 3267/www. thomasandmack.com). Bus 201A. **Tickets** $30-$40. **Credit** AmEx, Disc, MC, V. **Date** mid Mar.
Huge cars running over massive things. It's just too good to pass up, especially when one of the participants is the Transformer-like tank Megasaurus.

St Patrick's Day
Around Las Vegas. **Date** 17 Mar.
The celebrations kick off with a parade Downtown. The pace picks up at the Brooklyn Bridge replica near New York–New York (*see p83*), with a festival featuring bands, storytellers, food, *faux* Irish countryside (turf, peat moss) and – of course – booze. McMullan's Irish Pub (4650 W Tropicana Avenue, 247 7000) also hosts a day-long celebration.

World Series of Poker
Rio 3700 W Flamingo Road, at S Valley View Boulevard, West of Strip (367 9767/www.playrio. com). Bus 104, 202. **Hotel** p93. **Map** p317 X3. **Date** mid-late Mar.
The best poker players in the world – and a lot of chancers – get down to business during this two-week event, which has more prize money than any major sporting event. If you can't afford the buy-in, single-table satellites run the goings-on for all events around the clock. Sadly, the event has just been shifted from the atmospheric Binion's to the clinical Rio.

Extreme Thing Festival
Desert Breeze Skate Park, 8275 W Spring Mountain Road, at S Durango Drive (474 4000/www.extreme thing.com). Bus 203. **Tickets** $15.75 advance; $20 at the door. **Credit** AmEx, MC, V. **Date** late Mar.

Arts & Entertainment

James Woods looks for a good deal at the 2004 **World Series of Poker**. *See p202.*

An exhilarating event out in the west of the city that combines the best of extreme sport (skateboards, bikes or blades) with a music festival featuring ska and punk acts.

Viva Las Vegas

Gold Coast *4000 W Flamingo Road, at S Valley View Boulevard, West of Strip (1-562 496 4287/ www.vivalasvegas.net). Bus 104, 202.* **Admission** $65 advance; $90 on the door. **Credit** AmEx, Disc, MC, V. **Hotel** p102. **Map** p317 X3. **Date** Easter wknd.
Impeccably stylish fanatics of classic rock 'n' roll and rockabilly get together each year to drink, ogle each other's hot rods, brush back their quiffs and compare tattoos.

Clark County Fair & Rodeo

Clark County Fairgrounds, on I-15, Logandale (1-888 876 3247/www.ccfair.com). No bus. **Admission** *Fair* $5. *Rodeo* $9. *Season pass* $18. Free under-5s. **Credit** AmEx, Disc, MC, V. **Date** early Apr.
Southern Nevada's old-time county fair, located about an hour north of town, offers four days of food, rides, rodeos and unreconstructed entertainment.

Mardi Gras Celebration

Fremont Street, at Las Vegas Boulevard South, Downtown (1-800 249 3559/678 5777/www.vegas experience.com). Bus 107, 108, 109, 113, 207, 301, 302. **Map** p318 D2. **Date** early Apr.
In Vegas, Mardi Gras comes in April. Expect costumed performers, live music, plenty of beads and gallons of alcohol at this colourful street parade.

Native American Arts Festival

Clark County Heritage Museum, 1830 S Boulder Highway, between Horizon Drive & Wagon Wheel Avenue, Henderson (455 7955/www.co.clark.nv.us). Bus 107. **Admission** $1.50. **No credit cards**. **Date** early Apr.
Kick up your heels and learn some Native American dance at this three-day cultural festival. For the museum, *see p138.*

Ecojam

Sunset Park, E Sunset Road, at S Eastern Avenue, East Las Vegas (455 8200). Bus 110. **Date** mid Apr.

Vegas may not be known for its environmental awareness, but this annual Earth festival attracts more than 50,000 people to Sunset Park to check out the displays of electric cars and cool science projects.

Epicurean Affair

Location varies (878 9272/www.nvrestaurants.com) **Tickets** $100 advance; $125 at the door. **Credit** AmEx, Disc, MC, V. **Date** mid Apr.
This lavish do, part of the Las Vegas International Hotel & Restaurant Show, flaunts signature dishes from the valley's best restaurants. The crowd favourite, however, is Bar Alley, a giant outdoor nightclub that doesn't quit until very late.

UNLVino

Bally's *3645 Las Vegas Boulevard South, at E Flamingo Road (967 4111/www.unlvino.com). Bus 202, 301, 302.* **Admission** $50 advance; $75 at the door. **Credit** AmEx, DC, Disc, MC, V. **Hotel** p76. **Map** p320 A7. **Date** late Apr.
This tasting event brings more than 100 winegrowers from all over the world to town. The experience lasts only four hours, but you'll be amazed how many samples you can get through in that time. Designated drivers are available on-site.

Cinco de Mayo

Lorenzi Park, 3333 W Washington Avenue, at N Rancho Drive, Northwest Las Vegas (649 8553). Bus 106, 208. **Admission** $5; free under-12s. **No credit cards. Map** p317 X1. **Date** Sun closest to 5 May.
This traditional Mexican holiday is a good excuse for a massive party. The festivities, which include mariachi bands and fireworks, begin at 10am and last all day. Celebrations continue at a three-day fiesta on Fremont Street.

Race for the Cure

Fremont Street, at Las Vegas Boulevard South, Downtown (1-800 249 3559/678 5777/www.komen lasvegas.com). Bus 107, 108, 109, 113, 207, 301, 302. **Admission** $25. **Credit** AmEx, Disc, MC, V. **Map** p318 D2. **Date** early May.
Downtown hosts the Komen Foundation's annual fundraising 5km run, proceeds from which go to breast cancer research. A street fair follows.

Vegas Cruise

Fremont Street, at Las Vegas Boulevard South, Downtown (1-800 249 3559/678 5777/www. vegasexperience.com). Bus 107, 108, 109, 113, 207, 301, 302. **Map** p318 D2. **Date** late May-early June.

For three days, classic cars cruise the city before parking on the pedestrianised Fremont Street Experience in a show-and-shine. Glorious stuff.

Independence Day & Damboree Days Festival

Bicentennial Park, at Colorado Street & Nevada Highway, Boulder City (293 2034). Bus 116. **Date** 4 July wknd.

The best Independence Day celebration in the area features contests, music and fireworks. Back in Las Vegas itself, some local casinos host barbecues and small fireworks shows, but the biggest bash is presented by the Firemen's Benefit Association at Sam Boyd Stadium.

Star Trek Las Vegas Convention

Las Vegas Hilton *3000 Paradise Road, between Karen Avenue & Desert Inn Road, East of Strip (732 5111/www.creationent.com/cal/stlv.htm).* Bus 108, 203, 213, 301. **Tickets** $299 wknd pass. **Credit** AmEx, Disc, MC, V. **Hotel** p92. **Map** p319 C5. **Date** mid Aug.

If you're not a Trekkie, you'll live longer and prosper more if you stay away from the Hilton for these four days. Otherwise, however, you ought to buy

Viva Cindy Funkhouser

In Downtown Las Vegas, amid the wedding chapels and pawn shops and monthly-rent motels, a cultural revolution is going on. On one block sits the gallery- and studio-packed Arts Factory (*see p230*). Just up the street are two more galleries, Dust and Godt-Cleary Projects (*see p231*). A couple of blocks away, a pair of old buildings are being renovated and turned into more artists' spaces. And at the intersection of Colorado Avenue and Casino Center Boulevard are a series of eight gallery/work cottages, directly across from an antiques store called the Funk House (*see p182 and p230*).

Within the Funk House, amid mannequin torso lamps, psychedelic furniture and preserved bug specimens, Cindy Funkhouser sits in a cluttered office, answering her continually ringing phone. Funkhouser (yes,

it's her real last name, of German origin) with her shocking red hair and piercing light blue eyes, is one of the women behind (and often in front of) the growing Las Vegas arts scene. It was Funkhouser who initiated the **First Friday** street festival, taking place on the first Friday of each month, at which gallery spaces stay open late, streets are blocked off from cars, and local bars, restaurants and entertainers help transform a once dark and dreary area into a bright and bustling street scene.

The 46-year-old got the idea when she was visiting her son in Portland, Oregon, a few years ago, and came across a similar event called First Thursday. 'It just made sense to me that we would have that kind of event here, because we have the same population and I didn't understand why it wasn't your tickets early, as an all-star cast of guests draws Trekkies from miles around: Patrick Stewart, Jonathan Frakes and Armin Shimerman are frequent visitors, and both Shatner and Nimoy have stopped by in the past.

Las Vegas Harvest Festival

Cashman Field, 850 Las Vegas Boulevard North, at E Washington Avenue (1-800 321 1213/www. harvestfestival.com). Bus 113. **Admission** $7.50 3-day ticket. **Credit** AmEx, Disc, MC, V. **Map** p317 Y1. **Date** late Aug.

More than 250 exhibitors from across the US come out to hawk wood carvings, jewellery, food items, clothing, crafts and more. All items must meet stringent standards of quality; this is no flea market. A perfect start to your holiday shopping.

Autumn

Black & White Party

Palms *4321 W Flamingo Road, at S Valley View Boulevard, West of Strip (382 2326/http://afanlv. org).* **Tickets** $40. **Hotel** p92. **Map** p317 X3. **Date** mid Sept.

The B&W has become the main AIDS fundraiser in Vegas, a gigantic outdoor bash uniting the community. Local restaurants cook fresh food samples: gorge away while entertainment rages on the stage.

Las Vegas BikeFest

Fremont Street, Downtown, & around the city (1-866 245 3337/450 7662/www.lasvegasbikefest.com). **Tickets** $35-$40. **Credit** AmEx, Disc, MC, V. **Date** mid Sept.

happening,' she says. Never one to watch an opportunity go by, Funkhouser and friends Naomi Arin (co-owner of Dust) and Julie Brewer founded the non-profit Whirlygig, Inc, responsible for First Friday. The festival now draws up to 10,000 visitors a month.

During First Friday, Funkhouser's usually too busy selling antiques, chatting with friends and customers and sipping her signature Chimay to savour the fire-breathers and the bands, the psychics and the ice sculptors. But she makes sure she has an artist hang their work in her shop for their own show each month, keeping art within easy reach and providing opportunities local artists otherwise may not have. Between her lives as a businesswoman, a mother, a community leader and (most recently) an investor in real estate,

purchased to help keep rental prices low for artists, her time is at a premium.

Fortunately, home's not far away: Funkhouser's commute involves one flight of stairs. If she ever needs a break, or a moment of respite, she can simply walk above the shop to her apartment and gaze at her own collection of local art and artefacts: the '50s fixtures, the piano that inspires her cat to dance, and the series of drawings she traded with a guy at a local bar in exchange for a steady supply of beer. It's a funk-house life.

● *First Friday is held in the Arts District of Downtown Las Vegas, in and around the junction of Main Street and W Charleston Boulevard, from 6pm to 10pm on the First Friday of every month. For details, including a map, see www.firstfriday-lasvegas.org or www.whirlygiglasvegas.org.*

Arts & Entertainment

Rapidly becoming one of the biggest bike rallies in the West, BikeFest attracts bikers and their babes for four days of poker runs, wet T-shirt contests, classic rock shows and a custom bike show.

Greek Food Festival

St John the Baptist Greek Orthodox Church, 5300 El Camino Road, at E Hacienda Road, Southwest Las Vegas (221 8245). No bus. **Tickets** $5. **No credit cards.** **Date** late Sept-early Oct.

Started in 1972 to raise money to build the St John the Baptist church, this event is now the longest continuously running festival in Vegas, attended by nearly 20,000 people a year. Enjoy stalls, authentic Greek food, music and folk dancing.

Art in the Park

Bicentennial Park, at Colorado Street & Nevada Highway, Boulder City (294 1611). Bus 116. **Date** 1st wknd in Oct.

Hundreds of artists and craft-makers from throughout the Southwest set up shop for this art show, one of the largest events of the year in Boulder City. A wonderful day half-day in the state's only city without gambling. *See p261.*

Grand Slam for Children

MGM Grand *3799 Las Vegas Boulevard South, at E Tropicana Avenue (information 227 5700/tickets 474 4000/www.mgmgrand.com). Bus 201, 301, 302.* **Tickets** *Concert* $35-$85. **Credit** AmEx, Disc, MC, V. **Hotel** p80. **Map** p320 A9. **Date** early Oct.

Much-loved local Andre Agassi invites a group of his pals for an auction and dinner, followed by a concert at the MGM Grand Garden that's open to all.

San Gennaro Feast

Rio *3700 W Flamingo Road, at S Valley View Boulevard, West of Strip (286 4944/www.san gennarofeast.net). Bus 104, 202.* **Tickets** $7. **Credit** AmEx, Disc, MC, V. **Hotel** p93. **Map** p317 X3. **Date** 2nd wknd in Oct.

Pile on the pounds at the spaghetti-eating contest, and then work them right off again in the grape-stomping competition at this Italian foodfest.

Age of Chivalry Renaissance Fair

Sunset Park, E Sunset Road, at S Eastern Avenue, East Las Vegas (455 8200/www.lvrenfair.com). Bus 110, 212. **Date** mid Oct.

Gladiator battles, jousting competitions and other displays of horsemanship dominate this slightly comic display of mock Englishness. Avoid the major parking hassles and take public transport.

Professional Bull Riders Tour

Thomas & Mack Center, 4505 S Maryland Parkway, at E Tropicana Avenue, University District (information 1-719 471 3008/tickets 474 4000/ www.pbrnow.com). Bus 109, 201. **Tickets** $30-$60. **Credit** AmEx, Disc, MC, V. **Date** mid Oct.

If you can't wait for the National Finals Rodeo (*see p207*), check out this event, at which the world's top 45 bull riders compete over three days for $1 million and the title of World Champion Bull Rider.

Shakespeare in the Park

Henderson Pavilion, 200 South Green Valley Parkway, at Paseo Verde Parkway, Henderson (384 8427). Bus 217. **Admission** free-$25. **Credit** Disc, MC, V. **Date** mid Oct.

The best outdoor theatre event in town is out in Henderson, and sees a travelling troupe present a Shakespeare play (usually a comedy one year, a tragedy the next). Mimes, madrigal singers and jugglers complete the spectacle. For more outdoor theatre events, *see p251.*

Vegas Valley Book Festival

Henderson Pavilion & Paseo Verde Library, 200 South Green Valley Parkway, at Paseo Verde Parkway, Henderson (www.vegasvalleybookfest.org). Bus 217. **Date** mid Oct.

Vegas's literary community comes alive at this three-day feast of author visits, signings and workshops down in Henderson.

Las Vegas Balloon Classic

Silver Bowl Park, 6800 E Russell Road, at Boulder Highway, Southeast Las Vegas (452 8066). Bus 217. **Date** 3rd wknd in Oct.

Hot-air balloons fill the sky for this weekend of flying competitions. The Saturday sundown 'balloon glow' demonstration is a must-see.

Fetish & Fantasy Ball / Hallowe'en

Tropicana *3801 Las Vegas Boulevard South, at E Tropicana Avenue (739 2222/www.halloweenball. com). Bus 201, 301, 302.* **Tickets** $50. **Credit** AmEx, DC, MC, V. **Hotel** p90. **Map** p320 A8. **Date** 31 Oct.

Lace, leather and latex are the sartorial faves at this crazed event, though some make do with a tux or evening gown (and are subjected to a 'party pooper' fine). Nearly every nightclub and bar hosts a dress-up party for Hallowe'en, many crammed to capacity with adults exercising their innermost demon or slut fetish. Check *Las Vegas Weekly* or *CityLife* for event listings.

Las Vegas Odyssey

Various locations; visit www.lasvegasodyssey.com for full details. **Tickets** $150-$1,000. **Credit** AmEx, Disc, MC, V. **Date** early Nov.

Vegas is known for overindulgence, and that's certainly the case here. Learn to live the gourmand's lifestyle with seminars from local chefs, wine tastings and as much food as you can shovel in.

Motor Trend International Auto Show

Las Vegas Convention Center, 3150 Paradise Road, at Convention Center Drive, East of Strip (892 0711/www.motortrendautoshows.com/lasvegas). Bus 108, 112. **Admission** $8; $4 7-12s. **Map** p319 C5. **Date** late Nov.

Check out the latest models from all your favourite manufacturers at Vegas' biggest and best auto show. Free parking is available to all attendees at the Convention Center's Silver Lot 3.

New Year's Eve.

National Finals Rodeo
Thomas & Mack Center, 4505 S Maryland Parkway, at E Tropicana Avenue, University District (information 895 3900/1-719 593 8840/www.nfr-rodeo.com). Bus 201. **Tickets** $75-$775. **Credit** AmEx, Disc, MC, V. **Map** p317 3Y. **Date** early Dec.
Top cowboys and girls set Vegas ablaze for nine days. Tickets are distributed by lottery a year beforehand, but you can always watch proceedings on closed-circuit TV at the Gold Coast (367 7111). Buy western duds from the Cowboy Christmas Gift Show at the Las Vegas Convention Center, and party all night at Sam's Town (*see p103*; 456 7777).

New Year's Eve
Date 31 Dec.
The Strip and Fremont Street turn into a couple of big street parties, as more than a quarter of a million visitors – plus a relative handful of locals – gather to celebrate. Expect headline performers, a party at every casino, fireworks and a horrible shortage of hotel rooms. Don't attempt to get anywhere by car.

An American Trilogy
Cannery, 2121 E Craig Road, at Las Vegas Boulevard North, North Las Vegas (507 5700/ www.cannerycasinos.com). Bus 113. **Tickets** prices vary. **Credit** AmEx, Disc, MC, V. **Date** mid Jan.
The Cannery becomes all things King around Elvis's birthday (16 Jan). Guests have included Elvis photographer Ed Bonja, chief bodyguard Sonny West, the Sweet Sensations and impersonator Paul Casey. The buffet is transformed into a smörgåsbord of Elvis's favourite foods.

Las Vegas International Marathon & Half-Marathon
Around the city (876 3870/459 8314/www.lv marathon.com). **Date** late Jan.
Saturday sees the International Friendship 5km run, starting first thing at the Tropicana. The next day, a half-marathon leaves Sloan, Nevada, and heads to Vegas at about the same time as a 26-miler departs Jean, Nevada. Register online: the earlier you do it, the cheaper the fee.

African American History Month
West Las Vegas Library, 951 W Lake Mead Boulevard, at Concord Street, Northwest Las Vegas (507 3980/www.lvccld.org). Bus 105, 210, 215. **Date** throughout Feb.
A treasure trove of collections on African American culture throughout Las Vegas and the world, the library offers a gamut of activities – spoken word events, dance performances – in its amphitheatre.

High Rollers Scooter Weekend
Around the city (www.lvscooterrally.com). **Date** mid Feb.
Since 1998, up to 1,000 scooterists have coaxed their vintage Vespas and Lambrettas from as far away as England to Las Vegas for four days of music, meets, road trips and the inevitable frantic search for spares. It's a mod world all over again.

Winter

Magical Forest
Opportunity Village, 6300 W Oakey Boulevard, btwn S Jones Boulevard & S Torrey Pines Drive, West Las Vegas (259 3741). Bus 102, 205. **Tickets** $7; $5 3-12s. **No credit cards.** **Date** late Nov-late Dec.
This Christmas display contains a cool two million lights and a castle, complete with Santa, giant candy canes and a forest of decorated trees.

Ethel M Chocolates Light the Night
Ethel M Chocolates Factory, 2 Cactus Garden Drive, at Sunset Way & Mountain Vista Street, Henderson (458 8864/www.ethelm.com). Bus 217. **Admission** free. **Date** early Dec.
Ethel M's cactus garden is adorned with millions of multicoloured lights and carolers traverse the pathways full of good cheer. The switch is flipped at dusk, but be sure to get yourself into the factory by 7pm to sample a sweet treat. One of the prettiest – and tastiest – holiday events. For Ethel M, *see p138*.

Other light events include the Parade of Lights (Lake Mead Marina, Lake Mead National Recreation Area, 293 2034; mid Dec) when lighted boats sail around Lake Mead. A Gift of Lights (Sunset Park, E Sunset Road, at S Eastern Avenue, East Las Vegas; 455 8206; $10; mid-late Dec) involves a drive-through lights display illuminating the park. Some proceeds go to local charities.

Arts & Entertainment

Adult Entertainment

Sin is in… as long as it sells.

Thanks to the hefty advertising budget of the Las Vegas Convention & Visitors Authority, the world recently has come to think that 'what happens in Vegas, stays in Vegas'. Taking liberties with Sin City's mythic reputation as an adult-oriented free-for-all, the ads cheekily suggest more than the truth. Visitors do come to Vegas to go wild, even if 'going wild' means nothing more than sipping weak comp drinks at nickel slot machines. And sure, sex sells. Just as with greed, lust now shares equal billing with gluttony and pride as but one of the sins to which Vegas attends, and thus the sex aspect is often tamer than promised. Anyone hoping for Sodom and Gomorrah will be as disappointed as someone boarding Disneyland's Space Mountain expecting to be launched into orbit.

Still, there's naughty fun here. As the rest of America has sexed itself up, Las Vegas's increasingly playful sexuality is more attractive than ever. Numerous upscale strip clubs are located just off the Strip, attracting everyone from Midwestern conventioneer couples to the Hollywood elite. Even upscale casinos are testing the tease with pricey burlesque bars (see p244 **A nudge and a wink**), though pundit predictions of lap dance clubs in casinos still seems only a remote possibility.

Live adult entertainment is chiefly geared towards the straight male (and his girlfriend, as long as they arrive together). Despite more courting of couples, most strip clubs still refuse to allow women to enter without a male escort, purportedly to discourage prostitution. There are more than 40 places where nude or nearly nude women dance for dollars, but just a handful of spots where women can see men do the same (**Olympic Garden Cabaret**, the **Excalibur**'s *Thunder From Down Under*, the **Rio**'s newly revamped Chippendales show). Gay men may attend these shows, but they generally prefer to slip tips in the G-strings of the muscled go-go boys at **Gipsy** (*see p234*) or **Krave** (*see p235*).

Adult entertainment falls into four categories: casino clubs and revues; topless or nude clubs; adult stores; and swingers' clubs. Prostitution is illegal in Clark County, where Las Vegas sits. Those nearly nude girls in the pamphlets pushed at you every time you walk the Strip? Merely 'entertainers', who will come to your hotel room and dance for you. Naked. But nothing else. If they do, you'll both get busted. Officially.

Casino clubs & revues

Sour over millions in potential revenue lost to the strip-clubs, casino moguls have done what they can to keep horny visitors on site. Though they remain restricted by their gaming licences, there have been whispers of the casino lobby working to ease the restrictions on nudity in resorts. The recent spate of burlesque bars may

La Femme. *See p209*.

be a way for them to test the limits. Don't expect a modern strip-club experience when visiting a joint like Mandalay Bay's Forty Deuce: the performances hark back to the classic era of 1940s and '50s striptease, accompanied by a live jazz band, and neither tipping nor lap dancing are permitted. For more on these burlesque clubs, *see p244*.

There are, of course, the more traditional Vegas shows, such as the campy burlesque of the Riviera's **Crazy Girls** and **Jubilee!** at Bally's; others are sexy but tame, among them **Skintight** at Harrah's and the new **Aussie Angels** at the Hilton. A new wave of modern adult shows includes the lesbian-chic rock 'n' roll vampires of **Bite** at the Stratosphere. The Parisian-style **La Femme** at the MGM fancies itself as cultural, as does Cirque du Soleil's **Zumanity** at New York–New York. For these and other adult shows, *see pp213-214*.

Clubs & bars

Topless bars

Though a few seedy hangouts remain – among them the gloriously unpretentious **Larry's Villa** (2401 W Bonanza Road, 647 2713), like something from a Bukowski short story – Las Vegas's topless bars are now mostly upscale places. Many are crowded at weekends and during conventions (also, not coincidentally, when the best and best-looking dancers make the roster). But a quiet midweek visit can be more fun, as you won't have to scramble for a seat. A continuous parade of strippers shimmy to music, stripping down to a G-string, a pair of five-inch stilettos and, if you're lucky, a smile.

Topless dancers are more chatty than those in nude clubs, and the bars all serve alcohol and are open to patrons aged 21 and over. A word of warning, though. Most of these clubs are located in bleak areas, so you're best catching a cab both ways. Be sure to specify which club you want to visit: cabbies are paid kickbacks by door staff to drop tourists at particular venues.

 Adult clubs

For siliconophobes
Déjà Vu Showgirls. *See p211*.

For variety
Spearmint Rhino. *See p210*.

For couples
Sin. *See p210*.

Cheetahs Topless Club
2112 Western Avenue, between W Oakey Boulevard & W Sahara Avenue, West of Strip (384 0074/ www.cheetahstoplessclub.com). Bus 105, 204, 205. **Open** 24hrs daily. **Admission** $5 8pm-5am Mon-Fri; $10 8pm-5am Sat, Sun. **Credit** AmEx, Disc, MC, V. **Map** p319 B4.
Vegas's most relaxed topless bar offers a comfortable experience. Large enough to have five intimate stages, yet as homey as a neighbourhood sports bar, Cheetahs has a reputation as a locals' hangout. The place is packed during American football season, when Monday Night Football parties offer $10 'touch-down dances'. Girls have less silicone than at other clubs; bouncers and bartenders are friendly enough.

Crazy Horse Too Gentlemen's Club
2476 S Industrial Road, at W Sahara Avenue, Stratosphere Area (382 8003/www.crazyhorsetoo. com). Bus 105, 204. **Open** 24hrs daily. **Admission** $10 6.30pm-4.30am. **Credit** AmEx, Disc, MC, V. **Map** p319 B4.
Crazy Horse Too can be a frustrating experience. The two main rooms have only one stage each, in the centre of the room, making it look more like an illegal card room than a strip joint. It's nearly impossible to get a stageside seat. We can only guess that the party is better in the VIP Emperor's Room, where a pricey two-drink, four-dance minimum is in effect.

Girls of Glitter Gulch
20 Fremont Street, at Main Street, Fremont Street Experience, Downtown (385 4774). Bus 107, 108, 301. **Open** 1pm-4am Mon-Thur, Sun; noon-6am Fri, Sat. **Admission** 2-drink minimum. **Credit** AmEx, MC, V. **Map** p317 C1.
In the security-sanitised area beneath the Fremont Street Experience, this hold-out from the old days still draws in the punters. After watching the FSE's free light and music show, stroll inside for a performance with a different kind of sizzle. Glitter Gulch features average-looking women with enormous breasts lap dancing for average-looking men with enormous wallets. It draws a touristy crowd.

Jaguars
3355 S Procyon Avenue, at W Desert Inn Road, West of Strip (732 1116/www.jaguarsnv.com). Bus 104, 203. **Open** 24hrs daily. **Admission** $10. **Credit** AmEx, Disc, MC, V.
The $15 million spent on building this 25,000sq ft (2,300 sq m) club is evident in the decor: plush chairs, marble, Tuscan styling. However, the experience can be refreshingly egalitarian and very comfortable. The dancers are stunning, but the three stages are neither dancer- nor patron-friendly: dancers often stumble on the multi-level floors and patrons must stand to tip.

Olympic Garden Cabaret
1531 Las Vegas Boulevard South, at E Wyoming Avenue, Stratosphere Area (385 8987). Bus 301. **Open** 24hrs daily. **Admission** (incl 2 drinks) $20 non-residents. **Credit** AmEx, Disc, MC, V. **Map** p319 C3.

Arts & Entertainment

Dirty secrets

Adult stores were once the province solely of furtive men in trenchcoats; these days, it's not unusual to find their aisles filled with couples, bachelorette partiers and single women seeking a place to store their loose batteries. The dirty bookstore of legend may be a rare breed, then, but they've not totally vanished. In the edgy zone between the Stratosphere and the Fremont Street Experience are two sister stores, each with its own back room catering to loner horndog males with plenty of one-dollar bills in their wallets.

The **Talk of the Town** (1238 Las Vegas Boulevard South, 385 1800) is a brightly lit building that looks like its fancier cousins, until you notice the sign touting it as 'the home of the $5 lap dance'. Past the Swedish magazines and double-barreled love toys, a velvet rope, guarded by a mannequin dressed in police gear, blocks entry to a dark hallway. For a nominal fee (usually $10), you'll find yourself led into the most barren, smoke-filled din of misfit strippers the city has ever known. Clad only in prison tattoos and awkward piercings, the girls will give you a 40-second lap dance for your five-spot, but with a mind to engaging you in a fantasy-room romp out back. The rooms are equipped with cameras, and the naughtiness can only rise to the level of 'hot and bothered'. Prices depend on time and run in $40 increments.

While its big sister boasts a stage, the back room at nearby **Showgirl Video** (631 Las Vegas Boulevard South, 385 4554), this time guarded by a coin-operated turnstile, contains a number of private booths. The routine is straight out of a Madonna video: insert the dollar bill, get your lesson in gynaecology, smell the ammonia, the mop man only knocks twice. You can pay a little more for the same routine in a one-on-one situation, but the endgame is the same. Dress code: trenchcoat preferred.

A warehouse of sexuality. Though the incessant strobing and loud music can be overwhelming, the atmosphere is comfortable. The number of enhancements on show have earned the OG the nickname 'Silicone Valley', but the sheer number of performers should keep most happy. Upstairs is a VIP room and an all-male revue. Dress: no tank tops.

Sapphire

3025 S Industrial Road, at Stardust Road, Stratosphere Area (796 6000/www.sapphirelasvegas. com). Bus 105. **Open** 24hrs daily. **Admission** (incl 2 drinks) $10 locals; $20 non-residents. **Credit** AmEx, Disc, MC, V. **Map** p319 B5.
Built with a nightclub sensibility, this is the largest adult club in the world, boasting a huge main room and 13 private skyboxes (rental: $250 an hour). Run by the owners of Olympic Garden, Sapphire is OG to the nth degree: big bars, quiet VIP rooms, and hundreds of very attractive, very enhanced entertainers.

Sin

3550 W Quail Avenue, at Polaris Avenue, West of Strip (673 1700). No bus. **Open** noon-6am Mon-Sat; 6pm-6am Sun. **Admission** free locals; $20 non-residents. **Credit** MC, V.
Opened in late 2004, the newest topless club in town is also our favourite. Sin has the warehouse feel of Olympic Garden, the plush, velvet style of Jaguars, the varied music of Spearmint Rhino and marketing aimed squarely at couples: everyone here, from the bouncers to the dancers, is fawningly friendly.

Spearmint Rhino

3340 Highland Drive, at W Desert Inn Road (access via Spring Mountain Road), West of Strip (734 7336/www.spearmintrhino.com). Bus 105. **Open** 24hrs daily. **Admission** $10 locals; $20 non-residents. **No credit cards. Map** p319 A5.
A recent expansion has only enhanced the chic, intimate interiors of this chain adult club. It also sports the best food menu and one of the most daring playlists. Of course, Spearmint Rhino also has the expected stage and lap dancing antics, but what makes it unique is its diverse crowd, which usually includes a healthy number of style-driven couples.

Treasures

2801 Westwood Drive, at Highland Drive, West of Strip (257 3030). Bus 106, 204. **Open** 3pm-6am daily. **Admission** $20. **Credit** MC, V. **Map** p319 A4.
An ornate mansion-styled room filled with beautiful dancers, Treasures is what one imagines the *Playboy* mansion to be like. That said, the club only reopened at the end of 2004 after legalities regarding its licensing, and so holds its dancers to extremely strict rules of behaviour. Some visitors may find them inhibiting.

Nude clubs

Nude clubs are similar to topless bars save for one important difference: the full-nudity licence prohibits alcohol, and so the clubs (except for the Palomino) are open to anyone over 18. As a result, the clubs attract a different kind of patron (younger and less affluent) and a different kind of dancer (younger and more money-hungry).

One plus is that there's less silicone at nude clubs. Unfortunately, nude dancers also take their 'art' more seriously than topless dancers, even though most punters just want to see them wiggle, spread and show some personality. The lack of alcohol makes a significant impact: most nude clubs lack atmosphere, and often resemble tarted-up recreation halls .

Déjà Vu Showgirls

3247 Industrial Road, between Stardust Road & W Sahara Avenue, West of Strip (894 4167). Bus 105, 204. **Open** 11am-6am Mon-Sat; 6pm-4am Sun. **Admission** free-$10 locals; $10 before 6pm non-residents; $10 bar minimum after 6pm. **No credit cards. Map** p320 A5.

Dancers lean towards the pretty end of the scale, with a uniqueness hard to find in the land of silicone sameness. Look out for theme nights, from oil wrestling to shower parties; the ambience is frat party with strippers. Dress: no tank tops.

Little Darlings

1514 Western Avenue, at W Oakey Boulevard, Stratosphere Area (366 1141/www.showgirl.com). Bus 105. **Open** 11am-6am Mon-Sat; 6am-4am Sun. **Admission** $10 locals; $20 non-residents. *Women free.* **Credit** MC, V. **Map** p319 B3.

Stark lighting, annoying DJs and plastic drink cups are immediate challenges to the success of Little Darlings. Add the fact that most patrons are high-school kids and you'll wonder why we've listed it. Simple: most of the girls are gorgeous. Dances can get wild, but the performers aren't chatty: if you don't pay for a dance, they'll move on. Dress: no tank tops.

Palomino Club

1848 Las Vegas Boulevard North, at E Owens Avenue, North Las Vegas (642 2984). Bus 113. **Open** 2pm-4am daily. **Admission** $15 locals; $30 non-residents. **No credit cards. Map** p317 Y1.

The grandaddy of Vegas clubs is ragged, but merits its reputation as the city's most atmospheric nude club: it's the only one with a liquor licence (and so is over-21s only). Upstairs, an egalitarian roster of dancers work a small stage, while downstairs (open weekends and busy seasons) 'feature dancers' (adult film actresses, centrefolds) take to the catwalk.

Stores

For the new, female-friendly breed of adult stores, *see p199.* For the old-fashioned variety, *see p210* **Dirty secrets.**

Swingers' clubs

Adults of all sexual proclivities and relationship arrangements head to the city's swingers' clubs. The clubs don't offer gambling or alcohol (you can bring your own), but they often have pool tables, dancefloors and stripper poles. You pay an entrance fee (or 'donation') only. Aside from the fixed-location swing clubs, several groups (such as **Red Twilight**, www.red twilight.com) organise 'off-premises couples parties', essentially elite, PG-rated social mixers in nightclubs and bars. Look for adverts in the local weeklies.

As well as being notable for hosting some of the city's best ethnic eateries and gay bars, the down-at-heel Commercial Center on E Sahara Avenue contains three swingers' clubs within a few doors of each other: the **Green Door** (735 4656, www.greendoor.com) enjoys the top local name recognition; **Rendezvous** (732 2587, www.rendezvous-lasvegas.com) is especially friendly; and the **Fantasy Social Club** (893 3977, www.fantasysocialclub.com) has a less-social scene than the others. Admission is generally $40-$50 per single male, while single women get in free or for as little as $5. The **Red Rooster** in Henderson (451 6661, www.vegasredrooster.com) attracts an older, more local crowd, and just opened a satellite location in, of all places, Green Valley.

► For more on **sex in Vegas**, *see pp34-37.*

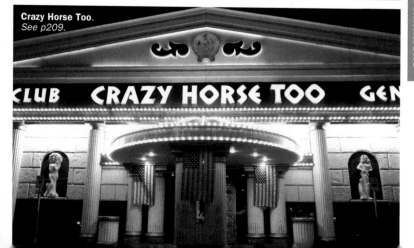

Crazy Horse Too.
See p209.

Casino Entertainment

Say… let's do the show right here!

The 2005 opening of **Kà** was greeted by hyperbole excessive even by Vegas standards. Local writers lined up to hail the show, widely regarded as Cirque du Soleil's most extravagant yet. However, more surprising was the praise bestowed on it by critics from other cities all with their own theatrical traditions. The man from the *Chicago Tribune* even seemed to regard the show's opening as some kind of baton-passing moment, Broadway handing on to Las Vegas Boulevard for a sprint towards a finish line labelled 'excess'.

Thanks mainly to the arrival of Cirque du Soleil, the standard of entertainment on the Strip has vaulted in the last decade. However, Cirque aside, Vegas is still more imitator than progenitor. The Broadway/West End shows that arrive here are tried and tested (**Mamma Mia!**, **We Will Rock You**); the musical headliners are all safe bets (**Barry Manilow**, **Celine Dion**); the best non-Cirque spectacles are old fashioned (**Jubilee!**, in the main); and the magicians, **Penn & Teller** excepted, are traditional. The presence on the Strip not just of four Cirque shows but of two more productions helmed by the company's associate Franco Dragone (who's behind **Celine Dion: A New Day** and **Le Rêve**, as well as Cirque's **Mystère** and **O**), with a fifth Cirque show scheduled for the Mirage in 2006, is proof that nothing succeeds here like impersonation. 'They've got one!' cries the casino. 'I want one too!' And, $100 million later, they have one.

Las Vegas is also nothing like Broadway because it resolutely prefers spectacle to storytelling, while New York is still very much the other way around. However, as you may already have gathered, no one does spectacle like Vegas. Settle back and enjoy the show.

INFORMATION AND TICKETS

Although most of the shows listed here are expected to run for the shelf-life of this guide, others open and close all the time. For the most up-to-date information, check 'Neon' in Friday's *Las Vegas Review-Journal*, free magazines such as *Showbiz* and *What's On*, the town's alternative papers (such as *Las Vegas Weekly* and *CityLife*) and www.vegas.com. In any given week, there are also a number of big-name acts working short engagements at the theatres listed in this chapter, complementing the resident shows reviewed below.

You're best off buying tickets at the hotel-casino box office where the show is being staged, either in person, by phone or online. If you get stuck, try **TicketMaster** (474 4000), but prepare to pay over the odds. There are also ticket brokers in nearly every casino but, like the agencies, they often charge a (hefty) commission on top of the ticket price. If you book by phone, pick up the tickets at the 'will call' window. You can find half-price tickets to some shows at **Tickets Tonight** (1-888 484 9264, www.tickets2nite.com) in the Showcase Mall (*see p115*); the booth opens at noon daily. Admission prices are high: many of the big shows sell their best seats for more than $100. However, there are bargains around. Lots of shows offer discounts with coupons found on flyers or in local magazines: two-for-one offers are not uncommon. If you're a heavy gambler, you might even get comped into a show in the casino in which you've been playing.

What's included in ticket prices also varies. Some quoted prices include tax, others don't; many shows include one or two drinks in their prices. For the sake of convenience, all prices in this chapter have been calculated to include tax, which is 10 per cent. Some shows, especially those with a degree of nudity, come with age restrictions; always check if you have kids in tow. It's best to book six weeks ahead for the really big shows. However, even if the show has sold out, it's worth calling the box office, especially midweek, to check for cancellations.

The best Shows

For tasteful erotica
La Femme. See p214.

For talented tributes
Legends in Concert. See p214.

For cheap tricks
Mac King. See p218.

For wordless wonder
Blue Man Group. See p220.

For amazing aquabatics
O. See p221.

Tickets for many shows allocate specific seats. However, it's not always the case. If you have tickets for a show that offers only 'general admission' (unnumbered) seating, arrive early if you want a good seat. If you're not satisfied with your seat's location, try discreetly tipping the maître d' $10 or $20. For music venues, *see pp236-240*, and for nightclubs, *see pp241-244*.

Resident shows

Las Vegas's first stage productions were known as 'floor shows'. When Sophie Tucker performed at El Rancho and Jimmy Durante played the Flamingo in the 1940s and '50s, they were preceded by a line of girls, a comic or magician, and a speciality act (a juggler, say). The Vegas floor show changed radically when the Stardust premièred Lido de Paris. With its big spectacle and topless showgirls the show itself was the star. The Stardust packed them in, and the Vegas-style show was born. A few, such as *Folies Bergère, Jubilee!* and **Splash**, are still around, hoisting the banner of classic Vegas entertainment despite their schlocky themes and feeble storylines.

Vegas entertainment staples also include magic shows (even with Siegfried & Roy gone, there's still plenty from which to pick); celebrity impersonator shows, in which lookalikes sing live or lip-synch in imitation of pop-culture heroes and heroines; and the full-on adult revue, featuring a parade of hardbodies taking it off for appreciative crowds of women and (more often) men. Those keen on straighter theatre can catch Broadway shows, either in short runs or in permanent homes (**Blue Man Group**, **Mamma Mia!** and, from late 2005 at Wynn Las Vegas, **Avenue Q**). And then there's Cirque du Soleil, which deserves a category all of its own. The four shows – *Mystère*, *O*, **Zumanity** and **Kà** – will be joined in 2006 by a new production at the Mirage based on the music of the Beatles.

Many casinos carry on the time-honoured tradition of booking celebrity headliners, giving visitors a chance to see their favourite stars up close and in the flesh. Among those resident here in Sin City are Celine Dion, **Gladys Knight** and **Rita Rudner**. However, everyone who's anyone, from Gwen Stefani to Jay Leno, passes through Las Vegas eventually. Check local listings to make sure you don't miss 'em. Unless you really, really want to, of course.

Adult revues

Other adult shows include topless vampire panto **Bite** (Stratosphere; 380 7777); truly preposterous rock 'n' roll stripfest **Erocktica** (Rio; 777 7776); the scantily-clad lovelies known as the **Aussie Angels** (Las Vegas Hilton; 1-800 222 5361); and their well-oiled male equivalent, the **Thunder from Down Under** (597 7600). Tickets for all shows cost in the region of $40 to $60.

Chippendales

Rio *3700 W Flamingo Road, at S Valley View Boulevard, West of Strip (1-888 746 7784/777 7776/www.playrio.com)*. Bus 104, 202. **Shows** 8pm Mon-Tue, Thur, Sun; 8pm, 10.30pm Fri, Sat. **Tickets** $38.45-$82.50. No under-18s. **Credit** AmEx, Disc, MC, V. **Hotel** p93. **Map** p317 X3.

Things can get quite touchy-feely in this provocative male revue. The updated show is ensconced in a brand new theatre that's complete with private lounge and retail boutique, where well-oiled guys bump and grind to popular pop tunes and the giddy delight of many a bachelorette party. Gals who venture onstage for their own close encounters should expect a hands-on performance. No wonder it's called 'the Ultimate Girls Night Out'.

Crazy Girls

Riviera *2901 Las Vegas Boulevard South, at Riviera Boulevard (1-800 256 6860/794 9433/ www.rivierahotel.com)*. Bus 301. **Shows** 9.30pm Mon, Wed-Sun. **Tickets** $45.50-$73. No under-18s. **Credit** AmEx, DC, Disc, MC, V. **Hotel** p87. **Map** p319 B5.

Bazza! *See p219.*

Arts & Entertainment

'Girls! Girls! Crazy girls!' goes the infernally catchy theme song. Well, crazy they ain't, and, if local legend is to be believed, the arses displayed in bronze outside the Riviera by way of advertisement aren't all female. Regardless, this low-budget titfest, now into its 18th year on the Strip, is a giggle: cheaper than any of its competitors and about as arousing as a kick in the teeth, granted, but lovers of Vegas camp will be in heaven. 'Girls! Girls!' Etc.

Fashionistas

Krave, 3663 Las Vegas Boulevard South, at Harmon Avenue (836 0833/www.fashionistasthe show.com). Bus 301. **Shows** 9.30pm Mon-Sat. **Tickets** $54.95-$65.95. **Credit** AmEx, DC, Disc, MC, V. **Map** p320 A7.

Robin Leach described this dance set-up as 'classy and sexy'; he must have been there on a different night, for the show we saw resembled a Victoria's Secret commercial minus the eroticism. Not even sexy latex fetish wear and ultra-bendy dancers can save this overwrought production that's strictly BTA – Better Than Ambien. The only thing more embarrassing than these dancers skittering around the stage is admitting you actually sat through it.

La Femme

MGM Grand *3799 Las Vegas Boulevard South, at E Tropicana Avenue (1-877 880 0880/891 7777/ www.mgmgrand.com/lv). Bus 201, 301, 302.* **Shows** 8.00pm, 10.30pm Mon, Wed-Sun. **Tickets** $59. No under-21s. **Credit** AmEx, DC, Disc, MC, V. **Hotel** p80. **Map** p320 A8.

The topless revue for *The New Yorker* set, this artsy import from the Crazy Horse in Paris features classically trained ballet dancers from the original company in a fabulous play of coloured, patterned light on skin that's about as erotic a show as you'll find on the Strip. Cheaper than a night at Cheetah's, too. A great night of entertainment.

Midnight Fantasy

Luxor *3900 Las Vegas Boulevard South, between W Tropicana Avenue & W Russell Road (262 4400/ www.luxor.com). Bus 105, 301.* **Shows** 8.30pm, 10.30pm Tue, Thur, Sat; 10.30pm Wed, Fri; 8.30pm Sun. **Tickets** $43.95. No under-21s. **Credit** AmEx, DC, Disc, MC, V. **Hotel** p80. **Map** p320 A9.

Mild girl-on-girl action? Check. Token bondage scene? Check. Muscular, shirtless tap-dancing bloke for the ladies? Uh, check. Midnight Fantasy is one of the new breed of nudie shows on the Strip, which means the girls shake 'em not to 'She Wears Red Feathers' but to the Eurythmics, and the show is broken up not by a conjuror but by a potty-mouthed comedian named Carol Montgomery. Progress, eh?

Zumanity

New York–New York *3790 Las Vegas Boulevard South, at Tropicana Avenue (1-866 606 7111/ 740 6815/www.zumanity.com). Bus 201, 301, 302.* **Shows** 7.30pm, 10.30pm Mon, Tue, Fri-Sun. **Tickets** $65-$125. **Credit** AmEx, DC, Disc, MC, V. **Hotel** p83. **Map** p320 A8.

The idea of granting Cirque du Soleil the freedom to compile their own adult revue was an unexpected one. In parts, they pull it off, most notably the more comic stretches and the two-women-in-a-fishtank section towards the start of the show. A little too often it seems unsure whether it's better off trying to dazzle or arouse the audience, but those on the love seats (or, as the box office coyly calls them, 'duo sofas') seem to go upstairs happy enough. And the flying midget is a show-stealer.

Celebrity impersonators

An Evening at La Cage

Riviera *2901 Las Vegas Boulevard South, at Riviera Boulevard (1-800 256 6860/794 9433/www. rivierahotel.com). Bus 301.* **Shows** 7.30pm Mon, Wed-Sun. **Tickets** $67.50-$78.50. No under-18s. **Credit** AmEx, DC, Disc, MC, V. **Hotel** p87. **Map** p319 B5.

It may look from the stalls as though 95 per cent of your ticket price has gone on the succession of increasingly preposterous frocks that Marlboro-voiced Vegas legend and host Frank Marino dons during the course of this long-running drag revue. What remains has been used to enlist a number of dolled-up queens who are lipsynching to J-Lo, Madonna and (a scarily convincing) Celine Dion. The show is entertaining enough, but you'll have more fun for a lot less expense at one of FreeZone's gay drag shows (*see p234*).

Danny Gans

Mirage *3400 Las Vegas Boulevard South, between Spring Mountain Road & W Flamingo Road (1-800 963 9634/796 9999/www.themirage.com). Bus 203, 213, 301, 302.* **Shows** 8pm Tue-Thur, Sat, Sun. **Tickets** $100. No under-5s. **Credit** AmEx, DC, Disc, MC, V. **Hotel** p68. **Map** p320 A6.

Fronting an ass-kicking (and, luckily for him, ass-covering) band, Gans misses more impressions than he hits in his tribute to musicians and actors that he hits, recycling material that's practically prehistoric and wrapping it up in an ending so treacly that the show should come with cavity warnings. Quite how he managed to land this prestigious headline slot is anyone's guess, though the greater puzzle is how he's managed to hang on to it.

'Downtown' Gordie Brown

Golden Nugget *129 E Fremont Street, at Casino Center Boulevard, Downtown (1-866 946 5336/386 8100). Bus 107, 108, 109, 113, 207, 301, 302.* **Shows** 7.30pm Mon, Tue, Fri-Sun. **Tickets** $60.50. **Credit** AmEx, DC, Disc, MC, V. **Hotel** p96. **Map** p318 C1.

The hardest-working impressionist in Vegas, Brown and his band set off at Porsche pace and never let up, mining even the most hackneyed material – Henry Fonda in *On Golden Pond*, for Chrissakes – to great success. It's worth it just to hear the diner skit, a musical roundelay involving everyone from Johnny Cash and Hootie and the Blowfish to Green Day and

James Brown, and the celebrity golf match, with Jack Nicholson facing off against DeNiro and Christopher Walken. Danny Gans should be very afraid indeed.

Legends in Concert

Imperial Palace *3535 Las Vegas Boulevard South, between Sands Avenue & E Flamingo Road (1-888 777 7664/www.imperialpalace.com). Bus 202, 301, 302.* **Shows** 7.30pm Mon-Sat. **Tickets** (incl 1 drink) $39.95-$59.95; $24.95-$44.95 2-12s. **Credit** AmEx, DC, Disc, MC, V. **Hotel** p79. **Map** p320 A6.
This show has been wowing audiences since the early '80s with its surprisingly bang-on impressions, among them Stevie Wonder, Rod Stewart, Gloria Estefan and (natch) Elvis, belting out 'Viva Las Vegas' in his white-jumpsuited pomp. Unlike many Strip tribute shows, these performers – backed by a fine band and surrounded by showgirls – actually sing, usually doing several numbers or a medley of top hits. The show changes every three months.

The Scintas

Rio *3700 W Flamingo Road, at S Valley View Boulevard, West of Strip (1-888 746 7784/777 7776/www.playrio.com). Bus 104, 202.* **Shows** 7.30pm Mon-Wed, Fri-Sun. **Tickets** $65.95. No under-5s. **Credit** AmEx, DC, Disc, MC, V. **Hotel** p93. **Map** p317 X3.
This family act from Buffalo, New York, serves up the usual suspects: Tom Jones, Dino, Joe Cocker, Kermit and Elvis, plus a fab Beatles medley. The revue's at its comic best when brothers Joe and Frank one-up each other for the audience's attention, and at its most maudlin when sister Chrissi takes the stage performing Whitney via Charo. Despite the overly sentimental finale, the Scintas are some of the best musical impersonators in town.

The Tribute to Frank, Sammy, Joey & Dean

Greek Isles, *305 Convention Center Drive, between Las Vegas Boulevard South & Paradise Road, East of Strip (1-800 633 177/737 5540/www.greekisles vegas.com). Bus 112, 301.* **Shows** 8.15pm Mon-Thur, Sat, Sun. **Tickets** $51.50-$68.25. No under-21s. **Credit** AmEx, Disc, MC, V. **Map** p319 B5.
The set-up's a bit artificial: God (Buddy Hackett, in a marvellous voiceover cameo) sends back the fantastic four (with a 'Happy Birthday'-singing Marilyn tagging along) for one night in Vegas, where they

Viva Sandy Hackett

The world is full of celebrity sons and daughters, born into show business but, more often than not, without the guts and the talent to fit in. A few succeed; most embarrass themselves and their parents. So how'd Sandy Hackett go from showbiz tagalong to fixture on the Vegas comedy scene? 'Let's start at the very beginning,' he trills, like Julie Andrews in *The Sound of Music.* 'It's a very good place to start.' A beat, perhaps two. 'I was born a poor black child.'

Back in the real world, Hackett was born in New York City and spent his early years in New Jersey. After his father, noted comic Bobby Hackett, took the family to LA while he filmed *It's A Mad Mad Mad Mad World* – 'And they moved to Beverly... Hills, that is,' sing-songs Sandy – he decided he was actually a Left Coast guy. It was Buddy who introduced his son to Vegas, getting him a summer job lifeguarding at the Stardust pool while Buddy himself played the Sahara. Instantly smitten, Sandy returned summer after summer, watching over swimmers by day and getting an education in showmanship from the best headliners – Flip Wilson, Jack Benny, Rowan and Martin, George Burns and, of course, his dad – by night. Though Hackett studied hotel management at UNLV, worked as a trainee at the Sahara and even dealt cards in the

casino, it was only a matter of time before he stepped on to the stage. How could he not? He'd made his showbiz debut on *Rowan and Martin's Laugh-In* at the tender age of 11. Entertainment's in his DNA.

Before he'd even finished college, Hackett caught his first break by creating a successful showcase for rising comics at the Sahara, which he hosted for a dozen years; since then, he's played all over the Strip. These days, when he's not doing corporate gigs, he juggles several projects at the Greek Isles. For starters, he's co-producer of the World's Greatest Magic Show and host of **Sandy Hackett's Comedy Theatre** *(see p223),* where newcomers and veteran comics perform nightly. And six nights a week, he portrays Rat Packer Joey Bishop – known to Hackett all his life as 'Uncle Joey' – in **The Tribute to Frank, Sammy, Joey & Dean** *(see above).*

It's not been easy for Hackett to make his own mark: for a short guy, the late Buddy Hackett casts a long shadow. But now in its fourth year, *Tribute* is, in fact, a giant wet kiss of a show that captures the Rat Pack gestalt with song parodies, bawdy banter and a swingin' band. And that laughter rolling through the theatre? Recognition, at last, that Hackett Jr's a wild and funny guy.

Arts & Entertainment

take when they go out.

 **LONDON'S WEEKLY LISTINGS BIBLE**

Actions speak louder than words for the **Blue Man Group**. *See p220.*

recreate their legendary Sands act. But complete with a nine-piece band, and all the off-colour jokes and locker-room razzing you remember, the show's a humdinger. *See p215* **Viva Sandy Hackett**.

Comedians

David Brenner

Las Vegas Hilton *3000 Paradise Road, between Karen Avenue & Desert Inn Road, East of Strip (1-800 222 5361/732 5755/www.lvhilton.com).* Bus 108, 112. **Shows** 8pm Mon-Wed, Fri-Sun. **Tickets** $55. **Credit** AmEx, DC, Disc, MC, V. **Hotel** p92. **Map** p319 C5.

Holding forth in the Shimmer Cabaret, the original observational comedian shows he's still on top with insightful, ripped-from-the-headline riffs that are part current-events discourse, part *Ripley's Believe It Or Not!* It's pretty darn hilarious, too: certainly, there's not another comedian in town who can work Serbia-Montenegro into a routine and get big laughs.

George Wallace

Flamingo *3555 Las Vegas Boulevard South, at E Flamingo Road (1-800 221 7299/733 3333/www. flamingolasvegas.com).* Bus 202, 301, 302. **Shows** 10pm Tue-Sat. **Tickets** $49.50-$60.50. **Credit** AmEx, Disc, MC, V. **Hotel** p77. **Map** p320 A7.

George 'I be thinking' Wallace ponders who 'needs their asses kicked', which is pretty much everyone in this pull-no-punches howler: from Martha to Jacko to Kobe to stupid people everywhere. Bonus: select audience members are gifted with freebies such as T-shirts, CDs, chocolates, diamonds, even $100 bills.

Rita Rudner

New York–New York *3790 Las Vegas Boulevard South, at W Tropicana Avenue (1-800 693 6763/ 740 6815/www.nynyhotelcasino.com).* Bus 201, 301. **Shows** 8pm Mon-Thur; 9pm Fri, Sat. **Tickets** $60.50. No under-5s. **Credit** AmEx, Disc, MC, V. **Hotel** p83. **Map** p320 A8.

With her observational riffs on relations, ageing, shopping, boob jobs, body piercing, being a new mom and the overall weirdness of living in Las Vegas, the author of *Tickled Pink* and now host of NBC's *Ask Rita* offers a howling good time.

Ronn Lucas

Rio *3700 W Flamingo Road, at S Valley View Boulevard, West of Strip (1-888 746 7784/777 7776/www.playrio.com).* Bus 202. **Shows** 3pm Mon-Thur, Sat, Sun. **Tickets** $32.95. No under-5s. **Credit** AmEx, Disc, MC, V. **Hotel** p93. **Map** p317 X3.

Short of reaching your credit limit, this 90-minute afternoon show is the perfect excuse for leaving the Rio's slots. Lucas, accompanied by his 'teenage' dragon Scorch and the gutter-minded cowboy Buffalo Billy, is a hoot: he throws his voice around to great effect in a performance that's cool for kids.

Dinner shows

Tony 'n' Tina's Wedding

Rio *3700 W Flamingo Road, at S Valley View Boulevard, West of Strip (1-888 746 7784/777 7776/www.playrio.com).* Bus 104, 202. **Shows** 7pm daily. **Tickets** $86.75. **Credit** AmEx, MC, V. **Hotel** p93. **Map** p317 X3.

Two kids are getting hitched, and you're invited to a wedding that's full of every Italian stereotype and cliché in the book (think *Saturday Night Fever* meets *My Big Fat Greek Wedding*). How much fun you have depends on how willing you are to immerse yourself in it, boogie-oogie-oogie-ing on the dance-floor, jockeying for the bouquet and bantering with the characters. The show could be more camp and many of the actors' interactions get lost in the rush, but there's still plenty of drama, and the actors do a good job of pulling guests into the story.

Tournament of Kings

Excalibur *3850 Las Vegas Boulevard South, at W Tropicana Avenue (597 7600/www.excaliburcasino. com).* **Bus** *201, 301, 302.* **Shows** 6pm, 8.30pm daily. **Tickets** $55. **Credit** AmEx, DC, Disc, MC, V. **Hotel** p86. **Map** p320 A8.

There aren't many places where you can pound the table, eat with your hands and then lick your fingers without Miss Manners coming down on your head. But at King Arthur's court, it's not only encouraged, it's demanded. Tear into a game hen and gulp some 'dragon's blood' (really only tomato) soup while cheering the kings as they race their mighty steeds around the arena, jousting and swordfighting. The stage violence is tame and the storyline silly, but the food's good and messy, and kids will dig the pageantry and pyrotechnics. Huzzah!

Magicians

The Amazing Johnathan

Riviera *2901 Las Vegas Boulevard South, at Riviera Boulevard (1-800 256 6860/794 9433/www. rivierahotel.com).* **Bus** *301.* **Shows** 10pm Mon-Wed, Fri-Sun. **Tickets** $47.95-$58.95. No under-12s. **Credit** AmEx, DC, Disc, MC, V. **Hotel** p87. **Map** p319 B5.

Remember the guy down the pub who could make you laugh no matter what else was happening? Well, he's now working in Las Vegas. Johnathan claims a magical heritage, but spends more time on the comedy than the illusions. In fact, the few tricks he completes often play more for laughs than mystery, but it matters not. His patter varies night to night, based on the audience and the reaction of his single volunteer (who's onstage for upwards of 45 minutes of the 90-minute show), but he usually pulls it off.

Lance Burton: Master Magician

Monte Carlo *3770 Las Vegas Boulevard South, between W Harmon Avenue & W Tropicana Avenue (1-877 386 8224/730 7160/www.lanceburton.com).* **Bus** *201, 301, 302.* **Shows** 7pm, 10pm Tue, Sat; 7pm Wed-Fri. **Tickets** $72.45-$66.45. **Credit** AmEx, DC, Disc, MC, V. **Hotel** p82. **Map** p320 A8.

Blessed with all the personal dynamism of a ventriloquist's dummy – his interaction with the audience is still mesmerically awkward, despite the fact that he's been performing professionally for upwards of two decades – Burton relies purely on his magic to keep the audience wrapped around his

finger. He just about manages it, too, pulling doves from napkins, coins from ears and geese – geese! – from all over the place. One for all the family.

Mac King

Harrah's *3475 Las Vegas Boulevard South, between Sands Avenue & E Flamingo Road (1-800 392 9002/369 5111/www.harrahs.com).* **Bus** *301.* **Shows** 1pm, 3pm Tue-Sat. **Tickets** $18.65. **Credit** AmEx, DC, Disc, MC, V. **Hotel** p78. **Map** p316 A6.

One of the real gems of Vegas's entertainment roster is also one of its cheapest shows. Sure, there are no big bangs or grand illusions here: the budget extends to a pack of cards, a box of Fig Newtons and a silly suit. But King's warm manner, gentle humour and quietly dazzling tricks fit this cosy showroom perfectly. Look out for discount coupons in the local magazines, but if you don't find 'em, this is well worth full price. A highly likeable afternoon.

Penn & Teller

Rio *3700 W Flamingo Road, at S Valley View Boulevard, West of Strip (1-888 746 7784/777 7776/www.playrio.com).* **Bus** *104, 202.* **Shows** 9pm Mon, Wed-Sun. **Tickets** $82.50. No under-5s. **Credit** AmEx, Disc, MC, V. **Hotel** p93. **Map** p317 X3.

Burly man-mountain Penn Jillette and the mute, mono-monikered Teller have become scourges of the Magic Circle by showing the audience how tricks are done, but they deserve equal credit for the pzazz with which they pull off the few illusions whose secrets they don't reveal. The closing bullet routine is the only one that falls flat, but with any luck, it'll get dropped when the show receives a sizeable (and overdue) revamp in 2005. An experience.

Showgirls of Magic

Hotel San Remo *115 E Tropicana Avenue, at Duke Ellington Way, West of Strip (1-800 522 7366 ext 6028/www.sanremolasvegas.com).* **Bus** *201, 301, 302.* **Shows** 8pm, 10.30pm Tue-Sun. **Tickets** $39. **Credit** AmEx, DC, Disc, MC, V. **Map** p320 B8.

The lights dim and the music starts. A beautiful girl dances on stage wheeling a large box in front of her. She's joined by five others, each more gorgeous than the last. The music swells, but there's no sign of a tuxedoed magician. That's because the magic is done by the girls. Topless. Yes, this is the *reductio ad absurdum* of modern Vegas: big illusions, plastic breasts and not much else. For most of the show, the girls make great use of naked misdirection to keep your eyes away from the gags. So? What of it?

Steve Wyrick

Aladdin/Planet Hollywood *3667 Las Vegas Boulevard South, at E Harmon Avenue (1-877 333 9474/785 5000/www.aladdincasino.com).* **Bus** *301.* **Shows** 7pm, 10pm Mon-Thur, Sat, Sun. **Tickets** $67.95-$89.95. **Credit** AmEx, Disc, MC, V. **Hotel** p76. **Map** p320 A7.

The most amazing thing about this hack magician, who recently moved from the Sahara to the newly renovated and renamed Steve Wyrick Theatre at the

Folies Bergère. *See p220.*

Aladdin/Planet Hollywood, is how he manages to continually pull audiences into his showroom and make their cash disappear. Sadly, there's no sign of him pulling off his own vanishing act any time soon.

Musical headliners

Barry Manilow: Music & Passion

Las Vegas Hilton *3000 Paradise Road, between Karen Avenue & Desert Inn Road, East of Strip (1-800 222 5361/www.lvhilton.com). Bus 108, 112.* **Shows** 9pm Wed-Fri; 7.30pm, 10pm Sat. **Tickets** $93.50-$159.50. **Credit** AmEx, Disc, MC, V. **Hotel** p92. **Map** p320 A7.

Now resembling a white-bread Rod Stewart, the man who writes the songs has joined the ranks of aging pop stars going Vegas, setting up shop in the house that Elvis built. All the classics are here: 'Mandy', 'Can't Smile Without You', a disco-meets-hip-hop version of 'Copacabana' that's weird but fun. Happily, the sugar is laced with Manilow's self-effacing charm and humor. He knows he's a muzak icon, and he's hip to the joke, cracking that he hopes his music 'will be ruined in elevators and dentist offices for years'.

When Bazza's not around (he plays only around half the year), other headliners take his place in the theatre, anyone from ZZ Top to Damon Wayans.

Celine Dion: A New Day

Caesars Palace *3570 Las Vegas Boulevard South, at W Flamingo Road (1-877 423 5463/866 1400/ www.caesarspalace.com). Bus 202, 301, 302.* **Shows** 8.30pm Wed-Sun. **Tickets** $87.50-$225. **Credit** AmEx, Disc, MC, V. **Hotel** p65. **Map** p320 A7.

Franco 'O' Dragone's staging is extravagantly dazzling but utterly without meaning. The musical material will not to be everyone's taste; or, in the case of an ill-advised tribute to vintage Vegas, anyone's taste. Ticket prices are very high. But Celine carries it off by old-fashioned means: she's a tremendously committed performer with the band and, linking the songs, an adorably goofy individual without them.

Dion's absences from the 4,000-capacity Colosseum are filled by a highly impressive array of headline acts, chief among them Elton John (with his terrific show *The Red Piano*) and Jerry Seinfeld.

Clint Holmes: Takin' it Uptown

Harrah's *3475 Las Vegas Boulevard South, between Sands Avenue & E Flamingo Road (1-800 392 9002/369 5222/www.harrahs.com). Bus 301.* **Shows** 7.30pm Mon-Sat. **Tickets** $65.95. No under-5s. **Credit** AmEx, DC, Disc, MC, V. **Hotel** p78. **Map** p320 A6.

Who? In fairness, Holmes, a genial singer who looks at least a decade younger than he is (he moves into his sixties in 2006), riffs on his obscurity during *Takin' it Uptown*, in a routine that leads up to a performance of his sole hit 'Playground in My Mind'. The rest of the set is a mix of unsurprising covers and rather watery originals, though Holmes, engaging throughout, gives it everything he's got, as does the fab backing band. You can't help but like him.

Gladys Knight

Flamingo *3555 Las Vegas Boulevard South, at E Flamingo Road (1-800 221 7299/733 3333/ www.flamingolasvegas.com). Bus 202, 301, 302.* **Shows** 7.30pm Tue-Sat. **Tickets** $71.50-$82.50. **Credit** AmEx, Disc, MC, V. **Hotel** p77. **Map** p320 A7.

This former Pip gives up a concert that raises the roof and brings down the house with a medley of Motown hits that includes a version of 'I Heard it Through the Grapevine' that somehow weaves in Michael Jackson, James Brown, Harry Belafonte and, uh, 'Who Let the Dogs Out?'. She'll do 'Midnight Train to Georgia' if you ask nicely.

When Knight's out of town, Frankie Valli and the Four Seasons step into the breach.

Production shows

Blue Man Group

Venetian *3355 Las Vegas Boulevard South, at Sands Avenue (1-800 258 3626/www.blueman.com). Bus 203, 213, 301, 302.* **Shows** 7pm, 10pm daily. **Tickets** call for details. **Credit** AmEx, Disc, MC, V. **Hotel** p73. **Map** p320 A6.

Surprisingly cast off by the Luxor after several years of busy houses and excellent reviews (it's a favourite show among locals, always a good sign), Blue Man Group relocated to the Venetian in the middle of 2005. The show'll change in the translation, but a similar set-up is to be expected: an exuberant, irresistible wordless pantomime of illusion, comedy and artful satire, all backed by the Strip's best band (some of whom play semi-regularly under the name Überschall at the Double Down Saloon; *see p169*).

Folies Bergère

Tropicana *3801 Las Vegas Boulevard South, at E Tropicana Avenue (1-800 829 9034/739 2411/ www.tropicanalv.com). Bus 201, 301, 302.* **Shows** 7.30pm, 10pm Mon, Wed, Thur, Sat; 8.30pm Tue, Fri. **Tickets** $49.45-$60.45. No under-16s for late show. **Credit** AmEx, DC, Disc, MC, V. **Hotel** p90. **Map** p320 A8.

This rather spartan feather and sequin show, a by-the-decades homage to women's attitudes and fashion (including the obligatory can-can), is looking its age. But it's still packed with gorgeous showgirls – in bikinis for the early show, topless for the late one – and juggler Wally Eastwood provides laughs doing extraordinary tricks with his balls.

Forbidden Vegas

Westin Casuarina *160 E Flamingo Road, at Koval Lane, East of Strip (1-866 212 7026/933 3300/ www.forbiddenvegas.com). Bus 102, 105.* **Shows** 8pm Mon-Sat. **Tickets** $46.95. **Credit** AmEx, DC, Disc, MC, V. **Hotel** p94. **Map** p320 B8.

A quartet of musical theatre pros and one versatile piano player make for a lot of mischief in this wicked parody of Vegas old and new. The cast lampoon everyone from Wayne Newton and Tom Jones to the Steve and Edie duo and a literally 'statuesque'

Marlene Dietrich. Celine Dion comes in from some particularly sharp skewering. It can be tough to follow if you don't know much about Vegas; if you do, it's funny and, eventually, tiresome.

Forever Plaid

Gold Coast *4000 W Flamingo Road, at S Valley View Boulevard, West of Strip (1-888 402 6278/ 251 3574/www.goldcoastcasino.com). Bus 104, 202.* **Shows** 7.30pm Tue-Sat; 3pm, 7.30pm Sun. **Tickets** $32.95. **Credit** AmEx, DC, Disc, MC, V. **Hotel** p102. **Map** p317 X3.

If we could turn back time, we'd be be-boppin' to the music of the 1940s and '50s, which is essentially what this Off-Broadway import is all about. Check out the era of Betty Grable 'dos and doo-wop at this nostalgic revue in the cabaret-style Gold Coast Showroom. Dinner and theatre packages are available for those wanting to make an evening of it.

Havana Night Club

Stardust *3000 Las Vegas Boulevard South, at Stardust Road (1-866 525 2077/732 6325/www. stardustlv.com). Bus 301.* **Shows** 7.30, 10.30pm, days vary. **Tickets** $54.95-$76.95. **Credit** AmEx, DC, Disc, MC, V. **Hotel** p89. **Map** p319 B5.

The disappearance, in April 2005, of local legend Wayne Newton from the schedules of the Stardust showroom that bears his name was not altogether unexpected: his singing voice was a gravelly husk of its former self, and his charisma was no longer enough to carry him through. His main replacement looks likely to be this Siegfried & Roy-sponsored show, which in late 2004 got off to an extraordinary start in the city when all 50 members of the Cuban cast sought asylum. The show itself isn't quite as dramatic, bringing a 21st-century showbiz zing to musical and dance numbers that pay homage to Cuba in the '50s, but it's proving popular. The motley assortment of acts who fill in during their absences are led by irascible comic George Carlin.

Jubilee!

Bally's *3645 Las Vegas Boulevard South, at E Flamingo Road (1-877 374 7469/967 4567/www. ballyslv.com). Bus 202, 301.* **Shows** 7.30pm, 10.30pm Mon-Thur, Sat, Sun. **Tickets** $55-$74. No under-19s. **Credit** AmEx, DC, Disc, MC, V. **Hotel** p76. **Map** p320 A7.

Jubilee!'s staging of the sinking of the *Titanic* and Samson's destruction of the Philistines in the temple are beyond lame. But the production numbers in this long-running spectacle, which feature endless parades of beauties wearing nothing more than outlandishly coloured feathers, headdresses and rhinestones, make it one of a kind.

Kà

MGM Grand *3799 Las Vegas Boulevard South, at E Tropicana Avenue (1-877 880 0880/891 7777/ www.mgmgrand.com/lv). Bus 201, 301, 302.* **Shows** 7.30pm, 10.30pm Mon, Tue, Fri-Sun. **Tickets** $99-$150. No under-5s. **Credit** AmEx, DC, Disc, MC, V. **Hotel** p80. **Map** p320 A8.

Having pushed the boat out for *O* (literally, in a couple of scenes), Cirque du Soleil really had to work hard to top it in this multimillion-dollar extravaganza for the MGM Grand. They gave it a damn good go, too. *Kà*, directed by theatrical notable Robert Lepage, differs from other Vegas-based Cirque shows in that it has a plot, though there's still not much of one: in a nutshell, the story involves two separated twins struggling to reunite. But this is still more about spectacle than story. *O* is the more gorgeous show, but *Kà* is a more impressive achievement. See one of 'em during your stay, at least.

Mamma Mia!

Mandalay Bay *3950 Las Vegas Boulevard South, at E Hacienda Avenue (632 7580/474 4000/www. mandalaybay.com). Bus 105, 301.* **Shows** 7pm Mon-Thur; 5pm, 9pm Sat, Sun. **Tickets** $49.50-$110. **Credit** AmEx, DC, Disc, MC, V. **Hotel** p67. **Map** p320 A9.

While the story – a youg woman trying to find her father on the eve of her wedding – plays a little too earnestly for the featherweight songs, fans of '70s group Abba will have a heap of fun seeing how and where their favourite tunes – among them 'Take a Chance on Me' and 'Gimme! Gimme! Gimme!' – pop up in this West End smash hit. Hang on in there: they'll get to 'Dancing Queen' eventually.

Mystère

TI (Treasure Island) *3300 Las Vegas Boulevard South, at Spring Mountain Road (1-800 392 1999/ 796 9999/www.treasureisland.com). Bus 203, 213, 301, 302.* **Shows** 7.30pm, 10.30pm Wed-Sat; 4.30pm, 7.30pm Sun. **Tickets** $95. **Credit** AmEx, DC, Disc, MC, V. **Hotel** p71. **Map** p320 A6.

The first Cirque du Soleil show to reach Vegas, *Mystère* holds up pretty well next to the more spectacular – and more expensive – siblings that have joined it in recent years. The reason? It doesn't take itself too seriously, and plays for slapsticky laughs (get there 20 minutes early) as much as it does for astonishment (taiko drumming, bunraku puppetry, dazzling did-you-see-that gymnastic exhibitions). The design is showing its age a little, but otherwise, this long runner is in rude health.

O

Bellagio *3600 Las Vegas Boulevard South, at W Flamingo Road (1-888 488 7111/796 9999/ www.bellagio.com). Bus 202, 301.* **Shows** 7.30pm, 10.30pm Wed-Sun. **Tickets** $93.50-$150. **Credit** AmEx, DC, Disc, MC, V. **Hotel** p63. **Map** p320 A7.

It's been surpassed in the extravagance stakes by *Kà* (*see p220*), but this is still the best Cirque du Soleil production in town, and maybe the best show on the Strip. *O* – a pun on *eau*, French for water – is a spectacle of Fellini-esque tableaux coupled with acrobatic feats performed by 70-plus swimmers, divers, aerialists, contortionists and clowns in, on, above and around a pool/stage containing 1.5 million gallons of water. None of which goes any way towards describing just how beautiful it all is.

Le Rêve

Wynn Las Vegas *3131 Las Vegas Boulevard South, at Spring Mountain Road (1-888 320 7110/770 1570/www.wynnlasvegas.com). Bus 203, 213, 301, 302.* **Shows** 7.30pm, 10.30pm Mon, Thur-Sun. **Tickets** $121. **Credit** AmEx, DC, Disc, MC, V. **Hotel** p75. **Map** p319 B6.

His track record is mixed: he created *O* (*see above*), which is among the most impressive theatrical shows on earth, but also staked his name to *Celine Dion: A New Day* (*see p219*), which simply isn't. Still, Steve Wynn, who hired him to create the former, has re-employed Franco Dragone in his new resort. Like *O*, it's set in the water; unlike *O*, the seating arrangement is intimate, with no seat more than 40 feet from the stage. This really could go either way.

Splash

Riviera *2901 Las Vegas Boulevard South, at Riviera Boulevard (1-800 256 6860/794 9433/www. rivierahotel.com). Bus 301.* **Shows** 7pm, 9.30pm Tue-Thur, Sat; 8pm Fri, Sun. **Tickets** $64.95-$79.95. No under-18s. **Credit** AmEx, DC, Disc, MC, V. **Hotel** p87. **Map** p319 B5.

If there was an award for the most Vegas-like of Vegas shows, *Splash* would be the hands-down winner. An extreme variety show that's part topless revue, part celebrity tribute and part comedy hour, it's the only production where you'll catch Russian ice skaters and daredevil motorcyclists racing around a 16-foot metal sphere. We can only guess at the size of the Riviera's liability insurance bills.

We Will Rock You

Paris Las Vegas *3655 Las Vegas Boulevard South, at E Flamingo Road (1-877 762 5746/www. parislasvegas.com). Bus 202, 301, 302.* **Shows** 8.30pm Mon-Wed, Fri; 7pm, 10.30pm Sat; 2pm, 8.30pm Sun. **Tickets** $49.50-$110. **Credit** AmEx, DC, Disc, MC, V. **Hotel** p69. **Map** p320 A7.

Proof that a famous name will sell any old crap, this laughable mess took London's West End by storm and has managed to hold its own in a crowded Las Vegas market where out-and-out rubbish doesn't usually last five more than minutes. Essentially, it does for Queen what *Mamma Mia!* has done for Abba, but with none of the wit, humanity and charm. Don't say you weren't warned.

Comedy

Comedians are as much a Vegas staple as magicians, showgirls and second-mortgage-inducing blackjack losses. In addition to marquee funnymen such as **George Carlin**, **Steven Wright** and **Jerry Seinfeld**, who make regular pilgrimages to Vegas's biggest showrooms, and acts such as **Rita Rudner**, **George Wallace** and **David Brenner** (for all, *see p217*), who all have nightly residencies in large casino theatres, the city boasts a number of comedy clubs. These

Arts & Entertainment

feature a revolving roster of comics who have honed their chops on the club circuit and on TV spots, so are generally pretty good. Shows typically run for about 80 minutes and feature a pair or trio of headliners.

Comedy Stop

Tropicana *3801 Las Vegas Boulevard South, at E Tropicana Avenue (1-800 829 9034/739 2714/ www.tropicanalv.com). Bus 201, 301, 302.* **Shows** 8pm, 10.30pm daily. **Tickets** (incl 1 drink) $19.95. **Credit** AmEx, DC, Disc, MC, V. **Hotel** p90. **Map** p320 A8.

The Comedy Stop is a fixture of the Las Vegas comedy circuit. It features 'three comics and a mike' in two separate shows every night. Jimmie 'Dy-no-mite!' Walker often hosts the performances. Smoking is not allowed during the early show.

Comedy Zone Showroom

Plaza *1 Main Street, at Fremont Street, Downtown (1-800 773 0992/www.plazahotelcasino.com). Bus 107, 108, 109, 113, 207, 301, 302.* **Shows** 8pm daily. **Tickets** $24.15. **Credit** AmEx, DC, Disc, MC, V. **Hotel** p99. **Map** p318 C1.

You'll find comedy here every night of the week, as a pair of comedians – typically one local and one import – entertain the Downtown crowds in a 60-minute show. The line-up changes weekly so check the website for the most up-to-date information.

Improv

Harrah's *3475 Las Vegas Boulevard South, between E Flamingo Road & Sands Avenue (1-800 392 9002 ext 5222/369 5111/www.harrahs.com). Bus 301.* **Shows** 8.30pm, 10.30pm Tue-Sun. **Tickets** $27.45. No under-21s. **Credit** AmEx, DC, Disc, MC, V. **Hotel** p78. **Map** p320 A6.

After more than 40 years in the funny business, the jokes here at the Improv are still pretty fresh. Expect to find three nationally known headliners in two 80-minute shows. The line-up changes weekly.

Laugh Trax

Palace Station *2411 W Sahara Avenue, at S Rancho Drive, West of Strip (1-866 264 1818/ 547 5300/www.palacestation.com). Bus 106, 204.* **Shows** 7pm Tue-Sat. **Tickets** $14.25. **Credit** AmEx, Disc, MC, V. **Hotel** p104. **Map** p317 X2.

Each week, a new pair of comics rolls into this locals' favourite lounge-cum-club. There's a one-drink minimum. On Fridays and Saturdays, stick around after the show for Sound Trax, which features live bands.

Lounge

Palms *4321 W Flamingo Road, at S Valley View Boulevard, West of Strip (1-866 725 6773/942 7777/www.palms.com). Bus 104, 202.* **Shows** 8pm, 10.30pm 1st Sat of the month. **Tickets** $27.50. No under-21s. **Credit** AmEx, DC, Disc, MC, V. **Hotel** p92. **Map** p317 X3.

Kà. *See p220.*

This normally dark lounge lights up one Saturday a month with the Hollywood Comedy Tour, featuring newcomers and established comics all bustin' their butts to make you laugh off yours.

Riviera Comedy Club

Riviera *2901 Las Vegas Boulevard South, at Riviera Boulevard (1-800 256 6860/794 9433/ www.rivierahotel.com).* Bus 301. **Shows** 8.30pm, 10.30pm daily. **Tickets** $26.75-$37.75. No under-18s. **Credit** AmEx, DC, Disc, MC, V. **Hotel** p87. **Map** p319 B5.

Sopranos star and *Goomba's Guide to Life* scribe Steve Schirripa books the acts, lining up three new comics a week. The venue's a little dreary, but the humour's first rate: stars such as Brett Butler, Ray Romano and Drew Carey have all dropped by.

Sandy Hackett's Comedy Theatre

Greek Isles, 305 Convention Center Drive, between Las Vegas Boulevard South & Paradise Road, East of Strip (1-800 633 177/737 5540/www.greekisles vegas.com). Bus 112, 301. **Shows** 9pm Mon-Thur, Sat. **Tickets** $17.55. **Credit** AmEx, Disc, MC, V. **Map** p319 B5.

Both a launching pad for rising stars and a welcoming environment for established performers such as Fats Johnson and Shui Edgar of the *Howard Stern Show.* Some nights you catch Sandy flexing his comic muscles. *See p215* **Viva Sandy Hackett.**

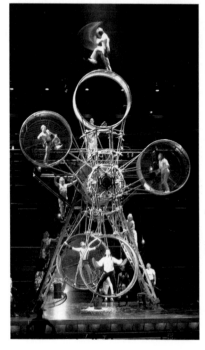

Second City

Flamingo *3555 Las Vegas Boulevard South, at E Flamingo Road (733 3111 ext 6663/www.flamingo lasvegas.com).* Bus 202, 301. **Shows** 8pm Mon-Wed, Sun; 8pm, 10.30pm Fri, Sat. **Tickets** $36.15. **Credit** AmEx, DC, Disc, MC, V. **Hotel** p77. **Map** p320 A7.

The razor-witted Chicago troupe ditches the stand-up/headliner format in favour of comedy sketches and improv games that riff on topical events and all sorts of Vegas wackiness. On Wednesdays, it's Second City Scriptless, a totally improvised show based on audience suggestions.

Showrooms

Many hotel-casinos have smallish showrooms that host touring productions, concerts and other special events. Prices vary wildly with performers: top stars such as David Copperfield will set you back around $100, while biggish names such as Neil Sedaka and Chicago will charge around $50, and covers bands ought to be free. In addition to the two Strip venues mentioned below, there's a strong programme of name-brand entertainment at theatres within several locals' casinos, chiefly the 800-seater **Orleans** (*see p102*), the larger 1,100 capacity **Sam's Town** (*see p103*) and the more intimate **Suncoast** (*see p103*), while the newish locals' casino **Cannery** (2121 E Craig Road, North Las Vegas, 617 5585, www.cannerycasinos.com) offers covers bands, from the Beatles to Santana, on weekends, and outdoor shows when the weather is good. For larger venues that host big-name bands and other single-night events, *see pp236-240*.

MGM Grand Hollywood Theatre

MGM Grand *3799 Las Vegas Boulevard South, at E Tropicana Avenue (1-800 929 1111/891 7777/ www.mgmgrand.com).* Bus 201, 301, 302. **Credit** AmEx, DC, Disc, MC, V. **Hotel** p80. **Map** p320 A8.

With its thrust stage and old-time movie-theatre ambience, the 740-seat Hollywood Theatre hosts a grab-bag of big-name entertainers, chief among them Howie Mandel, David Copperfield, Tom Jones, Paul Anka and the abominable Carrot Top.

V Theatre at Desert Passage

Aladdin (**Desert Passage** *3667 Las Vegas Boulevard South, at E Harmon Avenue (892 7790).* Bus 301. **Credit** AmEx, DC, Disc, MC, V. **Hotel** p76. **Map** p320 A7.

The former Sevilla steakhouse that once housed Charo's comeback tour has charred and burned; in its place has risen the V Theatre at Desert Passage, an intimate cabaret-style venue that showcases a trio of productions that once played other venues: these are adult revue *X*; *The Fab Four* Beatles tribute and *V: The Ultimate Variety Show.*

Children

Big kids, little kids: Vegas has it covered.

Chase the dragon at the **Adventuredome**. *See p226 and p121.*

Las Vegas leaves no stone unturned in its pursuit of omni-marketing. In the 1950s and '60s, the town was strictly for adults, a swingin' set that dressed up for dinner and a show. During the '70s and '80s, the city set its sights on Middle America, targeting lowbrow tourists who'd plug the slot machines day and night. But in the '90s, amid a frenzy of themed resort openings, Las Vegas advertised itself as a family destination, a place to bring the kids for a once-in-a-lifetime family vacation (and, oh yeah, maybe gamble a little bit while you're there).

The dawn of the new millennium saw the marketing focus change yet again, as the casinos played down the 'family destination' motif and promoted an edgier, more risqué image. The shift in focus is perhaps best exemplified by the formerly family-oriented Treasure Island's decision to rebrand itself 'TI' and morph its kid-friendly outdoor pirate pantomime into a mesmericallly ghastly piece of sub-MTV, wannabe-saucy nonsense. Still, while the casinos are no longer emphasising the family-friendliness of their facilities – and,

in a few cases, have canned them altogether – Vegas can still be an entertaining town if you've got kids in tow. Particularly if those kids like video arcades and rollercoasters.

THE LAW
State law sensibly, if sometimes rather irritatingly, forbids under-21s from lingering on casino floors. Kids are allowed to pass through the casino area when accompanied by an adult, but they cannot stay by any of the gaming tables or machines. If they do a security guard is likely to ask them – politely, but firmly nonetheless – to leave the casino. Parents are also not allowed to bet when they have youngsters in tow.

A Clark County curfew dictates that unaccompanied under-18s are not allowed on the Strip after 9pm on weekends and holidays. Off the Strip, the curfew is 10pm every night except Fridays, Saturdays and during school holidays, when it's midnight. Teenagers have the roughest time because, until you're 21, you can't drink or gain admission to the city's bars, nor to most of the clubs and showrooms.

Where to stay

The price of most hotel rooms in Las Vegas is reasonable, or at least as reasonable as you'll find in any big city. Many of the major hotel-casinos on the Strip have an arcade and/or a cinema to keep children entertained. That said, some resorts are more family-friendly than others: if you've got kids in tow, then the best of the bunch are **Circus Circus** (see p85), the **Excalibur** (see p86), the **Luxor** (see p80) and **Mandalay Bay** (see p67), all of which are owned by the Mandalay Resort Group. Described as a 'Bellagio for families' the **Monte Carlo** (see p82) is a good, low-priced option, while **New York–New York** (see p83) is recommended for concentrating as much on keeping the kids happy as the adults. The **Four Seasons Las Vegas** (see p105) doesn't offer any flashy attractions, but the service is extremely child-friendly (at least in part because there's no casino here).

Near the Strip, both the **Stratosphere** (see p90) and the **Palms** (see p92) have good childcare facilities, as do a number of the locals' casinos, particularly **Boulder Station** (see p103), **Santa Fe Station** (see p105), **Sunset Station** (see p105) and **Texas Station** (see p105) and **TI** (see p71). For full details on all the city's accommodation options, child-friendly and otherwise, see pp60-108.

Eating & drinking

The best restaurants for families in Las Vegas are, as they are in most towns, heavily themed and often quite loud. Chief among them is probably the **Rainforest Café** in the MGM Grand (see p80; 891 8580, www.rainforest cafe.com, open 8am-11pm Mon-Thur & Sun, 8am-midnight Fri & Sat), which is filled with fake foliage, life-size robotic animals and large aquariums with (real) fish. There's even an occasional 'thunderstorm' to cool things off. Sports fans will enjoy the Sahara's **NASCAR Café** (see p226; 734 7223, www.nascarcafe lasvegas.com, open 11am-9pm Mon-Thur, 11am-10pm Fri & Sat, 11am-8pm Sun), a noisy tribute to Middle America. But the most fun of all is **Quark's Bar & Restaurant** (see p170) in Star Trek: The Experience (see p126) at the Las Vegas Hilton.

Entertainment

Animals

Strictly speaking, there are no zoos in Vegas. However, if you put together all the numerous animal habitats along the Strip, you'd have a pretty good one, albeit a very old-fashioned, not-especially-politically-correct one. The magicians themselves may have been forced from the stage, but **Siegfried & Roy's Secret Garden** is still open for business at the Mirage (see p68). Check out the lions, tigers and a playful Asian elephant, before adjourning to the more relaxing confines of the **Dolphin Habitat**. There are more big cats over at the MGM Grand, whose **Lion Habitat** (see p115) is a brief but satisfying experience. Even if the lions are asleep, they'll probably be lying on top of a glass tunnel through which you can walk for a closer look. Wait around at both spots to see the animals being fed and played with by the informative staff.

Perhaps the best animal attraction on the Strip, Mandalay Bay's **Shark Reef** (see p115), features over 75 species of fish and reptiles, including golden crocodiles. The tropical adventure includes safe-distance encounters with water monitors, piranhas, sharks and eels; there's also a touch pool, where you can get your hands wet touching sharks, rays and horseshoe crabs. Finally, the **Wildlife Walk** at the Tropicana (see p90; 739 2222) shows off a menagerie of unusual creatures, including pygmy marmosets and toucans. There's also a free bird show in the Tropics Lounge most afternoons, during which you're likely to see birds ride a bike (not actual size), play basketball (they're not much cop from the free-throw line but get pretty good air during the lay-ups) and sing songs. Call for details of times.

Arcades

Most of the major casinos have games arcades, which are always a winner with kids. Some have little more than a room with a dozen video

Kids' stuff

For sharks (away from the gaming tables)
Mandalay Bay's **Shark Reef**. See p115.

For pure madness
Insanity – The Ride at the Stratosphere. See p122.

For a play for today
Rainbow Company Children's Theatre. See p227.

For hanging around
Trapeze acts at **Circus Circus**. See p226.

games (and, quite often, not altogether modern video games at that), but others hold superlative arcades with fairground entertainment to boot. The arcades at both the **Excalibur** (on the Fantasy Faire level; *see p86*) and **Circus Circus** (where the games surround a central ring with circus acts; *see p85*) are pretty decent, but the best of all are the **Coney Island Emporium** (*see p114*) at New York–New York, the **Games of the Gods** arcade at the Luxor and – especially – the non-casino **GameWorks** (*see p116*) in the Showcase Mall.

Attractions

Of the clutch of theme parks in the city, the indoor – air-conditioned – **Adventuredome** (*see p121*) at Circus Circus rules the roost. The variety of thrill rides and calmer attractions will keep both big and small kids happy for hours, yet it's never so busy that you'll spend the bulk of your time in queues. The Canyon Blaster is a short but furious double-loop, double-corkscrew rollercoaster; other exciting rides include the head-rushing Inverter and the Rim Runner water flume (yes, you will get wet). There are half a dozen low-intensity rides for young 'uns, plus carnival games, miniature golf and the Xtreme Zone, where you can test your mettle with rock climbing and bungee jumping.

There are a handful of rides in town, which range from the ridiculous to the absolutely heart-stopping. Arguably the most harrowing ride is the scream-inducing **Manhattan Express** rollercoaster (*see p115*), which twists and loops inside and outside the New York–New York hotel-casino. However, the Sahara's **Speed: The Ride** (*see p122*) is not far behind it in terms of thrill value: it races all over the property, even descending through an underground tunnel and zipping into the hotel's marquee. The roller coaster is accessible via the aforementioned NASCAR Café, which itself offers a ride of sorts in the shape of the **Cyber Speedway** race simulator. Further north is the Stratosphere, which hosts two monstrous thrill rides some 1,000 feet (300 metres) above the Strip. Though older kids may go for the **High Roller**, the **Big Shot** and the latest addition **Insanity – The Ride** (for all, *see p122*), the **Strat-o-Fair** (380 7777) is better for young kids. It features arcade games, a bucking bronco and a Ferris wheel.

Back on the Strip, the **Forum Shops** (*see p177*) at Caesars Palace are a kid-pleaser thanks to the free animatronic shows in the mall and two IMAX rides. Sci-fi-loving teens may prefer **Star Trek: The Experience** (*see p126*) at the Las Vegas Hilton. The motion simulator here gives riders a view of the action surrounding their simulated shuttlecraft.

The **Las Vegas Mini Gran Prix** (1401 N Rainbow Boulevard, just off US 95 (N), 259 7000, www.lvmgp.com) features an indoor arcade and carnival games, as well as a miniature rollercoaster. However, the main attractions here are the four go-kart tracks, the size and speed of whose vehicles match the increasing age and skill of the young drivers.

Height restrictions apply for many thrill rides in Vegas. Phone ahead to avoid disappointment.

Scandia Family Fun Centre
2900 Sirius Avenue, at S Rancho Drive, West of Strip (364 0070/www.scandiafun.com). Bus 105. **Open** *June-Sept* 24hrs daily. *Oct-May* 10am-10pm Mon-Thur, Sun; 10am-11pm Fri, Sat. **Rates** $4.95-$7.50 all-game pass. **Credit** MC, V. **Map** p319 A5.
This charmingly old-fashioned games centre is a family favourite despite its elusive location just west of the Strip. The attractions include an elaborate mini golf course, go-karts, bumper boats, batting cages and arcade games. However, it was threatened with closure in 2005, after the owner received an offer from developers who wanted to build – of course – a condo tower on the site. Call before setting out.

Film

There are cinemas all over Las Vegas. Many of the Station casinos have in-house movie theatres. **Sam's Town**, another locals' casino, counts an 18-screen multiplex among its selling points. For all, *see pp103-105* and *p229*.

Parks

There are numerous parks and recreational areas dotted around the Las Vegas Valley. **Sunset Park** (at E Sunset Road and Eastern Avenue), **Lorenzi Park** (at W Washington Avenue and N Rancho Drive) and **Floyd Lamb State Park** (on Tule Springs Road, off US 95 north of Las Vegas) are three large parks with rolling grass, lakes and volleyball; the former two also have tennis and baseball facilities. Kids can feed the ducks; don't forget to bring a loaf of bread. For more details, call 455 8200.

Sport

For family-friendly sports suggestions, such as ice rinks and bowling alleys, *see pp245-250.*

Theatre

Most of the shows on the Strip are adult-oriented, whether in terms of direct content or complex themes; many of those that are suitable for children, such as Cirque du Soleil's fabulous **Mystère** and **O** (for both, *see p221*),

Play at **GameWorks**. *See p226 and p116.*

can cost more than $100 a ticket. However, there are some bargains: magicians **Lance Burton** and **Mac King** (for both, *see p218*), and ventriloquist **Ronn Lucas** (*see p217*) all produce good, kid-friendly shows, the latter pair in the afternoons.

Rainbow Company Children's Theatre

229 6553/www.nevada.edu/~treed/rainbow.
Tickets $7; $3-$5 concessions. **Credit** Disc, MC, V.
Las Vegas's oldest theatre company – it's been going for nearly 30 years – is also, in many people's opinion, its best. Rainbow prides itself on creating children's theatre that doesn't insult young people's intelligence; its productions are always creative and well designed. Shows are held at the Reed Whipple Cultural Center and the Charleston Heights Arts Center (for addresses, *see p230*).

Services

Babysitters

There are several reliable agencies in Las Vegas offering licensed and bonded babysitters who have been cleared through the sheriff's department and by the FBI. Every hotel worth its salt can arrange babysitting services, and many even offer on-site babysitters.

Children's supplies

Baby's Away

1-800 560 9141/458 1019/www.babysaway.com.
Open 7am-9pm daily. **Rates** $10 delivery, plus rental. **Credit** AmEx, Disc, MC, V.
Baby's Away will rent, deliver and pick up baby supplies, including strollers, cribs, car seats and even VCRs and Nintendo games.

Nurseries & activity centres

Although many of the largest resorts – even those with family attractions – don't have childcare facilities, a few of the neighbourhood hotel-casinos do. They usually require written consent from the parents and may ask you to leave valid ID; they may also insist that the child is potty-trained and no longer in nappies. Most have a three-hour time limit, and only the person who drops off the children can pick them up. You don't have to be staying at the hotel, but you do have to be on the premises while your child is in the nursery.

In addition to **Kids Quest** (*see below*), there are **Kids Tyme** facilities at the Orleans (*see p102*) and Suncoast (*see p103*), which have licensed supervisors on hand to entertain the children with movies, toys and crafts. Each has a five-hour time limit.

Kids Quest

Boulder Station *4111 Boulder Highway, at E Desert Inn Road, East Las Vegas (432 7569/ www.kidsquest.com).* **Bus** 107, 112. **Open** 9am-11pm Mon-Thur, Sun; 9am-1am Fri, Sat. **Rates** $6/hr Mon-Thur; $7/hr Fri-Sun. **Credit** Disc, MC, V. **Hotel** p103.
Kids Quest has all manner of attractions including a Barbie area, a big cliff and jungle area (very popular, these) and, of course, computer games. Kids aged from six weeks to 12 years can be dropped off for up to three and a half hours, but parents must remain on site. There are also branches at Santa Fe, Sunset and Texas Stations (*see p105*), as well as at the Palms (*see p92*).

Trips out of town

For a rewarding day out away from the city, don't miss the assortment of natural and man-made attractions just outside town. **Hoover Dam**, **Valley of Fire State Park**, **Red Rock Canyon** and **Bonnie Springs/ Old Nevada** are all great for exploring with children (for all, *see pp260-265*). Further afield, **Primm** (at the California state line; *see p273*) has a trio of resorts: Buffalo Bill's, Whiskey Pete's and Primm Valley. Children love the Desperado rollercoaster and other rides at Buffalo Bill's.

Arts & Entertainment

Film

It's hooray for Hollywood in Vegas, but the independents are hanging in there.

Hollywood loves Las Vegas. With its images of long-legged showgirls, floating blackjack tables and gazillion watts of neon, no other city can convey such unapologetic indulgence with such high style. Beyond that, though, the town's round-the-clock energy attracts the Tinseltown elite every weekend, not for work but for play: Vegas is just a 45-minute flight from LAX, even faster if you've got your own jet.

The rest of us will have to build our own cinematic world around the town's multiplexes. Many are located in the casinos, but there are a few free-standing operations. Hollywoood rules the roost, but there are a few spots in which you can catch artier films. The better foreign and indie movies play at the **Regal Village Square 18** and the **Century Suncoast 16**, while the **Winchester Community Center** (3130 McLeod Drive, East Las Vegas, 455 7340, www.co.clark.nv.us) runs a tidy film series that concentrates on old, cultured movies. Tickets are just $3. In addition, the **Charleston Heights Arts Center Theater** (800 S Brush Street, Northwest Las Vegas, 229 6388) hosts a varied series of documentaries and foreign films every spring and autumn.

After many fits and starts, the city now boasts a major annual movie event: the **CineVegas International Film Festival**, which offers a mix of retrospectives, premières and curiosities when it plays at the **Brenden Las Vegas 14** for around ten days in June. The festival made a splash in 2002 when it became associated with the Sundance Film Festival; with help from Sundance's programmers, it's poised to become something of a satellite event for the festival of independent film. For full details, see www.cinevegas.com.

The best Cinemas

For mainstream fare

Brenden Las Vegas 14. *See p229.*

For indie flicks

Century Suncoast 16. *See p229.*

For previews and premières

CineVegas. *See p228.*

Downtown flicks at **Neonopolis**. *See p229.*

INFORMATION AND TICKETS

You'll find film listings in the *Las Vegas Sun*, the *Las Vegas Review-Journal*'s Friday 'Neon' supplement, at www.lasvegasmovietimes.com, and in *CityLife* and the *Las Vegas Weekly*. You can also contact MovieFone on 222 3456 for listings; the service uses zip codes to direct callers to their nearest cinema, so have yours to hand before you phone.

The phone numbers listed here offer only recorded information. Tickets can be bought in person from the respective box offices or via **Fandango**, either on 1-800 326 3264 (or 1-800 FANDANGO) or at www.fandango.com. Fandango accepts all major credit cards.

Cinemas

There are movie houses scattered all over the valley, but those listed opposite are the best and most interesting.

Brenden Las Vegas 14

Palms *4321 W Flamingo Road, at S Valley View Boulevard, West of Strip (507 4849/www.brenden theatres.com). Bus 104, 202.* **Admission** $6-$9; $5.50 concessions. **Hotel** p92. **Map** p317 X3.
Fourteen screens of digital sound and stadium seating makes this the nicest multiplex near the Strip. While the fare is typical Hollywood, the cinema hosts events like the CineVegas International Film Festival (*see p228*). There's also an IMAX cinema.

Century Orleans 18

Orleans *4500 W Tropicana Avenue, at Arville Street, West of Strip (227 3456/www.century theatres.com). Bus 104, 201.* **Admission** $6-$9; $5.50 concessions. **Hotel** p102.
The Orleans' cineplex features full THX on all screens and was the first to have stadium-style staggered seating; many other cinemas have since followed suit. The sound and projection is the best in town, and the location, close to the Strip, also helps.

Century Suncoast 16

Suncoast *9090 Alta Drive, at S Rampart Boulevard, Summerlin (341 5555/www.century theatres.com). Bus 207.* **Admission** $6-$9; $5.50 concessions. **Hotel** p103.
The Suncoast multiplex offers first-rate sound and projection, and is one of the few Valley spots to present non-Hollywood fare: at least two cinemas are reserved for art-house films each day. Since the theatres are narrow and steeply sloped, there's nary a bad seat in the house. The group also runs **Century 18 Sam's Town** (5111 Boulder Highway, East Las Vegas, 547 7469) and **Century Stadium 16 Rancho Santa Fe** (5101 N Rainbow Boulevard, Northwest Las Vegas, 645 5518).

Crown Theatres Neonopolis 14

Neonopolis, 450 E Fremont Street, at Las Vegas Boulevard South, Downtown (383 9600/www.crown theatres.com). Bus 107, 108, 109, 113, 207, 301, 302. **Admission** $5-$8.50. **Map** p318 D1.
Crown, on the third floor of Neonopolis, has brought movies back to Downtown, with steeply raked seating, a crowd-free environment and low prices, especially for matinees. Validation for parking in the mall's underground garage is available.

Discount Cinema

3330 E Tropicana Avenue, at S Pecos Road, East Las Vegas (434 8108/www.tropicanacinemas.com). Bus 111, 201. **Admission** $1-$2. **Map** p317 Z3.
Movies for a buck or so: independent flicks, foreign films and recent Hollywood fare that's just left the mainstream cinemas. On occasion, the prints are less than stellar, but the projectionists are always on their game and the clean restrooms, comfortable chairs and 50¢ hot dogs don't hurt.

Las Vegas Drive-In

4150 W Carey Avenue, at N Rancho Drive, Northwest Las Vegas (646 3565/www.century theatres.com). **Admission** $6. *Tue* $4.

Built in 1960, this is still a neat spot. Pay at the gate, park in front of the screen, turn your radio dial and enjoy. You can bring your own food and drink rather than paying the high multiplex prices.

Rainbow Promenade

2321 N Rainbow Boulevard, at Smoke Ranch Road, Northwest Las Vegas (225 4828). Bus 101, 211. **Admission** $9; $6 matinees, children.
Although there are ten screens at this suburban cinema, it's not unusual to find five Hollywood features playing on two screens each. Teenagers everywhere.

Regal Cinemas

Boulder Station 11 Boulder Station *4111 Boulder Highway, at E Desert Inn Road, East Las Vegas. Bus 107.* **Hotel** p103.
Colonnade 14 *8880 S Eastern Avenue, at E Pebble Road, Green Valley. Bus 110.*
Sunset Station 13 Sunset Station *1301 W Sunset Road, at N Stephanie Street, Green Valley. Bus 212, 217.* **Hotel** p105.
Texas Station 18 Texas Station *2101 Texas Star Lane, at N Rancho Drive, North Las Vegas. Bus 106, 208.* **Hotel** p105.
Village Square 18 *9400 W Sahara Avenue, at S Fort Apache Road, Northwest Las Vegas. Bus 204.*
All venues *221 2283/www.regmovies.com.* **Admission** $6-$9; $5.25-$7 concessions.
Although three of these operations are located in casinos, most Regal cinemas have a touch of the old movie palace about them: the Boulder cinema evokes an art deco train station, while the Sunset takes its inspiration from the tilework of Barcelona architect Antonio Gaudí. Village Square is popular with the indie-film set, but can get crowded on weekends.

United Artists Showcase 8

Showcase Mall, 3785 Las Vegas Boulevard South, at W Tropicana Avenue (740 4911/www.regmovies. com). Bus 201, 301, 302. **Admission** $6-$9; $5.25-$7 concessions. **Map** p316 A8.
The Strip's only cinema is in an alley next to the MGM Grand's parking garage. Location is a plus, but the sound, projection and seating are outdated compared to the Brenden theatres. Film-goers can park for free, with validation, in the Showcase garage.

IMAX cinema

Luxor IMAX Theatre

Luxor *3900 Las Vegas Boulevard South, at E Hacienda Avenue (1-800 557 7428/262 4000/ www.luxor.com). Bus 105, 301.* **Admission** $9.95. **Hotel** p80. **Map** p320 A9.
Science and nature films, most under an hour long. Tickets can only be purchased in person from the Pharaoh's Pavilion box office. The **Brenden Las Vegas 14** (*see above*) now has an IMAX theatre.

> ▶ For more on **how Vegas has been depicted in the movies**, *see pp30-33*.

Arts & Entertainment

Galleries

The art of the city.

Dust. *See p231.*

Las Vegas's arts scene is on the verge of something big. A few years ago, the town had a variety of venues, but the scene was split. On the one hand were high-end resorts (such as the Bellagio) with their own galleries. On the other was the bohemian Downtown scene, centred on the **Arts Factory** (www.theartsfactory.com). Interaction between these two discrete arenas was rare, meaning the arts community didn't much benefit from casino cash largesse.

Recently, however, things have changed. The shift began when the Mandalay Resort Group's President and CFO Glenn Schaeffer, who'd done out **THEhotel at Mandalay Bay** (*see p106*) with works by blue-chippers such as Warhol, shifted his **Godt-Cleary Projects** gallery from Mandalay Place to the Downtown Arts District. The move has been reflected in the wider range of people drawn to the area's monthly **First Friday** events (*see p204* **Viva Cindy Funkhouser**). As more people come to the area, so more galleries and shops open in it. And the recent creation of the **Young Collectors Council**, largely made up of young professionals and socialites, shows the new breed of Vegas art buff is rewarding itself by snapping up a masterpiece or two.

Galleries & art museums

Admission to all galleries is free unless stated.

Aerial Gallery
Las Vegas Boulevard South, between E Charleston Boulevard & E Fremont Street, Downtown.
Touted by the City of Las Vegas as a 'streetscape enhancement' project, the Aerial Gallery consists of dozens of seven-foot banners strung from lampposts on an unglamorous mile-long stretch of Las Vegas Boulevard. Local artists design the banners, which are changed every year or so and will be given over to centennial celebratory signage for part of 2005.

Art @ the Funk House
1228 S Casino Center Boulevard, at E Colorado Avenue, Downtown (678 6278/www.thefunkhouselasvegas.com). Bus 108, 206. **Open** 10am-5pm Mon-Sat; noon-5pm Sun. **Credit** AmEx, MC, V. **Map** p319 C3.
It's not a gallery *per se*, but space inside this antiques shop (*see p182*) is dedicated to art. Past the antique embalming table and Victorian-era gynaecologist's gurney is a back room where art is shown amid mid-century modernist furnishings in various states of repair. Shows feature mostly local artists.

City of Las Vegas Galleries
Charleston Heights Art Center *800 S Brush Street, between W Charleston Boulevard & Evergreen Avenue, Northwest Las Vegas (229 6383).* Bus 206. **Reed Whipple Cultural Center** *821 Las Vegas Boulevard North, at E Washington Avenue, North Las Vegas (229 6211).* Bus 113. **Map** p318 D1.
Both *www.artslasvegas.org.* **Open** 11am-9pm Tue-Fri; 10am-6pm Sat, Sun.
The City of Las Vegas puts a great deal of thought into the shows it exhibits in its municipal galleries. Both spaces offer satisfying exhibits by serious artists from across the US, many of whom demonstrate a decidedly academic bent. Artists without local representation who show at Reed Whipple will sometimes sell work at a considerable discount, owing to the space's non-profit status.

Contemporary Arts Collective
Arts Factory, 101 E Charleston Boulevard, at S Casino Center Boulevard, Downtown (382 3886/www.cac-lasvegas.org). Bus 108, 206. **Open** noon-4pm Tue-Sat. **Map** p318 C3.
The city's only artist-run, non-profit gallery splits its focus between the diverse work of its members and travelling shows. Every productive Las Vegas artist shows at the CAC at some point: it's the anchor of the Arts Factory, a complex housing studios, a theatre and design businesses.

Donna Beam Fine Art Gallery
Alta Ham Fine Arts Building, UNLV, 4505 S Maryland Parkway, between E Flamingo Road & E Tropicana Avenue, University District (895 3893/ www.unlv.edu). Bus 109, 201, 213. **Open** 9am-5pm Mon-Fri; 10am-2pm Sat. **Map** p317 Y3.
A bit tricky to find, this gallery is best visited on a weekday, when you're sure to run into an art student who can point you towards it. During the academic year (Sept-May), it hosts work by students and faculty of UNLV's fine art programme, along with the occasional travelling exhibit.

Dust
1221 S Main Street, at E California Street, Downtown (880 3878/www.dustgallery.com). Bus 113, 205. **Open** noon-6pm Fri-Sun. **Credit** MC, Disc, V. **Map** p319 C3.
When Dust opened a few years back, it breathed real life into Downtown's art scene. Today, together with the neighbouring Godt-Cleary Projects (*see below*), it provides the area's heartbeat. Rotating every six weeks, shows include everything from design abstraction to figural painting, from artists in New York, Los Angeles and Las Vegas. It's all good.

Gallery au Go-Go
Pussykat Tattoo Parlor, 4972 S Maryland Parkway, between E Tropicana Avenue & E Hacienda Avenue, University District (597 1549). Bus 109. **Open** hours vary. **Credit** AmEx, Disc, MC, V. **Map** p317 Y4.
Whether his canvas is paper or skin, inksmith Dirk Vermin is an artist. Located inside Vermin's tattoo parlour (*see p198*), Gallery au Go-Go mounts madly inclusive shows for local artists. Catch an opening to fully experience the grittily underground vibe.

Gallery of Fine Art
Bellagio *3600 Las Vegas Boulevard South, at W Flamingo Road (693 7871/www.bgfa.biz). Bus 202, 301, 302.* **Open** 9am-9pm daily. **Admission** $15; $12 concessions. **Credit** AmEx, DC, Disc, MC, V. **Hotel** p63. **Map** p320 A7.
The longest-standing gallery on the Strip. Recent exhibits have included bejewelled works from the House of Fabergé, paintings and decorative art from the Duke of Devonshire's Chatsworth House, and a wildly popular and surprisingly meaty Monet exhibit leased from the Museum of Fine Arts, Boston.

Godt-Cleary Projects
1217 S Main Street, at E California Street, Downtown (452 2200/www.godtcleary.com). Bus 113, 205. **Open** 10am-6pm Tue-Sat. **Credit** AmEx, Disc, MC, V. **Map** p319 C3.
The town's first blue-chip gallery, Godt-Cleary is where serious collectors go for original and limited edition works by Ruscha and Rauschenberg, as well as fine art *objets* by Koons *et al.* Director Michele Quinn has a New York pedigree, and it shows.

Guggenheim Hermitage Museum
Venetian *3355 Las Vegas Boulevard South, at Spring Mountain Road (414 2440/www.guggenheim lasvegas.org). Bus 203, 213, 301, 302.* **Open** 9.30am-8.30pm daily. **Admission** $19.50; $14.50-$16.50 concessions. **Credit** AmEx, Disc, MC, V. **Hotel** p73. **Map** p320 A6.
Designed by Rem Koolhaas, this is a joint project between the Guggenheim and the Hermitage Museum of St Petersburg. Shows, which draw on both institutions' collections as well as that of Vienna's Kunsthistorisches Museum, have included 'The Pursuit of Pleasure': designed for Sin City, it featured paintings depicting celebration, flirtation and gaming.

Las Vegas Art Museum
Sahara West Library, 9600 W Sahara Avenue, between S Fort Apache Road & Grand Canyon Drive, Northwest Las Vegas (360 8000/www.lasvegasart museum.org). Bus 204, 213. **Open** 10am-5pm Tue-Sat; 1-5pm Sun. **Admission** $6; $3-$5 concessions; free under-12s. **Credit** AmEx, Disc, MC, V.
Affiliated to the Smithsonian, the LVAM aims to be one of the area's most important galleries. Exhibitions can be inconsistent, but good ones, such as recent shows by Fernando Botero and monumental sculptor Frederick Hart, make it worth the trek.

S² Art Group Atelier
1 E Charleston Boulevard, at S Main Street, Downtown (868 7880/www.s2art.com). Bus 108, 206. **Open** 9am-5pm Mon-Fri. **Credit** AmEx, DC, Disc, MC, V. **Map** p319 C3.
S^2 reproduces fine art lithographs and sells them at various venues, including galleries at Mandalay Bay, the Venetian and the Fashion Show Mall. The 19th-century French and German presses turn out reproductions of posters by Mucha and Toulouse-Lautrec, vintage film ads and other old favourites, as well as contemporary works. Visitors can watch the presses while touring the large selection of prints.

Wynn Gallery
Wynn Las Vegas *3131 Las Vegas Boulevard South, at Sands Avenue (770 7100/www.wynnlas vegas.com). Bus 203, 213, 301, 302.* **Open** call for hours. **Admission** call for prices. **Credit** MC, V. **Hotel** p75. **Map** p320 B6.
Housed in Las Vegas's newest mega-resort, this collection includes two Matisses, two Manets, a Van Gogh, a Cézanne, a Gauguin and a Warhol triptych of Steve Wynn himself. In truth, though, Picasso's *Le Rêve* is alone worth the price of admission.

The best Galleries

For emerging artists
Dust. See p231.

For the already-emerged
Guggenheim Hermitage. See p231.

For total arts immersion
First Friday. See p204.

Arts & Entertainment

Gay & Lesbian

Come out, come out, wherever you are…

Pearly queens at the **Las Vegas Lounge**. *See p233.*

It might be Sin City for straights, but for gays Las Vegas was, for many years, not much more than Snooze Town. Still, if there's one thing of which you can be certain in Vegas, it's that change is around the corner, and so it's proved with the gay scene. The mainstream moves towards sexier nights out are spilling over into the more adventurous areas of the market for *l'amour*, the mayor is vocally pro-gay, and the Strip finally has an alternative club, **Krave** (*see p235*), bringing gay life out of the ghettos and on to the main drag. The gay action in Vegas is no longer just limited to drag shows sold to Midwestern coach parties: there are now hot offerings for gay and gay-friendly locals.

Off the Strip, there is no particular gay neighbourhood. However, most of the gay bars, nightclubs and bookstores are centred around two main areas. The **Fruit Loop** is located south of the Hard Rock Hotel on Paradise Road, a mile from the Strip, and includes the Vegas outpost of national chain **Hamburger Mary's** (*see p234*), bars such as **Buffalo** (*see p233*) and nightclubs including **FreeZone** and the ever-popular **Gipsy** (for both, *see p234*). Note that between the Hard

Rock and the Fruit Loop is a popular, posh strip club, **Club Paradise** (4416 Paradise Road, 734 7990), at which daring ladies have been known to enjoy lapdances from the female staff.

The **Commercial Center**, located on E Sahara Avenue, is a little sketchier in terms of kerb appeal, but buried between a wig store, several Asian karaoke bars and a swingers' club are a host of gay draws, from the **Center** (*see p295*), the anchor around which the city's gay community revolves, to **Hawk's Gym** (*see p234*). Also here is a new gay-themed coffeehouse and bookstore, **Pride Factory** (*see p234*), which brings metrosexual gay life to Vegas with sofas, large-screen televisions playing *Queer as Folk* and *The L Word*, internet access, clothing, jewellery, coffee and an X-rated DVD section.

For other socialising, check out the events held and/or advertised at the aforementioned Center. Among the more fun ways to see the town are the gay skate night on the third Monday of the month at the **Crystal Palace Skating Center** (4680 Boulder Highway, 458 7107, www.skatevegas.com); entrance (including skate hire) is $6 in advance, or $8 on the door. And if the hotel-casinos on the Strip are a little too straight for your taste, Las Vegas now has gay accommodation that extends to more than just B&B: the clothing-optional **Blue Moon Resort** (*see p295*) is a handsome, well-appointed hotel that's only a short cab ride away from the Commercial Center, the Fruit Loop and the Strip.

As Vegas's population continues to grow, it brings with it a more diverse mix and the gay community benefits from that. Although it's still a transient community in which gays and lesbians are not tightly knit, visitors will find a good time can be had at the bars and clubs. For the **Black & White Party**, *see p205*.

LESBIAN LAS VEGAS

Female readers shouldn't be discouraged by the apparent lack of lesbian bars and activities geared towards women. Most of the gay bars have a healthy mix of men and women at weekends; Tuesday at **FreeZone** (*see p234*) is ladies' night, while the **Backstreet Bar & Grill** (*see below*) has an unofficial ladies' night on Thursday. Check out, too, the **Bitch Bar** at **Krave** (*see p235*) every Friday, and **GirlBar** on the second Saturday of each month.

Vegas also has a women's social group called **Betty's Outrageous Adventures** (991 9929, www.bettysout.com), which organises movie nights, camping excursions, sporting events, pool parties and other non-bar fun. All ages and sexual orientations are welcome, including male friends (unless it's a women-only event).

Bars

As well as Vegas's dozen or so gay bars, a few places identify themselves as 'alternative', essentially proclaiming themselves as gay-friendly operations.

Backdoor Lounge

1415 E Charleston Boulevard, at S 15th Street, Downtown (385 2018). Bus 206. **Open** 24hrs daily. **Admission** $5 Fri, Sat. **No credit cards.** **Map** p318 E3.

A haven for local gay Latino men, the Backdoor boasts friendly bartenders, occasional slot and video poker tournaments, and regular drinks specials.

Backstreet Bar & Grill

5012 Arville Street, at W Tropicana Avenue, Southwest Las Vegas (876 1844). Bus 103, 201, 202. **Open** 24hrs daily. **No credit cards.**

A favourite haunt for Vegas cowboys and cowgirls and home of the Nevada Gay Rodeo Association, Backstreet has the busiest Sunday afternoon beer bust in town. Ladies: if you want to meet women of all ages and interests, git yerself down here every Thursday at 7pm for some line-dancing lessons. Non-dancers also welcome.

Badlands Saloon

Commercial Center, 953 E Sahara Avenue, between S 6th Street & S Maryland Parkway, East of Strip (792 9262). Bus 109, 204. **Open** 24hrs daily. **No credit cards.** **Map** p317 Y2.

This local hangout, while perfectly fine for a night out, is really nothing out of the ordinary, featuring the usual combination of country music, pool tables and nary a woman in sight.

Buffalo

Paradise Plaza, 4640 Paradise Road, between E Harmon Avenue & E Tropicana Avenue, East of Strip (733 8355). Bus 108. **Open** 24hrs daily. **No credit cards.** **Map** p320 C8.

Inside this legendary Levi's/leather bar in the Fruit Loop, you'll find the requisite pool-playing, recipe-swapping, friendly crowd of guys (and a few gals). Beer busts take place on Tuesdays and Fridays.

Las Vegas Eagle

Tropicana Plaza, 3430 E Tropicana Avenue, at S Pecos Road, East Las Vegas (458 8662). Bus 111, 201. **Open** 24hrs daily. **No credit cards.** **Map** p318 Z3.

Famous around the scene for its Underwear Nights (held on Wednesdays, Fridays and Saturdays), this is primarily a men's Levi's/leather bar, with regular beer busts and nightly drinks specials.

Las Vegas Lounge

Commercial Center, 900 E Karen Avenue, between Paradise Road & S Maryland Parkway, East of Strip (737 9350). Bus 109, 204. **Open** 24hrs daily. **No credit cards.** **Map** p317 Y3.

This mixed venue situated in the Commercial Center draws mostly queens, transsexuals, cross-dressers and their friends, fans and appreciators. There are regular shows from dancers, not to mention the requisite array of drinks promos.

Snick's Place

1402 S 3rd Street, between E Charleston Boulevard & E Oakey Boulevard, Stratosphere Area (385 9298). Bus 301. **Open** 24hrs daily. **No credit cards.** **Map** p317 Y2.

Snick's Place is Las Vegas's oldest gay men's bar. It's cruisey and slightly tatty, but is still a historic, must-see neighbourhood landmark.

The best Gay stuff

For fashion, fetish and cabaret
Krave. *See p235.*

For coffee and a read
Pride Factory. *See p234.*

For lassoing a cute cowboy
Backstreet Bar & Grill. *See p233.*

Spotlight

Commercial Center, 957 E Sahara Avenue, between
S 6th Street & S Maryland Parkway, East of Strip
(696 0202). Bus 109, 204. **Open** 24hrs daily.
No credit cards. Map p317 Y2.
Very much a locals' hangout, this Commercial
Center spot hosts regular liquor busts, free pizza on
Friday and a Jock Night every Saturday.

Cafés & restaurants

Hamburger Mary's

4503 S Paradise Road, at E Harmon Avenue, East
of Strip (735 4400/www.hamburgermarys.net). Bus
108. **Open** 11am-3am daily. **Credit** AmEx, Disc,
MC, V. **Map** p320 C8.
This national burgers 'n' booze chain has a lively
Vegas operation. Aside from the food, which is
pretty good, there's a variety of events put on for
punters each week, from karaoke to club nights.

Pride Factory

Commercial Center, 953 E Sahara Avenue, between
S 6th Street & S Maryland Parkway, East of
Strip (444 1291/www.pridefactory.com). Bus 204.
Open 10am-midnight daily. **Credit** AmEx, Disc,
MC, V. **Map** p317 Y2.
A sister to the coffee and novelty store in Fort
Lauderdale, Pride draws a mix of students and older
clientele, both men and women, for a variety of social
events including an open mic night once a month.

Clubs

The newer, glitzier, more entertainment-driven
casinos in Vegas house the city's most popular
nightclubs, all of which boast a 'mixed' or
'alternative' dance crowd. Some even have
special gay nights: check the local press for
details. For full nightclub listings in Vegas,
see pp241-244.

Flex Lounge

4371 W Charleston Boulevard, at S Arville Street,
Northwest Las Vegas (385 3539). Bus 206. **Open**
24hrs daily. **Admission** $5 Sat nights. **Credit**
AmEx, MC, V.
One of Las Vegas's few truly mixed clubs, the Flex
Lounge has become a neighbourhood favourite for
its drinks specials and great dancing. The programme of events that happen throughout the week
includes go-go boys on Wednesday nights.

FreeZone

610 E Naples Drive, at Paradise Road, East of Strip
(794 2300/www.freezonelasvegas.com). Bus 108, 213.
Open 24hrs daily. **No credit cards. Map** p320 C8.
Often seen as the alternative to Gipsy, FreeZone
caters for women only (on Tuesdays), men (on
Thursdays) and mixed karaoke fans (Sundays and
Mondays), and has one of the best drag shows in
town (every Friday and Saturday). The FreeZone
café serves food until 2am every night.

Gipsy

4605 Paradise Road, between E Harmon Avenue
& E Tropicana Avenue, East of Strip (731 1919).
Bus 108, 213. **Open** from 9pm daily. **Admission**
$5-$10. **No credit cards. Map** p320 C8.
Until the Strip's nightclub explosion, Gipsy was the
only place to go for the live-and-let-dance attitude
that is prevalent in most metropolitan nightclubs,
and it still draws a very mixed crowd. But be warned:
small by most standards, Gipsy becomes a heaving
wall-to-wall sweatfest by around 2am on Saturdays.
Renovated, there's now a video wall and some seats
for those who want to chill. Music ranges from
techno through R&B to gay-friendly neo-disco, while
scantily clad go-go boys work the corners.

GoodTimes Bar & Nightclub

Suite 1, Liberace Plaza, 1775 E Tropicana Avenue,
at Spencer Street, University District (736 9494).
Bus 201. **Open** 24hrs daily. **No credit cards.**
Map p317 Y3.
It's open all week, but GoodTimes is the only place
to be on Monday night, when a lively mixed crowd
and plenty of younger party-goers take advantage

Undo those buttons at **Gipsy**.

Arts & Entertainment

Take Pride

Las Vegas Pride celebrations have gone from strength to strength in recent years: the festival now runs for more or less a week, with a variety of entertainments from the sedate to the saucy. The main event is **Pridefest** on the Saturday afternoon (121 E Sunset Road, East of Strip), which has food booths, games, workshops and entertainers that go on until the evening. It's preceded on the Friday night by a big parade Downtown, and followed by a Saturday-into-Sunday after-party, usually at **Gipsy** (*see p234*). However, the fun doesn't stop there: also on the agenda are girls' and boys' parties in the week leading up to the festivities; an arts show at the **Center**; and even a tea dance at the **Blue Moon Resort** (for both *see p295*) on the Sunday night. Pride is usually held in May: check www.lasvegaspride.org for details.

of the best liquor bust in town, then dance into the morning on the only stainless steel dancefloor in Las Vegas. Late Saturdays cater to the Latino crowd.

Krave

3663 Las Vegas Boulevard South, at Harmon Avenue (836 0830/www.kravelasvegas.com). Bus 301. **Open** from 9pm Tue-Sun. **Admission** $10 members; $20 non-members. **Credit** MC, V. **Map** p320 A7.
In addition to John Stagliano's *Fashionistas* (*see p214*), Krave's nightclub and lounge spaces are home to a host of gay nightlife offerings. On Thursdays at 10pm, there's queer cabaret with acts by performers who feature in Vegas's other shows; Friday night caters to the ladies with Bitch Bar at 9pm, before Men of Vegas takes over, moving into the nightclub at midnight; and every other Saturday the girls will find more relief at GirlBar.

Cruising

Las Vegas's plethora of adult bookstores (including the **Adult Superstore**, for which *see p199*), theatres and video arcades are prime spots for cruising.

Apollo Health Spa

Commercial Center, 953 E Sahara Avenue, between S 6th Street & S Maryland Parkway, East Las Vegas (650 9191/www.apollospa.com). Bus 109, 204. **Open** 24hrs daily. **Admission** $25-$35. **Credit** MC, V. **Map** p317 Y2.
The Apollo is known worldwide through the notoriety of former co-owner Doc Ruehl, who owned the houseboat in Miami where gay serial killer Andrew

Cunanan took his own life. Nevertheless, the spa enjoys a healthy crowd most nights, including some tourists. It has a heated pool, jacuzzi, sauna, video room, gym and maze (darkroom) area.

Desert Books

4350 N Las Vegas Boulevard, at Craig Road, North Las Vegas (643 7982). Bus 113, 115. **Open** 24hrs daily. **Credit** MC, V.
If you like a man in uniform, this adult bookshop is conveniently close to the Nellis Air Force Base. Open since the 1980s, which qualifies as ancient history in Las Vegas, it attracts an older gay clientele during the day, while evenings draw browsing couples.

Gay beach

This clothing-optional gay men's beach is on Lake Mead, just outside the city. Although the site falls under federal jurisdiction, there's a state law against nudity 'with sexual intent', so cruise with caution. To get here, head east on Lake Mead Boulevard out of North Las Vegas (Highway 147) until you hit the lakeside road, then turn left (north) towards Calville and Overton Bays. After 4.8 miles (clock it or you'll miss it), turn right on to a dirt road; stay left at all forks, making all left turns. Park where it seems obvious, then head left over the hills and continue on the path for about five minutes: gays to the left, straights to the right. Beware: park rangers are on the lookout for people engaging in 'lewd and lascivious behaviour' and you could incur a fine.

Hawk's Gym

Commercial Center, 953 E Sahara Avenue, between S 6th Street & S Maryland Parkway, East of Strip (731 4295/www.hawksgymlv.com). Bus 109, 204. **Open** 24hrs daily. **Admission** $5 daily; extra charge for lockers and rooms. **No credit cards**. **Map** p317 Y2.
This spa has gym equipment, shower facilities and, as an employee put it, 'other different areas'. Word of mouth says the younger set prefers Hawk's to its more-established neighbour, Apollo (*see above*).

Shops

In addition to **Get Booked**, **Pride Factory** (*see p234*) sells a range of gifts, novelties, clothes and over 2,000 gay movies.

Get Booked

Paradise Plaza, 4640 Paradise Road, between E Harmon & E Tropicana Avenues, East of Strip (737 7780/www.getbooked.com). Bus 108. **Open** 10am-midnight Mon-Thur, Sun; 10am-2am Fri, Sat. **Credit** AmEx, Disc, MC, V. **Map** p320 C8.
This small shop located down on Paradise sells books, magazines, gifts, clothes, calendars, cards and videos (for rent or sale) for a mixed clientele.

▶ For details of **gay support groups** and other useful organisations, *see p295*.

Arts & Entertainment

Music

The sounds of the city.

Las Vegas's unenviable musical image is hinged around two types of performers: mildly talented lounge acts and washed-up pop stars. However, at least on the Strip, the city's continuing evolution has improved matters. The still-famous **Celine Dion** (*see p219*) has a residency at Caesars Palace; the casino has hired Elton John to fill in for her when she's on vacation. Enormous venues at the **MGM Grand** and **Mandalay Bay** host huge names year-round, while the **House of Blues** and the Hard Rock's **Joint** (for all four, *see p237*) offer more alternative fare. Be warned, though: casino shows come at a high price, and venue locations deep within their confines often mean a lengthy trek from the car. Arrive early to ensure getting inside the venue on time.

Non-casino music venues have a harder time, competing against the deep pockets and music industry ties that casinos use to their advantage; other Vegas venues have been sunk simply by inept management. Those that remain stage an eclectic range of offerings, but many nights are left unbooked. If a venue has video poker or any other gaming on-site, it's legally prevented from charging admission. However, that doesn't stop bands from asking for a donation. The sporadic nature of shows makes it difficult to stumble on an unexpected night of musical fun; researching event calendars in advance is advised.

Vegas isn't only about pop and rock: the town has increasingly purposeful classical and jazz organisations. It's particularly wise to join culture-savvy locals at the various events held under the auspices of the **Las Vegas Music Festival** (*see p240* **The classics**).

INFORMATION AND TICKETS
For information, consult *Las Vegas Weekly* or *CityLife*, or check online at www.vegas.com or www.yourlocalscene.com. Tickets can generally be bought direct from venues and/or through Ticketmaster (474 4000), and prices vary wildly. Shows in bars rarely come with a cover of more than $10, and many are free; **House of Blues** gigs can run from $10 up to six or seven times that; and the sky's the limit for big names at the **MGM Grand Garden Arena**.

A word of warning: Clark County has made all-ages events almost impossible due to strict rules regarding a venue's proximity to businesses with a liquor licence: with the

exceptions of the Joint and the House of Blues, where age restrictions vary, most rock venues cater only to over-21s.

Casino venues

Aladdin Theatre for the Performing Arts
Aladdin/Planet Hollywood *3667 Las Vegas Boulevard South, at E Harmon Avenue (736 0111/tickets 785 5000/www.aladdincasino.com). Bus 301.* **Tickets** $25-$150. **Credit** AmEx, Disc, MC, V. **Hotel** p76. **Map** p320 A7.
A $25-million renovation in 2000 made major improvements to both looks and sound at this 7,000-seater. Enrique Iglesias, Prince and Nelly have all played here, though the Planet Hollywood takeover may offer even more choices to a venue that already books mainstream pop, hip hop and R&B acts.

Beach
Mandalay Bay *3950 Las Vegas Boulevard South, at E Hacienda Avenue (632 7777/tickets 632 7400/www.mandalaybay.com). Bus 105, 301.* **Tickets** $10-$100. **Credit** AmEx, Disc, MC, V. **Hotel** p67. **Map** p320 A9.
Mandalay Bay's impressive pool area is also a sometime music venue populated by patrons with little on but their smiles. The B-52s, the Go-Gos and the Beach Boys have all played at the 11-acre facility. Concerts are in spring and summer only, so their events calendar doesn't start posting beach concerts until the weather heats up. Want to dress up? Get tickets to watch from Moorea, the outdoor lounge.

Golden Nugget Theatre Ballroom
Golden Nugget *129 E Fremont Street, at Casino Center Boulevard, Downtown (1-866 946 5336/385 7111/www.goldennugget.com). Bus 107, 108, 207, 301, 302.* **Tickets** $25-$100. **Credit** AmEx, DC, Disc, MC, V. **Map** p318 C1.

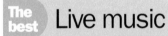

The best Live music

For megastars at mega-prices
MGM Grand Garden Arena. *See p237.*

For big stars at big prices
House of Blues. *See p237.*

For local acts with no cover
Double Down Saloon. *See p239 and p169.*

Arts & Entertainment

This tasteful 400-seat showroom is home most nights to 'Downtown' Gordie Brown (*see p214*), with free shows late on Monday and Saturday nights from Lon Bronson and the high-energy All-Star R&B and Rock 'n' Roll Revue. However, the Nugget also stages regular two- or three-night engagements by headliners from Tony Bennett and George Benson to Staind singer Aaron Lewis.

House of Blues

Mandalay Bay *3950 Las Vegas Boulevard South, at E Hacienda Avenue (632 7000/tickets 632 7600/ www.hob.com). Bus 105, 301.* **Tickets** $10-$70. **Credit** AmEx, Disc, MC, V. **Hotel** p67. **Map** p320 A9.
This nationwide franchise uses American 'outsider' (folk) art as the focal point for its design, and follows up with the most eclectic booking policy – blues, rock, metal, hip hop, electronica – of any venue in town. With the exception of four pillars, standing room on the first floor and tiered balcony seating on the second offer unobstructed views of the stage. Regular events include Rockstar Karaoke (pick your song and sing it with a live band) and shows from disco act Boogie Knights and hard-rock satirists Metal Shop.

The Joint

Hard Rock *4455 Paradise Road, at E Harmon Avenue, University District (693 5000/tickets 1-888 473 7625/www.hardrockhotel.com). Bus 208.* **Tickets** $20-$250. **Credit** AmEx, DC, Disc, MC, V. **Hotel** p91. **Map** p320 C7.
Morrissey, Elvis Costello, Mötley Crüe and Duran Duran are among the acts that have played here, the Vegas venue that most resembles a Los Angeles street club in attitude. General admission gets you on the three-levelled first floor, with reserved table seating on the second-storey balcony. Perhaps the city's leading rock venue.

Mandalay Bay Events Center

Mandalay Bay *3950 Las Vegas Boulevard South, at E Hacienda Avenue (632 7777/tickets 632 7400/ www.mandalaybay.com). Bus 105, 301.* **Tickets** $25-$200. **Credit** AmEx, Disc, MC, V. **Hotel** p67. **Map** p320 A9.
Another enormous arena, this events centre is a multi-use space catering to both public special events and private functions sponsored by attending conventions. The mixed use means musical events are widely spaced and varied: Latino acts, rock legends and musical awards ceremonies are all staged here. Check a calendar for events and arrive early for the long walk through the hotel.

MGM Grand Garden Arena

MGM Grand *3799 Las Vegas Boulevard South, at E Tropicana Avenue (891 7777/tickets 1-877 880 0880/www.mgmgrand.com). Bus 201, 301, 302.* **Tickets** $30-$250. **Credit** AmEx, DC, Disc, MC, V. **Hotel** p80. **Map** p320 A8.
The enormous arena is host to most of the big-name touring artists that pass through town, from U2 to Alan Jackson; its size also allows for large-scale

Cooler Lounge.
See p239.

productions. The hotel and the arena have different entrances that a car can drive up to, which may get a visitor in trouble. From the main entrance of the hotel to the arena is a ten-minute walk, accessible through the shops and restaurants area of the MGM.

Railhead

Boulder Station *4111 Boulder Highway, at E Desert Inn Road, East Las Vegas (432 7777/tickets 1-866 264 1818/547 5300/www.boulderstation.com). Bus 107, 112.* **Tickets** free-$50. **Credit** AmEx, Disc, MC, V. **Hotel** p104.

This locals' casino a little way out from the centre of town stages a mix of rock, jazz and dance, though most of the acts tend to be old-timers: Morris Day & The Time, Blue Oyster Cult and Maynard Ferguson have all played recently. The free shows staged here are mostly covers bands.

Roadhouse Casino

2100 N Boulder Highway, at Sunset Road, Henderson (564 1150). Bus 212. **Tickets** from $10. **Credit** AmEx, MC, V.

Viva Rob Ruckus

It wasn't his birthday. Nor, in fact, was it a special party of any sort. Yet on this random Wednesday evening at the Double Down Saloon (*see p169*), a huge mass of well-wishing friends, enemies and ex-lovers – including some folks who qualified in all three categories – greeted long-time Las Vegas bass-plucker Rob Ruckus with a hearty blast of vile profanity, peppered with healthy doses of genuine well-wishing.

For the first time that anyone could remember, the gravel-voiced thirtysomething punker was speechless. It didn't last. Standing in front of a makeshift banner emblazoned, perhaps inevitably, with the phrase 'fuck you Ruckus', he embarked on

a politically incorrect call-and-answer session with the gathered throng that – to paraphrase Morrissey, virtually the anti-Ruckus – would have made Caligula blush.

As the verbal affray diffused, Ruckus was presented with a new bass guitar, paid for by contributions from almost everyone in the bar, to replace his old one, which was destroyed by... well, it's a long, disgustingly graphic story involving a drunken ex-wife of another musician. Suffice to say, Ruckus was touched by this outpour of support from the local scene. So after a spur-of-the-moment roast ('What can I say about Ruckus that hasn't been reported in great detail to detectives over three generations?'), the man of the moment got ripping drunk, stripped butt-naked and struck up with his punk band the Vermin. You know, to give something back to the people.

You want to know how punk Ruckus is? He's so punk that in addition to the Vermin, he also plays in a goth band (Moonvine), a rock outfit (Jupiter Shifter) and a funky retro-lounge band (the Nines). Oh, and another punk group (the Showgirls), but they only do ripped-up versions of cheesy hits like the Cowsills' 'Flower Girl'. While dressed in thrift-store drag.

The common link with all Ruckus's bands is that his persona never changes. Always rude, usually crude, and often more or less nude. A force of nature, Ruckus is disgusting but smart, fearless but also tender. Heck, when a younger punker pointed out the absence of a comma between the words 'you' and 'Ruckus' on the banner behind him, the man with the movie-monster tattoos stopped the show and let the fellow, a schoolteacher by profession, insert the proper punctuation. Fitting for the exclamation point that Ruckus represents in any thoughtful discussion of Las Vegas rock 'n' roll.

Your choice at this venue: loud, louder or loudest. The Roadhouse generally sticks to metal and punk acts, with local productions group Revenge Therapy and record label Roadrunner responsible for bringing bands here regularly. The venue is also one of only a few in town to offer all-ages shows.

Whiskey Beach

Green Valley Ranch *2300 Paseo Verde Parkway, at S Green Valley Parkway, Henderson (617 7777/tickets 1-866 264 1818/547 5300/www.greenvalley ranchresort.com). No bus.* **Tickets** $25-$75. **Credit** AmEx, DC, Disc, MC, V. **Hotel** p104.
Run by the Whiskey (*see p244*), this outdoor venue has shows rain or shine, though poor weather is rare. Beautiful pools, cabañas, and a sweet Strip view aid the gigs, whether Hall & Oates or Sean Paul.

Non-casino venues

Leaving aside the major casino venues, which host pretty much all the touring bands to come through town, lovers of live music are not well served by Las Vegas. The local scene is fairly small, especially for a city of two million people, and while there are several great bars that stage live music, there are no great music bars; the music is usually an adjunct to the drinking and gaming, and few owners run their bars with the express purpose of showcasing bands.

That said, it's no desert. The circuit isn't huge, but it's enthusiastic. Among the local acts worth seeing are rock-lounge act the Nines, one of numerous acts featuring quasi-legendary local musician Rob Ruckus (*see p238* **Viva Rob Ruckus**); power-punk trio the Pervz; and Celtic rock covers act Killian's Angels, who feature Blue Man Group drummer Nan Fortier. Other members of the BMG's band play together as freeform tribal-rock act Überschall. For listings, consult *Las Vegas Weekly* and/or *CityLife*.

Aside from the venues detailed below, other establishments listed elsewhere also host music. At the **Fremont Street Experience** (*see p129*), bands often perform free sets on holidays and for other special events: in 2005, a Mardi Gras event featured Dr John and Buckwheat Zydeco. The **Double Down Saloon** (*see p169*), the king of Vegas dive bars, offers a regular calendar of bands, for which admission is always free. The **Ice House Lounge** (*see p170*), a little slice of Miami Beach in Sin City, occasionally hosts live music, as does **Dino's** (*see p169*), especially on First Friday. But perhaps the best place to see regularly scheduled bands is **Matteo's Underground** (*see p174*), beneath the Boulder Dam Hotel in Boulder City. Local music fan/patron Poizen Ivy both books the bands at Matteo's and publicises many of Vegas's other music happenings on her site, www.sincitysounds.com.

Aristocrat

850 S Rancho Drive, at W Charleston Boulevard (870 1977). Bus 106, 206. **Open** 24hrs daily. **Map** p317 X2. **Credit** AmEx, Disc, MC, V.
This dark and smoky strip-mall dive is found in a neighbourhood not known for either bars and music. Currently hosting erratic rock/punk shows and loud karaoke nights, it's popular among the city's tattooed and pierced population.

Cheyenne Saloon

3103 N Rancho Drive, at W Cheyenne Avenue, Northwest Las Vegas (645 4139/www.thecheyenne saloon.com). Bus 106, 218. **Open** 24hrs daily. **Credit** AmEx, Disc, MC, V.
Somewhere between nowhere and the northern suburbs, the Cheyenne is a long way from 'most everything. Still, it's trying hard to get people to travel, with a range of hard rock and metal bands. Pool tables separate the bar and the sunken dancefloor; there are nicely divided areas for dancing, watching and just drinking. One of the better small venues.

Cooler Lounge

1905 N Decatur Boulevard, at W Havelina Street, Northwest Las Vegas (646 3009/www. coolerlounge.com). Bus 103, 210. **Open** 24hrs daily. **No credit cards.**
Another dive bar in another strip mall. The difference is that not only bands play here, but the Babes in Sin Burlesque Troupe make this bar their home. The bartenders range from mildly disinterested to occasionally hostile. The programme is generally split between rock, rockabilly and punk bands, with DJs and MCs on Sundays and Tuesdays.

Garage-Ma-Hall

Northwest Las Vegas (www.garagemahall.com). **Open** *Shows* 8pm. **No credit cards.**
One of around a dozen Woodsongs Coffeehouses in the US (see www.woodsongs.com for details of this homespun folk scene), the Garage-Ma-Hall has the appearance of a party house, with comfortable sofas (capacity is 60) and a large apron/patio across the front of the garage. Shows, most often by singer-songwriters, are held roughly once every three or four weeks; check online for listings and book your place via email to betty@moonandeye.com, who'll pass the address on to you. A $10 donation is suggested for most shows.

Huntridge Theatre

1208 E Charleston Boulevard, at S Maryland Parkway, Downtown (477 7703/www.thehuntridge. com). Bus 109, 206. **Open** hrs vary. **Admission** call for details. **No credit cards. Map** p318 D3.
This historic art deco theatre has traditionally been the best place in Las Vegas to catch touring rock and punk bands. It's closed at present for renovation, and work has taken longer than expected. But nationally known groups such as the Beastie Boys love this place, and when it reopens, there's no reason to suspect it'll be anything less than the town's best non-casino venue.

Iowa Café

*300 E Charleston Boulevard, at S 3rd Street,
Downtown (366 1882). Bus 206, 301.* **Open** 8am-
3.30pm daily. **No credit cards. Map** p318 C3.
Maps of Iowa, pictures of corn and fleets of toy farm
tractors adorn the walls of this Downtown café. It's
generally open only during the day, but there are
occasional evening shows (check the weeklies for
details) and bands on every First Friday. With no
stage, performers just shove aside the furniture and
get on with it. The Italian sodas are great, too.

Jillian's

*450 Fremont Street, at Las Vegas Boulevard South,
Downtown (759 0450/www.jillians.com). Bus 301.*
Open 11am-midnight Mon-Thur, Sun; 11am-2am Fri,
Sat. **Credit** AmEx, Disc, MC, V. **Map** p318 2D.
Jillian's is making a go of catering to locals by staging some all-ages shows and some small bands on
national tours. The groups share the building with
bowling lanes and a large games area. Be ready to
rock with the young and the young at heart.

New York Café

*4080 Paradise Road, at E Flamingo Road, East of
Strip (796 0589). Bus 108, 202.* **Open** hrs vary.
Credit AmEx, Disc, MC, V. **Map** p317 3Y.
Another dive, this one is on the east side of the Strip
near the Hard Rock. The small, dark and loud bar
stages punk and rock bands; pizza is also available.

The classics

Vegas's small classical music scene is
dominated by the **Las Vegas Philharmonic**
(www.lasvegasphilharmonic.com), which
gives roughly two concerts a month at
UNLV's Artemus W Ham Concert Hall
(4505 S Maryland Parkway). Tickets cost
$25-$66, and can be bought from UNLV
on 895 2787. The **Nevada Chamber
Symphony** (433 9280) offers more
populist concerts than the Phil, playing
fairly regularly in the city's library venues
(*see p251*).

Otherwise, the landscape is highlighted
by a couple of festivals. UNLV's annual
Charles Vanda Master Series (895 2787,
http://pac.nevada.edu) brings assorted
notables to town each year from autumn
to spring; recent performers have included
violinist Itzhak Perlman and Samuel
Ramey. In summer, meanwhile, there's
the **Las Vegas Music Festival** (895 3949,
www.lasvegasmusicfestival.org). Run
by George Stelluto and the UNLV music
department, the event brings together
top professional and student talent from
around the city and across the nation.

Jazz & acoustic venues

Citywide venues

Neither jazz nor acoustic music is very well
represented here. Groups such as the **Las
Vegas Jam Band Society** had a scene going
for a while, but host venues close and aren't
readily replaced; much of the jazz offered in
casino lounges, meanwhile, is of the ambient
wine-bar variety. However, keep an eye on local
listings and you may get lucky. In addition
to the venues detailed below, check out the
Bootlegger Bistro (*see p160*), a gem of an
old Vegas haunt whose celebrity karaoke nights
on Monday often live up to their billing.

Acoustic Routes Theatre

*2753 S Highland Drive, at Presidio Avenue,
Off-Strip (385 1232/www.acousticroutes.com).
Bus 204.* **Open** *Shows* 8pm. **Admission** $10-$20.
Credit AmEx, Disc, MC, V.
New to the city, this 148-seat auditorium recently set
up in an office complex not far from the Strip. As the
name suggests, the speciality is acoustic music. Only
a few shows are scheduled each month, though the
owners also occasionally hire Whiskey Pete's in
Primm for larger shows.

Larry's Hideaway

*3369 Thom Boulevard, at N Rancho Drive, North
Las Vegas (645 1899). Bus 106.* **Open** 11am-2am
Mon-Thur, Sun; 11am-5am Fri, Sat. *Shows* 8.30pm
daily. **Admission** free. **No credit cards.**
Larry's Hideaway has been around for years,
and making locals happy for years. In a city that
caters chiefly to youth and secondly to middle age,
longstanding venue Larry's is loved by locals for
staging music tailored to an older set. Music runs
the gamut from polka to country and western.

Pepper's Lounge

*2929 E Desert Inn Road, at McLeod Drive, East
Las Vegas (678 6674). Bus 212.* **Open** 24hrs daily.
Admission free-$10. **Credit** AmEx, DC, Disc, MC, V.
This comfy bar regularly welcomes musicians for
jazz and jam sessions. There've been big band performances and dance lessons here in the past, and
there may well be again.

Pogo's Tavern

*2103 N Decatur Boulevard, at W Lake Mead
Boulevard, Northwest Las Vegas (646 9735). Bus
103, 210.* **Open** 10am-late daily. **Admission** free.
No credit cards.
This lovely, unassuming old local is one of the last
venues where one can regularly catch the music on
which, in a manner of speaking, Vegas was built.
Every Friday at 8pm, an assortment of pensionable
old local jazzers meet up to ramble through standards familiar and obscure, led by eightysomething
drummer and anecdotalist Irv Kluger. It's one of the
most charming nights in town.

Arts & Entertainment

Nightclubs

Expensive and exclusive, but with more variety than ever.

In the late 1990s, Vegas clubbing boasted an international reputation. Party jets on worldwide circuit tours would drop in, disgorging hundreds of 24-hour party people. Casino execs who had added nightclubs now found themselves facing associated challenges – drugs, underage drinking, rowdy behaviour – and, in a dispiritingly familiar way, blamed the music (electronica). Eliminate the clubbers and you eliminate the problems, they said.

True to form, Vegas followed the money, opting for safe pop music mixes and upping the antes. Many of today's most popular clubs pin themselves as 'ultralounges', a marketing term intended to suggest a more intimate, more manageable and, of course, more expensive environment to discourage the 'troublemakers'. Forget bouncing around to Fatboy Slim while nursing a bottle of water; if you're lucky, good-looking, connected or rich enough to blag your way past the velvet rope, you'll more likely be nodding your head to a Lynyrd Skynyrd/Outkast mash-up while sipping $15 Martinis, or worse (*see p242* **Bottling out**).

One positive change is that the number and variety of clubs and bars – not to mention those that straddle the line – is impressive. But the quantity of venues spreads crowds thin: it can be hard to find a vibe that's yours, especially when the music is no longer the thing. However, if you are all about the tunes, check *Las Vegas Weekly* and *CityLife* for information on special DJ nights at chic restaurants or bars.

Some ultralounges open their doors as early as 6pm, but others (and most clubs) open around 10pm and many have no fixed closing hour. For an updated listing of clubs operating, check www.vegas.com or the weeklies, but do

call before setting out: times and prices change often. Except for the (very) occasional special event, clubs refuse entry to under-21s. And here, as elsewhere, groups of women who approach the bouncer and/or host can often jump the queue and avoid cover charges.

Nightclubs

Beach

365 Convention Center Drive, at Paradise Road, East of Strip (731 1925/www.beachlv.com). Bus 108, 112. **Open** *Cabaña & sports bar* 24hrs daily. *Club* 10pm-4am Mon-Thur, Sun; 10pm-6am Fri, Sat. **Admission** $10-$20. **Credit** AmEx, Disc, MC, V. **Map** p319 C5.
Animal House meets *Beach Blanket Bingo* in this two-storey meat-market – big with the convention crowd – where hard-bodied servers of both sexes sport scanty beachwear. There's also a cabaña and sports bar that opens during the day, and occasional comedy events. Dress smart-casual.

Body English

Hard Rock *4455 Paradise Road, at E Harmon Avenue, East of Strip (693 5000/www.hardrock. com). Bus 108.* **Open** 10pm-5am daily. **Admission** $10-$25. **Credit** AmEx, DC, Disc, MC, V. **Hotel** p91. **Map** p320 C7.
In the subterranean space formerly occupied by Baby's, Body English competes with Pure as one of the newest dance clubs in town. Gone is the James Bond/Austin Powers look. Now, it's all *Playboy* mansion meets '60s Brit rock star: red velvet, dark wood and chandeliers. A top choice for visiting celebs.

Drai's After Hours

Barbary Coast *3595 Las Vegas Boulevard South, at E Flamingo Road (737 0555). Bus 202, 301, 302.* **Open** 11pm-8am Wed-Sun. **Admission** $20. **Credit** AmEx, Disc, MC, V. **Hotel** p85. **Map** p320 A7.
Drai's draws those who've had enough of the clubs up the street but not quite enough of them to retire. Its kitschy chic succeeds in making you forget that the sun may rise; deep house DJs enhance the illusion. Prepare to stand in line; tank tops, cut-offs or too-baggy clothing will have you turned away.

Godspeed

Mandalay Bay *House of Blues Foundation Room, 3950 Las Vegas Boulevard South, at E Hacienda Avenue (632 7777/www.hob.com). Bus 105, 301.* **Open** 11pm-5am Mon. **Admission** $30; $10 locals. **Credit** AmEx, Disc, MC, V. **Hotel** p67. **Map** p320 A9.

The best Clubs

For drinking in the view
Mix. *See p242*.

For celeb-spotting
Body English. *See p241*.

For proper club kids
Ice. *See p242*.

The handsome Foundation Room is a members-only affair except on Mondays, when you need just an adult ID. Michael Fuller and guests spin deep house and lounge while hip locals sip pricey Martinis and swan about looking sexy or self-important.

Ice

200 E Harmon Avenue, at Koval Lane, East of Strip (699 9888/www.icelasvegas.com). Bus 201, 202, 213. **Open** hrs vary Fri, Sat. **Admission** $10-$40. **Credit** AmEx, Disc, MC, V. **Map** p320 B7.

This old-school megaclub, run by Birmingham's Godskitchen, isn't in a casino, which gives DJs freedom to spin sounds other than safe remixes. In 2005, Donald Glaude started a Friday-night residency. The modish interior includes a huge dancefloor.

Light

Bellagio *3600 Las Vegas Boulevard South, at W Flamingo Road (693 8300/www.lightlv.com). Bus 202, 301, 302.* **Open** 10.30am-4am Thur-Sun. **Admission** from $20. **Credit** AmEx, DC, Disc, MC, V. **Hotel** p63. **Map** p320 A7.

Though it's upscale and a bit exclusive, Light is jumping most nights. The mix of mash-ups, hip hop, disco, house and R&B is populist: music changes in 20-minute rotations, resulting in a bizarre dancefloor turnover. The booths are essentially on the dancefloor, which can get crowded.

Mix

THEhotel at Mandalay Bay *3950 Las Vegas Boulevard South, at E Hacienda Avenue (632 7777/ www.mandalaybay.com). Bus 105, 301.* **Open** 5pm-2am Mon-Thur, Sun; 5pm-3am Fri, Sat. **Admission** $20-$25. **Credit** AmEx, Disc, MC, V. **Hotel** p106. **Map** p320 A9.

Attached to Alain Ducasse's elaborate rooftop restaurant (*see p147*), Mix has been tagged by locals as the new Ghostbar. Surrounded by 30ft windows (even in the restrooms), Mix offers a top view of the city taken in by a slightly older but no less beautiful crowd. Perks: comfortable VIP seating, a heated balcony, a champagne bar, and a strong food menu.

OPM

Caesars Palace (Forum Shops) *3570 Las Vegas Boulevard South, at W Flamingo Road (369 4998/ www.o-pm.com). Bus 202, 301, 302.* **Open** 10pm-6am Wed-Sun. **Admission** $10-$20. **Credit** AmEx, Disc, MC, V. **Hotel** p65. **Map** p320 A7.

The top floor of Wolfgang Puck's Chinois transforms into a lounge (with small dancefloor) bursting with Asian-inspired sensuality. Most nights, loungecore plays early and predictable house follows, but check the schedule for speciality nights that may include reggae or '80s. Food until 3am.

Plush

JW Marriott Las Vegas/Rampart Casino *221 N Rampart Boulevard, at Summerlin Parkway, Summerlin (992 7970/www.rampartcasino.com). Bus 207.* **Open** midnight Wed; 7pm-2am Thur; 7pm-4am Fri , Sat. **Admission** $10 men; free women. **Credit** AmEx, DC, Disc, MC, V. **Hotel** p100.

Bottling out

Las Vegas's recent ascension as a nightlife destination has been a long time coming. However, with fashion has come a dreadful exclusivity in the form of what bars call 'VIP bottle service': essentially, in order to book a table, you need to pay through the nose for your booze. To locals looking for a fun night out, it's a foolhardy waste: why pay a 1,000 per cent mark-up on a bottle of middle-shelf vodka just to sit behind a velvet rope?

However, to the cash-flush partier who arrives with reels of Rat Pack footage spinning through their head, VIP treatment allows them to be part of the Vegas myth, if only for a moment. There are advantages. A bottle-service reservation means no queues, no snobby stares from the host, and no cover for at least some of the party (all of them, if they're female). Men love VIP seating as a way to attract women; women love it as a way to escape men. But both pay dearly for the privilege: bottles of spirits cost $225 and up, sometimes with a two-bottle minimum.

However, as competition has increased, Vegas is again shifting towards becoming a buyer's market. Locals – unceremoniously dismissed by the hipster hotspots for five years – are once more being courted with free admission, plus comped bottle service on slow nights. Visitors, meanwhile, are discovering the locals' longtime secret: restaurant lounges. Eateries such as **Simon Kitchen & Bar** (*see p152*), **Fiamma** (*see p148*), **Fleur de Lys** (*see p144*) and the **Hookah Lounge** (*see p173*) contain lounges with proper drinks, comfortable seating and a good atmosphere, but no doormen, velvet ropes or bottle service.

Despite being run by the people behind the Key Club in West Hollywood, Summerlin's answer to the ultralounge has failed to draw a consistent crowd. Still, it's a nice place: inside its dark modern interior is an attractive bar, numerous VIP booths and a large dancefloor fronting a stage. The perfect place to disappear and chat up the suburban locals. DJs spin deep house some nights.

Pure

Caesars Palace *3570 Las Vegas Boulevard South, at E Flamingo Road (731 7873/www.caesars.com). Bus 202, 301, 302.* **Open** 10pm-4am Mon, Tue, Fri-Sun. **Admission** $20. **Credit** AmEx, DC, Disc, MC, V. **Hotel** p65. **Map** p320 A7.

At least at the moment, this megaclub is Vegas's most popular nightlife option. The large White Room serves as the main (hip hop/club mix) dance club, while the smaller Red Room is a more intimate (rock) lounge. A massive outdoor patio stares over the Strip to a deep house soundtrack; the Pussycat Dolls Lounge is the city's latest burlesque joint.

Ra

Luxor *3900 Las Vegas Boulevard South, at E Hacienda Avenue (262 4000/www.rathenightclub. com). Bus 105, 301.* **Open** 10pm-6am Wed-Sat. **Admission** $10 men; $5 women. **Credit** AmEx, Disc, MC, V. **Hotel** p80. **Map** p320 A9.

One of the oldest clubs in town (it opened in 1997) Ra is also one of the best for atmosphere, and packs in a Euro crowd. Caged dancers get their groove on in a room that boasts elaborate *Stargate* decor; the occasional theme night keeps things fresh. No-nos: baggy trousers, shorts, jeans, T-shirts and hats.

Rain in the Desert

Palms *4321 W Flamingo Road, at S Valley View Boulevard, West of Strip (992 7970/www.rainatthe palms.com). Bus 104, 202.* **Open** 11pm-4am daily. **Admission** from $20. **Credit** AmEx, Disc, MC, V. **Hotel** p92. **Map** p317 X3.

Once considered *the* place in Vegas to party for the young and beautiful, Rain's raw industrial style feels a bit sparse in the face of the newer plush velvet joints. Still, it remains, first and foremost, a club in which to dance. Water and fire features, sexy go-go gals and a variety of VIP booths and cabañas complete the scene.

Risqué

Paris Las Vegas *3655 Las Vegas Boulevard South, at E Flamingo Road (967 4729/www.parislas vegas.com). Bus 202, 301, 302.* **Open** 10pm-4am Thur-Sun. **Admission** free-$10. **Credit** AmEx, Disc, MC, V. **Hotel** p69. **Map** p320 A7.

Bigger than a bar but smaller than a nightclub, Risqué was the first venue to effectively straddle the line between the two. The New Yorky space boasts semi-private lounges, small balconies overlooking the Strip and too-brief nightly performances by a burlesque-style troupe. There's a nicely sized dancefloor.

Rumjungle

Mandalay Bay *3950 Las Vegas Boulevard South, at E Hacienda Avenue (632 7777/www.mandalay bay.com). Bus 105, 301.* **Open** 10.30pm-2am Mon-Thur, Sun; 10.30pm-4am Fri, Sat. **Admission** $20-$25. **Credit** AmEx, DC, Disc, MC, V. **Hotel** p67. **Map** p320 A9.

This pleasantly hip bar (*see p168*) morphs into Vegas's hottest club after hours. The dancefloor is tiny compared to the rest of the club, but its size does little to quell the spirits of the just-21s who flock here to hear DJs play music that's heavy on the Latin house and hip hop. The admission fee is waived for dinner guests. Dress smart-casual.

Seven/Club Rubber

3724 Las Vegas Boulevard South, at E Harmon Avenue (739 7744/www.sevenlasvegas.com). Bus 301. **Open** $10-$20. **Open** 10pm-4am Fri, Sat. **Credit** AmEx, Disc, MC, V. **Map** p320 A7.

The Strip's sole freestanding nightclub has battled with an identity crisis since opening several years ago; perhaps its 2004 alignment with Club Rubber, the SoCal promoters who sponsor the annual Pimp 'n' Ho Ball, will help. Paul Oakenfold has spun here, though it's more thanks to its location that it's usually busy on the weekends.

Studio 54

MGM Grand *3799 Las Vegas Boulevard South, at E Tropicana Avenue (891 1111/www.mgmgrand. com). Bus 201, 301, 302.* **Open** 10pm-3am Tue-Sat. **Admission** $10-$20 men; free women. **Credit** AmEx, DC, Disc, MC, V. **Hotel** p80. **Map** p320 A8.

Risqué.

A nudge and a wink

Take a drive along Industrial Road or Western Avenue. Think about how many free-spenders it must take to fill the myriad massive strip joints, then picture those same clubs packed to bursting on a Saturday night, which, despite their locations, they invariably are. Now do you see why casino executives are so eager to get into the adult entertainment game? Their first salvo has come with a series of burlesque joints that push the boundaries of what their gaming licences permit (nudity is banned), but rumours suggest they're working behind the scenes to see just how far they can go.

The trend started in 2000 with the Venetian's now-defunct Venus, before Paris Las Vegas's **Risqué** (see p243) began offering turns – a little dancing, a lot of posing – by a modernised burlesque troupe. However, things really began to take off in 2004. TI's sleek lounge **Tangerine** (212 8140) was the first to step out, breaking up DJ sets with winkingly retro bartop striptease (performances hourly 10.45pm-1.45am). It's packed most nights.

Soon after, sophisticated Hollywood club **Forty Deuce** (632 9442, www.fortydeuce.com) arrived in Mandalay Bay to cascades of hype. Sparkly ceilings, big chairs and a purpose-built stage make you feel as if you've stepped into a 1940s Manhattan speakeasy; when the stage rotates to reveal a jazz trio playing away while a Bettie Page lookalike grinds behind a beaded curtain, the illusion is complete. Of course, it's then shattered immediately afterwards, as the jazz trio spins away and 50 Cent booms from the sound system. But the point has been made.

In mid 2005, Caesars' Pure opened the **Pussycat Dolls Lounge** (212 8806, www. caesars.com), the first bar to bear the name of the celeb-laden troupe that kick-started the Hollywood burlesque revival. It's less sexy and more cheesy: indeed, next to Forty Deuce, it's virtually *Crazy Girls*. No matter: it's the next move for which everyone's waiting, the move that tips the Strip from saucy burlesque to something more risky and risqué.

This warehouse-styled reinvention of NYC's famed club has four levels, each with its own dancefloor, seating and bar. The sound and lighting are great, the go-go dancers (men and women) are sexy, and the high-energy mix of music from the 1970s to the present is fun. MGM guests get in for free Tuesdays to Thursdays. No baggy jeans or tennis shoes.

Tabú
MGM Grand *3799 Las Vegas Boulevard South, at E Tropicana Avenue (891 7183/www.mgmgrand. com). Bus 201, 301, 302.* **Open** 8pm-4am Tue-Sun. **Admission** free-$25. **Credit** AmEx, Disc, MC, V. **Hotel** p80. **Map** p320 A8.
The first club to self-consciously bill itself an 'ultralounge' (all the way back in 2003), the MGM's Tabú remains a glamorous fave. It's upscale and tastefully modern in decor (aren't they all?); the scene is hip, laid back and intimate early and on slow nights, but gets cramped thanks to a velvet rope tended with attitude and A-list overloading on weekends. There's no dancefloor.

Teatro
MGM Grand *3799 South Las Vegas Boulevard, at E Tropicana Avenue (285 8844/www.mgmgrand. com). Bus 201, 301, 302.* **Open** 5pm-2am Mon-Thur, Sun; 5pm-4am Fri, Sat. **Admission** free, except special events. **Credit** AmEx, DC, Disc, MC, V. **Hotel** p80. **Map** p320 A8.
Those who favour democratic door policies cheered Teatro's initial upscale Euro-lounge vibe and acid-jazzy soundtrack delivered *sans attitude*. That

lasted about two months: now, the service bar has been converted into a go-go stage and the couch area to a tiny dancefloor, and the clipboard and velvet rope are in full operation. Still fun, but what a shame.

Vivid
Venetian *3355 Las Vegas Boulevard South, at Sands Avenue (992 7970/www.venetian.com). Bus 203, 213, 301, 302.* **Open** 10.30pm-4am Wed-Sun. **Admission** $20. **Credit** AmEx, DC, Disc, MC, V. **Hotel** p73. **Map** p320 A6.
In late 2004, the retro-chic Venus was gutted and transformed into this adult-film-branded lounge. Dark and comfortable with 1970s design touches, it reads like a classic Vegas disco of the polyester era. The much-hyped PG-rated 'holographic projections' of girls feeling up each other are, however, rather overrated. Locals get in free on Thursdays.

Whiskey
Green Valley Ranch *2300 Paseo Verde Parkway, at Green Valley Parkway, Henderson (617 7777/ www.midnightoilbars.com). No bus.* **Open** 6pm-2am Mon-Thur, Sun; 6pm-3am Fri, Sat. **Admission** free. **Credit** AmEx, Disc, MC, V. **Hotel** p104.
Stylish suburban hangouts are becoming the norm as the city spreads, but Rande Gerber's far-flung outpost was one of the first. At weekends, the 1970s mod ski-lodge design is buried under a sea of Seven jeans and hip hop tunes. During warm weather, the bar opens on to Whiskey Beach, an eight-acre pool and outdoor concert venue. Gerber was planning a stylistic overhaul for late 2005.

Sports & Fitness

Blackjack, craps and video poker aren't the only games in town.

Ride 'em, cowboy: the **National Finals Rodeo**. *See p207 and p247.*

Contrary to popular belief, blackjack is not a sport. No, the 100-metre dash from bar to buffet doesn't really count as exercise. 'Work hard, play hard' doesn't have to involve sitting in front of a green baize table at 3am, nursing a beer and a broken bank account. So, blink the neon from your eyes, stumble into the daylight and discover a whole new side to Las Vegas, where the golf courses are verdant, the watersports are dazzling and the ski slopes inviting. All this in the middle of the desert.

If you prefer to watch, Las Vegas can help there. In addition to offering more sports books than anywhere else in the world (*see p56*), the city offers several minor league professional sports teams. Thanks to the transient nature of the population, the casino bosses' hatred of risk (gambling is a sure thing in comparison to running a sports franchise) and league owners' fears about a team becoming contaminated by the local sports book industries, there's no major league team in town. Still, Mayor Oscar Goodman wants one, and he usually gets his way. In other words: watch this space.

NOW... ABOUT THAT WEATHER

Las Vegans calmy offer, 'It's a dry heat.' Visitors reply, 'Christ on a bike, it's like an oven out here.' In summer, overnight lows are in the 80s, while the average daytime temperature is over 100. Drink plenty of water and, if you are doing any kind of outdoor exercise, wear good sunscreen and a hat, drink plenty of water, and do the exercise early in the morning or late at night; midday rounds of golf are for suckers.

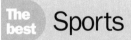

The best Sports

For natural desert scenery
Cycling in Red Rock Canyon. *See p247.*

For unnatural desert scenery
A round at **Desert Pines**. *See p248.*

For implausible near-desert snow
Skiing on Mount Charleston. *See p250.*

Making the bigs

Las Vegas's quest to upgrade its image from dirt patch with slots to world-class destination has been phenomenally successful. Some think, though, that until it attracts a big sports franchise, Sin City will remain a minor league town. With a showgirl on each arm, Mayor Oscar Goodman approached Major League Baseball about the possibility of moving the Montreal Expos to town in 2005, but baseball chose the moral quagmire of the nation's capital over Vegas. Back, then, to the drawing board: but which sport best fits the Las Vegas image?

THE SPORT	CAN YOU PLAY INSIDE?	IS IT SLEAZY ENOUGH?	WHAT ABOUT A MASCOT?	SO, WOULD IT FIT IN VEGAS?
National Football League (NFL)	Indoors is fine. Still, so much for the NFL's trademark postseason battles in the snow.	The bosomy cheerleaders and touchdown dances are tacky, but football still insists it's a serious sport.	Rowdy, a frat boy who gropes cheerleaders and makes lewd gestures at the crowd. Can be played by any male by the pool at the Palms.	Perhaps, though the obnoxious showmanship and high scoring of arena football are a better match.
Major League Baseball (MLB)	You can, but if that's what people wanted, the Expos would have stayed in Montreal.	If you ignore the steroids, the brawls and the jock-scratching, it's downright classy.	Dino, a tuxedoed drunk who, after every home run, dives headfirst into a giant Martini.	No. It's too slow for a city that considers nude girls in feathered headdresses quaint.
National Hockey League (NHL)	You'd better. The rink wouldn't last three minutes in the desert.	Not really. Still, the Eastern European players may lose control in a town of such unbridled capitalism.	Marcel, a broken-nosed Cirque du Soleil export who mimes classic brawls during breaks in the action.	The NHL might be as desperate for Las Vegas's cash as the city is for respect.
National Basketball Association (NBA)	You have to. The only people who play outdoors are kids at poor schools.	Scantily-clad dancers, free-spending loudmouths… It's either the NBA or a night at the Hard Rock.	Strippy, a topless dancer with a basketball for a head who gives lap dances to the referees during time outs.	It's the perfect match for Las Vegas. In fact, the city might grow to look dignified by comparison.

Spectator sports

American football

The **UNLV** team plays under coach Mike Sanford at **Sam Boyd Stadium** (Boulder Highway & Russell Road, 739 3269, http://unlv rebels.collegesports.com) from September to December. Tickets cost from $12 to $20; there are usually plenty of seats available. Sam Boyd also hosts the Las Vegas Bowl, which features the best of the Mountain West Conference.

The Arena Football League found a home in Las Vegas during 2002, and the **Las Vegas Gladiators** won a number of fans for their fast-paced, high-flying brand of football. Games are played on a shortened field in UNLV's **Thomas & Mack Center** (4505 S Maryland Parkway, at E Tropicana Avenue, 895 2787, www.thomasandmack.com) from February to May; tickets cost $6-$60 (739 3267, www. lvgladiators.com). From 2005 to 2007, the Gladiators' home field will also host the **Arena Bowl**, the AFL's championship game.

Baseball

The **Las Vegas 51s**, the AAA team of the Los Angeles Dodgers, play at **Cashman Field** (850 Las Vegas Boulevard North, at Washington Avenue) from April to September. The 12,000-seat stadium is rarely packed, though the 51s are among the most consistently successful teams in the Pacific Coast League. Call 386 7200 for tickets ($7-$12), or see www.lv51s.com. The ballpark opens for business in late February or early March with an exhibition game featuring selected major league stars.

Basketball

With coach Lon Kruger on the bench, look for UNLV's **Runnin' Rebels** men's basketball team eventually to make as many headlines as they did when they won the NCAA title in 1990. Games are played at the **Thomas & Mack Center** (4505 S Maryland Parkway, 739 3267, http://unlvrebels.collegesports.com) from November to May. In October, NBA teams may play exhibitions, but tickets go quickly.

UNLV's women's basketball team, the **Lady Rebels**, play at the **Cox Pavilion** (739 3269, http://unlvrebels.collegesports.com), next door to the Thomas & Mack. The team has been posting as many wins as the men of late; at $4, a game is one of the cheapest tickets in town.

Boxing

No city is as closely tied to boxing as Las Vegas. It's a relationship that makes perfect sense: both the sport and the city love winners and detest losers; both draw the richest of the rich and the poorest of the poor; and both present action that has a reputation for both excitement and seediness. Among the hotels used regularly for big bouts are **Mandalay Bay** (which also hosts numerous 'ultimate fighting' events; *see p67*), the **MGM Grand** (*see p80*) and **Caesars Palace** (*see p65*). Call each hotel or Ticketmaster (474 4000) ahead of the fight for tickets, which sell out quickly and can cost several thousand dollars apiece.

Golf

Each October the PGA Tour shows up in Las Vegas for the **PGA Michelin Championship** (www.pgatour.com), played at the TPC at Summerlin and the TPC at The Canyons. Daily tickets cost $15-$20; call 242 3000 to buy. The women's game returned to Las Vegas in 2003, with the **LPGA Takefuji Classic**, held at the Las Vegas Country Club ($15, 898 4653, www.lpgatakefujiclassic.com).

Ice hockey

The **Las Vegas Wranglers** (471 7825, www.lasvegaswranglers.com) take to the ice for 36 games each autumn at the 7,000-seat **Orleans Arena**. The squad, which competes in the West Division of the National Conference, is a feeder club for the NHL's Calgary Flames, though with the NHL Lockout in 2004/05, there hasn't been much feeding of late. Tickets cost $7 to $30.

Motor racing

The vast **Las Vegas Motor Speedway** complex (7000 Las Vegas Boulevard North, 644 4444, www.lvms.com) hosts the **Las Vegas 400** (*see p202*), a Winston Cup event in March, and an **NHRA drag racing** event in April. Tickets range from $16 to $140.

Rodeo

Held every December, the **National Finals Rodeo** (*see p207*) is the sport's most prestigious event. For the **Professional Bull Riders Tour**, *see p206*.

Active sports

Bowling

A few casinos have huge, 24-hour alleys, chief among them **Sam's Town** (56 lanes; *see p103*). There are also alleys at the **Gold Coast** (72 lanes; *see p102*), the **Orleans** (70 lanes; *see p102*) and **Santa Fe Station** (60 lanes; *see p105*). But call first: the popularity of local bowling leagues can put paid to an impromptu evening.

Bungee jumping

Don't jump! But if you insist, **AJ Hackett** (at Circus Circus, 385 4321, www.aj-hackett.com) will at least attach an elastic cord to you, and leave a net 210ft (64m) below. The first jump costs between $59 and $84 (and earns you a T-shirt and a certificate). Should you develop a taste for it, subsequent plunges are a mere $29.

Cycling

Some of the nation's best mountain bike single-tracks are within driving distance of Las Vegas, but only the most seasoned urban cyclists think about cycling in the central of the city (*see p292*). Rather, head west to **Escape Adventures** (Unit 101, 8221 W Charleston Boulevard, 596 2953, www.escapeadventures.com). The company conducts road and off-road

Arts & Entertainment

tours in **Red Rock Canyon National Conservation Area** (*see p263*), as well as further afield in the national parks of Utah, Arizona and California, but will also provide bikes, maps and supplies if you'd rather go it alone. Bike hire is from $28/day.

Aside from Red Rock, Escape is also within reach of the wide, marked bike lanes in the planned town of **Summerlin**, while Pueblo Park, at the north end of Rampart Boulevard, has several miles of paved paths that are separated from the traffic. Other popular routes include the eight-mile off-road **Cottonwood Valley Loop** near Red Rock: head west from town on Highway 160 and look for a dirt road six miles past the junction with Highway 159. The **River Mountain Peak** is a ten-mile route between Las Vegas and Henderson. To get to the head of the trail, drive along I-93/95 to Equestrian Drive, turning east.

An unofficial mountain bike trail sits on the north-west corner of Tropicana Avenue and Decatur Boulevard. This challenging, well-worn trail runs through one of the few undeveloped parcels of land in town: power your bike up and down steep sandstone formations and across a natural wash. Though used often by local gearheads, it's unsanctioned, so bike safely.

Fishing

There's fishing year-round at **Lake Mead** (*see p261*); it's stocked with half a million rainbow trout annually, and there are also plenty of black and striped bass. Head for the upper Overton Arm of the lake for crappie, bluegill and catfish. Further south, **Lake Mohave** (*see p261*) is good for rainbow trout, especially in its upper reaches in Black Canyon and at the Willow Beach south of the Hoover Dam. Katharine Landing, a few miles north of Davis Dam on the Arizona side, is the best place from which to plunder the lake's huge striped bass. You can fish in the city at **Lorenzi Park** (Rancho Drive, at Washington Avenue), **Sunset Park** (Sunset Road, at Eastern Avenue) and **Floyd Lamb State Park** (*see p265*).

To fish from any Nevada shore, you'll need a Nevada fishing licence ($18 a day, plus $7 per extra day). To fish from a boat on Lake Mead, you'll need a licence and a special-use stamp from Arizona (the two states share jurisdiction over the lake). An extra stamp is also required for trout fishing. For details on all aspects of fishing in Nevada, contact the **Nevada Division of Wildlife** (486 5127, www.ndow.org), check at a ranger station for the current hot spots or consult **Fish Incorporated** (565 8396, www.fish incorporated.com).

Golf

Las Vegas has about half the golf courses it needs to meet demand; call several weeks ahead and show up with a three-figure sum – less if you can bear the stifling heat on summer afternoons – if you want to play any of the better ones. **Las Vegas Preferred Tee-Times** (1-877 255 7277, www.lvptt.com) makes reservations at a number of area courses, most of which open 7am to dusk.

Badlands

9119 Alta Drive, at S Rampart Boulevard, Northwest Las Vegas (382 4653/www.badlandsgc.com). Bus 211. **Green fees** *Sept-May* $135-$190; $80-$95 twilight. *June-Aug* $75-$95; $50-$55 twilight. **Credit** AmEx, Disc, MC, V.
Whichever way you piece together these three nine-hole layouts, designed by Johnny Miller, they'll add up to one of the most unforgiving tracks in town.

Bali Hai Golf Club

5160 Las Vegas Boulevard South, at W Russell Road (450 8000/www.waltersgolf.com). Bus 301. **Green fees** *Sept-May* $245-$295; $169-$199 twilight. *June-Aug* $175-$195; $105-$125 twilight. **Credit** AmEx, Disc, MC, V. **Map** p320 A9.
This challenging 7,002-yard, par-72 track, the only one on Las Vegas Boulevard, features seven acres of water, 2,500 palm trees, Augusta white sand and more than 100,000 tropical plants.

Craig Ranch Golf Course

628 W Craig Road, between N Martin Luther King Boulevard & Losee Road, North Las Vegas (642 9700). No bus. **Green fees** $19; $5 juniors. **No credit cards.**
The highlights of this locals' favourite are the thousands of towering pine trees lining the fairways and the insanely cheap green fees. You're also likely to see an abundance of wildlife, including rabbits and roadrunners.

Desert Pines Golf Club

3415 E Bonanza Road, at N Pecos Road, East Las Vegas (366 1616/www.waltersgolf.com). Bus 111, 215. **Green fees** *Sept-May* $135-$175; $50-$100 twilight. *June-Aug* $80-$89; $40-$45 twilight. **Credit** AmEx, MC, V. **Map** p317 Z1.
Voted one of the best public courses in the US by *Golf Digest*, this tight, 6,810-yard, par-71 layout has narrow, tree-lined fairways and nine holes on water. The practice facility is the best in Las Vegas.

Las Vegas Golf Club

4300 W Washington Avenue, between N Decatur Boulevard & N Valley View Boulevard, North Las Vegas (646 3003/www.americangolf.com). Bus 103, 208. **Green fees** vary. **Credit** AmEx, Disc, MC, V.
This 6,319-yard, par-72 public course has always been popular, but recent improvements have made it play better than ever. Book ahead.

Home: the 18th at **Bali Hai**. *See p248*.

Legacy Golf Club

130 Par Excellence Drive, at Silver Springs Parkway, Henderson (897 2187/www.thelegacygc.com). **Green fees** *Sept-May* $100-$155; $70-$75 twilight. *June-Aug* call for details. **Credit** AmEx, DC, Disc, MC, V.
This handsome, 7,233-yard, par-72 course is host each year to US Open qualifying. It's also a popular choice among the public.

TPC at The Canyons

9851 Canyon Run Drive, at Town Center Drive (256 2500/www.tpc.com). **Green fees** *Sept-May* $205-$260; $140-$150 twilight. *June-Aug* $125-$150; $80 twilight. **Credit** AmEx, DC, Disc, MC, V.
One of two courses to host the PGA Michelin Championship, this 6,772-yard layout was co-designed by Bobby Weed and Ray Floyd.

Gyms & sports centres

Gold's Gym

Gold's Plaza, 3750 E Flamingo Road, at Sandhill Road, East Las Vegas (451 4222/www.goldsgym.com). Bus 202. **Open** 24hrs daily. **Rates** $15/day; $35/wk. **Credit** AmEx, Disc, MC, V. **Map** p311 Z3.
Touted as a no-frills gym, Gold's offers all the aerobics classes, free weights, weight machines and CV equipment an exercise buff could handle.
Other locations: throughout the city.

Las Vegas Athletic Club

2655 S Maryland Parkway, at Karen Avenue, East Las Vegas (734 5822/www.lvac.com). Bus 109. **Open** 24hrs daily. **Rates** $15/day; $35/wk. **Credit** AmEx, Disc, MC, V. **Map** p311 Y2.

All five Vegas locations have pools, saunas, jacuzzis, Nautilus, free weights and more than 200 weekly aerobics classes. This is the only 24-hour branch.
Other locations: throughout the city.

24 Hour Fitness

2605 S Eastern Avenue, at E Sahara Avenue, East Las Vegas (641 2222/www.24hourfitness.com). Bus 110, 204. **Open** 24hrs daily. **Rates** $15/day. **Credit** AmEx, Disc, MC, V. **Map** p311 Z2.
In addition to gym facilities, 24 Hour has a kids' club and rock climbing. The larger branches offer pools and basketball courts (check the website for details).
Other locations: throughout the city.

Hiking

The **Sierra Club** (363 3267, www.sierraclub.com), the grandaddy of environmental outfits, organises regular hikes – open to non-members – around Red Rock Canyon, Mount Charleston and the Lake Mead area. For information on the best hiking areas near Vegas, *see pp260-265*.

Horse riding

How better to see Red Rock Canyon than from the back of a horse? **Cowboy Trail Rides** (387 2457, www.cowboytrailrides.com) will saddle you up. The most popular excursion is the Sunset BBQ trip ($139). Rides are accompanied by a guide; first-timers are welcome. Booking is advisable for all tours and required for several.

Hunting & shooting

Call the **Nevada Division of Wildlife** (486 5127, www.ndow.org) for information on hunting dove, quail and waterfowl in the Lake Mead area. There's limited deer-hunting, and special seasons are scheduled for elk, antelope and bighorn sheep. A hunting licence for non-residents is $142.

The **American Shooters Supply & Gun Club** (3440 Arville Street, between W Desert Inn Road & Spring Mountain Road, 362 1223, www.americanshooters.com) has the only 50-yard (45-metre) indoor range in Las Vegas.

Ice skating

Outside, it's well over 100°, the sun is a ball of fire and even the insects are taking a siesta. Inside, you're trying out your double axles and triple salcos; or, at least, you are if you're at the **Sobe Ice Arena** at **Fiesta Rancho** (*see p103*; 2400 N Rancho Drive, between Lake Mead Boulevard & Carey Avenue, 647 7465, www.lvskating.com). Call to check skating times, as they vary with the Wranglers' ice-hockey schedule (*see p247*).

Pool & billiards

Pink E's

3695 W Flamingo Road, at S Valley View Boulevard, West of Strip (252 4666). Bus 202. **Open** 24hrs daily. **Cost** free-$3. **Credit** AmEx, MC, V. **Map** p311 X3.
A bright, colourful (the playing surfaces are pink) spot with 50 tables. No under-21s; decent food.

Rafting

Black Canyon River Raft Tours (294 1414, www.blackcanyonadventures.com) will take you on one-day guided raft trips along the Colorado River, from just below the Hoover Dam to Willow Beach, through a waterfall and hot springs, for $72.95 per person, or $105.95 with hotel pick-up. Similar trips are offered by **Down River Outfitters** (1-800 748 3702, 293 1190, www.downriveroutfitters.com).

Rock climbing

The rock-climbing opportunities are one of the area's least publicised attractions. In particular, **Red Rock Canyon** (*see p263*) offers some of the best year-round climbing in the US. The best guide is *Rock Climbing Red Rocks* by Todd Swain (Falcon Press, $30). Call the visitors' centre (363 1921) for information on regulations and stop at **Desert Rock Sports** (*see p200*) for gear and some practice on the indoor wall. You can also practise at the **Nevada Climbing Centers** (Suite 4, 3065 E Patrick Lane, 363 4533), **GameWorks** (*see p116*) and Circus Circus's **Adventuredome** (*see p121*).

Scuba & skin diving

Scuba divers should head to **Lake Mead** (*see p261*), where visibility averages 30 feet and can reach double that in winter. There are some unusual sights, including boat wrecks and an asphalt factory. The most popular diving area is **Scuba Park**, adjacent to Lake Mead Marina. You can rent equipment for around $35 a day from **American Cactus Divers** (3985 E Sunset Road, Henderson, 433 3483, www. americancactusdivers.com), the **Blue Seas Scuba Center** (4661 Spring Mountain Road, Southwest Las Vegas, 367 2822) and **Desert Divers Supply** (5720 E Charleston Boulevard, East Las Vegas, 438 1000).

Snow sports

It might feel odd packing skis for the desert, but there are two skiing areas close to the city. In good years, the season runs from November until April. Just 47 miles away, the **Las Vegas**

Ski & Snowboard Resort (645 2754, snow conditions 593 9500, www.skilasvegas.com) at Lee Canyon on Mount Charleston (*see p264*) offers action for all abilities, and has a half-pipe and terrain park. Lift passes cost $28 per day; a complete gear package will cost another $30. In season, the park is open 10am-4pm.

A three-hour drive from Vegas on I-15 and SR 145 is the **Brian Head Ski Resort** in Utah (454 7669, www.brianhead.com), which offers terrific skiing on two mountains and plenty of accommodation. Full-day lift passes are $39 or $46 during holidays.

Spas & health clubs

See p194 **Star spas**.

Swimming

Almost every hotel and motel in Las Vegas has a pool, some with elaborate waterfalls, slides and other features. All are for hotel guests only (though the Hard Rock opens its pool on Sundays for Rehab, a poolside party for anyone with the cash and the body), but some are worth a peek, even if you're not allowed to swim; among the poshest are at **Caesars Palace** (*see p65*), the vast **MGM Grand** (*see p80*), the **Rio** (with a beach for volleyball; *see p93*) and **Mandalay Bay** (*see p67*). Sadly, the majority of pools close at twilight: casino bosses would rather have their guests lounging in the casino than poolside. At the **Tropicana** (*see p90*), however, you can combine the two and lose your money at a swim-up blackjack table.

Tennis

Some hotels have courts that are open to the public, though guests are given priority. These include **Bally's** (ten courts, six lighted; *see p76*), the **Flamingo** (four lighted courts; *see p77*) and the **Monte Carlo** (four lighted courts; *see p82*). You can also play for $5 on **UNLV**'s 12 lighted courts (4505 S Maryland Parkway, 895 4489), for free at **Paradise Park** (4770 S Harrison Drive, 455 7513), or for $3/hr during the day or $5/hr after sundown at **Sunset Park** (2601 E Sunset Road, 260 9803). Facilities are also available at some local sports centres.

Water-skiing

Expansive **Lake Mead** (*see p261*) offers great water-skiing opportunities. **Tom's Water Sports** at Lake Mead Marina (558 0678, www.tomswatersports.com) rents equipment, organises trips to Tahoe and offers lessons in water-skiing, tubing and wakeboarding.

Theatre & Dance

There's plenty of drama away from the Strip.

It's rare to find the words 'quality theatre' and 'Las Vegas' in the same sentence. Few have ever bothered to pitch plays here with a storyline, decent actors or a solid two-act structure. However, things are changing. The big rooms are a popular stop for roadshows such as *Les Misérables*. And Wynn Las Vegas has plans to bring Tony-winning musical *Avenue Q* to town in late 2005, to compete against West End or Broadway hits such as *Hairspray* (at the Luxor) and *Mamma Mia* (at Mandalay Bay).

There's local theatrical talent here, too. The veteran **Rainbow Company Children's Theatre** (*see p227*) has been creating fine productions for three decades, and the quality of work at the various **UNLV** theatres is high. These venues have now been joined by upstart companies such as **SEAT** and the **Cockroach Theatre**, whose higher profiles are a reflection of the city's growing arts subculture. The dance scene, sadly, is less advanced.

For information, check the *Las Vegas Weekly* or *CityLife*, or Friday's *Las Vegas Review-Journal*. For casino shows, *see pp212-223*.

VENUES

The library district offers three relatively new spaces, all with fine sightlines and acoustics. The **Summerlin Library & Performing Arts Center Theatre** (1771 Inner Circle Drive, Northwest Las Vegas, 507 3860) and the **West Las Vegas Library Theatre** (951 W Lake Mead Boulevard, North Las Vegas, 507 3980) are both proscenium stages seating around 300 capacities, while the **Clark County Library Theatre** (1401 E Flamingo Road, East of Strip, 507 3400) is a 400-seater with a thrust stage. For details, see www.lvccld.org.

UNLV (*see p252*) has three good venues. Major shows are held in the 550-seat **Judy Bayley Theatre**, with smaller productions staged in the **Paul C Harris Theatre** and the intimate **Black Box** used for workshop-style and student-produced shows. Across from the JBT, UNLV's **Artemus W Ham Concert Hall** (*see p236*) hosts anything from touring lecturers to ballet companies. Other venues range in size from the small **Reed Whipple Cultural Center** (*see p230*), used regularly by local companies; on the other are the 7,000-seat theatre at the **Aladdin/Planet Hollywood** (*see p237*) and the huge **Orleans Arena** (*see p102*), which host blockbuster events.

Theatre companies

Asylum Theatre

Winchester Cultural Center, 3130 S McLeod Drive, at Desert Inn Road (604 3417/www.asylumtheatre.org). Bus 112. **Tickets** $7.50-$12.50. **No credit cards**. Asylum make their mission the staging both of full productions and readings of new plays. In the past, they've performed work by Davey Marlin-Jones, Rich Orloff and Evan Guilford-Blake.

Cockroach Theatre

743 3839/www.cockroachtheatre.com. Like its namesake, this risk-taking acting troupe is dedicated to survival. And also like the insect, the group crops up all over the Las Vegas valley. Shows, staged roughly monthly, are a mix of new, obscure and forgotten works; check online for details.

Las Vegas Academy

315 S 7th Street, at Bridger Avenue, Downtown (799 7874/www.lvacademytheatre.org). Bus 107, 301, 302. **Tickets** vary. **No credit cards**. **Map** p318 D2. Las Vegas's oldest secondary school was threatened in the 1990s with destruction, but was instead converted to a public magnet school for performing arts and international studies. The Downtown campus has earned accolades for its impressive shows (such as *Les Miserables*); the school opens a sparkling new state-of-the-art theatre in fall 2005.

Las Vegas Little Theatre

Schiff City, 3920 Schiff Drive, at Spring Mountain Road & S Valley View Boulevard, Southwest Las Vegas (362 7996/www.lvlt.org). Bus 104, 203. **Tickets** $10-$18. **Credit** (online only) AmEx, MC, V. Vegas's pre-eminent community theatre company recently relocated to new digs, a level of security that means it can afford to mix riskier productions in with popular fare. The edgier Insomniac Project

The best Theatre

For the family
Super Summer Theatre. *See p252*.

For the student
UNLV. *See p252*.

For the cultural adventurer
SEAT. *See p252*.

Nevada Ballet Theatre.

features midnight performances of plays that don't fit into the regular programme. The space also plays host to various scene nights and workshops.

Nevada Theatre Company

873 0191/www.nevadatheatreco.org.

The NTC, founded in 1998, has created a buzz for its productions of numerous children's plays as well as more adult fare. Some shows tour outside Las Vegas.

New City Theatre

2900 E Patrick Lane, at McLeod Drive, Southeast Las Vegas (795 0487/www.newcitytheatre.com). Bus 110. **Tickets** *vary.* **Credit** *call for details.*

This new theatre shut after only a handful of badly received productions in early 2003; when it reopened nine months later, allegations about it in the local press caused no little controversy. It's still going, though, with a range of classes and productions.

SEAT (Social Experimentation & Absurd Theatre)

Arts Factory, 103 E Charleston Boulevard, at S Casino Center Boulevard, Downtown (736 4313/ www.godsexandbowling.com/seat.html). Bus 108, 206. **Tickets** *$10.* **Credit** *MC, V.* **Map** *p319 C3.*

This edgy company is the liveliest in Las Vegas: they've had run-ins with the police for producing *Equus*, helped the local burlesque revival and incorporated video into their more forward-thinking pieces. Shows play Tue-Sat at 8pm and 10pm, with a special event at every First Friday (*see p204*).

Super Summer Theatre

Spring Mountain Ranch State Park, Red Rock Canyon (594 7529/www.supersummertheatre.com). No bus. **Tickets** *$7-$10.* **No credit cards.**

High-quality but low-cost musicals in a beautiful open-air setting. Since there are no set seats (chairs can be rented), get there early; gates open at 6pm, with curtain-up two hours later. Bring a picnic (and a jacket). The season runs June to August.

UNLV Department of Theatre

4505 S Maryland Parkway, between E Flamingo Road & E Tropicana Avenue, University District (895 2787/www.unlv.edu/colleges/fine_arts/theatre). Bus 109, 201, 213. **Tickets** *$5-$25.* **Credit** *AmEx, Disc, MC, V.* **Map** *p317 Y3.*

UNLV presents classic drama and recent musicals during spring and autumn in its Judy Bayley Theatre. The programme is run with the Nevada Conservatory Theatre, who bring professionals from all over the world to work with the classes. The more interesting productions are often found in the Black Box, where the MFA stage-writing programme workshops plays by students and faculty. The annual series of student one-act plays in spring and autumn is usually good for a gem or two.

Dance companies

Nevada Ballet Theatre

243 2623/www.nevadaballet.com.

Associated with UNLV, the Nevada Ballet Theatre is the city's only fully professional ballet company and tends towards classical works and certified crowd-pleasers. The majority of shows are held at UNLV's Judy Bayley Theatre (for address and box office, *see below*; tickets $25-$65), though in 2004, their annual production of *The Nutcracker* was staged in the Samba Theatre at the Rio.

UNLV Dance Theatre

4505 S Maryland Parkway, between E Flamingo Road & E Tropicana Avenue, University District (895 2787/www.unlv.edu/colleges/fine_arts/dance). Bus 109, 201, 213. **Tickets** *free-$25.* **Credit** *AmEx, Disc, MC, V.* **Map** *p317 Y3.*

UNLV's dance programming takes in performances by faculty, students and guest artists. Both classical ballet and modern work are well represented in its productions, generally held at the Artemus W Ham Concert Hall or the Judy Bayley Theatre.

Weddings

The permanent, the passing and the priceless.

In 1912, California passed a Gin Law requiring couples to wait for three days after acquiring a marriage licence before exchanging vows. The motive, as the nickname suggests, was to discourage intoxicated lovers from marrying when too mashed to make a sound decision. Nevada had no such hang-ups, welcoming couples, both drunk and sober, who wanted to get married in double-quick time. And in 1931, there was more progress of sorts: not only was gambling legalised, but the divorce laws were relaxed. You could – indeed, still can – divorce after residing in the state for just six weeks (which led to another cottage industry, the divorce ranch) and then remarry immediately.

Nevada came into its own during World War II, when large numbers of GIs wanted quick, effortless weddings before being stationed abroad. The city's marriage industry thrived, hitting its stride in the 1950s when celebrities started dropping by for high-profile hook-ups. Stars such as Rita Hayworth, Kirk Douglas, Paul Newman (with Joanne Woodward) and Frank Sinatra (with Mia Farrow) all took their vows in Vegas. The industry has barely paused for breath since then. Around 120,000 marriage licences are issued in Las Vegas each year, a figure that equates to around 330 every day. The flipside? In the same 12 months, some 12,000 divorces are also processed.

Well, marriage always was a gamble...

BEFORE YOU GET HITCHED

There are myriad ways to get spliced in Las Vegas, but whether you want the full glory-be or a quickie-drive-thru ceremony, the basics remain the same. Both bride and groom must appear at the Clark County **Marriage Bureau** (first floor, 200 S 3rd Street, 455 4415, www.co.clark.nv.us, open 8am-midnight Mon-Fri, 24hrs Sat & Sun) with $55 cash and a form of picture ID (a passport or photo driving licence will do). Proof of age is required for partners under 21; parental consent and a court order is necessary for would-be newlyweds under the age of 18. The licence is good for one year from the date of issue. No waiting periods or blood tests are necessary, but those wanting to marry their second cousin or cousin of half-blood should look elsewhere. There goes the last leg of the Confederacy.

Couples from outside the US who get spliced here may have to deal with extra paperwork to ensure the marriage is recognised in their home countries. Most countries want a certified copy of the certificate ($10 from the Marriage Bureau) and an Apostille of Certification ($20) from the Nevada Secretary of State, which can be sent directly to your home government.

Where to wed

If a quick service with the **Commissioner of Civil Marriages** will suffice, $50 is all you need. It's a short walk from the Marriage Bureau to the Office of Civil Marriages, Clark County Court House at 309 S 3rd Street (455 3156, then '5' for Marriage Bureau, '4' for Civil Marriages; open 8am-10pm daily). One witness is required by law; bring your own if you don't want to wait. No appointment is necessary. However, chances are you didn't fly or drive all the way here to get married in such unremarkable circumstances. Well, you're in luck: Vegas offers memorable weddings of every possible stripe and to suit every budget.

Car trouble

Two recently acquainted people stumble down Las Vegas Boulevard with a yard of Margarita in one hand and ads for in-room strippers in the other. Making out under the Eiffel Tower, inspiration strikes. The pair decide, after craps and blackjack and maybe another drink, to go full-on Vegas (baby!) and get hitched. A short ride to the Marriage Bureau ensues, followed by the filling out of applications, each party glancing over the other's shoulder to learn their partner's surname.

Handing back their golf pencils and turning in their forms, they glance around the tiny office and privately make bets as to which of the other swaying couples will 'make it'. The all-night clerk doesn't bother to check a most-wanted list for bicoastal bigamist killers stopping off from the desert leg of a cross-country rampage and, instead, turns the form into a licence.

So, where to go? How about the famous Little Church of the West? Perhaps one of the chapels whose signage inadvertently advertises random celebrity couplings, such as Joan Collins and Michael Jordan? Or maybe they could get married by Elvis! Yes! But, dammit, you have to book an Elvis in advance, and time seems short. Then, somehow, one of them remembers you can get married in Vegas without even leaving your car. You drive up, slap your vehicle into park, roll down the window and greet an internet-ordained minister leaning out to exchange electroplated wedding bands for cash.

The ceremony, long on brevity and short on belief structures, is pleasant enough but unlikely to be remembered in its entirety. A scant few items survive the haze: the wedding photo (the happy couple show off their rings from the front seat), a goth CD from an underground Arizona band that they used in place of a wedding march and a congratulatory gift pack from the chapel containing, among other things, a heart-shaped key ring and coupons for deodorant.

Las Vegas is beautiful in the morning, but with daylight comes sobriety, and a reminder that night is only night but daytime is Real Life. The legally bound strangers emerge from a Downtown motel, dry-mouthed and slightly confused, and take a long look at each other. Or a short one. Back in their respective home towns, bride and groom initiate divorce proceedings, surprised and disappointed to learn that there isn't a drive-thru for that, too, and, upon imparting their now-famous-among-friends Vegas story, are often asked: 'So, did you get fries with that?'

The most basic chapel services, offered mostly at the myriad chapels near Downtown, cost around $100, which may include pre-recorded music (you can often supply your own). Add photos (six to 12 prints), a video recording and a limousine, and the cost rises to nearer $300. Some places include the limo for a little less, but it will only take you to and from the hotel or marriage bureau and the chapel. Expect to pay a minimum of $100 to rent a gown, $75 to rent a tuxedo and $35 for a bouquet.

Note that most chapels reserve the right to provide all professional services (photos, flowers, video recording). All chapels provide a photographer, but he or she may keep the negatives in the hope that you'll return to buy more prints. You may even get a letter to remind you of this on your first anniversary. There are additional costs. The minister is rarely an employee of the chapel, so a $50-$75 'donation' for his services is expected on top of the chapel fee – check packages to see if this is covered – and a similar tip should be given to the driver of your limo. All chapel packages are subject to sales tax of 7.25 per cent.

With upwards of 30 freestanding chapels in the city, and a good number of the major casino resorts offering marriages, competition is fierce. So fierce, indeed, that it's led to some unsavoury behaviour by a few chapel owners. One way of reducing the mayhem is by making advance reservations and/or utilising the professional consultants that come as a part of most package deals struck with the casino resorts. Casinos can also accommodate wedding parties both large or small, have numerous reception options and provide the hallmark 24-hour debauchery that one travels to Las Vegas to enjoy. The drawback: the resorts spend hours determining the most effective ways to part patrons and their money, and getting married in one of them can be extremely costly.

If it's classic Vegas kitsch you want, choices abound. Shop carefully, check all prices twice and, if you go for a walk-in, look at the floor first: if it's freshly vacuumed (not all are), you've probably done all right. Though some are deceptive, chapel websites do offer some information on what's on offer, though you'll likely have to call for pricing information.

Independent chapels

A Christian Pastor 2U

(378 7000/641 9174/www.spiritofprophecy.org).
As well as performing full-dress dramatisations of the Sermon on the Mount, these guys will come to you wherever you want to take your vows: Red Rock, Valley of Fire, Lake Mead, even jetskiing.

Graceland Wedding Chapel

619 Las Vegas Boulevard South, at E Bonneville Avenue (1-800 824 5732/382 0091/www.graceland chapel.com). Bus 301. **Open** 9am-9pm Mon-Thur, Sun; 9am-midnight Fri, Sat. **Credit** AmEx, Disc, MC, V. **Map** p318 C2.
Thompson Twins Tom Bailey and Alannah Currie are among the celebs who've married at this well kept chapel; so much for the town's laws on not marrying into the family. There's a well-landscaped outdoor area and quaint indoor chapel. Packages range from $55 to $595 for the King's Elite. An Elvis impersonator can be supplied for $145.

Hearts & Roses Wedding Chapel

Liberace Plaza, 1775 E Tropicana Avenue, at Spencer Street (1-800 293 9212/451 0008/www. heartsandroseswedding chapel.com). Bus 201. **Open** 10am-6pm Mon-Sat; by appointment Sun. **Credit** AmEx, Disc, MC, V. **Map** p317 Y3.
Get married at the Liberace Museum! Prices range from $99 and $2,500.

Hey, little sister, what have you done?

Hitching Post Wedding Chapel

1737 Las Vegas Boulevard South, between S Main Street & E St Louis Avenue (1-888 540 5060/387 5080/www.hitchingpostweddingchapel.com). Bus 301. **Open** 24 hours by appointment. **Credit** AmEx, Disc, MC, V. **Map** p319 C4.
In business since 1926, the Hitching Post is the oldest chapel in Vegas. Packages start with the $48 I Do, I Do ceremony, but for $250, you can have an Elvis impersonator witness your wedding; for $420, the 'King' will walk the bride down the aisle.

A Hollywood Wedding

2207 Las Vegas Boulevard South, at E Sahara Avenue (1-800 704 0478/731 0678/www. ahollywoodweddingchapel.com). Bus 204, 301, 302. **Open** 10am-8pm Mon-Fri, Sun; 10am-10pm Sat. **Map** p319 C4.
This friendly business runs four wedding specials, running from $125 to a top-end $225 deal that includes limo, video, flowers, photos, minister fees plus tips, taxes and champagne.

Las Vegas Wedding Specialists

Suite A101, 4045 S Buffalo Drive, at W Flamingo Road, West Las Vegas (888 638 4673/496 2613/ www.lasvegasweddingspecialists.com). **Open** by appointment. **Credit** MC, V.
There's a bountiful costume shop for themed weddings, indoor chapels and a gazebo for traditionalists. Same-sex commitment ceremonies are given special attention. For $675 you can float above the desert in a hot air balloon as you say 'I do.'

Little Chapel of the Flowers

1717 Las Vegas Boulevard South, at E Sahara Avenue (1-800 843 2410/735 4331/www.little chapel.com). Bus 204, 301, 302. **Open** 8am-8pm Mon-Fri; 8am-9pm Sat. **Credit** MC, V. **Map** p319 C4.
One of the finest chapels in Vegas, with three chapels, a lovely gazebo, and a bridge. There's a florist and photography studio on-site. Prices start at $195; an off-site yacht wedding will cost $5,000.

Little Church of the West

4617 Las Vegas Boulevard South, at W Russell Road (1-800 821 2452/739 7971/www.littlechurchofthe west.com). Bus 105, 301. **Open** 10am-10pm daily. **Credit** AmEx, Disc, MC, V. **Map** p317 Y4
Voted 'Best Chapel in Las Vegas' seven times by the *Review-Journal*, the quaint Little Church has been a favourite of celebs including Angelina Jolie and Billy Bob Thornton, Bob Geldof and Paula Yates, and Noel Gallagher and Meg Matthews. Try not to take this as an omen. Reservations required.

Little White Wedding Chapel

1301 Las Vegas Boulevard South, at E Charleston Boulevard (1-800 545 8111/382 5943/www. alittlewhitechapel.com). Bus 206, 301. **Open** 8am-midnight Mon-Thur, Sun; 24hrs Fri, Sat. **Credit** AmEx, Disc, MC, V. **Map** p319 C3.
This Vegas original has been marrying couples since the '50s, including Frank Sinatra and Mia Farrow. However, high throughput means you may end up

Arts & Entertainment

waiting for your turn to say the magic two words. Options include the Tunnel of Love drive-up wedding, an outdoor gazebo, and Elvis impersonators.

Mon Bel Ami

607 Las Vegas Boulevard South, at W Bonneville Avenue (1-800 503 4400/388 4445/www.monbel ami.com). Bus 301. **Open** 8am-10pm daily. **Credit** MC, V. **Map** p318 C2.

Owned by a mother-daughter team, this chapel puts the spotlight firmly on the bride. Hair and make-up artists, a manicurist and massage therapist can be sent to your hotel room. Le Petit package starts at $79; the Crème de la Crème costs $1,699.

A Special Memory Wedding Chapel

800 S 4th Street, between W Bonneville Avenue & E Charleston Boulevard, Downtown (1-800 962 7798/ 384 2211/www.aspecialmemory.com). Bus 301. **Open** 8am-10pm Mon-Thur, Sun; 8am-midnight Fri, Sat. **Credit** AmEx, Disc, MC, V. **Map** p318 C2.

The original drive-through chapel costs a meagre $25 plus gratuity. If you get out of the car, the bride's dressing room exits onto a red carpeted staircase. Ceremonies run from $199 to $1,899.

Sweethearts Wedding Chapel

1155 Las Vegas Boulevard South, at E Charleston Boulevard (1-800 444 2932/385 7785/www.sweet heartschapel.com). Bus 206, 301. **Open** 10am-7pm Mon-Thur, Sun; 10am-8pm Fri, Sat. **Credit** Disc, MC, V. **Map** p319 C3.

This modest chapel seats 25 and has a bridal boutique on site. The $275 special includes a wedding gown, a headpiece, an underskirt, shoes and a tux.

Viva Las Vegas Chapel & Villas

1205 Las Vegas Boulevard South, at E Charleston Boulevard (1-800 574 4450/384 0771/www.vivalas vegasweddings.com). Bus 206, 301. **Open** 9am-7pm daily. **Credit** AmEx, Disc, MC, V. **Map** p319 C3.

The home of the themed wedding – Camelot, Elvis and Intergalactic, among others – for traditional and same-sex commitment ceremonies. Rooms, themed rooms and suites run from $75 to $225.

Wee Kirk o' the Heather

231 Las Vegas Boulevard South, between E Bonneville Avenue & Fremont Street (1-800 843 5266/382 9830/www.weekirk.com). Bus 301. **Open** 9am-10pm Mon-Thur; 9am-midnight Fri, Sat; 9am-8pm Sun. **Credit** AmEx, Disc, MC, V. **Map** p318 D2.

This spot was opened in 1940 by a Scottish minister, but all ministers are non-denominational. Prices range from $189 to $649.

Resort weddings

While independent chapels accept walk-ups, the big resorts usually require that you book.

Artisan

1501 W Sahara Avenue, at Highland Drive (1-800 554 4092/www.theartisanhotel.com). Bus 204. **Credit** AmEx, DC, Disc, MC, V. **Hotel** p107. **Map** p319 A4.

The Artisan exhibits superb taste in a calm, hip atmosphere. The exquisite hotel bar is perfect for an after-wedding drink or nine with pals.

Bellagio

3600 Las Vegas Boulevard South, at W Flamingo Road (1-888 987 3344/693 7700/www.bellagio.com). Bus 202, 301, 302. **Credit** AmEx, DC, Disc, MC, V. **Hotel** p63. **Map** p320 A7.

Bellagio's opulent South Chapel, seating up to 130, garners accolades for its gold and earth tones decor. The Amore package starts at $1,500 (Mon to Thur only). The Beautiful Thing wedding is $15,000.

Paris Las Vegas

3655 Las Vegas Boulevard South, at E Flamingo Road (1-877 650 5021/946 7000/www.parislas vegas.com). Bus 202, 301, 302. **Credit** AmEx, DC, Disc, MC, V. **Hotel** p69. **Map** p320 A7.

Whether you prefer Paradis, a cathedral-style venue for 90 guests, a ceremony for 12 atop the Eiffel Tower or a casual poolside cabaña pairing, Paris Las Vegas possesses bags of charm.

Rio

3700 W Flamingo Road, at S Valley View Boulevard (1-888 746 5625/777 7986/www.playrio.com). Bus 104, 202. **Credit** AmEx, DC, Disc, MC, V. **Hotel** p93. **Map** p317 X3.

The main reason for marrying here is the chance to say your vows on the 50th floor terrace with a view of the Las Vegas Strip. Pre-selected packages start at $150, but we recommend building your own from the extensive list of options.

Venetian

3355 Las Vegas Boulevard South, at Sands Avenue (1-866 548 1807/414 4280/www.venetianweddings. com). Bus 203, 213, 301, 302. **Credit** AmEx, DC, Disc, MC, V. **Hotel** p73. **Map** p320 A6.

You can wed on a gondola, on a bridge overlooking the canals or in a chapel. The upside: this *faux* Italian city is not sinking. The downside: it's actually a mall. Weddings range from $750 to $4,750.

Wynn Las Vegas

3131 Las Vegas Boulevard South, at Spring Mountain Road (1-888 320 7115/770 7400/www. wynnlasvegas.com). Bus 203, 213, 301, 302. **Credit** AmEx, Disc, MC, V. **Hotel** p75. **Map** p319 B6.

If you've got the money, try Las Vegas's hottest new resort. Expect the best, and a bill to match.

Outdoor specialists

Many chapels can organise outdoor weddings, but how about exchanging vows at the top of a bungee tower before taking the, uh, plunge. For $400, **AJ Hackett** (*see p247*) will take a video, pay the minister's fees and give you a helpful shove. For a more sedate experience, charter the 125-capacity *Desert Princess*, a Mississippi-style paddlewheel boat, from **Lake Mead Cruises** (*see p262*).

Trips Out of Town

Features

Getting Started

And you thought Las Vegas was in the middle of nowhere?

Though many test the idea when they come to Las Vegas, man cannot live on free cocktails and enormous buffet meals alone. After a while, iridescent sun will become more attractive than fluorescent striplights, and fresh air will appeal more than cranked-to-the-max a/c, even if, as is the case in summer, the temperatures outside are well in excess of three figures. Happily, the roads leading out of Las Vegas, from just north of Downtown and just south of the Strip, offer some terrific escape routes.

The options for day trips from Las Vegas are plentiful. Within 50 miles of the city you'll find desert parks (Red Rock Canyon, Valley of Fire), boating and fishing (on Lake Mead), man-made marvels (Hoover Dam) and even somewhere to ski (Mount Charleston). Further afield lie more possibilities: the deserts of Nevada (and, eventually, the lights of Reno) to the north; the breathtaking national parks of Utah and Arizona (including the Grand Canyon) to the east; and, to the west, the myriad glories of California, from Los Angeles to Death Valley.

GETTING AROUND

Though the **Greyhound** bus network (1-800 231 2222, www.greyhound.com) runs a service to many major towns and attractions, and though there are a number of companies offering tours to key sights such as the Grand Canyon (for details, *see p111*), by far the easiest and most comfortable way to travel from Las Vegas to the surrounding area is by car. The road connections from Vegas are good, with federal highways and interstates leading off at all points of the compass. The main roads leaving the city are I-15, which runs south-west towards Los Angeles and north-east towards Salt Lake City, and US 93 and US 95, which head, respectively, north into Nevada and south into Arizona and California. For details on renting a car while you're here, *see p292*.

THE DESERT

Lovers of the desert are drawn to the very starkness and nakedness that non-aficionados find so repellent. Compared to wetter, greener areas, deserts are easy to read: the 'bones' of mountains are laid bare before you, and views are long and unobscured. And Las Vegas is one of the best places in the US from which to explore the country's dramatic desertscapes: it lies slap bang in the middle of one, the Mojave,

and close to two others, the Great Basin and the Sonoran (also known as the Colorado desert).

The usual definition of a desert is that it receives less than ten inches (25 centimetres) of precipitation a year and has high evaporation, but this is a pretty wide definition. Lack of cloud cover is important, because it causes heat to reradiate – go back into the sky – rapidly after it gets dark, hence the often high variation between daytime and nighttime temperatures. All three deserts near Las Vegas share some characteristics, but they also exhibit great differences in landscape, vegetation and wildlife.

The **Mojave Desert** is the smallest, covering the lower quarter of Nevada and part of Southern California. It includes the lowest absolute elevation and highest temperature recorded in the US (both in Death Valley, California), and receives almost no rain during an average year. However, not every year is average, and when the rains do fall, the effects can be dramatic. The downpours that caused so much havoc in Death Valley during 2004 (*see p278*) also resulted in the most dramatic desert flowering in a generation: in March 2005, parts of the park were briefly carpeted with flowers.

Unless you venture far from Las Vegas, most of your driving will be in the Mojave Desert. You'll soon learn to recognise characteristic plants: the spidery creosote bush predominates, but its signature plant is the iconic, multi-armed Joshua tree, a yucca and a member of the lily family. Joshuas grow slowly and live up to 900 years, with an average height of 15 to 30 feet. In spring, the tips of the branches carry clusters

---

The best Trips

For deserted desert
Mojave National Preserve. See p277.

For crowded nightclubs
West Hollywood. See p274.

For a quick escape
Red Rock Canyon. See p263.

For a longer break
North Kaibab Trail in the **Grand Canyon**. See p266.

of creamy flowers, which open for one night only and smell like mushrooms. After blossoming, the branch forks, eventually giving the Joshua its many-limbed form. The most extensive forests locally are found in the East Mojave National Preserve (*see p277*).

The **Great Basin Desert**, which covers the northern three-quarters of Nevada and the western half of Utah, is the largest desert in the USA, extending over more than 158,000 square miles. It's described as a 'cold' desert as more than half its precipitation occurs in winter in the form of snow, and its northern position and high base elevations mean it experiences lower average temperatures than areas to the south. It doesn't look much like a desert: silvery green sagebrush, Nevada's state plant, blankets vast areas, and many desert plants of popular imagination – such as large cacti, agaves and yuccas – are conspicuous by their absence. The transition between the Great Basin and the Mojave deserts occurs north-west of Las Vegas, roughly between Beatty and Caliente.

The **Sonoran Desert** extends over part of southern California and the south-western quarter of Arizona. Like the Mojave, it's both lower and hotter than the Great Basin, and rain falls in both summer and winter. Unless you drive as far south as Joshua Tree National Park, you won't cross into the Sonoran.

The Colorado Plateau is a geological feature that includes southeastern Utah and the northeastern portion of Arizona. It's a mass of original continental crust whose colourful layers of sedimentary rock have been eroded into dramatic rock formations and stunning canyons, of which the Grand Canyon is the most magnificent.

DESERT SAFETY

Don't underestimate the dangers of travelling in the desert just because you'll be in an air-conditioned automobile: even the most modern cars can overheat and even break down under extreme conditions. If you're planning to drive any unpaved roads, check local conditions before you set out. Turn off air-conditioning on uphill stretches to lessen the strain on the engine. Leave a window slightly open if you park the car for any length of time in the heat, and use a fold-up windscreen shade. Out of your vehicle, wear lots of sunscreen and light-coloured, body-covering clothing. Don't exert yourself in the midday sun. In or out of your car, carry plenty of water: you need to take on at least one gallon (four litres) a day.

Tourist information

Arizona Office of Tourism
1-866 275 5816/1-602 364 3700/
www.arizonaguide.com.

California Division of Tourism
1-800 862 2543/1-916 444 4429/
www.visitcalifornia.com.

Nevada Commission on Tourism
1-800 638 2328/1-775 687 4322/
www.travelnevada.com.

Utah Travel Council
1-800 200 1160/1-801 538 1030/www.utah.com.

Trip planning

Lake Mead National Recreation Area/National Park Service
293 8907/293 8990/www.nps.gov/lame.

Nevada Division of State Parks
Southern Nevada park information 486 5126/
statewide office 1-775 687 4384/www.parks.nv.gov.

US Forest Service
Humboldt-Toiyabe National Forest main office 1-775 331 6444/Spring Mountain National Recreation Area 515 5400/www.fs.fed.us/r4/htnf.

Day Trips

A very different world awaits just minutes from the Strip.

Heading East

Hoover Dam

The bare facts are staggering enough. It's 726 feet (221 metres) high. At its base, it's 660 feet (200 metres) thick; at its crest, it's 1,244 feet (379 metres) wide. It weighs 6.6 million tons. The building of it used enough concrete to pave a highway between San Francisco and New York. Its reservoir is 110 miles long and around 500 foot (150 metres) deep, and can hold enough water to cover the entire state of Nevada six inches deep. So far, so impressive. But then you actually catch sight the Hoover Dam, and you can scarcely believe your eyes.

Without the Hoover Dam – née Boulder Dam, but renamed in 1947 for President Herbert Hoover, under whose administration the project was begun – much of the Southwest would not exist. The dam controls the Colorado River, providing electricity and water to more than 18 million people in Nevada, California and Arizona, and makes it possible for cities and farmland to flourish in one of the driest, hottest and most inhospitable regions of the world. In the early 20th century, the sheer power of the Colorado River made the building of the Hoover Dam both a necessary measure and a terrifying prospect. Black Canyon was chosen as the location for the project, which was overseen by the Bureau of Reclamation and came with four main aims: flood prevention, silt control, water storage and electrical energy generation.

Building it was a mammoth task. First, the Colorado had to be temporarily diverted so the dam wall could be constructed. The concrete would have taken 100 years to set if left under normal conditions, so the cooling process was sped up by pumping ice-cold water through a network of pipes laid into each block of concrete. Next, vast pipes some 30 feet in diameter, known as penstocks, were lowered from an overhead cableway 800 feet (250 metres) above the canyon floor and squeezed into tunnels blasted out of the side walls. A vast army of 16,400 workers – remember, the project was built at the height of the Depression – laboured day and night for four years, finishing in February 1935… two years ahead of schedule.

The dam straddles the border between Arizona and Nevada. US 93 passes over the top, although, to address both increased traffic and concerns about terrorism, a bypass bridge is planned. The main car park and the visitor centre are on the Nevada side. The latter is something of a necessary evil, through which the bulk of the 'Discovery' tour is conducted; booking is unnecessary, but early arrival is recommended to beat both crowds and traffic. (The 'Hard Hat' tours, which took visitors closer to the action, were suspended post 9/11 and seem unlikely to resume.)

The tour is a mixed bag. The films are informative, but the constant waiting in line is frustrating and the way in which visitors are herded in and out of cinemas and galleries like cattle, while no fault of the staff – it's to do with the hamfisted design of the centre itself – is an irritation. However, in between the movie and a so-so exhibition, you'll get to see inside the dam, specifically into a main hall on the Nevada side that contains eight huge generators.

Back outside, take your eyes off the big picture and note a few interesting features on or near the dam itself. Chief among them are two 30-foot sculptures, the Winged Figures of the Republic, which flank a flagpole above a terrazzo floor inlaid with a celestial map, marking Franklin D Roosevelt's dedication of the dam in September 1935. The white mark on the shoreline indicates the flood level in 1983 when the aforementioned reservoir, Lake Mead, rose to within seven feet of the top. But while these are nice diversions, they won't be what you remember. That'll be the sheer enormity of the place, one of the greatest man-made constructions on the planet and, despite the absence of neon and pzazz, as impressive a sight as anything Las Vegas has to offer.

Hoover Dam Visitor Center & Tours

1-866 291 8687/294 3517/www.usbr.gov/lc/hoover dam. **Open** *Visitor Center* 9am-5pm daily. *Tours* every 15mins 9am-4.30pm. **Admission** *Tour* $10; $5-$8 concessions. **Credit** AmEx, Disc, MC, V.

Getting there

To reach the Hoover Dam from Las Vegas, take US 93 south for 32 miles. You will pass through Boulder City en route.

Hoover Dam. *See p260.*

Boulder City

A few miles from the Hoover Dam is the green and pleasant town of Boulder City, built in 1931 to house the dam workers. Triangular in shape, it was the first 'model city' in the US, built according to progressive planning theories. The Bureau of Reclamation, government buildings and a park sit at the apex of the triangle, with the workers' houses radiating down from there. It was never intended to be a permanent settlement, but though its population dropped after the dam was finished, it recovered during World War II and is now flourishing.

Driving down US 93, you pass some small, old-fashioned motels and stalls selling Mexican pottery and other handicrafts. Only slowly do you realise that something's missing: there are no casinos. This is the only town in Nevada where gambling is illegal. If the atmosphere appeals, you can stay at the historic **Boulder Dam Hotel** (turn right at Arizona Street; 293 3510, www.boulderdamhotel.com), a white and green building that counts Howard Hughes among its former guests. The hotel houses a shop, galleries, a restaurant and the **Chamber of Commerce** (293 2034, www.bouldercity chamber.com, closed Sat & Sun), where you can pick up a map and a guide to walking tours. It's also home to the **Boulder City/Hoover Dam Museum** (294 1988, www.bcmha.org, closed Sun am, admission $1-$2), which shows a film on the building of Boulder City and the dam.

Boulder City is small town Americana, and the best eating option in that vein is **Two Gals from Cal** (1632 Nevada Highway, 293 1793), serving light lunches and sandwiches. For a touch of quirky sophistication, check out **Milo's Best Cellars** (538 Nevada Highway, 293 9540) in the old town, which offers outdoor seating, a lengthy wine list, and a nice menu of salads, sandwiches and cheese plates.

Getting there

Boulder City is 25 miles south of Las Vegas (seven miles west of Hoover Dam) on US 93. To see Boulder City's historic district, turn off at the business loop, which rejoins US 93 on the far side of the town.

Lake Mead

Lake Mead is the second most popular recreation spot in Nevada: around ten million visitors, most of them locals, come to its 550 miles of shoreline every year to sail, fish, swim, water-ski, camp, picnic and generally enjoy watery pleasures in the middle of the desert. Completely artificial, it was created when the Colorado was blocked by the Hoover Dam, and is an incongruous sight: a large blue splodge surrounded by barren mountains and canyon-tops.

It's the centrepiece of the huge **Lake Mead National Recreation Area**, which also includes Lake Mohave to the south (formed when the Colorado River was stemmed again in 1953 by the Davis Dam) and the desert east to the edge of Grand Canyon National Park (*see p266*) and north to Overton, from where you are within easy reach of the **Valley of Fire State Park** (*see p263*). There's a $5 permit fee per car (or $3 per person), which grants five days' access to the whole Lake Mead area.

Lakeside Scenic Drive (Highway 146) and Northshore Scenic Drive (Highway 167) skirt the western and northern sides of Lake Mead for nearly 60 miles. The route isn't in fact particularly scenic, but it's the access road for five concession-operated marinas along the Nevada shoreline. All have small ranger stations, grocery stores and some form of restaurant; some also have swimming beaches (without lifeguards), picnic sites, motels, showers, laundries and gas stations. **Lake Mead Marina** on Boulder Beach (293 3484, www.riverlakes.com) and the **Las Vegas Boat Harbour** (565 9111, www.lasvegasboat harbour.com) are the largest, closest and busiest marinas; further north are the **Callville Bay Marina** (565 8958, www.callvillebay.com), the **Echo Bay Resort** (394 4000, www.echo bay7c.com) and the **Overton Beach Resort** (394 4040, www.overtonbeachmarina.net).

On the water

The best way to explore the lake is by boat. There are numerous secluded coves, sandy beaches and narrow canyons accessible only by water, and the warm, clear lake is ideal for swimming: the water temperature averages 78°F (26°C) in spring, summer and autumn. You can hire a boat for daily use from the marinas around the lake. Rates vary; expect small fishing boats to cost around $20 to $40 for two hours or $60 to $120 a day, with large ski boats roughly three times the price. Alternatively, take a cruise on the *Desert Princess*, run by **Lake Mead Cruises** (293 6180, www.lakemeadcruises.com).

Lake Mead offers some of the best year-round sport fishing in the country (*see p248*). In addition, the clarity and warmth of the water and fascinating underground landscapes make it one of the country's top freshwater scuba diving destinations. You can't hire equipment at the lake, but dive shops in Las Vegas rent gear and run courses (*see p250*).

Where to stay & eat

Try the eaterie on the water at the **Las Vegas Boat Harbour House Café** (565 9111) or the grander **Tail o' the Whale** restaurant at Echo Bay (394 4000). **Seven Crown Resorts** (1-800 752 9669, www.7crown.com) runs motels at **Echo Bay** (394 4000, rates $60-$115) and **Boulder Beach** (293 2074, rates $75-$175), and also rents houseboats. There are campgrounds (293 8491, rates $10) at all marinas bar Overton and Willow Beach. Close by are the upscale resorts of **Lake Las Vegas** (*see p137*).

Getting there

The Alan Bible Visitor Center is 27 miles south of Las Vegas on US 93, at the junction with Lakeshore Scenic Drive (Highway 146). To reach Las Vegas Bay, Boulder Beach and Lake Mead marinas without going to the visitor centre, take Boulder Highway south from Vegas and turn left at Lake Mead Drive (Highway 146), or take I-15/US 93 north to exit 45 in North Las Vegas and turn on to Lake Mead Boulevard east (Highway 147). Both routes join the shore road.

Tourist information

Consult the NPS website (www.nps.gov/lame) for information about the Lake Mead Recreation Area. The **Alan Bible Visitor Center** (293 8990, 8.30am-4.30pm daily) on US 93 is basic, but has a useful map and details on fishing and other activities. Information stations are also located at Overton Beach, Echo Bay, Callville Bay, Las Vegas Bay and Temple Bar.

Border crossing

The flipside of Las Vegas's dazzling glamour can be found by taking US 95 south from the city for 70 miles, then taking Highway 163 ten miles east. It's here you'll find the town of **Laughlin**, founded in 1969 by Don Laughlin, an entrepreneur who somehow saw the commercial possibilities in a sweltering, scruffy patch of desert in the middle of nowhere. Except that, of course, it's not quite in the middle of nowhere at all: it's right on the border with Arizona, and extremely close to the California stateline. This might be inhospitable desert terrain, but its proximity to two states where gambling is hard to find has, especially over the past two decades, proven very lucrative indeed.

The chalk of Laughlin's casinos, among them the steamboat-themed Colorado Belle, don't stand comparison with the cheese of the Vegas Strip resorts. A closer comparison would be Downtown Vegas, but Laughlin lacks its charm. Two keys to its appeal are that the gaming's cheap and the rooms are cheaper, but in real-estate parlance, it's location, location, location that's made this funny little spot a low-roller heaven.

Valley of Fire State Park

An hour north-east of Las Vegas lies a natural marvel whose eroded red sandstone formations are just as spectacular as the neon-clad casinos on the Strip. Bounded by the grey limestone Muddy Mountains to the south and west, **Valley of Fire State Park** was the first state park in Nevada, and is still one of its most breathtaking.

The main attractions are the fiery Aztec sandstone formations, created from sand dunes deposited 135 to 150 million years ago and sculpted by wind and water into bizarre, often anthropomorphic shapes: in particular, look for **Elephant Rock** and **Seven Sisters** along Highway 169, the main east–west road through the park. A two-mile scenic loop road takes you past some of its most dramatic rock formations, nestled among which are two campgrounds; campsite B has the best pitches. Backcountry camping isn't allowed; nor, sadly, is camping in the three stone cabins constructed by the Civilian Conservation Corps in the 1930s to provide primitive shelter for travellers, and accessible via a short walk.

The park is easily explored in a day. Hiking is permitted throughout, but there are few marked trails, and all are very short. Get advice on hiking and a trails map from the visitor centre halfway along Highway 169 (397 2088, http://parks.nv.gov/vf.html, 8.30am-4.30pm daily, $6), stopping to check displays on the area's geology, ecology and human history. The road north from the centre offers a panoramic view of multicoloured sandstone at **Rainbow Vista** and ends at the White Domes picnic area. An easy three-mile trail from Rainbow Vista leads to spectacular rocks at **Fire Canyon**, from where you can see the spot where Captain Kirk met his doom in *Star Trek: Generations*.

Atlatl Rock on the scenic loop road has a number of petroglyphs, while others are visible on the short trail to **Mouse's Tank**, a natural water basin used in the 1890s as a hideout by a renegade Indian known as Mouse. Visit the **Lost City Museum** in Overton (397 2193, www.comnett.net/~kolson), eight miles north of the park, to learn about the Indian inhabitants, from the ancient Basketmaker people and the Puebloans (Anasazi) to the Paiute, whose descendants still live in Southern Nevada.

Summer highs top 110°F (43°C); as such, the best times to visit are spring and autumn. The cactus and wildflower blooms are usually at their peak in mid April. If you're lucky, you may spy a desert tortoise (Nevada's state reptile) and you're sure to see antelope ground squirrels (aka chipmunks). Don't feed or pet them: they are suspected of carrying the fleas that transmit bubonic plague.

Getting there

Head north on I-15 for 33 miles to Highway 169: it's 17 miles to the park's western entrance. You can also enter the park from Lake Mead, off Northshore Scenic Drive (*see p262*).

Heading West

Red Rock Canyon

A mere 20 miles from the gaming tables of Vegas is one of Nevada's most popular and beautiful outdoor areas. The cool, deep-cut canyons of the **Red Rock Canyon National Conservation Area** (515 5350, www.redrock canyon.blm.gov, 8.30am-4.30pm daily, $5) make it a popular hiking spot all year round, while climbers come here from all over to enjoy some of the best rock climbing in the US (*see p250*).

Red Rock Canyon is part of the Spring Mountains and has as its centrepiece a nearly sheer escarpment of Aztec sandstone, the remnant of ancient sand dunes that covered this area some 180 million years ago. About 65 million years ago, the Keystone Thrust Fault pushed older grey limestone over younger sandstone, reversing the normal layering and resulting in today's dramatic and unique landscape. The red and cream Calico Hills to the east are more rounded, as they are not protected from erosion by a higher limestone layer.

Because of the availability of water in the area, Native Americans have used Red Rock Canyon since about 3,500 BC: evidence remains in the form of rock art (etched petroglyphs and painted pictographs), as well as artefacts such as arrowheads and ceramics. More than 45 mammal species also inhabit the park, among them mountain lions, coyotes, kangaroo rats, mule deer and the near-mythical desert bighorn sheep, but you'll be lucky to spot any. The most visible animals are probably the non-native burros (donkeys), around 50 of which live around Red Rock Canyon. Observe from a distance and never feed them (it's illegal and dangerous). Humans are also a danger to burros; if they are encouraged to gather at roadsides, some will inevitably be injured by vehicles.

Stop first at the **Bureau of Land Management Visitor Center** (clearly signed) for information and a map, before exploring the one-way, 13-mile scenic drive through the canyon. It's popular with cyclists (*see p247*) and gives access to numerous hiking trails and three picnic sites. Some trails are not marked clearly and require some scrambling; best take a topo map (available at the visitor centre) and compass.

Monoliths both man-made and natural adorn **Red Rock Canyon**. *See p263.*

A good introduction to the **Calico Hills** that line the start of the scenic drive is the two-and-a-half-mile **Calico Tank** trail from Sandstone Quarry. Just above the tank is a fine view (smog permitting) of the valley and the Strip's casino monoliths. Other good short summer hikes include **Ice Box Canyon** and **Pine Creek Canyon**. For further details of the scores of other trails, pick up a copy of the BLM's trail leaflet, or Branch Whitney's *Hiking Las Vegas*, which also covers Mount Charleston. Guided hikes are led by park staff at the weekends and some weekdays, run by the Sierra Club (363 3267, www.sierraclub.org).

Around Red Rock Canyon

If you'd prefer something less physical, head further west on Highway 159 to the green oasis of **Spring Mountain State Park**, at the base of the dramatic Wilson Cliffs. Admission to the park includes entrance to the New England-style ranch house, where the $6 day-use fee is payable (875 4141, http://parks.nv.gov/smr.htm, house open 10am-4pm daily). Stroll around the historic buildings in the fenced grounds and picnic on a grassy meadow. There are walking tours year-round, open-air theatre and jazz performances in summer, and 'living history' programmes in the autumn.

Bonnie Springs Old Nevada

1 Gun Fighter Lane, off Highway 159, south of Red Rock Canyon (875 4191/www.bonniesprings. com). No bus. **Open** *May-Oct* 10.30am-6pm daily. *Nov-Apr* 10.30am-5pm daily. **Admission** $7-$10/ car. **Credit** MC, V.

South on Highway 159 sits this mock Wild West town, with a melodrama and hanging staged daily (times vary by season). It's rather dilapidated but good fun; visitors can take a horse ride ($30), and there's also a free petting zoo, a restaurant and a motel (875 4400, rates $60-$135).

Getting there

To reach the visitor centre, head west on Charleston Boulevard (Highway 159) for 20 miles. Alternatively, if you're staying near the southern end of the Strip, drive south on I-15, take Highway 160 (towards Pahrump) and then turn right on to Highway 159, passing Bonnie Springs and Spring Mountain State Park en route to Red Rock Canyon.

Mount Charleston

It's true: you can jet-ski near Las Vegas in the morning and snow-ski in the afternoon. A mere 45 minutes north-west of the city lies the Spring Mountain Recreation Area, more commonly known as **Mount Charleston**. It's part of the massive Spring Mountain range, dominated by Charleston Peak, the highest point in Southern Nevada at 11,918 feet (3,633 metres). In the winter, ski and snowboard at Lee Canyon; in summer, hike the forested slopes, substantially cooler than the city. There are also picnic sites and several campgrounds ($10, open mid-May to mid-Oct) in the area.

Watch the vegetation change as you climb into the mountains, moving from creosote, bursage and Joshua trees on the lower slopes to piñon and Utah juniper, through ponderosa pine and mountain mahogany, and finally to gnarled bristlecone pines where the tree-line peters out at 10,000 feet (3,000 metres). Due to the isolation of the Spring Mountain Range, around 30 species of flora and fauna are unique to this 'sky island'.

Exploring by car

There are two roads into the area, both off US 95. Nearest to Las Vegas is Highway 157 (Kyle Canyon Road), which ascends prettily through winding canyons and wooded slopes to the **Mount Charleston Hotel** (*see below*), a rustic-style lodge with a huge lobby warmed by an open fireplace. The road continues west for another few miles, past a small park office (872 5486, closed Mon & Tue in winter), terminating at **Mount Charleston Lodge** (*see below*). Here, you'll find a 24-hour bar, restaurant, riding stables and some delightful log cabins.

From the Mount Charleston Hotel, Highway 158 (Deer Creek Highway) heads north to the junction with Highway 156 (Lee Canyon Road). Seven miles along Highway 158, the short Desert View Trail leads to a spectacular view of the valley and the mountains. At the junction with Highway 156, turn left for the ski area, usually open between November and April. The elevation here is 8,500 feet (2,600 metres), with three chairlifts leading up another 1,000 feet (300 metres) to 13 slopes. (For more on skiing in the area, *see p250*). Drive back to US 95 on Highway 158 for a fine view of the desert below.

Hiking

The US Forest Service prefers hikers to stick to designated trails, but there are also numerous unmarked hikes around Mount Charleston (take a compass and a trail guidebook). The six-mile **Bristlecone Trail** provides worthwhile views of limestone cliffs and bristlecone pines. The short trail to **Mary Jane Falls** is more strenuous but more rewarding, with hikers climbing 900 feet (270 metres) to a waterfall. The mother of all hikes, though, is the 18-mile round trip to **Mount Charleston Peak**, a difficult and demanding trail that's not clear of snow until as late as July. From the summit you can enjoy a stunning view of southern Nevada, eastern California and southern Utah. For all hikes, you'll need warm clothing and water.

Around Mount Charleston

On your way to Mount Charleston, stop off at **Floyd Lamb State Park**, former site of Tule Springs Ranch, where prospective divorcees

waited out their six-week residency requirement in the 1940s and '50s. Located 15 miles from the city, though now surrounded by sprawl, its lush lawns, shady cottonwoods and four lakes make it a popular, year-round picnicking and fishing spot. It's best to avoid weekends if you don't like crowds. However, during the week, it's a positively serene spot, and a magnificent change from Las Vegas: not even the swankiest Strip hotel-casino can boast the peacocks that wander showily around the 1940s white ranch buildings. You can hire horses from the old stables ($20/hour). There's no camping, though: the park, for which admission costs $6 (486 5413, http://parks.nv.gov/fl.htm), is solely a day-use facility.

Further is the **Desert National Wildlife Refuge** (646 3401, http://desertcomplex.fws. gov), established in 1936 to protect the desert bighorn sheep, and its habitat. A gravel road leads to a self-service information centre, where you can pick up a leaflet on the refuge and stroll around the ponds of Corn Creek Springs. The refuge occupies 1.5 million acres and receives only about 20,000 visitors a year. The western half is used by the Nellis Air Force Range as a bombing area and is closed to the public, while the rest is a nature reserve, accessible by two unmaintained dirt roads: you'll need a high clearance or 4WD vehicle in order to gain access to them. Summer is the best time to spot the elusive bighorn sheep and the wildflowers are usually in bloom from March to May.

Where to stay & eat

Accommodation and eating options on Mount Charleston are few and far between. The **Mount Charleston Hotel** (1-800 794 3456, 872 5500, www.mtcharlestonhotel.com) has a cavernous dining room and 57 rooms (rates $109-$229), though a better bet is the characterful **Mount Charleston Lodge** (1-800 955 1314, 872 5408, www.mtcharlestonlodge. com), whose cosy log cabins (rates $125-$250) come with desks and offer wonderful views down over the landscape. Recent work added 36 new condo-style log cabins with lofts and decks. The restaurant serves solid American fare, and doubles as a bar in the evening. There are also several camping areas; midweek, you can often find a spot just by driving in, though in season, weekends book up early.

Getting there

Take US 95 north from Downtown for about 35 miles to reach Highway 157; Highway 156 is about 12 miles further on. In winter, you'll need snow chains on the mountain roads.

Arizona

Home of the Grand Canyon, nature's genuinely awe-inspiring way of getting Vegas excess into perspective.

Of Arizona's two main towns, **Phoenix** has little to offer the Vegas-based visitor save for a surfeit of fine golf courses, while the more characterful **Tucson**, 400 miles south-east of Las Vegas, is too far away to visit comfortably in a couple of days. No surprise, then, that most visitors to Arizona from Vegas head as directly west as the road network allows, towards one of the world's great natural wonders.

Arizona, like Las Vegas, is on Pacific Standard Time, but doesn't put the clocks back in summer, leaving it one hour behind.

Grand Canyon National Park

You'll have seen pictures, perhaps TV footage, or maybe even the IMAX film on one of their normally larger-than-life-size screens. You'll have read about it, heard about it, talked about it. You may feel like you know it before you've even ventured into it. And still nothing will prepare you for your first glimpse of the epic, breathtaking, unknowable Grand Canyon.

Grand Canyon National Park sprawls across a length of 277 miles, most of which is difficult to reach and rarely visited; just a tiny portion of it is accessible from the **South Rim**, where most visitors congregate. The canyon is also misnamed: it's not just one rip in the earth, but rather a series of canyons surrounding the central gorge cut by the Colorado River, a staggering 5,000 feet (1,500 metres) from top to bottom. At an average elevation of 7,000 feet (2,150 metres), the South Rim is not unbearably hot in summer, but temperatures at the bottom of the canyon, a mile down, can push 110°F (43°C). April, May, September and October are probably the best months to visit; most of the rainfall occurs in summer; from December to March, the upper canyon is generally snowbound and temperatures plummet.

Entrance to the park costs $20 per car ($10 per person for pedestrians and cyclists) and is valid for seven days. You'll need to stay at least two nights to give yourself enough time to properly explore the village, rim drives and various lookout points, to venture into the canyon itself, and then drive back to Vegas.

TOURIST INFORMATION

For general information, call the National Park Service on 1-928 638 7888, or check out the Grand Canyon's excellent website at www.nps.gov/grca/grandcanyon, which has information on accommodation, hiking, backcountry permits, maps of the area; everything you need to know to plan your trip.

En route to the South Rim

Some 150 miles west of the South Rim, the Grand Canyon forms the northern boundary of the Hualapai Indian Reservation, a 1,563-square-mile Wildlife Conservation Area. Although not as spectacular as the South Rim, the western canyon is much closer to Las Vegas and will give you a taste of the grandeur further east. Approaching from Vegas along US 93, you'll first hit **Kingman**, which marks the end of the longest surviving stretch of the iconic Route 66 (immortalised in song by Bobby Troup) with kitsch aplenty. Midway along the route to Williams, you'll reach **Peach Springs**, the gateway to the western canyon area and the location of the Hualapai tribal headquarters.

Permits for sightseeing, fishing and camping in the Diamond Creek area are available from **Hualapai Lodge** (900 Route 66, Peach Springs, AZ, 1-925 769 2419, www.grand canyonresort.com). The lodge also provides accommodation and dining facilities, and is the starting place for rafting tours down the Colorado River (1-928 769 2219). It also runs a variety of sightseeing and activity tours.

Continuing along I-40 will bring you to the town of **Williams**, 60 miles south of the National Park. Some use the town as a staging post en route to the canyon (a picturesque narrow gauge steam railway runs visitors to the canyon from here), while others prefer the larger **Flagstaff**, 35 miles east. Situated at the base of the **San Francisco Peaks**, the highest mountains in Arizona, this pleasant railroad and university town has motels, restaurants, cafés and a brewpub, as well as the **Lowell Observatory**, from which the planet Pluto was first spotted in 1930. More information on the town is available from the Chamber of Commerce (101 E Route 66, 1-928 774 4505, www.flagstaffchamber.com).

The South Rim

The majority of the annual five million visitors to Grand Canyon National Park head for the **South Rim** and the restaurants, shops and sights of **Grand Canyon Village**, on the edge of the canyon lip. Inevitably, it's crowded, but it remains remarkably untouristy; or, in some cases, pleasantly retro-touristy. It's also closer to the Colorado River than the North Rim and has much better views into the canyon.

If you have sufficient patience to avoid driving straight to the rim, park your car and take a free shuttle bus to the **Canyon View Information Plaza**, where you'll find a visitors' centre and bookstore (open 8am-5pm daily). Pick up a map of the National Park and a copy of *The Guide*, the park's newspaper, which has comprehensive information on sights, transportation, facilities and activities, before strolling to **Mather Point** for your first gob-smacking view of the canyon. The **Village Route** shuttle bus will then take you from the Information Plaza into Grand Canyon Village.

Grand Canyon Village

Travellers have been coming to gawp at the Grand Canyon since the 19th century, and the village is dotted with historic buildings. Many of the most interesting were built by pioneering female architect Mary Colter for the Fred Harvey Travel Company.

A leaflet describes a self-guided walking tour around the village's historic district, starting at the **Santa Fe Railway Station** (1909), the terminus for the **Grand Canyon Railway** (*see p270*). Across the road on the canyon edge is the luxurious **El Tovar Hotel**, a wooden building in hunting-lodge style, which cost a cool $250,000 to build in 1905. Next to it is the

Hopi House (open 8am-6pm daily), designed by Colter in 1904 as a showroom and salesroom for Indian handicrafts. Colter modelled the building on a terraced Hopi dwelling, using local stone and wood and employing Hopi builders. Nearby is **Verkamps Curios** (1906; open 9am-6pm daily), one of the canyon's oldest continuously operating stores.

Walking west from the hotel along the Rim Trail, you'll pass the modern **Kachina** and **Thunderbird** lodges and the pioneer-style stone and log **Bright Angel Lodge**, designed by Colter in 1935. If you're here in winter, warm your hands at the fabulous 'geological' fireplace, the design of which mimics the layers of rock in the Grand Canyon, from the hearth, made from stone from the bed of the Colorado River, right up to a layer of Kaibab limestone at the top of the chimney breast.

Beyond Bright Angel Lodge is **Bucky O'Neill's cabin**, which dates from the 1890s and is the oldest surviving building on the rim, and the **Lookout Studio** (Colter, 1914), which now houses a gift shop (open 9am-5pm daily). Perched on the edge of the precipice, the studio was designed as an observation building, from which visitors could view the canyon. Colter didn't want the building to detract from the beauty of the canyon, creating a stone structure that merges with the surrounding rock; from a distance, the building is almost invisible.

The **Kolb Studio** was built by pioneering photographers Ellsworth and Emery Kolb, who started snapping mule riders here in 1902. The lack of water on the rim meant the brothers were required to hike halfway down the canyon to their developing tent at Indian Gardens, process the photos, and get back to the top before the mules returned. (All water at the South Rim is still pumped up from inside the canyon; look for the trans-canyon pipeline on the Bright Angel trail.) The Kolbs were also the first to film a boat trip down the Colorado, in 1912. The studio houses a bookstore and gallery (open 8am-5pm daily), and has displays on the brothers' work. Beyond here is the head of the Bright Angel trail (*see p270*).

Along the South Rim

Two roads lead west and east from the village along the canyon rim, each providing very different views into the canyon. You can also walk along the very edge of the rim, on the newly extended, 12-mile, pedestrian-only **Rim Trail**. The village section of the trail is paved; elsewhere it can get rocky.

The eight-mile **Hermit Road** (previously called the West Rim Drive) is closed to private vehicles from March to November. Instead,

visitors are encouraged to take the shuttle bus that departs from the western edge of the village to **Hermit's Rest**, which was built by Mary Colter as a refreshment stop in 1914. The building, now in use as a gift shop (open 9am-5pm daily), is deliberately primitive in style so that it blends with its natural surroundings (fortunately, a Swiss chalet design was rejected). From here, you can set off on the Hermit Trail into the canyon (*see p271*).

The shuttle bus stops at various observation points on its way out, including the spectacular **Abyss**, where the Great Mohave Wall drops 3,000 feet (900 metres) to the Tonto Platform above the Colorado River. However, it only stops at Mohave Point and **Hopi Point** on its return. If you're planning to watch the sunset, check the time of the last bus before you leave to avoid a long, dark walk back to the village.

Along the east rim, **Desert View Drive** goes 26 miles in the opposite direction, as far as the park's eastern entrance. On the way, the road passes several excellent lookout points, with access to the **South Kaibab** and **Grandview Trails** (*see p271*). (However, note that the side road to the South Kaibab Trailhead and Yaki Point is closed to private vehicles Mar-Nov.) Near the end of the drive, there's an 800-year-old ruin of an Anasazi pueblo and the **Tusayan Museum** (open 9am-5pm daily), which provides somewhat scanty information on the history and culture of the canyon's Native American inhabitants. The drive finishes at **Desert View**, which offers the clearest views of the Colorado River. This is also the location of the **Watchtower**, a circular, 70-foot (21-metre) tower regarded as Colter's masterpiece. A remarkable re-creation of the ancient Indian towers Colter had seen at Mesa Verde and Canyon de Chelly, the ground-floor room is modelled after a kiva (or sacred ceremonial chamber), while the roof provides a panoramic view of the Grand Canyon, the Painted Desert and the San Francisco Peaks, 40 miles to the south. It's fitted with black-mirror reflectoscopes, which condense and simplify the views of the canyon while also intensifying the colours. But the centrepiece is the **Hopi Room**, decorated with vivid Hopi designs depicting various gods and legends.

To learn more about the geology, history and archaeology of the South Rim, join one of the Park Service's ranger-guided walks or activities. Check the park's website or *The Guide* for a programme schedule.

Where to eat

There are three restaurants, two self-service cafés and a takeaway snack bar in the Grand Canyon Village, all open daily. The splendid, dark wooden dining room with its large Indian murals at the **El Tovar Hotel** is very popular: you can take your chances at breakfast (6.30-11am) and lunch (11.30am-2pm), but must book for dinner (5-10pm; 1-928 638 2631 ext 6432); hotel guests take priority over non-guests.

Nearby are the less formal **Bright Angel Lodge** dining room (6.30am-10pm) and the **Arizona Room** steakhouse (4.30-10pm). **Maswik Lodge** has a sports bar (5-11pm) and inexpensive but rather institutional cafeteria (6am-10pm); there's a larger cafeteria at **Yavapai Lodge** (6am-9pm). Wherever you dine, have a drink in the lounge at the El Tovar (11am-11pm), decorated by the ubiquitous Colter. There are also snack bars at Hermit's Rest (9am-4pm) and Desert View (9am-4pm), and a deli at Market Plaza for picnic supplies.

Where to stay

There's plenty of accommodation in Grand Canyon Village, but demand is high, so to get what you want, book as far ahead as you can (we're talking months, not weeks). That said, there is sometimes accommodation available for walk-in visitors at Yavapai and Maswik Lodges, even in high season, if you arrive early. Book through **Xanterra Parks & Resorts** (1-888 297 2757, 1-303 297 2757, www.grandcanyonlodges.com).

The **El Tovar Hotel** ($129-$291), with its grand lobby adorned with stuffed animal heads, offers the most splendid lodging in the village. Try to get a room with a spacious private balcony overlooking the rim. Pricier are the 1930s **Bright Angel Lodge** ($55-$130) and more modern, motel-style **Kachina** and **Thunderbird Lodges** ($125-$135), also on the edge of the canyon. **Maswik** ($77-$124) and **Yavapai Lodges** ($96-$113) are located in pine forest a short walk away.

Also within the village are two campsites. **Mather Campground**, run by the Park Service (1-800 365 2267, 1-301 722 1257 from outside US, http://reservations.nps.gov), has 320 pitches ($15) and a trailer village for RVs (from $25). **Desert View Campground**, 25 miles east of Grand Canyon Village, is open from mid May to mid October on a first-come, first-served basis ($10 per site).

A few miles south of the village, just outside the park, is **Tusayan**, where you'll find the National Geographic Visitor Center, with its supremely superfluous IMAX playing films including *Grand Canyon: Hidden Secrets* (are there any other kind?), and a rather more useful park fee pay-station, so you don't have to queue on entry. There are also several motels, including the well-specced **Red Feather Lodge** (1-800 538 2345, www.red featherlodge.com), **Best Western Squire Inn** (1-928 638 2681, 1-800 622 6966, www. grandcanyonsquire.com) and a **Holiday Inn Express** (1-928 638 3000, www.grandcanyon. hiexpress.com). A free shuttle-bus service runs between Tusayan and the village. There are also plenty of motels in Flagstaff and Williams.

Getting there

By air
Several companies offer scheduled flights from North Las Vegas airport to Grand Canyon airport at Tusayan: try **Scenic Flights** (1-800 634 6801, 1-702 638 3300, www.scenic.com). The flight takes 1hr 15mins and a return ticket costs $149-$269. For details of aeroplane and helicopter sightseeing flights over the Grand Canyon, *see p271*.

Trips Out of Town

By bus

Bus service between Phoenix, Flagstaff and Grand Canyon Village is provided by **Open Road Tours** (1-800 766 7117, www.openroadtours.com; go to the Flagstaff link), which charges $39 one-way or $70 round-trip between Phoenix and Flagstaff and $25 one-way or $50 round-trip between Flagstaff and the Grand Canyon. **Greyhound** (1-800 531 9424, www.greyhound.com) runs bus services from Las Vegas to Flagstaff (5.5hrs; $49 single, $98 return).

By car

To reach the South Rim, head south on US 93 to I-40, then turn left on to Highway 64. It's 290 miles from Vegas and the journey takes about 5hrs. As an alternative, you can drive as far as Williams and board the Grand Canyon Railway (*see below*).

By rail

The **Grand Canyon Railway** (1-800 843 8724, 1-928 773 1976 from outside US, www.thetrain.com) runs train services from the depot in Williams (10am daily) to the old **Santa Fe Station** in the heart of Grand Canyon Village, returning at 3.30pm. In summer the train is pulled by an early-20th-century steam locomotive. There are various 'classes' of service in an assortment of historic carriages, and characters in Western costume entertain passengers on the journey. The trip takes 3hrs and tickets, which include the park entrance fee, cost from $73.72 to $177.78 per adult year-round.

Getting around

To encourage a more serene appreciation of nature, the park service has limited private-vehicle access in some areas and is expanding pedestrian and bicycle routes around the South Rim. The bus shuttles are an entirely pleasant and workable alternative to private transport.

By bus

A free shuttle-bus service operates on three interconnecting services around the South Rim: the **Village Route** (serving Canyon View Information Plaza and the main village destinations); **Hermit's Rest Route** (along the rim from the west side of the village to Hermit's Rest; Mar-Nov only) and **Kaibab Trail Route** (from Canyon View to Yaki Point). A route for visitors needing mobility assistance operates from Canyon View to Mather Point.

By car

Canyon View Information Plaza, Mather Point, Yaki Point Road (Mar-Nov) and Hermit (Mar-Nov) are all *not* accessible to private vehicles.

By coach

Choose from various Xanterra-run (*see p268*) sightseeing trips around the canyon rim, including the **Hermit's Rest Tour** ($16.75 per person), **Desert View Tour** ($29) and a popular 90min trip to watch the sunset from **Mohave Point** ($12.75). Call 1-303 297 2757 for reservations or visit the desks at Bright Angel, Maswik and Yavapai Lodges, or at Canyon View Information Plaza, to book your place.

By taxi

A 24hr taxi service can be booked on 1-928 638 2822.

Exploring the canyon

Hiking in the canyon

However limited your time may be, try to hike at least part of the way into the canyon. As jaw-dropping as the views are from the rim, it is almost too huge to take in the full extent of this unique environment. Really, you need to get closer to appreciate the stunning colours of the cliffs, to identify the different geological layers of rock, to see the turbulent brown waters and hear the roar of the Colorado River.

Just because the upper trails teem with crowds doesn't mean that you're at a theme park. The extremes of terrain and climate are dangerous: always seek and heed advice from rangers and make sure you are properly equipped and provisioned, as well as in decent physical shape. Overnight hikes require a backcountry permit. These are strictly limited and must be applied for in advance via the website (or you can take your chances on the day and turn up at the Backcountry Information Center at 8am – which is not a very good idea in high season).

Hikers should note that mule riders have priority on the **Bright Angel**, **South Kaibab** and **North Kaibab** trails. Stop walking when the mules approach, and follow the instructions of the rider leading the tour. For further details of mule rides, *see p271*.

Backcountry Information Center

Grand Canyon National Park, PO Box 129, Grand Canyon, AZ 86023 (1-928 638 7875 1-5pm Mon-Fri/fax 1-928 638 2125). **Open** 8am-noon, 1-5pm daily. **Rates** *Backcountry permit* $10, plus $5 per person per night. **No credit cards**.

Bright Angel Trail

Grand Canyon Village to Phantom Ranch. **Round trip** 19.2 miles. **Duration** 2 days.

This popular, maintained trail follows the line of a wide geological fault, which shifted the layering of the rock strata; as you descend you can see that the layers on the left are much higher than those on the right. Water is usually available (May-Sept) at the resthouses 1.5 miles and 3 miles from the trailhead (the first one also has toilet facilities). These are good day-hike destinations, but can get crowded; more experienced hikers could head for the campground at **Indian Gardens** (4.5 miles), whose tall cotton-woods, planted in the early 1900s, can be seen from the rim. From here you can take a detour to **Plateau Point** (6.1 miles) for a dramatic view into the river gorge, or continue on the River Trail to the east, crossing the **Bright Angel Suspension Bridge** to reach Phantom Ranch.

Grandview Trail
Grandview Point to Horseshoe Mesa. **Round trip** 6.4 miles. **Duration** 1 day.
This unmaintained trail is steep and should only be attempted by experienced hikers. There's no water en route, but there are toilet facilities at **Horseshoe Mesa**, the site of an abandoned mining works.

Hermit Trail
Hermit's Rest to Colorado River. **Round trip** 18.4 miles. **Duration** 2-3 days.
This difficult trail passes Hermit Gorge, Santa Maria Spring and the Redwall Formation en route to the Colorado River and is recommended for experienced desert hikers only. A precipitous side trail leads for 1.5 miles to **Dripping Springs**. There is no drinking water on the trail; spring water must be treated.

North Kaibab Trail
North Rim to Colorado River Bridge. **Round trip** 29.2 miles. **Duration** 3-4 days.
The North Kaibab trail starts about 1.5 miles from Grand Canyon Lodge on the North Rim and begins with a beautiful but steep hike through the trees. The **Supai Tunnel** (1.8 miles) is an ideal day hike with a great view of the canyon, plus water and toilet facilities. There is little shade beyond this point. More experienced hikers might make it to **Roaring Springs**, but should not attempt to go further than this and back in one day. Beyond Roaring Springs the trail continues to **Phantom Ranch** (13.8 miles) and the **Colorado River Bridge** (14.6 miles).

South Kaibab Trail
Yaki Point to Phantom Ranch. **Round trip** 12.6 miles. **Duration** 2 days.
This trail, which starts 5 miles east of Grand Canyon Village, is shorter but steeper than Bright Angel trail, dropping 5,000ft (1,500m) in a little over six miles. The route follows a series of ridge lines, crossing the Colorado at the **Kaibab Suspension Bridge** on its way to Phantom Ranch. There is no campground or water en route; you can hike to the tree-dotted plateau of **Cedar Ridge** (1.5 miles) if you're short of time.

Mule rides

Mule rides into the canyon are operated by **Xanterra** (*see p268*), and booking is essential. The **day trip** ($132 per person) takes you 3,200 feet (1,000 metres) down the Bright Angel trail to Plateau Point. On the **two-day trip** ($360 one person, $641 two people), you'll go down the Bright Angel trail, overnight in a cabin in the magical setting of Phantom Ranch and return on the shorter South Kaibab trail, allowing you to see the canyon from a different perspective. From mid-November to mid-March there are also **three-day trips**, with meals and two nights' accommodation at Phantom Ranch ($507 one person, $855 two people).

Plane & helicopter rides

Plane and helicopter rides over the rim are a major cause of air and noise pollution in the canyon, reducing visibility and disturbing the area's natural tranquillity. None are available from within the park. However, if you must get a bird's-eye view, various outfits operating out of Grand Canyon Airport in Tusayan will oblige. Plane rides start from around $100; helicopter rides are more expensive. For details of flights departing from Las Vegas, *see p111*.
Air Grand Canyon *1-800 247 4726/1-928 638 2686/www.airgrandcanyon.com.*
Grand Canyon Airlines *1-866 235 9422/1-928 638 2359/www.grandcanyonairlines.com.*
Papillon Grand Canyon Helicopters *1-800 528 2418/1-928 638 2419/www.papillon.com.*

River rafting

Follow in the wake of one-armed explorer Major John Wesley Powell, the first man to navigate the length of the Colorado River by boat (in 1869), by taking a river trip through the rapids of the Grand Canyon. It's a major undertaking:

Tips for the trail

To prevent yourself becoming one of the statistics of dehydrated or exhausted hikers picked up by rangers (the number of search and rescue missions each year regularly tops the 400 mark), take note of the following hiking advice:
● Know your limitations and choose a hike that is suited to both your ability and your fitness.
● Allow twice as much time to walk up as down. A three-hour canyon hike means one hour down, two hours up.
● Never attempt to hike from the rim to the river and back in one day.
● There is little shade in the inner canyon, so avoid hiking in the hottest part of the day; start early in the morning or delay your hike until after 4pm.
● Water supplies below the rim are very limited, so carry plenty (allow one gallon per person per day in summer).
● Eat high-energy food. A few granola bars or a bag of trail mix is not enough for a day's arduous hiking.
● Wear proper hiking boots and take a ten-minute rest every hour; if you begin to feel faint, raising your legs above the level of your heart will aid recovery.

you'll need at least eight days to travel the entire distance – 277 miles downriver from Lees Ferry at the far eastern end of the Grand Canyon to Pearce Ferry on Lake Mead – and you'll have to book months in advance. A list of approved operators is on the national park's website, under the 'River' heading.

The only way of doing a shorter trip is to hike in or out of the canyon; companies such as **Canyoneers** (1-800 525 0924 outside Arizona, 1-928 526 0924 within, www.canyoneers.com) also offer shorter trips that start or finish at **Bright Angel Beach**, near Phantom Ranch. Although these trips mean less time on the river, remember that you will also have to hike in or out of the canyon at the beginning or end of your trip.

For whitewater trips from **Diamond Creek** in Grand Canyon West (roughly a four-hour drive from the South Rim), *see p266*.

Staying in the canyon

Phantom Ranch, down at the bottom of the canyon, was designed by Mary Colter in 1922 and is a welcome oasis after the rigours of a strenuous hike. Hikers who stay at Phantom Ranch do not need backcountry permits, but will need to book their accommodation months in advance; the rustic log and stone cabins ($81 for two) and more modern dorms ($30 per person) are usually filled to capacity. Non-guests can eat at the ranch, but must book meals in advance ($17.50 breakfast, $10 packed lunch, $21-$32 dinner).

There are campsites at **Indian Gardens**, **Bright Angel** (next to Phantom Ranch) and **Cottonwood Springs** (open May to October, accessible from the North Rim on the North Kaibab Trail). You need a backcountry permit to use them; *see p270*.

The North Rim

From the South Rim you can see lightning forks hit the **North Rim** ten miles across the canyon, but to reach it you'll have to hike down to the bottom and up again, drive 200 miles or catch the rim-to-rim bus. The North Rim is 1,000 feet (300 metres) higher and only open mid-May to mid-October; it has fewer facilities and is less accessible than the South Rim, so doesn't get as busy. Many seasoned visitors prefer the North Rim for this reason; its tranquil atmosphere can still evoke what it may have been like to visit the canyon in the early days. That said, it can get crowded and you should book ahead for lodging. Facilities on the North Rim include a visitors' centre, a grocery, camping supplies shops and a post office.

Where to stay & eat

Grand Canyon Lodge (run by Xanterra; 1-303 297 2757, same-day reservations 1-520 638 2631) has rooms and cabins ($92-$116 double) and a dining room. There's also a campsite (1-800 365 2267, $15-$20 per night). Booking is advisable. Outside the park, there are lodging and eating facilities at **Kaibab Lodge**, 18 miles north (1-800 525 0925, 1-928 526 0924, www.kaibab.org) and **Jacob Lake Inn**, 45 miles north (1-928 643 7232, www.jacoblake.com).

Getting there

By bus

The only public transport to the North Rim is the **Trans Canyon Shuttle** bus service between the two rims; the journey takes about 5hrs and costs $6. Call 1-928 638 2820 for details.

By car

From Las Vegas, head north on the I-15, then east on Hwy 9, Hwy 59 and US 89A to **Jacob Lake**. The park entrance is 30 miles south of Jacob Lake on Hwy 67; the canyon rim is a further 14 miles. At a distance of 263 miles, the North Rim is nearer to Las Vegas than the South Rim, but the journey will take longer.

California

The wildest deserts and the hugest cities: welcome to the Golden State.

You'll see them every weekend, their California license plates and casual insouciance immediately marking your fellow gamblers, diners or drinkers as Angelenos escaping Los Angeles for a weekend in Sin City. However, as Las Vegas has grown in size, many of its own residents now drive down I-15 in the opposite direction, into California and towards LA.

The route between the two cities takes the driver through pioneer country, traversed in the 19th century by migrants travelling westwards, celebrated in the 20th century in Hollywood Westerns, and now offering 21st-century trippers a dramatic landscape. Just across the Nevada–California border lies the vast expanse of the **Mojave National Preserve**. Alternatively, head west to America's most infamous desert area, the starkly beautiful **Death Valley National Park**. Note that much of south-western California is remote, largely uninhabited and sometimes scorching, so take suitable precautions for desert driving and hiking (*see p259*).

Along I-15

You can throw the dice one last time at the mini-gambling resorts of Jean, a few miles from the Californian border, and tiny Primm, on the border itself. **Jean** is the older of the two, and feels like it. The visitor centre (874 1360) behind the Gold Strike, one of two casinos, provides information on Jean, Primm and other nearby attractions. Among them are the ghost town **Goodsprings**, which hit the headlines in 1942 when Clark Gable waited here for news of the plane crash that killed his wife, Carole Lombard.

Primm is a three-resort cluster of more modern aspect, making the most of its location on the Nevada–California state line to get first dibs on desperate inbound gamblers. The success of the Primm family's first casino-hotel, Whiskey Pete's, was so great they followed it with Primm Valley and Buffalo Bill's (1-800 386 7867, www.primadonna.com for all three). Continuing south, the I-15 passes through stunning scenery along the northern boundary of **Mojave National Preserve** (*see p277*). The small town of **Baker**, 90 miles south of Vegas, makes a convenient gateway to this vast swathe of wilderness, and is home to the world's tallest thermometer, which measures

134 feet (40 metres) top to toe. West, the I-15 continues through stark desert for 63 miles until it reaches **Barstow**, an unattractive town notable primarily for its location on historic Route 66 and the assortment of small heritage attractions in it. Beyond the high desert hick-town of **Hesperia**, I-15 takes you through the pine-capped wilderness of the San Bernardino Mountains until it hits the Los Angeles sprawl.

Los Angeles

If you haven't been to Los Angeles before, the first thing you need to know is that it doesn't really exist as an identifiable place. Los Angeles is a city, a county and a region; the county contains 88 cities merged into a single vast agglomeration more than 100 miles wide, of which the city of Los Angeles is the nominal heart. If you only have a short time, you should focus on the area between Downtown and the ocean, known as the LA basin, which includes the best-known beach areas and the fabulous burgs of the rich and famous. Note that LA merits far more space than we can grant it here; for the full story, pick up *Time Out Los Angeles*.

DOWNTOWN

Downtown LA is an odd stew of old and new, vibrant and stagnant, beautiful and ugly, circumscribed by a vast moat of freeways. Some of LA's most stunning architecture is here: at

For more on Los Angeles and California, see the 320-page **Time Out Los Angeles** (UK: Ebury £12.99; US: PGW $19.95) or the 416-page **Time Out California** (UK: Ebury £13.99; US: PGW $19.95).

the romantic **Union Station**, you almost expect to see Bogie and Bergman kissing a star-crossed goodbye, while the **Bradbury Building** (304 S Broadway) is an early 20th-century masterpiece that featured in *Blade Runner*. However, the recent regeneration of the area – new hotels and restaurants are opening here all the time, and people are starting to move here permanently in numbers for the first time in years – is also in evidence, never more so than in the distinctive shape of Frank Gehry's stunning **Walt Disney Concert Hall** (111 S Grand Avenue, 1-213 972 7211), home of the LA Philharmonic. Also of note are the **Museum of Contemporary Art** (MOCA; *see p276*) and two lively ethnic enclaves: **Chinatown**, at Downtown's northern extremity, and the Mexican-dominated area of **Broadway**. South, the **Staples Center** (1111 Figueroa Street, at 11th Street, www.staples center.com) stages NBA games and concerts. In Koreatown, the 1927 Mexican restaurant **El Cholo** serves as the home base for much of the MexiCali cuisine that followed.

HOLLYWOOD

The tourist authorities would have you believe that **Hollywood** has been undergoing a sort of renaissance. Certainly, it's a lot less sleazy than it once was, the X-rated cinemas having long since been replaced by souvenir shops. However, the recent rechristening of the area as the 'Hollywood Entertainment District' is a little optimistic, not to mention contrived. The Hollywood & Highland complex, the area's big new showcase attraction, is a bafflingly laid out jumble of shops and restaurants, and sights such as the **Hollywood Wax Museum** (6767 Hollywood Boulevard, 1-323 462 8860, www. hollywoodwax.com) are rather tacky. This isn't the centre of the movie industry, and don't let anyone convince you it is: most studios are in or near Burbank, and celebrities are conspicuous by their absence away from Oscars night.

Still, there are a few places well worth a stop: the historic **Mann's Chinese** and **El Capitan Theaters** (6925 & 6838 Hollywood Boulevard), the **Hollywood Roosevelt Hotel** (No.7000) and the beautiful **Pantages Theatre** (No.6233) among them. The **Walk of Fame**, with bronze stars embedded in the Hollywood Boulevard pavement paying tribute to over 2,000 show-biz greats (and not-so-greats who had some spare cash and a good publicist), extends from the corner of Vine Street and Hollywood Boulevard.

WEST HOLLYWOOD, BEVERLY HILLS AND BEL AIR

West of Hollywood lies, er, **West Hollywood**, through which is threaded the stretch of Sunset Boulevard known commonly as the **Sunset Strip**. The centre of LA nightlife since the 1920s, it's a little dowdy these days, its clubs past their prime, but there are a few spots worth seeking out. It's also home to some of LA's best hotels, most notably the Mondrian, the Standard and the perennially glamorous Chateau Marmont. South of here is **Melrose Avenue**: not as cutting-edge as it once was, it's still a mecca of LA cool, with restaurants, galleries, theatres and shops.

Hometown boy Frank Gehry's **Walt Disney Concert Hall**.

All the clichés about Beverly Hills are true: it's glamorous, star-packed, expensive, inaccessible, stylish and totally out of most visitors' league. Still, that doesn't stop them trying to make themselves at home along its wide boulevards and cosy shopping streets. Whether hard-core shopper or sociologist, you shouldn't miss a walk on and around **Rodeo Drive**. In the heart of the area, these few blocks embody conspicuous consumption at its best or worse. Trinkets sell for thousands, and men, women and kids don furs, silks and giant gemstones for a regular afternoon outing. Nearby, the university area of **Westwood** isn't nearly as interesting as it should be.

Bel Air, also home to the rich and famous, is a posh hillside community west of here. Known for its privacy and pretty views, the gated houses in this neighbourhood are visual feasts, though most of them are hidden from the public gaze. To get a closer look, stop in for tea at the ultra-exclusive Hotel Bel-Air (701 Stone Canyon Road, 1-800 648 4097, www.hotelbelair.com).

THE BEACH TOWNS

Beautifully framed by mountains and sea, affluent **Santa Monica** is the jewel of LA's Westside, the heart of bourgeois liberalism. Its centre is the four pedestrianised blocks that make up the 3rd Street Promenade. Hordes of Angelenos mill around the stores on weekends, entertained by street performers. The area's handy for the beach, with ample parking on 2nd and 4th Streets. There's good shopping and food on Main Street between Edgemar and Rose Avenues.

Turning south off Venice Boulevard on to Dell Avenue, about a quarter of a mile back from the beach, you'll find **Venice**. At the end of the 20th century, builders, the government and, notably, the tobacco magnate Abbot Kinney transformed this area into the 'Venice of America', complete with canals, bridges, gondolas and a bohemian spirit. The first three have all gone, but the vibe just about remains: Venice as a whole is a mixed and magnetic community of post-1960s hippies, the elderly and the artistic. Abbot Kinney Boulevard is good for food and window-shopping. And, of course, there's (in)famous **Venice Beach**.

Major sights & attractions

Disneyland

1313 S Harbor Boulevard, between Katella Avenue & Ball Road, Anaheim (1-714 781 4000/recorded information 1-714 781 4565/www.disneyland.com). **Open** daily. Hours vary by season: call or check online for full details. **Admission** *One park for one day* $53; $43 discounts; free under-3s. Combination tickets also available. **Credit** AmEx, DC, Disc, MC, V.

A spectacular piece of pop art that's as bright or dark as you'd like it to be. Incorporating two parks – the 50-year-old **Disneyland**, split into seven themed areas (Fantasyland, Main Street USA, etc), and the newer **Disney's California Adventure** – with the outdoor shopping and dining mall, **Downtown Disney**, between them. The resort calls itself 'The Happiest Place on Earth'. If you bring the right mood to it, it certainly can be. It's not so much a park as its own separate world; there are even three Disney-operated hotels here. The main drawback to spending time here, once you've budgeted for food, lodgings and souvenirs, is the sheer expense: the fun sure don't come cheap.

Hollywood Museum

1660 N Highland Avenue, at Hollywood Boulevard, Hollywood (1-323 464 7776/www.thehollywood museum.com). **Open** 10am-5pm Thur-Sun. **Admission** $15; $5-$12 discounts. **Credit** AmEx, MC, V.

First known as the Hollywood Fire & Safe Building, this structure was converted in 1928 into a beauty salon by Max Factor. A refurbishment seven years later turned it into an art deco classic; a recent five-year renovation has restored it to something like its former glory. Since 2002 it's housed this museum, which surveys the last century of movie-making.

Los Angeles Zoo

5333 Zoo Drive, Griffith Park (1-323 644 4200/ www.lazoo.org). **Open** *July-Labor Day* 10am-6pm daily. *Labor Day-June* 10am-5pm daily. *Last entry* 1hr before closing. **Admission** $10; $5-$7 concessions; free under-2s. **Credit** AmEx, Disc, MC, V.

Take the Safari Shuttle on a loop of the excellent LA Zoo before venturing on foot for a closer look; the

TV tapings

LA is the best place on earth for TV junkies to get their fix. What's more, tickets are free: you can score them from clipboard-toting 'brokers' on Venice Beach, Universal CityWalk or Hollywood Boulevard, or by writing to the studios. But the easiest way to snag a seat is on the internet from **Audience Associates** (1-323 653 4105, www.tvtix.com), which has tickets to such shows as *The Price is Right* and *The Tonight Show with Jay Leno*; **Audiences Unlimited** (1-818 753 3470 ext 810, www.tvtickets.com), which doles out tickets to more than 30 shows during peak season (Aug-Mar); and **Hollywood Tickets** (1-818 688 3974, www.hollywoodtickets.com). Allow up to three or four hours of taping time. All shows have minimum age requirements.

Trips Out of Town

Mojave National Preserve.

perspective will help you (and your kids) figure out what you want to see. The $6.5 million Red Ape Rainforest, where orang-utans live in an imitation Indonesian rainforest, is popular, but was overshadowed in summer 2004 by a new sea lion habitat and kids' Discovery Center at the front of the zoo.

Museum of Contemporary Art & Geffen Contemporary

MOCA *250 S Grand Avenue, at 3rd Street, Downtown.* **Geffen Contemporary** *152 N Central Avenue, at 1st Street, Downtown.* **Both** *1-213 621 6222/www.moca.org.* **Open** 11am-5pm Mon, Fri; 11am-8pm Thur; 11am-6pm Sat, Sun. **Admission** Combined ticket $8; $5 concessions; free under-12s. Free to all Thur. **Credit** AmEx, MC, V.

A premier showcase for post-war art, the Museum of Contemporary Art splits its life between the Geffen Contemporary, a humongous bus barn, and a newer building a block from the Civic Center. Upwards of half a dozen shows can be viewed at any single time between the two venues; MOCA stages the more mainstream exhibits, leaving the Geffen to concentrate on more esoteric art.

Universal Studios & CityWalk

100 Universal City Plaza, Universal City (1-800 864 8377/www.universalstudios.com). **Open** daily. Hours vary by season: call or check online for full details. **Admission** $53; $43 concessions; under-3s free. **Credit** AmEx, DC, Disc, MC, V.

Once you've run the gauntlet of CityWalk, crammed with souvenir hawkers and junk-food retailers, you'll find an attraction whose entertainment value is more than the sum of its parts. The rides, while fun, aren't as exciting as one might expect; you're here for the illusion of glamour. The pick of the themed attractions, for both adults and kids, is the *Shrek 4-D* movie. The studio tour is cheesy but enjoyable; the rest is mush. Arrive early to avoid the worst crowds.

Where to stay, eat & drink

A string of high-concept restaurants appeared in LA in the 1980s, putting the city on the culinary map; things have only improved since then. It can be dizzying for visitors: consult *Time Out Los Angeles* for reviews of the latest hotspots.

For places to stay, contact the **Los Angeles Convention & Visitors Bureau** (*see below*). For hotel contacts, *see p53* **The chain gang**.

Getting there

By car

Los Angeles is around 300 miles from Las Vegas; the journey can take 4-8hrs, depending on traffic and how closely you observe the posted speed limits.

By bus

Greyhound operates a frequent service between Las Vegas and LA, costing $39 one-way or $75 return.

By air

Fares vary tremendously, depending on availability and time of year, but usually the earlier you book, the better the price. For airlines, *see p290*.

Tourist information

For insider information on LA, pick up *Time Out Los Angeles*. Online, consult www.at-la.com.

Los Angeles Convention & Visitors Bureau

685 S Figueroa Street, between 7th Street & Wilshire Boulevard, Downtown, LA, CA 90017 (1-213 689 8822/www.lacvb.com). I-110, exit 9th Street east. **Open** 8am-5pm Mon-Fri; 8.30am-5pm Sat. **Other locations**: 6541 Hollywood Boulevard, at Hudson Avenue, Hollywood (1-213 689 8822).

Mojave National Preserve

Covering a gigantic rectangle bordered by I-15 to the north and I-40 to the south, the 2,500-square-mile **Mojave National Preserve** is a Cinderella park: it has no honeypot attractions, low visitorship and few facilities, and is really best approached as a giant and fascinating desert sampler. The meeting point of three of the four types of North American desert – Mojave, Great Basin and Sonoran – it contains a variety of terrains, features and ecosystems, including the human. Because its protected status is recent (it was upgraded from a Scenic Area to a National Preserve in 1994), historical relics of inhabitants and would-be conquerors, from early man right through to 20th-century ranchers, dot the landscape. Spanish explorers, western pioneers and routefinders, soldiers, navvies and settlers passed this way, leaving behind roads and railroads still in use today.

Mojave National Preserve has been developed only minimally: there are just four paved roads and three marked trails, and gas and lodging are available only on its borders. You can see plenty by car and on short walks, but for those with 4WD, it's truly an off-road paradise: numerous unpaved roads include the 140-mile east–west Mojave Road, a Native American track developed by successive users (see *Mojave Road Guide* by Dennis Casebier). Go off-road, and you take your safety into your own hands. The best times to visit are spring or autumn; it's brutally hot from mid-May to mid-September, often over 110°F (43°C).

A good starting point from I-15 is the small town of Baker. Fill up on gas and drinking water while you're here. If you've only a few hours, a 67-mile triangular drive from Baker, via the Kelbaker Road, Kelso-Cima Road and Cima Road, to rejoin I-15 at the end of the trek, is a good introduction to the sights.

You pass the reddish humps of over 30 young volcanic cones before reaching **Kelso**, which used to be a major passenger stop on the Union Pacific Railroad. The grand, Spanish Mission-style depot, built in 1924 and closed in 1985, is in the process of being turned into a visitor centre, due to open in late 2005; when it does, the Desert Information Center in Baker, located beneath the giant thermometer, will close. If you want to detour to the 500-foot (150-metre) Kelso sand dunes, continue south from Kelso on the Kelbaker Road and turn right after about seven miles on to a signed dirt road. These 10,000- to 20,000-year-old dunes support a remarkable variety of plant and animal life, including the rarely seen desert tortoise.

Back in Kelso, turn left towards Cima, passing the 7,000-foot-high (2,150-metre) Providence Mountains en route. At Cima, you have a choice. Either take Cima Road towards I-15, past the gently swelling Cima Dome, which has the largest stand of Joshua trees in the world, or go up Morning Star Mine Road to Nipton Road up the Ivanpah Valley, then either take a left to I-15 or a right to tiny **Nipton** (population 40), just outside the preserve's northern edge. Here you'll find a railroad crossing, an old-fashioned store, a town hall and the charming **Hotel Nipton** (*see p278*).

If you've time, you could take the Essex Road to the **Providence Mountains State Recreation Area**, which is far cooler than the desert floor. Multi-branched cholla, spiky Mojave yucca, round barrel cactus, spindly Mormon tea and the flat pads of prickly pears share the upland slopes with juniper and piñon trees, creating a stunning geometric display. There are great views south from the visitor centre. This park within a park also houses the dramatic limestone **Mitchell Caverns**, which remain a cool 65°F (18°C) year round, good to know in summer. There are tours of the caves ($4 adults, $2 children) daily from Labor Day to Memorial Day, and Saturday and Sunday the rest of the year; call 1-760 928 2586 for details.

Another diversion from I-40 is a stretch of the old Route 66, featuring the kind of bleak desert landscapes beloved of cinematographers and the similarly iconic astro-googie Americana of photogenic **Amboy**. To the east, 66 crosses I-40 and dips back into the preserve to visit **Goffs**, a lonely spot despite – or perhaps because of – being 'the Desert Tortoise Capital of the World'. Further south is **Joshua Tree National Preserve**, worth a look in its own right.

Where to stay & eat

On the edge of the park, Baker has a clutch of pretty basic non-chain motels, but the pick of the park-side accommodation is the **Hotel Nipton** (1-760 856 2335, www.nipton.com, rates $69), an early-century hotel in splendid desert isolation (except, that is, for its wi-fi internet access); the nearby **Whistle Stop Oasis** (1-760 856 1045) serves good Italian-American food. The landmark grub is back in Baker at the rammed and rated **Mad Greek Diner** (1-760 733 4354), where fast food both Greek and American is served up. It is practically a criminal offence to leave without ordering the strawberry milkshake.

In the preserve itself, the new visitor centre at Kelso will have a lunch counter. Of the two campgrounds ($12, no reservations), **Mid-Hills** is usually cooler than **Hole-in-the-Wall**, and always much prettier. You'll need to drive some reliable but not always comfortable dirt roads to get here; Hole-in-the-Wall is accessible on blacktop from I-40.

Getting there

By car
Baker is 90 miles south of Las Vegas on the I-15. Nipton is located on Hwy 164, accessible via the I-15 or Hwy 95, 63 miles south of Las Vegas. To reach Joshua Tree National Park, take Kelbaker Road through the Mojave National Preserve and head south via Amboy until you reach Twentynine Palms; it's 130 miles from Baker to the park.

Tourist information

Chamber of Commerce
PO Box 241, Baker, CA 92309 (1-760 733 4469). **Open** 9am-5pm daily.

Desert Information Center
72157 Baker Boulevard, Baker, CA 92509 (1-760 733 4040). **Open** 9am-5pm daily.

Death Valley National Park

Enlarged and redesignated a national park under the 1994 Desert Protection Act, Death Valley is now the largest national park outside Alaska, covering more than 5,156 square miles. It's also, famously, one of the hottest places on the planet. The park's website calmly offers that 'Death Valley is generally sunny, dry and clear throughout the year'. True, but the word 'generally' masks a multitude of curiosities. Air temperatures regularly topping 120°F (49°C) in July and August (50 per cent higher on the ground), fearsome by anyone's standards.

However, while the park is generally parched – in an average year, it receives fewer than two inches of rain – it's not immune from water. In August 2004, terrifying flash floods hit Death Valley, killing two tourists and destroying parts of Highway 190 into the park. As of late 2005, the road between the small settlement of **Death Valley Junction** and Furnace Creek was closed for long-term reconstruction work, affecting the accessibility of **Dante's View**, a wonderful viewpoint some 5,475 feet (1,669 metres) above sea level, and **Zabriskie Point**, famed for the eponymous 1970 Antonioni film but recognisable to all by its ragged, rumpled appearance. For directions to the park, *see p279.*

Your first stop should be the **Death Valley Visitor Center** (*see p279*) at **Furnace Creek**, where you'll find an excellent bookshop, decent exhibits, a useful orientation film and helpful staff. Stop in for advice on current weather and road conditions (some tracks are only accessible to 4WD vehicles), pay your fee of $10 per car and take the opportunity to fill up at one of the park's three expensive gas stations.

Heading back north from Furnace Creek offers a greater variety of sights. The remains of the **Harmony Borax Works** have been casually converted into a short trail; there's a similarly simple walk, less historic but more aesthetically pleasing, at nearby **Salt Creek** (look out for pupfish in the stream in spring). Following the road around to the left will lead you past the eerie **Devil's Cornfield**, the frolicable **Sand Dunes**, which rise and dip in 100-foot (30-metre) increments, and on to the small settlement at **Stovepipe Wells**; taking a right and driving 36 miles will take you to the extravagant **Scotty's Castle** (1-760 786 2392); built in the 1920s for Chicago millionaire Albert Johnson, it was named after Walter Scott, his eccentric chancer of a friend. Costumed rangers tell the story during 50-minute tours from 9am to 5pm, usually hourly ($8; $4-$6 discounts).

If Highway 190 has reopened south of Furnace Creek, there'll be plenty more to see. At **Golden Canyon**, there's a straightforward two-mile round-trip hike that's best walked in the late afternoon sunlight: you'll see how the canyon got its name. Continuing south, the landscape gets plainer. Nine miles down the road is the **Devil's Golf Course**, a striking, scrappy landscape formed by salt crystallising and expanding; a few miles further is bleak, eerie **Badwater**, just two miles as the crow flies from Dante's View but over 5,000 feet (1,524 metres) lower. Nearby but inaccessible is the lowest point in the Western Hemisphere, 282 feet (86 metres) below sea level. It's only 85 miles from the highest point in the US, the 14,494-foot (4,420-metre) Mount Whitney in the Sierra Nevada. An annual bicycle race takes place between the two.

Alive in **Death Valley**.

It's often too hot to hike, but there are plenty of trails in Death Valley, short and long. The options include the 14-mile round-trip to the 11,000-foot (3,353-metre) summit of **Telescope Peak**, a good summer hike (the higher you climb, the cooler it gets). Starting at Mahogany Flat campground, you climb 3,000 feet (914 metres) for some spectacular views of Mount Whitney. In winter only experienced climbers with ice axes and crampons should attempt it.

Where to eat

Culinary pickings are a bit slim in these parts – there are restaurants at Furnace Creek Ranch, Stovepipe Wells Village and Panamint Springs – and the food tends to be fairly ordinary. The exception is the dining room at the **Furnace Creek Inn** (*see below*; closed mid May-mid Oct), where the upscale Californian food is much better than it has a right to be. The Inn also has a handsome bar; the watering hole at the related **Furnace Creek Ranch** is fun but more basic.

Where to stay

Set into the hillside above Furnace Creek Wash, 1930s **Furnace Creek Inn** (1-760 786 2345, www.furnacecreekresort.com, closed mid May-mid Oct, rates $250-$395) is the luxury option. **Furnace Creek Ranch** ($105-$182) has 200 motel-style rooms and cabins, as well as a pool, tennis courts and the world's lowest golf course. **Stovepipe Wells Village** has 83 rooms (1-760 786 2837, www.stovepipewells.com, rates $83-$103). Most of the park's nine campgrounds cost $10 a night; Furnace Creek (1-800 365 2267) and a few others are open all year.

Getting there

By car
With parts of Hwy 190 closed, the quickest way into Death Valley is to take the US 95 to Beatty and then head south on Hwy 374. If Hwy 190 has reopened, then the shortest route is via Pahrump. Go south on I-15 towards LA, exit on to Blue Diamond Road (at Silverton), then head west on Hwy 160 up and over the Spring Mountains. A few miles after Pahrump, take Bell Vista Road to Death Valley Junction and Hwy 190 into the park (120 miles). (Returning to Vegas via Death Valley Junction, note that Bell Vista Road is labelled State Line Road.) Call the Visitor Center or check online for the latest on Hwy 190's reopening.

Tourist information

Death Valley Visitor Center
Furnace Creek, Death Valley National Park, CA 92328 (1-760 786 3200/www.nps.gov/deva). **Open** 8am-5pm daily.

Nevada

Would you like to see the desert menu, sir?

See p282.

Those who claim that there's plenty more to Nevada outside Las Vegas are overstating their case a little. Those who aver that there's plenty more *of* Nevada outside Las Vegas, on the other hand, are right on the money. Although the state is the seventh largest in the Union, almost three-quarters of its residents live within 40 miles of Las Vegas, with half the remainder in the Reno-Sparks urban area. That leaves an awful lot of not very much.

Yet after Vegas, an awful lot of not very much can be just what one needs. The under-visited **Valley of Fire State Park** (*see p263*) is truly stunning, offering the kind of absolute and carefree escape from civilisation that **Red Rock Canyon** (*see p263*), on the edge of the city, fails quite to provide as the city continues to creep west, ever closer to it. The drive north-west from Vegas to **Reno** on I-95 offers desert landscape alternately bleak and beautiful under skies as big as you'll ever see. The smattering of towns along it are scruffy but fascinating, all in thrall to the prospectors and chancers who established them a century ago. And then there's the **Extraterrestrial Highway**, named after the many extraordinary tales of UFO sightings and other sinister goings-on at Nevada Test Site's infamous Area 51.

The road to Reno

US 95 leaves the lights of Las Vegas behind in a hurry. As the road roars out through the city's north-western corner, the landscape visible from the driver's seat empties from urban sprawl into endless desert. Get used to the view. You'll have seen a lot like it by the time your 450-mile ride from Vegas to Reno is complete. Soon, you'll be rolling past **Mount Charleston** (*see p264*). On the right sits **Nellis Air Force Range**, a vast tract of desert that, with an area of 5,200 square miles, is slightly larger than state of Connecticut.

From 1951 until 1995 the US government, which owns over 80 per cent of the land in Nevada, used the **Nevada Test Site**, which is flanked on three sides by the Nellis Range, to test atomic weapons, both above ground and beneath it. Famously, Vegas treated the blasts as an excuse to party. Day-long tours of the site are now available to those prescient enough to book two months ahead and prepared to supply all manner of information to get themselves through security, tight before 9/11 and now even tighter. Details can be found at www.nv.doe.gov, or from 295 0944.

Shortly after Indian Springs, you'll leave Clark County and enter Nye County. At 18,147 square miles, it's the third largest county in the US, but it's also one of the emptiest: the 2000 census tagged the population at 34,075 people. Signs of life are few and far between. At **Amargosa Valley**, close to the junction of US 95 and SR 373 (leading towards **Death Valley**, for which see p278), a thoroughly unprepossessing complex of buildings houses a bar, a gas station and a brothel, making it perhaps America's ultimate travellers' rest area. Across the road sits another bar; nearby, on SR 373, sits Jackass Airport, named for the animal rather than the idiocy of the local pilots. And that's more or less it.

The area has been in the news lately after the government suggested that **Yucca Mountain**, just north of Amargosa Valley, would be the perfect spot in which to dump America's nuclear waste. But while the citizens of Las Vegas, 80 miles away, have been up in arms about the plans, locals are ambivalent, balancing health concerns with optimism that the site might bring more business to the area's saloons, stores and whorehouses. Tours of the mountain, which sits inside the Nevada Test Site, are available, though you'll need to book several months ahead to get a place; call 821 8042 for details.

Head 30 miles north-west of Amargosa Valley and you'll find **Beatty**, established – as were so many towns at the turn of the 20th century – by prospectors ambitious to make their fortunes. When word got around that Ed Cross and Frank 'Shorty' Harris had discovered a goldmine in the hills, hundreds of hopefuls descended on the area, leading Walter Beatty to set up a town on his homestead. The volunteer-run **Beatty Museum** (417 Main Street, 1-775 553 2967, www.beattymuseum.com, open 10am-2pm daily) offers exhibits and anecdotes on these early days.

Beatty is now a ramshackle collection of casinos and bars, but at least it's still a town, which is more than can be said for nearby **Rhyolite**. An archetypal gold rush town, it sprung up after gold was found in August 1904. The first lots were sold in February 1905; by 1908, 10,000 locals were served by schools, hospitals, 50 bars, an opera house and a huge red light district. But by 1910, all but a few hundred had moved on to the next boomtown, leaving the town to crumble. Today, a handful of buildings sit in various states of disrepair, weather-beaten and neglected but refusing to vanish; hand-drawn street signs remind visitors that these desert tracks were once busy thoroughfares. It's a fascinating, melancholy place. To reach it, take SR 374 south from Beatty (towards Death Valley) for about four miles, then take a right. Also here is the **Goldwell Open Air Museum** (www.goldwellmuseum.org), a haunting spot which comprises a half-dozen works by Belgian artists who settled in the area 20 years ago. Look out for Albert Szukalski's striking sculpture *The Last Supper* – although, to be honest, it's pretty hard to miss.

Some 50 miles north of Beatty sits **Goldfield**, another former mining town whose population surged from nothing to 10,000 between 1902 (when gold was discovered here) and 1907, and then doubled in the following three years. It didn't last, but Goldfield refused to die: a population of 500 makes it a sizeable settlement for this part of the world. If several grand stone buildings, including the Goldfield Hotel, the courthouse and the imposing former fire station (now a putative fire museum), are poignant reminders of the town's heyday, the shambling Mozart Club and Santa Fe Saloon offer evidence that not everybody got lucky.

It's 26 miles from Goldfield north to **Tonopah**, which sits on US 95 at about the halfway point between Vegas, 208 miles to the south, and Reno, 235 miles north-west of here. It's another town built on the hopes of a sole prospector: Jim Butler found silver here in 1900, and over the next 15 years (until the lode ran out) almost $150 million of ore was dug from the small mines that dot the area. The **Central Nevada Museum** (1900 Logan Field Road, 1-775 482 9676, www.tonopahnevada.com, closed Mon & Tue) details this history, though if time's tight, you might be better off heading for the **Tonopah Historic Mining Park** (520 McCulloch Street, 1-775 482 9274, www.tonopahnevada.com, closed Mon & Tue Oct-Mar, admission $3) instead and wandering the century-old buildings on the self-guided tour there. Certainly, there's not much else likely to detain you in this edgily charming but still fairly archetypal crossroads town at the junction of US 95 and US 6.

From here, the landscape gets plainer. Settlements seem further apart – the next town of any note, **Hawthorne**, is 100 miles down the road – and there's little to engage the senses save the freedom of an open road. Until, that is, a few miles after Hawthorne, when you find US 95 narrowing and curving – quite a shock after 300 miles of mainly straight highway – as it forces its way around a sizeable body of water.

Trips Out of Town

In prehistoric times, **Walker Lake** covered much of western Nevada. These days, though still 20 miles long, it's in decline, dropping 100 feet (30 metres) since 1930 as the Walker River was diverted for irrigation purposes. Although not spectacularly beautiful, the lake and the state park that frames it are popular spots for swimming, boating and camping; call the state park on 1-775 867 3001 for more details on park activities, or see http://parks.nv.gov/walk.htm.

About 30 miles north of Hawthorne is **Schurz**, a town every bit as unbecoming as its name, after which there are several routes to Reno. The quickest is to take US 95 north to Fallon, then pick up US 50 and Alternate US 50 to the surprisingly picturesque I-80, and head west on the Interstate into Reno. A slightly slower, slightly more scenic option is to head west on Alternate US 95 at Schurz, via the pleasant town of **Yerington** and the enjoyably green **Fort Churchill Historic State Park** in Silver Springs (1-775 577 2345, www.parks. nv.gov/fc.htm, admission $4), and then pick up I-80 to Reno near Fernley. The slowest option is to take this latter route as far as Silver Springs, then take US 50, SR 341 and US 395 into Reno via cutesy **Virginia City** (*see p285*). Our advice? Take the speedy run into Reno, but return to Vegas via Virginia City.

Where to stay, eat & drink

In Tonopah, choose from numerous motels along the main street. The large **Tonopah Station** casino (1100 Erie Main Street, 1-775 482 9777) has a dark, cramped gaming area, rooms, a restaurant and a wonderful collection of old chrome slot machines in the basement next to the toilets. **El Marques** (1-775 482 3885) serves decent, good-value Mexican food.

Hawthorne has a number of motels and one casino, the **El Capitan** (540 F Street, 1-775 945 3321). **Maggie's Restaurant** (US 95 at E Street, 1-775 945 3908) is a clean place that serves burgers, salads and sandwiches.

Tourist information

For information about **Tonopah**, contact the Chamber of Commerce at 301 Brougher Avenue (1-775 482 3859/www.tonopahnevada.com).

Reno

Popular culture flags the differences. In song, Las Vegas is the town that set Elvis's soul on fire; Reno is where Johnny Cash shot a man just to watch him die. On film, Vegas always looks glamorous, stealing scenes from every actor dumb enough to compete with it. The finest

Reno movie is Paul Thomas Anderson's *Hard Eight* (aka *Sydney*), a bleak, edgy tale set in the shadows of the town's gaming industry.

To visitors, especially those from abroad, Reno can't compete with Las Vegas. The casinos are smaller and shabbier, the neon less dazzling, the dining not as varied and the entertainment decidedly wearier. But to suggest that Reno is Vegas in miniature is to do it a disservice. In any case, if Reno can't compete with Las Vegas – both are gambling towns, so, to that extent, the comparison's a fair one – it only has itself to blame. In the 1950s the city fathers passed a law that limited gambling to downtown Reno, and watched for two decades as Vegas exploded in popularity, population and wealth. The law was repealed in 1978, but it was too late: Reno's been playing a half-hearted game of catch-up ever since. Still, locals are proud of their town and disparaging about their putative rival. Just as the famed **Reno Arch**, which bridges N Virginia Street at the junction of W Commercial Row, advertises Reno as 'The Biggest Little City in the World', so some locals pin Vegas as the littlest big city in the world, a gag as wry as it is inaccurate. Either way, there's little love lost between Renoites and Las Vegans.

In truth, gambling aside, the two cities have little in common. Where Vegas is an anything-goes, 24-7 kind of town, Reno's slower, prettier and more conservative. The flow of the Truckee River through downtown is attractive, and if the Riverwalk that's been built around it doesn't differ wildly from the formula that's been applied in countless other American cities (a few shops, a handful of restaurants), it's no less pleasant for its lack of originality.

Reno also benefits from the variety of its seasons. Winter can be viciously cold, but you won't hear a word of complaint from the skiers who jam the slopes of the 20-plus resorts within an hour of town. Summer, meanwhile, is usually balmy, with outdoor events galore. The biggest is **Hot August Nights** (www.hotaugust nights.net), a 1950s-themed mix of classic cars and rock 'n' roll, but **Street Vibrations** in September (www.road-shows.com), the Harley-Davidson equivalent, keeps pace with it.

Casinos

Though there are a handful of casinos out of the centre, notably the monstrous **Reno Hilton** (2500 E 2nd Street, at US 395, 1-800 501 2651, www.renohilton.com) and the colourful **Peppermill** (2707 S Virginia Street, at W Grove Street, 1-866 821 9996, www.peppermillreno. com), Reno's gambling is mostly downtown, around the junction of N Virginia Street and E Second Street. Some of the names in lights

Trips Out of Town

The prospectors replaced by tourists, **Virginia City** still thrives. *See p285.*

will be familiar to gamblers fresh from Vegas, among them the characterless **Harrah's** (219 N Center Street, at E 2nd Street, Reno, 1-775 786 3232, www.harrahs.com) and the family-friendly **Circus Circus** (500 N Sierra Street, at W 5th Street, 1-800 648 5010/1-775 329 0711, www. circusreno.com).

Other casinos, though, are unique to Reno. The **Eldorado** (345 N Virginia Street, at W 4th Street, 1-800 648 5966, 1-775 786 5700, www.eldoradoreno.com) is the most pleasant downtown operation, while the upscale **Silver Legacy** (407 N Virginia Street, at W 4th Street, 1-800 687 8733, 1-775 325 7401, www.silver legacyreno.com) boasts a lobby filled with treasures from Tiffany's. It's in stark contrast to the **Cal-Neva Virginian** (140 N Virginia Street, at E 2nd Street, 1-877 777 7303, 1-775 323 1046, www.clubcalneva.com): anyone for 99¢ ham and eggs?

Sights & attractions

The newish **Nevada Museum of Art** (160 W Liberty Street, 1-775 329 3333, www.nevada art.org, closed Mon, $1-$8), housed in a striking black building, has a strong permanent collection, the majority from the last century. There's also a programme of temporary shows: check online for details.

The **National Automobile Museum** (10 S Lake Street, 1-775 333 9300, www.automuseum. org, $3-$8) isn't just the best museum in Reno: it might also be the best museum in Nevada. The building holds over 200 cars from a timeframe of over a century, from an 1892 Philion Road Carriage – imagine a throne stuck on top of an outsized perambulator – to assorted altogether

less dignified Ed Roth Kustom creations. The cars, including 1940s Lincolns, a 1930s Mercedes and a divine 1957 Cadillac, are all beautifully maintained.

From the sublime, then, to the **National Bowling Stadium** (300 N Center Street), a $35-million, 78-lane, 2,000-capacity arena that has turned Reno into – *please* stop giggling – the Bowling Capital of the World. The stadium is reserved for tournaments, but the public can tour the building for free when there's no action, or for a small charge when a tournament is on.

Reno's other attractions sit on the University of Nevada campus north of downtown. At the **Fleischmann Planetarium** (1650 N Virginia Street, 1-775 784 4811, http://planetarium.unr. nevada.edu), star shows run alongside 70mm nature films, while a stone's throw away at the **Nevada Historical Society** (1-775 688 1190), there's a fine primer on the history of the state and a well-stocked bookstore.

Where to eat & drink

Stay in or near a casino, as almost all visitors to Reno do, and you'll probably eat a number of your meals there. Of the downtown spots, the **Eldorado** and **Harrah's** offer the best dining, while out of the centre, the **Reno Hilton** and the **Peppermill** are among the strongest for food (for all, *see above*). Elsewhere, find fine and messy Mexican food at **Bertha Miranda's** (336 Mill Street, at Holcomb Avenue, 1-775 786 9697), absurdly heavy traditional Basque scran at **Louie's Basque Corner** (301 E 4th Street, at Evans Avenue, 1-775 323 7203) and splendid coffee at **Java Jungle** (246 W 1st Street, at S Arlington Avenue, 1-775 329 4484).

Trips Out of Town

Reno's not overburdened with excellent bars. Of the casino imbiberies, **Brew Brothers** at the Eldorado (*see p283*) has a fine beer menu. Sadly, it chooses to accompany it with the music of horrible bar bands. More microbrews can be sunk at the infinitely more attractive, slightly tucked-away **Silver Peak** (124 Wonder Street, at Holcomb Avenue, 1-775 324 1864, www.silverpeakbrewery.com), which serves nice upscale bar food.

Where to stay

Roughly 25,000 rooms are available in Reno, running the pricing gamut from dirt-cheap to sky-high. Prices peak in August (it's worth booking) but are cheap in winter: you can often get a room in one of the downtown casinos or motels for under $30. Contact the Reno–Sparks Convention and Visitors Authority (1-800 367 7366, www.visitrenotahoe.com) or any of the casinos listed above for more details. Note that rooms in casinos that have a sister Vegas hotel won't necessarily be in an identical mould.

Tourist information

Reno's visitor centre is in the lobby of the National Bowling Stadium. Alternatively, phone the information line at the Reno–Sparks CVA (*see above*).

You're fired

To say the **Burning Man Festival** isn't really like most other events in Nevada is to say that Las Vegas isn't really like most other cities in the US. Each year, in the week leading up to Labor Day, around 30,000 people gather in the isolated Black Rock Desert to build a temporary, self-contained city, the physical, spiritual and symbolic centre of which is a 50-foot man who's set aflame at the end of the event. What goes on beforehand defies both belief and easy description. Suffice to say that the event will be unlike anything you've ever experienced before. Self-expression is prized above all else – one participant pinned Burning Man as a non-stop, week-long piece of performance art – with self-reliance a close second (temperatures can range from 0°C to 40°C (32°F to 104°F). Either way, for one week you'll be part of the world's most eccentric and fascinating community. For more, see www.burningman.com.

The **Extraterrestrial Highway** runs through Rachel (*right*). *See p286.*

Around Reno

Carson City

As state capitals go, **Carson City**, 30 miles south of Reno on US 395, is not one of the more demonstrative. Still, what it lacks in pomposity it makes up for in quaintness, a quaintness albeit balanced by a string of casinos on Carson Street, the town's main drag and also US 395.

Cynics suggest that the real balance of power in Nevada is held by the casino owners in Las Vegas, but the politicos of Carson City can still pack a punch when they need to. The centres of their activity are the **Nevada State Capitol** (N Carson Street, at Musser Street), a handsome domed structure dated 1871, and the **State Legislature**, a dreary building erected nearby a century later. The Kit Carson Trail, a two-mile walk detailed on a map available from the Chamber of Commerce (1900 S Carson Street, 1-775 882 1565, www.carsoncitychamber.com), offers a decent overview of the town's history.

Most of these buildings are closed to the public, but one that isn't is the suitably grand old US Mint Building at 600 N Carson Street, which for the last 60 years has served as the eclectic **Nevada State Museum** (1-775 687 4810, www.nevadaculture.org). The state's historic railroad comes under the microscope at the **Nevada State Railroad Museum** (2180 S Carson Street, 1-775 687 6953, www.nsrm-friends.org). Rides on old trains are offered most weekends outside winter. Still,

the few casinos aside, there's not much nightlife here, and Carson City's best taken in during a day-trip from Reno or Lake Tahoe.

Virginia City

A pleasant half-hour drive from Reno, south on US 395 for eight miles, then east on SR 341 for another eight miles, will take you to one of the most authentic historic mining towns in the West, where the discovery of gold and silver in nearby mines on the land of Henry Comstock sparked a furious bonanza in the 1860s. Of course, **Virginia City** is now also one of the most touristy towns in the West, its thin main drag soaked with themed bars, tatty museums – the **Julia C Bullette Red Light Museum** (5 N C Street, 1-775 847 9394) is a classic of the genre, and makes the likes of **The Way It Was Museum** (118 N C Street, 1-775 847 0766) look like the Smithsonian – photo studios and other less easily categorisable attractions ('See the Suicide Table!').

That said, provided you avoid summer weekends, when C Street can get claustrophobic with tourists, it's good fun. If you take the time to wander off the main drag, it's even a little bit more than that. The Walking Tour, available from the town's visitor centre, takes in the town's most fascinating buildings, among them the newly regenerated **Piper's Opera House** (1 N B Street, 1-775 847 0433 and **The Castle** (70 S B Street, 1-775 847 0275), a handsome mansion dating from 1868 and open for tours

six months a year (many of the town's sights close during the bitterly chilly winters).

Eating and drinking options in Virginia City are hardly varied, but you can wash down your sandwich or burger with a beer or a Coke in any number of establishments. There aren't too many places to stay, reflecting Virginia City's status as a day-tripper's paradise; in fact, you're best off driving back to Reno to find a bed for the night. And if you've time, take the long way round – south on SR 341, then west on US 50 and back north on US 395 – in order to stop in at the magnificent **Chocolate Nugget** candy factory (56 SR 341, 1-775 849 0841) and pick up a couple of bags of sugar-rush.

Lake Tahoe

After driving through hundreds of miles of desert, Reno's verdant trim comes as a pleasant surprise. But it's as nothing compared to **Lake Tahoe**, which sits on the border between Nevada and California a 45-minute drive from Reno (south on US 395 for eight miles, then west on SR 431 for 25 miles). Some 22 miles long and 12 miles wide, it's one of the world's most beautiful alpine lakes.

Tahoe's two main settlements are at either end of the lake, both within a few miles of the state line. **Incline Village**'s population of 7,000 is swelled in winter by skiers (the slopes of **Mount Rose–Ski Tahoe** and **Diamond Peak** are nearby, with **Northstar-at-Tahoe** and the well regarded **Squaw Valley USA** just across the state line), in summer by the hiking and other outdoor sports, and year-round by the socialising. Three miles west in **Crystal Bay**, on the state line, are a handful of casinos, from the super-smart **Cal-Neva** (1-800 225 6382, www.calnevaresort.com) to the more approachable **Tahoe Nugget** (1-775 831 0455).

South Lake Tahoe, meanwhile, also has its casinos, temptingly positioned on the Nevada edge of the state line. Among those offering accommodation are **Caesars Tahoe** (1-888 829 7630, www.caesars.com), **Harrah's** (1-775 588 6611, www.harrahs.com), and its relation **Harveys** (1-775 588 2411, www.harrahs.com). On the California side sit a string of restaurants, bars and motels. Skiers flock here in winter – **Heavenly**, **Kirkwood** and **Sierra-at-Tahoe** are the nearest slopes – while summer brings a more demure holiday-maker.

The Extraterrestrial Highway & Area 51

Of course, you won't see anything. No one ever does. And if you're thinking about walking into the desert for a closer look, think again: you may find yourself greeted by employees of the US government wielding the kind of weaponry that'll encourage you to turn around in a hurry.

Still, SR 375 continues to draw tourists year-round. A few are here to plane-spot the military aircraft that roar overhead. A handful are on their way north to Ely, albeit taking the long way around. But the reason most people are ploughing up and down SR 375 is its now-official nickname, and what reputedly rests just a few miles west of the road.

If you've taken US 95 north to Reno, you'll already have skirted the western edge of the Nellis Air Force Range (*see p280*). Well, if you take SR 375, a plain-as-day desert road that links US 93 with US 6 in central Nevada, you'll be edging along its eastern perimeter. No one gave this much thought until the late 1980s, when physicist Bob Lazar, in a series of interviews with local news gadfly George Knapp, claimed he had worked at Papoose Lake, inside the range, on alien spaceships. He also gave details – scant, but enough to light the touchpaper of America's conspiracy theorists – of a previously unknown facility: the dry-bedded Groom Lake, allegedly a test site for top-secret new military aircraft and, even more contentiously, the centre of government investigations into alien life. After the numbered grid square in which the base sits on maps of the test site, it's become known as Area 51; as a result of its notoriety, SR 375 has been nicknamed the **Extraterrestrial Highway**.

The US government refuses to acknowledge the existence of Area 51. Rumours persist that the notoriety of the base forced the government to move its operations from here to Utah during the 1990s. Either way, tourists are undaunted. Sightings of UFOs near the road are predictably common, but hard evidence of their existence remains scant.

Take care when approaching Area 51; someone is watching your movements. Don't cross into the military zone: you'll be arrested, questioned and fined. Armed guards are authorised to use 'deadly force' on trespassers. The border is not marked on maps and is often hard to detect: it's defined by orange posts, some topped with silver globes, and occasional 'restricted area' signs, but no fence.

The only town on SR 375 is Rachel, a scruffy collection of houses and huts that's home to a little under 100 people. This number is swelled by tourists staying at the **Little A'Le'Inn**, a shabby, eccentric motel-bar-restaurant combo stocked with cheaply made, dearly priced alien ephemera and staffed by slightly scary people unafraid of engaging you in a conversation about politics (tip: if you're a Democrat, keep your mouth shut).

Since 1995, when the military annexed more land, the only view of Area 51 is from Tikaboo Peak, 26 miles from the base. You get superb views of the desert, but even with binoculars, all you'll see of the base is a few distant buildings. It's a strenuous hike, best done in summer (snow can last until April) and early in the morning, before heat haze distorts the view. The best route is via a dirt road off US 93 at milepost 32.2, south of Alamo. It's just over 22 miles to Badger Spring and then a two-hour hike to the summit, but it's easy to get lost. For more, read Glenn Campbell's *Area 51 Viewer's Guide* ($15 from www.aliensonearth.com).

Where to stay

Little A'Le'Inn
HCR 61 Box 45, Rachel, NV 89001 (1-775 729 2515/www.aleinn.com). **Rates** $40 double.
Seven rooms located in cosy, if dilapidated, trailers: you get a shared bathroom, a communal kitchen-cum-living room and yet more UFO photos.

Getting there

By car
Take US 93 north for 107 miles to the junction with SR 375, aka Extraterrestrial Highway. Rachel is 36 miles north-west of the junction. When driving, watch not so much for aliens but for wandering cows: much of the road is an open range, and collisions occur regularly.

Utah

Where the monoliths are natural.

It'll come as a culture shock after Las Vegas. In southern Utah, it can be hard just to find a bar that serves alcohol or a restaurant that stays open past 9pm. If Las Vegas is a 24-hour city, then Mormon-dominated Utah – suspicious of outsiders and deeply mistrustful of its Nevada neighbours – is a 12-hour state. But Southern Utah is a unique place: National Park follows National Recreation Area follows National Monument, hulking rock formations giving way to vistas by turns peculiar and pretty. And **Zion National Park** is a bit of both.

Zion National Park

A few hours north from Las Vegas lies **Zion National Park** (www.nps.gov/zion), a glorious introduction to the canyon country of south-east Utah. Zion's 2,000-foot (600-metre) cliffs and towering rock formations were discovered by early Mormon travellers in the 1880s. Originally called Mukuntuweap (roughly 'like a quiver', a description of the canyon's shape), its name was changed to Zion, an ancient Hebrew word meaning 'place of refuge', when it became a national park in 1919. With more than 2.5 million visitors annually, Zion is busy all year. Try to avoid it in winter, when snow and ice make the park's trails tough to negotiate, and summer when temperatures top 110°F (43°C). Visit instead in spring (wild flowers are at their best in May) or autumn.

The main entrance to Zion National Park is in the south, near the pretty town of Springdale (admission $20/car, valid for seven days). Just beyond the entrance are the park's two campgrounds (*see p288*) and visitors' centre (staff are wonderfully helpful), with the tidy new **Zion Human History Museum** a further half-mile inside.

The majority of the park's sights and trails are accessible or visible from the six-mile dead-end **scenic drive** (closed for part of the year; for details, *see p288*), which starts at the main entrance and winds through the Virgin River gorge. The names of the vividly coloured Navajo sandstone monoliths along the drive echo the first visitors' religious sensibilities: the **Great White Throne**, **Angel's Landing**, the **Three Patriarchs**, the **Pulpit** and the **Temple of Sinawava**. Scan the sheer rock faces and you may see the ant-like figures of climbers; routes are detailed in Eric Bjourstad's *Desert Rock: Rock Climbs in the National Parks* (Chockstone Press).

East from Springdale and the scenic drive, you will travel along the twisting **Zion–Mount Carmel Highway**, an engineering miracle when it was built in 1930. The impressive route leads through two long, narrow tunnels, passing scenery that is completely different from the landscapes of Zion Canyon. This is slickrock country: vast white, orange and pink rock formations, eroded into domes and buttes and marked with criss-cross patterns, loom next to the road. You can't miss the huge white monolith of **Checkerboard Mesa**.

Kolob Canyons, which is located in the park's north-western corner, has its own entrance (at exit 40 off the I-15) and visitors'

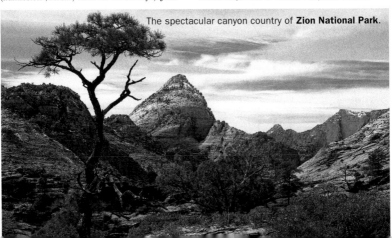
The spectacular canyon country of **Zion National Park**.

Trips Out of Town

centre, from where a stunning five-mile drive leads into the red-rock **Finger Canyons**. There are also two hiking trails to embark on from here; the longer trail culminates at **Kolob Arch**, which is possibly the world's largest natural arch reaching 310 feet (95 metres).

Where to eat

Springdale has plenty of cafés and restaurants, but – this is Utah, folks – a shortage of bars. The closest you'll find is the **Bit & Spur** (1212 Zion Park Boulevard, 1-435 772 3498), a Mexican restaurant with outdoor seating. **Oscar's Café** (612 Zion Park Boulevard, 1-435 772 3232), just off the main drag, does decent pizzas and pastries, while the family-friendly **Bumbleberry Restaurant** (897 Zion Park Boulevard, 1-435 772 3224, www.bumble berry.com) has a nice line in breakfasts.

Where to stay

There are many places to stay in Springdale, ranging from the cheap (the friendly, ten-room **El Rio Lodge**, 995 Zion Park Boulevard, 1-888 772 3205, 1-435 772 3205, www.elriolodge. com, rates $49-$54) to the top-dollar (the 40-room **Cliffrose Lodge & Gardens**, 281 Zion Park Boulevard, 1-800 243 8824, 1-435 772 3234, www.cliffroselodge.com, rates $64-$179). For details, contact the **Zion Chamber of Commerce** (PO Box 331, Springdale, UT 84767, 1-888 518 7070, www.zionpark.com). Not all the town's lodgings open in winter, but you should be able to find a room without having booked. However, it's essential to book during the peak summer season.

Inside the park are **three campgrounds** (one closed in winter, one open only in summer and one operational year-round; 1-800 365 2267, http://reservations.nps.gov, rates $16-$20) and the rustic-style **Zion Lodge** (1-888 297 2757, 1-435 772 3213, www.zionlodge.com, rates $132-$148 Mar-Nov, $73-$119 Dec-Feb), built in 1925 by the Union Pacific Railroad. Accommodation at Zion Lodge includes six suites, 40 cabins and 76 motel-style rooms on the Zion Lodge site; you'll need to book at least six months in advance for a room between April and October.

Getting there

To reach the park (164 miles from Vegas), take I-15 north (watch your speed once you leave Nevada) through the pleasant Mormon town of St George and turn right at exit 16 on to Highway 9 to Springdale. To visit the Kolob Canyons area of the park, continue for 25 miles on I-15 until you eventually reach exit 40.

Getting around

By car & bus

The volume of visitors is such that the **Zion Canyon scenic drive** is closed to private vehicles from April to October. Cars are then left at the south entrance or in Springdale, and visitors catch a (free) bus into the park. The rest of the park is open to private cars, but vehicles wider than 7ft 10in (2.39m) or higher than 10ft 4in (3.15m) must be escorted through the **Zion–Mount Carmel tunnel** ($10/vehicle), which can lead to delays.

By bike

The **Pa'rus Trail**, a short cycle path along the Virgin River, connects Zion Canyon to the visitors' centre. You can rent bikes from **Springdale Cycles** (1458 Zion Park Boulevard, 1-800 776 2099, 1-435 772 0575, www.springdalecycles.com, $35-$45 per day, less for three- or five-day rentals), who offer tours.

Hiking

There are plenty of hiking trails off the scenic drive. The busiest are the short easy routes along the valley floor, such as **Weeping Rock** and the **Riverside Walk**, but the best views are at the end of the two-mile **Watchman Trail** – beware: shade is minimal – and the five-mile trail to **Angel's Landing**. Don't even attempt the latter if you're afraid of heights: the last half-mile follows a steep, narrow ridge fitted with chains. Perhaps the most spectacular hike is through the 16-mile **Narrows**, with canyon walls up to 2,000ft (600m) high and at times only 20-30ft apart. Be prepared to wade (or swim) through cold water and check conditions at the visitors' centre: there can be flash floods in summer.

Tourist information

Kolob Canyon Visitors' Center

3752 E Kolob Canyon Road, New Harmony, UT 84757 (1-435 586 9548/www.nps.gov/zion). **Open** *Summer* 7am-7pm daily. *Winter* 8am-4.30pm daily.

Zion Canyon Visitors' Center

Springdale, UT 84767 (recorded information 1-435 772 3256/www.nps.gov/zion). **Open** 8am-7pm daily in summer; closes earlier in winter.

Beyond Zion

At **Mount Carmel Junction**, east of the park, Highway 9 joins up with US 89 for access to the rest of Utah and Arizona, and scenery that is arguably even more spectacular than in Zion. North on US 89 then east on SR 12 takes you to **Bryce Canyon National Park** (1-435 834 5322, www.nps.gov/brca), whose landscape of vast rock hoodoos is breathtakingly odd. North up SR12, through **Dixie National Forest**, brings you to the **Capitol Reef National Park** (1-435 425 3791, www.nps.gov/care), and the US 89 south to the **Grand Canyon** (*see p266*).

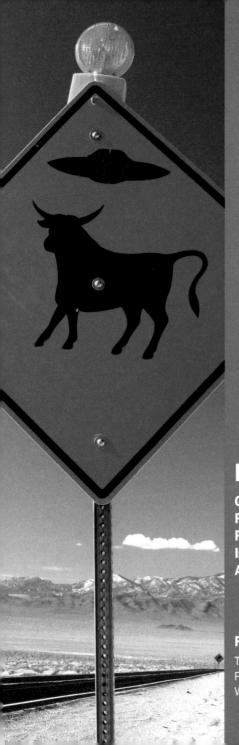

Directory

Features

Directory

Getting Around

Arriving & leaving

By air

McCarran International Airport (261 5211, www.mccarran.com) is just five minutes from the south end of the Strip, which makes the trip from airport to hotel relatively painless. The airport itself is clean and modern, and takes first (and last) tilt at the tourist dollar with halls of slot machines and video poker.

There are hundreds of internal flights to Las Vegas each week. However, direct international flights are limited; from the UK, for example, only Virgin Atlantic (from London Gatwick) and BMI (from Manchester) fly direct. Most flights to and from Europe require passengers to change at an East Coast airport or in Los Angeles.

Public bus routes 108 and 109 run north from the airport: the 108 heads up Swenson Avenue and stops at the Las Vegas Hilton; the 109 goes along Maryland Parkway. Shuttle buses – from several companies, including **Bell Trans** (739 7990, www.bell-trans.com), **Grayline** (739 5700, www.grayline.com) and **ODS** (876 2222) – run to the Strip and Downtown hotels 24 hours a day. They cost less than $5 each way to the Strip, slightly more to Downtown.

Taxis can be found outside the arrivals hall. There's a $1.20 surcharge on all fares originating at McCarran; bearing in mind, expect to pay $10-$15 to get to most hotels on the Strip, or $15-$20 to Downtown (plus tip).

Airlines

Air Canada *1-888 247 2262/ www.aircanada.com.*
Alaska Air *1-800 252 7522/ www.alaskaair.com.*
America West *1-800 235 9292/ www.americawest.com.*
American Airlines *1-800 433 7300/www.aa.com.*
British Airways *1-800 247 9297/ www.britishairways.com.*
Continental *domestic 1-800 523 3273/international 1-800 231 0856/ www.continental.com.*
Delta *domestic 1-800 221 1212/ international 1-800 241 4141/ www.delta.com.*
Northwest *domestic 1-800 225 2525/international 1-800 447 4747/ www.nwa.com.*
Southwest *1-800 435 9792/ www.southwest.com.*
United Airlines *domestic 1-800 864 8331/international 1-800 538 2929/www.united.com.*
US Airways *domestic 1-800 428 4322/international 1-800 622 1015/ www.usairways.com.*
Virgin Atlantic *1-800 862 8621/ www.virginatlantic.com.*

By road

Greyhound
200 S Main Street, at Carson Avenue, Downtown (1-800 231 2222/384 9561/www.greyhound. com). Bus 108, 207. **Open** *24hrs daily.* **Credit** *AmEx, Disc, MC, V.* **Map** *p318 C1.*
Greyhound covers around 2,000 destinations nationwide, including Los Angeles ($40 one-way, $75 round-trip; 5-7hrs) and Reno ($75 one-way, $150 round-trip; 11hrs). No reservations required.

Getting around

If you're based on the Strip, a mix of buses, taxis, monorails and feet will get you around. However, automobile hire is affordable in Vegas: a car is recommended if you're staying away from the Strip or want to visit off-Strip attractions, and essential if you plan to visit any out-of-town destinations.

CAT bus services

Information

The bus system is run by **Citizens Area Transit (CAT)**. For a map, *see p315.*

Downtown Transportation Center
300 N Casino Center Boulevard, at Stewart Avenue, Downtown (228 7433/www.rtcsouthernnevada.com). Bus 106, 107, 108, 109, 113, 207, 301, 302. **Open** *7am-5.30pm daily.* **Map** *p318 D1.*
The DTC is the main transfer point for most bus routes.

Fares & tickets

Most **CAT** routes cost $1.25, or 60¢ for over-62s, 6-17s and the disabled. Use exact change; you must have a photocard (available from the DTC) to get a concessionary fare. The 301 route along the Strip costs $2 for all. Transfers are free, if you ask for one when you pay.

A 30-day **reduced fare pass** costs $30, but **tokens** are a better bet for short-term visitors. They're sold in bags of 40 for $20; you need two tokens for an adult fare (four on route 301) and one for kids, a saving of about 25 per cent.

Routes

CAT buses run 24-7 between Downtown and the Strip, and roughly 5.30am-1.30am elsewhere. The buses are safe and relatively comprehensive in their coverage of the city. All take both bicycles and wheelchairs. Bus stops are marked by white, green and purple signs with the feline CAT logo; most have shelters to provide relief from the sun.

Bus 301

The most useful bus for tourists is the 301, which travels the length of Las Vegas Boulevard from the DTC in the north to just by I-215 in the south, stopping in front of all major casinos (every 7½min, 5.30am-1am; every 15min 1-5.30am). 301s are often packed, especially at night.

Strip Trolley

The Strip Trolley (run by Bell Trans, 382 1404) heads along the Strip (with a detour to the Las Vegas Hilton) every 15min from 9.30am to 1.30am. The Trolley picks up and drops off passengers at the front door of some hotels, rather than on the street outside as the CAT does. Ask your hotel front desk if it's on the route. The fare (exact money only) is $1.75.

Monorails & shuttle buses

After teething problems, the **Las Vegas Monorail** is now running a reliable service along Paradise Road behind the Strip. However, it hasn't displaced the numerous hotel shuttle buses and monorails.

Las Vegas Monorail

699 8200/www.lvmonorail.com.
The monorail runs from the **Sahara** to the **MGM Grand**, stopping at the **Las Vegas Hilton**, the **Las Vegas Convention Center**, **Harrah's**, the **Flamingo** and **Bally's**), but it's projected to carry 19 million passengers a year. The journey time from end to end is usually around 15 minutes. Single-ride tickets cost $3, though the ten-ride package ($20) and day pass ($10) offer better value.

Other monorails

Free, 24hr monorails, separate to the Las Vegas Monorail link the **Monte Carlo** and the **Bellagio**; the **Mirage** and **TI**; and **Excalibur**, the **Luxor** and **Mandalay Bay**. For all of them, it's often quicker to walk.

Shuttle buses

The **Barbary Coast** runs a shuttle bus to the **Gold Coast** on Flamingo Road (also useful for the **Rio** and the **Palms**), and to the **Orleans**. The Rio's own shuttle runs from a small building on the east side of the Strip, just south of the **Aladdin**.

The **Stratosphere** runs a shuttle to and from the Strip, while the **Hard Rock**'s shuttle travels in a loop to the **Stardust**, Fashion Show Mall and the Forum Shops. The **Sam's Town** bus, to the Fremont, Bourbon Street, the California and the Stardust, is the most efficient, and gives you access to just about every other shuttle in town. Useful places to pick up shuttles are the **Fashion Show Mall** and the **Tropicana**.

Taxis & limos

There are **taxi ranks** outside most hotels; restaurants and bars will be happy to call a cab for you. Technically, you're not allowed to hail a taxi from the street, although it's usually OK to approach an empty cab with its light on if it has stopped in traffic. Meters start at $3.20, and increase by $1.80 per mile. If you have a complaint about a registered taxi, note the cab number and call the **Nevada Taxicab Authority** (486 6532, www.taxi.state.nv.us). For lost property, *see p297*.

Limousines are a flash and popular way of getting around. The rides vary from the basic black stretch ($40/hr) to huge SUVs with hot tubs, disco balls and the like ($100/hr). Many limos are available for hire outside hotels and the airport; if you're in a large group on a busy night, the cost is worth it to avoid the long taxi queue. In order to protect the taxicab trade, limo drivers are not allowed to solicit passengers, but you are perfectly at liberty to approach them for a ride.

Cab companies

Yellow Checker Star Cab *873 2000/www.ycstrans.com.*
Desert Cab *386 4828.*
Whittlesea Blue *384 6111.*

Limousine companies

Bell Trans *385 5466/ www.bell-trans.com.*
Las Vegas Limo *736 1419/ www.lasvegaslimo.com.*
Presidential *731 5577/ www.presidentiallimolv.com.*

Driving

The Las Vegas streets get very congested in the morning and evening **rush hours** (7-9am, 4-6pm), as well as at weekends, when traffic is awful in tourist areas after 4pm.

The Strip is slow-going most of the time and turns into a virtual car park when the town is busy. The nearby parallel streets – Industrial Road and Frank Sinatra Drive to the west and Paradise Road to the east – move faster, and provide access to several casinos. For north–south journeys longer than a block, it's often worth taking I-15, which runs parallel to the Strip. If you're trying to get east–west across town, take the Desert Inn arterial, a mini-expressway that runs under the Strip and over I-15 (no junctions at either).

I-15 intersects with the east–west US 95 north-west of Downtown. US 95 connects to the 53-mile beltway at the edges of the valley, which leads commuters around the entire region. For local road conditions, call 486 3116 or log on to www.ci.las-vegas.nv.us.

Speed limits vary in Nevada. In general, the speed limit on freeways is 65mph; on the highway, it's either 65mph or 70mph. Limits on main urban thoroughfares (such as Tropicana Avenue) are 45mph; elsewhere, limits are 25mph or 35mph. Look for signs in construction zones and near schools, which often enforce a reduced limit. Unless otherwise specified, you can turn right on a red light, after stopping, if the street is clear. U-turns are not only legal (unless specified) but, often, a positive necessity given the length of the blocks.

In case of a **car accident**, call 911; do not move the cars involved in the accident until the police ask you to do so.

In Nevada, you can be arrested for driving under the influence if your blood alcohol level is 0.08 or higher. If you're pulled over, the police can legally give you a drink-driving test on the spot. If you refuse, you'll be taken to jail for a blood test, which will be taken by force if necessary.

Breakdown services

American Automobile Association (AAA)

3312 W Charleston Boulevard, east of S Valley View Boulevard, Northwest Las Vegas (870 9171/emergencies 1-800 222 4357/www.aaa.com). **Open** 8.30am-5.30pm Mon-Fri. The Triple A provides maps, guidebooks and campsite listings – and they're free if you're a member or belong to an affiliated organisation, such as the British AA. **Other locations:** 601 Whitney Ranch Drive, Henderson (458 2323); 10860 W Charleston Boulevard, Summerlin (360 3151).

Fuel stations

Gas is cheaper than in Europe, but pricey for the US. There are stations by Circus Circus and across from Mandalay Bay; gas stations abound on (among others) Paradise Road, Maryland Parkway, Tropicana Avenue and Flamingo Road. For mechanics and full-service gas stations, see 'Automobile repair' in *Yellow Pages*.

Insurance

Drivers must have vehicle insurance supplied by a state-licensed insurance agent. Carry a **proof of insurance** card in your vehicle at all times, otherwise you risk a fine of up to $500. If you hire a car, make certain your agency provides proof of registration and insurance. Consider buying additional insurance if your credit card does not automatically provide it.

Parking

Most hotel-casinos have **valet parking**, which is convenient, safe and free (apart from the $2 tip on your way out). If you see a sign saying the valet car park is full and you're in a luxury car, stay put: chances are they'll find a spot. Hotel guests also get preferential treatment; when the attendant asks to see your room key, $5-$10 will

often substitute. **Self-parking** is free at every Vegas resort (Downtown casinos require a validation stamp), but the convenience of lots is variable.

Vehicle hire

Most car-hire agencies are at or near the airport. Call around for the best rate, booking well in advance if you're planning to visit over a holiday weekend or for a major convention. When business renters are scarce, though, you should get a good rate, and maybe – if you ask nicely – an upgrade.

Almost every firm requires a credit card and matching driver's licence; few will rent to under-25s. Prices won't include tax, liability insurance or collision damage waiver (CDW); US residents may be covered on their home policy, but foreign residents will need to buy extra insurance.

Car rental companies

Want to make your entrance in style? **Rent-a-Vette** (1-800 372 1981, www.rent-a-vette.com) rents Corvettes, Porsches and the like. The Vegas franchise of **Rent-a-Wreck** (474 0037, www.rentawreck.com) has year-old models at great prices.

Alamo *US: 1-800 462 5266/263 8411/www.goalamo.com. UK: 0870 400 4562/www.alamo.co.uk.*
Avis *US: 1-800 230 4898/261 5595/www.avis.com. UK: 0870 606 0100/www.avis.co.uk.*
Budget *US: 1-800 527 0700/736 1212/www.budget.com. UK: 0870 153 9170/www.budget.co.uk.*
Dollar *US: 1-866 434 2226/1-800 800 3665/www.dollar.com. UK: 0800 085 4578/www.dollar.co.uk.*
Enterprise *US: 1-800 261 7331/365 6662/www.enterprise.com. UK: 0870 350 3000/www.enterprise.com/uk.*
Hertz *US: 1-800 654 3131/220 9700/www.hertz.com. UK: 0870 844 8844/www.hertz.co.uk.*
National *US: 1-800 227 7368/261 5391. UK: 0116 217 3884. Both: www.nationalcar.com.*
Thrifty *US: 1-800 847 4389/896 7600/www.thrifty.com. UK: 01494 751600/www.thrifty.co.uk.*

Motorcycle rental

Eaglerider *876 8687/www.eaglerider.com.*
Harley-Davidson of Southern Nevada *431 8500/www.lvhd.com.*

RV rental

Renting a recreational vehicle (camper van) costs approximately $400 for three days or $800-$1,200 for a week. **Cruise America** (1-800 327 7799, 456 6666, www.cruiseamerica.com) has everything from 18ft (5.5m) camper homes to 30ft (9m) RVs.

Cycling

In a word: don't. You can just about get away with it on the Strip on weekend nights, when traffic has slowed to a crawl. At other times, the drivers on the three- and four-lane roads in the city simply aren't looking for cyclists: you're taking your life in your hands.

Walking

Pedestrians are rarely seen off the Strip in Vegas, and even there they face considerable dangers from carefree and often careless drivers. The intersection bridges on the Strip help, but it's still a tricky business. **Jaywalking** here is so deadly that police regularly issue citations. Laws favour the driver: never put yourself in the path of cars that have the green light.

The safest places to cross are the overhead **pedestrian bridges** at several key Strip locations, bridges that (of course) guide you past the entrances of the casinos on each corner. You can find them at Tropicana Avenue, at Flamingo Road, and at Spring Mountain Road near Wynn Las Vegas. Where there are no bridges, closely follow all traffic signals and check both directions twice before stepping into the street.

It's possible to take short-cuts from one Strip hotel to the next, but you're likely to get trapped in a maze of service roads. Use our maps to guide you (*see pp317-320*) and don't underestimate distances: the Strip is longer than it looks, and walking it end to end will take at least 90 minutes.

Directory

Resources A-Z

Addresses

Written addresses follow the standard US format. The room and/or suite number usually appears after the street address (where applicable), followed by the city name and the zip code. Note that Las Vegas Boulevard South is the official name of the Strip. For details on street-numbering and orientation, *see p110*.

Age restrictions

Las Vegas is a carefree city of hedonism and wild abandon, but only if you're old enough.

Admission to nude clubs 18 (except Palomino).
Admission to topless clubs 21.
Buying/drinking alcohol 21.
Driving 16.
Gambling 21.
Marriage 16 (with parental consent) or 18 (without).
Sex 16 (heterosexual) or 18 (homosexual).

Attitude & etiquette

As a tourist city, Vegas is as formal or informal as you want it to be. During the warmer months, shorts and T-shirts are accepted wear along the Strip as well as on the gaming floors of most casinos, though dressing up to a minimum of smart-casual has become the norm for a night out. Some lounges, nightclubs and restaurants have dress codes (sports shoes, T-shirts and jeans may be prohibited), and dining can be quite formal.

Business

Gambling and tourism remain the dominant enterprises, in terms of both revenue and employment. However, the climate and favourable tax structure have helped the state's economic development authorities to attract hundreds of companies to the city.

But a stronger input into the Vegas economy comes from the five million business travellers who come to town each year for conventions. As a result of all this traffic, most major resorts offer excellent business services: faxing, photocopying and shipping services are standard; phone and computer hire is common, as are the presence of private conference rooms; and in-room high-speed internet access and/or wireless access are growing in popularity.

Conventions & conferences

Vegas is the convention capital of the US. Most conventions and trade fairs are held at the three locations listed below, with smaller shows held at other resorts and at the Cashman Center a short drive north of Downtown.

Las Vegas Convention Center

3150 Paradise Road, at Convention Center Drive, East of Strip (892 0711/www.lasvegas24hours.com). Bus 108, 112. **Map** p319 C5.

The largest convention facility in the US is still growing, and now contains 3.2 million sq ft (300,000sq m) of meeting and exhibition space. The 16 exhibit halls are separated by moveable walls; the 144 meeting rooms range in capacity from 20 to 7,500. The on-site business centre provides access to computers, faxes, telephones and courier services. Parking is relatively limited, so either walk or use hotel shuttle buses.

Mandalay Bay Convention Center

3950 Las Vegas Boulevard South, at E Hacienda Avenue (632 7777/www.mandalayconventions.com). Bus 105, 301. **Map** p320 A9.

Opened in 2003, this impressive facility contains around 1 million sq ft (90,000sq m) of exhibition space, along with state-of-the-art business services and loads of meeting rooms.

Sands Expo & Convention Center

210 Sands Avenue, at Koval Lane, East of Strip (733 5556/www.sandsexpo.com). Bus 203, 213. **Map** p320 B6.

Second in size to the LVCC and connected to the Venetian, this facility offers the same excellent amenities, with even worse parking.

Convention dates

The LVCVA website (*see p301*) provides a search engine that enables you to find conventions by date, keyword or venue. Below we've listed the town's most sizeable conventions and their dates (some confirmed, some provisional). Hotel rooms will be hard to find during these periods.

Travel advice

For up-to-date information on travelling to a specific country – including the latest news on safety and security, health issues, local laws and customs – contact your home country government's department of foreign affairs. Most have websites packed with useful advice for would-be travellers. For vital information for travellers to the US, *see also p300* **Passport regulations**.

Australia
www.smartraveller.gov.au
Canada
www.voyage.gc.ca
New Zealand
http://mfat.govt.nz/travel

Republic of Ireland
http://foreignaffairs.gov.ie
UK
www.fco.gov.uk/travel
USA
www.state.gov/travel

Consumer Electronics Show (CES) (120,000 delegates) 5-8 Jan 2006; early Jan 2007.
World of Concrete Exposition (80,000 delegates) 17-20 Jan 2006; mid Jan 2007.
Nightclub & Bar Convention (40,000 delegates) early Mar 2006; early Mar 2007.
National Association of Broadcasters (90,000 delegates) Apr 2006; Apr 2007.
World Shoe Association (35,000 delegates) 4-7 Aug 2005; 10-13 Feb 2006; early Aug 2006; early Feb 2007.
Associated Surplus Dealers/ Associated Merchandise Dealers (ASD/AMD) (52,000 delegates) 14-18 Aug 2005; 5-9 Mar 2006; 13-17 Aug 2006; early Mar 2007.
Automotive Aftermarket Products Expo (AAPEX) (130,000 delegates) 1-4 Nov 2005; early Nov 2006.
Speciality Equipment Marketing Association (SEMA) (130,000 delegates) 1-4 Nov 2005; early Nov 2006.

Couriers & shippers

Most conventions have on-site drop-off boxes. Many of the big hotels also have business centres with courier services.

DHL *1-800 225 5345/www.dhl-usa.com.* **Credit** AmEx, DC, Disc, MC, V.
Federal Express (FedEx) *1-800 463 3339/www.fedex.com.* **Credit** AmEx, DC, Disc, MC, V.
United Parcel Service (UPS) *1-800 742 5877/www.ups.com.* **Credit** AmEx, MC, V.

Office equipment & services

Bit-by-Bit
3400 Desert Inn Road, at S Pecos Road, West of Strip (474 6311/ www.bit-by-bit.com). Bus 112. **Open** 9am-5pm Mon-Fri. **Credit** AmEx, MC, V. **Map** p317 X2.
Computers and other kit for hire.

FedEx Kinko's
395 Hughes Center Drive, at Paradise Road, East of Strip (1-800 546 5674/951 2400/www.kinkos.com). Bus 108, 202, 203, 213. **Open** 24hrs daily. **Credit** AmEx, Disc, MC, V. **Map** p320 C7.
America's most prominent chain of copy shops, recently bought by its most prominent courier, has eight branches in the Las Vegas area; this is one of three that are open 24hrs. (The other very central branch is

Downtown at 830 S 4th Street; 383 7022.) Services include typesetting, printing, fax and phone facilities, as well as courier service via FedEx.
Other locations: throughout the city.

Officemax
2640 S Decatur Boulevard, at W Sahara Avenue, Southwest Las Vegas (1-800 788 8080/221 0471/ www.officemax.com). Bus 103, 204. **Open** 7am-9pm Mon-Fri; 9am-8pm Sat; 11am-7pm Sun. **Credit** AmEx, Disc, MC, V.
Each Officemax store carries a full line of office supplies, computers, furniture and business machines.
Other locations: throughout the city.

Useful organisations

For the **Las Vegas Chamber of Commerce** and the **Las Vegas CVA**, *see p301.*

Consumer

For complaints about casinos, contact the Enforcement Department of the **Gaming Control Board** (555 E Washington Avenue, Las Vegas, NV 89101, 486 2000, www.gaming.state.nv.us). For general consumer enquiries and complaints, see below.

Better Business Bureau
2301 Palomino Lane, Las Vegas, NV 89107 (320 4500/www.vegasbbb.org).
Private agency that reports on the background of businesses and reviews written complaints.
Nevada Department of Business & Industry, Consumer Affairs Division
1850 E Sahara Avenue, Las Vegas, NV 89104 (486 7355/www.fyi consumer.org).
The state division overseeing correct business practice.

Customs

Travellers arriving in Vegas on an indirect international flight will go through Customs and Immigration at the airport in which they change planes. This involves reclaiming baggage at the transfer airport, taking it through Customs and then checking it in again. Connection times should take account of this process.

On US flights, non-US citizens are given two forms – one for Immigration, one for Customs – which must be filled in and handed in at the appropriate desk on landing.

US Customs allows foreign visitors to import the following items duty-free: 200 cigarettes or 50 cigars (not Cuban; over-18s only) or 2kg of smoking tobacco; one litre (1.05 US quart) of wine or spirits (over-21s only); and up to $100 in gifts ($800 for returning Americans). You can take up to $10,000 in cash, travellers' cheques or bank drafts in or out of the country tax-free. Anything above that must be declared, or you risk forfeiting the lot. Depending on the state in which you land, you may need to declare and possibly forfeit any plants or foodstuffs that you have with you. Check the **US Customs** online brochure before travelling (www.cbp.gov/xp/cgov/travel).

UK Customs & Excise allows returning travellers to bring in £145 of goods bought abroad. Citizens of other countries should check the rules in their country.

Disabled travellers

Vegas is a disabled-friendly city. Strip resorts are fully wheelchair-accessible, from pools, spas and restrooms to gambling facilities (things are a little harder in the older Downtown properties). A few casinos, notably Caesars Palace, offer games for sight- and hearing-impaired players. Disabled parking is found almost everywhere; buses and many taxis are adapted to take wheelchairs (though be sure to ask when you book).

The **Society of Accessible Travel and Hospitality** (1-212 447 7284, www.sath.org) offers advice for disabled people planning trips to all corners of the United States.

Southern Nevada Center for Independent Living

6200 W Oakey Boulevard, at S Jones Avenue, Northwest Las Vegas (889 4216/www.sncil.org). Bus 205. **Open** 8am-5pm Mon-Fri.
Advice, information, transport and equipment loans (including wheelchairs).

Drugs

The use of illegal drugs, including clubbing drugs such as ecstasy, is quite prevalent in Sin City. Dealers will approach you all over town, but take care. In addition, watch your drinks: illicit, hard-to-trace drugs are sometimes slipped into unattended glasses.

The local authorities have a strict zero-tolerance policy on drug use and trafficking. If you're implicated in a drug sale or purchase, you will be arrested and subject to trial, and if convicted could receive a maximum sentence of five to ten years in prison.

Electricity & appliances

The US uses a 110-120V, 60-cycle AC voltage. Except for dual-voltage flat-pin shavers, most foreign visitors will need to run appliances through an adaptor. Most US TVs and DVDs use a different frequency from those in Europe.

Embassies & consulates

The only countries with Vegas consulates are Italy (385 6843) and Germany (734 9700). Nationals of other countries should contact their consulate in Los Angeles or San Francisco.

Australia *19th Floor, Century Plaza Towers, 2049 Century Park East, Los Angeles, CA 90067 (general 1-310 229 4800/consular 1-310 229 4865/passports 1-310 229 4828/fax 1-310 277 2258).* **Open** 9am-5pm Mon-Fri.

Canada *9th Floor, 550 S Hope Street, Los Angeles, CA 90071 (1-213 346 2700/fax 1-310 620 8827).* **Open** 8.30am-4.30pm Mon-Fri.
New Zealand *Suite 1150, 12400 Wilshire Boulevard, Los Angeles, CA 90025 (1-310 395 7480/1-310 395 5453).* **Open** 9am-5pm Mon-Fri.
Republic of Ireland *Suite 3830, 44 Montgomery Street, San Francisco, CA 94104 (1-415 392 4214).* **Open** 9am-5pm Mon-Fri.
South Africa *Suite 600, 6300 Wilshire Boulevard, Los Angeles, CA 90048 (1-323 651 0902/fax 1-323 651 5969).* **Open** *Office* 8am-4.30pm Mon-Fri. *Consulate* 9am-noon Mon-Fri.
United Kingdom *Suite 1200, 11766 Wilshire Boulevard, Los Angeles, CA 90025 (1-310 481 0031/24hr emergencies 1-877 514 1233/fax 1-310 481 2960).* **Open** 8.30am-5pm Mon-Fri.

Emergencies

In an emergency, dial 911 (free from public phones) and state the nature of the problem.

Gay & lesbian

Help & information

Q-Vegas (formerly the *Las Vegas Bugle*) is the leading resource for the GLBT community, with a wide range of news, reviews and features. You can pick up the magazine, which emerges every two weeks and boasts a 15,000 circulation at, among others, **Get Booked** (*see p235*). It's online at www.qvegas.com; also useful is gay events website www.gayvegas.com.

The Center

Commercial Center, 953 E Sahara Avenue, between S 6th Street & S Maryland Parkway, East of Strip (733 9800/www.thecenter-lasvegas. com). Bus 109, 204. **Open** 10am-7pm Mon-Fri; 10am-5pm Sat. **Map** p317 Y2.
A support organisation for the gay, lesbian, bisexual and transgender communities, relocated in 2002 to this capacious building. The Center organises a wild variety of social events (*see p232*), from miniature golf tournaments and bowling leagues to leather nights and HIV counselling, and is a meeting place for a variety of groups; check its website for a full calendar of events.

Accommodation

Blue Moon Resort

2651 Westwood Drive, at W Sahara Avenue, West of Strip (1-866 798 9194/361 9099/www.bluemoonlv. com. Bus 204. **Rates** vary. **Credit** AmEx, Disc, MC, V.
Las Vegas's premier gay hotel sits close to the Strip. There are two types of room: 400sq ft deluxe rooms and 800sq ft parlor suites. Amenities include a clothing-optional pool, a steam room and a coffee house.

Health

Doctors are available around the clock in emergency rooms and at some UMC Quick Care locations, and by appointment during regular business hours. Most hospitals accept major insurance plans, but – unless it's an emergency – you should call ahead to check. Large hotels have access to on-call doctors, though you may have to pay cash for this service.

Ambulances

Several ambulance companies operate in Las Vegas. If you are injured and conscious, you can choose which ambulance company you'd like to service you. If you're unconscious, the first ambulance on the scene will take you to the closest hospital ER available.

Complementary medicine

The city's few practitioners of complementary medicine enjoy a healthy business, as do aromatherapists and herbal healers. All of the major hotel spas include some form of aromatherapy. The city even has its very own popular purveyor of Chinese medicine: **T&T Ginseng** (*see p196*).

Doctors & dentists

Clark County Medical Society (739 9989, www.clark countymedical.org) provides information on and referrals to local doctors, including Medicaid and Medicare practitioners. The **Nevada Dental Association** (www.nvda.org) will make referrals to registered local dentists, including Medicaid and Medicare practitioners.

Family planning

Planned Parenthood

3220 W Charleston Boulevard, between Rancho Drive & Valley View Boulevard, Northwest Las Vegas (878 7776/www.pprm.org). Bus 206. **Open** (appointment only) 9am-5pm Mon, Wed; 11am-7pm Tue, Thur; 9am-4pm Fri; 9am-2pm Sat.
This non-profit organisation can supply contraception (including the morning-after pill), treat STDs, perform abortions and test for AIDS (results take a week).
Other location: Suite 54, 3320 E Flamingo Road (547 9888).

Hospitals

All the hospitals listed below have a 24-hour ER, although only **Sunrise** and **UMC** have out-and-out trauma centres.

Desert Springs Hospital *2075 E Flamingo Road, at Burnham Street, East Las Vegas (733 8800/www. desertspringshospital.net). Bus 202.*
Lake Mead Hospital Medical Center *1409 E Lake Mead Boulevard, between Las Vegas Boulevard, North & Eastern Avenues, North Las Vegas (649 7711/www.lake meadhospital.com). Bus 113, 210.*
St Rose Dominican Hospital *102 E Lake Mead Drive, at Boulder Highway, Henderson (616 5000/ www.strosecares.com). Bus 107, 212.* A non-profit hospital that never turns patients away.
Summerlin Hospital Medical Center *657 N Town Center Drive, at Hualapai Way, Northwest Las Vegas (233 7000/www.summerlin hospital.org). No bus.*
Sunrise Hospital & Medical Center *3186 S Maryland Parkway, between E Sahara Avenue & E Desert Inn Road, East Las Vegas (731 8000/www.sunrisehospital.com). Bus 109.* Nevada's largest hospital has a kids' facility and a poisons centre.
University Medical Center *1800 W Charleston Boulevard, at Shadow Lane, West Las Vegas (383 2000/ www.umc-cares.org). Bus 206.* The only hospital that by law must treat all applicants. The ER entrance is on the corner of Hasting and Rose Streets.

Valley Hospital Medical Center *620 Shadow Lane, off W Charleston Boulevard, between S Rancho Drive & S Martin Luther King Boulevard, West Las Vegas (388 4000/www. valleyhospmedcenter.com). Bus 206.*

Pharmacies

Both over-the-counter and prescription drugs are readily available all over town. Most hotel gift shops carry a variety of non-prescription painkillers for the most common ailments, although you are likely to be charged outrageous prices. It's best, for that reason, to use specialist drugstores.

All-night pharmacies are plentiful in Las Vegas: they're listed in the *Yellow Pages* and include all branches of **Sav-On**. The closest branches to the Strip are at 2300 E Tropicana Avenue (736 4174) and 1360 E Flamingo Road (731 5373). For details of other pharmacies – such as **Walgreens**, many of whose local locations can fulfil prescriptions 24-7 – *see p199*.

Prescriptions

Doctors in Las Vegas generally insist on giving you a physical exam before they'll write a prescription. Take the prescription to a licensed pharmacist, who'll usually be able to provide the medication within minutes.

STDs, HIV & AIDS

Nevada ranks 12th in the United States for AIDS cases per capita and second for alcohol consumption. Combine these sobering statistics with the fact that the town attracts 37 million visitors a year, and it becomes obvious that Las Vegas is not only a pleasure zone but a danger zone too. To state more of the obvious, always practise safe sex.

For specific information on HIV/AIDS, local resources, various support groups and

free, confidential tests, contact **Aid for AIDS of Nevada**. For treatment of STDs and free AIDS tests, visit **Planned Parenthood** (*see above*).

Aid for AIDS of Nevada (AFAN)

Suite 211, Sahara Rancho Medical Center, 2300 S Rancho Drive, between W Sahara Avenue & W Oakey Boulevard, West of Strip (382 2326/hotline 842 2437/www.inside afan.org). Bus 106. **Open** 8am-noon, 1-4pm Mon-Fri.
In addition to offering free advice and testing, this support group raises money and awareness through large-scale events, including a benefit walk Downtown each spring.

AIDS Information Line

Clark County Health District, 625 Shadow Lane, at W Charleston Boulevard, Northwest Las Vegas (759 0743/www.cchd.org). Bus 206. **Open** 8am-4.30pm Mon-Fri.

Helplines

For AIDS helplines, *see above*. For information on what to do in an emergency, *see p295; see also pp295-296* **Health**.

Alcoholics Anonymous *598 1888.*
Gamblers Anonymous *385 7732.*
Narcotics Anonymous *369 3362.*
Poison Control Center *732 4989.*
Rape Crisis *366 1640.*
Suicide Prevention *731 2990.*

ID

Vegas checks IDs frequently: you'll need to prove your age when buying tobacco and alcohol, gambling and entering nightclubs. Legal IDs include passports, driver's licences and state ID cards. UK citizens are advised to get a photo driving licence, so they can keep their passport secure at their hotel.

Insurance

Non-nationals should arrange baggage, trip-cancellation and medical insurance before departure. Medical centres will ask for details of your insurance company and your policy number; keep them with you at all times.

Internet

Hotels are increasingly keen to keep guests connected. Many have high-speed connections wired into every room (around $10 a day), and some have wireless access. All Starbucks and Borders locations have T-Mobile wireless access (for a fee), but the savvy laptop owner can link to free wifi at the Coffee Bean & Tea Leaf as well as in the Fashion Show Mall near the Apple Store. You can even check your email from any of the display Macs.

For those without a laptop, the pickings are slimmer. A few convenience stores have terminals (there are two by the Hawaiian Marketplace, on the east side of the Strip north of Tropicana Avenue), but prices are high. Public libraries (*see below*) offer free, time-limited access, and **FedEx Kinko's** (*see p294*) has access at 20¢ a minute. But the best bet for dedicated surfers is **Cyber Zone** (*see below*), where access costs a mere $2 an hour. If you need a local ISP, try **Cox** (383 4000) or **Sprint** (244 7400). For useful websites, *see p303*.

CyberZone

4400 S Maryland Parkway, at E University Avenue, University District (732 2249). Bus 109, 202, 203. **Open** 11am-7am daily. **Map** p317 Y3.

Left luggage

The lockers at McCarran are unavailable due to security concerns. Most major hotels will allow you to leave luggage with the bellmen for a nominal fee (a tip of $5 per bag, say).

Legal help

If you are arrested, contact either your insurance company's emergency number, your consulate or the Lawyer Referral Service on 382 0504. If you do not have a lawyer, the court will appoint one for you.

Libraries

Las Vegas–Clark County Library District

www.lvccld.org. Libraries open 9am-9pm Mon-Thur; 10am-6pm Fri-Sun.
Clark County Library *1401 E Flamingo Road, University District (733 7810).* **Map** p317 Y3.
Enterprise Library *25 E Shelbourne Avenue, South Las Vegas (507 3760).*
Green Valley Library *2797 N Green Valley Parkway, Henderson (507 3790).*
Las Vegas Library *833 Las Vegas Boulevard North, North Las Vegas (382 3493).* **Map** p318 D1.
Rainbow Library *3150 N Buffalo Drive, North Las Vegas (243 7323).*
Sahara West Library *9600 W Sahara Avenue, Northwest Las Vegas (360 8000).*
Spring Valley Library *4280 S Jones Boulevard, Southwest Las Vegas (507 3820).*
Summerlin Library *1771 Inner Circle Drive, Northwest Las Vegas (256 5111).*
West Charleston Library *6301 W Charleston Boulevard, Southwest Las Vegas (878 3682).*
West Las Vegas Library *951 W Lake Mead Boulevard, West Las Vegas (507 3980).*
Whitney Library & Recital Hall *5175 E Tropicana Avenue, East Las Vegas (454 4575).*

Lied Library

4505 S Maryland Parkway, between E Flamingo Road & E Tropicana Avenue, University District (895 3531/www.library.nevada.edu). Bus 109, 201, 213. **Open** 7.30am-midnight Mon-Thur; 7.30am-7pm Fri; 9am-6pm Sat; 11am-midnight Sun. **Map** p317 Y3.
This $40-million facility houses 1.8 million volumes.

Lost property

McCarran Int'l Airport

Terminal 1 (261 5134). **Open** 6.30am-1am daily. **Map** p320 B9.

Public transport

600 Grand Central Parkway, at Alta Drive, Downtown (228 7433). Bus 207. **Open** 8am-5pm Mon-Fri. **Map** p318 C1.

Taxis

Checker/Star/Yellow Cab *3950 W Tompkins Avenue, at S Arville Street, Southwest Las Vegas (873 8012).* **Open** 9am-3.30pm daily.
Whittlesea *2030 S Industrial Road, at W Sahara Avenue, West of Strip (384 6111).* **Open** 10am-4pm daily. **Map** p319 B4.

Media

Daily newspapers

As well as the city's two daily papers, the *Los Angeles Times* (50¢) is widely available, and most Strip hotels will also carry the *Wall Street Journal* (75¢) and the *New York Times* ($1). International media is harder to find, though **Tower** (*see p198*) has a well-stocked periodicals section.

Las Vegas Review-Journal

www.reviewjournal.com. The *R-J* (50¢, $2.50 on Sunday) offers bland but serviceable coverage of local and national stories. John L Smith is the must-read columnist for local politicos; Norm Clarke covers gossip. The *R-J* also has an entertainment guide (the Friday 'Neon' section), which gives listings for movies, shows and restaurants.

Las Vegas Sun

www.lasvegassun.com. The *Las Vegas Sun* (50¢, Mon-Fri) used to offer a populist alternative to the conservative *R-J*, reflecting the style of its maverick founder, Hank Greenspun. It's declined since Hank's death in 1989; after cash troubles, it entered a joint operating agreement with the *R-J*. Jon Ralston's column is a draw, but the *R-J* outsells the *Sun* by five to one.

Weekly newspapers

CityLife

www.lasvegascitylife.com. One of two free so-called 'alternative news weeklies', *CityLife* was bought out in March 2005 by the Stephens group, publishers of the *R-J*, who then merged the *Las Vegas Mercury* into it. It's too early to tell how this change will affect the stance of the paper, but if the editors favour the *Mercury*'s savvy, leftist writing over *CityLife*'s often sneery contrarianism, it should do fine.

Las Vegas Weekly

www.lasvegasweekly.com Established in 1992 as *SCOPE*, and purchased in 1998 by the Greenspun family, the *Weekly* has gone through several transitions, but seems to be returning to *SCOPE*'s arts and entertainment roots. It's the most impressively presented free paper in town, but its writing isn't as strong as perhaps it could be.

Directory

Free tourist guides

Numerous freebie mags – including *Today in Las Vegas*, *Showbiz Weekly* and *What's On: The Las Vegas Guide* – are distributed at hotels and other tourist spots. The editorial is uncritical, with articles and reviews often reading disturbingly like press releases; it's also not entirely comprehensive. However, each contains a cornucopia of handy facts and numbers, plus coupons for free or discounted admission to shows.

Magazines

City-wide magazines

There are several glossies in Las Vegas, including the *Las Vegan*, *Las Vegas*, *Vegas* and *Las Vegas Life*. The latter is the best of the bunch.

State-wide magazines

Nevada (bi-monthly) contains an events calendar for Las Vegas, Reno and the bits in between; articles tend to appeal to older readers.

Business magazines

Business news is covered by the *Nevada Business Journal* (monthly), the *Las Vegas Business Press* (weekly) and the Greenspun Media Group's *In Business Las Vegas* (biweekly). All provide coverage of Nevada's business scene with an emphasis on non-gaming industries. *Las Vegas Business Press* is the most comprehensive. For gaming news, check out *Casino Journal* (quarterly), the *Las Vegas Advisor* (monthly) and *Gaming Today* (weekly).

Television

The Las Vegas affiliates of the four major American networks are **KVBC 3** (NBC), **KVVU 5** (Fox), **KLAS 8** (CBS) and **KTNV 13** (ABC). UPN and WB are represented by **KTUD 25** and **KVWB 21**, while the Greenspun Media Group and **KLAS 8** operate Las Vegas ONE channels 1 and 39, with lots of Vegas-oriented news and programming. Las Vegas's public broadcasting affiliate is **KLVX 10**. Every hotel TV will get these stations; most will also carry cable networks such as **CNN** (news), **ESPN** (sport) and **HBO** (movies). Daily TV listings can be found in the *Sun*, the *R-J*, *Showbiz*, *What's On* and *TV Guide*.

Radio

FM radio in Vegas has become a bland parade of hackneyed playlists suitable only for splicing together ads for car sales and topless joints. Public stations are far better: try KNPR, one of two national public radio affiliates.

On AM, news and sports dominate. Art Bell still runs the 'Coast to Coast' national show on KDWN, featuring a catch-all of paranormal *X-Files* type guests. All the major national hosts are syndicated here, among them Rush Limbaugh (KXNT 840 AM; 9am-noon Mon-Fri).

Radio stations

KCEP *88.1 FM/www.power88lv.com.* Urban contemporary tunes.
KNPR *89.5 FM/www.knpr.org; affiliate of National Public Radio.* Classical music, news and talk.
KUNV *91.5 FM/http://kunv.unlv.edu; affiliate of National Public Radio.* Jazz and NPR news.
KOMP *92.3 FM/www.komp.com.* Mainstream rock.
KMXB *94.1 FM/www.kmxb.com.* Adult alternative and 1980s hits.
KWNR *95.5 FM/www.kwnr.com.* Country and western.
KKLZ *96.3 FM/www.963kklz.com.* Classic rock; lots of Led Zeppelin.
KXPT *97.1/www.point97.com.* Adult rock, on the lighter side
KLUC *98.5 FM/www.kluc.com.* Top 40 hits, often dancey.
KJUL *104.3 FM/www.kjul.net.* Ballad after ballad.
KSNE *106.5 FM/www.ksne.com.* Light rock and pop.
KVGS *107.9 FM/www.v108fm.com.* Hip hop hits.

Money

The US dollar ($) is split into 100 cents (¢). Coins run from the copper penny (1¢) to the silver nickel (5¢), dime (10¢), quarter (25¢), the less common half-dollar (50¢) and the rarely seen dollar. Notes ('bills') are all the same green colour and size, but come in denominations of $1, $5, $10, $20, $50 and $100.

Las Vegas is not as cheap as it once was. Hotels remain good value, but in the end you get what you pay for: the top shows and restaurants cost a fair penny. What's more, you may spend a large amount on gambling, so stick to a budget. If you go broke, call **Western Union** on 1-800 325 6000 and arrange for someone to wire money to you. Otherwise, there are pawnbrokers Downtown.

ATM/cash machines

ATMs are ubiquitous here. Either withdraw money on your credit card, or use global networks such as Cirrus to withdraw money directly from your account. Foreign visitors may not have to pay the stated charge, though their bank may levy its own fee.

Banks

If you forget your PIN and need to get cash on a credit card – something you can do in a casino, but for which you'll be charged a premium – there are banks all over town (but none on the Strip). In addition to the main branches, usually only open 9am to 6pm Monday to Friday, some full-service branches in stores are open until 7pm or 8pm during the week, as well as part of the weekend. **Bank of America** (1-800 388 2265) has a branch in Vons, and **Nevada State Bank** (1-800 727 4743) has one in Smiths Food & Drug.

Credit & debit cards

Major credit cards are accepted in almost every hotel, shop and restaurant, but do keep cash on hand just in case (and for tips). The card networks mentioned above are also linked to the Maestro (Cirrus) and Delta (Plus) debit networks.

Currency exchange

Some casinos have their own bank or bureau de change; all have a 24-7 cashier's cage where you can cash most US bank and travellers' cheques, and exchange most major currencies. Indeed, the casinos tend to offer better rates on currency than **American Express** desks. At non-casino hotels, you should be able to cash travellers' cheques at the front desk. You may need photo ID in order to cash them. There's also a **Travelex** bureau at the airport.

American Express

Fashion Show Mall, 3200 Las Vegas Boulevard South, at Spring Mountain Road (739 8474/www.americanexpress.com). Bus 203, 213, 301, 302. **Open** 9am-9pm Mon-Fri; 10am-8pm Sat; 11am-6pm Sun. **Map** p320 A6. The one AmEx office in town. If you lose your AmEx card (*see below*), ask for the replacement to be issued here.

Lost & stolen cards

American Express *1-800 992 3404/travellers' cheques 1-800 221 7282/www.americanexpress.com.*
Diners Club *1-800 234 6377/ www.dinersclub.com.*
Discover *1-800 347 2683/www. discovercard.com.*
MasterCard *1-800 622 7747/www. mastercard.com.*
Visa *1-800 847 2911/www.visa.com.*

Tax

Sales tax is 7.5%; food (groceries) purchased in stores are exempt. Room tax is 9%, except Downtown (11%).

Natural hazards

The most obvious hazards are the heat and intense sunshine (*see p301*). Summer visitors should be prepared for other severe weather conditions, too. Las Vegas receives a fair bit of rain in July and August, often causing flash floods that are dangerous and rather deeper than they first appears.

Opening hours

The casinos, their bars and at least one of their restaurants or coffee shops are open all day, every day. Grocery stores, dry-cleaners and gas stations are also open 24 hours a day.

On a local level, Las Vegas still keeps small-town hours. Many eateries close at 10pm; non-chain shops may shut at 6pm and won't open Sundays. Government hours are 9am to 5pm, give or take half an hour.

Police stations

Police

400 Stewart Avenue, at Las Vegas Boulevard, Downtown (795 3111). Bus 107, 108, 109, 113, 207, 301, 302. **Open** 24hrs daily. **Map** p318 D1. For non-emergency enquiries only.

Postal services

US mailboxes are red, white and blue. There is usually a timetable of collections and a list of restrictions inside the lid. Packages over 16 ounces must be taken to a post office counter (*see below*). For couriers and shippers, *see p294*.

Stamps are sold in shops and from machines. Contract stations (there's one at Allstate Ticketing in the Forum Shops) can send international mail, but will charge a supplement.

Post offices

For most transactions, contract stations in Albertsons stores should suffice. General delivery mail (*poste restante*) can be collected from the Downtown station (to: General Delivery, Las Vegas, NV 89101). You'll need to show photo ID when you collect it. For your nearest post office, call 1-800 275 8777 and quote the zip code.

Main post office *1001 E Sunset Road, between Paradise Road & S Maryland Parkway, East of Strip (1-800 275 8777). Bus 212.* **Open** 7.30am-9pm Mon-Fri; 8am-4pm Sat. **Map** p317 Y4.
Downtown station *201 Las Vegas Boulevard South, between Fremont Street & E Bonneville Avenue (1-800 275 8777). Bus 301.* **Open** 8.30am-5pm Mon-Fri. **Map** p318 D1.
Strip station *Industrial Road, at Stardust Way, West of Strip (1-800 275 8777). Bus 105, 301.* **Open** 8.30am-5pm Mon-Fri; 10am-2pm Sat. **Map** p319 A5.

Religion

For your nearest **Lutheran** church, contact 456 2001; for **Episcopal**, call 737 9190; and for **Methodist**, 369 7055. For others, consult the phone book.

Congregation Ner Tamid *2761 Emerson Avenue, East Las Vegas (733 6292). Bus 112.* **Map** p317 Z3. Jewish Reform.
First Baptist Church *4400 W Oakey Boulevard, West Las Vegas (821 1234). Bus 104.*
First Presbyterian Church *1515 W Charleston Boulevard, West of Strip (384 4554). Bus 206.* **Map** p319 B3.
Guardian Angel Cathedral *336 Cathedral Way, E Desert Inn Road (735 5241). Bus 301.* **Map** p319 B5. The Catholic diocese of Reno-Las Vegas.
Islamic Center of Las Vegas *3799 Edwards Avenue, Northwest Las Vegas (395 7013). Bus 106.*
Latter-Day Saints Las Vegas Temple *827 N Temple View Drive, East Las Vegas (452 5011). Bus 208.* The Church of Jesus Christ of Latter-Day Saints (Mormons) only.
Temple Beth Sholom *10700 Havenwood Lane, Summerlin (804 1333). Bus 211.* The city's oldest Jewish congregation.

Safety & security

There's relatively little crime in Vegas. Casinos have such elaborate security systems that few serious offences take place within them. However, on the streets, especially outside tourist areas, pickpockets and muggers strike more often than the city would like. Be careful in the seedier-looking areas of Downtown.

● Only take out what you need: leave the bulk of your money and travellers' cheques in a room safe or in a safety deposit box at the hotel.
● Keep a note of the numbers and details of your passport, driving licence, travellers' cheques, cards and insurance policies, along with the phone numbers you'll need to report their loss (*see above*). Leave the same list with someone at home.
● Take the usual precautions with your wallet or handbag, especially on buses and at bus stops. Don't keep valuables in your pockets.
● If you're threatened with a weapon, give your assailants what they want. Then find a phone and call the police (911).

Smoking

Puff away! In Vegas, smoking is tolerated almost everywhere. Most restaurants, especially in major casinos, have smoking and non-smoking sections.

Study

Many local colleges feed the service and gaming industry. Those looking to learn how to become a dealer or croupier must attend one of the city's specialist dealer schools.

PCI Dealers School *920 Valley View Boulevard, West of Strip, Las Vegas, NV 89102 (877 4724/www. pcidealerschool.com)*. **Map** p317 X2.

Telephones

Dialling & codes

There are two area codes for Nevada: 702 for Clark County (including Las Vegas) and 775 for the rest of the state. Within Vegas, there's no need to use 702: just dial the seven-digit number. Outside this area, calls are long distance: dial 1, then the area code, then the number. The 1-800, 1-866, 1-877 and 1-888 codes denote toll-free numbers; many are accessible from outside the US, but you'll be charged for your call.

Making a call

Most hotels charge a flat fee of between 50¢ and $1 for calls to local and toll-free numbers. You can get around this at some hotels by using a house phone and asking the operator to connect you. Alternatively, you should find payphones in the lobby or by the restrooms. Long-distance and international calls can be very pricey if direct-dialled from a hotel. You're better off using a US phonecard, whether tied to a domestic account or bought as a one-off. Drugstores and convenience stores sell them in various denominations.

Passport regulations

The United States now requires visitors travelling under the Visa Waiver Program (VWP) to present a machine-readable passport in order to be admitted to the country. VWP countries include the UK, Australia and New Zealand. Machine-readable passports contain either a magnetic strip or barcode. The standard-issue EC/EU maroon passport is machine readable. Each traveller, including all children, need their own passport, which must be valid for at least a further six months.

Passports issued to VWP travellers on or after October 26 2005 must contain biometric data: for the US's purposes, index finger prints and a digital photo. Officials will be 'enrolling' VWP travellers whose passports were issued prior to this date by taking fingerprint scans and a photo. This can result in long queues at immigration. Whether the countries concerned can sort out the technology required to issue biometric passports by this date, and the US to read them, is still subject to question: one deadline extension has already been necessary.

Before you travel, visit http://travel.state.gov/visa and click on 'Temporary Visitors' to check the current situation.

To use a public phone, check for a dialling tone and then put in your change (35¢ for a local call; long-distance, dial first and wait to be quoted a cost). Operator and emergency calls are free. Payphones at the airport and at some casinos accept credit cards.

Operator services

Collect calls (reverse-charge) 0.
Local directory enquiries 411.
National directory enquiries 1 + [area code] + 555 1212 (if you don't know the area code, dial 0 for the operator).
International calls 011 + [country code] + [area code] + [number].
International country codes UK 44; New Zealand 64; Australia 61; Germany 49; Japan 81.
Emergencies 911.

Mobile phones

Vegas, like most of the US, operates on the 1900 GSM frequency. European travellers with dual-band phones will need to rent a handset.

Cellular City *4720 S Polaris Avenue, at Tompkins Avenue, West of Strip (873 2489). Bus 203.* **Open** 10am-7pm Mon-Sat. **Credit** MC, V. **Map** p317 X3.

Time

Nevada operates on Pacific Standard Time, eight hours behind GMT (London). Clocks go forward by an hour in late April, and back in late October. (Note: neighbouring Arizona has no daylight saving.)

Tipping

Limo drivers ($10-$25 per ride), valet parking attendants ($1-$2), cocktail waitresses (50¢-$1), housekeepers ($1 a night) and even desk clerks ($10-$20 if you're looking for a better room) all ride the tip gravy train. For detailed information on tipping in casinos, *see p43*.

Tourist information

You will see many self-styled tourist offices on the Strip, but only those listed below are official. For the Nevada Commission on Tourism's contact details, *see p259*.

Las Vegas Chamber of Commerce

Hughes Center, 3720 Howard Hughes Parkway, between Sands Avenue & E Flamingo Road, East of Strip, Las Vegas, NV 89109 (735 1616/www.lvchamber.com). Bus 108, 203. **Open** 8.30am-5pm Mon-Thur; 8.30am-1pm Fri. **Map** p320 C6.
Advice, brochures, maps and a few coupons are available if you visit in person; there's also a good phone information service, and you can write in advance for a visitor pack.

Las Vegas Convention & Visitors Authority

3150 Paradise Road, opposite Convention Center Drive, East of Strip, Las Vegas, NV 89109 (892 0711/www.visitlasvegas.com). Bus 108, 202, 203, 213. **Open** 8am-5pm Mon-Fri. **Map** p319 C5.
A comprehensive and helpful office. Write to the LVCVA for a visitor pack that includes lists of hotels, a brochure, a map and the regularly updated *Showguide*. In the UK, contact Cellet Travel Services for details on Vegas (01564 794999, www.visitlasvegas.co.uk).

Visas & immigration

Citizens of the UK, Australia, New Zealand, Japan and most West European countries do not need a visa for stays in the US of less than 90 days (business or pleasure) if they have a passport valid for six months beyond the return date and a return (or open standby) ticket. Canadians and Mexicans do not need visas but must have legal proof of their residency. All other travellers must have visas.

Full information and visa application forms can be obtained from your nearest US embassy or consulate. UK travellers should check the US Embassy's website at www.usembassy.org.uk, or call their helpline on 09055 444 546 (£1.30 a minute).

When to go

Though there's no off-season in Las Vegas, it's slightly quieter (and hotel prices are lower) between Thanksgiving and Christmas, and during the heat of July and August. Public holidays are always busy. If you're planning a short visit, try to avoid weekend crowds (and higher prices). The convention schedule has a major effect on hotel prices and availability. For a list of the major conventions, *see p293*.

Public holidays

1 Jan New Year's Day; **3rd Mon in Jan** Martin Luther King Jr Holiday; **3rd Mon in Feb** President's Day; **late Mar/early Apr** Easter Sunday; **last Mon in May** Memorial Day; **4 July** Independence Day; **1st Mon in Sept** Labor Day; **last Fri in Oct** Nevada Day; **2nd Mon in Nov** Veterans' Day; **4th Thur in Nov** Thanksgiving; **25 Dec** Christmas Day.

Climate

Las Vegas has blue skies and little rain all year round (the percentage of sunny daylight hours runs from 77 per cent in December and January to 92 per cent in June). Daytime temperatures can get burning hot: afternoon temperatures can reach 110°F (43°C) in July and August, remaining above 90°F (32°C) at midnight. However, they can also get pretty chilly: temperatures can approach freezing in December and January, though 50-60°F (10-15°C) is more usual during the day. Don't plan on doing too much exercise in summer. Drink lots of water and wear a hat, sunglasses and sunscreen. Note that hotel swimming pools (outdoors only) close from roughly October to March, the same time you may need to wear a jacket.

Women

Las Vegas is an interesting contradiction in feminist politics. On the one hand, women are objectified in the entertainment industry; on the other, they fare well in the job market. There's no women's centre; the **UNLV Women's Studies Office** (895 0837) is a good first contact.

Work

To work in the US, non-nationals must be sponsored by a US company and get an H-1 visa. They also have to convince US Immigration that no American is qualified to do the job. Contact your US embassy for details.

Weather report

Month	Ave high	Ave low	Rainfall
January	58°F (14°C)	37°F (3°C)	0.59in
February	63°F (17°C)	41°F (5°C)	0.69in
March	69°F (21°C)	47°F (8°C)	0.59in
April	78°F (26°C)	54°F (12°C)	0.15in
May	88°F (31°C)	63°F (17°C)	0.24in
June	99°F (37°C)	72°F (22°C)	0.08in
July	104°F (40°C)	78°F (26°C)	0.44in
August	102°F (39°C)	77°F (25°C)	0.45in
September	94°F (34°C)	69°F (21°C)	0.31in
October	81°F (27°C)	57°F (14°C)	0.24in
November	66°F (19°C)	44°F (7°C)	0.31in
December	57°F (14°C)	37°F (3°C)	0.40in

Average rainfall: 4.5 inches per year
Average sunshine: 294 days per year
(211 clear, 83 partly cloudy)

Directory

Further Reference

Books

Non-fiction

Al Alvarez
The Biggest Game in Town
It's more than two decades old, but Alvarez's account of the World Series of Poker still fascinates.

Frances Anderton & John Chase *The Success of Excess*
Gorgeous large-format photo book on Vegas's theme-park architecture.

Thomas A Bass
The Newtonian Casino
Can casinos be beaten? With a bit of computer geekery, the answer's yes.

Fred E Basten & Charles Phoenix *Fabulous Las Vegas in the 50s: Glitz, Glamor & Games*
A nostalgic full-colour collection of photographs, menus and postcards from the lost glory days of Vegas.

Susan Berman *Easy Street*;
Lady Las Vegas: The Inside Story Behind America's Neon Oasis
By the daughter of a Mob insider, made all the more creepy by her murder in 1999.

Eric Bjourstad *Desert Rock: Rock Climbs in the National Parks*
A useful desert companion.

Jeff Burbank *License to Steal*
A detailed exposition of the legal side of Nevada gaming control and how it participated in building Las Vegas.

Deke Castleman
Whale Hunt in the Desert: The Secret Las Vegas of Superhost Steve Cyr
A fascinating glimpse into the world of the high roller, via one of the town's most powerful casino hosts.

Sally Denton & Roger Morris
The Money and the Power: The Making of Las Vegas and Its Hold on America
Investigative history of how Vegas was shaped and corrupted.

Pete Early *Super Casino: Inside the 'New' Las Vegas*
Fizzing, journalistic account of the 1990s revolution in resort-building.

William L Fox
In the Desert of Desire
The nature of culture and the culture of nature in Las Vegas.

Jeff German
Murder in Sin City: The Death of a Las Vegas Casino Boss
Reporter German explores the 1998 murder of Ted Binion.

Mark Gottdiener, Claudia C Collins & David R Dickens
Las Vegas: The Social Production of an All-American City
A fascinating look at the social phenomenon of Vegas, from how a city grows in the desert to what it means to live off the tourist dollar.

AD Hopkins & KJ Evans (eds)
The First 100: Portraits of the Men and Women Who Shaped Las Vegas
A thought-provoking, well-written encyclopaedia.

Stephen Ives & Michelle Ferrari *Las Vegas: An Unconventional History*
… Of an unconventional town.

Shaun Levy *Rat Pack Confidential*
A modern, funky appraisal of the Rat Pack years and beyond.

Andrès Martinez
24/7: Living It Up and Doubling Down in the New Las Vegas
An attorney and journalist spends his $50,000 advance in this modern-day *Fear and Loathing*.

Robert D McCracken *Las Vegas: The Great American Playground*
A mix of history and commentary, and a great read to boot.

James McManus *Positively Fifth Street: Murders, Cheetahs, and Binion's World Series of Poker*
McManus was sent on assignment to cover the 2000 World Series of Poker, but ended up taking part. Fun stuff.

Eugene P Moehring & Michael S Green
Las Vegas: A Centennial History
The best of the centennial books.

Dick Odessky *Fly on the Wall*
Amusing anecdotes and insider accounts told by a long-term Vegas reporter and publicity man.

William F Roemer *The Enforcer: Spilotro – The Chicago Mob's Man over Las Vegas*
Vegas attorney Oscar Goodman kept Tony 'The Ant' Spilotro out of jail for a decade. Now Goodman is mayor and Spilotro is dead, beaten to death and buried in an Indiana cornfield.

Hal Rothman
Neon Metropolis: How Las Vegas Started the 21st Century
UNLV history professor deconstructs Las Vegas's myth and reality.

Geoff Schumacher
Sun, Sin and Suburbia: An Essential History of Modern Las Vegas
Editor of *CityLife* surveys the last few decades in readable fashion.

Cathy Scott *Murder of a Mafia Daughter: The Life and Tragic Death of Susan Berman*
Journo investigates the murder of the mafia daughter-turned-author.

Lora Shaner
Madam: Inside a Nevada Brothel
The author was a full-time madam before setting up her own PR firm.

John L Smith *No Limit – The Rise and Fall of Bob Stupak & Las Vegas' Stratosphere Tower*; *Running Scared: The Life and Treacherous Times of Las Vegas Casino King Steve Wynn*
Savvy *R-J* columnist dishes the dirt on two major casino players.

Lyle Stuart
Howard Hughes in Las Vegas
This history of a Vegas maverick gets behind the legend.

David Thomson *Into Nevada*
Musings on Nevada – its mining, nuclear and gambling history – by an expat Brit-Californian.

Nick Tosches *Dino*
Scorching biog of the Rat Packer.

Mike Tronnes (ed)
Literary Las Vegas
An excellent anthology of journalism from 1952 to the late 1990s.

Robert Venturi, Steven Izenour & Denise Scott Brown *Learning from Las Vegas: The Forgotten Symbolism of Architectural Form*
Fascinating study of the auto-driven architecture of the Strip.

Mike Weatherford *Cult Vegas: The Weirdest! The Wildest!*
The Swingin'est Town on Earth
Offbeat movies, ornery characters, unforgettable trivia, all explained in gossipy detail by an *R-J* columnist.

Branch Whitney *Hiking Las Vegas: 60 Hikes Within 60 Minutes of the Strip*; *Hiking Southern Nevada*
Clear instructions, good detail.

WR Wilkerson III
The Man Who Invented Las Vegas
Think Bugsy Siegel built Vegas? Learn about Billy Wilkerson, from whom Siegel stole the Flamingo, and stand corrected. By his son.

Fiction

Larry McMurtry *Desert Rose*
The *Terms of Endearment* writer turns his attention to the portrayal of a washed-up showgirl.

John O'Brien *Leaving Las Vegas*
Love, loneliness and alcoholism in the city of fun. Better than the film.

Wendy Perriam *Sin City*
Personal drama played out against an impersonal city.

Nicholas Pileggi *Casino: Love and Honour in Las Vegas*
Book of the film: a cracking read.

Tim Powers *Last Call*
A fantasia on the Las Vegas myth, in which Bugsy Siegel is the Fisher King and tarot cards the deck of choice at the Flamingo's poker tables.

Mario Puzo *Fools Die*
The *Godfather* author returns with another 'sweeping epic'. Lots of casino colour.

Hunter S Thompson
Fear and Loathing in Las Vegas
The drug-crazed classic is always worth re-reading.

Michael Ventura
The Death of Frank Sinatra
Cracking private-eye story set among the implosions of the early 1990s.

Gambling

Gambling guides are many and varied, but a sizeable number are poorly researched and dangerously misleading. We recommend ordering material direct from renowned gambling experts **Huntington Press** (1-800 244 2224, www. huntingtonpress.com), who publish all the books listed below.

Ian Andersen *Burning the Tables in Las Vegas: Keys to Success in Blackjack and in Life*
A high-stakes blackjack player reveals how he gets away with it.
Bob Dancer
Bob Dancer Presents WinPoker
Software tutor (PC only) on proper strategies for video poker. A must for anyone who plays these machines.
Max Rubin *Comp City: A Guide to Free Gambling Vacations*
Classic text on casino comps, now in its second edition. A hilarious read.
Jean Scott *The Frugal Gambler*
How to get the most from the least. A classic text.
Olaf Vancura & Ken Fuchs
Knock-Out Blackjack: The Easiest Card-Counting System Ever Devised
Former astrophysicist's 'unbalanced' count, which eliminates most of the mental gymnastics of other systems. Not easy, but doable.

Film

In addition to these movies, recent TV shows worth catching (either on TV or on tape) include **American Casino**, **Casino**, **CSI**, **Las Vegas** and **The Real World: Las Vegas**.

America's Sweethearts (2001)
Filmed in Lake Las Vegas. Stars Billy Crystal. Abysmal.
Bugsy (1991)
Witty script (James Toback), classy direction (Barry Levinson) and great performances (Beatty, Bening).
Casino (1995)
Martin Scorsese's three-hour mishmash of gambling and the Mob, voiceovered to death.
The Cooler (2004)
Set in Vegas (but filmed mostly in Reno). William H Macy stars.
Diamonds Are Forever (1971)
Bond (Connery, this time) in Vegas. Silly gadgets abound.
Fear and Loathing in Las Vegas (1998)
This relentless adaptation of the Thompson classic was a cult movie before it was even released.
Go (1999)
Doug Liman's follow-up to *Swingers* seems a little forced, but there are some good bits of business.
Honeymoon in Vegas (1992)
Nicolas Cage in engagingly oddball comedy mode.

Leaving Las Vegas (1995)
This Mike Figgis masterpiece stars Cage as a self-destructive alcoholic.
Meet Me in Las Vegas (1956)
Problem gambler hooks up with Strip dancer in a familiar plot, brightened by Cyd Charisse as the dancer.
Ocean's 11 (1960)
With all the Rat Pack present, this kitschy, corny film has become the *de facto* video history of a romantic Vegas era. Soderbergh's 2001 *Ocean's Eleven* deploys George Clooney and chums in a surprisingly vigorous high-tech remake.
One From the Heart (1980)
Coppola's Vegas love story, flawed but still somehow winning. Tom Waits and Crystal Gayle (duetting!) provide the beautiful soundtrack.
Rain Man (1988)
Dustin Hoffman's autistic Raymond – and brother Charlie (Tom Cruise) – finds his ability to remember numbers comes in handy in Vegas.
Showgirls (1995)
Some films that are universally panned on release benefit from a later reappraisal. Paul Verhoeven's Vegas misadventure still isn't one of them.
Swingers (1996)
First feature by Doug Liman: 90 minutes learning how not to pick up girls. Vince Vaughn is still trading off the kudos.
Viva Las Vegas (1963)
Fun film for those nostalgic for the old, swanky Vegas and the young, svelte Elvis. Ann-Margret co-stars.

Music

Crystal Method *Vegas*
This techno duo studied at UNLV; the cover photo is from the Binion's Horseshoe parking garage.
David Holmes *Ocean's Eleven*
Funky, spunky soundtrack to the Steven Soderbergh remake of the Rat Pack classic. Excerpts of the original soundtrack are available on the box set *Sinatra in Hollywood*.
The Killers *Hot Fuss*
Indie-rock from Vegas; the first band from the town to make it big in aeons.
Wayne Newton
Wild, Cool and Swingin'
Back when he still had a voice.
Elvis Presley *Live in Las Vegas*
As Elvis got fatter, his shows got glammier. This box set is all the fat Elvis you'll ever need, and then some.
Louis Prima *Collectors Series*
Glorious, hard-swingin' lounge stuff from the 1950s.
Frank Sinatra *Sinatra at the Sands*
Classic recording of Frank backed by the Count Basie Orchestra.
Various Artists
The Rat Pack: Live at the Sands
The definitive audio record of Dino (on top form), Sammy and the Chairman of the Board.

Websites

www.cheapovegas.com
An excellent guide to the casinos of Vegas, slanted towards cash-poor travellers but with enough useful information (and fine writing) for all. Run by Big Empire, who supplement it with a guide to Vegas on 25¢ a day (www.bigempire.com/vegas).
http://crecon.com/vintagevegas
Nothing here but images of classic Vegas matchbooks, postcards and gambling chips. Isn't that enough?
www.firstfriday-lasvegas.org
Information on Vegas's highly successful monthly cultural event.
http://gayvegas.tripod.com
Gay-friendly establishments, from nightclubs to restaurants, plus a list of resources and an events calendar.
www.intercomm.com/koala
The Nevada Movie Page is a wide-ranging look at the more than 500 movies made in or about the state.
www.knpr.org
Run by the local NPR affiliate, this site has a great local programming archive that includes transcripts as well as audio files.
www.lasvegas.com
Operated by the *Review-Journal*, this provides links to local news, event listings and other resources.
www.lasvegasadvisor.com
The latest gambling tips, plus a very active forums section.
www.lasvegas2005.org
Information on the city's centennial celebrations will be posted here.
www.lasvegas24hours.com
The official consumer website of the Las Vegas Convention & Visitors Authority (there's a business-oriented one at www.lvcva.com).
http://lvartsandculture.blogspot.com
Robert Kimberly's readable, insightful and sometimes gossipy musings on the local culture scene come with a hugely useful sidebar of local links.
www.lvstriphistory.com
Both design and editing illustrate that this is a small, homespun effort, but the information is invaluable.
www.reviewjournal.com
Your first stop for Vegas news. The weekly eNeon newsletter is a useful entertainment resource.
www.vegas.com
This all-encompassing Vegas portal site for visitors includes reviews of bars and restaurants, listings of shows, films and nightlife, and access to hotels. Not all the criticism is quite sharp enough, but as a database, it's very useful.
www.weddinginvegas.com
Planning to get hitched in Vegas? Find information and ideas here.
www.yourlocalscene.com
News and reviews of local bands.

Directory

Index

Index

Advertisers' Index

Please refer to the relevant pages for contact
details.

Place of interest	▨
Casino hotel	▨
Non-casino hotel	■
Park or forest	▨
One-way street	→
Interstate highway	🛡75
US highway	⬡41
State or Provincial highway	64

Maps

Trips Out of Town

Pyramid Lake

80

395

RENO
(p282)

Fallon

Virginia City

Lahontan Lake

50

80

Lake Tahoe (p285)

Carson City
(p284)

95

N E V

SACRAMENTO

505

80

Yerington

ALT 95

Schurz

361

376

5

SAN FRANCISCO

50

Walker Lake

580

Hawthorne

359

280

MODESTO

Yosemite National Park

120

167

Mono Lake

95

6 95

Tonopah

5

395

6

Goldfield

95

41

Bishop

Scotty's Junction

267

Death Valley National Park

Rhyoli

Monterey

Salinas

FRESNO

Kings Canyon National Park

374

180

Stovepipe Wells

19

Mt Whitney
(14,494ft)

Furnace Creek

198

Badwater
(-282ft)

Ballarat

C A L I F O R N I A

395

178

46

PACIFIC OCEAN

BAKERSFIELD

M O J A V

Barsto

5

15

Hesperia

San Bernardino Mtns

LOS ANGELES
(p273)

Disneyland

215

10

Inset map

Vancouver

Calgary

Regina

Winnipeg

C A N A D A

Québec

Seattle

Minneapolis

Montreal

Ottawa

Salt Lake City

Denver

Detroit

Chicago

Buffalo

Boston

New York

Philadelphia

Pittsburg

San Francisco

Kansas City

St Louis

Washington

Las Vegas

U S A

Los Angeles

Phoenix

Oklahoma City

Memphis

Atlanta

Charleston

San Diego

Dallas

M E X I C O

Houston

New Orleans

Miami

CUBA

0   40   80 miles

0   100 km

© Copyright Time Out Group 2005

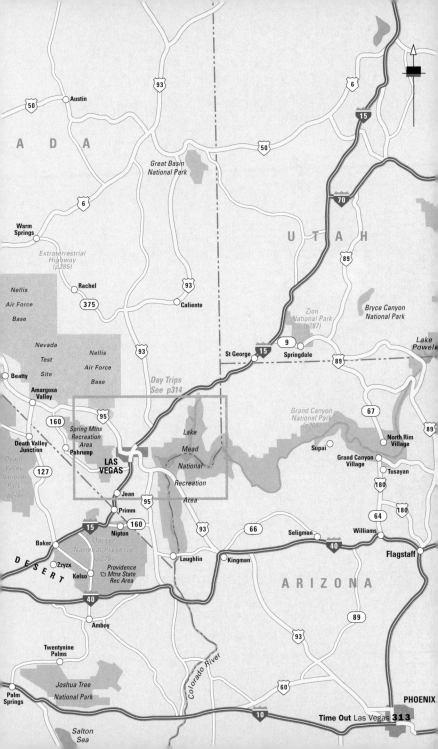

Time Out Las Vegas **313**

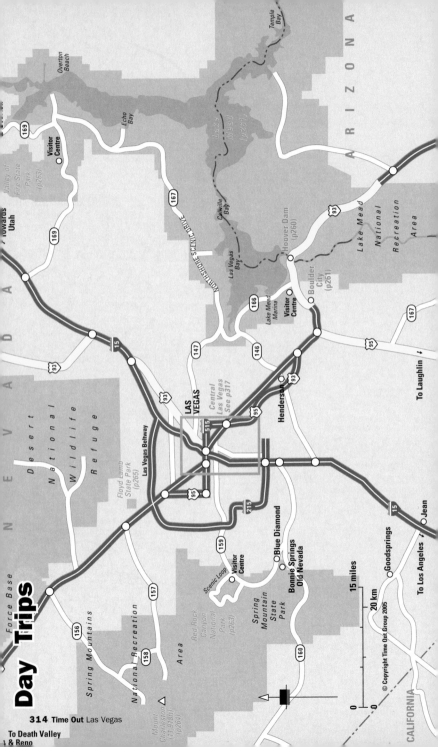

Day Trips

**To Death Valley
& Reno**

N E V A D A

Desert National Wildlife Refuge

Spring Mountains National Recreation Area

Floyd Lamb State Park (p265)

Las Vegas Beltway

LAS VEGAS

Central Las Vegas See p317

Red Rock Canyon National Conservation Area (p263)

Scenic Loop

Visitor Centre

Spring Mountain State Park (p263)

Mount Charleston (11,918th) (p264)

Blue Diamond

Bonnie Springs
Old Nevada

Valley of Fire State Park (p263)

Visitor Centre

Echo Bay

Overton Beach

Lake Mead (p261)

Temple Bay

NORTH SHORE SCENIC DRIVE

Callville Bay

Las Vegas Bay

Hoover Dam (p260)

Boulder City (p261)

Lake Mead Marina

Visitor Centre

Lake Mead National Recreation Area

A R I Z O N A

Henderson

To Laughlin

Jean

Goodsprings

To Los Angeles

CALIFORNIA

15 miles

15 km

20 km

© Copyright Time Out Group 2005

To Howards Utah

Nellis Air Force Base

169

169

93

15

93

167

167

147

166

146

93

95

95

515

95

215

159

157

156

158

160

169

93

167

95

93

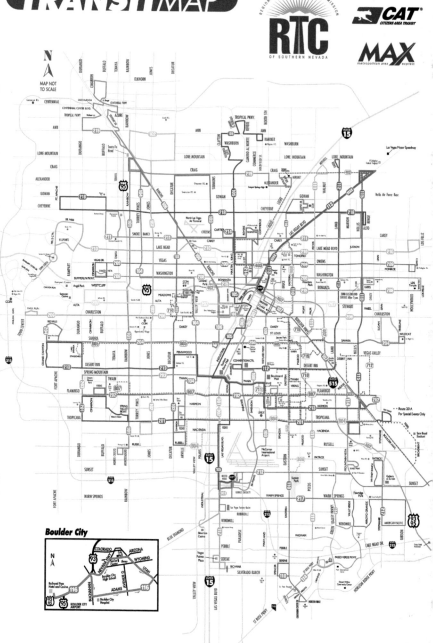

Street Index

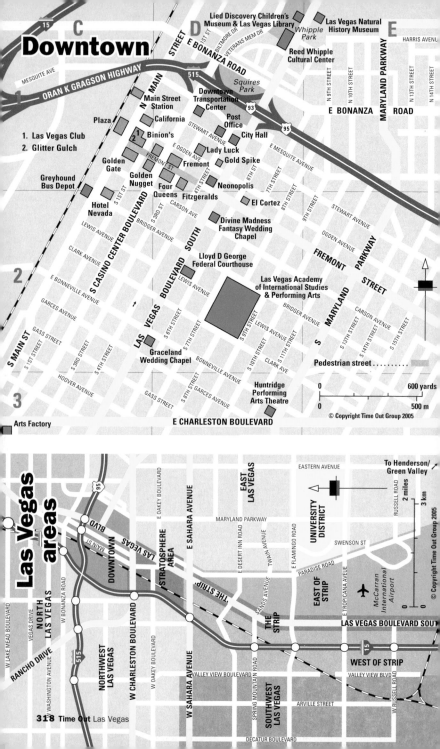

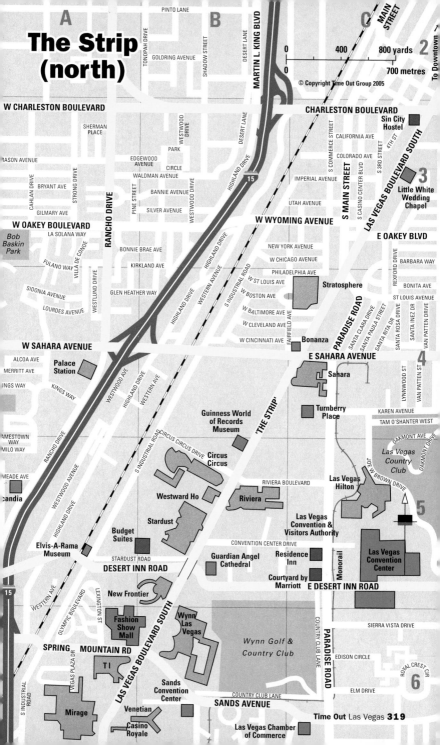

The Strip (north)

A · B · C

© Copyright Time Out Group 2005

0 · 400 · 800 yards
0 · 700 metres

PINTO LANE

TONOPAH DRIVE
GOLDRING AVENUE
SHADOW STREET
DESERT LANE

MARTIN L. KING BLVD

MAIN STREET

To Downtown

W CHARLESTON BOULEVARD
CHARLESTON BOULEVARD

Sin City Hostel

SHERMAN PLACE
MASON AVENUE
CAHLAN DRIVE
BRYANT AVE
STRONG DRIVE
GILMARY AVE

PARK
EDGEWOOD AVENUE
CIRCLE
WALDMAN AVENUE
BANNIE AVENUE
PINE STREET
SILVER AVENUE

WESTWOOD DRIVE

DESERT LANE

HIGHLAND DRIVE

15

S COMMERCE STREET
CALIFORNIA AVE
COLORADO AVE
4TH ST
S 3RD ST
S CASINO CENTER BLVD

IMPERIAL AVENUE

UTAH AVENUE

LAS VEGAS BOULEVARD SOUTH

Little White Wedding Chapel

RANCHO DRIVE

W OAKEY BOULEVARD

Bob Baskin Park

LA SOLANA WAY
VILLA DE CONDE
FULANO WAY
BONNIE BRAE AVE
KIRKLAND AVE
SIDONIA AVENUE
LOURDES AVENUE
GLEN HEATHER WAY
WESTLUND DRIVE

WESTWOOD DRIVE

HIGHLAND DRIVE

WESTERN AVENUE

S INDUSTRIAL ROAD

W WYOMING AVENUE

NEW YORK AVENUE
W CHICAGO AVENUE
PHILADELPHIA AVE
W ST LOUIS AVE
W BOSTON AVE
W BALTIMORE AVE
W CLEVELAND AVE
W CINCINNATI AVE

FAIRFIELD AVE

E OAKEY BLVD

REXFORD DRIVE
BARBARA WAY
BONITA AVE
ST LOUIS AVENUE
SANTA INEZ ST
VAN PATTEN ST

Stratosphere

Bonanza

W SAHARA AVENUE
E SAHARA AVENUE

ALCOA AVE
MERRITT AVE
KINGS WAY
KINGS WAY

Palace Station

PARADISE ROAD
SANTA CLARA DRIVE
SANTA PAULA STREET
SANTA RITA DR
SANTA ROSA DRIVE
VAN PATTEN ST
LYNNWOOD ST

Sahara

Turnberry Place

KAREN AVENUE
TAM O' SHANTER WEST
OAKMONT AVE
OAKMONT DR

JAMESTOWN WAY
MILO WAY
MEADE AVE
candia

WESTWOOD AVENUE

HIGHLAND DRIVE

WESTERN AVE

S INDUSTRIAL ROAD

CIRCUS CIRCUS DRIVE

Guinness World of Records Museum

'THE STRIP'

Las Vegas Country Club

JOE W BROWN DRIVE

Circus Circus

RIVIERA BOULEVARD

Las Vegas Hilton

Westward Ho

Riviera

Stardust

Budget Suites

RANCHO DRIVE

HIGHLAND DRIVE

Elvis-A-Rama Museum

STARDUST ROAD

DESERT INN ROAD

CONVENTION CENTER DRIVE

Guardian Angel Cathedral

Residence Inn

Courtyard by Marriott

Las Vegas Convention & Visitors Authority

Monorail

Las Vegas Convention Center

E DESERT INN ROAD

WESTERN AVE

15

New Frontier

SPRING MOUNTAIN RD

OLYMPIC BOULEVARD
LEXINGTON ST
VEGAS PLAZA DR

Fashion Show Mall

Wynn Las Vegas

Wynn Golf & Country Club

PARADISE ROAD

SIERRA VISTA DRIVE

EDISON CIRCLE

ROYAL CREST CIR

T I

LAS VEGAS BOULEVARD SOUTH

COUNTRY CLUB LANE

ELM DRIVE

Mirage

S INDUSTRIAL ROAD

Sands Convention Center

Venetian

Casino Royale

SANDS AVENUE

COUNTRY CLUB LANE

Las Vegas Chamber of Commerce

Time Out Las Vegas **319**

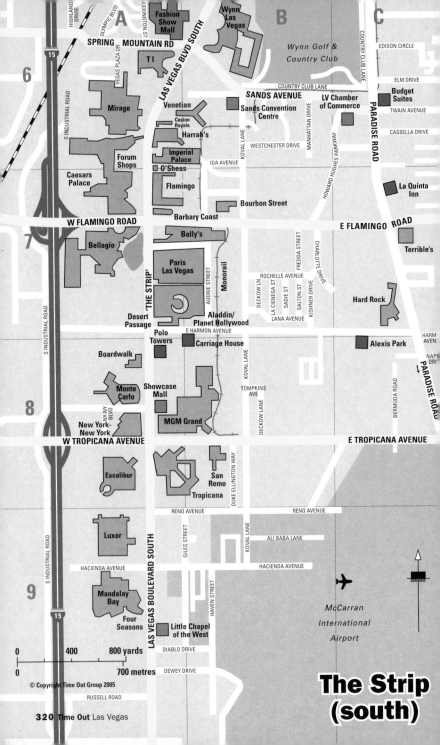

The Strip (south)

© Copyright Time Out Group 2005